THE PROCESS OF PARENTING

THE PROCESS OF PARENTING

FIFTH EDITION

JANE B. BROOKS

Mayfield Publishing Company

Mountain View, California
London • Toronto

To my grandparents and parents,
my children and their children

Library of Congress Cataloging-in-Publication Data
Brooks, Jane B.
    The process of parenting / Jane B. Brooks. — 5th ed.
        p.   cm.
    Includes bibliographical references and index.
    ISBN 0-7674-0215-4
    1. Parenting — United States.   I. Title.
    HQ755.8.B75 1999
    649′.1 — dc21   98-39378
                                                              CIP

Manufactured in the United Sates of America
10 9 8 7 6 5 4 3 2 1

Mayfield Publishing Company
1280 Villa Street
Mountain View, California 94041

Sponsoring editor, Franklin C. Graham; production, Greg Hubit Bookworks; manuscript editor, Molly Roth; design manager, Jean Mailander; cover designer, Andrew Ogus; photo researcher, Roberta Spieckerman; manufacturing manager, Randy Hurst. The text was set in 10.5/12 Berkeley Oldstyle Medium by ColorType and printed on 45# Highland Plus by Malloy Lithographing, Inc.

Credits: Cover photo, Britt Erlanson/The Image Bank. Pp. 1, 2: Definitions of "parent" and "process" reproduced with permission from *The American Heritage Dictionary of the English Language.* Copyright © 1981 by Houghton Mifflin Company. Pp. 51, 185: from *Between Generations: The Six Stages of Parenthood* by Ellen Galinsky. Copyright © 1981 by Ellen Galinsky. Reprinted by permission of Times Books, a division of Random House, Inc. Pp. 68, 71, 76; from *Children: The Challenge* by Rudolf Kreikurs, M.D., with Vicki Soltz, R.N. Copyright © 1964 by Rudolf Dreikurs, M.D. Used by permission of Dutton Signet, a division of Penguin Books USA Inc.

Photo credits: © Jose Carrillo/PhotoEdit, p. 225; © Elizabeth Crews, pp. 31, 88, 131, 244, 302, 341, 463; © Elizabeth Crews/Stock, Boston, p. 42; © Myrleen Ferguson/PhotoEdit, p. 280; © Joel Gordon, pp. 72, 457; © Phiz Mezey, p. 329; © Jeffry W. Myers/Stock, Boston, p. 19; © Okoniewski/The Image Works, p. 400; © Kent Reno/Jeroboam Inc., p. 194; © Frank Siteman/Jeroboam Inc., p. 176; © Kathy Sloane/Jeroboam Inc., p. 259; © Robert Ullmann/Design Conceptions, p. 60; © Ulrike Welsch, p. 105; © Gale Zucker/Stock, Boston, p. 251.

 This book is printed on acid-free, recycled paper.

CONTENTS

CHAPTER 2

ENCOURAGING GROWTH   27

CHAPTER 3

ESTABLISHING CLOSE EMOTIONAL RELATIONSHIPS
WITH CHILDREN   54

CHAPTER 4

MODIFYING CHILDREN'S BEHAVIOR   80

PART II PARENTING AT DEVELOPMENTAL STAGES

CHAPTER 5

BECOMING PARENTS   102

CHAPTER 6

THE FIRST YEAR OF LIFE   127

CHAPTER 7

TODDLERHOOD: THE YEARS FROM ONE TO THREE   156

CHAPTER 8

THE PRESCHOOL YEARS 189

CHAPTER 9

THE ELEMENTARY SCHOOL YEARS   220

C H A P T E R   1 0

EARLY ADOLESCENCE: THE YEARS FROM ELEVEN TO FIFTEEN   256

CHAPTER 11

LATE ADOLESCENCE: THE YEARS FROM FIFTEEN TO NINETEEN   286

PART III PARENTING IN VARYING LIFE CIRCUMSTANCES

CHAPTER 1 2

PARENTING AND WORKING   325

CHAPTER 13

SINGLE PARENTING AND STEPPARENTING   350

CHAPTER 14

CHAPTER 15

CHAPTER 16

SUPPORTS FOR PARENTS AND CHILDREN   453

PREFACE

"For most adult humans, parenthood is still the ultimate source of the sense of meaning. For most adults the question 'What does life mean?' is automatically answered once they have children; better yet it is no longer asked,"[1] writes the psychologist David Gutmann after testing and interviewing men and women about the impact of parenthood on their lives.

Do people get training to succeed in this central life activity? No! Anyone who cuts hair for pay or drives a car must have a license and demonstrate a certain level of skill before being permitted to engage in these activities independently. But nowhere does society require systematic parenting education, which may matter most of all.

This book attempts to fill this educational gap. Like the earlier editions, the fifth edition of *The Process of Parenting* shows how parents and caregivers can translate their love and concern for children into effective parenting skills. The book strives to bring to life the child's world and concerns, so parents can better understand what their children may be thinking and feeling. The book also describes the myriad thoughts and feelings—positive and negative—that accompany parenting, so parents can better understand themselves.

The book is divided into three parts. Part I, General Concepts, Goals, and Strategies, includes Chapters 1 through 4. Chapter 1 describes the roles and interactions of the three participants in the process of parenting—the child, the parent, and the social system—and the ways social and historical forces shape parenting. Chapter 2 describes the role of parenting in lifespan development, parents' goals in rearing children, and the ways people learn to be parents. The two basic tasks of parenting are detailed—creating close emotional relationships (Chapter 3) and establishing effective limits (Chapter 4).

Part II, Parenting at Different Ages, describes how general concepts and basic strategies are applied to children of different ages. This part begins with a chapter on how parents make the transition to parenthood, focusing on how past experiences with one's own parents, as well as the present social context of marriage, work, and social relationships, influence the transition.

The next six chapters apply the general concepts to children in infancy, toddlerhood, the preschool years, the elementary school years, and early and late adolescence. Each chapter presents updated information on children's physical, intellectual, and personal-social development for the six age periods, focusing on the ways parents can promote positive behaviors. In this edition, I pay particular attention to understanding and promoting children's capacity for emotional regulation, which underlies children's competence in many areas.

A portion of each of these six chapters focuses on problems children experience at the given age. Because each child is a unique individual, parents require a variety of strategies and techniques for handling problems, depending on the child and the circumstances. The strategies of Haim Ginott, Thomas Gordon, and Dorothy Briggs emphasize communicating feelings and establishing relationships with children. Rudolf Dreikurs and the behaviorists emphasize ways of changing behavior. Parents can find solutions among these approaches if they adopt a problem-solving method that consists of defining the problem exactly, making certain that the problem is the child's and not the parent's, considering alternative actions, taking action, evaluating the results, and starting over again if necessary.

In addition to describing what parents do, the book describes how parents feel as they raise children. Stages of parenthood are identified, and interviews with parents provide information about what parents wish they had known about parenting before they started. The book also emphasizes the joys that parents experience. In 1948, Arthur Jersild and his colleagues wrote that most research on parenting was focused on the problems parents experience and little attention was given to "the cheerful side of the ledger."[2] Because this is still true today, I try in this book to address this imbalance.

Part III, Parenting in Varying Life Circumstances, describes how parents adapt parenting strategies to meet the common challenges of everyday life — both parents' working, single parenting and stepparenting, trauma striking a family, and having children with special needs. Chapters 12 through 16 describe the demands life circumstances make on parents and children and how parents with supportive help can meet such demands.

Throughout, the book describes programs that support parents. The final chapter takes this further, describing a systematic framework for understanding the roles supportive people and programs play in the process of parenting.

The book discusses cultural and social factors affecting parenting. As in the two previous editions, the fifth edition pays attention to the experiences of ethnic groups as they relate to special topics such as the formation of ethnic identity and bicultural identity and ways to combat prejudice. I do not have a separate chapter describing specific ethnic groups individually, in terms of particular beliefs and strategies. Individuals and subgroups within larger ethnic groups vary so widely it is difficult to construct a composite portrait that does justice to both individuals and the group. Further, I believe what unites us as parents is much greater than what distinguishes us. Though ethnic groups may stress different values and emphasize differing strategies, all groups rear children by forming relationships with them, setting limits, and shaping behavior when it does not conform to group standards. As such, we can all learn from basic principles and strategies.

The fifth edition follows the same structure as that of the fourth, but it includes updated information, expanded coverage, and new sections within chapters. Information on children's development has been updated from research described in the fifth edition of *The Handbook of Child Psychology,* published in 1997.

In addition to emotional regulation, particular attention is given to language development, social development, and the promotion of healthy behaviors in adolescence. Chapter 9 contains an expanded and revised section on the school's influence on children's lives and ways parents can form alliances with school authorities to promote learning.

New sections contain information on the impact of infertility on parenting and on ways to engage fathers, especially single fathers, in parenting. There is a new interview with James Levine on this latter topic. Chapter 14 includes a new section on preventing violence in children's lives, and Chapter 15 contains a large section on the special needs of children who are poor.

I have written this book from the point of view of a parent, a clinician, a researcher, and a teacher of parenting. I hold the firm conviction that anyone who wishes to invest attention and effort in becoming a competent, caring parent can do so in his or her own way. The only prerequisites required are a desire to succeed and a willingness to invest the effort to do so. The results are well worth the effort. Having seen children face many difficult situations, I am impressed that children can live fully and happily even when temporarily engulfed by trauma, provided they have the loving support of a reliable caretaker.

Children are not the only ones enriched by adults' efforts to be effective parents. Helping children grow is an intense, exciting experience for parents in all areas of functioning. Parents' physical stamina, agility, and speed increase to care for infants and toddlers. Emotional stamina grows to deal with intense feelings toward children and to help them learn to express and modulate their feelings. Intellectual skills grow to answer young children's questions and, later, to help them with school subjects. In helping new life grow, we gain for ourselves an inner vitality and richness that affect all our relationships. Summarizing the importance of parenthood. Jersild and his colleagues conclude, "Perhaps no other circumstance in life offers so many challenges to an individual's powers, so great an array of opportunities for appreciation, such a varied emotional and intellectual stimulation."[3] This book is written to help readers take advantage of such opportunities.

ACKNOWLEDGMENTS

Writing acknowledgments is one of the pleasures of completing a book. As I read galleys and page proofs, I am constantly reminded of all the people who have helped make this book a reality.

I wish to thank all the clinicians and researchers who gave generously of their time not only for the interviews themselves but also for the time later to review the excerpts and clarify points: Jay Belsky, Andrew Billingsley, Judy Dunn, Susan Harter, Barbara Keogh, Claire Kopp, Anneliese Korner, James Levine, Jacqueline Lerner, Richard Lerner, Susan McHale, Paul Mussen, Emily Visher, John Visher, Jill Waterman, Carol Whalen, Emmy Werner, and Steven Wolin.

I thank the following people for a review of the fourth edition of this book, as their comments enabled me to make more insightful revisions: Rochelle Dalla, University of Nebraska at Omaha; Mary Jo Graham, Marshall University; Cary E. Lantz, Liberty University; and Cheryl Mueller, University of Southern Mississippi.

Special appreciation goes to Robert Kremers, Chief of the Department of Pediatrics of Kaiser Medical Center, for his willingness to place questionnaires about the joys of parenting in the waiting rooms. I thank the many anonymous parents who completed them there and in parenting classes. Most particularly, I express my gratitude to all those parents whom I interviewed about the joys of parenting and the ways they changed and grew through the experience. I gained valuable insights about the process of parenting, and their comments enliven the book immeasurably. These parents are Wendy Clinton, Mark Clinton, Judy Davis, Robert Rosenbaum, Linda Dobson, Douglas Dobson, Jill Fernald, Charles Nathan, Otie Gould, Warren Gould, Caryn Gregg, Robert Gregg, Michael Hoyt, Henrietta Krueger, Richard Krueger, Patricia Landman, Jennifer Lillard, Chris McArtor, Robert McArtor, Kathy Malone, Jean Oakley, Paul Opsvig, Susan Opsvig, Sherry Proctor, Stewart Proctor, Iris Yotvat-Talmon, Moshe Talmon, Raymond Terwilleger, Patricia Toney, Anthony Toney, Steven Tulkin, Barbara Woolmington-Smith, and Craig Woolmington-Smith.

My co-workers at the Kaiser Medical Center at Hayward were supportive and helpful throughout. Cynthia Seay, the medical librarian, obtained all the books and articles I requested. Pediatricians and pediatric advice nurses have given helpful information about parents' concerns. I greatly appreciate the leadership at Kaiser, especially Annabel Anderson Imbert, the Physician-in-Chief, and Jerome Rauch, the Chief of Psychiatry, who promote an atmosphere in which creativity flourishes.

The staff at Mayfield Publishing Company deserve special appreciation for the care and diligence they exercise in transforming the manuscript into a book. Franklin Graham has brought his enthusiasm and critical skill to the task of producing a book students will enjoy and use. His interest and knowledge of the area are invaluable. April Wells-Hayes has given careful consideration to all aspects of the book. Greg Hubit, of Greg Hubit Bookworks, has worked quietly and efficiently to move the manuscript, seemingly magically, to book form. Molly Roth has taught me much about writing through her careful editing of the manuscript, always keeping the reader very much in mind. Her enthusiasm and support for the book are greatly appreciated.

I wish to thank Paul Mussen for his suggestions and interest in my writing over the years. In particular, he recommended using comments from researchers to make material more vivid for students. His concern with the social forces impinging on parenting has continued to influence my thinking.

Finally, I wish to thank my family and friends for their thoughtfulness and their company. I want to thank my patients for sharing their lives and experiences with me. I hope they have learned as much about life from me as I have learned from them. Most particularly, I want to thank my children, who are now grown and live away from home. They are very much in my mind as I write, and I relive our experiences together as I explore the different developmental periods. I find that I have learned the most important truths of parenting from our interactions. I believe that when I have paid attention, they have been my best teachers.

FOREWORD

The author of this book, Jane Brooks, has had a wide variety of professional and personal experiences that qualify her as an expert in child development. She is a scholar, researcher, and writer in the discipline of child psychology; a practicing clinician working with parents and children; and a mother. Drawing on the knowledge and insights derived from this rich background of experience, she has produced a wise and balanced book that parents will find valuable in fostering the optimal development of their children—helping them to become secure, happy, competent, self-confident, moral individuals. Dr. Brooks offers guidelines that are explicitly linked to major theorists (for example, Freud, Piaget, Erikson) and findings of scientific research in child development, so that the reader is also presented with a wealth of information on physical, cognitive, social, and emotional development. Students of human development and all who work with children professionally, as well as parents, will profit greatly from reading this book.

Brooks' approach to parenting incorporates many noteworthy features. Her coverage of the fundamental tasks and issues in childrearing is comprehensive. Included are tasks shared by all parents (for example, preparing for the birth of the infant, feeding, toilet training, adjusting to nursery school or kindergarten, the adolescent's growing interest in sex) as well as special, although common, problems (such as temper tantrums, delinquency, use of drugs, and physical or mental handicaps). Critical contemporary experiences such as divorce, single parenting, and stepparenting are also treated with insight and sympathy. Brooks' suggestions for ways of dealing with these problems are reasonable, balanced, and practical; her writing is straightforward, clear, and jargon-free.

Authorities in child development generally agree that the principal theories and accumulated findings of scientific investigations are not in themselves adequate to provide a comprehensive basis for directing parents in childrearing. Given the limitations of the present state of knowledge, guidance must be based on established principles of human development *plus* the cumulative wisdom and insights of specialists who have worked systematically and successfully in child-guidance settings. Yet many, perhaps most, academically trained child psychologists pay little attention to the writing of such clinicians as Briggs, Dreikurs, Ginott, Gordon, and Spock, regarding them as unscientific "popular" psychologists. This is not true of Dr. Brooks. After careful and critical reading of their work, she concluded that, as a consequence of their vast clinical experience, these specialists have achieved some profound insights about children and have thus developed invaluable techniques for analyzing and dealing effectively with many problems that parents face. Furthermore, Brooks believes that parents themselves can successfully apply some of these techniques to resolve specific problems. Some of the experts' suggestions are therefore incorporated, with appropriate acknowledgment, where they are relevant.

The book is not doctrinaire or prescriptive, however; the author does not advise parents simply to unquestioningly adopt some "system," plan, or set of rules. On the contrary, Brooks stresses the uniqueness of each individual and family, the complex nature of parent-child relations, and the multiple determinants of problem behavior. In Brooks' view, each problem must be placed in its developmental context, and evaluated in terms of the child's level of physical, cognitive, and emotional maturity. The processes of parenting are invariably bidirectional: Parents influence children *and* children influence parents. Furthermore, families do not function in isolation; each family unit is embedded in a wider network of social systems that affect its functioning. Successful childrearing depends on parents' accepting these complexities, yet also attempting to understand themselves and their children and maintaining a problem-solving orientation.

It is a pleasure to note the pervasive optimistic, yet realistic, tone of the book. The author has recognized that promotion of children's welfare and happiness is one of the highest parental goals, and she communicates her confidence that most parents *can* achieve this. Underlying this achievement is parents' deep-seated willingness to work hard and to devote thought, time, energy, and attention to their children's development and their problems. Reading this book will increase parental understanding and thus make the difficult tasks of parenting easier.

Paul Mussen
Professor Emeritus of Psychology
Former Director, Institute of Human Development
University of California, Berkeley

PARENTING IS A PROCESS

C H A P T E R 1

Parenthood transforms people. After a baby comes, parents are no longer the same individuals they were. A whole new role begins, and they start a new way of life. What does parenting really mean? What are the joys and responsibilities of being a parent? How has being a parent changed in the last fifty years? How does society help or hinder parents? This chapter explores parenting as a cooperative venture between parents, between parents and their child, and between parents and society. It defines parenting, describes the roles of parents and the environment in rearing children, and focuses on how society can help both parents and children.

Four million babies are born in the United States each year.[1] The challenge for parents and society is to rear children to attain their full potential in adulthood. How parents do this under varying family and social conditions is the subject of this book. The aim of the book is to open up the potential of parenthood for all adults by giving information on how children grow and develop and how parents' actions influence children's feelings, behavior, and growth.

WHAT IS PARENTING?

The American Heritage Dictionary of the English Language[2] defines *parent* in several ways—as a father or mother; an organism that generates another; guardian or protector. Combining these definitions, one can define a parent as a person who fosters all facets of a child's growth—nourishing, protecting, guiding new life through the course of development.

The words *protecting* and *guiding* are vague. Social scientists translate these terms into the context of everyday life and describe parents' main functions as (1) procreating, (2) providing basic resources such as food, shelter, and clothing that ensure physical safety and survival, (3) giving affection and caring, (4) teaching society's core values, and (5) helping children develop competencies that enable them to become functioning adults in society.[3]

1

Identifying a child's parents would appear to be a simple matter. Usually, *biological parents* provide the egg and sperm to produce new life and serve as caregivers for the child as well. But this is not always the case. *Adoptive parents* become parents through action of the court. *Surrogate mothers,* most often inseminated with the father's sperm, provide the gestational womb for children they will give to that father and his wife. Parenthood by *artificial insemination* involves a woman's being impregnated through the mechanical introduction of sperm. The sperm may be that of her husband or another man.

In recent years, complex legal issues have arisen over the question of who is the parent. Does a surrogate mother have any rights to maintain a relationship with the child she bears for another couple? Does a biological father have a right to a child the mother denies is his and has given up for adoption? Can a teenage child choose to live with a nonrelated parent even when biological parents seek custody of the child? In the absence of abuse or other high risk to the child, the courts have generally favored giving a very young child to the biological parent or parents, even if the parents are not married or one parent objects to the other's having the child. Further, courts are reluctant to terminate a biological parent's contact and, in the Baby M case, permitted the surrogate mother to have continuing visitation with her biological child, who resides with the father and his wife.

The following excerpt from a newspaper column shows the complexity of defining a parent today in our society:

> Jaycee Louise Buzzanca is not exactly an orphan. Nor is she, if you will excuse the expression, a bastard. But the two-year-old from Orange Country, California, started out her life with five parents. Now, she has none.
>
> Her story began with an infertile couple, Luanne and John Buzzanca, aka *the intended parents.* Having been on a roller coaster of fertility treatments, they set about having a child the new-fashioned way.
>
> Then there were *the genetic parents.* A sperm donor and an egg donor, anonymous and unrelated, produced Jaycee's genetic material. These two had a fateful meeting in a petri dish.
>
> Next came *the gestational mother,* a woman whose cottage industry was growing babies. This surrogate offered up her womb for rent.
>
> But a not-so-funny thing happened while Jaycee was still in the womb. The intended father changed his intentions. He left the intended mother. When Jaycee was born, Luanne brought her home anyway and became *the rearing mother.* But John denied any responsibility including need I add, child support, on the grounds that he wasn't the father.
>
> The small offspring of reproductive and marital dispute was left in legal limbo.
>
> Last week, it was revealed that a family court judge in Orange County sided with John. No, the judge said, he didn't owe child support because he wasn't the father. This judge went even further to say that Luanne wasn't the mother either. He called her the "*temporary custodial person.*" This is how Jaycee, daughter of five, became officially a parentless child.[4]

Parenting Is a Process

The American Heritage Dictionary of the English Language defines *process* as a "system of operations"; "a series of actions, changes, or functions that bring about a desired end."[5] The word emphasizes that the end result depends on numerous actions or changes occurring in a systematic way over time.

Parenting in general can be described as a series of actions and interactions on the part of parents to promote the development of children. Parenting is not a one-way street in which parent influences child day after day. It is a process of interaction between the two, influenced by cultural and social institutions. The interaction changes all the contributors.

Jay Belsky describes three major influences on the process of parenting: (1) the child's characteristics and individuality, (2) the parent's personal history and psychological resources, and (3) the context of stresses and supports.[6] Currently, controversy centers on the rights and responsibilities of each of the participants in this process of parenting, and we will touch on these conflicting views in our discussion. The description of these roles—child, parent, and society—will draw on Urie Bronfenbrenner's views regarding the ecology of development and on developmental protective and risk factors.

THE ROLE OF THE CHILD

Children bring to parenting their individual needs, gender, birthorder, temperaments, and patterns of growth. These influence parents' behavior and are, in turn, influenced by parents and their larger social context.

Children's Needs

Children's immature state at birth requires that parents and society nurture them and meet their needs so they can survive. Meeting these needs reorganizes parents' lives and makes demands on society as well.

According to Bronfenbrenner and Pamela Morris, a child grows [through] "progressively more complex reciprocal interaction [with] persons, objects, and symbols in its immediate external environment." Further, "to be effective, the interaction must occur on a fairly regular basis over extended periods of time." A father feeding a baby and a child exploring a toy are just two examples of such interactions. The interactions must include "one or more other persons with whom the child develops a strong, mutual, irrational attachment, and who are committed to the child's development, preferably for life." The maintenance of the caregiver-child relationship depends on the attachment and involvement of a second adult "who assists, encourages, spells off, gives status to, and expresses admiration and affection for the person caring for and engaging in joint activity with the child."[7]

Bronfenbrenner and Morris believe interactions must continue on a regular basis so activities can become more complex and stimulate further development. The child need not be biologically related to his or her parent nor live in a two-parent family, but the caregiver must have a long-term, "irrational" attachment and love for the child and receive the emotional support and respect of at least one other adult.

Individual Characteristics

Children significantly influence the process of parenting in that their specific qualities both affect what parents do and determine the impact of what parents do. For example, highly fussy babies demand more soothing behavior from parents than do easy-going infants; in turn, they often make parents feel ineffective by responding negatively to parents' interventions. In addition, children of differing temperaments respond in different ways to the same parental action. For instance, maternal stimulation can increase exploration and competence in less active toddlers but decrease exploration in highly active toddlers.[8]

Further, parents' perceptions of their children's individual qualities and the "goodness of fit" between the child's qualities and parents' and society's expectations and values also affect parenting.[9] For example, when parents have unrealistically high expectations of children, they see their children as functioning poorly even when objective observations indicate otherwise.[10] Or, if a child has a high activity level, she or he will fit in well with an active family but may feel out of place in a family where most members are slow-moving and quiet.

Protective and Risk Factors

Social scientists have noted that children, families, and societies have qualities they term *protective* and *risk factors*.[11] Risk factors are variables significantly associated with a poor outcome of some sort — poor health, poor growth. Protective factors are conditions or qualities related to positive outcomes even in the face of increased risk.

Protective factors within the child include such objective characteristics as normal birth weight, sex (e.g., being a boy is a protective factor for a child of an adolescent mother), and age (e.g., being young can help protect a child during parental divorce). Protective factors also include personal qualities, such as an easy temperament, as well as personal experiences, such as having good friends.

The risk factors of children include objective qualities such as perinatal complications, prematurity, sex (e.g., boys are more at risk than girls for attentional problems), and age (adolescents face a greater risk of difficulty than younger children when their single mothers remarry). Risk factors also include personal experiences such as neglect or physical abuse. See Box 1-1 for other risk factors stemming from the child, the parents, and the larger environment.

The Importance of Children to Parents

Accustomed to thinking about parents' importance to children, most of us fail to recognize children's importance to parents. Children, however, meet many of their parents' basic psychological needs.

In recent surveys, two-thirds of men and women report that their families and love life provide the most satisfying parts of their lives.[12] Parents of all ethnic backgrounds cite the love and emotional closeness they experience with children as the most important reason for having children.[13] Further, parents talk about the special quality of this love. Bronfenbrenner and Morris refer to an "irrational attachment."[14] Tracy Gold announces her feeling about her baby on the cover of *People* magazine: "You never imagined you could love someone this much."[15] Parents also enjoy watching and helping their children grow and develop. Children give parents a sense of being responsible, mature adults; link their parents to the rest of the community; and can even provide a sense of immortality.[16]

BOX 1-1
GENERIC RISK FACTORS

1. Ecological Context

Neighborhood disorganization
Racial injustice
Unemployment
Extreme poverty

2. Constitutional Handicaps

Perinatal complications
Sensory disabilities
Organic handicaps
Neurochemical imbalance

3. Family Circumstances

Low social class
Family conflict
Mental illness in the family
Large family size
Poor bonding to parents
Family disorganization
Communication deviance

4. Skill Development Delays

Subnormal intelligence
Social incompetence
Attentional deficits

Reading disabilities
Poor work skills and habits

5. Emotional Difficulties

Child abuse
Apathy or emotional blunting
Emotional immaturity
Stressful life events
Low self-esteem
Emotional dyscontrol

6. Interpersonal Problems

Peer rejection
Alienation and isolation

7. School Problems

Academic failure
Scholastic demoralization

From John D. Coie et al., "The Science of Prevention: A Conceptual Framework and Some Directives for a National Research Program,"
American Psychologist 48 (1993), p. 1022.
Copyright © 1994 by the American Psychological Association. Reprinted with permission.

The Importance of Children to Society

We shall examine the importance of society to children in a later section, but here
we focus on the vital role children play in society. Children ensure that a society will
continue. They maintain traditions and rituals, and they pass on societal values. In
addition, they grow into economic producers who support the aging members of society as well as their own children. In a society like ours, in which children represent a smaller and smaller percentage of the population, every child is a valued
participant.[17]

THE ROLE OF THE PARENT

Parents bring a complex personal history and a richly patterned social life to the
parenting process. When they become parents, they have to adapt their personal
qualities to their new role. Further, they need to adjust to the changes in this role
that social change brings.

A Short History of Parental Roles

Until late in the nineteenth century, parents were more concerned with the physical survival of their children than with effective parenting. Because of children's precarious hold on life, parents focused on their moral state, strictly punishing any transgressions. A parent's role was guardian of the body and soul of the child.[18]

In the early twentieth century, behaviorism taught that children were blank slates, so a parent's role was to teach children good habits through appropriate rewards and punishments. The 1930s and 1940s saw a welcome change from strict habit training. Freudian psychoanalysis and Arnold Gesell's observations of the healthy development of upper-middle-class children indicated that a parent's role was to understand children's needs, gratify them in socially appropriate ways, and permit the process of growth to occur as naturally as possible.

Insights from Jean Piaget and the ethologists shifted the role of parent from gratifier to facilitator of development. Piaget noted that children must act on the world in order to construct an intellectually complex view of life experience.[19] It is a parent's job to provide the experiences children need to develop. Similarly, the ethologists, who study human behaviors in terms of their adaptive qualities, emphasized that an organism requires environmental stimulation to develop fully.

A recent influence on limiting parents' role comes from the behavior geneticists, who study the relationship between genetic factors and people's behavior.[20] They believe that genetic makeup plays a major role in determining many personality qualities. Family environment, and particularly parenting, has a limited influence on the development of children's personality and intelligence unless that environment is extreme—for example, abusive or deprived or neglectful.

All the parental role behaviors described here appear appropriate for parents today. Parents' tasks are to ensure the physical survival of the child, teach good habits, gratify needs, and stimulate all facets of development by providing enriching experiences.

How Parents Influence Children

Ross Parke and Raymond Buriel believe parents meet role expectations and socialize children in three ways: (1) as an interactive partner with the child, (2) as a direct instructor, and (3) as a provider of opportunities that stimulate children's growth.[21]

We can classify parents' behaviors as having direct or indirect influences on children's behavior.[22] For example, teaching tooth brushing and healthy eating habits has a direct influence on children's physical health. Indirect influences consist of parental actions that affect the child in general and increase the likelihood of competent behavior in a given area. For example, when parents use reasoning to influence children's behavior—that is, give pertinent information and reasons for following parental requests—children are more likely to develop self-reliance and a sense of responsibility, which are in turn associated with children's carrying out positive health behaviors.

While past research has focused on how parents relate to children—how they teach and socialize them—current research indicates that many parent-child interactions previously unrecognized as significant may greatly affect children's growth and development. For example, the kinds of fantasy play that parents engage in with children impact children's learning to regulate and control their emotions.[23] The form of the questions parents ask and the style of their comments also influence children's language development and later cognitive functioning.[24] So, children learn from all kinds of interactions with parents.

Influences on Parents' Behavior

Many factors shape parents' behavior. As we saw earlier, children's temperaments and individual qualities shape what parents do, but many other influences also come into play. As we shall see in Chapters 2 and 5, parents' early interactions with their own parents mold how they interact and respond to their babies and to the other parent. A person's marriage, work, and overall support network also affect his or her parenting behaviors.[25] Finally, parents' cultural and social heritage influences their goals and how they go about accomplishing them. I describe this in greater detail in Chapter 2.

Protective and Risk Factors

Like children, parents' characteristics, personal qualities, and earlier experiences can serve as protective or risk factors.[26] Often, the same factor can potentially either harm or help, depending on circumstances. For example, family income, when average or above, serves as a protective factor, but when it remains at poverty level, it becomes a risk factor for many problems. A happy marriage can promote effective parenting, but a marriage in chronic conflict is one of the greatest risk factors for a child's overall development. (See again Box 1-1).

The Importance of Parents to Children

As just noted, behavior geneticists underscore the importance of a child's genetic makeup as determiner of development, given the sufficiently supportive environment most parents provide. Sandra Scarr writes, "Being reared in one family rather than another, within the range of families sampled, makes few differences in children's personality and intellectual development."[27]

In response to the behavior geneticists' claims, Diana Baumrind enumerates the many ways parents influence children's development.[28] Parents' ways of reasoning with children, their strategies of discipline, and their styles of communicating relate to such diverse areas as children's cognitive development, social competence, and responsible behavior from preschool years through adolescence. Baumrind makes her points in detail because she is concerned that parents will attribute their children's behavior to genetic makeup and, as a result, be less willing to use many of the strategies found to be so important in fostering children's development. Other researchers, such as Jacquelyne Jackson, have expressed concern that society will make fewer interventions in children's lives at the precise time that societal support is so necessary for parents and children.[29]

Jerome Kagan and his colleagues document that sensitive caregiving in the first years of life can affect the expression of a temperamental bias.[30] Highly reactive infants showing fretful crying and much motor activity at four months were followed for two years. When mothers of these reactive infants were firm and set reasonable limits with their babies, the babies were less fearful as toddlers, even though the general tendency is for highly reactive infants to be fearful toddlers. Mothers who were responsive to the child's fretting and did not set limits had toddlers who were more fearful. The latter kind of maternal behavior did not have the same effects with low-reactive infants. The researchers speculate that the mothers who did not reinforce the crying enabled their highly reactive infants to learn other coping strategies when they were upset so that in new situations they were less likely to cry and fuss.

Clinicians have emphasized the long-term consequences of certain kinds of early experiences, and now researchers are identifying specific behavioral styles that are transmitted across two or three generations of a family. Gerald Patterson and D. M. Capaldi show how styles pass from grandparents to parents to children.[31] Abusive and irritable grandparents whose disciplinary techniques involve explosive behavior tend to rear antisocial, impulsive children. When such children grow up, they have less education, get lower-paying jobs, and experience more life stress because of unemployment and divorce. When they become parents, they are relatively poor disciplinarians and monitors of children's behavior, so their children have problems as well. Such problems are reversible when parents use more effective discipline and more consistent monitoring of children.

Within the childhood period, early positive attachments with parents may pave the way for later positive interactions with others.[32] In a sample of poor families, children with positive attachments to their mothers in the infant/toddler years showed better adaptation in the elementary school years than did those who had insecure attachments, even though both groups of children had displayed problems in the preschool period. The early positive experience may have given the children an advantage by providing early internal models of care and self-worth that stimulated these children to seek out similar experiences in later years. As you can see, many kinds of research indicate how parents play a critical role in childhood development.

The Importance of Parents to Society

The direct caregivers for children, parents are responsible for helping them develop so they can be meaningful members of society. Society grants parents certain rights. In return, parents must feed, clothe, shelter, and educate their children, but they also have discretion in how they carry out these responsibilities.

Currently, there is debate over the extent to which society can limit parents in rearing their children.[33] Federal legislation, as well as a constitutional amendment introduced in twenty states, gives parents the right to direct the upbringing and education of their children as they see fit. Opponents of such laws question whether parents should have the right to remove their children from school classes they do not like or discipline children in severe ways.

At present, at least theoretically, society steps in when there is evidence of physical, sexual, or emotional abuse of children. But societal institutions do not easily substitute for inadequate care by parents. The recent death of six-year-old Elisa Izquierdo in Manhattan illustrates the problems society faces in supervising and caring for children when parents fail to do so.[34] Elisa was living with her father because her mother abused substances. When Elisa was four, her father died, and

THE JOYS OF FAMILY GENERATIONS

"At her christening party, we had a tape recorder, and each guest taped a little message into the recorder. When she began to sing, she would sing into the recorder, and when her grandmother was alive, she sang the old Norwegian songs into the recorder so we have that on tape. And every year at various times, at birthdays or holidays, we would all talk into the tape recorder about what our lives had been like and what had gone on since the last time we did it. We have her singing 'Silent Night' with all the words wrong, and that has been a real thread. We have a sort of oral history, and it's a real pleasure for us." MOTHER

"Thomas Wolfe wrote *You Can't Go Home Again*, but James Agee said you do go home again in the lives of your children. It is a sort of reexperiencing what you experienced when you grew up—they're reading the same books you read, the conflicts they have are the ones you remember having with your parents, or issues that mattered to you as a child are issues for them. When you have time to reflect on them, they bring you back over and over again to issues in your own childhood that I guess you have a second opportunity to resolve. You have a different perspective on them than you did before." FATHER

"One of the interesting things was when we took our children back to Ohio. Before she could crawl, one used to scoot around on her rear end and tuck one knee under the other, and she wore out all the seats of her pants. Her great-grandmother was alive then and said, 'Oh, that is just the way her grandfather did it.' We never knew that and it was just amazing. One of our girls is so like her great-aunt who never had any children of her own and was such a lovely woman. It would have pleased her so much to see my daughter grow up. Our son looks like my father and is so much like him in every way. He has his build. My father always had a joke at dinner every night and our son has always loved jokes. As soon as he could read, he had a joke book and was always telling us jokes at dinner. Our other son looks just exactly like his father and his grandfather." MOTHER

"One of my great joys was the first time my parent came to visit us, very proudly handing my son to my father and saying, 'Here's my boy!' That was a real highlight, a great thrill. I get choked up saying it now." FATHER

"I like having my family around. For the first time in my life, I want my mother to be here. There is a basic need to have your family around you. My husband's family and cousins are here, and I have a really strong urge to have everyone around. I was not really prepared for that." MOTHER

"Being a parent has helped me to see into myself. It's very illuminating in a personal way. It brings back a lot of memories, good and bad." FATHER

though his relatives petitioned the court for custody of Elisa, the judge returned her to her mother under the supervision of the Child Welfare Department. Elisa subsequently was found tortured, sexually abused, and beaten to death; her mother is charged with her murder.

A state review of the case revealed failures in the system at several levels.[35] For example, a court-ordered evaluation of the mother's home was not completed during a custody battle. Records were lost when Elisa's mother moved from Brooklyn to Manhattan. Record-keeping was lax, and follow-up lacking even after Elisa was admitted to a hospital with a fractured shoulder. Many times, Elisa's condition came to the attention of teachers, doctors, caseworkers, and other social workers, but no action was taken to remove her from the home.

The errors in this case led to an audit of 369 cases at the end of 1995.[36] Inadequate investigation occurred in 13 percent of cases; children were not interviewed face-to-face in 20 percent of cases; previous abuse reports were not reviewed in 40 percent of cases; and investigations did not occur within 24 hours, as required by law, in 10 percent of cases.

Extensive public criticism of the lax procedures in dealing with abusive families prompted many suggestions for change. Douglas Besharov believes that crack addiction underlies much current abuse and requires a different application of social resources to protect children.[37] For example, home supervision for children of crack addicts should extend for years because parents may only temporarily give up crack. Children who live with relatives of crack addicts should be monitored carefully because these relatives often have significant problems. In addition, formal licensing of these arrangements needs to be implemented. If adoption or placement with relatives is not possible, then authorities must find some other arrangement in which children can live until adulthood.

Richard Wexler, the president of the National Coalition for Child Protection Reform, warns of the problems that can ensue when government agencies rush in to remove children from abusive families following the death of a child.[38] In the fourteen months following the 1993 death of a Chicago three-year-old from abuse at home, concern about abusive families was so great that the population of foster children grew by 30 percent. Shelters became overcrowded, and some children had to sleep in welfare offices. Some children were placed with inadequately screened foster parents, and, in 1994, five children died in foster homes.

A torrent of child abuse reports created 4,000 cases for investigation. A 1995 Illinois study revealed that one-third of the foster children surveyed could have been cared for at home. In many at-risk families (as many as a third in a Washington, D.C., study), the basic problem is not abuse, but poverty, and the solution is financial help for adequate housing and food.

Just as society holds parents responsible for their treatment of their children, it also holds parents accountable for their children's misbehavior. Recently, a couple in Michigan were fined and ordered to pay court costs because they were judged to be lax in supervising their law-breaking sixteen-year-old son.[39]

As our society grows ever more complex, it becomes clear that parents who care for their children perform a role that society cannot easily fill.

THE ROLE OF SOCIETY

Parenting occurs in a social context. Children live in families, and families belong to social groups in a larger society that, in turn, influences how parents carry out their

---

◆
BOX 1-2
THE ECOLOGICAL ENVIRONMENT

Microsystem*   Immediate settings that a child develops in and patterns of daily
                   activities or interactions a child has in those settings (e.g., at
                   home, at school, in the neighborhood)

Mesosystem*   Interrelationships between two or more settings in which a child
                   participates (e.g., interrelationships between parents at home and
                   teachers at school).

Exosystem*   System that influences a child but with which the child does not
                   directly interact (e.g., parent's work, government agencies)

Macrosystem*   Broad cultural contexts in which mesosystems and exosystems
                   exist—culturally shared blueprints about how things are done
                   (e.g., how children are cared for)

Chronosystem[†]   Changes and continuities over time that influence a person's
                   development (e.g., school entry, puberty, marriage)

*From Urie Bronfenbrenner, *The Ecology of Human Development: Experiments by Nature and Design*
(Cambridge, MA: Harvard University Press, 1979).
[†]From Urie Bronfenbrenner, "Ecology of the Family as a Context for Human Development," *Developmental Psychology* 22 (1986): 723–742.

---

tasks. In this section, we look at the social context in terms of the levels of interaction the child has with the environment, forms of social influence on parenting, protective and risk factors in the social context, and society's views of parents and children as well as the importance of society to the child and parents.

The Ecology of the Environment

I described Bronfenbrenner's view that children's development requires daily interactions with persons and objects that stimulate increasing complexity in behavior. Here, I describe Bronfenbrenner's analysis of the environment and relate this to the material that will be presented in the rest of the book.[40]

The pattern of activities and daily interactions children experience with objects and with people—parents, caregivers, teachers, coaches, peers—Bronfenbrenner calls the *microsystem* (see Box 1-2). This is what I shall discuss in most chapters the daily interactions children have with other people and objects. The *mesosystem* consists of the interactions and interrelationships between parents and other people who care for children—parents and teachers (see Chapter 9), parents and day care providers (see Chapter 12), and parents and coaches (see Chapter 15).

The *exosystem* includes agencies and institutions that influence children's daily life but do not include children as participants—parents' work (see Chapter 12), and community and government agencies (see Chapter 16). For example, parents' work can promote positive parent-child relationships by allowing time off for children's illnesses or activities.

The *macrosystem* is the broad cultural context in which children, parents, institutions, and agencies exist. The social system provides a set of beliefs about what parents must do and how they must do it. The *chronosystem* refers to major changes occurring over time that influence development, such as entering school, leaving home, or getting a job.

Kinds of Social Influence

Community influences on parenting consist of such factors as a neighborhood's safety and the number of services the community provides. You will see these described from time to time throughout the text and particularly in Chapter 16.

We can subdivide society and culture in several useful ways. Culture provides a set of beliefs about (1) the importance of parenting, (2) the roles of extended family members and the community, (3) the goals of parenting, (4) approved methods of discipline, and (5) the roles of children in society. Our diversified culture has many ethnic groups with varying beliefs on these topics.[41]

Ethnicity "refers to an individual's membership in a group sharing a common ancestral heritage based on nationality, language, and culture. Psychological attachment to the group is also a dimension of ethnicity, referred to as ethnic identity."[42] Culture includes shared views of the world, values, and conduct that are passed down from one generation to the next. Each cultural group has its own social system based on some combination of parents' occupations, education, and income. Like culture, social position influences parents' goals and ways to achieve them, as we shall see in the next chapter.

Protective and Risk Factors

Like children and parents, society can also be described in terms of protective and risk factors. Society provides protective factors such as access to good health care, good education, high-quality day care, and wages that will support families. Society presents such risks as neighborhood disorganization, racial injustice, prejudice, poor employment opportunities, poor health care, and poor educational and recreational facilities.[43]

Examining the environment in terms of risk and protective factors can help us understand continuities in children's behavior. In the Rochester longitudinal study, there was a slightly greater consistency in the measures of risk factors for children from ages four to thirteen than there was in measures of individual behavior. Looking at only a child's behavior obscures the consistent influence of the environment. This study shows that the accumulation of risks rather than any one risk alone led to a poor outcome. From the Rochester study, Arnold Sameroff concludes, "Whatever the capabilities provided to a child by individual factors, it is the environment that limits the opportunities for development."[44]

Society's View of Children and Parents

Our society as a whole presents an ambivalent attitude toward children and parents. As individuals, we often write books and give speeches about the value and importance of children and families. The birth of a child is termed a "blessed event." Mother's Day and Father's Day are honored holidays.

At the same time, we also demonstrate a negative view of children and parents. A May 1996 survey of 2,600 adults (nonparents and parents of European-American, African-American, and Hispanic-American backgrounds) reveals that only a small percentage (12 to 17 percent) of U.S. citizens describe children and adolescents as friendly and respectful. A much larger majority (30 to 50 percent) see them as wild and disorderly, undisciplined and uncontrolled in public. These qualities are applied to children of all socioeconomic groups.[45]

Fears concerning the violence of many young teens have led the public to take a more punitive, less understanding attitude toward teen violations. Many teens are being charged and sentenced as adults in the courts. One California six-year-old who beat an infant was charged, as an adult would be, with attempted murder, a charge later reduced to assault and suspended until he can participate in his own defense.[46]

The treatment of this child sharply contrasts with that of two schoolchildren who had murdered a toddler in California twenty-five years earlier.[47] In that case, people saw the children needing help. A gag order on the case kept the names of the children from the public, including the victim's family. Sent to foster care, the children did not acquire a criminal record.

Nonparents and parents alike tend to blame parents for children's and teens' problems.[48] Almost two-thirds of U.S. citizens believe that parents have children before they are ready for the responsibility, and half feel that parents discipline children inappropriately, spoiling their children. Only 22 percent of the general public and 19 percent of parents feel that it is very common for parents to be good role models who teach children right from wrong. While critical of parents, the public does recognize that parents today must play a harder role because the world is more dangerous than before and children face more drugs and alcohol, more sex and violence on TV, and more gangs in school.

Survey responses indicate a deep distrust of government programs to help children and families. This may explain why, as a society, we do far less for children than other Western industrialized countries, which typically provide health care for children, child care for children ages three to five or six, and a child or family allowance based on number of children, not on income.[49] The United States shows a higher rate of poverty among children than most Western nations, and the living conditions of poor children in the United States rank fifteenth among eighteen industrialized countries.[50] Currently, the government is cutting back even those services it does provide children; proposed cuts will likely push another 1–2 million more children into poverty.

The public's attitude about government programs for children, however, demonstrates a definite ambivalence.[51] While people believe government programs aimed at improving the health and economic circumstances of children and families will not solve the problem of parents' failure to teach children appropriate behavior, the public turns to other government programs for solutions. They believe improving schools, increasing community recreational activities for children, and more involvement by volunteer organizations like the YMCA and Boys Scouts will help parents rear their children better. In another survey, 73 percent favor spending more tax dollars on children, and only 10 percent want services to children cut.[52]

The Importance of Society to Children

Judith Harris believes that society, not parents, socializes children to become adult members.[53] Like Sandra Scarr, Harris believes parents' interactions with children and the home environment they provide for them have little lasting effect. While Scarr turns to a child's genetic makeup as the major role in determining development, Harris believes that peer groups and socialization outside the home account for children's becoming functional members of society.

While this is not yet a widely held belief, most people believe that the social system is children's main hope when parents fail to nourish and protect them. This system includes extended family members as well as private, local, state, and federal agencies that provide basic resources such as shelter, food, and clothing. As detailed earlier, society may have to provide alternative living settings in which children without functional parents and relatives can live. Under what conditions and how society intervenes remains a matter of debate.

The Importance of Society to Parents

Chapter 16 details the kinds of support services that individuals and private and public agencies provide for parents to help them rear the next generation. These services, directly or indirectly, improve the quality of children's lives by enhancing parents' abilities to provide for their children.

An absent but critical benefit society can confer on parents is public acknowledgment of what parents contribute to society. Jay Belsky and John Kelly, summarizing observations from Belsky's study of new parents, write:

> As I watched our couples cope with financial concerns and with all the other challenges of the transition, I found myself deeply moved. The quiet dignity and courage of our new fathers and mothers—especially our employed mothers—was inspiring to behold. But as I watched them, I also found myself deeply troubled by how little public acknowledgment, how little public support and gratitude they and other new parents receive for their selflessness and devotion.
>
> In its better moods our society now treats the family with benign neglect; In its darker moods, as a source of parody. None of our participants complained about the lack of public support for their family building, but it affected them—in many cases by making the routine sacrifices of the transition that much harder. It is difficult to sacrifice oneself when the larger society says the overriding purpose in life is devotion to self, not devotion to others. And in a few cases it made those sacrifices too far to go. The rising divorce rate, falling school grades, widespread drug use—all ills that plague the American family today—are complex and have many sources. But I think one major source is that our society no longer honors what I witnessed every day of the Project—the quiet heroism of everyday parenting.[54]

INTERACTIONS AMONG CHILD, PARENT, AND SOCIETY

We have seen that children, parents, and society play their own vital role in the process of parenting, and each is affected by the actions of the other two.

TABLE 1-1
RELATIVE PROBABILITY OF A CHILD'S DEVELOPING COMPETENTLY

Probability of Child Competence	Conditions of the Parental Subsystems*		
	Parent's Personal Resources	Subsystems of Support	Child's Characteristics
High	+	+	+
↑	+	+	−
	+	−	+
	−	+	+
	+	−	−
	−	+	−
↓	−	−	+
Low	−	−	−

*(+) stands for supportive mode; (−) stands for stressful mode.

From J. Belsky, E. Robins, and W. Gamble, "The Determinants of Parental Competence: Toward a Contextual Theory," in *Beyond the Dyad,* ed. Michael Lewis (New York: Plenum, 1984), p. 253. Reprinted by permission.

A further level of complexity exists because the effect of one of the participants may depend on the relationship between the other two participants. Bronfenbrenner and Morris call these *interaction effects.*[55] We need to consider them because they indicate that what may be quite important for understanding a certain group of children and families may have little relevance to other families. For example, low birth weight and birth complications are developmental risk factors when parents are poor and have few resources to deal with these problems. In more advantaged families, however, these factors have little effect on later development, because parents have the emotional and financial resources to handle them.

Jay Belsky and his colleagues provide a model of how children, parents, and society interact to predict the probability of child competence—a combination of abilities reflected in the child's feeling emotionally secure, having the capacity for independent behavior, demonstrating social skills with peers, and showing intellectual achievement at school.[56] (See Table 1-1.) When all factors are supportive, the probability of child competence is high. When two of the three factors are supportive, there is still a good probability of child competence. For example, if a child has a learning disability but the parents' personal resources are strong and the school personnel provide practical help and emotional support, the probability of child competence is high.

Conversely, even when the child has many skills and positive qualities, a lack of social support and parental involvement lowers the probability of child competence. Belsky and his colleagues believe that even when all goes wrong, if the parent brings his or her personal resources to bear on behalf of the child, there is a good chance that the child will develop average competence.

◆

BOX 1-3
TRENDS IN FAMILY VALUES IN THE LAST FIFTY YEARS

Traditional Familism (Mid-1940s to Mid-1960s)

1. Couples with children dominated.
2. Birthrates were high.
3. Divorce rates were low.
4. The degree of marital stability was high.
5. Economic factors affecting the family included a strong economy with a high standard of living and an expanding middle class.
6. Cultural values emphasized conformity to social norms, different gender roles for men and women, and idealization of family life.

Individualism (Mid-1960s to Mid-1980s)

1. The population was more diverse.
2. The single lifestyle was created.
3. Marriage was postponed.
4. The birthrate declined.
5. The divorce rate rose.
6. Economic factors affecting the family included women's increasing participation at work and the idealization of work.
7. Cultural values emphasized self-expression as the source of meaning in life and a decline in definite gender roles for men and women.

New Familism (Mid-1980s to Present)

1. The birthrate increased.
2. The divorce rate leveled off.
3. Economic factors affecting the family included a leveling-off of women's participation in the workforce but a decrease in the number of adequate-paying jobs.
4. Cultural values included a shift from self-expression to greater attachment to family but with less conformity than in the traditional period.

Barbara Dafoe Whitehead, "The New Family Values," *Utne Reader,* May–June 1993.

PARENTING AT A PARTICULAR HISTORICAL TIME

The process of parenting takes place at a particular historical time that influences children, parents, and society. Economic, political, and social events affect how families live and what they value. Box 1-3 summarizes broad social changes in family values over the last fifty years. Table 1-2 shows how these changes have affected children's lives. We discuss briefly what contemporary family life is, given these changes.

TABLE 1-2
COMPARING THE STATE OF CHILDREN

A study of American children shows that their environments have changed in several important areas.

	1960	1990
Children born to unmarried mothers	5%	28%
Children under 3 living with one parent	7%	27%
Children under 3 living with both parents	90%	71%
Children under 3 living with a divorced parent	2%	4%
Children under 18 experiencing the divorce of their parents	less than 1%	almost 50%
Mothers returning to work within one year of a child's birth	17%	53%
Children under 18 living in a one-parent family (approx.)	10%	25%
Infant mortality (deaths before first birthday)	28/1,000	9/1,000
Children under 18 living below the poverty line	27%	21%
Married women, with children under 6 years old, in labor force	18.6%	60%

Carnegie Corporation Report; U.S. Census Bureau; The Urban Institute; National Center for Children in Poverty. Reprinted from Susan Chira, "Study Confirms Worst Fears on U.S. Children," *New York Times,* April 12, 1994. Copyright 1994 by the New York Times Company. Reprinted by permission.

Contemporary Families

Families today are more varied than ever before. Table 1-3 lists the diverse family forms in which today's children live. Because the Census Bureau does not give data in exactly this form, we do not know the percentages of children in the last two categories.

Day care arrangements add to the diversity of children's life experience. In the majority of families, both parents have paid employment. Parents may work split shifts so children are always in the care of a parent, but these families rarely are together as a unit, and parents see little of each other. Other children are cared for by relatives, so that they live in an extended family. Still other children have some form of day care, expanding their contacts with people outside the family.

Although children may be involved with many people, contemporary families are small. Most families with children under age eighteen have only one or two children. Only 10 percent of all families in the United States have three or more children. Some ethnic groups—for example, Hispanic Americans—have a higher percentage (19 percent) of families with three or more children. Even so, their average family size is 3.81, compared with 3.17 for the whole population.[57]

In 1995, 69 percent of children lived in two-parent families and 31 percent lived with a single parent. Most often this single parent is the mother (26 percent), but a

TABLE 1-3
CONTEMPORARY FAMILY LIVING ARRANGEMENTS OF CHILDREN

Family Form	Percentage of Children
Two-parent family	74%*
Intact nuclear (and biological)	61%
Intact nuclear (adoptive)	2%
Intact biological mother/stepfather	11%
Intact biological father/stepmother	1%
Single-parent family	26%*
Mother only	22%*
Father only	4%*
Grandparent(s)	1.7%
Other family (aunts, uncles)	Unknown
Foster care, group homes, residential placements	Unknown

*These statistics differ from those in the text; those here were collected two to three years earlier, though reported in 1995.

From U.S. Bureau of the Census, *Statistical Abstract of the United States: 1995,* 115th ed. (Washington, DC: U.S. Government Printing Office, 1995).

growing number of children are living with single fathers (5 percent).[58] Although single mothers are most often separated or divorced, there are a growing number of single mothers who have never married. This group includes teenage girls who cannot or do not want to marry the father, older women who fear they will not marry in time to have children and so choose to conceive a child anyway, and lesbian couples who have children by artificial insemination.

Ever more Americans are living alone. In 1995, about 25 million people or about 12 percent of the population, live alone.[59]

Social Factors Influencing Contemporary Family Life

Many interacting social factors account for both the changes observed in family life over the past four decades and the great diversity in contemporary lifestyles.

Employment   Women's work participation increased as childbearing took up less time in the adult lifespan and as women became aware of life satisfactions attainable outside the home. Women not only joined the labor force in increasing numbers but also sought higher-status occupations in business and the professions.

When these women married and had children, they stayed at work, and the work force today includes many mothers of young children. Fifty-nine percent of married women with children under a year old and 76 percent of women with children older than six work outside the home.[60] Employment figures for single mothers are even higher. So the mother is no longer full-time caregiver for children, and families have adapted to her transformed role.

Single divorced fathers increasingly are rearing their young children alone.

The decrease in adequate-paying jobs has also impacted families. Because fewer jobs enable a single wage earner to support a family, the incomes from two parents are required; where there is only one parent, poverty is more likely.

Divorce   The high divorce rate has profoundly affected both adults and children. Though parents are divorcing, they are marrying again, blending families in a variety of ways. Children become part of a larger network of stepparents, half-siblings, stepsiblings, and stepgrandparents. Thus, the family unit, as well as the number of role models, has greatly expanded for children.[61]

Ethnic Diversity   Our country's growing ethnic diversity has resulted in the incorporation of different traditions and new values that bring richness to our society. Because of immigration and a higher reproductive rate in some groups, the proportion of various ethnic group members is increasing.

The main ethnic groups in this country are European Americans (74 percent), African Americans (12 percent), Hispanic Americans (10 percent) Asian Americans (3 percent), and American Indians (0.7 percent).[62] Just as European Americans trace their origins to different cultures in Europe, so other ethnic groups consist of several subgroups, each with its own set of values. For example, Hispanic Americans from Mexico differ from Hispanic Americans from Cuba. Asian Americans from Vietnam have different traditions from Asian Americans from China.

We use the term *predominant culture* or *majority culture* to refer to that set of beliefs emphasizing initiative, independence, achievement, individualism, ownership of material goods, mastery, and planning. The ease with which any new ethnic group fits in with the predominant culture depends on many factors—the circumstances of its members' arrival in this country and the similarity of their characteristics, such as skin color, language, and values, to those of the majority culture. Each subgroup will have its own experience with the majority culture.

Nevertheless, reviews of the literature describing the attitudes and values of minority families reveal that they use common strategies, though in differing degrees and combinations, to survive and flourish in the majority culture. Relying on the extended family, becoming bicultural (functioning well in more than one culture and using whatever behavior is adaptive to the situation), developing role flexibility, and drawing strength from ancestral or spiritual worldviews are ways people adapt traditions to a majority culture that stresses competitive individualism.[63]

Though the majority culture sometimes equates differences in family life with deficiencies, in 1976 Diana Baumrind pointed out in a discussion of cultural variations in social competence that the continued survival of African-American and Hispanic-American families in our highly industrialized society is "proof of their outstanding and durable competence."[64] As we move toward a new century, we do not know what strategies will be most adaptive. We may need different values and find ourselves drawing on the strengths of our minority cultures—for example, by incorporating the more cooperative approaches these groups favor.

As we shall see when we examine resources and strengths for individuals in times of trouble, the values of the extended family, role flexibility, and a spiritual orientation all promote resilience in people. Recent research suggests that the most understanding and perceptive parents are those who go through the process of integrating two cultures into a meaningful whole. For instance, Mexican-American mothers attached equally to their Mexican heritage and to U.S. culture have a broader, more understanding view of their children's development than do mothers attached to only one culture.[65]

Poverty   Poverty affects children more than any other age group in U.S. society and puts them at risk for chronic problems such as malnutrition, poor health, and school failure. In 1994, 12 percent of Americans over sixty-five lived below the poverty level. The comparable figure for the entire population was 14.5 percent, but 21 percent of children under eighteen were living below the poverty level—more than one in five children in our society.[66] The poverty rate in 1994 was higher for children of certain ethnic groups. For white children it was 16 percent, but for African-American children it was 43 percent, and for Hispanic-American children 41 percent.[67]

Even more disturbing are figures showing that African-American children experience more persistent poverty than any other group. Longitudinal data from 1968 to 1982 reveal that 24 percent of these children were poor for at least ten years of the fifteen-year period, and 5 percent were poor the entire time. Less than 1 percent of non-African-American children were poor for ten years, and none were poor for fifteen years.[68]

Poverty has increased with the rise in single-parent households. In 1993, the median family income for married couples with children under eighteen was $45,548, and for single female heads of household, $13,472. For single male householders, the median income was $22,348.[69] Poverty is also related to other economic changes such as the decline in higher-paying manufacturing jobs, the rise in lower-paying service jobs, and changing governmental policies that have taxed low-income families more and provided fewer support programs.

Economic hardship affects parenting. Vonnie McLoyd has developed a model of how poverty affects parents and, in turn, children.[70] Rand Conger and his colleagues have demonstrated a similar process in low-income rural families.[71]

Financial pressures create day-to-day problems and cause parents to experience increased irritability, depression, and demoralization. McLoyd found that the pressures followed the poverty, not vice versa. Parents under stress are less likely to support each other, are more irritable with children, and give them less affection. As a result, children suffer more emotional problems. Conger and his associates found that both parents' reactions had an impact on children's behavior.

Violence   Violence has become a matter of concern as well. Recent research indicates that fewer children than in the past die from accidental injuries, but increasing numbers die from violent causes.[72] Among children under age nineteen, fatal accidents like drowning dropped 39 percent from 1978 to 1991, but deaths due to nonaccidental injuries rose by 47 percent. Homicide increased 67 percent, and suicide rose 17 percent.

In 1985, approximately 3,000 children and adolescents died from firearms. In 1989, this figure rose to over 4,000, and in 1991, to over 5,000 children and adolescents.[73] Because of this violence, many children live in fear that this may happen to them. In a 1994 poll of high school students, 19 percent of European Americans and 37 percent of African Americans identified violence as their biggest concern in school.[74]

Substance Abuse   Substance abuse has increased dramatically in the United States, with dire consequences for children.[75] In 1960, there were fewer than 30,000 drug arrests, but in the thirty years since then, the number of annual arrests has grown to more than a million. Beginning in 1989, incarcerations for drug offenses have exceeded those for violent crimes, and most violent crimes involve substance abuse as well. Although drug arrests do not provide a clear indicator of the amount of substance abuse in this country, such figures do highlight the phenomenal increase in a form of behavior associated with physical and psychological problems for children.

Although systematic research has not yet detailed the ways various forms of substance abuse affect specific parent-child interactions, we can make some general observations on how substance abuse affects children. However, it is not always clear whether the effects are the result of the substance abuse itself or are due to preexisting problems on the part of the parents that led to the substance abuse.[76]

Substance abuse is associated with pregnancy and birth complications. Pregnant women who abuse substances are less likely to be in good health and less likely to seek prenatal care, compounding potential problems with pregnancy and delivery.

Their babies may be born prematurely and be small for their gestational age. Substance use during pregnancy affects children's prenatal development directly and can lead to fetal damage and to ongoing health problems after birth.[77]

Infants born to heroin and morphine addicts are born addicted to these substances, further complicating the process of nurturing these children. Because these children have not yet been followed through adolescence to adulthood, definitive answers are not available on the long-term consequences of mothers' drug use. But there are indications that these children are more likely to have impairments in arousal, activity level, attention modulation, and motor and cognitive development. The kind and severity of impairment will depend on the type, amount, and timing of the substance abuse during pregnancy.[78]

Fetal alcohol syndrome (FAS) serves as an example of the kind of damage a substance, even a legal one, can do. FAS is a condition that applies to a group of babies who are the children of alcoholic mothers. These babies are stunted in growth and development and are hyperactive. Their faces may be deformed, with asymmetrical features, low-set eyes, and small ears, and their intellectual growth is retarded. Worst of all, the damage is not reversible. When FAS was first identified, experts believed that a steady, daily consumption of 3–6 ounces of alcohol by the mother was necessary to produce abnormalities. But more recent research suggests that smaller doses have been related to such problems as low birth weight, sucking difficulties, and developmental delays.

Substance abuse not only produces long-lasting physical and intellectual impairments in children but also puts them at risk for other problems.[79] Parents who abuse substances are more prone to violence—toward both adults and children. They are more likely to physically or sexually abuse, neglect, or abandon their children. Parents' substance use may make it necessary for children to live with other relatives or out of the home, thus weakening the bond between parent and child.

Summary   The social changes we have just discussed make the job of raising the next generation more difficult than before. First, parents have less time with children. Both parents frequently work, and many parents do not live with their children, as a result of separation or divorce. Second, many parents also face stress from new work and family responsibilities, poverty, and community violence. These cause them to be more worried and less able to be accepting and understanding of children than were parents in the past.

Critics blame such problems on the decline of the nuclear family, women's increasing participation in the labor force, day care, divorce, and poverty. But Arlene Skolnick, the author of *Embattled Paradise: The American Family in an Age of Uncertainty,* argues that economic factors are the major sources of children's difficulties.[80] These are controllable when society views the family as fragile and provides support, as European countries do, in the form of allowances for children and for housing and benefits for working parents such as parental leave, child care, and flexible work schedules. Some programs exist that support families, teach new skills, and provide hope that problems are solvable, but their numbers are decreasing as a result of recent congressional action.

FIGURE 1-1
THE PROCESS OF PARENTING IN A PARTICULAR HISTORICAL TIME

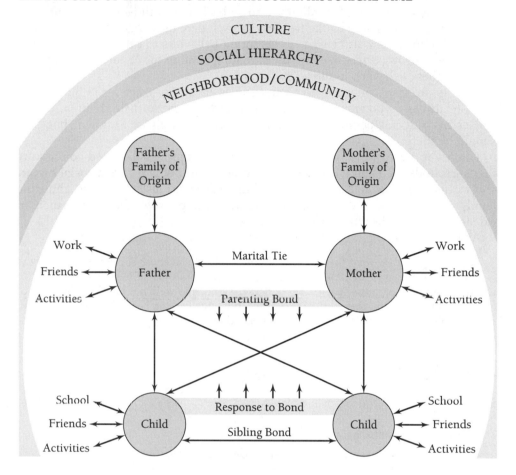

PARTNERSHIP FOR CHILDREN

We have discussed forces that affect social organization, parents, and, in turn, children. Coping with all the changes and their many effects on the process of parenting requires that all members of society work together to promote the well-being of the next generation.

Figure 1-1 presents a schematic diagram summarizing the relationships of the participants in the process of parenting, the activities and institutions and the social, cultural, and historical factors that influence these relationships. At the heart of the process are the mother and father, who are usually married to each other. They form a parenting bond that continues even if the marital tie dissolves and each marries someone else. Sometimes, a single parent has no ties to another partner either because the child was adopted or there was a donor involved.

Children in families develop what is called *sibling bond*. When a marriage dissolves, the relationship or bond between siblings may provide the most continuous, steady family relationship for children who go back and forth between parents.

As shown in the figure by the two-way arrows, parents form direct relationships with each child. They also engage in parenting behaviors to care for their child—the one-way arrows extending from the parenting bond to the children. Children respond to these behaviors in turn.

Parents are also connected to their families of origin—parents, siblings, and other relatives—who are in turn connected to them and to their children. (Space and clarity did not permit arrows from families of origin to children, but they should be there.)

Parents relate to work, friends, and activities in the neighborhood-community that surrounds the family. The neighborhood/community is part of a social hierarchy within a specific cultural context within a particular historical time. Thus, the family is nested in several social layers that provide support for the family which, in essence, serves as the vital nucleus of society.

As David Hamburg writes, programs that provide basic support to children

> have to be seen for what they are—a responsibility of the entire society. Not just of the federal government, but of other levels of government; not just of business, but of labor; not just of light-skinned peoples, but of darker-skinned as well; not jut of the rich, but of the middle-class and the poor. We are all in this huge leaking boat together. We will all have to pay and reason and care and work together.[81]

MAIN POINTS

Parenting is

- guiding, nourishing, and protecting new life
- providing basic resources, love, attention and values

The parent's role traditionally has been to

- develop the child's moral nature and good habits
- gratify the child's needs and facilitate development
- permit genetic predisposition to develop

The process of parenting involves

- ongoing interaction among children, parents, and society
- children having their own needs and temperaments and meeting important needs of parents and society
- parents having rights and responsibilities to rear children, meeting children's and society's needs
- society as a source of support or stress for children and parents
- risks and protective factors within all three participants

- now are smaller and more varied in composition
- involve many important figures outside the home

Social changes affecting the family setting include

- later marriage and smaller families
- women's increasing commitment to work
- a rise of divorce and remarriage
- a rise in the ethnic population
- a rise in poverty, violence, and substance abuse

Partnership for children involves

- parents and communities working together to help children develop
- a role for public and private agencies

EXERCISES

1. From the year you were born, trace the social influences acting on your parents as they raised you. For example, for the 1980s, influences might have been the high rate of women's participation in the workforce, the high rate of divorce and remarriage, the drop in skilled-labor jobs, and the instability of jobs in corporate America. Show the effects of social change on your daily life and the ways your parents cared for you—for example, mother's working resulting in specific day care, divorce leading to your being in two homes, remarriage introducing more adults into your life, increased violence causing greater restrictiveness.

2. Based on the material in this chapter, write a job description for a parent. You may want to revise the job description as you read future chapters.

3. Suppose that parents had to obtain a license in order to have a child, much as they do to get married or drive a car. What would you require for such a license?

4. Read the newspaper for one week and cut out all the articles of interest to parents, including news and feature articles, and describe what these articles tell you about parenting experience in the 1990s. The articles might focus on solving certain kinds of behavioral problems or providing opportunities for children's optimal development (certain play or educational activities). Or they might consider laws relating to parents' employment benefits and to the rights of parents and children in courts when parents divorce or must pay penalties because of children's behavior.

5. In California, a surrogate mother petitioned the court for the baby she bore even though the child was not genetically related to her. Who are the parents of the child—the genetic parents or the parent who carried the child in utero?

ADDITIONAL READINGS

Hamburg, David A. *Today's Children*. New York: Times Books, 1992.

Harris, Judith Rich. *The Nurture Assumption*. New York: The Free Press, 1998.

Hewlett, Sylvia Ann, and West, Cornell. *The War Against Parents*. Boston: Houghton Mifflin, 1998.

Konner, Melvin. *Childhood: A Multicultural View*. Boston: Little, Brown, 1991.

Louv, Richard. *Childhood's Future*. New York: Doubleday, 1991.

Skolnick, Arlene. *Embattled Paradise: The American Family in an Age of Uncertainty*. New York: Basic Books, 1991.

ENCOURAGING GROWTH

C H A P T E R   2

Parents face the daunting responsibility of promoting children's healthy growth. It's a big job — to provide the loving care and the opportunities that will lead the child to competence and self-esteem — and there is no job description. What are the duties? Will they come naturally or are they learned? If learned, where do the ideas come from? What makes us effective parents? If parents cause change in children, do children cause change in parents. Because parents go through their own stages while their children develop, encouraging healthy growth is a difficult and ever-changing parental task.

Parents create the environment in which children develop. In this chapter, we look at development in broad terms — first in terms of psychological development over the lifespan and then in terms of the development of specific competencies. This information provides a general framework for understanding the more specific parent-child interactions of given age periods presented later in the book. This chapter also presents key points about children's development and about the sources of parents' beliefs about parenting. Let's turn now to Erikson's lifespan scheme of psychological development, which describes both children's and parents' stages of growth.

EIGHT STAGES OF GROWTH

Erik Erikson, a Freudian psychoanalyst with a strong interest in cross-cultural research and the social and cultural determiners of personality, has created a scheme for understanding lifespan psychological development based on his clinical experiences with patients, insights from his longitudinal research with healthy children, and his cross-cultural research.[1]

Erikson describes growth as a series of eight stages, as shown in Figure 2-1. In each stage, the individual has specific physical and psychological needs. Each stage has a developmental crisis that must be met and resolved. People have positive and negative experiences in satisfying needs, and both kinds of experiences are important for optimal development. If we have only positive gratifications, we never learn

FIGURE 2-1
ERIKSON'S EIGHT STAGES OF GROWTH

1.	2.	3.	4.	5.	6.	7.	8.
							Integrity vs. Despair (Wisdom)
						Generativity vs. Stagnation (Care)	
					Intimacy vs. Isolation (Love)		
				Identity vs. Identity diffusion (Fidelity)			
			Industry vs. Inferiority (Competence)				
		Initiative vs. Guilt (Pupose)					
	Autonomy vs. Shame, doubt (Will)						
Trust vs. Mistrust (Hope)							
1. 0–1	2. 1–3	3. 3–5	4. 5–12	5. 12–19	6. 19–	7.	8.

Years

Adapted from Erik H. Erikson, *Childhood and Society,* 2d ed. Copyright 1950, © 1963 by W. W. Norton & Co., Inc., renewed © 1978, 1991 by Erik H. Erikson. Reprinted by permission of W. W. Norton & Company, Inc.

how to cope with difficulties. However, for healthy growth, the balance should favor the positive side. When this occurs, a strength or virtue develops.[2]

Erikson does not believe that we solve each crisis once and for all. Later experiences can change earlier resolutions, for better or for worse. For example, stress during adulthood can disrupt mature ways of coping, so that for a brief period the individual may seem immature. Positive experiences in adulthood can reverse mistrust or doubt developed in childhood.

Let's look at each of the stages in Figure 2-1. In the first year of life (stage 1), when caregiving is sensitive and reliable and the balance of experience is positive, children develop a sense of trust and a feeling of hope about life. In the toddler years (stage 2), when children receive opportunities and encouragement for self-direction, they develop a sense of autonomy, the ability to act independently, and strength of will—the ability to make free choices and to act with self-control.

In the preschool years (stage 3), children acquire more skills and initiate more complex activity. When the sum of experiences is positive, they develop a sense of purpose, the ability to set and pursue goals, free of fears of failure, punishment, or criticism. In the elementary school years (stage 4), children attend school and are industrious and productive. If experiences of success and accomplishment outweigh experiences of frustration and inferiority, children develop a sense of competence, the feeling that they can apply their skills to accomplish goals.

In adolescence (stage 5), teens incorporate sexuality into their evolving sense of self and develop an identity, a sense of sameness and continuity of self. Erikson emphasizes that we incorporate social values in our individual identities. For example, we all incorporate, in our own ways, society's views of what men are, what women are, what members of our ethnic group and religion are.

Individuals need to have their identities validated and confirmed by their parents and society. If teenagers cannot integrate previous life experiences with their emerging capacities and obtain confirmation from others that they are who they think they are, role confusion results. They remain uncertain of who they are and where they are heading. When life events and family members have not been supportive, an individual may develop a negative identity. He or she may become a delinquent, a dropout, a person who feels unable to do anything positive. When the balance of the experiences falls on the positive side and a sense of identity is formed, the virtue that develops is fidelity—what Erikson describes as faithfulness and loyalty to one's choices, whether they be persons, goals, or ideals.

The first stage of adulthood (stage 6) is the establishment of intimate personal ties. Intimate relationships involve the mutuality and surrender of the self to the other person and the relationship. The ability to be close to other people leads to the virtue of love—sharing of identities between friends and partners. This is a freely chosen, active love and involves transferring the love experienced in the developing years of childhood to adult relationships actively sought by and mutually important to the two partners.

The second stage of adulthood (stage 7) is the initiation of generativity, or the creation of new life. In the past, women have most often experienced this in the family setting, in creating home and children; men have done so in their work, in creating new products and new ideas. However, parenting and work now are significant activities for both sexes. The virtue that develops in this period is care—concern for and attention to what has been created, even if this requires sacrifice.

In the final stage of life (stage 8), the focus returns to the individual and the development of a sense of ego integrity. People must come to terms with their lives and be satisfied with who and what they are and what they have done. The virtue or strength that develops during this period is wisdom, a deep understanding of life that is enriched by coming to terms with the prospect of one's own death. Erikson points out that children will be able to face life if elders can face death.

Examining the ego qualities and the virtues of each stage, we can see that Erikson describes the growth of active, adaptive individuals who are independent, giving, and concerned with other people and the world around them. Erikson believed that children grow best when they experience reliable and trustworthy caregiving, opportunities for self-directed activity, and parental and social confirmation that what they make and do is valuable. In Erikson's scheme of development, parenting is important to both the child who receives it and the parent who gives it.

THE GROWTH OF COMPETENCIES

Parents have three broad goals in rearing children: (1) ensuring the physical health and survival of the child, (2) preparing the child to become an economically self-sustaining adult, and (3) encouraging positive personal and social behaviors — for example, psychological adjustment, intellectual competence, and social relations with friends.[3]

The desire to protect the child from harm and ensure survival is the strongest long-term goal for parents, and perhaps the clearest.[4] In socializing children to be economically productive and socially responsible members of society, however, parents seek a broad array of competencies. The priority given to competencies depends on parents' social and ethnic backgrounds. For example, parents in the majority culture in U.S. society emphasize goals of academic achievement and cognitive skills, whereas several minority cultures emphasize goals of social skills, harmony, sharing, and cooperation within the extended family.

Parents typically encourage the development of several forms of competence in their children: self-esteem and physical, intellectual, emotional, social, and moral competence. Before examining how parents encourage competencies, we need to be aware of three key points.

First, as we saw in Chapter 1, parenting is a process influenced by the contributions of parent, child, and society. Here, we focus on what parents do to encourage growth in a variety of areas. In later sections, we discuss children's contributions and the interaction between parent and child.

Second, as we also saw, parents exert both direct and indirect influences on children.[5] In this chapter, we shall discuss these influences more fully. For example, indirect influences tend to be highly similar for all the competencies.[6] Parents who form secure attachments with children; who provide a home atmosphere free of unresolved conflict, intense anger, or severe stress; who use reasoning and positive rewards to increase valued behaviors; and who avoid physical and harsh discipline indirectly encourage all forms of competent behavior.

Third, we can view the development of competencies as a complex interaction of constitutional factors within children and environmental forces in their daily lives.[7] Genes provide one major source of constitutional differences within the child. Events during pregnancy, labor, and delivery can also result in physical or physiological characteristics that influence development. Environmental forces include characteristics of the parents and other caregivers as well as of the larger social system.

In Chapter 1, we touched on views insisting that one factor — either constitutional or environmental — is more important than the other. Here and throughout the book, I shall emphasize the view many developmentalists espouse — namely, that the interaction of these two factors is complex and may differ depending on the behavior of in-

Because children observe, imitate, and model the behavior of their parents, parents have the opportunity to exert both positive and negative influences over their children.

terest.[8] Thus, in understanding any particular behavior, the question centers on how these two factors interact to affect jointly the development of a specific behavior.

Recent Changes in Research Emphases

New research is changing how we view the parent-child relationship. As we saw in Chapter 1, Urie Bronfenbrenner has described a network of forces surrounding the parent-child interaction. New research is telling us more about both what goes on within the child and the complex environmental forces that interact with the child.

Advances in Neuroscience   Recent studies in neuroscience and brain development have led to an increased concern about the environmental stimulation children receive.[9] We used to think that genes determine how the brain develops, and brain development determines how we interact with the world. Though some scientists considered the effects of nutrition and other environmental events on brain development during pregnancy, people generally thought that apart from extreme circumstances, genetic determiners account for brain development.

Recent advances in research tools, such as imaging techniques, have taught us, however, that much supposedly genetically determined brain development actually involved input from the environment. Beginning with conception, environmental factors such as nutrition, physical surroundings, care, and stimulation influence "how the intricate circuitry of the human is 'wired.' " [10] After birth, environmental input and stimulation establish and strengthen connections among brain cells, thus shaping the architecture of the brain. The absence of such stimulation means such connections may not be made. While some researchers emphasize the importance of stimulation in the first three years of life, William Greenough[11] believes, on the basis of his and others' works, that environmental stimulation increases brain development through adolescence and most likely throughout life.

One neuroscientist summarizes the importance of experience for brain development as follows:

> The amazing capacity of the human brain to develop in a "use-dependent" fashion, growing, organizing, and functioning in response to developmental experience, means that the major modifier of all human behavior is experience. . . . Indeed, it is the primary caretaking relationships of infancy and childhood that determine the core neurobiological organization of the human individual, thereby allowing this incredible social specialization. Early life experience determines core neurobiology.[12]

Insights from Anthropology and Cultural Psychology   A second major advance in our understanding of how competencies grow comes from increased research on how parents' cultural values and beliefs shape both the kinds of competencies they seek to promote in their children and how they go about promoting them. Formerly, much research on the development of competencies focused on European-American, middle-class families; researchers have had to be cautious in generalizing the results of these studies to all ethnic groups. Diana Baumrind reports, for example, that the authoritarian parenting style linked with withdrawn, inhibited behavior in European-American, middle-class girls led to competent, mature behavior in her small sample of African-American girls. In African-American culture, strict control seemed to be interpreted as a sign of caring and involvement rather than a sign of the cold rejection it seems to be in European-American culture.[13]

Interpreting research on ethnic issues can be tricky, because in too many instances differences attributed to ethnic values actually stem from educational or social differences. Luis Laosa found that ethnic differences between Mexican-American and European-American mothers' helping children to make a toy disappeared when he used as subjects groups of mothers with equal amounts of schooling.[14]

Our increasing desire to understand our diverse ethnic population and the influences of cultural patterns on parenting has led to a growing body of knowledge on the many, often subtle, ways that culture influences parenting. You will see more on this later in this chapter and throughout the book.

Focus on Regulatory Processes   In the past, research on regulation centered on such topics as parental control and discipline, children's resistance to temptation, and delay of gratification.[15] More recently, studies in this area emphasize different kinds of regulatory processes: (1) the infant's ability to soothe and regulate the physiological system, (2) the ability to shift and control attention, (3) the control of the arousal and expression of feelings, (4) the control of behavior, (5) the optimal conditions for developing self-regulation, and (6) the relationship of temperamental qualities to the capacity for self-regulation. Several of the competencies discussed in this chapter and throughout the text depend on some form of regulation, such as regulation of one's own feelings, of behavior to meet moral standards, or of social relationships. We can thus see how certain competencies relate to each other in terms of the regulation that underlies them.

The Unit of Study   Past research often focused on the individual. In the area of parenting, this usually meant the parents—what they did to, for, or with children. Then, attention shifted to the child's influence on the parent. Currently, research centers on the relationship, activity, or interaction as the unit.[16] This difference may seem small at first, but it is quite significant. The interaction of two or more individuals forms a unit that one cannot reduce to separate individuals; participation in a joint activity transforms both partners. So, whenever I speak of shared meaning created between parent and child, intersubjectivity or shared state, or co-regulation or mutual regulation, I mean to imply that two individuals create a state or relationship that includes them both and forms a unit.

We turn now to parents' contributions to particular forms of competence. In later chapters, we shall look in greater detail at the parent-child interactions of specific age periods.

Physical Competence

Physical competence has two aspects—physical health/well-being and motor competence. In their direct role, parents model healthy behavior in their lives—eating nutritious meals, exercising, avoiding harmful habits like smoking and excessive alcohol consumption, and getting preventive health care in the form of routine checkups. They also teach healthy behaviors—dental hygiene, proper diet, and so on. Further, they provide resources for healthy behavior, making sure their children get checkups, immunizations, and dental care.[17]

In addition to ensuring physical health, parents provide experiences so children develop motor competence and motor skills. Early psychologists developed norms concerning the timely appearance of various motor skills such as crawling and walking. They believed these skills developed automatically; as the brain matured and the proper connections formed among brain cells, the skills appeared.[18]

However, exciting new work in the area suggests that motor competence develops as a result of real-life experience rather than maturation of inborn abilities.[19] Infants and children integrate sensory perceptions and motor movements and form a multisensory map of experience. From their experience, they select and retain movements that help them accomplish their goals. For example, young infants who seek an

THE JOYS OF BEING A PARENT

"It has changed my priorities, my perspective. I am much more protective. If I see someone driving like an idiot, I get much more upset. I feel more like a regular person, more grown up." FATHER OF TODDLER

"Now I'm officially grown up. It's kind of funny because I am a forty-year-old person who is just feeling grown up. For me, it's being less caught up in myself, more unselfish, I don't do everything I want to do all the time, and that's changing and it's okay. I used to resent that. I am less self-centered, less concerned with myself and how I'm doing, how I'm feeling, what's up. Now I am thinking more about him. For both my husband and me, I don't know whether this is going to change, but we are more oriented toward the future." MOTHER OF TODDLER

"My own personal sense of the meaningfulness of life, in all aspects, has really gone through a dramatic change. It's just been so gratifying and meaningful and important to have this other little life, in a sense, in my hands, to be responsible for it." MOTHER OF TODDLER

"It has changed my sense of the past. I appreciate more of what my parents must have gone through for me. No matter what their problems or shortcomings, gee, they had to do all this for me." FATHER OF TODDLER

"It's that overused word, *maturity*. It happened for both of us, my husband and me. We look back on how our lives were before our son and afterwards. Our whole lives were what we wanted every hour of every day. Along came the baby and, by choice, there was a reverse, almost 100 percent. We don't get to go out like we used to. It seems like an agony sometimes, but we are growing as a couple and as a family. It's very enriching." MOTHER OF TODDLER

object across a room use whatever movements—rolling, pulling themselves, crawling, crabbing, walking—are available to them depending on their size and strength. Successful movement patterns that achieve goals are strengthened and, with use, lead to further refinements.

Successful motor patterns lead to further exploration and change in a process of repeated cycles of perception, action, selection, and retention of successful movements. Perception and action, not inborn genetic structure, lead to motor competence.

Neuroscientists now hypothesize that the brain provides a "rough palette" for human experience but that experience determines the selection and retention of certain neural connections.[20] The brain makes certain behaviors possible, but the actual connections among brain cells are made and strengthened by experience.

This gives both the environment and caregivers a more important role in promoting motor competence than was once believed. They provide opportunities for experience in the world that leads to neural change and motor competence. Some may question the importance of motor abilities, but motor competence, particularly in the early years, fosters cognitive and social development. Increasingly skilled

"It has changed me for the better. It matured me, really at the core. I am much more responsible because I want to be a good example for them, provide stability for them. It has helped me to see into myself. I recall things I did as a child, and I understand better what was happening then. It has changed the kinds of things I think of as fun." FATHER OF ELEMENTARY SCHOOL CHILD AND EARLY ADOLESCENT

"I wish I could say it has made me more patient, but it has intensified my emotions; and if something really difficult has happened, as it did today when she destroyed something I took a lot of time to make for her, because she didn't follow a simple rule, then I am amazed at how furious I feel. Yet a little while later, the great love I have for her made forgiveness easy, and I sat down and started to make the whole thing over. So now I have extremes of feeling from great love to great anger."
MOTHER OF ELEMENTARY SCHOOL CHILD AND EARLY ADOLESCENT

"Having children makes you more patient, more humble, better able to roll with the punches because life is not so black and white. You can't just base your life on platitudes. You have the experience of having things go not the way you would have them go, having your children do things you would not have them do; and you have to roll with that. You learn it; it either kills you or you go on, and you have a different view of life. You become more patient and, I think, more kind."
MOTHER OF EARLY AND LATE ADOLESCENTS

"I want to be a good father so it makes me evaluate what I do and say; I look at mistakes as you would in any important and intense relationship, so it certainly makes me more self-examining and more aware of myself and how I am being experienced by the other person. It is also a challenge to be tolerant when I don't feel very tolerant. So in developing certain interpersonal skills, I think being a parent has helped me to become a better person." FATHER OF ELEMENTARY SCHOOL CHILD

movements enable infants and children to explore their world in greater depth. They share their discoveries with others who name them, adding to their knowledge. Exploration also triggers social interactions. With greater ability to move, infants and toddlers can initiate social interactions with parents. Older children expand their social world as they move around even more independently, and they can enjoy social interactions centered on games and sports.

As yet, little research has examined exactly how the environment and caregivers can intervene to promote motor competence. We have learned, though, that interventions will be most successful when behaviors are in transition and the child "has sufficient flexibility to explore and select new solutions."[21]

Intellectual Competence

Just as motor competence develops out of repeated cycles of perception, action, selection, and retention, so cognitive development occurs. Jean Piaget, the Swiss psychologist, deepened our understanding of how children's minds grow and develop when he emphasized the importance of the child's active construction of knowledge.[22] Intellectual competence is a dynamic process in which the child explores the world, takes in information, and organizes it into internal structures called *schemes*. The process of taking in and organizing information is termed *assimilation*.

As children obtain new information, they find their internal schemes inadequate and modify them to account for the new information. The process of changing internal schemes to incorporate new facts is called *accommodation*.

Intellectual growth is a constant interplay of taking in new information (assimilation) and modifying it (accommodation) to achieve balance or equilibrium between the individual's structure of the world and the world itself. *Equilibration* is the active process by which the individual achieves this effective balance.

Piaget believes that intellectual growth is not just a matter of adding more and more refined schemes. Growth also results from new ways of responding to experience and organizing it. Piaget describes intellectual growth in terms of four major periods that include substages. In the first two years, the *sensorimotor stage,* perceptions and motor activity are the sources of knowledge, and schemes consist of action patterns. In the *preconceptual period,* from two to seven years of age, symbols such as language and imitative play lead to knowledge. The child reasons intuitively but not logically. In the period of *concrete operations,* from seven to about eleven years of age, the child structures knowledge symbolically and logically but is limited to concrete objects and events that are seen and manipulable. In the last stage, the period of *formal operations,* from age twelve through adulthood, the individual reasons logically and can go beyond what is present to consider hypothetical and abstract situations.

While Piaget emphasizes individual action and maturing capacities, the Russian psychologist Lev Vygotsky, born in the same year as Piaget, emphasizes the social aspect of intellectual growth.[23] He believes that knowledge, thought, and mental processes such as memory and attention all rest on social interactions.

Whatever children learn they first experience at the social level in a social interaction with someone and then internalize it at the individual psychological level. For example, an infant watches how an adult shakes a rattle or plays with a toy and then carries out the same action. Later, the child independently performs the activity.

Social interactions rest on the organization of the individual's culture and society. Every culture has a view of the world and the way to solve problems. Language, writing, art, and methods of problem solving all reflect this social worldview. Adults use these societal forms in interacting with children, and children internalize them.

Social interaction not only conveys societal knowledge of the world but also plays an important role in stimulating children to learn that knowledge. Vygotsky describes a unique concept called "the zone of proximal development." There is a range of actions a child can perform alone, demonstrating a capacity that is clearly internal. This is what most of us would consider the child's level of ability. But Vygotsky points out that the child's behavior in this area can improve. When a more experienced person guides or prompts the child with questions, hints, or demonstrations, the child can respond at a more mature level not achieved when the child acts alone. So, the child has potential that emerges in social interaction. For example, a child learning how to talk may use a particular number of words spontaneously. That would be the child's verbal ability. A mother, however, might increase the number of words by prompting the child to remember what she called an item when she used it or by waiting for the child to add an action to an object he just identified, saying, "The doggie?" and waiting for "runs" or "goes bow-wow."

This zone of behavior, extending from what the child can do alone to what the child has the potential to do when guided, is the zone of proximal development. Vygotsky's interest goes beyond what the child can do to what the child's learning potential is. Teaching has the greatest impact, he believes, when it is directed to the child's potential at the high end of the zone of proximal development. The experienced person helps the child do alone what he or she can initially do only with guidance.

Like Piaget, Vygotsky believes that the child is an active learner, but he focuses on the strategies children use to become proficient and to learn more efficiently. Teaching encourages children to develop and use strategies to learn a task. For example, children can use strategies to remember material, and part of teaching involves helping them develop and use these strategies.

Language plays a significant role in mental development. Language develops from social interaction and contact and initially is a means of influencing others. Adults talk to children, influencing their reactions or behavior. Children initially guide their own behavior with external language similar to that already heard. They talk to themselves as others have and guide their behavior with their speech. Many a young toddler will say "No, no" to herself as a way of stopping forbidden action, with varying degrees of success. As the child matures, the speech that guides behavior becomes internal or inner speech. Such inner speech becomes thought in the older child.

The theories of Piaget and Vygotsky suggest that parents' role is (1) to provide opportunities for independent exploration and action in the world and (2) to interact with children, serving as a model and guide in the world, helping them reach their potential.

Robert Sternberg and Wendy Williams describe how parents can stimulate children's intellectual growth.[24] In their view, intellectual competence rests on children's capacity for independent action and hard work. Children select areas to pursue, actively seek out information by asking questions, take risks, and assume responsibility for successes and failures. Parents are supportive as they encourage children to work hard, delay gratification, and set desired goals without using self-limiting phrases like "I can't." Sternberg and Williams believe that the most important lesson parents teach is that children can achieve their goals if they are willing to work long and hard. In this process, parents serve both as a coach giving guidance and a fan giving support.

Emotional Competence

In his best-selling book *Emotional Intelligence,* Daniel Goleman argues that learning to modulate and control the arousal and expression of feelings is now more important to both individuals and society than is intellectual competence.[25] He points to the relationship between the capacity to deal with emotional feelings and success at work and in relationships with families and friends. He expresses concern at the increase in personal psychological problems like depression, eating disorders, and anxiety attacks that ensue when individuals cannot effectively modulate their feelings and the effect of these problems on work and family life. Of equal importance is the cost to society. Poorly controlled individuals can react in aggressive and destructive ways that harm others as well as themselves.

Psychologists use the term *emotional regulation* to refer to "the ability to respond to the ongoing demands of experience with the range of emotions in a manner that is socially tolerable and sufficiently flexible to permit spontaneous reactions as well as the ability to delay spontaneous reactions as needed."[26] Researchers agree with Goleman that the capacity to regulate the arousal and expression of feelings underlies effectiveness in close relationships, in cognitive tasks requiring attention and the controlled pursuit of long-term goals, in the management of stressful experiences, and in the ongoing maintenance of a positive mood.[27]

In addition, emotional regulation underlies moral development. Robert Emde and his colleagues believe that the moral self, present in the child by age three, grows out of reciprocal relations with parents in the first year of life.[28] Responsive caregivers appropriately regulate the child's feelings — encouraging interest in the surrounding world, maintaining positive affect, and soothing the child when upset. These interactions give children a sense of how things happen in the world, of how people interact with one another. The child internalizes these routines and rules, which then guide his or her behavior.

Parents play a crucial role in directly helping children develop emotional regulation. First, research suggests that parents' physical presence serves as an external regulator of young children's physiological functioning.[29] When a caregiver leaves, physically or emotionally, one can see changes in children's physiological functioning, in their eating and sleeping patterns, in their play patterns, and in their moods. These changes last until the parent returns. Similar responses to parents' absence have been observed in the young of many other species as well.[30]

Second, parents' sensitive, accepting, and responsive caregiving minimizes the arousal of negative affect, helps infants shift from negative or neutral moods to positive and engaged ones, and prevents children from being overwhelmed by intense feelings.[31]

Third, parents provide, and then encourage children to develop, strategies for controlling their feelings once aroused. They model ways to handle frustration and anger as well as love and caring. As children develop their own strategies, parents provide support and encouragement in refining the strategies. In subsequent chapters, I describe precisely how they do this.

Conversely, when parents expose children to atypical levels of stress, they put them at risk for being overwhelmed by feelings they cannot control.[32] Conflict in the home, extreme and abusive discipline, parents' severe psychological problems — all present children with stress that not only disorganizes their behavior but requires stronger coping skills even as they have fewer resources.

Recent evidence suggests that these positive early parent-child interactions are critical for still another reason. In promoting the child's emotional regulation, parents also promote the development of certain connections in the frontal area of the brain that, in turn, increase the capacity for emotional control. So these early experiences have a powerful impact on later emotional control.[33]

TABLE 2-1
DOMAINS OF THE SELF-CONCEPT AT EACH PERIOD OF THE LIFESPAN

Early Childhood	Middle/Late Childhood	Adolescence	College	Adult
Cognitive competence	Scholastic competence	Scholastic competence	Scholastic competence	
			Intellectual ability	Intelligence
			Creativity	
		Job competence	Job competence	Job competence
Physical competence	Athletic competence	Athletic competence	Athletic competence	Athletic competence
	Physical appearance	Physical appearance	Physical appearance	Physical appearance
Peer acceptance	Peer acceptance	Peer acceptance	Peer acceptance	Sociability
		Close friendship	Close friendship	Close friendship
		Romantic relationships	Romantic relationships	Intimate relationships
			Relationships with parents	
Behavioral conduct	Behavioral conduct	Conduct/ morality	Morality	Morality
			Sense of humor	Sense of humor
				Nurturance
				Household management
				Adequacy as a provider
	Global self-worth	Global self-worth	Global self-worth	Global self-worth

Susan Harter, "Causes, Correlates, and the Functional Role of Global Self-Worth: A Life-Span Perspective," in *Competence Considered,* ed. J. Kolligian and Robert Sternberg (New Haven, CT: Yale University Press, 1990), p. 73. Reprinted by permission.

Self-Esteem

Parents want children to feel good about themselves, to have self-esteem. Susan Harter describes the domains of the self-concept at each stage of development;[34] Table 2-1 traces these domains. Across the lifespan, the self-concept becomes increasingly differentiated though the basic dimensions remain surprisingly similar. Young children do not verbalize global feelings of self-worth, but they do express them in behavior.

Global feelings of self-worth are related to two independent factors: (1) one's feelings of competence in domains of importance and (2) the amount of social support one receives from others. Those highest in self-worth feel good about the abilities they value and also feel that others support and accept them. Those lowest in global self-worth feel they lack competence in domains deemed important and report that they receive little social support. Harter notes that no amount of social support can directly counteract one's perception of incompetence; conversely, no amount of competence can completely overcome feelings of lack of social support. So, to increase self-esteem, one has to increase both social support and feelings of competence in valued domains.

High-self-esteem children, ages three to seven, had two qualities—confidence in approaching situations and resilience when frustrated or upset.[35] These are also the qualities of children securely attached to their caregivers. Parental experiences that foster secure attachment are most likely those that help develop high self-esteem. Parental support, then, is a more important determinant of early self-esteem than is competence per se. In later childhood, both support and feelings of competence are important in determining self-worth.

The specific areas of competence that contribute most to feelings of self-worth are physical appearance and social acceptance by others—namely, parents and peers. Surprisingly, physical appearance and social support continue to be salient across the lifespan for individuals from eight to fifty-five years of age.

Which comes first—do children and adolescents base their self-esteem on others' social approval and others' perceptions of their attractiveness, or do children and adolescents high in self-esteem believe that others like them and find them attractive?[36] According to questionnaire responses, about 60 percent of children and adolescents say their self-esteem depends on others' views of them and about 40 percent say they like themselves and feel others approve of them. Those in the first category have lower self-esteem because they depend on the shifting regard of others. Those who like themselves and assume others do too have higher self-esteem that is more stable because it is an internal quality.

Though self-esteem depends on the early positive regard given by parents and caregivers, this regard does not fix it for life. Levels of self-esteem can increase over time as individuals become more competent in areas of importance to them or as they receive increased support from others. Self-esteem decreases under the reverse conditions.

Times of change and transition—entrance into kindergarten or junior high or college, moves to new schools or new neighborhoods—can trigger changes in self-esteem. New skills to develop, new reference groups for comparison, and new social groups for support provide the stimulus for change. People maintain self-esteem most successfully when they join or create positive social support or when they increase in other areas of competence.

Social Competence

Parents take a direct role in encouraging social competence when they choose residential neighborhoods where playmates are available and where flat areas, parks, and playgrounds make play possible.[37] Parents promote social skills when they organize

INTERVIEW
with Susan Harter

Susan Harter, a professor of psychology at the University of Denver, has spent twenty years studying the development of the self and self-esteem and has written numerous articles and chapters on the subject.

You have done a great deal of research on self-esteem. More than any other quality, I would say, parents hope to help children develop self-esteem. What can they do to promote it in their children?

We have identified two broad themes that impact children's self-esteem. First, the unconditional support and positive regard of parents and others in the child's world are particularly critical during the early years. What do we mean by support? It is communicating to children that you like them as people for who or what they are.

That sounds relatively easy but is in fact extremely difficult. Most of us as parents are far more skilled at providing conditional regard or support for children even though we are unaware we are doing it. We approve of our child if he cleans up his room or shares or doesn't hit his brother. So our support is conditional on his conduct. However, it isn't perceived by children as supportive at all. Basically it specifies how the child can please the parents. That does not feel good to children.

Unconditional regard validates children as worthy people and lets them know they are appreciated for who they are, for their strengths and weaknesses. It also involves listening to them, which is very validating to children as well as adults. So many well-meaning parents, and I make the same mistake, preach at their kids because we think we have a lot to say. We think we're teaching when we are really preaching. We don't refrain from talking; we don't shut up, listen well, and take the child's point of view seriously.

With unconditional support early on, children internalize positive regard so that when they are older, they can approve of themselves, pat themselves on the back, give themselves psychological hugs—all of which contribute to high self-esteem.

Another major part of self-esteem, beginning at about age eight, is feeling competent and adequate across the various domains of life. One does not have to feel competent in every domain in order to experience high self-esteem. Rather one needs to feel competent in those domains that he or she judges to be *important*. Profiles of competence for two children in the different areas of athletic, social, and intellectual competence can look very similar, but one child can have high self-esteem while the other can have low self-esteem. They both can feel competent in the same areas and feel inadequate in the same other areas. What distinguishes the *low*-self-esteem child is the fact that areas of incompetence are very important to one's feeling of being worthwhile; thus the child doesn't feel good about himself or herself. The *high*-self-esteem child feels the low areas are very unimportant and so still feels good about himself or herself.

When parents describe their own feelings and what causes them, children are more sympathetic and understanding of others.

both informal and play group activities for their children and supervise them to ensure that positive interactions occur. For toddlers and preschoolers, parents' active participation has a beneficial impact on play. As children grow older, parents may supervise from the sidelines and intervene only to promote positive interaction. As children mature still further, parents influence social competence by consulting with children before and after social activities and by offering guidance on how to handle problematic situations.

A parent's role is both direct and indirect when she or he creates a family atmosphere conducive to positive interactions with people in general. Creating secure attachments with children, modeling positive interactions with family members, arranging and reinforcing pleasurable sibling interactions—all promote children's trust in other people, their skills in understanding and dealing with others, and their overall enjoyment of social activity.

Research suggests fathers' behavior may be particularly important in promoting children's social development.[38] For example, physical play with their fathers may help children learn to use signals to regulate others' behavior. A father's ability to accept his children's anger and sadness and to help them cope with these feelings at age five are related to his children's social skills at age eight. When fathers respond to children's negative feelings with anger of their own, their children will more likely be aggressive and avoidant of others than will children of more accepting fathers.

Children from families under chronic stress are less socially skilled than those not under stress. Poverty, for example, exerts a negative impact on social competence. Children in low-income families have a great need for social group activities, but both the physical environment and parental resources restrict access to play. Low-income neighborhoods often are not safe for outdoor play, and parents have less time to organize peer contacts, so there are fewer of them.

Other stressors that decrease social competence include parental unemployment, marital conflict, and divorce. Parental abuse, depression, and alcoholism further decrease children's abilities to interact positively with others.

Moral Competence

Moral competence refers to several aspects of children's behavior: (1) carrying out positive acts that are voluntary, helpful, and beneficial to others; (2) avoiding disruptive or negative behaviors, like lying, stealing, and physical aggression, that are harmful to others; (3) developing a conscience or internal standards that direct behavior; and (4) acquiring the capacity to make moral judgments.[39] Moral competence rests on the capacity for self-control and concern for others, and thus is related to emotional and social competence.

Helpful behavior springs from early caregiving experiences. In his book *The Moral Sense,* James Q. Wilson, like Robert Emde, points to the important contribution of early parent-child relations to moral development:

> Our moral senses are forged in the crucible of this loving relationship and expanded by the enlarged relationships of families and peers. Out of the universal attachment between child and parent, the former begins to develop a sense of empathy and fairness, to learn self-control, and to acquire a conscience that makes him behave dutifully at least with respect to some matters. Those dispositions are extended to other people (and often to other species) to the extent that these others are thought to share in the traits we find in our families.[40]

Parents also exert a direct influence on children's helpful behaviors by encouraging empathy for others. Parents verbalize concern for others and induce children to understand others' points of view with statements such as, "See, you made Joey cry." They also take an active role in modeling and teaching children how to be helpful and in conveying standards of behavior that they hope children will meet. Warmth and nurturance in the absence of moral standards are less effective than such actions in promoting helpful behavior.[41]

The emotional climate of the home influences children's level of sympathy and concern for others.[42] In homes where parents fight, children have sympathy for mothers and siblings but less concern for peers outside the family. When mothers express tension, sadness, and fear at home but help their children understand these feelings, the children's sympathy increases.

Children tend to be more sympathetic and prosocial when they have parents who help them with their negative feelings. Listening to children's negative emotions, talking about them, and helping children find ways to manage them are all related to children's being more sympathetic to others' distress and more likely to take action to comfort others.

Parents increase children's hurtful behaviors when they enforce harsh discipline, show little concern for the child's needs, and reflect inconsistent and fleeting interest in their children's behavior. When parents fail to supervise and monitor children's actions consistently, the children are more likely to be aggressive toward and unconcerned about others.[43]

We know more about parents' influence on helpful and hurtful behaviors than about their role in promoting the internalization of rules and moral reasoning. Toddlers do not develop internal standards of accomplishment until about age three. At that time, they take pride in their successes and feel sadness at their failures. But not until the elementary school years do children feel guilt, a sense of having done something wrong and wanting to make amends for it. Parents help children internalize family values by conveying standards of behavior and making nonpunitive, supportive statements to help the child understand the other's point of view and act in accordance with what is best for all.

The capacity to reason about moral issues and make moral judgments depends, in part, on the child's cognitive skills, but parents can help this capacity develop in several ways. When parents are supportive of children's opinions and views of situations, when they ask questions and elicit children's opinions in real-life situations, and when they present higher levels of moral reasoning for consideration, then children achieve more advanced levels of moral reasoning. Criticizing children's opinions, challenging their views, and correcting them with new information are not associated with children's moral growth.[44]

The Role of Authoritative Parenting

The parental behaviors associated with competencies in several areas center on what Diana Baumrind terms *authoritative parenting*. In studying children in the preschool years and following their development, she identified three parenting styles.[45]

Authoritative parents exercise firm control over the child's behavior but also emphasize the independence and individuality in the child. Although the parents have a clear notion of present and future standards of behavior for the child, they are rational, flexible, and attentive to the needs and preferences of the child. Their children are self-reliant and self-confident and explore their worlds with excitement and pleasure.

Authoritarian parents employ similar firm control but in an arbitrary, power-oriented way without regard for the child's individuality. They emphasize control without nurturance or support to achieve it. Children of authoritarian parents, relative to other groups of children, are unhappy, withdrawn, inhibited, and distrustful.

Permissive parents set few limits on the child. They are accepting of the child's impulses, granting as much freedom as possible while still maintaining physical safety. They appear cool and uninvolved. Permissive parents sometimes allow behavior that angers them, but they do not feel sufficiently comfortable with their own anger to express it. As a result, the anger builds up to unmanageable proportions. They then lash out and are likely to harm the child more than they want to. Their children are the least independent and self-controlled and could be best classified as immature.

So, respecting individuality, providing warmth and nurturance accompanied by standards of behavior, monitoring and supervising children, and actively teaching desired behaviors are all related to competencies in several areas.

PARENTING BELIEFS AND BEHAVIOR

Parents have not only long-term goals about the behaviors they want their children to develop, but also ideas and theories about how to accomplish their goals.[46] We now look at how parents develop their ideas about how to rear children effectively, how these ideas influence their behavior, and how they go about changing their ideas.

Origins of Parenting Beliefs

Direct experience with children appears to produce fewer differences in beliefs about children than one might expect,[47] and so we turn to other influences on parents' beliefs and behavior.[48]

Culture   Sara Harkness and Charles Super believe that culture provides a "developmental niche" in which children develop. This niche includes (1) the physical and social settings the culture provides for parents and children, (2) the child-rearing practices the culture recommends, and (3) the psychological characteristics of the caregivers.[49] So, culture shapes a broad range of parental behaviors, from the more general values parents teach to the concrete daily aspects of life such as where children sleep.

Often, parents daily communicate general values to their children from the earliest days of life. For example, many cultures that emphasize family closeness throughout life begin with the family members' sleeping together until the child is several years old.

Patricia Greenfield and Lalita Suzuki describe two cultural models — the independent and the interdependent — that provide a framework for organizing and understanding what parents think matters and what they do with children.[50] (See Table 2-2.) These models apply to many different cultural and social groups; they do not reflect any ethnic group in particular.

In the independent model, parents help children to become self-sustaining, productive adults who enter into relationships with other adults by choice. In many ways, Erikson's chart of lifespan development (Figure 2-1) illustrates the independent model. The child received nurturance to develop autonomy, competence, and a freely chosen identity that in adulthood merges with others outside the family.

In the interdependent model, parents help children grow into socially responsible adults who take their place in a strong network of social relationships, often within the family, that place obligations on the adult. Parents indulge the young child, but as children grow older, they are expected to internalize and respect the rules of parents and other authorities. Parents and relatives are respected and obeyed, and family and group needs matter more than individual ones.

While cultural beliefs and values are deeply ingrained and often invisible, they are not fixed and unchangeable. The anthropologist Jean Briggs writes,

> The notion that meaning inheres in culture and that people receive it passively as dough receives the cookie cutter, is rapidly being replaced by the idea that culture consists of ingredients, which people actively select, interpret, and use in various ways, as opportunities, capabilities, and experience allow.[51]

TABLE 2-2
CONTRASTING CULTURAL MODELS OF PARENT-CHILD RELATIONS

	Developmental Goals	
	Independence	Interdependence
Developmental trajectory	From dependent to independent self	From asocial to socially responsible self
Children's relations to parents	Personal choice concerning relationship to parents	Obligations to parents
Communication	Verbal emphasis	Nonverbal emphasis (empathy, observation, participation)
	Autonomous self-expression by child	Child comprehension, mother speaks for child
	Frequent parental questions to child	Frequent parental directives to child
	Frequent praise	Infrequent praise
	Child negotiation	Harmony, respect, obedience
Parenting style	Authoritative: controlling, demanding, warm, rational	Rigorous and responsible teaching, high involvement, physical closeness
Parents helping children	A matter of personal choice except under extreme need	A moral obligation under all circumstances

From Patricia M. Greenfield and Lalita K. Suzuki, "Culture and Human Development: Implications for Parenting, Education, Pediatrics, and Mental Health," in *Handbook of Child Psychology,* ed. in chief William Damon and vol. ed. Irving E. Sigel and K. Ann Renninger, vol. 4: *Child Psychology in Practice,* 5th ed. (New York: Wiley, 1997), p. 1085. Reprinted by permission of John Wiley & Sons, Inc.

James Youness describes a series of studies showing that parents who immigrate can identify the cultural values of their new country and socialize their children to fit in while the parents maintain their more traditional beliefs.[52] Youness reviewed studies of two groups who emigrated from Croatia to the United States. One group lived very much as a self-contained community, stressing their traditional values, customs, and language. The other group became assimilated into the new culture. Yet, both groups socialized their children to be more independent, questioning, and self-directed than the parents had been raised to be. This helped the children fit into their new culture.

Many children in our multicultural society are exposed to two sets of cultural values and develop what is termed a *bicultural identification,* an identification with the values of two groups. For example, one can harmonize the values of the independent and interdependent models and become an independent adult who belongs to a strong family network. One can both respect parents, showing consideration for their needs, and become an achievement-oriented, self-sustaining person.

For this reason, Ross Parke and Raymond Buriel warn against making overly sharp distinctions that only promote stereotypes. Parke and Buriel emphasize the importance of considering both individual and collectivist features when one tries to understand child rearing in any type of family.[53]

Cultural models influence not only what parents do in their homes but also the qualities children take with them into the larger society.[54] Children more easily adapt to the larger culture when the home culture is the same as that of the larger society. Problems can arise when the home culture conflicts with that of the school. For example, teachers and schools operate on the independent model, emphasizing individual effort to achieve knowledge. Questions and expressions of opinion are encouraged and seen as signs of intellectual curiosity. Children's quiet acceptance of the teachers' statements may be interpreted as lack of interest or lack of intelligence. So, we need to recognize that children may live in a home culture that differs from the culture in school and the larger society. Throughout the text, we shall further explore cultural influences on parenting.

Socioeconomic Status Every cultural group contains a social hierarchy. Erika Hoff-Ginsberg and Twila Tardif state that socioeconomic status (SES), like culture, provides a developmental niche for children.[55] Social position partly prescribes the settings children live in, their parents' child-rearing practices, and the psychological characteristics of their parents.

Three variables—parents' occupation, education, and level of income—make up socioeconomic status. Because the three variables, though correlated, can vary, SES is a complicated concept. Thus, one middle-class family may have an average income, education, and occupational status, while another middle-class family of average income and occupational status may have a higher educational status. Even if the two families had different values, both would be considered middle class.

While income at or below the poverty level affects parenting (see Chapters 1, 12, and 15), above the poverty level, income appears less influential in shaping parenting beliefs than do education and occupational status. One study in China indicates that people with the same income may exhibit values that differ greatly. In the United States, too, studies indicate that values may remain the same though income varies.

Like that of culture, the influence of social status is not fixed. For example, parents' occupations may change as the result of increased education, or a family may find great success in some endeavor and income may rise sharply. Conversely, income and social status may drop as a result of unemployment. Further, parents change their ideas about parenting as a result of new information. In one study, mothers of all educational levels provided their young children with books and read to them most likely because of strong advice to read to children. However, the mothers with only a high school education had few books and read far less than college-educated mothers.

As one reviews the influences of SES on parenting, three main findings stand out. First, whether one compares college-educated and high-school–educated parents or middle-class and working-class parents—the higher the SES, the more likely the parents will have a child-centered orientation to parenting. Parents with this orientation seek to understand children's growth and development, to understand children's feelings and motivations, to use reasoning and negotiation to solve problems. Such parents approach children in an egalitarian manner. The lower the SES status, the more likely parents will be parent centered in their approach to children, to want obedience and conformity to the rules without discussion or explanation. Parents seek to direct and control activities rather than to understand them or negotiate with their children. Melvin Kohn[56] speculates that working-class parents are more likely to stress obedience and conformity because their jobs require these qualities, whereas higher-status occupations permit more autonomy, initiative, and independence.

A second major finding is that differences in SES correlate with more differences in verbal than nonverbal interactions between parents and children. A third finding is that higher-status parents talk more to children and elicit more speech from them. They also show more responsiveness when children do speak, and they supply more labels to children.

The description of such differences may sound uninteresting and unimportant, but an unusual study has documented the profound impact of these differences in young children's lives. Betty Hart and Todd Risley recorded the words spoken to and by children in their homes from the ages of one to three years.[57] Investigators visited the homes of forty-two families of professional, working-class, and welfare background for an hour each month.

They found that all children had quality interactions with parents and experienced caring expressed in many different ways. The higher the status of the family, however, the more time parents spent interacting and talking with children. In professional families, parents spent 30–40 minutes per hour interacting with their children; in welfare families, parents spent 15–20 minutes; and in working-class families, parents spent 20–30 minutes per hour. Further, higher-status families were more active and outgoing with friends and in the community. Welfare families were more isolated, sometimes without a phone or transportation.

The higher the status of the family, the more words parents directed to children, with professional parents making 481 utterances per hour, in contrast to working-class parents, who made 301 utterances, and welfare parents, who addressed 178 utterances per hour to their children.

Families did not differ in the number of words per utterance or the number of questions asked, they did differ in the numbers of positive statements and prohibitions they gave to children. Professional parents gave their children positive feedback every other minute or 30 times per hour and gave them prohibitions only twice an hour. Working-class parents gave positive statements 15 times per hour and prohibitions 5 times per hour. Welfare families, though, gave positive statements about 6 times per hour but gave prohibitions about 10 to 12 times per hour. So, children of professional parents receive much of the unconditional positive support that Harter believes leads to high self-esteem, while children of welfare parents receive much less positive information about themselves and their skills.

Parents' Own Socialization Experiences   Parents' experiences with their own parents provide a major source of beliefs about parenting. From their childhood experiences, parents have internalized a working model of how people relate to each other, how trustworthy others are, and how much control one has over interactions with other people. This internal model influences how parents perceive their children and interact with them.

Interviews with parents about their feelings concerning childhood experiences with their parents yield information on parents' current state of mind regarding their attachment to their parents.[58] Securely attached parents, even those who experienced traumatic events, value these early attachments and place negative childhood events in perspective so they can think about and understand the effects of these events on their lives. Insecurely attached parents who also dismiss the importance of these early events and attachments minimize the influence of these events on their present lives. They see themselves as independent and strong adults. Insecurely attached parents preoccupied with past events seem confused about their experiences with early attachment figures. They remain entangled in feelings of anger, helplessness, conflict, or fearfulness, and they cannot gain insight or closure regarding these early experiences.

Securely attached parents are direct and open in their dealings with others and not inclined to misperceive situations.[59] Toward their children, they are emotionally supportive, sensitive, and responsive, yet they can set clear and consistent limits.

Insecurely attached, dismissive parents emphasize their independence and strength in the face of parental rejection, and they remain cool and remote from their children. As they do not believe their parents mattered in their lives, they do not try to help or support their children emotionally. Confident of their abilities, they have few doubts about their parenting effectiveness. They report few negative thoughts about children in difficult child-rearing situations.

Insecurely attached, preoccupied parents behave in a confusing and inconsistent manner with their children. Warm and gentle at times, they become angry and forcing with children at other times. They have many negative thoughts about children in difficult child-rearing situations, blaming the problems on the child's personality. Clearly, parents' views of children and their styles of relating to them stem from a general way of perceiving and relating to people based on early life experiences.

Influence of Parenting Beliefs on Behavior

Research documents that parents' beliefs influence many aspects of their behavior.[60] Here, I offer just a sampling of these findings. When parents believe it is important to read to children and to allow them freedom to explore their world, they do these things. When mothers state it is important to encourage gender-typed activities, they engage in more active play with boys than with girls. When parents believe a child's effort determines success, they encourage a child's effort. Those parents who believe parenting affects a child's development exert greater effort and provide more supportive environments than those who think parenting practices have little influence on development.

These findings suggest that beliefs lead to direct action in a conscious, reflective manner. Reading matters, so parents read to children. This is clearly the case with some beliefs. Other research suggests, however, that beliefs can lead indirectly to action by shaping parents' interpretations of children's behavior and parental response to that behavior.

Sometimes these beliefs are so deeply ingrained that parents act on them automatically, without any awareness of how these beliefs, rather than their children's behavior, shape their responses.[61] For example, parents who believe that adults control adult-child interactions experience little stress when a child is unresponsive. Because they do not see themselves as powerless, such parents do not react with negative affect or change their behavior.

When parents believe adults have little control over adult-child interactions, they quickly feel threatened and stressed at a child's unresponsiveness. They respond with negative affect and attempts either to ingratiate themselves with or to dominate the unresponsive child. So, beliefs about who controls the parent-child interaction affect a parent's interpretations of and emotional responses to children's behavior.

Relation between Beliefs and Affect   As we shall see in the next chapter, emotions greatly determine what parents do with their children, in part because they shape parents' interpretations of children's actions. Yet, we have just seen that beliefs shape parents' interpretations and, in turn, their emotional responses. What is the relationship between beliefs and affect? Ann McGillicuddy-De Lisi and Irving Sigel summarize the relationship in this way:

> We prefer to think of affect as entwined with cognition, regardless of whether affect precedes or derives from cognition. The indissociability of cognition and affect can be approached in terms of a figure-ground metaphor. The figure will vary from time to time to the degree that cognitive or affective features are highlighted. In the course of solving an emotional problem, affective features of the situation may be pronounced with the cognitive aspects in the background.[62]

For example, dealing with a child's problem with lying might arouse strong feelings of concern and hurt on the part of the parent, and these feelings might be the determining factors in how a parent deals with the lying. If a child were having a problem learning math at school, a parent's cognitive problem-solving skills might be the determining factors in finding a solution even though a parent might also be worried about the school difficulty.

Changing Beliefs

Parents revise their beliefs about children and the way they grow. Understanding the process of this change has practical and important implications because advisers to parents wish to encourage effective parenting behaviors and discourage those known to create problems for children.[63] For example, understanding how parents change would help advisers counter parents' impulses to use frequent physical punishment.

Though psychologists have not studied this process in detail, we do know that changes in beliefs are most likely to occur when they are in line with parents' sense of identity and social position. Parents are less likely to adopt beliefs if the beliefs decrease parents' self-esteem or if they are contrary to what others in parents' social groups believe.

Parents may have to change their actions first, and changes in beliefs will follow.[64] For example, parents may have to stop spanking their children and use other methods of discipline before they adopt the belief that these other methods work. Parents may have to give children opportunities to make decisions before they come to believe that children have the necessary skills to make decisions.

HOW PARENTS CHANGE

Parents continually develop new behaviors as they rear their children and as they deal with their frustrations as parents. So, it is not surprising that creating these new responses leads to permanent changes in parents themselves. Yet, there has been relatively little research on parents' changes as a result of parenting.

Ellen Galinsky, a consultant and lecturer on child development, found herself changing after her children were born. Curious about the meaning of her feelings, she consulted books and research reports to see what other parents were describing. Finding little to inform her, she began forming groups of parents of young children. She then interviewed 228 parents with different experiences of parenthood—married, divorced, step-, foster, and adoptive parents. These parents did not represent a random sampling but were a broad cross-section of the population.

Galinsky has divided parenthood into six stages in which parents focus their emotional and intellectual energy on the task of that period.[65] These stages differ from most in that a parent can be in more than one stage at a time with children of different ages. The first stage, occurring in pregnancy, she terms the *image-making* stage. It is a time when parents prepare for changes in themselves and in their relationships to others. The second, *nurturing,* stage goes from birth to the time when the child starts to say "no," about eighteen to twenty-four months. As parents become attached to the new baby, they arrange their lives to be caregivers, balancing their own and their child's needs and setting priorities. The third, *authority,* stage lasts from the time the child is two to four or five. Parents become rule givers and enforcers as they learn that love for children goes hand in hand with structure and order. From the child's preschool years through adolescence, parents are in the *interpretive* stage. Children are more skilled and independent, and parents establish a way of life for them, interpret outside authorities such as teachers, and teach values and morals. In brief, they teach children what life is all about.

When their children are adolescents, parents enter the *interdependent* stage. They form new relationships with children, and, though they are still authorities, their power becomes shared with children in ways it was not in past years. In the sixth stage, *departure,* parents evaluate themselves as their children prepare to leave home. They see where they have succeeded and where they might have acted differently.

Galinsky summarizes her views of how parenthood changes adults:

> Taking care of a small, dependent, growing person is transforming, because it brings us in touch with our baser side, it exposes our vulnerabilities as well as our nobility. We lose our sense of self, only to find it and have it change again and again. We learn to nurture and care. We struggle through defining our own rules and our own brand of being an authority. We figure out how we want to interpret the wider world, and we learn to interact with all those who affect our children. When our children are teenagers, we redefine our relationships, and then we launch them into life.
>
> Often our fantasies are laid bare, our dreams are in a constant tug of war with realities. And perhaps we grow. In the end, we have learned more about ourselves, about the cycles of life, and humanity itself. Most parents describe themselves as more responsible, more accepting, more generous than before they had children.[66]

MAIN POINTS

Erikson's lifespan developmental theory describes

- eight stages of growth, each having a developmental crisis that must be resolved (e.g., trust versus mistrust)
- the parenting role as a major source of growth in adulthood

Parents encourage children's competencies in all areas when they

- model competent behavior themselves
- form positive attachments and maintain a harmonious home atmosphere in which feelings are expressed in a regulated way
- provide opportunities for independent exploration and action in the world
- guide children's actions so children achieve their goals
- provide emotional support for children's efforts
- arrange appropriate experiences to stimulate social and moral development
- use reasoning and positive rewards and avoid harsh, physical punishments

New research affecting how we see the parent-child relationship includes

- advances in neuroscience, which emphasize how environment affects the brain
- anthropology and cultural psychology
- a focus on regulatory processes
- a shift in whom we study

Specific competencies of children

- include physical, intellectual, emotional, social, moral competence as well as self-esteem
- depend on parents' direct involvement in providing opportunities for growth in each competency
- stem from parents' own competency and modeling
- are affected by parenting style: authoritative, authoritarian, or permissive

Parents' beliefs about parenting

- are based on cultural, social, and personal values
- may emphasize values of an independent model or an interdependent model
- shape what they do with children
- are often subtle and impact parenting indirectly

As they raise children, parents go through the stages of

- image making, nurturing, and being authorities
- interpreting the world to and being interdependent with children
- departure

EXERCISES

1. Review Erikson's theory of lifespan development and look at your own life in terms of the positive qualities and strengths Erikson presents. What positive qualities have you developed? What virtues or strengths? Can you describe the kinds of family experiences that led to your positive qualities?

2. Rate yourself on the dimensions Susan Harter says college students use to describe themselves. (See Table 2-1.) For each dimension, rate yourself on a seven-point scale (1 = low; 7 = high) in terms of where you want to be on these dimensions and where you think you are. Note where you have strong feelings of competence. Also rate yourself on global self-worth on a seven-point scale. What dimensions seem to be most strongly related to your feelings of global self-worth?

3. Describe how you think you and your siblings have changed your parents as individuals. If possible, interview your parents about how they changed in the course of rearing you and your brothers and sisters.

4. To get an idea of the range of values in rearing children, interview a classmate or interview parents of different ethnic groups in the community to determine their values in childrearing: (a) What kind of child do they want to raise? (b) How much help do they anticipate from family and friends? (c) Will caregivers outside the family be used? (d) How much contact will there be with different generations? (e) What disciplinary techniques do they think they will use? (f) Do they have very different expectations about raising boys and girls? (g) How much independence will they encourage in their children?

5. Interview classmates about the three competencies they most want their children to develop. Why do they think these are the most important qualities to have? Do they think other competencies will be more valuable later? What are they?

ADDITIONAL READINGS

Erikson, Erik H. *Childhood and Society.* 2d ed. New York: Norton, 1963.

Galinsky, Ellen. *The Six Stages of Parenthood.* Reading, MA: Addison-Wesley, 1987.

Goleman, Daniel. *Emotional Intelligence.* New York: Bantam Books, 1995.

Guarendi, Ray, with Eich, David. *Back to the Family.* New York: Simon & Schuster, 1991.

Wilson, James Q. *The Moral Sense.* New York: Free Press, 1993.

ESTABLISHING CLOSE EMOTIONAL RELATIONSHIPS WITH CHILDREN

C H A P T E R 3

The first parenting task—establishing a close emotional relationship with a child—sounds easy enough. But how do parents create close ties with their children? What happens if the child is unwanted or has a difficult temperament? What do parents do when they feel angry? How do they reduce stress and maintain harmony in the family?

There's no foolproof recipe for a good parent-child relationship because the essential ingredients and environmental conditions are unique to each relationship. This chapter reviews what experts on parenting as well as current research suggest as methods to enhance communication and strengthen the bond between parent and child.

PARENTING EXPERTS REVIEWED

This book identifies basic strategies of parenting drawn from the work of Haim Ginott,[1] Thomas Gordon,[2] Dorothy Briggs,[3] Rudolf Dreikurs,[4] and the behaviorists.[5] Ginott, Gordon, and Briggs are clinical psychologists who focus on feelings. Dreikurs, a psychiatrist, focuses on changing behavior using the principles of Alfred Adler. The behaviorists—including Wesley Becker, Robert Eimers, and Robert Aitchison—use principles of experimental learning studies to modify children's behavior.

Table 3-1 summarizes the similarities among these strategies. The major goal of parenting, the importance of modeling, communication of positive feelings, respect for children, the importance of praise, avoidance of ridicule and shaming, criticism of the idea that love is enough—these are features of all the methods. Making impersonal statements of rules, offering choices to children, being consistent in demands, emphasizing the needs of parents, and viewing the child in a positive light are agreed on by most of these strategists. The main disagreements lie in the use of external rewards and punishments, parents' expression of their anger at children, differing emphases on the uniqueness of the child, and the use of preventive statements to ward off trouble.

TABLE 3-1
COMPARISON OF STRATEGIES OF PARENTING

Specific Aspect	Ginott	Gordon	Briggs	Dreikurs	Becker	Eimers and Aitchison
Goal of responsibility	•	•	•	•	•	•
Parent as model	•	•	•	•	•	•
Child's ability to learn	•	•	•	•	•	•
Respect for child	•	•	•	•	•	•
Communication of feelings	•	•	•	•	•	•
No ridicule or shaming	•	•	•	•	•	
Importance of time, attention	•	•	•	•	•	•
Critical of idea love is enough	•	•	•	•	•	•
Use of praise	•	•	•	•	•	•
Democratic living	•	•	•	•		
Impersonal statement of rules	•		•	•	•	•
Consistency	•		•	•	•	•
Needs of parents	•	•	•	•		
Use of specified rewards					•	•
Use of specified punishment					•	•
Positive image of child	•	•	•	•		
Use of choice	•		•	•		•
Parental expression of anger		•			•	•
Distinction between deed and doer	•		•	•		
Uniqueness of child			•	•		
Preventive measures		•				•

These strategies share a common problem — they give only limited attention to the effects of the child's age, sex, and temperament on the parents' behavior. This book distills and synthesizes these strategies and shows how one can apply them to the problems children experience at different ages. I have also included ideas about how to facilitate children's development.

FAMILY ATMOSPHERE

As we saw in Chapter 1, both men and women of all ethnic groups find their deepest satisfactions in family life. Parents' main joy in having children is the close emotional relationships that develop. These ties not only bring parents pleasure but also stimulate infants' and children's healthy psychological growth.

56

CHAPTER 3
Establishing
Close
Emotional
Relationships
with Children

I N T E R V I E W
with Emmy E. Werner

Emmy E. Werner is research professor of human development at the University of California, Davis. For three decades, she and her colleagues Jessie Bierman and Fern French at the University of California, Berkeley, and Ruth Smith, a clinical psychologist on the Hawaiian island of Kauai, have conducted the Kauai Longitudinal Study, resulting in books such as Vulnerable but Invincible, The Children of Kauai, Kauai's Children Come of Age, *and* Overcoming the Odds.

From your experience of watching children at risk grow up on Kauai, what would you say parents can do to support children, to help maximize their child's potential? From your work with children at risk, what helps children survive and flourish even when faced with severe problems?

Let me say that, in our study, we studied the offspring of women whom we began to see at the end of the first trimester of pregnancy. We followed them during the pregnancy and delivery. We saw the children at ages one, two, and ten, late adolescence, and again at thirty-two and forty years. We have test scores, teachers' observations, and interview material at different times on these people. We have a group of children who were at high risk because of four or more factors. They were children who (1) experienced prenatal or perinatal complications, (2) grew up in poverty, (3) lived in a dysfunctional family with one or more problems, and (4) had a parent with alcohol or mental health problems.

You ask me to comment on parenting and what parents can do, but first I would like to urge that we redefine and extend the definition of parenting to cast a wider set and include people who provide love in the lives of children. I like to talk about *alloparenting,* the parenting of children by alternate people who are not the biological parents — they can be relatives, neighbors, siblings.

In our study of vulnerable but invincible children, we found that a major protective factor was that at least one person, perhaps a biological parent, or a grandparent, or an older sibling, accepted them unconditionally. That one person made the child feel special, very, very special. These parent figures made the child feel special through acts. They conveyed their love through deeds. They acted as models for the child. They didn't pretend the child had no handicap or problem, but what they conveyed was, "You matter to me, and you are special."

Now, another theme in our findings is that the parent figure, whoever he or she was, encouraged the child to reach out to others beyond the family — to seek out a friendly neigh-

Close Emotional Relationships

Parents begin to form a positive parental relationship when they love the child as a special person. Dorothy Briggs describes the psychological climate that enables children to feel their parents' love: "Nurturing love is tender caring — valuing a child just because he exists. It comes when you see your youngster as special and dear — even though you may not approve of all that he does."[6] Parents attend to children's unique qualities "with a special intensity born of direct personal involvement."[7] Children are

bor, a parent of one of their boy or girl friends, and, thus, learn about normal parenting from other families.

The resilient child was temperamentally engaging. He or she encouraged interaction with others outside the home and was given the opportunity to relate to others.

I had no preconceptions about this protective factor, but what came through was that somewhere along the line, in the face of poverty, in the face of a handicap, faith has an abiding power. I'm not referring to faith in a narrow, denominational sense, but having someone in the family or outside of it who was saying, "Hey, you are having ups and downs, this will pass, you will get through this, and things will get better."

Another thing was that these children had an opportunity to care for themselves or others. They became nurturant and concerned, perhaps about a parent or a sibling. They practiced "required helpfulness."

Now, another protective factor is whether the children were able to develop a hobby that was a refuge and gave them respect among their peers. One of our study members said later, "If I had any doubts about whether I could make it, that hobby turned me around." The hobby was especially important as a buffer between the person and the chaos in the family. But it was not a hobby that isolated you from others; it nourished something you could share with other people.

As many of the children looked back, they describe how a positive relationship with a sibling was enduring and important. As adults they commented with surprise how supportive the relationship was and how these relationships were maintained despite great distances and despite dissimilarity in life and interests.

What did adults say they wanted to pass on to their own children?

Looking back as an adult, they felt that some sort of structure in their life was very important. Even though the family life was chaotic, if a parent imposed some reasonable rules and regulations, it was helpful.

They emphasized faith as something to hang on to and make this clear to their children. As parents now they are quite achievement motivated. They graduated from high school, and some went back and got additional training. They encourage their children to do well in school.

The main theme that runs through our data is the importance of a parent figure who says "you matter" and the child's ability to create his or her own environment. The children believed they could do it, someone gave them hope, and they succeeded against the odds.

loved simply because they exist—no strings attached, no standards to meet. This is the unconditional love that Susan Harter refers to in her interview in Chapter 2.

Parents express their love in a variety of ways—tone of voice, smiles, hugs, humorous comments, special time together. The child's temperament, discussed in greater detail in Chapter 6, partly shapes how the parent expresses love. The quality of parents' daily caregiving conveys love as well. Looking after children, playing with them, taking them places, and talking to them all indicate to children that they matter.

58

CHAPTER 3
Establishing
Close
Emotional
Relationships
with Children

What qualities do children value in parents? Preschoolers interviewed about the qualities of a good and a bad mommy and daddy suggest that good parents are physically affectionate and nurturant, especially in the area of providing food for children. In addition, good parents like to play games with their children and read to them, and they discipline them — that is, they keep children from doing things they should not, but they do not spank them or slap them in the face. Bad parents have the opposite qualities. They don't hug or kiss, don't fix food, don't play games. They hit and don't let children go outside. Bad parents are also described as generally irresponsible — they go through red lights, throw chairs at people, and don't read the newspaper.[8]

As children grow older, they continue to value nurturance and affection, but they also appreciate qualities reflecting psychological nurturance. Mothers' good qualities include "understanding feelings and moods," "being there when I need her," and "sticking up for me." Children continue to emphasize the limit-setting behaviors in a good mother — "She makes us eat fruit and vegetables," "She yells at me when I need it" — but they want their mother to consider their needs and wishes in setting the rules. Older children still enjoy mutual recreational time — playing, joking, building things together. Finally, as children get older, they appreciate the teaching activities of the good mother.[9]

The Power of Positive Feelings

In Chapter 2, we saw that positive attachments are powerful stimulants of competent behavior in parents and children. When parents have positive attachments to their own parents and to each other, they are more likely to have secure attachments to their children. These secure attachments promote children's competent behavior in a variety of areas. When people are happy with each other, they are more likely to be understanding and sympathetic.[10]

Although closeness is enjoyable for and helpful to children, some parents may not feel good about themselves or some of their own qualities, causing them to wonder if their children might not be better off remaining distant from them. They fear their children will pick up their bad qualities. Research on close and nonclose relationships among adolescents and their parents revealed that children who feel close to their parents are less likely to take on the parents' negative qualities than are children who feel distant. Negative parental qualities are more potent influences on children when parents and children are not close.[11] Thus, even when parents have many self-doubts and self-criticism, closeness with them and all their failings is still a positive experience for their children.

Good feelings come from one's own actions and successes as well as from relationships. Kirk Felsman and George Vaillant, following the development of a sample of men from early adolescence to late middle life, identified boyhood competence as an important forerunner of adult mental health. Boyhood competence — a summary measure of working part-time, having household chores, participating in extracurricular activities, getting school grades commensurate with IQ, participating in school activities, and learning to make plans — generates feelings of effectiveness. Felsman and Vaillant write, "Perhaps what is most encouraging in the collective portrait of these men's lives is their enormous capacity for recovery —

evidence that the things that go right in our lives do predict future successes and the events that go wrong in our lives do not forever damn us."[12]

We do not always have a recent accomplishment to treasure, but studies reveal that if children simply think of some pleasant event for a short time, their performance improves and their behavior becomes more friendly, responsive, and responsible. These children resist temptation more successfully and respond to unfair treatment with fairness and generosity.[13]

Happy feelings serve as an inoculation against the effects of negative events. These good feelings are not just fleetingly helpful. Longitudinal research shows that how one spends leisure time, how one has fun in childhood, is more predictive of later psychological health than is the presence or absence of problems in childhood.[14] So parents are wise when they follow Dreikurs's advice to remind children of their progress and accomplishments and to build recreational activities into children's everyday lives.

The Disruptive Effects of Negative Feelings

We have long known that emotional extremes in parents, such as violent anger or clinical depression, affect children's behavior. We are increasingly aware as well that negative moods in the course of daily life can have adverse effects on parents' interactions with children and on children's behavior.

Everyday Anger   Many researchers have documented that when children are exposed to different forms of anger, they respond with emotional arousal that changes heart rate and blood pressure,[15] as well as the production of hormones.[16] Whether the angry interaction is actually observed or only heard from another room, or only angry silence is observed, young children react in a variety of ways.

A majority of children show signs of anger, concern, sadness, and general distress that can disrupt play, lead to increased aggressiveness, or result in attempts to end the conflict or comfort the participant.[17] Almost half of children primarily feel distress with a strong desire to end the fight. Slightly over a third of children are ambivalent, revealing both high emotional arousal and upset, but at the same time reporting that they are happy. A small percentage (15 percent) give no response. The ambivalent child is the one who becomes more aggressive in behavior.

Not surprisingly, then, children exposed to parents' fighting at home have strong physiological and social reactions to anger.[18] They are more likely to comfort the mother if she is involved in an angry exchange in a laboratory setting. With their friends, they characteristically play at a less involved level; and when anger occurs, they find it very hard to handle.

Children are particularly upset when arguments center on child-related issues or when parents imply children are to blame for the argument.[19] If parents reassure them that they are not to blame, children are less distressed. But when children feel conflict is their fault, they are likely to intervene to try to stop it. Even children as young as four believe they can reduce parental anger, and, in part, they are right.[20] Parents say they are more likely to stop fighting when young children ages four to six intervene. Older children believe there is less they can do to stop parents from fighting—and they are right, because parents pay less attention to their pleas.

60

CHAPTER 3
Establishing
Close
Emotional
Relationships
with Children

Resolving disagreements so that both parents are satisfied with the solution reduces stress for parents and children.

Does this mean that parents should never fight or disagree in front of children? No. Conflict is a natural part of life when people live closely together, and children may need to observe how conflicts are settled to learn these skills themselves. In their work, Mark Cummings and his associates found that children who viewed angry adults finding a compromise to a situation had emotional reactions that were indistinguishable from their responses when viewing friendly interactions.[21] They had the most negative reactions to continued fighting and the "silent treatment." Their responses to submissions or changes in the topic indicated they did not consider the situation resolved. So, what is most important to children is whether adults achieve a fair compromise to settle conflicts after they erupt.

Even when there is no particular distress, family members, both parents and children ages five to fifteen, see themselves a major cause of angry feelings in others.[22] Fathers (for whom there is limited information because they were not questioned in as much detail) and children of all ages saw themselves as the major cause of mothers' anger. Although mothers cited more general reasons like violence and poverty, when asked to keep diaries of what made them angry on a daily basis, they most often cited the noncompliance, destructiveness, and demanding nature of children. Thus, the children's perceptions appear accurate.

Children cited the family as the major source of their own anger and saw their happiness as coming from experiences outside the home with friends and personal accomplishments. In contrast, mothers thought children's happiness came from the family, and their anger from other experiences. This is how mothers attribute their own feelings—the family providing major positive feelings and other experiences providing anger—and they assume children view life in the same way.

Equally important, all family members believed they could change other members' feelings even when anger was involved. The majority of children believed they could alter their mothers' feelings—68 percent said they could make happy mothers angry, 68 percent said they could make sad mothers happy, and 63 percent said they could make angry mothers happy. Here there is agreement. Mothers said children could change their feelings dramatically, but they believed that they could alter children's feelings as well. Behavioral and verbal strategies were most frequently used by adults and children, but children also included material reward strategies.

All family members saw anger as very much a part of family life. Children appeared the most accurate in seeing their behavior as a major cause of family anger—though on any given occasion they could be mistaken—and the family routines and demands as the major source of their own irritations.

Everyday Negative Moods   Minor daily hassles at work or with children contribute to parents' negative moods that, in turn, affect parenting and children's behavior. Negative moods bias what parents recall about children's past behaviors, shape parents' interpretations of current behavior, and cause parents to discipline children more harshly.[23]

Hassles do not have to be intense or prolonged. Even a briefly induced negative mood reduced mothers' positive comments and verbal interactions with their children during play and laboratory tasks.[24] Being distracted by a simple task involving anagrams resulted in parents' being less positive, more irritable, more critical of and more interfering with their preschoolers.[25]

The hassles that generally trigger a negative mood are the daily challenges of parenting rather than major difficulties with children.[26] Hassles fall into two broad categories: (1) the effort required to rear children—continually cleaning up messes, changing family plans, running errands to meet children's needs—and (2) the challenge of dealing with irritating behaviors like whining, sibling fights, and constant demands.

Parents' personality characteristics, their coping styles, and the amount of support available to them can intensify or decrease stress.[27] Outgoing, sociable, optimistic parents are less likely to respond to hassles with negative moods. Parents who use avoidant coping styles, who wish stress would go away so they wouldn't have to deal with it, experience increased stress. Parents who use positive reappraisal of the situation, who feel they are learning from the situation and becoming more skilled, experience decreased stress and retain their self-confidence.

AFFECTIVE PROCESSES IN PARENTING

Theodore Dix presents a model of parenting that gives a central role to emotions in organizing parents' behavior with children.[28] As we have just seen, parenting involves strong positive and negative feelings. Children arouse parents' warmth and love, but they also trigger conflicts that can occur as many as fifteen times in a hour when children are young. These feelings determine whether parents will view children's behavior in a positive or negative light.

62

CHAPTER 3
Establishing
Close
Emotional
Relationships
with Children

FIGURE 3-1
DIX'S MODEL OF AFFECTIVE PROCESSES IN PARENTING

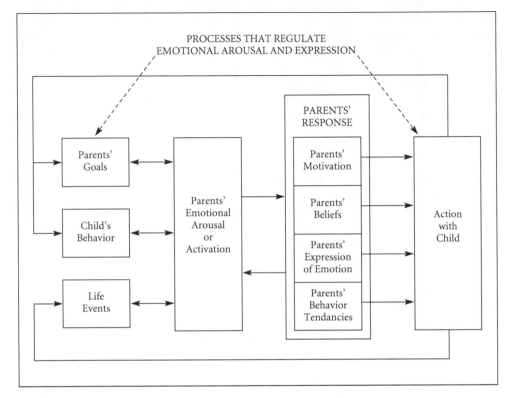

Parents' emotional states also determine the type, consistency, and effectiveness of the discipline they use. When angry, they may resort to physical punishment and carry it out more forcefully than they would otherwise. Dix concludes, "Thus, perhaps more than any other single variable, parents' emotions reflect the health of parent-child relationships. They are barometers for the quality of parenting, the developmental outcomes that are likely for children, and the impact that environmental stresses and supports are having on the family."[29]

Dix identifies three sources of parents' emotions: (1) parents' concerns/goals, (2) children's behavior, and (3) life events/social factors. The emotions, in turn, influence parents' motivations and beliefs about children and organize and energize parental behavior. Parents regulate and modulate emotional reactions so they are appropriate to the situation. Figure 3-1 depicts this model of affective parenting.

The following example illustrates Dix's model. A father has goals of raising an independent, curious child. On a particular day, however, he is frustrated and angry because his boss ignored his suggestions and gave impractical orders. When his four-year-old son asks numerous questions and insists on answers, the father, in his frustrated mood, views the child's behavior as defiance of his request to wait until later for the answers. He then punishes the child and feels worse because now he feels inadequate as a parent.

He talks his work situation over with his wife, makes positive plans, and feels better. When his persistent four-year-old returns in a few hours with new questions, the father, in a good mood, interprets the behavior as curiosity about the world and goes to the encyclopedia to look up the answers. The father feels good about taking the time to help his child. In each of the two situations, the father's goals and the child's behavior were the same. But the father's mood, negative in one instance and positive in the other, influenced his interpretation of the boy's behavior and his own response to it.

STRATEGIES FOR PROMOTING A HARMONIOUS FAMILY ATMOSPHERE

Strategies for creating the positive relationships with family members that are so important for development and well-being include (1) communicating feelings, (2) maintaining a democratic family, (3) providing respect and encouragement for children, and (4) providing opportunities for self-expression. We turn first to strategies for communicating feelings, which is at the heart of the parenting process.

Communicating Feelings

In a comprehensive survey concerning people's feelings about family life, participants described their families as loving and caring, but they felt they themselves lacked the skills to communicate these feelings to other family members, and as a result, families were not as close and supportive as they could be. The ways to express feelings described in this section give parents the tools for expressing their positive as well as their negative emotions.[30]

Haim Ginott describes emotions as follows:

> Emotions are part of our genetic heritage. Fish swim, birds fly, and people feel. Sometimes we are happy, sometimes we are not; but sometimes in our life we are sure to feel anger and fear, sadness and joy, greed and guilt, lust and scorn, delight and disgust. While we are not free to choose the emotions that arise in us, we are free to choose how and when to express them, provided we know what they are. That is the crux of the problem. Many people have been educated out of knowing what their feelings are. When they hated, they were told it was only dislike. When they were afraid, they were told there was nothing to be afraid of. When they felt pain, they were advised to be brave and smile. Many of our popular songs tell us "Pretend you are happy when you are not."
>
> What is suggested in place of this pretense? Truth. Emotional education can help children to know what they feel. It is more important for a child to know what he feels than why he feels it. When he knows clearly what his feelings are, he is less likely to feel "all mixed up" inside.
>
> How can we help a child to know his feelings? We can do so by serving as a mirror to his emotions. A child learns about his physical likeness by seeing his image in a mirror. He learns about his emotional likeness by hearing his feelings reflected by us.[31]

When parents feed back children's feelings, children feel understood, important, and valuable as individuals. As their responses receive attention, their self-esteem grows. How does one go about feeding back feelings? First, one pays attention and listens to hear what the feelings are, then restates those perceptions in simple language.

CHAPTER 3
Establishing
Close
Emotional
Relationships
with Children

Active Listening *Active listening* is Thomas Gordon's term for what parents do when they reflect their children's feelings. Parents listen to children's statements, pay careful attention to the feelings expressed, and then frame a response similar to the child's statement. If a child says she feels too dumb to learn a school subject, the parent feeds back that she feels she is not smart enough. Ginott might feed back a response about the child's fear, worry, or frustration. Gordon gives examples of feeding back responses about deeper feelings, so the difference between the two strategies is minimal. Following are Gordon's examples of active listening.

CHILD: I don't want to go to Bobby's birthday party tomorrow.
PARENT: Sounds like you and Bobby have had a problem maybe.
CHILD: I hate him, that's what. He's not fair.
PARENT: You really hate him because you feel he's been unfair somehow.
CHILD: Yeah. He never plays what I want to play.

CHILD: (Crying) I fell down on the sidewalk and scraped my knee. Oh, it's bleeding a lot! Look at it!
PARENT: You're really scared seeing all that blood.[32]

If the parent's response is accurate, the child confirms the feedback with a positive response. If the parent's interpretation is wrong, the child indicates that and has a chance to correct the misinterpretation by expanding on feelings. The parent can continue active listening and gain greater understanding of what is happening to the child.

Active listening has many advantages. First, it helps children express feelings in a direct, effective way. As feelings are expressed and parents accept them, children feel understood and learn that they are like everyone else. In the process of being understood, children gain a feeling of being loved and cherished. When parents talk about feelings and help their children pay attention to others' feelings, their children understand and get along better with people.[33]

Second, as feelings are expressed, parents and children together learn that the obvious problem is not necessarily the real or basic problem. Like the rest of us, children use defenses and sometimes start by blaming a friend, a parent, or circumstances for what they are feeling. Sometimes, they initially deny that they are upset. As parents focus on the feelings, children gradually come to identify the underlying problem and discover what they can do about it. Children feel increasingly competent and become responsible problem solvers. A positive cycle is set up, in which parents are accepting of children and trust them to behave responsibly, and children learn to act independently, thus reinforcing the parents' beliefs.

A third advantage is that listening to children's feeling sometimes resolves the problem. Often when we are upset, frustrated, sad, or angry, we simply want to express the feeling and have someone respond, "Yes, that's frustrating," or "It is really painful when a friend walks off with someone else and leaves you behind." The response validates the feeling as being justified and important, and frequently that is all we want.

What qualities must parents have to do active listening? Gordon warns parents not to attempt active listening when they are hurried or when they are preoccupied. It takes time and effort to determine whether a joking comment is covering up a deeper sadness over some disappointment, whether a critical remark is hiding a feeling of rejection, or whether a casual remark about a success is covering up real pleasure at a difficult achievement. Parents need to think carefully, to phrase and time their words with sensitivity, to make the comment that will move the dialogue along and facilitate expression of true feelings.

Active listening requires persistence, patience, and a strong commitment to attend to both the child's words and accompanying behavioral clues. Is the child's attitude casual, or is there an emotional intensity that is inconsistent with the words? Is the child fidgety, uncomfortable, withdrawn, silent, or distracted and thinking about something else? In the beginning, conversations may seem unnatural, stilted, even contrived, but they improve with practice—and active listening works with partners and friends as well as with children.

There are times when active listening is not appropriate. If a child asks for information, give the information. If a child does not want to talk about feelings, respect the child's privacy and do not probe. Similarly, if active listening and the dialogue have gone as far as the child is willing to go, then a parent needs to recognize that it is time to stop. And finally, active listening should not be started if a parent is too busy or too preoccupied to stay with it and really hear and respond to the child's feelings.

One of the mothers in Ginott's group raised the question of reflecting back feelings of great sadness over a loss.[34] Is this wise? Does it help children? Might not such feelings overwhelm them? Ginott responded that parents must learn that suffering can strengthen a child's character. When a child is sad in response to a real loss, a parent need only empathize, "You are sad. I understand." The child learns that the parent is a person who understands and sympathizes. Research documents the value for children of learning to express feelings.

I-Messages   When a parent is angry, frustrated, or irritated with a child, the parent communicates his or her feelings constructively with an *I-message* rather than nagging, yelling, or criticizing. The I-message contains three parts: (1) a clear statement of how the parent feels, (2) a statement of the behavior that has caused the parent to feel that way, and (3) a statement describing why the behavior is upsetting to the parent. For example, a parent frustrated with a teenager's messy room might say, "I feel upset and frustrated when I look at your messy room because the family works hard to make the house look clean and neat, and your room spoils our efforts."

An I-message is a very effective means of communication, but one that is not, in the beginning, easy to use. Developing skill with I-messages requires concentration and practice. But when they finally come easily, I-messages facilitate communication. I-messages help children to understand their parents as individuals. When parents use I-messages and feel free to express their individuality, they serve as models that encourage children to react openly, too.

Parents need to spend time analyzing their feelings and becoming more aware of exactly how they feel. Gordon points out that, often, when a parent communicates anger at a child, the parent may actually be feeling disappointment, fear, frustration, or hurt. When a child comes home an hour late, the parent may launch into a tirade. The worry that grew into fear during the hour of waiting is transformed into relief that the child is safe, and that relief is then translated into angry words intended to prevent a recurrence of this disturbing behavior. Similarly, a parent may complain

CHAPTER 3
Establishing
Close
Emotional
Relationships
with Children

about a child's behavior when, in reality, what is disturbing the parent is a problem at work. The parent who has learned to use accurate I-messages is less likely to misplace anger and use a child as a scapegoat.

What should a parent do if a child pays no attention to I-messages? First, be sure the child can pay attention to the I-message. Don't try to communicate feelings when the child is rushing out of the house or is already deeply immersed in some other activity. If an I-message is then ignored, send another, more forceful message. And be sure that the feeling tone matches the feelings.

I-messages have several benefits. First, when parents use I-messages, they begin to take their own needs seriously. This process benefits all family relationships because parents feel freer—more themselves—in all areas of life. Second, children learn about the parents' reaction, which they may not have understood until the I-message. Third, children have an opportunity to engage in problem solving in response to I-messages. Even toddlers and preschoolers have ideas, not only for themselves but also for others. Siblings often have good ideas about what may be bothering another child in the family. They think of things that might have escaped the attention of parents.

Sometimes, a child responds to an I-message with an I-message. For example, when a parent expresses distress because the lawn is not mowed, the daughter may reply that she feels annoyed because mowing interferes with her afterschool activities. At that point, the parent must "shift gears," as Gordon terms it, and reflect back the child's frustration by using active listening.

I-messages not only express parents' frustrations and unresolved feelings but also can convey appreciation—"I feel pleased when you help me with the dishes because then we have time to go to the store for your school supplies." I-messages are also useful in heading off problems and in helping children see that their parents have needs, too. These messages, termed *preventive I-messages,* express parents' future wants or needs and give children an opportunity to respond positively. For example, if a parent says, "I need quiet so I can drive the car," the child learns what to do to be helpful.

While parents use I-messages most often to describe their feelings about children's behavior, parents can also use such statements to describe their reactions to other events. This does not mean discussing intimate details of adult life that may upset children; rather, it means discussing parents' reactions to important daily concerns. In the discussion of moral competence in Chapter 2, we saw that when parents describe their own feelings and what causes them, children are more sympathetic to others. Parents' honesty and openness may help children better understand and be more involved with others.

Effects of Emotional Coaching   Recent research indicates that when parents coach their five-year-old children in how to deal with feelings, the children function better physically and psychologically when they are eight years old. They perform better academically and are socially more competent with peers. They are physically healthier as well, perhaps because coaching helps children modulate their emotional reactions, which, in turn, helps their physiological system function better.[35]

Coaching involves all those behaviors recommended by Ginott and Gordon—listening to children's feelings, accepting and validating them, using I-messages regarding one's own feelings, and helping children solve problems while maintaining acceptable limits concerning the expression of feelings.

This study finds that parents differ in their attitudes and thoughts about how important feelings are in life. Some parents have heightened awareness of their own and their children's feelings and a strong conviction that feelings are a central part of life. Feelings signal that change is required. Anger serves to initiate action in frustrating situations, and sadness slows a person down to have time to cope with loss.

These parents feel comfortable with their feelings, and they consider that a major parental task is to help their children live happily with their own emotional reactions. They do this by coaching children to label their reactions, validating the importance of their feelings whatever they might be, and teaching their children strategies for expressing the feelings appropriately. Feelings do not frighten these parents. Rather, parents see such feelings as opportunities to become closer to their children through sharing the strong reactions and teaching ways to handle them.

Other parents feel uncomfortable with feelings and seek one of three ways to handle the discomfort.[36] *Dismissive* parents minimize the importance of feelings, making light of or ignoring them because they believe the feelings may make matters worse. *Disapproving* parents criticize, judge, and punish children for the expression of feelings. These parents do not usually disapprove of all feelings, just a subgroup such as anger and sadness, or just under certain conditions such as a "minor event." Children of dismissive and disapproving parents have a hard time trusting their own judgment. By learning their feelings are wrong, they come to believe there is something basically wrong with *them* for having the feelings. Because they have little experience in acknowledging and dealing with their feelings, they often have difficulty controlling them and solving problems.

A third subgroup of parents who feel uncomfortable with dealing with feelings are termed *laissez-faire*. They accept all feelings and often comfort the child when the child experiences a negative emotional reaction, but they do little to teach or guide the child in how to express feelings appropriately. Parents seem to believe that expressing the feelings in any form will take care of the problem. Their children do not learn to cope with feelings constructively and have difficulty concentrating and learning in school and in making friends.

So, the two extremes of response—ignoring or criticizing feelings so they occur as little as possible and accepting all expressions of feeling without providing guidance for expression—lead to similar kinds of problems, such as the inability to regulate feelings and to feel comfortable with themselves and others. Coaching children not only helps children deal better with their feelings and with social and cognitive endeavors, it also frequently brings parents and children closer together because parents feel they really understand their children.

Establishing Democratic Family Living

Thomas Gordon and Rudolf Dreikurs both emphasize the importance of a democratic family atmosphere, but each gives a slightly different meaning to the concept.

In *Teaching Children Self-Discipline,* Thomas Gordon describes his great concern about authoritarian families, in which parents control children through rewards and punishment.[37] He is highly critical of parents who manipulate children in order to

CHAPTER 3
Establishing
Close
Emotional
Relationships
with Children

change them into what the parents think is desirable. He dislikes the concept of praise because it implies that the parent is judging and evaluating the child in terms of some external standard. He also disapproves of punishment because it allows a powerful person to take advantage of a less powerful person, and he especially condemns physical punishment for children because it belittles them, makes them angry at and fearful of the parent, and does not work.

Gordon also criticizes a permissive atmosphere as disorganized and even chaotic. He encourages a democratic atmosphere in which children are accepted as they are, with important needs and wishes that at times conflict with others' needs. When there is a problem, parents send I-messages, reflecting their own thoughts and feelings, and do active listening to get the child's point of view. If a solution does not arise, then parents and children engage in the mutual problem solving described in the next chapter.

According to Gordon, parents should never dictate solutions, but should work cooperatively with children to form a plan that meets everyone's needs. Working together this way frees children from feeling judged, evaluated, or manipulated. Children and parents become partners in solving the hassles of life.

Dreikurs, too, believes that democratic family living provides an encouraging atmosphere in which the needs of children and parents receive equal respect and consideration. Everyone has responsibilities as well. Parents provide food, shelter, clothes, and recreation for children. Children, in turn, contribute to family functioning by doing chores and running errands. Material rewards are not given for doing a particular number of chores. When mutual respect among equal individuals is the rule in a family, members work together to do the jobs that are necessary for the welfare of all. To deny children the opportunity to do their share is to deny them an essential satisfaction in life. Democratic living ensures freedom for family members but does not imply an absence of rule. Dreikurs strongly favors structure in family life and believes that providing boundaries gives a child a feeling of security.

To help children follow routines, parents serve as models. They also teach children how to do routine tasks. Parents often expect children to be able to learn self-care and do household chores without any instruction, so they do not spend the time needed to teach children. How many parents have taught a child, step by step, how to make a bed or how to get dressed and then observed as the child increased in skill, giving added coaching as needed? An encouraging parent helps children to be both self-sufficient and involved with other people.

Making Mistakes   In all families, children make mistakes. In democratic families, parents accept mistakes without dwelling on them. Dreikurs describes parents' tendencies to overemphasize the errors children make. Parents want so much for children to grow up and do well that they sometimes point out every minor mistake and continually tell children what they must do to improve. Under such a regime, children may feel they have to be perfect to be accepted. That fear may immobilize the child. As Dreikurs observes,

> We all make mistakes. Very few are disastrous. Many times we won't even know that a given action is a mistake until after it is done and we see the results! Sometimes we even have to make the mistake in order to find out that it is a mistake. *We must have the courage to be imperfect* — and to allow our children also to be imperfect. Only in this way can we

function, progress, and grow. Our children will maintain their courage and learn more readily if we minimize the mistakes and direct their attention toward the positive. "What is to be done now that the mistake is made" leads to progress forward and stimulates courage. Making a mistake is not nearly as important as what we do about it afterward.[38]

Effective parents separate the deed from the doer when responding the mistakes and make clear that the child is not a failure but simply is unskilled and in need of teaching. In coping with a mistake, parents remain problem oriented—looking at the situation, seeing what needs to be done, and helping the child function well by giving encouragement and guidance. For example, when a junior high school student gets a poor grade, the parents sit down with the child and help figure out what the trouble is and how the child might improve. Parents guide the child to select the actions that will bring improvements.

Mistakes are a natural part of life and need not have lasting ill effects. When children learn a healthy attitude toward mistakes early on, they are freer to explore and act; as a result, they learn and accomplish more. A healthy attitude consists of believing that mistakes are an expected part of life; though often accidental, they do have causes and many times can be prevented. So children and parents can learn to look at mistakes carefully and find out what to do differently the next time. Mistakes are proof that the child is trying to do something but may not be quite ready to achieve the goal. Mistakes are incompletions, not failures. The child can take more time learning the activity or perhaps practicing to achieve the goal.

Though unfortunate in the sense that they take up time and sometimes cost money, mistakes are rarely disastrous or damaging. To the contrary, they are very often valuable experiences because a child learns what is not effective. In addition, many warm family memories center on mistakes that were overcome.

Research supports Dreikurs's advice on handling mistakes and documents the power of parents' explanatory style in shaping children's way of thinking about themselves and their abilities.[39] Some children, at a very early age, show vulnerability to criticism. After receiving criticism about a single mistake, they generalize the criticism to their overall ability and feel helpless and inadequate. Vulnerable children five to six years of age who lack a clear concept of ability interpret the criticism as a comment on their goodness or badness as a person. When children feel helpless and inadequate, they give up and find it very hard to improve. Sensitive children are more likely than confident children to report that parents make critical comments about their mistakes. Sadly, even very young children internalize these comments and feel helpless and inadequate when they make a mistake.

Martin Seligman, who has studied the widespread effects of optimistic and pessimistic attitudes toward adversity, advises parents to teach children how to dispute global, pessimistic beliefs or interpretations of mistakes and difficulties.[40]

Parents must teach children that a negative event has many causes, some beyond their control. For example, a student may get a poor grade on a test because she did not study enough, the test was unusually hard, the class has many bright students and grading was on the curve, the teacher came late and allowed less time for the exam, or the student was nervous and could not organize her answers as well. The student might blame herself, saying she is stupid, is going to fail the class, and won't be able to take more courses in that area. She is "latching onto the worst of these possible causes—the most permanent, pervasive, and personal one."[41]

70

CHAPTER 3
Establishing
Close
Emotional
Relationships
with Children

◆

BOX 3-1
DEALING WITH ADVERSITY

Adversity: My teacher, Mr. Minner, yelled at me in front of the whole class, and everybody laughed.

Belief: He hates me and now the whole class thinks I'm a jerk.

Consequences: I felt really sad and I wished that I could jut disappear under my desk.

Disputation: Just because Mr. Minner yelled at me, it doesn't mean he hates me. Mr. Minner yells at just about everybody, and he told our class we were his favorite class. I guess I was goofing around a little, so I don't blame him for getting mad. Everyone in the class, everyone except for maybe Linda but she's a goody-goody, but everyone else has been yelled at by Mr. Minner at *least* once, so I doubt they think I'm a jerk.

Energization: I still feel a little sad about being yelled at, but not nearly as much, and I don't feel like disappearing under my desk anymore.

Martin E. P. Seligman, *Learned Optimism* (New York: Pocket Books, 1990), p. 241.

Parents teach their children to dispute pessimistic interpretations with questions like "What is the evidence for my belief?" "What are other, less destructive ways to look at this?" "What is the usefulness of this belief?" Seligman advises, "Focus on the changeable (not enough time spent studying), the specific (this particular exam was uncharacteristically hard), and the nonpersonal (the professor graded unfairly) causes."[42] Then parents and children can generate alternative explanations and future actions. Seligman calls his method the ABCDE—Adversity, Belief (usually negative), Consequences (usually negative), Disputation, Energization—method. This method is illustrated in Box 3-1.

Providing Respect and Encouragement

Dreikurs believes that children have built-in capacities to develop in healthy, effective ways.[43] Because children seek to be active and competent, a parent's main task is to provide an environment that permits this development to occur. The child's strongest desire is to belong to a group, and from infancy the child seeks acceptance and importance within the family. Children's deepest fear is of rejection, but each child develops a unique path to family acceptance. The child accomplishes this task by using innate abilities and environmental forces to shape dynamic relationships with other family members.

Do parents usually help children discover their own strengths and abilities? No, says Dreikurs. Most often, parents tear down children's confidence with such comments as "What a mess you make," or "I can do it for you faster," or "You are too little to set the table." Dreikurs recommends that parents use encouragement to help children develop their abilities. He defines encouragement as a "continuous process aimed at giving the child a sense of self-respect and a sense of accomplishment."[44] Encouragement is expressed by word and deed.

A parent's facial expressions, tone of voice, gestures, and posture all tell children how the parent feels about them. In many different ways—warm cuddling, active play, gentle nurturing—a parent can communicate that children are worthwhile and capable of participating in social living. How does a parent provide encouragement for development? First, by respecting the child and, from infancy, permitting self-sufficiency in all possible situations. Babies, for example, are encouraged to entertain themselves; they are left alone at times to explore their fingers and toes, play with toys, and examine their surroundings. As soon as possible, they feed themselves. Children as young as one or two are included in family chores and responsibilities as soon as they show any interest in helping. Even a toddler can empty a wastebasket and carry small nonbreakable items to the dinner table.

Second, parents foster development by giving verbal encouragement, telling children specifically what they do well—"I like your painting with all the bright colors" and "You certainly picked up all your toys quickly and that helps Daddy when he vacuums."

Third, parents offer encouragement when they teach children to ask for what they want. Children need to learn that parents cannot read their minds and that they must take an active role in saying what they want. As children try out new activities, parents wait until children ask for help before giving it. If children ask for help, parents can start off helping or request that children begin without them and say they will be available later if the children cannot proceed. When parents give encouragement, they call attention to the challenge of the task—"It's hard practicing now, but you'll master the keys and really enjoy playing the piano as you get more experience."

Finally, parents encourage development when they emphasize children's gains. They show children how far they have come since starting the activity. Encouraging comments often refer to the completed task. But children soon learn that enjoyment comes from the process as well as from final success.

Importance versus Self-Sufficiency When children feel discouraged and unable to make positive contributions to the social group, they seek other ways to feel important and competent. Misbehavior results from the pursuit of goals that give feelings of importance instead of feelings of self-sufficiency and social integration. Dreikurs identifies four "mistaken" goals of behavior—mistaken because they do not bring genuine feelings of competence and participation. These goals are attention, power, revenge, and inadequacy. The parent's task is (1) to understand which of the four mistaken goals is motivating the child's behavior and (2) to act so that the purpose is no longer achieved. Thus, the parent must understand the child's underlying feelings, but instead of reflecting back feelings, Dreikurs advises action to modify the child's behavior.

A child is seeking mistaken goals when his or her behavior conflicts with the needs of the situation. For example, a child may seek *attention* by being talkative and charming. This behavior can be pleasant and endearing rather than annoying, but when such behavior prevents others from talking, it becomes misbehavior.

When attention is denied, a child may hunt for an issue to use in the struggle of *power*. For example, a three-year-old may insist that he does not have to go to bed at 7:30 p.m. If he persists, running around the house and causing his mother to spend

CHAPTER 3
Establishing
Close
Emotional
Relationships
with Children

Becoming a parent gives meaning and purpose to life.

time chasing him down, the child is struggling for power. Sometimes, parents find it hard to tell whether a child is seeking attention or power. Dreikurs points out that children usually stop the mistaken behavior after the first request if they are seeking attention, but not if what they want is power. Attempts to stop the behavior only aggravate children's attempts to gain power.

When problems continue, children may intensify the power struggle and seek *revenge* and retaliation. Here, children have lost hope of getting approval through positive behavior and feel they have nothing to lose, so they seek revenge as a means of feeling important. Children are determined to feel important even if they have to hurt others physically.

Dreikurs notes that this form of misbehavior is particularly sad because the children who need the most encouragement are the ones most likely to be punished. Parents need to offer warm understanding and sympathetic acceptance so that children can express their own positive qualities. Unfortunately, punishment intensifies anger and guilt, leads to further attempts to provoke the parents, and sets up a vicious cycle.

Children who claim *inadequacy* to explain poor performance in some activity also pursue a mistaken goal. Dreikurs gives the example of an eight-year-old boy who was having school difficulties. The teacher told the mother he was a poor reader, was slow in all subjects, and showed no improvement despite the teacher's extra efforts. She asked the mother what he did at home. The mother replied that he did not like chores and did them so poorly that she had stopped asking him. The child had developed a low opinion of his abilities over a period of time and found it easiest to claim incompetence. Feelings of helplessness exaggerate any real or imagined problem. In such a situation, a parent can demonstrate the chores and work with children until they feel competent to function alone. Encouragement helps children persist until they are able to finish a job independently.

Providing Opportunities for Self-Expression

Family relationships are most harmonious when both children and parents have outlets for expressing feelings. Activities such as daily physical exercise, drawing, modeling clay, painting, and cooking all serve as outlets to drain off tensions and irritations and provide individuals with additional sources of pleasure and feelings of competence. Wise parents provide children with a variety of outlets so that they develop many skills. Research indicates that childhood leisure activities, especially a wide variety — such as painting, reading, and athletics — are more predictive of psychological health in adulthood than are the child's own personality characteristics in childhood. These activities promote self-confidence and self-esteem, which increase psychological health.[45]

STRATEGIES FOR DEALING WITH NEGATIVE FEELINGS

Active listening and I-messages help parents and children deal with negative feelings once they are aroused. But preventing stress is a major way to decrease negative feelings. Strategies to minimize hassles and negative feelings in the family include (1) creating family time, (2) developing a support system, (3) maintaining realistic expectations, and (4) learning ways to manage negative feelings.

Creating Family Time

Adults have identified lack of time with the family as the biggest stress on families today, and economic pressures as the main reason for this lack of time.[46] When both parents work, families simply have less time together.

Parents cannot create hours in the day, but they can shift priorities to ensure that available time is used to promote family closeness. Parents can decide to change housekeeping routines and standards so that family time is more important than

74

CHAPTER 3
Establishing
Close
Emotional
Relationships
with Children

cleaning house or preparing elaborate meals. In addition, parents can involve children as joint partners in meeting household responsibilities so that chores are opportunities for parent-child time together. Working together enables parents and children to converse and share common experiences, creating closeness and increasing understanding.

Developing a Support System

When parents get support from friends, relatives, and each other, they experience less stress and fewer negative moods. The support may come from organized parenting groups like those attended by the couples in Carolyn Pape Cowan and Philip A. Cowan's study.[47] Those groups, which included both husband and wife, met over a long period and decreased couples' stress.

Joseph Procaccini and Mark Kiefaber outline an extended program to provide parents with varied kinds of support to prevent *parent burnout,* defined as "a downward drift toward physical, emotional, and spiritual exhaustion resulting from the combination of chronic high stress and perceived low personal growth and autonomy."[48] Parents feel worn out by meeting seemingly endless family needs, especially those of children, and they lose enthusiasm for parenting.

Enthusiastic, devoted parents actually are the ones most likely to burn out because they invest so much of themselves in the parenting process and want to be perfect. Procaccini and Kiefaber propose a six-week program of daily exercises to deal with burnout by substituting positive attitudes for negative ones and by changing behavior slowly. Woven into the program are eight important ingredients for reducing burnout: (1) getting information about children and parenting skills from books, (2) connecting with a significant other for support (spouse, relative, friend, minister), (3) becoming part of a small social group, (4) engaging in some goal-oriented activity (athletics, artistic pursuit, hobby), (5) gaining knowledge of self, (6) having access to money or credit, (7) developing spiritual or intellectual beliefs that provide meaning to life, and (8) maintaining self-nourishing activity. All eight are needed to buffer a parent against burnout. Note that only one ingredient, the first, bears directly on rearing children. All the rest focus on helping the parent to become a competent, integrated person and on forging interpersonal connections with other people.

Research supports the findings of Procaccini and Kiefaber.[49] Parents who received training in parenting skills and in techniques of reducing parental distress were more effective in managing their children's behavior than were parents who received information only on parenting skills.

Maintaining Realistic Expectations

We all approach new experiences with expectations of what they will be like. Expectations are built from what authorities tell us and what we and other people we have observed have actually experienced. If expectations are realistic, they can help us prepare for the event, function at our best, and elicit the most positive results for all who are involved.

Realistic expectations prevent the stress that results when the experience differs vastly from what was expected. Violated expectations lead to self-questioning and

---

♦

BOX 3-2
EIGHT WAYS TO DEAL WITH PARENTAL ANGER

1. Exit or wait—taking time out is a way of maintaining and modeling self-control.
2. Make "I," not "you," statements to help the child understand your point of view.
3. Stay in the present—avoid talking about the past or future.
4. Avoid physical force and threats.
5. Be brief and to the point.
6. Put it in writing—a note or letter is a way of expressing your feelings in a way that the person can understand.
7. Focus on the essential—ask yourself whether what you are arguing about is really important and worth the energy involved.
8. Restore good feelings—talk over what happened calmly or give hugs or other indications that the fight is over.

Adapted from Nancy Samalin with Catherine Whitney, *Love and Anger: The Parental Dilemma* (New York: Penguin Books, 1992).

---

self-doubt. For example, for new parents, violated expectations are associated with lowered energy and lack of confidence as a parent.[50]

Parents' expectations also play a role in defining a hassle. For example, parents who grew up with siblings and have a realistic view of how much arguing siblings do are less stressed when their own children squabble. Having realistic expectations of children based on an understanding of their individual qualities and needs prevents parents from feeling stress because children are not performing as the books say they should or as the parents did as children.[51]

Parents develop realistic expectations from reading, from observing their own and other children, from talking to other parents and sharing problems with them, and from their own experiences as a parent.

Managing Negative Feelings

Because anger, stress, frustration, and guilt are all part of rearing children, parents need to find their own strategies for controlling the expression of these feelings. When these feelings lead to criticism, nagging, yelling, and hitting, both parents and children suffer. Children are hurt and discouraged; parents feel guilty and inadequate.

Nancy Samalin, who runs parent groups on dealing with anger, suggests that families compile lists of acceptable and unacceptable ways for parents and children to express anger.[52] Acceptable ways include such actions as crying, going for a walk, and yelling, "I'm mad." Unacceptable ways include destroying property, hitting, spitting, and swearing.

Of course, I-messages are the most direct way to express anger, but sometimes people want more physical outlets such as work or exercise. Box 3-2 lists a variety of ways to deal with anger.

CHAPTER 3
Establishing
Close
Emotional
Relationships
with Children

To parents who feel guilty about or frustrated with the mistakes they have made, Jane Nelson, using Dreikurs's guidelines, suggests following a three-step recovery program: (1) recognize the mistake, (2) reconcile with the child by apologizing, and (3) resolve the problem with a mutually agreed-on solution.[53] Nelson advises parents to view mistakes as opportunities for learning. Seeing mistakes in that way reduces parents' self-criticism and their resistance to recognizing them. Apologizing is a behavior children can emulate when they have made a mistake. It also enables parents to experience children's quickness to forgive.

Dreikurs emphasizes that, like children, parents must develop the courage to be imperfect. He writes,

> The importance of courage in parents cannot be overemphasized. Whenever you feel dismayed or find yourselves thinking, "My gosh, I did it all wrong," be quick to recognize this symptom of your own discouragement; turn your attention to an academic and impersonal consideration of what can be done to make matters better. When you try a new technique and it works, be glad. When you fall back into old habits, don't reproach yourself. You need to constantly reinforce your own courage, and to do so, you need the "courage to be imperfect." Recall to your mind the times that you have succeeded, and try again. Dwelling on your mistakes saps your courage. Remember, one cannot build on weakness—only on strength. Admit humbly that you are bound to make mistakes and acknowledge them without a sense of loss in your personal value. This will do much to keep your courage up. Above all, remember that we are not working for perfection, but only for improvement. Watch for the little improvements, and when you find them relax and have faith in your ability to improve further.[54]

THE JOYS OF PARENTING

The challenges, hassles, and frustrations of parenting often obscure the real joys in rearing children. Yet it is the joys that compensate for, and at times completely eliminate, all the negative feelings. Despite their importance, little has been written about the joys of parenting. In a remarkable study fifty years ago, Arthur Jersild and his colleagues interviewed 544 parents about the joys and problems of child-rearing. They introduce the book with the following comments:

> There has been relatively little systematic study of the cheerful side of the ledger of child-rearing. Studies of characteristics that bring headaches to a parent have not been matched by surveys of characteristics that warm a parent's heart. . . . The fact that the emphasis has been so much on the negative side is perhaps no more than one should expect. Behavior that is disturbing to the parent or to others usually calls for action or for a solution of some sort, and as such it also attracts the research worker. On the other hand, what is pleasant can be enjoyed without further ado.[55]

When Jersild and his associates talked to parents, they learned that by and large parents experience many more joys than difficulties, though the latter certainly exist. They found that children bring what parents hope they will—affection, companionship, enjoyment of the child as a special person, and delight in development and increasing competence. About parenthood, Jersild and his colleagues conclude, "Perhaps no other circumstance in life offers so many challenges to an individual's powers, so great an array of opportunities for appreciation, such a varied emotional and intellectual stimulation."[56]

Keeping an eye on the "cheerful side of the ledger" reduces stress and increases everyone's well-being and pleasure in life.

MAIN POINTS

Parenting experts reviewed here

- include Ginott, Gordon, and Briggs, who focus on communicating feelings
- include Dreikurs and the behaviorists, who focus on changing children's behavior
- agree on the importance of modeling, communicating positive feelings, respecting children, and avoiding ridicule and shaming
- disagree mainly on the importance of external rewards and punishments, the expression of parental anger, and the use of preventive statements to ward off trouble

Close emotional ties rest on the parent's love for the child

- as a unique person
- expressed in physical affection as well as in sensitive daily care
- and the mutual expression of feelings and thoughts

Happiness comes from

- feelings of love, affection, and concern others direct to us
- activities that lead to feelings of accomplishment and competence

When adults express unresolved anger in the presence of children, the anger

- produces feelings of sadness, anger, and guilt in children
- makes it hard for children to learn to express their own anger—some become overly passive and others become overly aggressive
- makes children feel they are the cause of anger and should fix the situation
- has minimal impact when parents resolve conflict fairly

Dix presents a model of the process of parenting that describes

- emotion at the center as an organizing, directing force in parenting
- child's characteristics, parents' goals, and life events as the main activators of parents' emotions
- emotion as determiner of parent's view of the child's behavior and the parent's response to it
- regulatory processes that modulate and control parents' emotions

78

CHAPTER 3
Establishing
Close
Emotional
Relationships
with Children

When parents listen to the child's feelings and reflect them,

- the child becomes increasingly able to identify feelings and to understand what their causes and consequences are
- the child learns his or her own feelings are important
- parent and child learn the obvious problem is not always the real problem

When parents express their feelings, they send I-messages that

- help parents clarify their own feelings
- state how the parent feels, what behavior aroused the feelings, and why the behavior affects the parent
- convey a message about a problem, about a good act the parent likes, or about a possible problem in the future
- help children understand parents' wishes and point of view

Emotional coaching

- involves the behaviors recommended by Ginott and Gordon
- is avoided by parents who instead are dismissive, disapproving, or laissez-faire

Close relationships grow when parents

- encourage the child and give the child a sense of self-respect and accomplishment by allowing as much independence as possible
- avoid criticism that discourages the child and instead help the child deal with mistakes
- teach children to communicate their needs
- create a democratic family atmosphere of mutual respect and cooperation in accomplishing family tasks and resolving problems that arise

Strategies for dealing with negative feelings include

- creating family time
- developing a support system
- maintaining realistic expectations
- learning to deal with negative feelings

EXERCISES

1. Imagine a time when you were a child and felt very close to one of your parents (if you like, you can do the exercise for each of your parents), and describe your parent's behavior with you. What qualities did your parent show that made for closeness? Share these qualities with class members. Is there a common core? If you do this exercise with each of your parents, note gender

differences. Do your mother and father at times show different qualities of closeness with you? Do your classmates experience differences in mothers' and fathers' behavior toward sons and daughters?

2. Imagine a time when you were a child and felt very distant from one of your parents (again, you may do this for each of your parents), and describe your parent's behavior with you. What qualities did your parent show that created distance? Again, share these qualities with class members and find the common core. Are these qualities the opposite of qualities that lead to closeness or do they represent a variety of dimensions? Do the qualities you discovered in Exercises 1 and 2 support what clinicians and researchers say is important?

3. Take turns practicing active listening with a classmate. This can be done in many formats. Have a partner active-listen as you do the following, then you active-listen as your partner does the same: (a) Describe a time when you were upset as a child. (b) Describe negative feelings in a recent exchange. (c) Describe scenes you have witnessed between parents and children in stores or restaurants. (d) Follow directions your instructor hands out for what one child in a problem situation might say.

4. With a classmate, practice sending I-messages. Again, choose from a variety of formats: (a) Recall a situation when a parent was angry at you when you were growing up and describe I-messages your parent might have sent. (b) Recall a recent disagreement with a friend or instructor and give appropriate I-messages for that. (c) Describe public parent-child confrontations you have witnessed and devise appropriate I-messages for the parents. (d) Devise I-messages for problem situations presented by your instructor.

5. (a) Recall one of your minor faults or weak points. When did you first become aware of this fault? In many instances, it goes back to what your parents said to you when you were a child. Use Martin Seligman's ABCDE method of dealing with negative beliefs to give different interpretations to that quality. (b) Recall a recent example, no matter how minor, in which you confronted adversity and felt negative emotions. Follow Seligman's recommendations for dealing with them.

ADDITIONAL READINGS

Briggs, Dorothy. *Your Child's Self-Esteem.* Garden City, NY: Doubleday, 1970.

Faber, Adele, and Mazlish, Elaine. *How to Talk So Kids Will Listen and Listen So Kids Will Talk.* New York: Rawson Wade, 1980.

Ginott, Haim G. *Between Parent and Child.* New York: Avon Books, 1969.

Gordon, Thomas. *P.E.T.: Parent Effectiveness Training.* New York: New American Library, 1975.

Gordon, Thomas. *Teaching Children Self-Discipline.* New York: Times Books, 1989.

Seligman, Martin E. P. *Learned Optimism.* New York: Pocket Books, 1990.

MODIFYING CHILDREN'S BEHAVIOR

C H A P T E R   4

Modifying children's behavior with fair and firm limits challenges parents. Deciding what is "fair" is no simple task. What are realistic expectations for that particular child of that particular age? What behaviors are appropriate? Getting the child to meet the expectations that are set can be even more difficult. How do parents effectively communicate what they expect and what the limits are? What if expectations are clear but the child fails to meet them? To establish firm boundaries, parents must enforce limits by using appropriate problem-solving techniques to modify behavior.

Children do not naturally do all the things parents want them to do. This chapter focuses on ways of shaping children's behavior so they adapt to family and social standards. As in many other areas of parenting, parents change their own behavior to ensure children will follow guidelines. In this chapter, we cover ways of (1) establishing realistic expectations, (2) structuring the environment to help children meet them, (3) teaching new, socially approved behaviors to children, (4) setting limits, and (5) enforcing limits.

THE LEARNING PROCESS

When children are infants, crying and whining and fussing are their only means of drawing attention to what they need—food, dry diapers, a burp, a hug. Their crying brings caregivers who satisfy their needs, thus reinforcing the crying. As children's skills increase, they develop more positive means to get what they want—asking, gaining cooperation from others, doing it themselves. Their parents' task is to encourage new behaviors to replace the coercive (forcing/pressuring) behaviors so natural to the infant.[1] In this chapter, I describe the many steps parents take to do this.

Children learn in several ways. They learn by observing models and imitating them. Models may be parents, siblings, or playmates. Children tend to imitate models who are warm, nurturant, and powerful. When such models are unavailable, children will imitate a cold, rejecting model.

Children also learn by the consequences of their actions. A reward or positive consequence increases the chance an action will occur again. Rewards may be pleasurable internal feelings that are not observable. For example, children run, jump, and solve puzzles simply because they enjoy the activities themselves. Often, rewards are external—getting attention, earning privileges, achieving a goal. When behavior leads to no reward or a negative consequence, then the behavior is less likely to occur than positively reinforced actions. Consequences are most effective when they immediately and consistently follow the behavior.

When parents use low-power strategies such as reasoning and helping children understand the consequences of their actions, their children are more likely to internalize parents' rules and values than children of parents who use high-power strategies.[2]

Such low-pressure strategies also enable children to learn the procedures and behavioral scripts of everyday life. Children can then more easily think through the outcomes of different actions; they can run through a mental simulation of what will happen and make appropriate choices. As a result, children increase their understanding of their own behavior and others' reactions to them.[3]

In contrast, when parents use high-power strategies such as threats and physical punishment, children may conform quickly, but they are less likely to internalize the rules and more likely to follow them only as long as a powerful external authority is present. Further, they are likely to become angry and resistant to high-power strategies.

As we saw in Chapter 2, parents have many different goals in socializing their children. Sometimes, parents want children to learn specific behaviors—staying out of the street, listening to parents—and sometimes, they want children to learn general values—being considerate toward older people, avoiding physical aggression.[4] These values vary according to parents' social and ethnic backgrounds. Whatever their goals, parents use specific processes to encourage the internalization of rules and values.

Teaching approved behaviors and values is a two-pronged process: (1) Parents send a clear, direct message to the child of what they want, its importance to the parents, and the expectation the child will comply with the request and (2) children accept the message, consider the request fair, and fulfill it without feeling a loss of autonomy or self-respect.[5]

Parents take many steps to encourage children's cooperation with their requests. First, many parents create an atmosphere of *receptive compliance,* defined as a "generalized willingness to cooperate with (or perhaps, 'exchange compliances with') a partner.[6] Sensitive parents, responsive to their children's needs, form secure attachments to their children, as described in Chapter 6, and create a climate in which children tend to comply because parents attend to their needs and wishes as well.

Second, parents structure situations to prevent problems. For example, when going to the grocery store, they give a child food in advance and find ways for the child to be helpful and busy so power struggles do not arise.[7]

Third, parents facilitate children's compliance by structuring the environment (e.g., providing storage space for children to put toys in and hooks children can reach to hang their clothes), by establishing routines so children can learn more easily, and by monitoring children's behavior to note difficulties in compliance.

Fourth, parents tailor their interventions to the child's temperament. For example, inactive babies need more stimulation and interaction before they will engage in exploration and play with toys whereas active babies explore most widely when parents give little stimulation.[8]

Fifth, parents modify their teaching behaviors as children grow. Eleanor Maccoby describes how the parent's role changes with the child's age.[9] With infants, parents are primarily caregivers who help infants regulate their physiological functioning. In the preschool years, parents help children control their emotions by showing them ways to deal with their emotional outbursts and by monitoring the amount of stimulation they receive. In the elementary school years, parents monitor children's self-monitoring, giving them much direct feedback. In the adolescent years, parents monitor teens' behavior as they spend more time away from home. And throughout childhood, parents provide guidance and consultation as the child moves into the larger society.

Finally, parents maintain a relatively calm emotional atmosphere with the strategies described in Chapter 3. It is difficult for children to receive clear messages when parents are upset, angry, or threatening. It is also difficult for them to understand parents' requests and reasoning when they themselves are angry, frustrated, or irritable.

Learning principles help parents teach children how to behave in approved ways. Rudolf Dreikurs comments that parents seem to expect that children will naturally observe what is correct.[10] It is indeed true that a first rule of parenting is that parents model the behaviors they wish children to have. Parents, however, must go beyond this simple model and take a more active role, teaching children new skills and limiting behavior. First, though, parents must decide on realistic expectations for children.

ESTABLISHING REALISTIC AND APPROPRIATE EXPECTATIONS OF CHILDREN

Unrealistic expectations of children's behavior are a major source of parents' frustration. With no one correct way to rear children at each stage of development, how do parents make their expectations realistic? What is realistic, given the variety of family settings that parents and children live in?

Realistic expectations are those that take into account the child's age and characteristics, the pattern of family living, social standards, parents' individual characteristics, health and safety factors, and daily events. Parents use the child's age as their first guide. For example, they do not expect toddlers to obey quickly, because they know toddlers are beginning to explore the world and assert their individuality. Parents learn what to expect at different ages by experience, reading, joining parent groups, and talking to other parents.

Having considered the child's age, parents then consider the child's own individual characteristics. Some children develop exactly by the book; their parents can base their expectations on what is typical for children of that age. Other children may have special needs to take into account. For example, parents of shy children will expect their children to need more than average support when meeting new people in a strange setting. Parents of gregarious, outgoing children will have dif-

THE JOYS OF PARENTING

"I have made deals with her. We always call it, 'Let's make a deal. This is what I want. What do you want?' We would come to some agreement, and as long as she was clear about it, she would do it. This was from early, early, early. So now on just about anything, we can negotiate. She wants to watch two programs, and we want to watch something else, and she'll come up with an idea. 'How about you let me watch this, and you tape that? Then I'll go do this.' We have tried a few democratic family meetings which is a little early, and we have done only a few, but she likes them. She'll see a problem and say, 'I think we need a meeting,' "
FATHER OF PRESCHOOLER

"We don't have sidewalks, and I have always put a chain at the end of the driveway whenever he is riding his bike so he doesn't go out. The other day he got his bike out to ride and then went and put the chain up. I thought, 'Good for him! He's learning to protect himself; he's learning these adaptive skills of safety for himself.' It made me feel proud of him. It was a good moment." FATHER OF PRESCHOOLER

"Another great joy is like painting a good picture or taking a good jump shot. It's doing something that is just right for your kids. It just hits the target. It might be, after reprimanding him and sending him to his room, going up and talking to him, telling him you love him and to come downstairs now. Just knowing how good a thing that is, how appropriate it is. It may be buying the fishing rod for a child that he desperately wanted. It is the pleasure of pleasing someone you care about and pleasing him on the basis of personal knowledge you have about him."
FATHER OF ELEMENTARY SCHOOL CHILDREN

ferent expectations than parents of shy children about how often friends can come to spend the night. So parents should always ask themselves whether a specific expectation is realistic for their child at a given stage.

Having taken the child's special characteristics into account, parents arrive at expectations based on their own and their family's overall needs. For example, in families where both parents work outside the home and children are in day care after school, it may be important for children to do chores before school because there is little time before dinner.

Parents' personal expectations can play a role in framing expectations for children. Parents may expect children to follow in their footsteps—parents who were school achievers may expect very good grades from children. Other parents expect children to achieve what they did not—the shy parent who wants a popular child or the early-working parent who wants the child to enjoy childhood. These expectations based on parents' lives are reasonable if they can be abandoned when a child cannot or does not want to meet them.

Parents also base expectations on their own social values and the social standards of the community. Parents in certain ethnic groups may have expectations about sharing or independence or about participation in extended family activities that differ from those of the predominant culture.

Expectations must be tailored to meet health and safety needs. When families live near busy streets, there will be firm expectations that very young children stay out of the streets. Health needs dictate reasonable amounts of sleep per night, a nutritious diet, toothbrushing, and so on. Children can be expected to follow these guidelines even though they do not want to.

Daily events also influence the nature of realistic expectations—and precisely in this area parenting becomes an art. If a child had a stressful day, expectations may have to be changed. For example, if a child lost a pet, it might be realistic and understanding to be tolerant of the child's irritability or inability to perform chores.

Finally, when they assess the appropriateness of their expectations, parents must ask themselves if this is something they expect from themselves or a friend. Parents will occasionally demand that children do things they themselves do not do. For example, parents may demand that children not eat between meals while snacking themselves. Sloppy parents may expect neat children. When parents themselves do not perform behaviors they expect of children, they should not be surprised when children follow suit.

All these factors—children's age and special characteristics, parents' characteristics, family lifestyle, community standards, health and safety needs, daily events—influence parents' realistic expectations. In general, children do best when expectations are consistent from one day to the next, especially in matters of importance. Though parents may make occasional allowances for special events and stresses, consistent expectations for the child lead to greater compliance.

HELPING CHILDREN MEET EXPECTATIONS

Having established realistic expectations, parents help children meet them in several ways. First, they structure the child's physical environment. Parenting is easier when the family house can be structured to meet children's needs with play space available outdoors and furniture, rugs, and decorations selected with an active family in mind. Thomas Gordon notes that many parents refuse to take fragile objects off tables or put them out of children's reach because they believe children should learn early on not to touch certain objects.[11] When asked, however, most of these same parents said they would quickly modify their homes if an elderly parent were coming to stay! Gordon believes that if an aging parent with mature faculties needs the home adjusted, all the more so do young children, who are not mature. Putting dangerous substances out of the way, having locks on drawers containing knives, clearly marking sliding glass doors—all these changes minimize the opportunities for children to harm themselves, helping children lead safe, healthy lives. Figure 4-1 presents additional suggestions for childproofing a house.

A second major way parents help children meet parental expectations is by establishing a regular daily routine. A regular routine makes a habit of certain behaviors that children learn to do automatically. In addition, most of us function better with a regular routine of eating, sleeping, and exercising.

FIGURE 4-1
CHILDPROOFING THE HOUSE

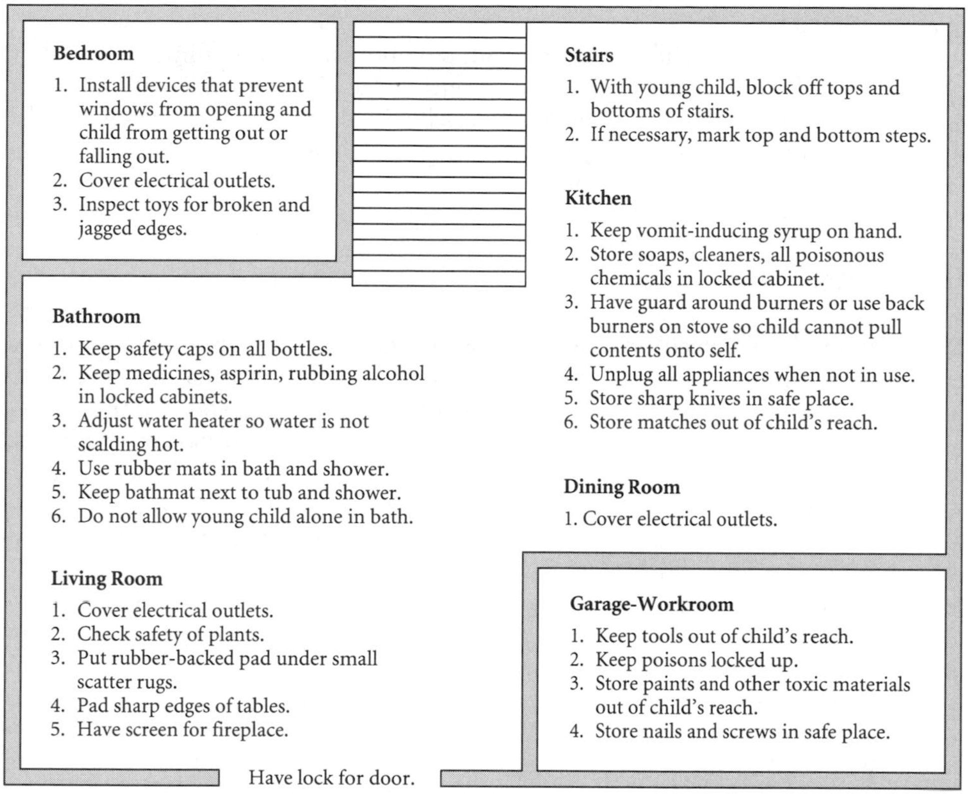

Bedroom
1. Install devices that prevent windows from opening and child from getting out or falling out.
2. Cover electrical outlets.
3. Inspect toys for broken and jagged edges.

Bathroom
1. Keep safety caps on all bottles.
2. Keep medicines, aspirin, rubbing alcohol in locked cabinets.
3. Adjust water heater so water is not scalding hot.
4. Use rubber mats in bath and shower.
5. Keep bathmat next to tub and shower.
6. Do not allow young child alone in bath.

Living Room
1. Cover electrical outlets.
2. Check safety of plants.
3. Put rubber-backed pad under small scatter rugs.
4. Pad sharp edges of tables.
5. Have screen for fireplace.

Stairs
1. With young child, block off tops and bottoms of stairs.
2. If necessary, mark top and bottom steps.

Kitchen
1. Keep vomit-inducing syrup on hand.
2. Store soaps, cleaners, all poisonous chemicals in locked cabinet.
3. Have guard around burners or use back burners on stove so child cannot pull contents onto self.
4. Unplug all appliances when not in use.
5. Store sharp knives in safe place.
6. Store matches out of child's reach.

Dining Room
1. Cover electrical outlets.

Garage-Workroom
1. Keep tools out of child's reach.
2. Keep poisons locked up.
3. Store paints and other toxic materials out of child's reach.
4. Store nails and screws in safe place.

Have lock for door.

General
1. Install smoke alarms in house.
2. Have fire extinguishers.
3. Plan fire escape routes.
4. Keep poison control, fire, police department numbers by telephone.

Adapted from *Working Mother,* October, 1995.

Here again, however, children's individual tempos must be taken into account. Some children are slow to wake from sleep and so need more time in the morning to get started. Other children need more time to wind down at night, so their bedtime routines may have to be started earlier than usual. Children also have different patterns of eating—some eat a lot in the morning and taper off by dinner while others have the opposite pattern. A child can be expected to come to the table for some sort of food, but portions can be varied so that the child's individual needs are kept in mind.

A third way parents help children meet expectations is by monitoring the amount of stimulation children receive. For example, they schedule their children's activities in such a way that children do not become overly tired or overly excited. Parents do not take a preschool child shopping all morning then send the child off to a birthday party in the afternoon, because the child may well be irritable and overly stimulated.

Parents also prepare children for difficult situations or changes in routine. They may calmly rehearse a visit to the dentist, letting the child practice with a doll or stuffed animal, so the child will be much less likely to feel overwhelmed when the real event occurs. Parents can use rehearsal to prepare children for other changes in routine, like a vacation or a change in day care.

PROVIDING REWARDS

Once parents have agreed on realistic expectations and structured their children's environment, they reward children for appropriate behavior when it occurs. *Rewards* or positive reinforcers are actions that increase the likelihood that the behavior will occur again. Rewards are always present when a behavior continues, whether we recognize them or not. As we have seen, rewards can be pleasurable internal feelings. For example, children often draw because such activities are enjoyable in themselves. External rewards, which other people give, fall into three general categories: (1) *social* rewards of attention, smiles, approval, praise, and physical affection; (2) *material* rewards of food, presents, and special purchases; and (3) *privileges* and activities, such as trips, special outings to the zoo, or permission to stay up late. Parents are wise to notice the kinds of rewards that appeal to their children and to make a list of activities and privileges that are particularly appealing to each child in the family. Sometimes, the reward is allowing the child to continue the pleasurable activity he or she initiated. When parents supply external rewards, behaviorists suggest that they rely most heavily on social rewards, because those bring the family closer together and create an atmosphere of warmth and trust. Within this category, however, individual preferences exist. Some children enjoy hugs and kisses while others like verbal compliments.

When behavioral patterns are being established, parents give rewards immediately after each successful act. Once the behavior occurs regularly, they can give rewards only occasionally. For example, when one boy first started picking up his clothes and putting them in the hamper, his mother commented every day about how helpful he was. As he continued, his mother remarked on it only when he did it rapidly.

Sometimes, praise alone is not effective. Children may not want to carry out an activity no matter what. A schoolchild may dislike math and refuse to work hard, even for social rewards. In this situation, tokens or a point system can be useful in motivating the child to take an interest. A token system is one in which children earn tokens or points that they can exchange for privileges or other rewards; Box 4-1 gives a sample reward menu. If a child avoids math homework, parents may want to establish a program in which the child can earn one token for every correctly complete math problem. At the end of the week, the child presents the homework, corrected by the math teacher, to the parent. The number of math problems correctly done determines the number of tokens earned.

◆

BOX 4-1
REWARD MENU

Extra snack	5 tokens	Card game with parents	5 tokens
Extra story read	5 tokens	Extra hour of outside play	10 tokens
Extra game with parents	10 tokens	Trip to park	10 tokens
Trip to library	10 tokens	Movie	15 tokens
Special dinner	15 tokens	Special hike	15 tokens

As children improve their behavior, they must do more and more to obtain tokens. For example, as math performance improves, the child might earn only half a token for each problem correctly done in a week. Robert Eimers and Robert Aitchison recommend giving social rewards of approval along with tokens and eventually switching to social rewards alone.[12] When the child's math skills are firmly established, the entire system can be phased out.

Parents must be careful not to take approved behaviors for granted. They must continue to comment on the chores completed on time, the good report card, the clothes picked up. In the rush of everyday life, it is easy to forget the desirable behaviors performed by all members of the family. The sensitive parent continues to make comments on well-learned but much-appreciated behavior.

Are rewards a form of bribery? This is a charge often made about the use of external rewards. Behaviorists reply that if rewards are increased when the child refuses to carry out an act, then the reward is a bribe. Giving regular rewards for desirable behavior, however, is nothing more than giving a realistic payoff, a common motivation for adults as well as children. For example, a paycheck is a payoff for work; a compliment to a co-worker expresses appreciation of some positive act. Why should we not do this with our children? To the extent that behaviorists rely on the social rewards of attention, smiles, and praise, they are conveying positive feelings to the children in the same way that Gordon, Haim Ginott, and Dorothy Briggs recommend. Reflection of feelings and I-messages are not considered bribes but rather social rewards that increase communication between child and parent.

TEACHING ACCEPTABLE NEW BEHAVIORS

The most effective way to teach children is to have parents model the behavior. However, because children may not spontaneously do what parents want them to do, parents must actively teach children what they model or desire them to do. When the behavior is already within the child's capacity, parents show the child what they want done. They move very young children through the necessary steps, verbalizing each step as they go — "This is how you put on your shirt." Parents can break the task into separate units and describe what is being done while the child

Because children may not spontaneously do what parents want them to do, parents must actively teach them desirable behavior.

does it. Parents offer encouragement and praise after each step. After the child has thoroughly learned the behavior, only occasional praise is needed.

In some situations, the child is not able to carry out the behaviors the parents want to reward, so the parents must *shape* the child's existing behavior. For example, suppose a parent wants her five-year-old to begin making his bed, and he does not know how. The first step for the parent is to decide what behaviors come closest to the specific behavior she wants the child to learn. Then she rewards these. As these increase in frequency, she demands a higher level of performance before the reward is given. Shaping behavior is a useful approach with schoolchildren who get poor report cards. Parents can reward the highest passing grade on the first report card. They can contract with children for rewards after the next report card if there are specific improvements. Because report periods are usually six weeks long, parents may reward good test performance during that period or contract to give small regular rewards for teacher reports of acceptable work. Parents may not want to give a child rewards only for superb performance measured by report cards, because these rewards may be a very long time coming; in this situation, rewarding improvements in homework and test grades may be more effective.

Theoretically, it is possible to raise children using only rewards and ignoring all misbehavior, which theoretically becomes extinguished for lack of reward. In everyday life, however, parents usually must deal with behavior that violates rules. When the child actively does something not approved, parents have two tasks before them: (1) stating limits effectively and then (2) enforcing them.

STATING LIMITS EFFECTIVELY

When rules are clearly and specifically stated, children are more likely to follow them than when rules are not clear. Say, "I want you to play outside for a while," not, "Be good this afternoon." Phrase the rule, if possible, in positive form, also stating its purpose. For example, say, "Carry your coat so it stays clean," not, "Don't drag your coat on the floor." Children respond well when rules are phrased in an impersonal way. "Bedtime is at eight" or "Dinner at six" is more likely to result in compliance than "You have to go to bed now" or "You have to be home for dinner at six."

Parents get the best results when they give only one rule at a time. As they give the rule, they gain the child's attention, standing close to the child and making good eye contact. Young children can be walked through the desired behavior. For example, as parents say, "It's time to pick up the toys," they can hold the young toddler's hand and show her how to put teddy on the self, guiding her hand through the movements.

When possible, give the children options—"You can have hot or cold cereal" or "You can take the trash out now or right after dinner." Having choices gives children some control over what is happening. Parents also give options when they prepare for changes in behavior. For example, they might say, "In five more swings, it is time to leave the park." This gives children a chance to get ready to follow the rule. Having options and having time to prepare for a change boost children's self-esteem as they see their feelings and wishes respected.

Ginott suggests four steps in stating limits: (1) Accept the child's wish without criticism or argument, (2) state what the rule or limit is, (3) when possible, describe how the child can obtain the wish, and (4) accept any irritation or resentment the child feels over being denied a request.[13] For example, with an elementary school child, a parent might say, "I understand that you want to watch an extra hour of TV tonight, but you know the rule is only one hour per day and you have already watched the one hour. If you want to give up tomorrow's hour, you can watch the extra hour tonight." If the child refuses to accept this, the parent can say, "I know you're unhappy you can't watch TV tonight."

Parents might like to see many changes in their children's behavior, but parents are most effective when their rules have priorities. Health and safety rules are most important—staying out of the street, always telling parents where they are, not hurting other people. Next are what might be called rules that ease social living—rules that make being together easier. This category includes rules against destroying other people's property or hurting their feelings deliberately and rules of general consideration (such as being quiet when others are sleeping or being helpful with chores).

Third in priority come conventional rules—how to use a napkin and silverware, how to answer the telephone, what social routines to follow. Even young preschoolers are aware of the difference between rules that concern kindliness and basic consideration of others and rules having to do with social convention.[14] Significantly, they are more impressed with the importance of kindness to others than with social conventions.

Last on the list are rules governing behaviors that can be choices for children. What clothes to wear, what games to play, and so on are, in most cases, matters of the child's individual preference unless there is a safety issue involved. Parents need not expend enormous energies getting children to do things just as they would like them to in these areas of individual preferences.

Once they have set priorities on the rules, parents must deal with children's failure to abide by them.

ENFORCING LIMITS

When rules have been stated clearly but children do not follow them, then parents need to enforce them. Before acting, however, parents must do two things. First, they must ask themselves whether their children continue to break the rule because, in some subtle way, parents are rewarding the rule-breaking behavior. Parents sometimes tell children to stop running or stop teasing but then undermine themselves with a chuckle and a shake of the head to indicate that the child has a lot of spirit and that they admire that spirit. So the child continues. Parents must first check whether they are unintentionally rewarding behavior they do not condone and either stop the reward or change their minds about the behavior.

Second, parents must be sure they are in general agreement about enforcing the rules. If there are big differences between them, parents should negotiate the differences with mutual problem-solving techniques. If parents frequently disagree, they may want to delay setting the consequence for a particular behavior until they have a chance to talk with each other, because children view such parental conflicts as justification to do what they want to do.

Parents have many options in enforcing limits, as the following sections explore.

Mutual Problem Solving

Using Gordon's mutual problem-solving technique is a useful first step.[15] Employing this approach, parents identify the rule breaking as a problem to them, a problem they want children to help them solve so that children, too, will be satisfied with the outcome. Parents solicit their children's opinions and work together to find a win-win solution agreeable to all concerned. For example, when children are consistently late for dinner or do not come to the table when called, parents present this as a problem they all must solve. The underlying assumption is that the family working together can find an alternative that satisfies everyone. There are six steps to the problem-solving process: (1) defining the problem, (2) generating possible solutions, (3) evaluating possible solutions, (4) deciding on the best solution, (5) implementing the decision, and (6) doing a follow-up evaluation.

Parents begin by explaining to children the exact problem that is troubling them and its effect on them, and then say that they are going to try a new method to solve the problem so that everyone's needs are met. Children may be skeptical at first, thinking that this may be another way for their parents to get them to behave. But as children realize that their needs are being considered, they become more active participants. Gordon advises parents and children to spend the most time on defining the nature of the problem and exchanging possible solutions.

Parents and children may disagree about a problem. For example, parents may feel upset by the continual mess in the kitchen on weekend mornings as children trail in one after another and get breakfast at odd times without cleaning up. The children, in turn, may feel the problem is that Mom won't serve weekend breakfasts at a reasonable time, like 10 or 11 A.M., because she wants to be out doing errands. Active listening by everyone and a willingness to listen to suggestions can result in agreement.

Gordon advises holding these problem-solving sessions frequently but not letting the discussion last too long. If the list of problems is long, the most important ones should be discussed first. As family members talk about each proposed solution, they should try to figure out how it will work. Once a solution is selected, the family should consider how the results will be evaluated and make sure to allow enough time for it to succeed. During the process of proposing solutions and picking one, each family member needs to listen actively to the suggestions of all family members. In this situation, as in so many, family members need to be able to trust one another and to recognize one another's needs.

Once a solution is agreed on, parents may find that children don't follow through. Children break agreements for a variety of reasons — they may not have had enough experience in self-direction, they may forget, they may test the limits to see what will happen, or they may have accepted an unworkable solution just to end the session. When an agreement is broken, parents must send a strong I-message of disappointment and surprise as soon as possible. Perhaps the child can be helped to keep the agreement. Or perhaps another problem-solving session is needed.

Parents might be tempted to build punishments into the problem-solving agreement — "If you don't carry out the garbage, your allowance will be reduced by twenty-five cents." Gordon advises against the use of penalties to enforce agreements. Parents should assume children will cooperate instead of starting with a negative expectation expressed in the threat of punishment. Children frequently respond to trust.

The contracting sessions devised by behaviorists are similar to Gordon's mutual problem-solving sessions. Contracting sessions are an expansion of the token system. When parents use tokens, they may do so to change one specific behavior or to reward the child for doing a particular chore. When parents want to reach agreement on several matters, and children are also asking for some changes, the family holds a contracting session. Contracting sessions are most appropriate with elementary school children and teenagers, but verbal preschoolers can also participate.

Suppose parents wish to decrease their seven-year-old son's messiness. It is decided that he should do four things: hang up his coat, clean and put away his lunchbox, put away his toys, and put his dirty clothes in the hamper. The behaviors are clearly stated. Before proposing a contract, however, the parents should observe the boy's behavior and count how many times a week he does these things. Eimers and Aitchison suggest a chart to record behavior over a seven-day period; Box 4-2 shows a sample chart.[16]

One mother, after observing and counting for a week, discovered that her son had hung up his coat only once and at no time put his dirty clothes in the hamper

◆

BOX 4-2
BEHAVIOR LOG

Behavior	Sun	Mon	Tue	Wed	Thurs	Fri	Sat
1. Hang up coat							
2. Clean and put away lunchbox							
3. Put away toys							
4. Put dirty clothes in hamper							

or put his toys away. When she told him what rewards he could earn with a point system, the child was excited and eager to try. Mother and child used the same form to record successful completion of each task. After the system went into effect, the mother noticed dramatic differences in the child's behavior. After seven weeks, the child was picking up his toys and putting his dirty clothes in the hamper. The system was gradually phased out after the habits were established.

Some behaviorists disapprove of elaborate programs of special incentives because they are more formalized and less personal than social rewards and can be financially costly. If a child has not responded to other strategies, however, special incentives may produce the desired results.

Natural and Logical Consequences

The terms *natural consequences* and *logical consequences*[17] are used jointly and interchangeably but have slightly different meanings. Natural consequences are those that occur directly as the result of a physical act. For example, if you do not eat dinner, you experience hunger. If you stay up late, you become tired.

Logical consequences refer to those events that follow a social act. For example, if you lie, other people will not believe you. If you misuse the family car, parents will not trust you with it. Natural and logical consequences are those that are directly related to the act itself and are not usually imposed by others. Exceptions exist, however. A natural consequence of running in the street is being hit by a car. Instead of risking that, parents generally use a logical consequence. If a child starts toward the street, the child's movement are restricted and he or she must play in the house.

Logical consequences differ from punishment in several ways. Logical consequences are directly related to what the child has done—if children do not put their clothes in the laundry, they have no clean clothes. A punishment may have no logical relationship to what the child has done—a spanking is not the direct result of being late for a meal but is the result of the parent's authority. The method of logical consequences does not place moral blame or pass moral judgment on the child. The child has made a mistake and pays the price. The parent stands by as an adviser rather than acting as a judge. Punishment implies that the child has committed a "wrong" act and must atone for the offense.

The method of logical consequences is not always as simple as standing by and letting the natural outcome of the act teach the child not to repeat the act. Parents must sometimes take a more active role. They must be careful not to turn the consequences into punishment by the comments they make. They must not criticize the child or angrily label the child. If a parent, for example, seems gleeful when a child suffers consequences—"You did not finish your homework and now you are paying the price! What did I tell you?"—the value of the method is lost. Children then experience the consequences as punishment, and they resent the parent's reaction.

Taking Action

When reflecting feelings, voicing limits, and allowing natural consequences have not worked, parents can take action. Ginott does not believe in punishment, which he defines as punitive action by a powerful person against a child. Taking action is different because the parent uses some form of behavior to enforce an existing limitation.[18] For example, if house rules include not bouncing a ball in the house and a child continues to bounce the ball after being given the choice of going outside to bounce or staying in and not bouncing, then parents act. They either send the child outside with the ball or take the ball away and permit the child to remain in the house. With teenagers, parents might remove the privilege of using the car if children do not observe the family curfew.

Punishments

If the preceding methods have not worked, parents will have to use punishments. Punishment means giving a behavior a negative consequence to decrease the likelihood of its recurrence. Punishments require varying degrees of effort on the parents' part. Before describing these, let us look at six general principles for using punishments: (1) Intervene early. Do not let the situation get out of control. As soon as the rule is violated, begin to take action. (2) Stay as calm and objective as possible. Sometimes, parents' upset and frustration are rewarding to the child. Parents' emotions can also distract the child from thinking about the rule violation. (3) State the rule that was violated. State it simply, and do not get into arguments about it. (4) Use a *mild* negative consequence. A mild consequence has the advantage that the child often devalues the activity itself and seems more likely to resist temptation and follow the rule in the future. (5) Use negative consequences consistently. Misbehaviors continue when they are sometimes punished and sometimes not. (6) Reinforce positive social behaviors as they occur afterwards; parents do not want children to receive more punishments than rewards.

The following punishments range from mild to severe. First, *ignoring* might seem the easiest punishment, in that the parent simply pays no attention to what the child says or does. It requires effort, however, because the parent must keep a neutral facial expression, look away, move away from the child, and give no verbal response

◆
BOX 4-3
USING TIME OUT FOR MISBEHAVIOR

1. Make a request in a firm but pleasant voice. Do not beg or shout.
2. Count silently to 5. Do not let the child know you are counting.
3. If the child has not started to comply in 5 seconds, look the child in the eye and say firmly, "If you don't _____, then you are going to stand in the corner."
4. Count silently to 5. Do not let the child know you are counting.
5. If the child has not begun to comply, take the child firmly by the hand or arm and say clearly and loudly, "You did not do as you were told, so you will have to stand in the corner."
6. No matter what the child promises, begs, screams, or yells, he or she goes directly to the corner. There is no going to the bathroom or getting a drink. Do not argue with the child.
7. Face the child to the wall and say, "Now you stay here for _____ minutes." If the child leaves the corner, return the child to the corner and stand behind him or her so that leaving the corner is not possible.
8. When the time is up, say "Now you may _____" (state the positive behavior).
9. If the unacceptable behavior recurs, start the process again.
10. Following the punishment, praise the next positive behavior with positive feedback. Never punish more than you praise.

Where should the corner be? Choose a dull corner—in the hall or dining room where there are no toys or distractions and no TV. You should be able to see the child.

How long in the corner? Young children under four can spend a few minutes. Children between the ages of five and eight can spend 5 to 10 minutes, and children over eight may require between 10 and 30 minutes. A general rule is that the child spends the same number of minutes as his or her age. While he or she is in the corner, the child misses whatever is happening—a meal, TV.

Russell A. Barkley, *Hyperactive Children* (New York: Guilford Press, 1981), pp. 328–330.

or attention to what the child says or does. Ignoring is best for behaviors that may be annoying but are not harmful to anyone. For example, children's whining, sulking, or pouting behavior can be ignored. Some experts put temper tantrums in the category of behavior that is best ignored. Children can frighten themselves with the intensity of a tantrum, so parents may choose to be more active and use the strategy of time out, described later in this section.

A second punishment is *social disapproval*. Parents express in a few words, spoken in a firm voice with a disapproving facial expression, that they do not like the behavior. For example, when a child dawdles, rather than clearing the table after dinner, a parent can say firmly, looking directly at the child with a serious expression, "It's time for the table to be cleared." For change to occur, parents' words, tone of voice, physical gestures, and facial expression must consistently make the point that the behavior is not approved.

When children continue disapproved behavior, parents can institute a *consequence* — removing a privilege, using the time-out strategy, or imposing extra work. When families have contracts, children agree to carry out specified chores or behaviors in exchange for privileges. When certain behaviors do not occur, children lose privileges. For example, TV time is linked to the completion of chores or homework. When homework or chores are not finished by a certain time, there is no TV. When a child brings home a report of unacceptable classroom behavior, time with friends is limited.

Time out is a method best reserved for aggressive, destructive, or dangerous behaviors. It serves to stop the disapproved behavior, giving the child a chance to cool off and, sometimes, to think about the rule violation. There are variations on the time-out method: The child can be requested to sit in a chair in the corner, but many children get up. If the child is required to face the corner, parents can keep the young child in the corner for the stated time. With older children, parents may want to add the rule that if the child does not comply with time out for one parent during the day, making the presence of both parents necessary, then the child will spend twice the amount of time in time out. Box 4-3 outlines one method of time out.

Sending a child to his or her room or being grounded there is not effective punishment, because the child can find many enjoyable things to do there. So, as children get older, extra work and chores may be substituted for grounding.

It is best to have only two or three behaviors requiring time out at any one time. Otherwise, a child may spend a great deal of time in the corner for too many different things. Further, it is important that both parents and all caregivers agree on the two or three things that will lead to time out so the child gets consistent punishment.

The last punishment we will consider is also the most controversial — *physical punishment* like spanking or hitting. Many parents and most experts *strongly* advise against spanking. Spanking children presents a model of adults using physical force on a smaller person, a model we do not want children to imitate. Experiencing physical punishment also increases children's own aggressiveness. Further, spanking and hitting do not lead to children's having internal controls of behavior, the goal of most discipline. Instead, physical punishment is associated with the child's behaving well only when a punishing adult is present. Finally, an angry parent can lose control with physical punishment and abuse the child.

Still, the majority of parents spank at one time or another.[19] In a survey of 150 middle-class families, 148 reported spanking at least once.[20] In a national survey, caregivers for 60 percent of children said they used physical punishment like spanking or hitting.[21] Seventy percent of those nominated as outstanding parents used spanking for getting children's attention for a serious misbehavior like a dangerous act or disrespect.[22]

Even children agree that spanking is acceptable. In response to survey questions, preschoolers, eleven- and twelve-year-old children, and mothers reported that spanking was acceptable punishment to reinforce safety rules and rules regarding treatment of others.[23] While preschoolers believed that physical punishment was acceptable for all misdeeds, older children and mothers did not believe that it was permissible for enforcing social conventions. Although mothers and older children believed that only parents or a designated adult should be permitted to spank, preschoolers believed that anyone should be permitted to spank a child.

INTERVIEW
with Paul Mussen

Paul H. Mussen is professor emeritus of psychology at the University of California, Berkeley. A former director of the Institute of Human Development on the Berkeley campus, he has coauthored many books, including The Roots of Prosocial Behavior in Children *with Nancy Eisenberg in 1989. He is also an editor of* The Handbook of Child Psychology, *1983 edition.*

Parents are very interested in moral development. What can they do to promote this in their children?

With my bias, modeling is of primary importance. It is *the* single most important thing parents can do. Parents create a nurturant environment in which the child wants to imitate the parents' behavior and the parents behave in an altruistic way so that there is an identification with the parents. Parents also can try to get the child to participate when they are doing something for someone else.

Then parents use empathy-eliciting disciplinary procedures in which they make the child aware that he or she has hurt someone. In the early years with toddlers, it is a disciplinary technique that involves showing clearly and emphatically that you disapprove, but at the same time making clear that someone else was harmed by what the child has done — "You pulled her hair. Don't ever do that again. You really hurt her."

In general, I think the disciplinary practices are very important. Studies show the empathy-eliciting techniques — so-called induction and reasoning as opposed to power-assertion (spanking and threatening) — are important because they focus not on punishing the child but on pointing up the consequences of what is done. So, first eliciting empathy, then later reasoning with the child are important.

Rewarding altruistic behavior when it occurs is important. The research evidence here is not as strong as one might like, but it does suggest this.

Discussing moral issues at home is critical both from the point of view of moral thinking and from the point of view of moral behavior. Older studies showed that the model's behav-

Reviewing her own and others' cross-cultural work, Diana Baumrind concludes:

The short- and long-term effects on child outcomes of any disciplinary practice within the normative range are moderated by cultural and childrearing contexts. The extent to which spanking or any other form of aversive discipline is part of a harsh parenting pattern or is conditioned by warmth and the use of reason determines its meaning to the child and its consequent beneficial or detrimental effects. . . . It should be the concern of professionals who work with parents to respectfully offer them alternative disciplinary strategies, using carefully evaluated intervention programs, rather than to condemn parents for using methods consonant with their own, but not with the counselor's beliefs and values. Parents who choose to use punishment often seek guidance in using it efficaciously. Efficacious punishment is contingent upon the child's misbehavior, as well as upon the parents' responding in a prompt, rational, nonexplosive manner and with knowledge and consideration of the child's developmental level and temperament.[24]

ior was the critical thing, not what the model said. More recent studies show that verbal responses can be helpful also. You are giving the child some codes or rules that the child can then apply later on when various situations arise. So the discussion and what, for lack of a better word, we used to call preaching—in effect, discussing problems, making principled statements—can be helpful.

Giving children assignments of responsibilities fairly early at the child's level is also useful. For example, in the schools, a young fifth-grader can help a second-grader, and at home, older siblings can help younger siblings. Having chores and assigning tasks in such a way that children get satisfaction from accepting responsibility is important.

Those are the important disciplinary techniques—modeling, a nurturant milieu so the child identifies with the modeling, reasoning, discussing rules and principles so the child can use them later, rewarding positive behavior when it occurs, and giving opportunities for satisfaction from accepting responsibility.

What are the things parents should avoid doing?

One thing to avoid is behaving immorally themselves. Another is being inconsistent—occasionally not reacting to misbehavior that harms someone else and at other times punishing it and at still other times rewarding it. Inconsistent patterns of reaction should be avoided. Also be very alert in terms of inconsistency with respect to what the parent says and what the parent does.

In general, I feel that power-assertive techniques (like spanking) should be avoided because they produce the wrong orientation. They give the impression that authority can do whatever it wants and the rest of us just have to go along. They result in less independent moral judgment, and they make the point that aggression can be a successful means of getting what you want.

Avoid underestimating children's understanding, because I think they are a lot more sensitive to these issues than we might think. And I don't think they should be babied or patronized when you are handling something. Let them be involved in making decisions. Assume that they can understand when you are trying to use inductive techniques. Parents sometimes feel they have to play down to children, and I don't think that's true.

Ineffective Forms of Discipline

A review of over three hundred studies[25] identifies four kinds of problems in disciplining children: (1) inconsistent discipline, referring to inconsistency both on the part of one parent and between two parents; (2) irritable, harsh, explosive discipline (frequent hitting and threatening); (3) low supervision and low involvement on the part of the parent with the child; and (4) inflexible, rigid discipline (use of a single form of discipline for all transgressions regardless of seriousness). All four forms of ineffective discipline are related to children's aggressive, rule-breaking behavior that frequently leads to social difficulties with peers.

Discipline is also ineffective when it does not match the child's age and capacity. One study revealed that depressed mothers tended to mistime their interventions.[26] With toddlers, they used fewer commands and reprimands and more verbal explanations; with five-year-olds, however, they used commands even though these children were better able to respond to verbal explanations. Their mistiming resulted in their avoiding giving commands to resistant toddlers and not giving explanations to inquiring older children.

THE PROBLEM-SOLVING APPROACH

Parents often wish they had a single solution to each kind of problem—one way to handle temper tantrums, one way to deal with teenagers' rebelliousness. Unfortunately, there is no one formula that all parents can use to raise all children, because each child, as well as each parent, is a unique individual.

When parents have difficulties, a seven-step problem-solving approach combining Gordon's mutual problem-solving method with the behaviorists' focus on specificity and Dix's attention to parental emotions seems most useful. The approach allows parents to choose interventions that take into account the child's age and temperament and the family's social values and living circumstances. It also enables parents to encourage the qualities that they and their ethnic group value. Here are the seven steps:

1. Identify the problem specifically; observe when and how often it occurs.
2. Question yourself on the reality of the problem.
3. Get the child's point of view.
4. Spend pleasurable time daily with the child.
5. Carry out an intervention.
6. Evaluate the results of the intervention.
7. Start over again if necessary.

How do parents select interventions? Most use a combination of the techniques just described to enforce limits, but parents develop beliefs about the effectiveness of low-power, authoritative methods as opposed to high-power, authoritarian methods.[27] Often, parents react in terms of these beliefs.[28] As noted in Chapter 3, however, a parent's affect is perhaps a more important determiner of the choice. When parents are under stress, angry, or upset, they tend to assert power. This is true of depressed mothers as well. According to one study, even though many such mothers believed in the importance of low-power techniques, their resentment of the child and the parenting role determined the choice of their parenting behaviors, not their beliefs.[29]

The complexity of using childrearing strategies increases when we realize that children may not be learning by the strategy parents are using. Jane Loevinger, in a perceptive and humorous article, illustrates this problem with the example of a five-year-old who hits his younger brother.[30] The parent who punishes the older child with a spanking may actually be teaching that child that it is permissible to use physical aggression to obtain one's ends. The parent who uses reason and logic in dealing with the older boy may find that the child, seeing that no punishment follows hitting, is likely to do it again.

Why use a strategy—why not just do whatever comes to mind at the time? Because, says Loevinger, those children who have the most difficulties growing up and functioning are raised by parents who are impulsive, self-centered, and unable to follow a set of guidelines. "The chief value of a parental theory," writes Loevinger, "may well be in providing a model for the child of curbing one's own impulses out of regard for the future welfare of another."[31]

When we combine the problem-solving approach with the parental qualities and behaviors all strategies advise—modeling of desired traits, respect for the child's and parents' own needs, confidence that the child can learn what is necessary, sharing of problems and solutions in family meetings—then parents can effectively foster the growth and development of their children. Each individual has a unique potential to discover and develop. Arnold Gesell and Frances Ilg state it well:

> When asked to give the shortest definition of life, Claude Bernard, a great physiologist, answered, "Life is creation." A newborn baby is the consummate product of such creation. And he in turn is endowed with capacities for continuing creation. These capacities are expressed not only in the growth of his physique, but in the simultaneous growth of a psychological self. From the sheer standpoint of creation this psychological self must be regarded as his masterpiece. It will take a lifetime to finish, and in the first ten years he will need a great deal of help, but it will be his own product.[32]

Parents have the privilege of serving as guide and resource as their child creates a unique "psychological self."

MAIN POINTS

Parent set the stage for learning by

- developing realistic expectations of the child
- helping children meet expectations
- rewarding approved behaviors consistently
- setting limits with clear, positive statements of what they want

To enforce rules, parents can

- use mutual problem solving
- let natural consequences of the act teach the child
- take action
- use punishments to decrease the disapproved behavior

Spanking as a punishment

- is used by most parents at one time or another
- derives its meaning from the quality of the relationship between parent and child
- is best supplanted by other forms of negative consequence

Ineffective forms of discipline include

- inconsistent discipline
- harsh, explosive discipline
- low supervision of the child
- rigid, inflexible discipline

The advantages of the seven-step problem-solving approach are

- parents can take into account the child's individuality
- parents can retain their own goals and values for their children's behavior

To help children develop caring, prosocial behavior, parents

- provide a nurturant, ethical, warm home atmosphere
- use reasoning in talking about rules
- reward caring behavior with attention
- discuss moral issues and actions so the child learns a code of rules that can be applied in new situations

EXERCISES

1. Write a description of the disciplinary techniques you recall your parents used with you in the elementary and high school years. How would you characterize your parents' methods and your response to them?

2. Choose some behavior you want to increase—for example, regular exercise—and work out a reward system to increase that behavior. Chart the frequency of the desired behavior before and during the reward period. If time permits, observe the frequency for a week after you stop the reward system. Share your experiences with classmates. What kinds of rewards have most successfully helped you and other students increase desired behavior?

3. Choose some behavior you want to decrease. Chart the occurrence of the behavior before any intervention. Then, choose a negative consequence that will occur after every repetition of the undesired behavior. If you wish, choose to reward a substitute behavior at the same time. Then monitor the occurrence of the undesired behavior. If time permits, observe the frequency of the behaviors after you have stopped the consequences. For example, you may decide you want to decrease procrastination in going to the library. Decide that every time you postpone going to the library for 5 minutes or longer, you will have to stay at the library an extra 30 minutes. If you go to the library on time, permit yourself to leave 10 minutes early.

4. Observe parents and children together at a playgound or in the grocery store or other public place. Select pairs of children of approximately the same age and contrast how their parents treat them. Do the parents show similar behavior? What theories of learning do they appear to be using? What parental

behaviors seem effective with the children? Observing 5 minutes with each child, time how often the parent intervenes to maintain or change the child's behavior.

5. Select a friend's behavior that you wish to change. Devise a system of rewards or a system of positive/negative consequences to change the behavior, then carry it out for 5 weeks and note the change. For example, you might decide to change a friend's habit of being late for meetings or of not calling when she says she will.

ADDITIONAL READINGS

Becker, Wesley. *Parents Are Teachers*. Champaign, IL: Research Press, 1971.

Dinkmeyer, Don, and McKay, Gary D. *The Parent's Handbook*. Circle Pines, MN: American Guidance Service, 1989.

Dreikurs, Rudolf, with Soltz, Vicki. *Children: The Challenge*. New York: Hawthorn, 1964.

Nelson, Jane. *Positive Discipline*. New York: Ballantine Books, 1987.

Patterson, Gerald R. *Living with Children*. Rev. ed. Champaign, IL: Research Press, 1977.

BECOMING PARENTS

C H A P T E R   5

Why do people want to have children? How do they go about deciding to have children? Does it matter if you have children when you are younger or older? Are people without children as happy as people who have children? How do parents adjust to the changes after a baby arrives?

This chapter describes how people become parents. It talks about what they hope to experience with their children and how they decide when they are uncertain. It looks at how couples' relationships change as they incorporate a baby into their lives.

THE PROCESS OF BECOMING PARENTS

Each individual who becomes a parent does so within unique circumstances. Some plan enthusiastically; others become parents without deciding to do so. Factors including the parent's age, career and social status, economic situation, extended family, and community support system make the process of anticipating, having, and raising a child special for each.

Reasons for Having Children

In Chapter 1, we saw that children meet parents' basic needs for having close emotional relationships with others and give parents the satisfaction of helping them grow and develop.[1] Box 5-1 lists seven major reasons men and women, parents and nonparents alike, give for having children. In general, these reasons are listed in similar order in different ethnic groups, with the exception that African Americans, rural residents, and people with less education are more likely than other groups to view children as providing economic utility and security in old age.[2]

Reasons for not having children center on three broad factors—restrictions (loss of freedom, loss of time available for other activities, increase in workload), negative feelings evoked by children (worries concerning children's health and wellbeing, difficulties of discipline, disappointments in children or in self as a parent), and

---

BOX 5-1
PARENTS' REASONS FOR WANTING CHILDREN

1. Love and satisfying, close relationship with others
2. Stimulation and excitement of watching children grow
3. Means of self-development — becoming more responsible, more sensitive, more skilled in relationships
4. Way of achieving adult status — parenthood is "proof" of being mature
5. Sense of creativity and achievement in helping child grow
6. Expression of moral, religious belief
7. Utility — belief that children will care for parents when parents are older

Adapted from Lois Wladis Hoffman and Jean Denby Manis, "The Value of Children in the United States: A New Approach to the Study of Fertility," *Journal of Marriage and the Family* 41 (1979): 583–596.

---

concerns about the child being poorly cared for. Research suggests that prospective parents, while aware of the costs, plan children on the basis of the positive experiences they anticipate rather than limit the number because of the difficulties.[3]

Although only about 10 to 15 percent of adolescent mothers plan their pregnancies, their decision to continue the pregnancy is related to their values for having children and is thus important to understand.[4] In a study of how adolescent mothers rank order the value of children, Gerald Michaels found that their ordering of the values for having children is similar to that of adults.[5] Adolescent mothers are more likely to see children as a source of power and influence and less likely as a measure of adult status; still, like adults, adolescent mothers want children because they see children as sources of love, fun, stimulation, and achievement.

Adolescent mothers are more likely to view children positively when these mothers have few outlets for need gratification.[6] For example, adolescent mothers who did not work or who did not feel very independent or self-sufficient were likely to have a high desire for children. These feelings, combined with the example of their own mothers, who also had children early, increased the value they placed on children. Viewing children positively, however, was related only weakly to subsequent parenting.

The Decision to Parent

About two-thirds of children are actively planned.[7] Among adolescent parents, only about 10 to 14 percent are planned. Here we shall discuss the ramifications of the process of this decision.

Couples   Carolyn Cowan and Philip Cowan write,

> Much of what happens after the birth of the baby is shaped by what is happening in couples' lives before the baby comes along. And one of the most important things that happens in the prebaby period is the way the couple goes about deciding whether to become parents in the first place.[8]

The Cowans identified four decision-making patterns. *Planners* (52 percent) discussed the question and made a definite decision to have or not have a child. *Acceptance of fate* couples (14 percent of those expecting) had unplanned pregnancies that they accepted either quietly or, in many cases, enthusiastically. *Ambivalent* couples (about 26 percent) expressed both positive and negative feelings about being parents, with one parent leaning in one direction and the other parent leaning in the other direction. *Yes-No* couples, (about 10 percent) were in marked conflict about having or not having a child.

The couples' decision-making process regarding pregnancy was related to their problem-solving skills in other areas.[9] Yes-No couples were less effective in solving everyday problems, just as they were less effective in deciding about the pregnancy. The decision-making process regarding pregnancy was also related to marital satisfaction over time. When couples plan the decision, regardless of whether they do or do not have a child, their marital satisfaction remains high following the birth or an equivalent time period. Couples who accept an unplanned pregnancy have a drop in marital satisfaction, but their initial level is so high that they are still as satisfied as the parents who plan the decision.

Marital dissatisfaction is most marked among couples who are ambivalent or in conflict but still have a baby. Ambivalent couples are not as high as the other couples in their initial satisfaction levels, and these levels drop when they have a baby. Ambivalent couples who do not have a child retain a high satisfaction level. The yes-no couples have the least satisfaction. Of nine yes-no couples who had a child, seven divorced by the time the child entered kindergarten. In all seven cases, the husband did not want a child. The two women who did not want to have children seemed better able to adjust, and their marriages continued.

Single Women   Each year, one-third of babies are born to unmarried women;[10] a third of these babies, mostly unplanned, are born to teenagers.[11] About one-third are born to unmarried women between ages twenty and twenty-five, many of whom started their families as unmarried teen mothers.[12] About 19 percent are born to women between twenty-five and thirty, and 16 percent to women over thirty. Babies born to women over thirty are the most likely to be planned.

Surveys of adolescents and of older women indicate that half the women would consider having a child alone if they were childless by the time they reached their late thirties and forties.[13] The percentage of educated business and professional women who have chosen to have a child without marriage increased from 3 percent in 1980 to 8 percent in 1990.[14] These women are older and have achieved occupational stability. Strong desires for babies along with the feeling that they have lost the opportunity to have a child under the ideal circumstances of marriage to a loved partner spur women to consider this option.

We do not know precisely the stages single mothers go through in making their decisions. Merle Bombardieri, a social worker who holds workshops and counsels single women about having a child, estimates that about a third of the women who initially consider such an option decide not to have a child on their own.[15] In her counseling work, she encourages women to mourn unresolved grief about not having a child in marriage and about the deaths of parents or similar losses. She believes that feelings of loss may cause the desire for a child; as such, when the loss is

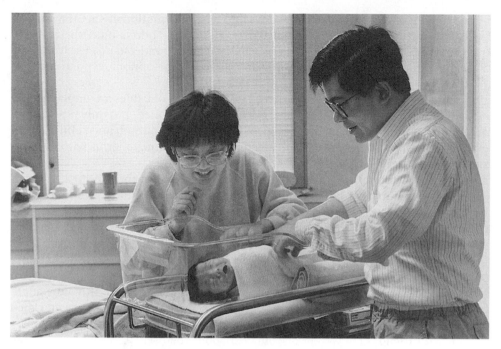

Becoming a parent gives meaning and purpose to life.

mourned, the desire for a child decreases. Whether a mother seeks formal counseling or not, she usually talks to friends, family, and whoever else will support her.

Jane Mattes, who decided to have a child as a single mother seventeen years ago,
found a need for support after the birth of her son. She organized an informal group
of other single mothers who had babies. The group grew and attracted media attention so that within a year they formed a national organization, Single Mothers by
Choice (SMC), that offers support and information to single mothers.[16]

In addition, this group holds sessions for prospective mothers and urges them to
consider a variety of issues — their ability to support a child financially, their ability
to mesh family life and work life, their psychological readiness to rear a child on
their own, and their conviction that they can provide a stable, loving home in the
absence of a father. Like Ms. Bombardieri, this group also suggests mourning the
loss of the ideal pregnancy prior to conception. One study done in the 1970s indicates that unmarried mothers are most likely to decide to have a child when they
can build a support system that enables them to combine work with rearing children. In the 1970s, some lived in communes, while others received support from
family and friends.[17]

In addition to planning whether to have a child, these single mothers must also
plan how to have children. There are many options. Some decide to become pregnant
by a known lover or friend. In these cases, the father has the same legal rights to the
child that he would have in marriage. Some women use anonymous donor sperm for
intrauterine insemination. Since many single mothers are older, they may seek the
help of fertility clinics, described later. Still other mothers decide to adopt a child,

often an older one. Such mothers are described as more emotionally mature and less easily frustrated than most.[18] A woman may try several options until she finds the one that produces a child for her. At this point, we do not understand clearly the psychological mechanisms involved in women's choice of one option over another.

Unplanned Children   As noted earlier, about one-third of babies are unplanned. In one study, however, 39 percent of first babies were unplanned, but only 5 percent of second babies were unplanned.[19] Most couples who had an unplanned child felt the nine months of pregnancy gave them an opportunity to come to terms with the baby and accept the child at birth.

Although most unplanned children are welcomed by the time of birth, actively unwanted children may have a more difficult time. In one study, children whose mothers had twice requested abortions to terminate that particular pregnancy had significantly more problems and less enjoyment in life than children whose parents wanted them.[20] The unwanted children, seen in elementary school, had fewer friends, more behavior problems, and poorer school performance even though they had equally high intelligence.

In adolescence, the difference between the two groups widened. In young adulthood, individuals unwanted before birth were less happy with their jobs and their marriages. They had more conflict with co-workers and supervisors and less satisfaction with friends. They were discouraged about themselves and their lives, but many took the positive step of getting help for their problems. So, being definitely unwanted during gestation is related to fewer satisfactions in work, friendships, and marital relationships in adulthood.

Thus, agreement on having children helps not only the couple and their relationship but also the long-term well-being of the child.

Getting Pregnant

Many couples and single women decide to have a child but find that they do not conceive as easily as they had hoped. Only 20 percent of women conceive in the first month of trying.[21] Infertility is considered a possibility if conception has not occurred after a year of unprotected sexual intercourse. Overall, one in twelve couples must deal with this problem, but the incidence increases with the age of the prospective parents.[22] About 14 percent of those ages thirty to thirty-four, 25 percent of those thirty-five to thirty-nine, and 27 percent of those forty to forty-four report difficulties conceiving. Miscarriage rates also rise with age, from 25 percent at age thirty-five to 50 percent at forty-five.[23]

A thorough medical workup can often determine the source of the problem and the best form of intervention. Depending on the diagnosis, interventions can vary from intrauterine insemination to surgery and the highly complex methods of Assisted Reproductive Technology (ART).[24] This chapter cannot go into the varieties of help in detail. Initially, help usually takes the form of supporting natural processes by insemination and by giving drugs that would stimulate the ovaries to produce more eggs. With more advanced methods, one can fertilize the egg in a petri dish and place the egg in the uterus, helping women who have blocked fallopian tubes. Currently, one can fertilize eggs and freeze them for use at later dates if conception has not taken place or the eggs can be given to another woman. It is thought now that young women may be able to freeze their eggs, as men freeze sperm, to be used at a later date.

This is an important advance. Research has revealed that the age of the egg, rather than the age of the uterus, limits a woman's fertility. Infertile women who receive a donor egg from a young woman greatly improve their likelihood of conceiving. For example, a forty-four-year-old woman using her own egg has a 3.5 percent chance of conceiving but a 50 percent chance if she uses a donor egg.[25] In the future, then, a woman may, if she is not pregnant by the age of thirty, decide to freeze her eggs for later use.

Ethical and Social Issues Such technological advances imply potentially large social ramifications. Many couples and single women who in the past would have remained childless can today conceive with donor eggs and donor sperm. For example, donor eggs make it possible for women in their fifties, and even those in their early sixties, to bear a child. Donor sperm has made it possible for lesbian couples and single women to have children. The use of surrogate mothers and gestational mothers has expanded the possible solutions to fertility problems. *Surrogate mothers* are impregnated with the sperm of the biological father and carry the child for him and his wife. *Gestational mothers* agree to carry the child of an egg and sperm fertilized outside her body — sometimes the egg of the biological mother fertilized by the sperm of the biological father, and sometimes a fertilized donor egg or sperm.[26]

Legal and ethical questions arise in the area of fertility treatments.[27] Thirty-five states have laws about the rights and responsibilities of sperm donors — anonymous donors generally have none, but known donors may have the same rights as other biological fathers — however, few states have laws about the rights and responsibilities of egg donors. If they insist, surrogate (biological) mothers may receive visiting privileges after the birth. Legal issues arise around who has the rights to frozen fertilized eggs if the parents divorce.

Unique ethical issues have been raised about the ages of mothers. For instance, is it right to have a woman in her sixties bear a child whom she may not live long enough to raise?[28] One such woman lied about her age and said she was in her fifties. What should the upper age be? Most clinics use the age at which menopause occurs naturally. Is it ethical to sell the frozen fertilized eggs of one woman to another? Do infertility clinics have a right to refuse to help some people such as lesbian couples or single women? Clearly, such issues will need to be addressed.

Dealing with Stress Despite their specific problems, all individuals who experience difficulty conceiving a child suffer severe stress. Potential parents have strong emotional reactions to the fact that they cannot produce a child easily.[29] Further, they have to undergo awkward physical examinations and reveal their intimate habits to strangers. The stress of not having the child so longed for and having to deal with the medical technology can strain an individual's sense of identity and well-being as well as a couple's relationship. Both couples and single women having this difficulty report feeling alone and isolated; surrounded by a populace that reproduces without a thought, they cannot accomplish what they so much desire.

People find help in support groups and in counseling. RESOLVE is one support group for people experiencing difficulty in conceiving.[30] Many find it a relief to talk with other people who have the same difficulties they do—finally, they no longer feel different or weird.

One counselor who works with couples and women dealing with infertility, Sherry Wilson, helps them grieve the loss of their dream of having a child easily.[31] She believes they go through a process of grieving unique to each person but consisting of predictable stages: shock and denial, anger, bargaining, depression, and acceptance. Though people differ in which order and what pace they go through the stages, everyone who grieves must deal with these basic emotional reactions. Wilson emphasizes listening and accepting the other person's feelings as well as one's own. She believes good communication skills are essential to couples' coping well with fertility problems.

Some physicians report a rate of success as high as 70 to 75 percent with their infertile patients.[32] This still means, though, that 25 to 30 percent have to accept that they cannot conceive a biological child. One doctor writes,

> For the minority of couples who go home without a baby, infertility is a tragedy. It is a loss—and one that is not easy to accept. When a patient leaves my care without a child in her arms after trying to conceive for years, it hurts. In fact, after working with infertile couples for almost thirty years, I still get angry and sad just thinking about the unfairness of infertility.[33]

Many couples go on to adopt children, a choice we shall look at more closely in Chapter 15. For those who do conceive, the stress and strain of infertility problems can make the parents fear that something else may go wrong, both before and after the birth. One mother says,

> The hardest thing to accept has been that this would not be the pregnancy I had wished for and imagined for so many years. I could never breeze through this, like those women who got pregnant easily or accidentally, and act as if nothing dramatic was taking place. In my second month I made the dreadful mistake of running (horrors!) to meet my husband, only to find him furious with me for taking such a "chance." This pregnancy was too precious for us to take nonchalantly.[34]

Even so, the effort to conceive may give parents a particular appreciation for their child. As one mother says,

> Yet feelings linger that those who conceive easily don't understand. Every night I stand in each of my children's rooms for a few minutes, watching them sleep, and recall the terrible childless years. I came so close to never having them. I am humbled by, and deeply thankful for, the miracle of my children.[35]

The Timing of Children

When is the best age to have children? Does it matter? Pamela Daniels and Kathy Weingarten[36] compared parents who had their children *early* (when they were on average 20.5 years old) and those who had children *later* (when they averaged 30.5). They found that although the number of problems parents experienced was about the same in both groups, the content of the problems differed for the two. Those parents who had children quickly in their early twenties found themselves rearing children before they themselves had firm identities. They were less established in work roles and were generally less experienced out in the world. The partners had not had time to become thoroughly acquainted with each other and settled as a couple. This group was nurturing children before they felt mature; women in this group had, however, less difficulty adjusting to the wife's role as mother and caregiver.

Late-timing couples had established themselves as individuals out in the world. They had work they enjoyed. They had had time to focus on their relationship, to learn about each other's reactions, to establish routines or working together and accomplishing tasks. When the baby came, late-timing couples were ready to nourish new life, but they had difficulty with the disruption of their intimate connection and established ways of doing things.

Many of the early-timing parents, if they had it to do all over again, would have postponed having children, whereas none of the late-timing parents would have had children earlier. Individual "readiness" to be parents is the critical factor. When individuals have a clear sense of who they are, what they like, how they relate to other people, when they can care for themselves and when they have established patterns of intimacy with the other parent, then they are ready to nourish new life.

Parents over Thirty-Five

A still older group is the *over-thirty-five* parents, who have increased dramatically since 1970. In 1992, 350,000 babies were born to women over thirty-five.[37] Feminism, a general postponement of childbearing, the large number of baby boomers in childbearing age, advanced contraception, better health for women, and advances in obstetrical care account for these growing numbers. While there have always been women over thirty-five having children, in the past these older mothers were having the *last* of several children. Now, many are mothers for the *first* time.

Older mothers, as already noted, have many advantages—higher education, higher status jobs, and, as a result, higher incomes with more money spent on child-related items like child care.[38]

Further, these parents have a lower divorce rate, are more stable, and are frequently more attentive and sensitive parents. Yet parents' work and community responsibilities may make it more difficult for them to incorporate an unpredictable, time-consuming young child into their lives.

Andrew Yarrow wondered what it is like for children to have older parents.[39] He obtained a volunteer sample of adults who described their experiences growing up with older parents. Many reported appreciating older parents' greater patience, broader outlook on life, and the more comfortable, settled lifestyle. Many, however, had numerous worries about parents' possible illness and death, feelings of being isolated from a larger family network because grandparents were often dead, and feelings of being isolated from peers whose parents were younger, more playful, and physically active with them. Some felt they were cheated of childhood and had to grow up too fast because they were around adults so much. Further, they had to assume responsibility for aging parents just as they were entering young adulthood. (*Note:* Today, children with older parents may not have the same experiences, because society is more accepting of the older parent.)

◆

BOX 5-2
GUIDELINES FOR OLDER PARENTS

1. Be open with children about your age and reasons for postponing children. Lying and avoiding the issue give children a sense of shame or embarrassment about parents' age.
2. Make a special effort to understand your children's world, as it may seem very different from the one in which you grew up.
3. Connect your children to extended family members. If this is not possible, provide an extended support network of friends who serve as uncles, aunts, grandparents.
4. Stay physically fit and energetic so you can share physical activities like hiking and camping with your children. If you cannot participate, then see that children join friends and other adults in these activities.
5. Most important, balance the time you spend on work and nonfamily commitments with your family's needs so children feel they are important parts of your lives.

Adapted from Andrew Yarrow, *Latecomers* (New York: Free Press, 1991).

Older parents can become sensitive to their children's feelings (see Box 5-2). Children will then be able to enjoy the benefits of older parents with a minimum of the problems.

Teenage Parents

While older parents are viewed positively, teenage parents are often viewed negatively. Certainly teenage mothers face many problems, but the authors of a seventeen-year study of very young mothers in Baltimore write that *diversity of outcome* was their most striking finding. Many adolescent mothers overcome their problems, despite public perceptions:

> The invidious stereotype of the adolescent childbearer underestimates young mothers' chances of recovery. . . . Ironically, part of the handicap of being a teenage mother may come from a widespread perception that failure is virtually inevitable—a belief that may become a self-fulfilling prophecy.[40]

In 1993, roughly 500,000 babies were born to teenage mothers, about two-thirds of whom were unmarried. While the number of babies born to teens decreased from the 1970s to the mid-1980s, it now appears to be on the rise again.[41] The 1989 rate for births to women fifteen to seventeen equaled that of teens in 1975.[42] The increasing birthrate occurs anomalously in the context of a general societal increase in the age of mothers at first birth. In 1957, 52 percent of women had a child by age twenty-two; in 1989, 52 percent of women had a child by age twenty-six. This four-year difference enables women to become more economically secure and more psychologically mature. So, today, the increasing number of teenage mothers stands in sharp contrast to the societal norm for age at first birth.[43]

Special Problems Births to adolescent mothers are associated generally with problems at several levels—biological, economic, social, and psychological—but specific outcomes are diverse, depending on the ethnic background of the mother and a host of other factors. Researchers in the area of adolescent pregnancy consider birth to a teenage mother one factor in a chain of events that predicts difficulty.[44]

Women who become teenage mothers generally already have psychological and economic problems before the birth of the baby. They are more economically disadvantaged and less psychologically mature than older mothers. The birth predisposes adolescent mothers to more problems than the average parent must meet, and they have far fewer resources for meeting them.[45]

First, teenage mothers suffer more pregnancy complications and have babies with problems more often than do older mothers. Prematurity and low birth weight—which increase the likelihood of cerebral palsy, mental retardation, and epilepsy in these babies—occur most often in the babies of teenage mothers. Two explanations have been advanced. One is that a true age difference is in effect—physiological immaturity on the part of the mother results in more problems in the baby. The other explanation cites psychosocial causes. Young mothers are a disadvantaged group with a less healthy lifestyle and poorer access to prenatal care, and these factors, not age itself, are related to outcome. Prenatal care improves outcome, but age still appears to be a factor.[46]

Biological risk depends somewhat on the ethnic background of the mothers. Whereas an early childbearing age is related to greater risk in European-American mothers, later childbearing (meaning from ages eighteen to thirty-four) is related to greater risk in African-American mothers, perhaps because their health declines as they get older.[47]

Second, there is greater likelihood that adolescent mothers and their children will live in poverty, with all the problems that involves. Because the majority of adolescent mothers are single, they face considerable risk for poverty for that reason alone, but adolescent single motherhood appears to confer an additional disadvantage to mother and child. The exact causes of this are not known, but two possible reasons are identified: lower educational attainment of adolescent mothers and their smaller likelihood of entering a stable marriage that provides economic support. Teens who marry in adolescence have less stable marriages, and single teen mothers are less likely to be in stable marriages in their twenties.[48]

Again, ethnic origins seem to make a difference. Delaying motherhood to age twenty-five resulted in economic gain among European-American women but not among African-American women. Being single at the time of birth presents an economic disadvantage that continues into their twenties for African-American women but not for European-American women, for whom only current marital status seems to matter.[49]

Certain characteristics of adolescent mothers create difficulties in child rearing. Compared with older mothers, adolescent mothers are less able to provide stable living arrangements, so their children experience more moves and more changes in caretakers and in male support figures.[50] These mothers are also less psychologically mature than their age mates. A study comparing adolescent mothers with a matched control group of teenagers also at high psychosocial risk found that adolescent mothers are less independent, less certain of themselves, and less trusting of others. They have a diffuse sense of their own identities, lower self-esteem, and greater susceptibility to depression.[51]

Such psychological immaturity creates difficulty in caregiving. Though as warm as older mothers, adolescent mothers view their infants as more difficult, and they are less realistic in their expectations of children.[52] They foster premature independence in their infants, pushing them to hold their bottles, sit up too early, and scramble for toys before they can get them. Yet, as infants become toddlers, these mothers reverse their behavior and become overly controlling, not letting toddlers explore freely, not giving them choices in activities.[53] Adolescent mothers also fail to provide a stimulating home environment conducive to learning, and they offer less verbal stimulation.[54]

Joy Osofsky and her co-workers explore how the mother's ability to regulate feelings affects her children.[55] They note that adolescent mothers are often depressed and emotionally unstable. Further, these feelings can lead to the negative interpretations of children's behavior and mothers' inability to respond in a controlled way. These mothers are less available to their children both in infancy and toddlerhood, and the lack of nurturing sensitivity and availability to children may account for the lower levels of secure attachments found in children of adolescent mothers.

Infants and toddlers of adolescent mothers do not differ from children of older mothers in cognitive measures; however, by the time such children reach preschool age, differences begin to emerge and continue into elementary school years.[56] Children of adolescent mothers face a greater likelihood of academic difficulties, school failure, and behavioral problems. Teens of adolescent mothers are also more likely than their peers to become teenage parents. Factors that promote positive development include the mothers' improved circumstances. If a mother goes off welfare between her child's preschool and adolescent years, she reduces the risk of her being retained a grade. When a male figure is present, adolescent offspring have fewer behavioral problems than those with no such figure.

The child's sex and temperament interact with other risk/protective factors to influence parenting.[57] Adolescent mothers appear more involved with sons than with daughters. When babies have easy, adaptable temperaments, adolescent mothers are more successful with them and feel better about themselves as parents. Conversely, if the child has a difficult temperament, does not adjust well, and is hard to soothe, adolescent mothers may have a more difficult time because it is hard for them to be patient. See Table 5-1 for other risk/protective factors.

Though these findings come largely from studies of African-American teenage mothers, work with other samples yields similar findings. Judith Musick has studied samples with a broader representation of poor adolescent mothers of African-American, Hispanic-American, and European-American backgrounds living in small towns and rural areas as well as urban areas in the Midwest and Southeast. In these samples, she finds similar difficulties in the maturity level of all the mothers and in their abilities to translate their love for their children into supportive, nurturing

TABLE 5-1
RISK AND PROTECTIVE FACTORS FOR CHILDREN OF ADOLESCENT MOTHERS

Risk Factors

1. Living in poverty with attendant problems of frequent residence changes, of living in high crime and violence areas, and experiencing changes in caretakers and male support

2. Birth complications: prematurity, low birth weight

3. Poor parenting from mothers

4. Behavior and school problems

5. Less social support from relatives/friends

Protective Factors

1. Being a boy

2. Having an easy, adaptable temperament

3. Having intelligence and problem-solving skills that lead to better coping

4. Mother continuing her education

5. Mother limiting number of subsequent children

6. Mother entering a stable marriage

7. Mother having high self-esteem

Adapted from Joy D. Osofsky, Della M. Hann, and Claire Peebles, "Adolescent Parenthood: Risks and Opportunities for Mothers and Infants," in *Handbook of Infant Mental Health*, ed. Charles H. Zeanah, Jr. (New York: Guilford Press, 1993), pp. 106–119.

care.[58] She too finds diversity of outcome with some mothers making heroic efforts to raise their children under very difficult circumstances.

Perhaps more importantly, her work has uncovered problems of a different sort—namely, that 65 percent of the adolescent mothers surveyed in one study were sexually abused in childhood or early adolescence, and 61 percent were abused by numerous perpetrators. She believes that these young girls feel helpless, unprotected, inferior, and unworthy of care; as a result, they fail to develop self-protection skills and are vulnerable to predatory or uncaring men. Further, they carry these feelings and difficulties into their role as parent, and often cannot protect their own children from sexual abuse. In Chapter 14, we shall explore the effects of sexual abuse in greater detail.

Other studies, comparing African-American adolescent mothers with Hispanic-American mothers, find that in both groups teenage mothers are more depressed, do less child care, and provide less stimulating environments than older mothers of the same ethnic backgrounds. However, African-American adolescent mothers receive more support from family and friends and are less strict than Hispanic-American mothers.[59]

Adolescent parenting also affects other family members, especially the teen's parents. Most adolescent mothers are single at the time of conception. Only about one-quarter marry in the first two years after the birth, and when they do, the marriages are highly unstable Thus, many adolescent mothers turn to the family of origin as their main source of support.[60]

Many teens continue to live with their mothers. This appears to have positive effects if teens are young or if the infant has a special problem and needs more care, perhaps because the young mother has a chance to develop skills and is willing to learn from her own mother and because especially stressful circumstances require two parental figures. When mothers reach young adulthood, however, living with their mothers appears to have negative ramifications, perhaps because the young mothers are less receptive to their own mothers' help.[61]

While they undoubtedly face many problems, adolescent mothers are often committed to their children, and many raise them successfully. Unfortunately, we pay less attention to the successes. For example, 75 percent of the mothers in the Baltimore study were employed and not involved with social services; yet, we focus on the 25 percent who receive services.[62]

Who are the successful mothers? They are women who use contraceptives and control their fertility. They stay in school or return to school and complete their education. They maintain a high level of motivation and high educational goals for themselves. The most successful of them entered stable marriages with men who provided support and help.

Help for Teenage Mothers   Two kinds of programs attack the problems of teenage pregnancies: (1) those that postpone the birth of the fist child by means of effective education and birth control and (2) those that help mothers once they have had children. Both programs emphasize effective birth control while encouraging teens to develop a sense of confidence about their ability to make and carry out future goals for themselves.[63]

Although help for mothers includes help with parenting, continuing education, and meeting responsibilities, research suggests that mothers also benefit from programs that help them sustain positive relationships with their children and their families. Because the adolescent mothers tend not to trust others, they need help in developing trust both in themselves as competent caregivers and in the relationships they form with their children. They require help in building their own self-esteem to help them survive the irritations and frustrations that occur in rearing children. They also need practice in empathizing with their babies so they can read babies' cues and better meet their needs. Videotaping interactions helps mothers recognize their powerful role in their babies' lives.[64]

Joy Osofsky and her co-workers conclude, "We feel that an emphasis on positive mental health — that is, a focus on what may go right rather than wrong with adolescent mothers and their infants — will lead us forward toward the development of more effective preventive interventions."[65]

The Fathers   Discussions of adolescent parenthood have focused primarily on the mother, in part because a significant number of fathers (estimated to be 50 percent) are older and are not teenagers. Though typically less involved with their children, adolescent fathers are often not completely absent. Though only about 25 percent of adolescent fathers live with their infants, a national survey suggests that about 57 percent visit weekly in the first two years of life. The percentage of those visiting drops as the children grow older—40 percent when the child is between two and four-and-a-half, 27 percent when the child is four-and-a-half to seven, and 22 percent when the child is over seven.[66]

African-American fathers are more likely to be involved than are European-American and Hispanic-American fathers. Only 12 percent of African-American fathers have no contact with their children, whereas 30 percent of European-American fathers and 37 percent of Hispanic-American fathers have no contact.[67] Adolescent fathers are more likely to be involved when other people in the environment support their involvement. (See the interview in this chapter with Dr. James Levine.)

Agencies are forming programs to encourage active fatherhood for these young men. In Cleveland, for example, Charles Ballard has founded a private National Institute for Responsible Fatherhood and Family Development.[68] Growing up without a father and with anger because of his lack of a positive male role model, he has established programs to help men learn responsibility so they can care for their children and be positive forces in their lives. As a social worker helping single adolescent mothers, he decided to go out on the streets and look for the fathers. He organized groups to discuss paternal responsibility. He raised money to support a small staff and formed the Teen Father Program. Fathers in his program have three requirements: they must (1) legitimize the child, (2) be in school or a General Education Development (GED) program, and (3) have a job. With the exception of the first, these are the same actions that mothers are encouraged to take. This program has been extended to young mothers and grandparents with the aim of strengthening the entire family. Now it is expanding to other cities, and Ballard believes there are applications to other social groups as well. "The problem is not exclusive to African-Americans and to poor people. A lot of men who have children in their homes—doctors, lawyers, politicians—are not taking care of their kids. When fathers get closer with their children, communities will become safer for all of us."[69]

Nonparents

Some couples actively decide not to have children. Some women know from an early age that they do not want children, but most report going through a sequence similar to the following four-step sequence: (1) postponing children for a definite period, (2) postponing children for an indefinite period, (3) considering the possibility of not having children, and (4) making a definite decision not to have children.[70]

Some couples want children very much and cannot have them. Even so, not all of these people feel frustrated and unhappy. Involuntarily childless wives are more likely than mothers or voluntarily childless wives to report feeling a lack of fulfillment and purpose in life, but they report especially close and supportive relationships with their husbands and their families. As a result, their overall sense of well-being is the same as that of mothers and voluntarily childless women.[71] Marital happiness and overall well-being are related to the quality of adult relationships, and a woman can be happy with a husband and extended family whether she does or does not have children.

INTERVIEW
with James Levine

James Levine is the director of the Fatherhood Project at the Families and Work Institute. He served as a principal consultant to Vice Present Al Gore in drafting the federal initiative on fatherhood, created by executive order in 1995.

As a result of your work regarding fathering, do you think that, on average, fathers bring special qualities to parenting?

That's a difficult question in the field. Do they bring something different, and if they do, is this culturally or biologically determined? I think what fathers bring that is different centers on two dimensions. First, there is a fair amount of research that fathers' interactive style with young children is different from mothers'. With young children, they have a more rough-and-tumble style. On average, dads whoop it up with little kids. They chase them, throw them up in the air, roll around with them. Ross Parke has a theory that this type of interaction has some relationship to how children relate to the social world outside the family.

The second dimension I think is really important is father is a man and knows what it is like to be a man in this society, what it takes. While my wife and I can guide our children in terms of basic values, there are some ways I can talk to my son about what the world expects of him and what it has felt like to me to be a man in this society, what the expectations are of men and women. I also share that perspective with my daughter. So my wife and I bring a different storehouse of experience to parenting, different ways of being in the world based on the way the world expects us to play roles as men and women.

What are the best ways to get men involved in parenting?

There are several issues. I think the absolute key is the couple's expectations of what the father's role will be. If the mom doesn't expect the dad to be involved, and the dad doesn't expect to be involved, that's a prescription for noninvolvement. If Mom doesn't expect dad to be involved and Dad might want to be involved, he won't be involved. The mother is the gatekeeper in the relationship. Many women say they want husbands to be involved, but in effect, they want them to be involved as sort of mom's subordinate or assistant. Mom's the manager, telling Dad how to be involved as opposed to assuming Dad will be involved and will learn the skills to be a father. It is important for mothers to back off and be in the background, and let fathers be with children.

So, one key to involvement is the couple's dynamics. I don't mean to blame Mom, but there is a system here — men and women as a system — and one starts here in terms of making a supportive system for fathers' involvement.

Then let's look at men in terms of men and the system outside the couple. All the research we've done shows that men today define success on two dimensions — being a good provider and equally important is having good relationships with children. So if you look at the values men bring to parenthood, there are generally agreed-upon desires to have close relationships with their children. But, aside from the couple relationship, there are two obstacles. Men sometimes feel incompetent as to how to do this; they need skills. And, second, their work sucks them up in spite of their best intentions to give time to relationships with children. They spend a lot of time working, not to avoid forming relationships with children but as a way of caring for children.

A key to change is changing the cultural clues men get about being fathers. Looking at this from an ecological and systems point of view, we can ask, "What are the cues that men get about parenting across the life cycle?" The expectations others have about them have a lot to do with shaping their behavior. For example, prenatally if men get expectations from the health care system they are expected to be at prenatal visits, they will be there. Mostly, however, they get the message they have no role during the pregnancy. Yet, research has shown that one of the best predictors of good prenatal care for the mother is whether the partner is involved with prenatal care.

We have found in our work with low-income men that when men understand how vital their role is even before the child is born, they can change their level of involvement. Knowing how important their role is with their babies increases the motivation of low-income men to be involved.

So at the time of birth and afterwards, if the pediatrician sends messages that he or she wants both parents at visits—"I need to know both of the baby's parents. I want to see you both, not just the mother"—that message shapes the father's behavior. Same thing at preschools or day care. They can also send messages that they want both parents, not just mothers, to be involved.

So it is the expectations that are embedded in daily interactions that are the real keys to fathers' involvement. If you look at the face-to-face interactions with maternity nurses and pediatricians, embedded in dialogues with doctors, health care providers, and teachers are messages about expected involvement. If more messages expect fathers to be involved and daily interactions offer support for fathers' involvement, fathers will be involved.

To give a specific example, West Virginia wanted to increase the rate at which fathers established paternity of children born to single mothers, and the question was how to do that. One could think about a big public-information campaign with messages to encourage involvement, but the key was the maternity nurse, who had the most influence on both the young man and the young woman. The father would come and look at the baby, and if the nurse assumed he was some bad guy and chased him away, if she did not invite him in to be involved with the baby, he would disengage and disappear. They increased the rate of paternity establishment by increasing the dialogue with fathers and also by changing what the nurse said to mothers. The nurse told mothers it is important for children to be involved with their fathers even if mothers decide not to marry the fathers. In two years, the rate of establishing paternity went from 15 percent to 60 percent of fathers who claimed paternity of babies born to single mothers.

The overall message to fathers was we want you here, we want you to establish paternity and be fathers to your children. Changing expectations encoded in daily interactions are the important elements in increasing fathers' involvement with their children.

TRANSITION AND ADJUSTMENT TO PARENTHOOD

The arrival of a baby changes every aspect of married life, from finances to sex life, sleeping habits, and social life. Although many first-time parents report that nothing could have adequately prepared them for the experience, knowing what to expect in advance can still help parents cope.

Parents' Preparenting Personal Characteristics

There tends to be continuity between parents' preparenting characteristics and their relationships with their own infants, which, in turn, affects the infant's subsequent development. The kinds of early experiences that promote effective parenting in men and women include those that promote adaptiveness, autonomy, and flexibility in both parents.[72] When parents feel secure and competent as individuals and worthy of care themselves, they are more likely to be responsive, caring parents. For example, according to research, pregnant women who had positive relationships with their parents envisioned themselves as confident mothers; later, they interacted with their babies in such a way that the babies grew more competent in social and motor skills.[73] Also, as we saw in Chapter 2, parents who had continuing positive attachment with their own parents were more likely to be responsive caregivers with their own children.[74]

Parents may worry if they read statements connecting childhood experiences with later adult parenting. Most parents want a fresh start with their children. They do not want to feel doomed to poor parenting by events of their own past. And, in fact, they are not. Recent research reveals that parents who come to terms with their own negative childhood experiences do not repeat the unhappy interactions with their own children. Mothers and fathers who understand and accept their feelings that their own parents could not give them what they wanted are able to create new kinds of relationships with their sons and daughters. Parents who describe difficult times but deny any emotional reaction like anger, sadness, or frustration in response to their parents, or parents who remain preoccupied with these feelings, are most likely to carry over negative patterns in their day-to-day contact because they have not worked through their feelings about their childhood.[75]

Coming to terms with one's early experiences appears to have an additional benefit of increasing self-reflection and the ability to understand others' complex psychological states. Such sensitivity to others enables parents, particularly mothers, to be more responsive caregivers with their babies.[76]

The Power of a Positive Marital Relationship

Throughout this book, we shall see that a positive marital relationship sustains both parents as they care for their children. Further, a positive marriage is related to children's healthy growth.

When mothers and fathers feel support from each other, they are more competent parents and interact with the baby more effectively. Father-infant interactions and fathers' competence, particularly, are related to feeling support from mothers. Even basic activities are influenced by the quality of the marriage. Mothers experience

I T ' S   N E V E R   T O O   L A T E

Knowing my interest in parenting, Harry Sirota, a Chicago optometrist, shared these anecdotes from his own life.

He was playing on the floor with his visiting grandchildren—four, seven, and eleven—when he looked up and saw his daughter looking at him from the corner of her eye. He asked her what was the matter. She said, "Nothing," but he persisted, and finally she asked, "Why didn't you ever play with us that way when we were growing up?"

Harry stopped and said, "I'm sorry, my father wasn't around to play. He didn't have a relationship with me. I grew up in a family where my father was angry, yelling at me, critical, yelling at me. When I was seventeen, I left home. What did I know about being a good father? I was glad I didn't have boys because I did not know how to be a father, the importance of a father playing and being around. I did the best I could and, over time, I have learned what to do. I didn't know when you were young how important it is to play with children, but now I know. I am a *grand* parent because I have learned and mellowed."

Harry said to me, "It's never too late to learn and to change. And you can even be a parent to your parent. When my father was 89, he had a big birthday party, and I went home for it. There were lots of guests, but my father was sitting off to the side of the garden. He motioned me over to him and said, 'Sit down, I want to talk to you. I want to apologize for all the things I did when you were growing up. I wish I had been a different father.'"

"What did you do?" Harry asked his father.

"You know what I did. Why are you hurting me by making me tell you now?"

"I know that *I* know, but I want to know what you're apologizing for."

His father stopped, thought, then talked for half an hour about all the things he did. When he was through, he concluded, "I didn't mean to hurt you. I love you."

Harry replied, "I hated you for doing those things, but I want to thank you for apologizing to me. If I had to do it to my children, I would find it very difficult."

His father said, "I want you to know I loved you then, I love you now, and I always will love you."

"Why are you telling me these things now?" Harry asked.

His father explained, "I'm sitting here looking at all these children and how parents behave with them, and I realize I made some terrible mistakes with you."

Harry said to me, "There was a great release from the anger I carried all those years." His father died a year later. Harry then went on to tell me how he had changed his mother's behavior.

"In all my childhood she never told me she loved me. So when she was about 90, I thought I would give her what she couldn't give to me. I called every week, and it was usually a superficial conversation, "How are you?" What are you doing?" At the end of one phone conversation, I took a deep breath, and said, 'I . . .' It was so hard to say, I almost gave up, but I gritted my teeth and blurted out, 'I love you, Mom.' And she replied she loved me. Each week it was a little easier.

"Then about the sixth week, no sooner had I got into the conversation, she said, 'You know, son, I really love you.'"

"Giving them what they could not give to me has been healing for them and healing for me."

fewer feeding difficulties when their husbands are supportive and view them positively, whereas marital distress is related to inept feeding by the mother.[77]

Intimate emotional spousal support is related also to parents' satisfaction with themselves in the parental role and with the baby. When parents are happy with each other, they smile at the baby more and play with the baby. Babies profit from this atmosphere of positive regard, are more alert, and have more motor skills. Conversely, a conflicted marital relationship decreases both partners' ability to function effectively as parents, which in turn affects their children.[78] We shall discuss this in greater detail in the next chapter.

Just as positive attachment to one's own parents promotes effective behavior with infants, so it promotes secure attachment to the marital partner.[79] However, an imperfect relationship exists between early childhood experience and attachment to the partner, and frequently one partner can influence the behavior of the other partner in the direction of becoming more secure. Philip Cowan and Carolyn Cowan found that when a person who had an insecure attachment to his or her parents in childhood married someone with a secure history, the insecure partner took on the parenting style of the more secure partner and became calmer, warmer, and more positive. This is most likely to happen when an insecure mother is married to a secure father. An insecure father is less likely to pattern himself after his wife.[80]

What constitutes a positive marital relationship? One contributor to marital satisfaction is related to parents' agreement on role arrangements.[81] It does not matter whether couples are traditional or egalitarian in their division of tasks, but satisfaction increases when couples have similar ideologies.

A second contributor to marital satisfaction is a couple's ability to communicate with each other — to express thoughts, feelings, and needs in ways each partner can hear and respond to. Communication does not have to be verbal. A look, a gesture, a touch, or an action can communicate support, agreement, or the need for further conversation. When so much that is new is happening, parents must be able to let each other know how they feel. Parents who have communicated well before gestation find time in crowded schedules to touch base and talk. They may not need a lot of time, because they are skilled at picking up how the partner feels, but they do take time to stay close.[82]

Parents who focus on what is good about the situation or the action of the other person, who avoid negative criticism and angry exchanges, feel less stress and create less stress for each other. These parents discuss different points of view and express themselves forcefully, but they stay focused on how they can make needed changes and improve the situation and they avoid assigning blame for problems.

Changes the Baby Brings

A great deal goes on during the early months. Parents are highly involved in the nurturing stage of parenthood,[83] caring for the child, and accepting their new role as parents. They worry, "Am I doing okay?" "Am I the kind of parent I want to be?" Gradually, parents incorporate other parts of their lives — work, extended family, friends — into their caretaking activities.

It may be difficult, however, for parents to give each other the support that is so crucial in coping during this period. A significant number of new mothers report specific problems, including (1) tiredness and exhaustion; (2) loss of sleep, especially in the first two months; (3) concern about ignoring husband's needs; (4) feeling inadequate as a mother; (5) inability to keep up with housework; and (6) feeling tied down.[84] Mothers did not anticipate the many changes that would occur in their lives when their babies arrived, in part because they did not realize how much work is involved in caring for an infant. Fathers had a similar ordering of complaints: (1) loss of sleep for up to six weeks; (2) need to adjust to new responsibilities and routines; (3) disruption of daily routines; (4) ignorance of the amount of work the baby requires; and (5) financial worries (62 percent of the wives were employed prior to the child's arrival and only 12 percent afterward). Husbands make such comments as "My wife has less time for me" and "Getting used to being tied down is hard."

The new father may see the infant as a threat to his relationship with his wife and to their lifestyle. Concern about the amount of time, money, and freedom the baby will surely consume can obscure the joy he expects — and is expected — to feel. No more candlelit dinners, or even impromptu decisions to go to a movie or to make love, not for a while. The father has not had the physical experience of carrying the baby for nine months, nor is he as likely to be as involved as the mother in the care of the newborn. And for a while, at least, the needs of the baby will come before the wishes of the husband — and those needs will be frequent and unpredictable, delaying meals and interrupting sleep. But almost all fathers and mothers find that emotional attachment to their babies grows and deepens if they are patient and caring.

In the first few weeks after birth, obstetricians advise restraint from sexual intercourse. During this period, the new mother is especially vulnerable to infection, her energy has been drained by pregnancy and birth, and her days and nights are devoted to care of the newborn. She is fulfilling the demands of an inarticulate and very dependent creature and must perform many unfamiliar tasks along with the usual household and personal routines. The fact that lovemaking, a source of pleasure in marriage, is interrupted adds to the feelings of stress felt by both parents after childbirth. During this early period of physical and emotional adjustment, the wife — particularly the working wife — needs time to regain her stamina and to establish new routines. The following section examines the way parents cope with all these issues.

Dimensions Underlying the Transition

Two longitudinal studies — one carried out at the University of California, Berkeley, by Carolyn Pape Cowan and Philip Cowan,[85] and the other by Jay Belsky at Pennsylvania State University[86] — yield remarkably similar findings on the basic dimensions underlying the adjustment process. Although these findings emerged from studies of couples, they apply, with modifications, to single parents as well.

First, a major determiner of the ease of the adjustment process is the parent's ability to balance his or her needs for autonomy and self-care with the need to be close and intimate with other people, particularly spouse and child. A parent who balances concerns for "me" and for "you" and creates an "us" relationship that has priority over the needs of the individual faces an easier transition. He or she puts aside

TABLE 5-2
DIMENSIONS UNDERLYING THE TRANSITION TO PARENTHOOD

1. Capacity to balance individuality and mutuality
2. Communication skills of both parents
3. Attitude (positive/negative) in confronting situations and people
4. Expectations about what the baby will bring
5. Ability to devise sharing of workload that is compatible with couple's beliefs/ideologies concerning appropriate behavior for men and women
6. Ability to come to terms with patterns of behavior learned in family of origin
7. Ability to manage conflict effectively

Adapted from Jay Belsky and John Kelly, *The Transition to Parenthood* (New York: Delacorte, 1994); Carolyn Pape Cowan and Philip Cowan, *When Partners Become Parents* (New York: Basic Books, 1992).

immediate wants in order to help the partner because that improves their relationship. A husband may put aside his desire to go visiting as a family, because his wife is tired and needs to rest, and he wants them both to feel good about the outing. Or a wife may not ask her husband to skip his evening jog to help with the baby, because she feels he needs to unwind from work, and she wants a relaxed family atmosphere when he is with the baby.

Other dimensions, listed in Table 5-2, include creating a positive marital relationship, having realistic expectations of the baby and themselves, and having skills to resolve problems when they arise. Those parents most at risk for difficulties are unrealistic about the changes a baby will bring, have negative views of the partner and their marriage, and are pessimistic about solving the problems. They take no action to arrive at mutually satisfying solutions to their difficulties.

Both Belsky and the Cowans agree that transitions vary by gender. Although men and women have many common experiences—both find the baby irresistible, both worry about bills and the increased work, and both feel better about themselves as a result of parenthood—still, they experience the transition in different ways. The experience is a much more physical one for women. Because women have a biological connection with the child during the pregnancy, labor, and delivery, the child is a greater reality to them, and the whole experience of birth and child care is totally absorbing. Following the birth, their bodies must recover from the effects of the labor and delivery, and from the upheaval in their hormonal system. Further, many maintain the intimate physical connection with the child by breast-feeding. Men experience the pregnancy and the early months after birth from a greater distance and often feel left out. Lacking the close physical connection with the child, fathers often need more time to form a strong attachment with the baby.

In most instances, couples navigate the transition well, not because they have fewer or less serious problems than the couples who experience difficulties, but because they have developed effective ways to cope with changes and resolve conflicts.

These domains were identified through studies of couples, but they apply to the transitions of single parents as well. Single parents have to form a supportive network of individuals who can help. Although the emotional attachments may not be so intense among friends as in couples, the domains are useful to consider. Whether their support group is made up of friends or family, single parents have to share with these individuals the parent's expectations and feelings; they must all find ways to divide the workload, manage conflict, and avoid negative outbursts.

Ways to Ease the Transition

Both the Cowans and Belsky write movingly about the difficulties young couples face as they have babies, and all these researchers agree on what produces the problems. Society is in a state of transition regarding men's and women's roles. Economic factors require most women with infants and young children to work outside the home, so couples must share child-care and family responsibilities as well as outside work. There are no agreed-on rules about how this should be done. We have few role models for couples working out conflicts. Further, society does little to give young parents support by providing or subsidizing high-quality day care.

Young parents often live far from their families of origin, so their parents and other relatives are often not around to help. These young people have fewer social supports and resources. Thus, they have more to do than parents in the past, with fewer guidelines and less help.

Support Groups   The Cowans have found that couples groups were very helpful to new parents.[87] Six groups of four couples each met weekly for six months, beginning in the last trimester of the pregnancy. These groups, led by husband-wife pairs, provided ongoing support for parents. The groups also sent an important message to fathers that they were essential participants in the parenting process.

Meetings typically began with a check-in that enabled each person to discuss a pressing matter or raise an important question. Following that, discussion centered on a topic chosen by the group or the leaders. Such topics included hopes and dreams of the couples, changes in their relationships to each other, their decision-making processes, their work lives, and their relationships to their parents. Prior to the birth, topics focused on the couple's expectations of parenthood, and after the birth, on actual experiences as parents. Table 5-3 lists some suggestions for making the transition to parenting less stressful.

Couples discussed the stresses of adjusting to parenting and found reassurance in learning that others have similar problems. The couples discussed activities or attitudes that reduced stress and that produced well-being and closeness between parents. In following the families, the Cowans found that all the couples who were in the six-month groups at the time of the birth were still together when the child was three years old, whereas 15 percent of couples who had not been in the groups were divorced. When children were five years old, the divorce rate was the same for the two groups.

When parents conceive a child and bring him or her into the world, they embark on possibly the most life-changing experience of their lives. Whether well or poorly planned, the child elicits new behaviors from parents and at the same time brings a host of new pleasures to them. When parents can work together with each other or with supportive friends and relatives, when they communicate expectations,

TABLE 5-3
RECOMMENDATIONS TO COUPLES FOR EASING
THE TRANSITION TO PARENTHOOD

1. Share expectations.

2. Give yourselves regular checkups on how each is doing.

3. Make time to talk to each other.

4. Negotiate an agenda of important issues; if one partner thinks there is a problem, there is.

5. Adopt an experimental attitude; see how solutions work and make modifications as necessary.

6. Don't ignore sex and intimacy.

7. Line up support for the early stages after the birth.

8. Talk with a friend or co-worker.

9. Find the delicate balance between meeting your needs and the baby's needs; children grow best when parents maintain a strong positive relationship.

Adapted from Carolyn Pape Cowan and Philip Cowan, *When Partners Become Parents* (New York: Basic Books, 1991).

experiences, and feelings as they care for the baby, the baby brings parents and friends and relatives closer together to share life experiences in a more intense, meaningful way than previously known. Babies demand a great deal, but they give much in return.

MAIN POINTS

People's reasons for wanting children include

- love, affection, and stimulation
- creative outlet, proof of adulthood, and a sense of achievement
- proof of moral behavior and economic utility

The decision to be a parent involves

- assessing parental readiness in terms of time and psychological resources
- couples' planning children and resolving differences
- single adults' planning children
- accepting a child if unplanned
- resolving ambivalence so the child is wanted, not rejected

Getting pregnant

- presents stress to 8 percent of couples and single women who have trouble conceiving

- can involve various kinds of help for couples with infertility problems
- via new technologies means people who would have been childless in the past can now have children

Timing of children

- is best when both parents want children and are personally ready to take on their new responsibilities
- depends on the psychological qualities of parents rather than their age
- affects a child's later adjustment — if parents are not mature, a child may develop later problems, as happens with children of adolescent mothers
- has resulted in negative stereotypes of teenage mothers and positive views of older ones

Nonparents

- usually decide in stages not to have children
- are as happy as couples who have children

Babies bring such changes as

- new routines, new responsibilities
- great pleasures

Dimensions underlying a parent's transition to parenthood include

- balancing individuality and mutuality
- communication skills
- positive attitudes
- agreed-on division of labor
- parents coming to terms with their own childhood experiences

Parents experience greater ease in the transition when they

- maintain intimate bonds with their partner or a supportive friend/relative
- share expectations, feelings, and workload with partners
- line up support from friends and relatives
- adopt an experimental attitude toward solutions — try them and see if they work

EXERCISES

1. Think about why and when you want children. List factors influencing your decision — school, health, financial, and work considerations of yourself and your partner. What will be your positive reasons for having children? What

supports will you need? Do you think it will be as hard for you to be a parent as it was for your parents?

2. Describe your expectations of parenthood. What changes will it require of you? Do you think your expectations are realistic? Describe the activities that you do now that might prepare you for being a parent—taking a course in parenting, learning to solve conflicts in a positive way, practicing communication skills with friends, learning about children and their needs. Are there other things you could be doing?

3. Plan out the support system you would organize for yourself and your partner if you were having a baby in three months. Whom would you include? How involved would relatives be? How much extra expense would such a system cost?

4. Imagine you are a fifteen-year-old girl who becomes pregnant and wants to keep her child. Investigate the resources in your community that would enable you to keep the child, remain in school, get a job. Visit the programs or day care center where your child would be cared for. Are services adequate?

5. Imagine you are married to someone with a gender ideology very different from your own. How would you go about arriving at compromises? What areas could you not compromise on? Do you and prospective spouses talk about these kinds of issues?

ADDITIONAL READINGS

Barrett, Nina. *I Wish Someone Had Told Me*. New York: Simon & Schuster, 1990.

Belsky, Jay, and Kelly, John. *The Transition to Parenthood*. New York: Delacorte, 1994.

Cowan, Carolyn Pape, and Cowan, Philip. *When Partners Become Parents*. New York: Basic Books, 1992.

Furstenberg, Frank F., Brooks-Gunn, J., and Morgan, S. Philip. *Adolescent Mothers in Later Life*. New York: Cambridge University Press, 1987.

Yarrow, Andrew. *Latecomers*. New York: Free Press, 1991.

THE FIRST YEAR OF LIFE

C H A P T E R 6

What are babies like? What do they see, hear, smell, taste, need? How soon will they recognize parents? play with them? How do parents form positive relationships with babies so babies get off to a good start? What do babies bring to parent-child relationships that shape what parents do? How can parents encourage competence in babies as they grow?

This chapter begins with a brief summary of how babies grow and develop in the first year. Such knowledge can help us understand the important and subtle contributions parents make to children's growth.

THE NEWBORN

What can parents expect of their new baby? Well, first, babies are not just asleep or awake as older children or adults are. Peter Wolff has identified six stages of consciousness in infants: (1) *regular sleep,* in which the child is relaxed and still; (2) *irregular sleep,* in which the eyes are closed but the child is somewhat active; (3) *drowsiness,* in which the eyes flutter and the child has a glazed look; (4) *alert inactivity,* in which the eyes are open and the child is alert; (5) *waking activity,* in which the child is alert and physically active; and (6) *crying,* in which the child cries and moves about.[1] Babies vary in how much time they spend in each activity. The average newborn spends 16 hours each day sleeping, though some sleep as little as 10 hours, and others sleep as much as 20 hours a day.

All human beings have biological cycles of sleep, wakefulness, activity, hunger, and fluctuations in body temperature and hormonal secretions. These cycles, repeating about every 24 hours, are called *circadian rhythms.* During the newborn period, body rhythms are not organized. Neonates sleep, wake, and eat every few hours. Their systems are irregular, gradually settling into a more organized pattern in the first three months, with most achieving a stable pattern at about six months. As we shall see, parents can help babies settle into regular patterns.[2]

WHAT I WISH I HAD KNOWN ABOUT INFANCY

"I remember when we brought him home from the hospital, and we had him on the changing table for a minute, and I realized, 'I don't know how to keep the engine running.' I wondered how could they let him go home with us, this little package weighing seven or eight pounds. I had no idea of what to do. I kind of knew you fed him, and you cleaned him and kept him warm; but I didn't have any hands-on experience, anything practical. In a way I would have liked them to watch me for a day or two in the hospital while I change him to make sure I knew how to do it. It's kind of like giving me a car without seeing whether I could drive it around the block." FATHER

"I didn't have enough information about breast-feeding for two months. I almost gave up because it was so painful. I found a good breast-feeding nurse who showed me two things, and it changed the whole experience. It made such a difference, and breast-feeding became a joy." MOTHER

"I wish we had known a little more about establishing her first habits about sleeping. The way you set it up in the beginning is the way it is going to be. Having enough sleep is so important. We went too long before we decided to let her cry for five minutes. Then she got into good sleep habits." FATHER

"I had no idea how tired I would be. I'm not sure anyone can describe the level of tiredness you feel. I am getting eight hours of sleep now but I always sleep lightly and could wake up in an instant. When I wake up in the morning now, I don't feel refreshed. I'm still tired even though he is sleeping through the night." MOTHER

"I wish I had known how it would change things between me and my husband. The baby comes first, and by the time the day is over and he is in bed, we have two hours together, but I just want to curl up and take care of myself." MOTHER

Senses

For years, psychologists thought newborn babies were incompetent creatures who were unable to comprehend the world around them. Because infants cannot tell us what they see, hear, taste, smell, and feel, our understanding of newborns' abilities was limited until complex equipment enabled us to detect babies' physiological responses to what they sense. As we have learned about their abilities, we have grown more impressed, with competent behavior displayed by babies just a few hours old.

Newborns are sensitive to light and to changes in brightness immediately after birth. They can distinguish objects, although they see things in a hazy blur rather than as clear images.[3] A newborn sees most clearly what is about 8 inches from his face, often the mother's or father's face. Babies are more interested in patterned ob-

"I wish I had known about how much time babies take. It is like he needs twenty-four-hour attention. For an older parent who is used to having his own life and is very set in his ways, it is hard to make the changes and still have some time for your own life." FATHER

"I bottle fed him, and I wished I had had better information about bottle feeding. I didn't know you weren't supposed to put nipples in the dishwasher because the holes get filled sometimes. I think it may have contributed to his waking up so much to eat the first several weeks, and it took him a long time to get full. I finally ran into a friend who said, 'Oh, get this kind of nipple because it is really the best.' I got it, and it really helped. Things like that were a problem. I think he was having a lot of trouble just getting milk, working too hard." MOTHER

"For me I had knowledge about feeding and what he would be like, and what the days would be like. I wish I had known what only experience can give you. I wish I had known how I would respond and how stressed I would be. I was sleep-deprived, and that was not easy for me. I wish I had had a mother who could be here and give me the benefit of her experience, to say, 'This is all normal, this is part of having a baby.' My mother died in the beginning of the pregnancy, and I had sisters and friends I called." MOTHER

"She had this periodic crying at night in the beginning, and you are caught in the raging hormones and somehow I thought if I just read Dr. Spock again or if I read more, I'd understand it better. And we joked about reading the same paragraph in the book over and over. We needed reassurance it would end, and at three months it ended. That was the hardest part." MOTHER

"I wish I had known enough to take advantage of the naps and sleep. You want to have some semblance of order, getting back to normal, and it's a big thing in the beginning to figure out that you can't do it all." MOTHER

jects—for example, faces or concentric circles—than in solid-colored circles. They tend to focus on the edges, however, perhaps because that is where contrast is sharpest. This may be disconcerting to the new mother, who wants her baby to look at her eyes, not at her forehead or chin. But within a few weeks the child will make eye contact. By the age of six months, the child's vision is similar to that of the adult.

Babies may well hear muffled sounds before birth.[4] Tests done a few hours after birth suggest that babies can tell the difference between sounds of different pitch, loudness, and duration. Babies sleep and eat better when they hear rhythmic sounds reminiscent of the heartbeat—a metronome, for example.[5] They are most sensitive to the human voice and to sounds in the voice range.[6] Babies a few days old will respond differently to various odors and can recognize the smell of their mothers' breast milk.[7] Though difficult to assess accurately their sense taste, babies appear to like sweet substances and dislike sour, bitter, and salt.

Social Responses

The newborn is not as isolated and self-centered as so often described by psychologists.[8] A one-day-old infant cries empathetically in response to another baby's cry, but not to a synthetic cry. When less than a week old, a newborn can imitate an adult's facial expressions. After seeing an adult stick out her tongue, flutter her eyelids, or open and close her mouth, very young babies imitate these movements. This suggests that (1) a newborn has a rudimentary sense of self as a human being capable of imitating a person and (2) the baby has sufficient motor control to do it. Babies also imitate adults' facial expressions of emotion.

A fascinating study of the social capacities of newborns reveals that babies move their bodies in harmony with meaningful speech, both live and recorded, but not in response to tapping or to meaningless vowel sounds.[9] This kind of adult-child interaction, in which the baby responds in a specific way to what the adult does, may be critical to development. If infants are not born with this ability to respond to what the mother does, the mother may become discouraged or depressed and eventually withdraw from the baby.

At about two weeks of age, babies will look at their own mothers more frequently than at strangers. When a voice that seems to come from the mother is that of a stranger, the baby will avert her gaze and refuse to look at the "mother" with a strange voice. Thus, very early in life, babies have sensory knowledge of the mother.[10]

Parents who are aware of babies' capacities to respond to human beings and the immediate capacity for learning that help the baby adapt and flourish in a variety of situations are less likely to be tense and worried about their new responsibility. They can relax and enjoy this new little person—babies are made of sturdy stuff.

Individual Differences

In Chapter 1 we saw that a baby brings his or her own temperament to the parenting process. *Temperament* is defined as "constitutionally based individual differences in emotional, motor, and attentional reactivity and self-regulation."[11] Though research suggests that temperamental traits are consistent across situations and stable over time, it has not yet identified the specific neurophysiological processes thought to underlie temperamental differences. These differences among newborns appear hours after birth in such behaviors as the amount of crying, ability to soothe oneself and be soothed by a caregiver,[12] and enjoyment of being hugged and cuddled.[13]

Though investigators differ on the specific dimensions of temperament, a thorough review of studies indicates six basic aspects of temperament: (1) *fearful distress,* emphasizing the baby's fearfulness and poor adaptability to new situations; (2) *irritable distress,* emphasizing fussiness, irritability, and distress at limitations; (3) *positive affect,* including laughing, smiling, and approaching objects and stimuli; (4) *activity level;* (5) *attention span,* or persistence; and (6) *rhythmicity,* or predictability of behaviors.[14] Parents are curious to know to what degree these differences persist. Some children showing certain temperamental qualities early on do not continue to show them later, but others do. For example, vigorous neonatal movements in the nursery were related to high activity levels at ages four and eight,[15] and activity level at twelve months predicted activity level and extroverted

Babies show a remarkable capacity for social interactions, including moving their bodies in rhythm to the meaningful speech of adults. This kind of adult-child interaction may be crucial to development.

behavior at six and seven years.[16] High physiological reactivity to stimulation at four months was related to inhibition in behavior in the toddler years, which, in turn, was related to being less outgoing and expressive in early adolescence.[17]

While early crying and fussiness did not endure, irritability at seven months tended to endure for the next year or two. Difficult temperament (which included negative affect, lack of rhythmicity, and persistence in behavior) measured at six months predicted difficult temperament at thirteen and twenty-four months and behavior problems when the child was three.[18] Stability from infancy to ages seven and eight has been found for such qualities as approachability and sociability, rhythmicity, irritability, persistence, cooperativeness and manageability, and inflexibility.[19] Behavioral differences in impulsivity at age three have been linked to measures of impulsivity, danger seeking, and aggression at age eighteen.[20]

Temperament influences parenting, but the relationship is inconsistent.[21] For example, difficult temperament stimulates greater parental involvement and attention in some mothers who later become frustrated and uninvolved, and in other mothers a negative and uninvolved approach from the start. Early high reactivity stimulates in some mothers a very soothing and solicitous approach, but in other mothers a firm insistence that the infants learn to soothe themselves.[22] There are no studies showing that a positive, sociable baby stimulates a negative reaction in parents.[23]

How much can parents influence temperamental qualities? Parenting can help children overcome early temperamental difficulties.[24] Sensitive, responsive caregiving can help irritable babies, who are more likely to have insecure attachments, develop positive attachments to parents. Early limit-setting can help highly reactive infants learn self-soothing strategies and become less inhibited as toddlers.[25] Clearly, no one set of interventions will help all children. Rather, parents should be sensitive, flexible caregivers who target their behaviors to provide a "good fit" with their child's temperamental qualities.

Sybil Escalona uses the term *effective experience* to describe what parents provide each child—the kind of experience that helps the child develop optimally.[26] For example, active children do not require stimulation to explore, but quiet children may require encouragement to explore and play with toys. Responding to the individuality each child brings to the relationship enables parents to create positive experiences and environments for each.

CULTURAL INFLUENCES ON PARENTING IN INFANCY

In Chapter 2 we discussed two general cultural models—one stressing independence and the other stressing interdependence. These two models encourage different parenting practices in infancy.[27]

The interdependent model emphasizes close physical contact and a very close relationship between caregiver and child. The infant is held or carried much of the time, nursed often, and at night frequently sleeps in the same bed with the mother. Mother and child are considered a unit, and babies grow with an intuitive understanding of what parents want.

The independent model emphasizes the child's growing independence and interest in the world. There is less carrying, less holding, more toys to manipulate, and more devices, like strollers and playpens, that emphasize separation between parent and child. Children are more likely to be bottle-fed and at night are expected to sleep alone in their own cribs, often in their own rooms.

As examples of the independent model, parents in the United States present an interesting contrast to parents in Japan, who follow the interdependent model.[28] The contrast is especially revealing because both countries are child centered and industrialized, with similar standards of living. Japanese mothers focus on closeness and dependency within the parent-child relationship. They indulge infants and encourage social responsiveness and interaction. When they play with their infants, they focus on being social partners. Mothers encourage early emotional control, social sensitivity, and responsiveness to others.

Mothers in the United States are more likely to encourage independence, verbal assertiveness, and exploration of the world. When they play with children, those mothers stimulate their interest in objects and the external world.

While many parents in the United States emphasize the independent model, many U.S. families practice cultural traditions that rely more on the interdependent model. Even parents who emphasize independence want close, mutually regulated relationships with infants. As we shall see later in this chapter, people in this country have moved toward the interdependent model; for example, many use Snugglies for carrying babies and having close physical contact for extended periods of time.

PHYSICAL DEVELOPMENT

On average, the baby grows from about 21 inches at birth to about 28 inches at the end of the year, and birth weight triples. Growth, however, involves more than an increase in size and weight; it includes increasing organization of behavior.

At about three months, changes occur in the nervous system. Increased myelination of nerves in cortical and subcortical neural pathways and an increase in the number of neurons improve the child's sensory abilities and bring greater stability and control of behavior. The nervous system appears more integrated. Babies seem to settle down with greater organization of bodily functioning. Voluntary, coordinated behaviors replace reflexes as the latter gradually disappear. Babies are more awake during the day and at night drop into a quiet sleep before dreaming.

Eight months brings changes in physical development that underlie several changes in behavior. Increased myelination of neurons occurs in the motor area, in areas of the brain controlling coordination of movement, and in areas responsible for organization of behavior. At about this same time, most babies develop the capacity to sit alone. Next comes control of the trunk, which leads to creeping and crawling. Babies now can move rapidly in all directions. Finally, walking replaces crawling sometime between ten and eighteen months.

Locomotion has an enormous impact on babies' exploratory and social behavior.[29] When babies crawl and move around their environment, they can look at, touch, and manipulate objects. Exploration triggers new social reactions to babies. When infants reach out for objects, mothers often begin to name what they are touching and to describe features of the objects, and so babies' language increases. Because babies can now initiate interactions with others more easily, locomotion also brings social changes. Crawling babies often get close to adults, crawl in their lap, and smile and vocalize more at them, and so locomotion is a reorganizer of babies' experiences.

INTELLECTUAL DEVELOPMENT

Physical and intellectual development are closely intertwined in the early months and years. To learn about the world, the child must be able to come in contact with it by getting around, exploring objects, and seeing how they work.

According to Jean Piaget,[30] in the first two months of life the child's own actions are the focus of his or her attention. The child acts—kicks legs, plays with fingers—for the sake of the activity, not to accomplish anything. In subsequent months, activity is directed outward toward the environment. From four to eight months, the child repeats an act to observe a change in the environment. The baby kicks a mobile to make it go or reaches to move an object. Each act is not organized with a purpose; rather, the goal is discovered accidentally in the process of activity. From eight to twelve months, the child uses responses to solve a problem and achieve some goal. For example, to reach a matchbox, the child brushes away the father's hand, which is an obstacle. The child knows what he or she wants and uses action to get it.

INTERVIEW
with Jacqueline Lerner and Richard Lerner

Richard Lerner is Anita L. Brennan Professor of Education at Boston College, and Jacqueline V. Lerner is a professor of education at Boston College.

Parents are interested in temperament and what this means for them as parents. What happens if they have a baby with a difficult temperament that is hard for them to deal with? Is this fixed? Will they have to keep coping with it?

R. Lerner: We don't believe temperament necessarily is fixed. We believe that temperament is a behavioral style and can, and typically does, show variation across a person's life. We're interested in the meaning of temperament for the person and the family in daily life.

J. Lerner: Although we know temperament is present at birth, we don't say that it is exclusively constitutionally derived. Temperament interacts with the environment. We find children who do seem to stay fairly difficult and children who stay fairly easy. Most children change, even from year to year. Given this, we can't possibly believe that temperament ever becomes fixed unless what happens in the family becomes fixed.

R. Lerner: What we are concerned with are individual differences. They are identifiable at birth, but they change, we believe, in relation to the child's living situation. We find that what one parent might call difficult is well below the threshold of another parent's level of tolerance for difficulty. What some people find easy, others find quite annoying.

In fact, you can find in our case studies examples of how difficult children ended up developing in a particular context that reinterpreted their difficulty as artistic creativity. One girl picked up a musical instrument at age thirteen or fourteen and began playing. She had a gift for that. Prior to that, she had a difficult relation with her father, who found her temperamental style totally abhorrent to him. As soon as she had this emerging talent, he said, "Oh, my daughter is an artist. This is an artistic temperament." They reinterpreted the first thirteen years of their relationship, believing they had always been close.

We believe the importance of temperament lies in what we call "goodness of fit" between the child's qualities and what the environment demands. The child brings characteristics to the parent-child relationship, but parents have to understand what they bring and how they create the meaning of the child's individuality by their own temperaments, and their demands, attitudes, and evaluations. Moreover, I think parents should understand that both they and the child have many other influences on them—friends, work, or school.

When you think about the fit with the environment, how do you think about the environment, what is it?

R. Lerner: We have divided demands from the environment into three broad categories: physical characteristics of the setting, the behavioral characteristics of the environment, and the behavioral and psychological characteristics of the other important people in the child's life.

J. Lerner: The setting has physical characteristics, and the people have behavioral characteristics and demands, attitudes, and values.

R. Lerner: Parents need to understand the demands of the context (the living situation) they present to the child by means of their own values and behavioral style. Even the features of the physical environment the parents provide can affect the child's fit with the context. Parents need to understand there are numerous features of the context; and because of the child's individuality, a better or lesser fit will emerge. For example, if your child has a low threshold of reactivity and a high intensity of reactions, you don't want to put that child's bedroom next to a busy street. If you have a choice, you'll put that child's bedroom in the back of the house or won't let the child study in any part of the house where he or she will get distracted.

A poor fit also occurs if you have a child who is very arrhythmic and you demand regularity, not necessarily as a verbal demand but perhaps in the way you schedule your life. You begin to prepare breakfast every morning at 8:00, the bagel comes out at 8:05 and disappears at 8:15, and some days the child makes it and some days not. The parents have to see how they may be doing things that create poorness of fit. It's not just their verbal demands but also their behavioral demands and the physical setup of the house.

J. Lerner: Some parents don't see what they are reinforcing and what they are teaching their child through their demands. There has to be consistency between the demands and the reinforcements. Sometimes you don't want to be too flexible. I learned this the hard way. My nine-year-old tells me about what I have done in the past. "But when I did this last week, it was okay and now it isn't."

In actively trying to get the child to behave or in trying to change a temperamental quality, parents need to focus themselves on what behaviors they want reinforced and what ones they don't. They need to be perceptive on both ends of the response — the demands they are setting up and what they are actually reinforcing. If you know a child is irregular in eating in the morning and you want to change the pattern because you know he'll get cranky and won't learn well if he doesn't have a full stomach, be consistent. "You don't walk out the door unless you have had at least three bites of cereal and a glass of juice." But if you let it go one morning, you can expect the child to say, "Well, yesterday you didn't make me do that."

From your research, do you see areas that can be supports for children as they are growing up?

R. Lerner: More and more children experience alternative-care settings, and this has to become a major support. The socialization of the child is moving out of the family more and more, and we are charging the schools with more of the socialization duties. Throughout infancy and childhood, the alternative caregiving setting is the day care, the preschool, and, obviously, the school. These settings have to be evaluated in terms of enhancing the child's fit and the ability to meet the demands of the context.

During the first year of life, the infant comes to understand the permanence of objects. This milestone is essential to the development of the concept of a coherent world. A newborn's ability to remember is very limited; only gradually do infants become able to recall an object or person. It is easier for parents to empathize with the crying of a newborn baby when they remember that "Out of sight, out of mind" is almost literally true for infants. Gradually, babies come to realize that objects and people exist even when they cannot be seen.

Piaget's theory emphasizes action in the development of thinking and reasoning powers. He believes babies and children have natural desires to approach the world and interact, to explore and learn.

As we saw in Chapter 2, Lev Vygotsky believes social interactions are the source of knowledge about the world.[31] When we discuss attachment behavior, we shall see that from their social interactions with caregivers, babies learn how the world works, how people interact with each other, what is expected of them, what they can expect of others, and how much influence they have over others. So, intellectual growth comes from what an individual does in the world and from the nature of his interactions with others.

Playing

Much of what infants learn about the world they learn through exploration and play. As a baby matures during her first year, parents find that the ways they play with the baby also change.[32] In the early months, parents play games with lots of touching to capture the child's attention and provide laughter. When babies are older, games like pat-a-cake and peek-a-boo include more physical activity and more interaction.

Beginning at about six months, babies are interested in the physical aspects of objects—the more things there are to investigate about an object, the longer a baby will interact with it. Once familiar with a toy, a baby will put it aside for a while and then return to it later with renewed enthusiasm.

As babies mature, they spend less time putting things in their mouths and more time manipulating objects. If the object makes noise, wiggles, or moves, the baby will elicit these responses over and over. If a toy is too simple or too complex, the infant will lose interest in it quickly or ignore it altogether. By the end of the first year, children go beyond the sensory qualities of toys and try to figure out what they can do with objects. They try to dial a telephone and talk, or they try to stack a set of plastic donuts. They play more imaginatively with toys for longer periods of time.

LANGUAGE DEVELOPMENT

Lois Bloom believes language enables people to express their intentions (their thoughts, feelings, desires) to achieve intersubjectivity—mutual or shared understanding—with others important to them.[33] In her view, the child's drive for expression is the motivating force for language development. Since language involves the communication of thoughts and feelings to important people, the development of language is closely intertwined with social, emotional, and cognitive development.

Bloom characterizes her model as a developmental perspective on language growth because it views language as an integral part of the child's overall development, subject to the same principles of growth as other aspects of development such as cognitive or social skill. Although babies do not speak words until the end of the first year, much that happens in the early months of infancy — in social relationships and in exploration of their world — contributes to babies' developing verbal skills.

Babies initially make known their feelings and desires through their emotional reactions — crying, smiling, frowning, kicking with excitement. When these communications receive positive responses from caregiver (e.g., crying leads to being fed) babies learn that communication "gets results" and is worthwhile. Babies not only communicate, but they also focus on and respond to the communications of others. I shall describe this process more fully in later sections on emotional development and parent-child relationships.

At birth, the baby is able to cry, and parents can distinguish a cry of anger from one of pain or hunger. Babies do not vocalize in the early weeks of life; rather, they make noises related to eating and mouthing. By the second month, they begin cooing. Gradually, babbling appears at six to nine months. Babies repeat syllables, often the same one, such as "mamama" or "dadada." During these months, a baby can make all the sounds of all the languages in the world, but the sounds eventually become more characteristic of the language the child hears.

In the earliest months, parents and babies develop a social dialogue. They gaze at each other and take turns vocalizing. In the social interplay, babies learn to capture adult attention. They also learn the rules of communication — one person "speaks" at a time, and each gets a turn. So, babies engage in meaningful exchanges with others before they know words. In this social dialogue, babies learn to imitate the sounds of words before they learn their meanings.

Even before babies begin to use words, the sounds they make have inflections that express happiness, requests, commands, and questions.[34] A baby who first begins to say words may use the same word as a statement, a command, or a request. "Mama," for example, can be a question, an order, an endearment, or a plea for help.

Language development in the first year depends on intellectual growth. Babies have to learn that objects and people exist whether they see them or not, that people, things, and events have names that they can use to communicate with others. Babies need to be able to remember words that go with objects, and they need to be able to recall the event they want to name.

As the result of cognitive development, babies have more mental representations to communicate, and single words develop at about age one to express these thoughts.[35] While emotional expression continues to be the most frequent form of communication, early words describe what the feelings are about — the reasons or source of feelings. So, language, the second form of communication for children, explains the child's emotional states.

EMOTIONAL DEVELOPMENT

From the beginning, feelings are a part of life and are babies' primary tools for communicating what they need. We focus here on the nature of babies' feelings, how infants deal with them, and how parents can help them manage their feelings. As we saw in Chapters 2 and 3, the regulation of emotions underlies children's abilities to control their behavior and function competently in many areas, and this regulation is also related to brain development.

Emotional reactions are a central part of babies' lives; even in the earliest months, infants have a range of facial expressions that change every 7 to 9 seconds.[36] As we saw in discussing temperament, infants have characteristic emotional responses like joy or irritability, some of which persist over time.

Infants and parents develop a complex emotional-communication system. Babies signal what they need, often persistently, until parents respond. They cry until picked up; they reach for a toy until the adult gives it to them. But parents do more than respond to babies' emotional reactions.

Using verbal and nonverbal techniques, mothers begin to guide and shape babies' emotional reactions in the first three months of life.[37] They avoid negative emotional reactions the baby can copy; instead, they emphasize positive emotions. Verbally, they encourage positive feelings with such phrases as "Give me a smile," or "Laugh for Mommy." At the same time they discourage negative reactions with such phrases as "Don't fuss now" or "Don't cry." Mothers of boys appear more responsive to them than to daughters and match their sons' behaviors more often as well.

Babies respond to others' emotional reactions and pattern their own after what they observe. Infants as young as ten weeks mirror mothers' emotional expressions and change their own moods. They respond with joy and interest to mothers' happy faces, anger and a form of fear to mothers' angry faces, and sadness to mothers' sad faces.[38] Babies pattern their moods after mothers on a more ongoing basis as well. Over time, mothers' positive expressions are related to increases in babies' smiling and laughing.[39] Babies of mothers with lingering depressions become more withdrawn and less active.[40]

Babies not only pattern their moods after parents' reactions but also modify their behavior on the basis of adults' emotional reactions. Confronting what appears to be a visual cliff, ten-month-old babies look to mothers' facial expressions for guidance. When mothers smile, babies continue to crawl, but when mothers look fearful, they stop.[41] When mothers look at toys in a disgusted manner, babies refuse to play with them.[42]

Positive and appropriate levels of emotional stimulation along with opportunities to learn to modify their reactions are important to babies because such experiences influence brain development. Babies of mothers with ongoing depression after the babies are six months old, as just noted, are more withdrawn and less active, have shorter attention spans, and are less likely to master new tasks, compared with infants of mothers who are not depressed. Further, the brains of about 40 percent of infants of depressed mothers show reduced brain activity, particularly in the area of the brain associated with the expression of such emotions as joy and anger.[43] When mothers' depression lifts because of treatment or spontaneous remission, their babies' brain activity level returns to normal. So, positive and well-regulated emotional reactions early in life have important implications for brain development as well as social and emotional development.

PERSONAL AND SOCIAL DEVELOPMENT

The greatest source of comfort and positive feelings in the world of babies is people. The infant is introduced to the world of human beings by the quality of social experiences in the first year of life. These experiences help the infant develop a sense of self and other.

Bonding

The first meeting of parents and child is an important occasion. In the first hour after birth, babies are more alert and visually attentive than they will be for the next three or four hours. During that first hour, they may be most responsive to contact with parents.[44]

While early contact is pleasurable and starts the relationship between parents and child on a positive note, Michael Rutter is critical of the concept of bonding that suggests physical contact is essential to strengthen the attachment.[45] He points out that relationships are multifaceted and not dependent on a single sensory modality such as skin contact. Relationships develop over time, and strong attachments can be formed with caregivers even if the early bonding is not possible for some reason.

Early Parent-Infant Interactions

In early infancy, the primary caregiver is usually the mother who nurtures the infant with food, clothing, warmth, and affection. Close physical contact with the mother serves to regulate the infant's physiological functioning—heart rate, vagal tone, hormonal levels, sleep patterns, and eating.[46] For example, when premature babies receive stroking and movement of their limbs for three 15-minute periods per day for ten days, they gain more weight, are more active and alert, and score higher on measures of developmental functioning than those who do not receive this attention.[47] In the first few weeks of life, infants who receive extra carrying in Snugglies cry less than other babies and are more visually and aurally alert.[48] When mothers of average babies are absent or unavailable because of trips or hospitalizations, such babies do not eat, sleep, or function physically or socially as well as before.[49]

A social dialogue between parents and babies begins in the very earliest months of life when parents give direct physical care and meet the physiological needs of the baby. From birth, sensitive mothers adjust their behavior to the rhythm and tempo of the baby. They look for periods of alertness and readiness to respond. When eating, for example, babies suck and pause in their eating. When babies pause, mothers talk to them, stroke or juggle them. When babies are eating, mothers are quiet and wait for the next pause. Parents alter their facial expressions, and slow down and exaggerate their speech. The range of their choices is expanded. When speech is slowed and stimulation exaggerated, the baby can process it more effectively.[50]

Babies' temperaments and emotional reactivity influence the social dialogue. When babies adjust well to change and are easily soothed when upset, parents can regulate the babies' environments and conditions reliably and consistently. When babies are fretful, however, easily upset by change and difficult to soothe, parents find it harder to provide this consistent regulation, and both partners in the dialogue are frustrated.[51]

At about four months, babies' babbling increases the impression of sociability,[52] and babies send parents signals by means of facial expressions, vocalizations, and motor activity. When babies seem happy, parents engage in play; when infants seem interested, parents provide toys and objects; but when babies are distressed, parents simply soothe them. Babies initiate activity and parents follow their leads. In face-to-face interactions, parents wait for babies to look at them before talking to the babies. Parents may talk, tickle, or physically stimulate their child or play games like pat-a-cake. They often imitate their baby's behavior — grimaces, frowns. Babies may enjoy the imitation, then imitate the parents' behavior in turn. Parents often highlight or interpret babies' activity, giving a running account of what is happening — "You were hungry. You had a nice, big bottle, Now you are ready for clean diapers."

The caregiver's role is to read the baby's signals and provide optimal levels of stimulations for the infant by following the baby's rhythm or by modifying the baby's behavior through her or his response to the child. Synchrony in the interaction, however, also rests on the baby's matching the caregiver's mood and behavior and being a partner in the interactive dance. The terms *attunement* or *entrainment* describe the synchronous coordination of behavior in caregiver-infant interactions. Attunement is associated with the physiological and emotional regulation of the infant's system.[53]

Attachment to Parents

After the first few months of life, babies respond positively to primary caregivers, initiating contact and interaction and giving joyful kicks, gurgles, and laughs to engage the parent in play.

Early in life, babies have no fear of strangers, but by four to five months, they show signs of apprehension in the presence of strangers — freezing, lying or sitting still, barely breathing. By seven or eight months, they show a pronounced fear, sometimes crying as an unknown person approaches them. This fear occurs at about the same time babies understand that mother exists even when she is not with the baby, and it is followed by a fear of separation from mother and other important people.

By seven or eight months, babies show attachments to parents. *Attachment* is defined as a strong psychological bond to a figure who is a source of security and emotional support. The baby seeks out the parent, is fearful when the parent leaves or strangers come, and uses the parent as a safe physical base from which to move into the world. [54]

When parents are accepting of the baby, emotionally available, sensitive to the baby's needs, and cooperative in meshing activities with the child's tempo, a strong *secure attachment* develops. Infants with secure attachments explore more and are more persistent in tasks than are other babies. About 65 percent of babies in middle-class families are described as securely attached.[55]

Insecure attachments are revealed in one of three ways. When parents are intrusive and overstimulate the child, babies form *anxious avoidant attachments* and avoid the parent after separation. When parents are insensitive to babies' cues and often unavailable, babies form *anxious resistant attachments* and alternately cling to the parent and push the parent away.

More recently, a third form of insecure attachment has been identified as *disorganized/disoriented attachment*. Babies with such attachments show unpredictable alterations in their behavior with the parent. At times, they happily approach the parent as a securely attached infant would, and at other times they avoid the parent.

Thus, their attachment is considered disorganized. They show signs of conflict by "freezing" or "stilling" when they are near the parent. They appear confused as to how to respond; thus the term *disoriented* is used to describe them.[56]

Such attachments are found in families where a parent appears frightened or traumatized and, as a result, may appear frightening to the child. These classifications are made for a small number of babies in low-risk families (13 percent), but the percentage increases in babies in high-risk families—28 percent in multi-problem families receiving supportive services, 54 percent in families of low-income depressed mothers, and 82 percent in families whose members mistreat babies.[57]

Other groups at risk of insecure attachments include adolescent and depressed mothers (of all incomes). Adolescent mothers are less attuned to babies' needs than are adult low-income mothers. Adolescent mothers expect infants to do more for themselves than the babies can do. As we have seen, they expect the infant to drink from a bottle that is propped up rather than held; they expect the child to scramble for toys. It is not surprising that infants of adolescent mothers often have avoidant and disorganized/disoriented attachments to them.[58]

Depressed mothers are less engaged and more negative in interactions with their infants; the infants are less positive and more negative with these mothers. They are more likely to have insecure attachments than are infants of nondepressed mothers.[59]

Social and Cultural Influences on Attachment   Social and cultural influences shape attachment behaviors. In a laboratory setting, infant attachment is most frequently measured at twelve months. Observers note the quality of the mother-infant interactions and the infant's reactions to the mother's leaving the room and then returning.

Securely attached infants protest when mothers leave and are happy and seek closeness when they return. About 60 to 70 percent of babies in U.S. samples are described as securely attached.[60] About 20 percent are described as having *anxious-avoidant* attachments—being unconcerned when mothers leave and uninterested in their return. About 10 to 20 percent are described as having *anxious-resistant* attachments—strong protests when mothers leave and difficulties establishing closeness on return—alternately seeking the mother and resisting closeness.

In Germany, where early independence is strongly encouraged once babies are mobile, about 49 percent of babies show avoidant attachments, 33 percent show secure attachments, and 12 percent show resistant attachments.[61] When encouraged to spend time separated from the mother, babies show less protest at mothers' going and less clingy, dependent behavior on her return than American babies.

In Japanese culture, where a close relationship between mother and child is encouraged and separations from the parent rarely or never occur, babies almost never demonstrate avoidant attachments but are much more likely than babies in other cultures to protest mothers' leaving and find it so stressful that they cannot adjust easily to their return. Japanese babies have about the same rate of secure attachments as U.S. babies, but avoidant attachments are rare or absent, and resistant attachments occur in about 30 percent of babies.[62]

Separation history then appears to affect children's responses to mothers' leaving and returning. Within U.S. culture, babies of working mothers are less likely to protest their leaving the room and less interested in their return, presumably because they have had more experience with temporary separations and adjust to them. In Japan, babies of working mothers show attachment patterns similar to those of U.S. babies, presumably because their experience of separations is similar to babies in this country.[63]

Attachment to Both Parents Until recently, the mother-child bond was considered the only attachment of importance in infancy. As researchers have observed parent-child interactions and attachments more carefully, however, they have found that babies become attached to both parents. The quality of the relationship with each parent determines the attachment. Although it is possible to be securely attached to one parent and insecurely attached to the other, attachment classifications are most often the same for both parents. Though attached to both parents, babies still seek comfort from mothers when the infants are distressed.[64]

Parents interact differently with babies. First, even though a high percentage are employed in the workforce, mothers spend more time with infants. Even in families with fathers staying at home at least part of the time and mothers going off to work, studies indicate that mothers were with children more than fathers.[65]

Mothers and fathers differ not only in the quantity of time but also in the way they spend time with babies.[66] Mothers, even when working, are significantly more engaging, responsive, stimulating, and affectionate. They are more likely to hold babies in caregiving activities and to verbalize more than fathers. Fathers, on the other hand, are more likely to be attentive visually and to be playful in physically active ways than are mothers. Though fathers spend less time than mothers with infants, they are sensitive caregivers and are as perceptive as mothers in adjusting their behavior to babies' needs. Fathers are most likely to be highly involved in caregiving and playing when the marital relationship is satisfying and wives are relaxed and outgoing. Both fathers and mothers give mostly care and physical affection in the first three months, when babies are settling in. As babies become less fussy and more alert at three months, both parents become more stimulating and reactive.[67]

Although mothers and fathers interact differently with babies, recent observations indicate that parents do not treat sons and daughters differently in routine caregiving activities at home during this early period. When mothers and fathers are observed at home interacting with their infants, they give sons and daughters equal amounts of affection, stimulation, care, and responsiveness. We cannot rule out possible differences in narrower measures of parent-child interaction (such as touching, frowning, physical closeness), but in these wide-ranging measures, including overall engagement with the child, modern parents treat their sons and daughters equally.[68]

Stability of Attachment Secure attachments are more stable over time than are insecure attachments, perhaps because satisfying relationships tend to keep going. Unstable attachments are often associated with mothers' having stressful life experiences that they find hard to manage, changes in availability of mothers because of employment, and changes in mothers' personality.[69]

When attachment classifications were first studied in the 1970s, researchers found a 70 to 80 percent rate of stability in attachment from twelve to eighteen months. In

◆

BOX 6-1
WAYS TO ENCOURAGE SECURE ATTACHMENTS

Because early attachments are so important for babies, we want to do all we can to encourage their formation. When parents support each other, they make a positive contribution to themselves, to their marriage, and to babies, who flourish in a happy marital atmosphere. Parents get practical help and support from meeting regularly with other parents, as we saw in Chapter 5.

The encouragement of early physical contact between mother and infant has greatly promoted secure attachments between them.[71] The day after the birth of their children, one group of low-income, inner-city mothers received Snugglies in which to carry their babies; a control group of mothers received an infant seat. Mothers used their gifts regularly. At three and thirteen months, mother-child interactions were assessed. At three months, mothers who had used Snugglies were more vocally responsive with infants, and at thirteen months, most of their infants (83 percent) had secure attachments to them; only 38 percent of the control group infants had secure attachments. Insecure attachments were observed in 61.5 percent of control group infants but only 17 percent of infants who had increased physical contact with mothers.

The increased carrying helped mothers to become more sensitive and responsive to their babies. The mothers had the capacity to be caring, and the increased contact gave them all the information they required to respond appropriately. These mothers received no extra teaching, coaching, or demonstrations.

Teaching programs given in hospitals at the time of the birth can provide information that increases parents' competence in caring for their babies.[72] The information focuses on babies' states and their repertoire of behaviors, the ways they send signals to parents, and how parents learn to understand and respond to the signals. Especially helpful are tips on when to "engage" with babies (when they are fed and alert), when to "disengage" (when babies turn away, fall into a drowsy state), how to feed infants, and how to deal with crying.[73]

Workers in extended visiting programs have gone into high-risk homes to promote appropriate parenting skills and have had success in establishing secure attachments between mothers and infants. These programs involved weekly visits for a year from professionals who model positive interaction patterns as well as offer instruction to parenting groups. Such programs have successfully stimulated secure attachments; in one study, 61 percent of the mother-infant pairs showed this relationship, similar to the percentage of secure attachments found in middle-class samples.[74]

Two extensive reviews of such programs indicate they help both low- and high-risk parents become more effective caregivers.[75] While some of the programs are intensive and expensive in terms of time and level of professional help, many, like those advocating the use of Snugglies, giving information in hospitals, or sponsoring parenting groups, are highly effective without being costly.

recent large-scale studies, however, the rate has dropped to about 50 percent.[70] Many changes in the patterns of infant lives may account for the lower stability in the 1990s. Many more mothers of infants work, more fathers are involved in child care, more tensions exist because of the greater instability of parents' employment. See Box 6-1 for ways parents can promote attachment in the face of these changes.

Importance of Attachment   Psychologists speculate that strong attachments to parents and fear of strangers are important because they help the infant survive.[76] Secure attachment ensures that the child will remain responsive to the parent's guidance so the parent can continue to protect the child as the child becomes more independent. Further, Thomas Bower presents another reason for the importance of attachment.[77] He believes the baby develops a communication system with a partner, usually the mother but possibly a twin or other adult. A complex individual style of relating develops with shared vocalizations and gestures. Without the partner, the baby feels lonely and isolated. No one pays attention in the same way, and the fear of separation develops. The baby fears no loss of food or of love, but solitude and loneliness. Bower speculates that if shared communication is the basis of separation anxiety, then such fear should decrease as the child develops speech and can communicate with others. And indeed, it does diminish as speech develops.

Psychologists believe that experiences in attachment relationships provide a framework for babies' understanding of the world.[78] From these relationships, babies build internal models of how people relate to one another. Babies develop expectations of how well others will understand and respond to them, how much influence they have on others, and what level of satisfaction they can expect from other people.

From these relationships, babies also develop a sense of their own lovability and competence. When others respond positively to their overtures, babies feel valued and influential and anticipate similar responses from adults in new situations. When babies are ignored or rejected, they may develop a sense of unworthiness and helplessness.

When interactions make up a consistent pattern, babies acquire a sense of order and predictability in experience that, in turn, generalizes to daily activities and to the world at large. Babies develop expectations about family routines and activities, and, as we have seen, they pattern their interest in toys and in exploration on their caregivers' emotional reactions.

The benefits of early attachments extend to the future. Securely attached one-year-olds are more curious later in childhood than are insecurely attached ones.[79] They attack a problem vigorously and persistently, but accept help from others and are not aggressive. Children with insecure attachments at one year tend later to be more anxious and more likely to have tantrums when presented with problems.

Development of the Self

Just as they gain information about the world from their own actions in the world and from their social relationships, so babies develop a sense of themselves from these same sources. We have just discussed how others' reactions to babies give them a sense of themselves; babies also develop a sense of who they are from their own actions in the world.

Integrating current research and theory, Susan Harter describes how the self begins to evolve in the first years of life.[80] From birth to four months, the infant gradually establishes predictable, satisfying patterns of eating, sleeping, quieting, and arousal. Responding to a caregiver, reacting to the surrounding world, the infant develops a rudimentary organization and integration of the perceptual and sensorimotor systems and gains a first sense of self and others.

In the period from four to ten months, the infant becomes more differentiated from the caregiver in social interplay and begins to develop an interpersonal self. As this period progresses, infants form attachments to caregivers, thus experiencing an increasing connectedness to others. At the same time, infants act on the world in more complex ways and begin to get a sense of their own ability to affect objects—make a mobile move, shake a rattle. Caregivers who react positively to babies' bids for attention increase babies' sense of control over events. The regularity and consistency of babies' feelings in response to others' behaviors—for example, delight from tickles and being thrown in the air—or in sharing emotional states with others help babies develop a sense of themselves and what they can expect in interactions with others.

From ten to fifteen months, babies become increasingly differentiated from caregivers and find a greater sense of themselves as agents who make things happen. Though attached to parents, they move off, using parents as secure bases for exploration in the world.

As we shall see in the next chapter, this is a period of sharing intentions and experiences with others. The I-self (the agent, the doer) is growing, but there is also a "we-self," the internalization of the relationships with the caregiver. The "we-self" may be what sustains infants in parents' absence.

In summary, babies are active agents strongly connected to others. The infants' sense of self depends on their actions and their relationships with others.

Development of Self-Regulation

Claire Kopp has described phases children go through as they develop the capacity for self-regulation and flexible self-control.[81] Self-control begins to develop in the earliest days of life. In the first three months of life, infants gain a form of control over their physiological functioning; they regulate arousal states of wake and sleep and the amount of stimulation they get. They also soothe themselves. The role of caregivers at this time is to help infants regularize their functioning by providing routines and social interactions.

From three to approximately nine months, infants modulate sensory and motor activities. They possess no conscious self-control yet, but they do use motor skills to gain parental attention and social interaction. As they reach out, form intentions, and develop a rudimentary sense of self, their capacity for control begins to emerge.

From nine to eighteen months, infants show awareness of social or task demands and begin to comply with their parents' requests. As infants act, investigate, and explore, their sense of conscious awareness begins to appear. These trends continue in the second year.

Researchers observing year-old babies' obedience to their mothers' commands in the home, found that babies obey their mothers' commands when the mothers accept and are sensitive to babies' needs.[82] Mothers who establish harmonious relationships with their babies, who respect them as separate individuals and tailor daily routines to harmonize with the children's needs, have babies who are affectionate and independent, able to play alone, and (even at one year) able to follow their mothers' requests. Thus, at this early age, a system of mutual cooperation between mother and child is established and maintained as each acts to meet the requests of the other.

Peers

Does an infant interact with other children? Babies respond positively to children ages three to four.[83] Infants also respond to each other and initiate contact in play sessions in the first year of life. In one study, a researcher observed nine-month-old babies who played together once a week for ten weeks.[84] She found that the play of the babies became increasingly complex when they were in their own homes and presumably feeling more comfortable. When they played in another baby's home, the babies tended to be more interested in toys and objects. This lessened interest in peers when away from home may explain why, in the past, psychologists failed to note babies' interest in each other—until recently psychologists have usually observed babies away from home, in laboratories.

TASKS AND CONCERNS FOR PARENTS OF INFANTS

Marc Bornstein describes four main tasks for the parents of infants:[85]

- Nurturant caregiving: providing food, protection, warmth, and affection
- Material caregiving: providing and organizing the babies' world with inanimate objects, stimulation, and opportunities for exploration
- Social caregiving: engaging and interacting with infants—hugging, soothing, comforting, vocalizing, playing
- Didactic caregiving: stimulating infants' interest in and understanding of the world outside the dyadic relationship by introducing objects, interpreting the surrounding world, and giving information

Besides these general tasks, parents face several common routines and problems in their baby's first year of life. For example, feeding problems can be a source of real anxiety to parents. Because these particular difficulties can reflect specific needs of the baby or parent, they are best discussed with a nurse, physician, or breast-feeding coach. The three problems we focus on here, however, are sleeping, crying, and limit setting.

Sleeping

Sleep disturbances are considered among the most common problems in infancy. The way people sleep in the United States, with its emphasis on independence, provides an interesting contrast to the practices of the interdependent model favored by much of the world's population.

In middle-class U.S. families, babies usually sleep alone in bassinets or cribs, though in the early months they may sleep near their mothers.[86] By the age of six months, however, most middle-class babies sleep in rooms of their own. The rest of the world does not follow this practice. Instead, babies sleep in the same room and often in the same bed (called *co-sleeping*) with the mother for the first few years of life. Co-sleeping is thought to have physical benefits, as it helps regulate the infant's physiological functioning, and psychological benefits, allowing the babies to feel more secure, attached, and close to the parent. Parents in other countries believe their babies understand what is wanted of them better because they are so close to the parent.[87]

In the United States, middle-class parents believe an infant needs to sleep in his or her own room to develop independence and autonomy.[88] So, sleep habits and bedtime routines are more a matter of concern for them. In other countries, everyone may go to bed at the same time or a baby may stay with the family until he or she falls asleep in the midst of activity. The matters discussed here are not central issues for these families.

To ensure good sleep patterns, Richard Ferber, who directs the Center for Pediatric Sleep Disorders at Children's Hospital in Boston, recommends that parents develop a regular, enjoyable, nighttime ritual that prepares the child for going to bed. It may include songs, rocking for infants, or a bath and story for older children.[89] Parents must then put the child in the crib alone to fall asleep. By the time the child is five or six months old, he or she will sleep most of the night. If the child is not sleeping through the night, the source of the problem may lie in the way the child is put down. Perhaps she has come to rely on rocking or nursing to get to sleep and cannot duplicate these conditions in the middle of the night when, like most children and adults, she wakes up briefly and must put herself back to sleep. Parents must emphasize a pleasant bedtime ritual and going to bed alone. If crying persists, parents can use the behavioral methods detailed in Chapter 7 to help the child sleep through the night.

Other sleep problems include infants who sleep 6 hours during the day and then wake up for long periods during the night. Parents can handle this problem by waking the child earlier and earlier from the long day sleep so it gradually becomes a nap rather than a major sleeping period. Waking up earlier in the afternoon will help the child to go to sleep earlier and sleep longer at night.

Other sleep problems can be related to intake of fluids. Ferber believes that unless there are special circumstances, a child over three months of age does not need a middle-of-the-night feeding. The awakening for milk can be eliminated using behavioral techniques of shaping behavior by reducing the amount gradually until the child receives no milk at night.

In the early months, colic often disturbs sleep; babies cry and cannot be consoled. For a colicky baby, Ferber, like Marc Weissbluth,[90] recommends soothing strategies. If these fail, he recommends letting babies cry for 15 to 30 minutes and then trying again. By letting the child cry, he comments, parents are responding to then child's need to cry. Nevertheless, they must make the attempt to soothe the child first. Although colic disappears at about three months, colicky infants often develop chronic sleep problems. These may seem the same as in the colicky period, but they are not. Colicky babies who have been rocked, walked, or soothed to sleep may have learned to expect this treatment for every night waking and come to expect it long after the colic is gone. Parents must wait until the colic has ended to stop these middle-of-the-night attentions, but this is not easy to determine, because colic often clears up gradually. If the child does not seem to be in pain, and if he or she is soothed when rocked, carried, or patted on the back and falls back to sleep quickly, then colic is not the reason for the sleep problem. The problem is that the child has learned to fall asleep only with parental attention, and this pattern must be changed. Parents must teach their children to fall asleep alone, both

THE JOYS OF PARENTING INFANTS

"I love babies. There is something about that bond between mother and baby. I love the way they look and smell and the way they hunker up to your neck. To me it's a magic time. I didn't like to baby-sit particularly growing up, and I wasn't wild about other people's babies, but there was something about having my own; I just love it. And every one, we used to wonder, how are we going to love another as much as the one before; and that is ridiculous, because you love every one."
MOTHER

"There is joy in just watching her change, seeing her individualize. From the beginning it seemed she had her own personality—we see that this is not just a little blob of protoplasm here, this is a little individual already from the beginning. She has always had a real specialness about her. It was exciting to see her change."
FATHER

"I think it's wonderful to have a baby in the house, to hear the baby laugh, sitting in the high chair, banging spoons, all the fun things babies do. They seem to me to light up a household. When there's a baby here, a lot of the aggravations in the household somehow disappear. Everyone looks at the baby, plays with the baby, and even if people are in a bad mood, they just light up when the baby comes in the room. I think there is something magical about having a baby in the house."
MOTHER

"What I've discovered about parenting is there is a constant process of loss and gain. With every gain you give up something, so there is sadness and joy. The joy comes when he does something new, different. He crawls and that's great, but the loss is

for naps and for night sleep. Develop a pleasant ritual—but put the child in the crib and leave him alone.

Crying

Helping babies regulate emotional behavior requires an understanding of crying. All babies cry and appear distressed some of the time. They show great individual differences in crying, however. In newborn nurseries, babies cried from 1 to 11 minutes per hour. The average daily total per baby was about 2 hours of crying. Researchers who classified reasons for babies' crying found that hunger was a significant cause, as well as wet or dirty diapers. The largest single category, however, was "unknown reason." It may be that crying expressed a social need for cuddling, warmth, or rhythmic motion.[91]

Babies' crying increases to about 3 hours at six weeks and decreases to an average of 1 hour per day at about three months. Though hunger seems a predominant reason, unknown causes remain the second highest category. As crying increases, it comes to be concentrated in the late afternoon or evening hour, with little during the day.

"you no longer have to get him something or carry him there. Now I have to do less for him. My role shifts the less I do for him. So, it's a mixed thing. He's growing up too fast. I want to hold on to each phase; I like the new phase, but I want to hang on to each one too." MOTHER

"As he gets older, I relate more, play more. He is more of a joy. Some of the joys are so unexpected. I would stop myself and open up and think, 'Oh, this is my son, he's so joyful. He's smiling for no particular reason.' I am not that joyful, but he's joyful for no reason. He reminds me of joy." FATHER

"It's the first time in my life, I know what the term 'unconditional love' means. The wonder of this little girl and nature! I have never experienced anything like that. It is 'Yes,' without any 'Buts.' " FATHER

"I enjoy seeing her and her father together, hearing them talk, seeing him so happy with her all the time." MOTHER

"Crawling was just so wonderful for me, it just seemed to reveal something about his personality, his persistence. It was strenuous for him physically. I would be across the room, and he would start out across the room; and you could hear him, breathing, kind of panting, working and working and working to get himself across the room. There was something about that, so valiant. And his laughter; he loves to laugh, and he had such joy, such a sense of accomplishment he communicated when he got across the room." MOTHER

"When I was ten years old, my school had a program in which we spent a few hours a week with babies and toddlers. I will never forget the eyes of the babies. They were so clear and trusting. I felt good every time I looked in their eyes."
PROSPECTIVE FATHER

Sylvia Bell and Mary Ainsworth conducted a thorough study of crying in the first year of life and found that babies had as many crying episodes at the end of the year as at the beginning, but they spent much less time in each episode.[92] Mothers tended to be consistent in how much they ignored the baby's crying, and there were marked differences among the mothers. One mother ignored only 4 percent of the cries, while another ignored 97 percent. Although each mother's behavior was consistent from quarter to quarter, the crying of each baby was not consistent until the last two quarters.

In the first quarter, there was no relationship between the baby's crying and the mother's behavior. In the second quarter, a trend appeared that became significant in the third and fourth quarters. Those mothers who responded immediately to the cries of the baby had babies who cried less! Conversely, ignoring a baby's cries seemed to increase the amount of crying, measured by frequency and duration. Those mothers who responded most at the beginning of the year had less to respond to at the end of the year.

What strategy is most effective in terminating crying? Picking up and holding the baby stopped the crying in 80 percent of the situations in which it occurred. Feeding, which involves physical contact, was almost as effective. The least effective method was to stand at a distance and talk to the child.

Judy Dunn reviews ways of providing comfort to crying babies and finds that caregivers around the world soothe by "rocking, patting, cuddling, swaddling, giving suck on breast or pacifier."[93] Effective techniques provide a background of continuous or rhythmic—as opposed to variable—sensations for the child. For example, constant temperatures, continuous sounds, and rhythmic rocking at a steady rate reduce the amount of time the infant cries. Effective soothing techniques also reduce the amount of stimulation the baby receives from his or her own movements. Thus, holding and swaddling reduce sensations from the child's flailing arms and legs and thus decrease crying.

Urs Hunziker and Ronald Barr recently speculated that U.S. babies might be more content and cry less if they were carried more, as babies are in other cultures.[94] They studied two groups of mothers and babies: One group consisted of mothers who received infant carriers (Snugglies) and carried babies 3 extra hours per day, when babies were not crying as well as when babies were crying; the other was a control group of mothers who carried their babies as usual. They monitored crying of the babies from three to twelve weeks and found that the supplemental carrying eliminated the peak of crying that usually occurs at six weeks, reduced crying overall, and modified the daily pattern of the crying so there was less in the evening hours. For example, at six weeks, those babies who received extra carrying cried 43 percent less overall than the control group, and 51 percent less than that group in the evening hours. At twelve weeks, the crying in both groups decreased, but the carried babies still cried 23 percent less. Equally important, babies who were carried more were more content and more visually and aurally alert.

Another recent suggestion for soothing crying babies takes a different approach. In his clinical and research training, William Sammons has observed many different kinds of babies and gradually developed the belief that babies have the ability to calm themselves, given the opportunity to develop this skill.[95] Babies suck on fingers, wrist, or arm; get into a certain body position; or focus on certain visual forms like walls, objects, or light to soothe themselves. In his pediatric practice, Sammons has encouraged parents to engage in a mutual partnership with babies so that the infants can find their own ways to calm themselves.

Parents can combine these two latest solutions to the crying problem by increasing the amount of carrying they do and, at the same time, letting the infants find ways to calm themselves when they do cry and fuss without an identifiable cause.

Colic is a parent's nightmare. It is generally defined as "inconsolable crying for which no physical cause can be found, which lasts for more than three hours a day, occurs at least three days a week or more, and continues for at least three weeks."[96] Colic occurs in about 20 percent of babies. It begins at about two weeks of age; if the child is premature, it begins about two weeks following the due date, not the birth date. Colic disappears at about three to five months. Birth order, sex, allergy, parental social class and the mother's intellectual ability and personality are not related to the condition.

Marc Weissbluth emphasizes that colic occurs in healthy babies who continue to thrive. It will pass; parents are not to blame—but there are ways to intervene. Weissbluth debunks what he considers the myths of colic. Colic is not a gastrointestinal problem caused by indigestion or the mother's diet; the gas that such babies experience is probably due to swallowing air during prolonged crying. Also, colic is not caused by the mother's anxiety, inexperience, or personality.[97]

Weissbluth believes colic is an extreme form of normal crying behavior: Colic occurs at two to twelve weeks, just when the average baby is fussiest, and disappears at about the same time that average crying decreases. Fussy, irritable babies with difficult temperaments appear most prone to colic. Colicky crying in the evening is possibly related to distorted or mixed-up biological rhythms; irregularities in the sleep-wake cycle, hormone secretions, temperatures, and breathing rhythm may cause the baby distress that results in inconsolable crying. Thus, more than one reason may underlie the distress. A physical cause is strongly suggested by the fact that premature babies develop colic about two weeks after their due date. If it were solely related to environmental causes, onset should occur two weeks after the birth date.[98]

There are many ways for parents to cope with colic. In addition to the remedies already mentioned for crying, Weissbluth recommends that parents try to synchronize their actions with the baby's tempo. If she is sobbing, rub her back in rhythm with her breathing. All remedies work for a while or at particular times. When no remedy works, parents may want to put the child down in the crib for 15 or 30 minutes and then try a soothing activity again. Some experts believe the child may need to "cry it out"; if consolation were really wanted, the child would respond to the attempts to soothe.

All experts, and parents of formerly colicky babies, advise suffering parents not to lose hope. Babies grow out of it, and many turn into infants with wonderful dispositions. Weissbluth suggests loving babies whether they are crying or happy.

Setting Limits

Thomas Gordon urges parents to cooperate with children by listening to their needs, responding to them, and modifying the environment so that children can explore safely.[99] Parents should remove things that are of value, such as fragile glassware and books. These changes create a safe environment in which the child is free to explore — one in which both parents and child can relax.

Even so, the child will inevitably want to play with something that is dangerous or that parents want to preserve. When this happens, Gordon suggests that parents "trade" — find a different but safe activity to offer as a substitute. He uses the example of the child whose mother substituted a pair of stockings with runs for a new pair the child had found to play with. The child could still enjoy the texture and tug at the stockings, and the mother's needs were also met.

Trading and finding acceptable substitutes requires ingenuity. Gordon describes how one mother wanted her baby to stay in the playpen while she cleaned the house, but the baby wanted to be out, crawling around and exploring. The mother put the child in the playpen. She wrapped a trinket in a box with ribbons, then gave it to the baby. The package immediately caught the baby's attention. He stopped crying and spent half an hour undoing the box and playing with the trinket, and the mother was able to do her housework.

Dreikurs, talking about the same situation, sees the cause of the problem differently.[100] The baby has always been held and wants to be amused by the mother.

Dreikurs says it is important for the baby to learn to play alone at least a portion of each day. Parents should provide toys and leave children to their own resources for definite periods each day. The tone sounds stern, but the main difference between Gordon and Dreikurs here is the amount of time the mother will spend searching for appealing toys to satisfy the child's need for novelty.

The behaviorists suggest another way of setting limits. John Krumboltz and Helen Krumboltz talks about developing an unpleasant association with a forbidden object or act to stop unacceptable behavior.[101] They give the example of a young child who visited a relative who builds model ships. The father sounded an old-fashioned automobile horn each time the child approached one of the fragile models. The child was startled, and after six sounds of the horn she stopped approaching the ships. If the parents had also said "no" just before sounding the horn, this experience would have helped the child learn the meaning of that important word.

Parents have to be careful not to create unpleasant associations with the wrong things. Krumboltz and Krumboltz give the example of a baby who is sitting on the floor crying because she wants crackers. If the mother puts this child in her playpen every time she cries for crackers, the child may stop this behavior, but she will also begin to dislike the playpen.

PARENTS' EXPERIENCES

As we saw in Chapter 5, when parents move from the image-making stage of pregnancy to the nurturing stage of infancy,[102] they must adjust the images they created of their anticipated baby and of themselves as parents to the reality of their infant and their actual skill in caring for the baby. Adjustments are painful when expectations have been unrealistic.

Parents interviewed about easing the transition to parenthood identified six basic ingredients in promoting parental well-being: (1) giving up the illusion of being a perfect parent, (2) looking for information you can apply to your child and your living situation rather than exact prescriptions of what to do, (3) learning the art of making decisions and setting goals (setting priorities on what is most important to do and following through on your priorities helps restore a sense of effectiveness), (4) considering parenthood as a series of tradeoffs and realizing that decisions to fill one member's needs may mean that someone else has to wait, (5) not trying to assume the role of parent without support from others, and (6) looking after yourself.[103]

Sometimes, even with good self-care, mothers feel depressed. Physicians and nurses who work in hospitals report that 80 percent of new mothers have crying spells and postpartum blues at some time during their hospital stay.[104] In the weeks after the baby is born, the mother may, from time to time, experience sadness, discouragement, and crying spells. These feelings are a natural part of the stress of incorporating a new baby into the family.

If sadness persists and is accompanied by early morning awakening, loss of appetite and weight, apathy, or inability to concentrate and remember, then the new mother should seek both a thorough medical checkup and psychological counseling.

Awareness of the difficulties of the postpartum period and of specific ways of reducing stress have helped mothers deal with the emotional upset at the time. Husbands and friends can provide emotional support and can be available if the mother wants to talk about her worries, concerns, and frustrations. The mother needs the kind of thoughtful care she gives her infant. She, too, must have enough rest. And she needs at least a little time she can spend alone or in a special, personal pursuit. A stable and serene environment helps to diminish stress. This is not the time to move or take on a new job if these events can be avoided.

Although it is difficult to have all aspects of your life change, parents find babies sufficient reward for all their efforts. Parents fall in love with these little people and are engrossed by their smiles, their delight in the world, and their open affection and attachment to their parents.

MAIN POINTS

Newborns

- are equipped with sensory, intellectual, and social abilities that enable them to make discriminations and learn new stimulus-response patterns
- are born with individual temperaments that influence parents' behavior

In the first year, babies

- gain control over their bodies and learn to sit alone, crawl, stand, and sometimes walk
- take a lively interest in the world around them, reaching out to grasp and explore objects
- develop language gradually from cooing and babbling in the early months to a few words at the end of the year
- develop a wide range of emotional reactions so that at the end of the year they express anger, fear, joy, pleasure, curiosity, and surprise and are learning to control their emotions

Attachment

- is a bond the baby forms with a caregiver
- is secure when parents are accepting and sensitive in meeting the baby's needs
- is insecure when parents are either unavailable and uninvolved or intrusive and controlling or experiencing trauma or loss
- is the basis for the baby's sense of being lovable and worthwhile

Babies

- begin to develop a sense of self in the last half of the first year
- begin to develop self-control, first over their physiological functioning, then over their motor activities, so that by the end of the first year, they can cooperate in following simple rules

Parents

- are nurturant, material, social, and didactic caregivers
- synchronize their behavior with the child's individual characteristics to meet babies' physiological needs
- form enduring attachments with infants
- reinforce regular schedules of eating and sleeping
- soothe babies when they cry by responding to them quickly, by carrying them more, and by giving them a chance to soothe themselves
- examine their own behavior to see how it creates a demand for adaptation on the part of the child
- stimulate babies' development when they play and converse with them
- interact with babies in different ways, with mothers holding babies more and doing more caregiving and fathers being more playful and physically stimulating
- are influenced by cultural and social factors in their care of infants

As they incorporate babies into family life, parents

- often do not anticipate the stress produced by all the changes
- learn to set priorities and make decisions in terms of them
- seek support from each other and their social network
- seek expert help if mothers' postpartum depression continues without change
- experience many joys

Problems discussed center on

- meeting babies' physiological needs
- beginning to set limits

EXERCISES

1. Read the father's statement on page 128 in which he admits that he knew so little about babies he should not have been permitted to take one home from the hospital. Should parents be required to take some kind of instruction prior to taking a baby home from the hospital? What would such a course include?

2. Have students interview either mothers or fathers of infants and ask about how much time they spend each day with the baby. What are their activities with the baby? Do mothers work? Does this change the pattern of their activities with babies? Does mother's working change father's patterns of time? What do they most enjoy doing with their infant?

3. Go to a supermarket or a park on a weekend and observe parent-infant interactions. Note how babies respond to the environment around them, to par-

ents, to passersby. Try to find two infants and compare their response to the same environment. Observe parenting behaviors and describe their effect on the child. Note how siblings, if present, respond to the infant.

4. Go to a toy store and spend an imagined $150 on toys for an infant from six to twelve months of age. Justify your choices.

5. Go to local hospitals and find out what kinds of instruction classes and hands-on training in the care of babies they provide for parents of newborns. Do you think this is sufficient? What would you add?

ADDITIONAL READINGS

Bing, Elizabeth, and Colman, Libby. *Laughter and Tears: The Emotional Life of New Mothers.* New York: Holt, 1997.

Brazelton, T. Berry. *Touchpoints.* Reading, MA: Addison-Wesley, 1992.

Brott, Armin A. *The New Father: A Dad's Guide to the First Year.* New York: Abbeville Press, 1997.

Eisenberg, Arlene, Murkoff, Heidi E., and Hathaway, Sandra E. *What to Expect the First Year.* New York: Workman, 1996.

Greenspan, Stanley, and Greenspan, Nancy Thorndike. *First Feelings: Milestones in the Emotional Development of Your Baby and Child.* New York: Penguin, 1985.

TODDLERHOOD: THE YEARS FROM ONE TO THREE

C H A P T E R   7

How do parents incorporate active, busy toddlers with minds of their own and a surplus of energy into family life with its routines, rules, and chores? How do they maintain positive relationships with toddlers when they have to say "No" so often? How do parents help them learn to regulate their feelings and behavior? How do parents deal with their own feelings about being authorities with children?

Life with toddlers is busy. They walk, run, explore, and question. In the years from one to three, language skills and understanding of the world grow rapidly. Children develop greater self-awareness and begin to understand what it means to be a boy or a girl. They start to learn what is considered right and wrong, and they make strong efforts to comply with these rules even though they have their own goals to pursue. Parents play a powerful role in helping children develop skills as they explore the world; at the same time, parents help children modulate and control their exuberant behavior to comply with others' wishes.

PHYSICAL DEVELOPMENT

By the end of the first year, the tiny newborn has become a little person who can probably stand alone and possibly walk. The average one-year-old stands between 27 and 29 inches tall and weighs about 21 or 22 pounds. By the end of the third year, height has increased to about 36 inches and weight to about 35 pounds. Though slower than during infancy, growth in the second and third years is quite rapid—about twice that of the years from three to five. Growth in this period is related to such environmental factors as quality and amount of food, absence of chronic illness, medical care, and family socioeconomic status.

Motor abilities begin to be more fine-tuned after the first year. Walking and running become automatic; reaching for and grasping objects become more refined. Better and more skills enable toddlers to explore the environment more carefully than before.

WHAT I WISH I HAD KNOWN
ABOUT TODDLERHOOD

"There are a couple of things. Most of the time he is okay about going to sleep, but sometimes he has a hard time; and reading a book gave me permission to put him in the crib while he was crying. He cried a little, made a few peeps, and went to sleep, but the book gave me permission to do that. Also being reminded to look at things from the child's perspective instead of the adult's is very helpful. You may know that it is not a great thing to pick up a toilet brush, but he does not know or understand that. I have found myself yelling at him, and I have to remind myself to look at it from his point of view." MOTHER

"Someone said when you have a child, it's like two appointment books—his appointment book and yours. And first you do everything in the kid's appointment book; and then when you're done, you do everything in the kid's appointment book again. I wish I had known they weren't joking. I knew that it would be a challenge, and in some ways I wish I had known more. But in other ways I think if I had really known exactly how hard it would be sometimes, I might have been more reluctant or waited longer, and that I would really have regretted—not doing it." FATHER

"I wasn't prepared for all the decisions. Is it okay if he does this or not? He's trying to do something; shall I step in so he doesn't hurt himself or shall I let him go? It's making all those choices, making sure what I feel." MOTHER

"There is anxiety, a feeling of vulnerability I have never felt before. If he gets sick, what are we going to do? If he has a little sickness, we just hope the doctor is doing the right thing. We went through a great deal in the past few weeks choosing a nursery school for him, and we hope we have done the right thing, but is this the one for him?" FATHER

"I wish I had known what to do about climbing. He climbs all over everything. I have the living room stripped bare, but I wonder if this is the right thing." MOTHER

"I wish we had—because he is our first child—more of a sense of the norms. What is okay versus what is a problem and what is really bad? Is this normal, is this just kids being kids? He pushed someone at school three times; is this par for the course or is this a problem? We don't know when we are reacting and when we are overreacting." FATHER

"I wish I had known how much time they needed between one and two. They are mobile, but they are clueless about judgment. I think it was one of the most difficult times. Even though she did not get into a lot of trouble, sticking her finger in the light sockets, still she takes a lot of time and watching, so the transition to two was great." MOTHER

INTELLECTUAL DEVELOPMENT

From twelve to eighteen months, children's interest goes beyond their bodies and focuses on objects. A toddler understands that objects have an independent, permanent existence, and he or she is curious about them. The toddler experiments with them—feeling their texture, watching how they drop, noting what can be done with them. In this period, toddlers can imitate more complex behaviors. For example, they imitate a parent's behavior when they push a teddy bear in a stroller or feed and care for a dolly.

According to Jean Piaget, around eighteen to twenty-four months, children begin to use symbols to represent their experience.[1] Up to this point, they have been limited to their immediate experience of things and people—what is present in the moment. Now, they can use language to symbolize objects or people who are not there, and they retain mental representations of what they see. Because their language is still rudimentary, however, toddlers do not have enough words for complex verbal representations of what they see. Piaget suggests that children store memories of motor movements associated with visual images. For example, a child who sees a bicycle stores a visual image of the bicycle along with an image of its movements. From two to three, children's skills in language increase, and their ability for imaginative play and complex imitation increases as well.

Drawing on Vygotsky's theory of social interaction as the source of knowledge in the world, Barbara Rogoff points to the ways parents help toddlers respond to the environment.[2] They draw children's attention to objects of interest and promote learning by choosing and structuring toddler activities. Parents serve as partners who engage the child's interest in a task, simplify the task to fit the child's skills, and motivate the child to control frustration and exert consistent effort to achieve their goals.

The availability of stimulation and emotional support in the home in the first three years predicts cognitive development, as measured by standardized ability tests, more strongly than do ethnic or social status variables.[3] Parental responsiveness and availability as well as access to stimulating toys foster the support that enhances toddlers' cognitive growth.

LANGUAGE DEVELOPMENT

In years one through three, babies go from speaking a few single words to having a vocabulary of about nine hundred words and forming sentences. The main events in language development in these years are the appearance of words and acquiring a basic vocabulary in the second year, putting two words together in the latter half of the second year, and elaborating more complex sentences in the third year.[4]

Developmental Trends

There is no agreed-on theory of how children acquire language. Some suggest that children have an inborn ability to learn language, while others emphasize the importance of modeling, teaching, and stimulation by others in the social environment.

Still others acknowledge the importance of both the child's contribution and that of the social context.

Lois Bloom emphasizes that we cannot separate language development from social, emotional, and cognitive development, because language serves to express the child's thoughts to other people, and thoughts change with cognitive growth.[5] Emotional experience is also significant because children seem to learn words and sentence structure most easily in a neutral emotional atmosphere. High levels of intense feelings, particularly negative ones, may make too many demands on the child's cognitive resources, so that the child cannot attend to the words. Those toddlers who maintain a neutral affect learn words earlier than those who become emotionally expressive at the time word learning is occurring. The emotionally expressive toddlers increase their vocabularies later, but when they get more words, their emotional expressiveness decreases. So, neutral affect may lead to learning words more easily, and learning words may help to maintain a more neutral affect.

Children's first words pertain to objects, people, and experiences important to them. Words describe what their feelings are about. They also usually refer to events in the present. With advances in cognitive development, words refer to past and future experiences as well. Bloom believes children learn words according to three principles — relevancy, discrepancy, and elaboration.[6] Children learn words relevant to their interests, their focus of attention, and their level of understanding. They also learn words when there is a discrepancy between their experience and what they want to convey. For example, they learn words to express future or past events that cannot be surmised from the present context. Finally, children learn more words to elaborate on the increasing complexity of their thoughts and responses.

From the beginning, children use words to explain feelings, but they do not label their feelings until about age two. By the beginning of the third year, toddlers talk about positive feelings such as being happy, having a good time, feeling good, and being proud. They talk about negative emotions as well — being sad, scared, or angry. They talk about uncomfortable physical states — being hungry, hot, cold, sleepy, and in pain.[7] Aware of others' feelings as well, toddlers develop ideas about what actions cause feelings and what actions change feelings. Following are examples of comments from twenty-eight-month-olds: "I give a big hug, Baby be happy." "Mommy exercise. Mommy having a good time." "I'm hurting your feelings 'cause I mean to you." "Grandma's mad. I wrote on wall." "You sad, Mommy. What Daddy do?" Toddlers also learn that one person's feelings can stimulate another person's actions. "I cry. Lady pick me up." "I scared of the shark. Close my eyes."[8]

Cognitive development provides children with more-complex thoughts to communicate. In the second year, children begin to conceptualize relationships between objects — for example, they use a spoon to feed the dolly or place a figure on the horse — and they require more than single words to express their intentions, thoughts, and reactions. Thus, Bloom believes, the two-word sentence emerges to enable children to communicate such responses to the world.[9] The *two-word sentence* is a telegraphic communication that omits such words as *the* or *a* and emphasizes the actor-action-object dimensions. Toddlers can convey several meanings with two words, changing the inflection to change the meaning. "Mama go" may identify the mother's leaving, the child's desire to be taken along, or the child's desire to leave a place.

In the third year, thoughts and reactions to the world become more complex. Children begin to understand causation, to be concerned about the past and the future. Thus, they need to be able to link simple sentences with connective words such as *and, when,* and *because.* Greater complexity in sentence structure reflects a more elaborate understanding of the world.

Conversations between parent and child provide opportunities to acquire complex grammar and syntax. Some believe that parents shape and guide their child's speech to more developed levels through conversation, but Bloom believes that the child is the active partner who initiates the conversation and learns from the parent's responses. The child's strong desire to express intentions to others determines how the child learns complex language. In these conversations children learn not only language but also social rules, others' expectations of them, and general guidelines for solving social problems.

Developmental Variations

Individual Differences   Individual differences show in both the rate of learning words and the order in which speech patterns emerge. For example, some two-year-olds learn actor-action sequences ("Kitty meows") before identification patterns ("Doggy there"). Some emphasize possessives first; others refer to place.

Differences in learning language are, in part, related to gender (girls excel in verbal abilities from the first year of life) and to characteristics of the parents and homes in the child's first three years. Home and family characteristics that predict language growth are similar to those that predict cognitive development.[10] A strong positive emotional tie with the caregiver—enhanced by the amount and quality of the time she or he spends talking to the child, asking questions, and responding to what the child says—increases the child's verbal skills. Language does not develop as rapidly, however, when the home contains many people who reduce the amount of time mothers speak directly to infants.[11] By providing many opportunities for exploration and play, as well as a structured atmosphere, parents facilitate children's verbal skills.

Differences Based on Social Group   The most detailed study describing the differences in homes with parents of different social and educational levels involved monthly, hour-long observations of children from ten to thirty-six months of age.[12] Observers recorded all language spoken in the home and emphasized what the child said and was doing.

The children in the study were European American or African American. Their parents were classified as professional, working class, or on welfare. Results indicated no gender or racial differences in language acquisition, but they did reveal large differences based on social group.

All children in the study experienced quality interactions with their parents; all heard diverse forms of language spoken to and around them; and all children learned to speak by the age of three. However, the differing amounts and kinds of language heard in the homes surprised the investigators.

First, professional parents spoke about three times as much to their children as welfare parents did, and about one and a half times as much as working-class parents did. Children in professional families heard about 487 utterances per hour; children in working-class families, 301; and children in welfare families, 178.

The emotional tone of the conversations also reflected startling differences. In professional families, children received affirmative feedback (confirming, elaborating, and giving explicit approval for what the child said) about 30 times an hour or every other minute. In working-class families, children received affirmative feedback 15 times an hour or once every 4 minutes. In welfare families, children received positive feedback 6 times an hour or once every 10 minutes. Professional parents gave prohibitions about 5 times an hour, and welfare parents about 11. Children in welfare families heard twice as many negative comments as positive ones, whereas children in professional families heard primarily positive comments with negative ones being rare. These findings have important implications for the development of self-concept and general mood as well as for language development.

Language differences in the home strongly predicted vocabulary growth and intellectual development for the next five years. The most important predictors of vocabulary and intellectual competence were emotional tone of the feedback and the amount of linguistic diversity the child heard.

Encouragingly, the study shows that all parents have the capacity to promote language and intellectual development, because they already have the ability to speak and interact with children effectively. Of course, some parents need to increase certain kinds of behavior—namely, their verbal interactions with their children—and provide more positive feedback to them.

EMOTIONAL DEVELOPMENT

By the end of the first year, babies express interest, surprise, joy, sadness, anger, fear, and disgust. In the second and third years, feelings related to self-awareness and self-evaluation develop—embarrassment, empathy, pride, shame, and guilt.[13] The development of these emotions requires that children be aware of themselves and assess their actions in terms of some standard. Thus, emotional development is closely connected with development of the self.

Pride and Shame

In the second year of life, toddlers gain a clearer sense of themselves as individuals. They take pleasure in their activities and feel joy from their accomplishments. Unconcerned with others' reactions to what they do, they do not appear to make judgments about the value of their own actions. Thus, before age two, children do not experience pride or shame.[14]

At about eighteen to twenty months, toddlers begin to make self-descriptive statements that may be neutral in tone—"I have curly hair," or may be self-evaluative—"good girl." Children show that they have expectations about what ought to happen. They look for recognition when they have done something well, and they look or turn away when they have not succeeded at a task. They show distress and try to make repairs if something breaks, even accidentally. So, they have a beginning sense of standards. Even so, though they will look for adult approval or disapproval, they are still most concerned with their own pleasure and delight in what they do.[15]

By their third birthdays, toddlers have internalized standards for accomplishment and show pride (big smiles, proud posture) when they succeed on tasks, particularly difficult tasks, and shame (sad faces, dejected body postures) when they fail.[16] They are most concerned about their performance when the task is one an adult gives them to complete. They are less concerned if the task is a competition, like a race, where someone must fail. Thus, toddlers' behavior indicates that by age three, they judge themselves by internal standards and are upset when they violate them and pleased when they meet them.

Empathy

Empathy develops in stages during the toddler period.[17] At ten to twelve months, babies respond to other children's distress by crying with agitation. In the second year, however, they take action—touching, cuddling, or rubbing the injured party. Upset by her baby brother's crying, one eighteen-month-old girl brought him a diaper to hold, because she liked to carry a diaper for comfort.

Between eighteen months and two years, children begin to imitate the emotional reactions of the hurt individual, mimicking facial expressions of pain. Many go through a process of referring the pain to themselves. If a mother bumps her arm, the child rubs the mother's elbow and then his own. Compassionate action follows the self-referencing behavior. Investigators suggest that true kindness may depend on the ability to relate the other's distress to oneself.

Because toddlers have a clearer sense of themselves and other people than do babies, they develop a better understanding of how others feel. When they witness distress, they are more likely to intervene to ask what is the trouble, express general concern, comfort the person, or remedy the problem. While girls and boys help equally often, girls express more concern when they see distress.[18]

Toddlers do not express as much concern when they are the cause of others' distress. They intervene to help, but they also show aggression, personal distress, or enjoyment. Their attempts to repair the situation occur in an atmosphere of emotional upset and turbulence. While they make restitution, then, they do not appear to feel guilty for causing the distress. Toddlers' concern is most frequently directed to members of the immediate family, particularly to mothers, who receive much of their toddlers' comforting and helping.

What qualities in parents stimulate empathy in a toddler? Children who are kind and helpful in response to the suffering of others have mothers who are warm, caring individuals concerned with the well-being of others. These mothers expect children to control aggression, and when they do not, the mothers show disappointment—"Children are not for hitting," "Stop! You're hurting him." Mothers of empathetic children model kindness, but they go beyond that to teach children how to do what is expected. They maintain high standards and continue a warm, caring relationship with children.

We saw that infants as young as three months react to the emotional expressions of mothers. Toddlers, too, are highly responsive to the emotional reactions of anger between parents. In one study, the most immediate response to anger was distress that increased with each exposure to the anger.[19] Children cried, frowned, and seemed upset. When anger continued, children attempted to help parents — to mediate or settle the argument, or to distract the parents by coming between them. When toddlers witness aggression among adults, they tend to vent angry feelings on peers. They may be imitating parents' aggressive behavior, they may be so distressed by the anger that they have less frustration tolerance with peers, or they may be expressing anger intended for adults. Regardless of the reasons, children who witness anger tend to express it with peers even though they remain solicitous of the adults themselves.

Toddlers also empathize with depressed mothers and, even at age two or three, may take excessive responsibility for mothers' depressed feelings and be very careful in relationships with others, including those with peers. They are more likely to apologize for behavior and to suppress any negative emotion than are toddlers of nondepressed mothers.[20]

Anger

Parents want most to understand children's anger. Florence Goodenough found that many factors influence the occurrence of anger.[21] Outbursts peak in the second year and are most likely to occur when children are hungry or tired (just before meals and at bedtime) or when they are ill. Thus, when reserves are down for physical reasons, tempers flare. Outbursts are usually short-lived — most last less than 5 minutes — and, with young children under three, the aftereffects are minimal. With increasing age, children tend to sulk and to hold on to their angry feelings. From one to three years, the immediate causes of anger seem to be conflict with authority, difficulties over the establishment of habits (eating, baths, bedtime), and problems with social relationships (wanting more attention, wanting a possession someone else has). With older children, social and particularly play relationships trigger more outbursts. After the second year, boys seem to have more outbursts than girls.

In the study, parents of the children who had the fewest outbursts were more consistent, used a daily schedule as a means to an end, and had a more tolerant, positive home atmosphere. They were consistent and fair in the rules they established. With realistic expectations that children would be independent, curious, and stubborn, they anticipated problems and found ways to prevent them. These parents tried to help children conform by preparing them for changes in activities. They announced mealtimes or bathtimes in advance so children had 10 minutes or so to get ready. In these homes, parents focused on the individuality of the child. When a real conflict arose, however, they were firm.[22]

Parents of children with many outbursts were inconsistent and unpredictable, basing decisions on their own wants rather than the child's needs. These parents tended to ignore children's needs until a problem forced them to respond. In some of these families, parents imposed a routine regardless of the child's activity of the moment and forced the child to act quickly in terms of their own desire. Criticism and disapproval characterized the home atmosphere.

In short, when children are tired, hungry, or sick, they are likely to respond with anger. Parental behaviors that reinforce attachment — acceptance, sensitivity to children's needs, and cooperativeness — minimize temper outbursts.

Happiness and Affection

Toddlers get much pleasure from achieving their goals in activities of their choice. They feel joy in learning and the free use of their abilities. While they most enjoy pursuing their own goals, they also enjoy meeting adults' expectations. In one laboratory study, toddlers played in a mildly interested way with toys, but when adults asked them to do easy, interesting tasks, like arranging the toys in a certain way, the toddlers did so quickly and enthusiastically.[23] Later, when allowed to play freely with no adult involved, they happily repeated the tasks. The researchers concluded that toddlers derive great pleasure from matching their actions to the words of another, and the pleasure of accomplishing a goal is a powerful motive for their obeying commands.

Affection also increases in this period. Toddlers give love pats, strokings, and kisses to parents, particularly mothers. They are also affectionate to animals and younger children.

Ways to Handle Negative Feelings

Toddlers have several ways to handle negative feelings. They use words to express their feelings and to get feedback from parents about how to manage them.[24] They enlist parents' and caregivers' help in resolving the negative feelings and different situations they cannot handle. They also call or pull parents to what they want fixed. In the third year, they wait less time for getting parents to move a barrier, get a prized possession, or in general "solve the problem." They seem to have a greater understanding of when they may need help and call for it more quickly.[25] Toddlers also use objects to handle negative feelings. They frequently have transitional objects like stuffed animals, blankets, pieces of cloth, or dolls to provide comfort in times of distress. The use of such objects peaks in the middle of the second year, when as many as 30 to 60 percent of children have them.[26]

DEVELOPMENT OF THE SELF

Recall that in Chapter 6, we discussed Susan Harter's integration of research and theory in her formulation of self-development.[27] From ten to fifteen months, a sense of an I-self who wills, acts, and explores develops. While becoming more differentiated from others and more assertive, infants this age are highly responsive and attached to caregivers.

From fifteen to eighteen months, a "me-self" develops. Toddlers begin to internalize how others respond to them — that is, they start to react to themselves as others do. Children at this age recognize themselves in a mirror, identify photographs of themselves, and respond strongly to others' responses to them.

From eighteen to thirty months, toddlers develop a greater understanding of what influences others to act; as a result, they gain a greater sense of the separation between the self and others. Developing language enables toddlers to describe themselves and what they do. By age two, they use pronouns such as *I, me,* and *mine,* and describe their physical appearance and actions — "I run," "I play," "I have brown hair." Besides reflecting a growing self-awareness, describing one's looks and actions also actually increases self-awareness.

Toddlers' self-evaluations are positive. They do not distinguish between their present performance and their ideal, and they are not sufficiently mature to make comparisons with other children. Though they do not compare themselves to other children, they do perceive caregivers' reactions to their behaviors. They understand what pleases or displeases caregivers, and they experience personal distress when they fail to gain others' approval. Responding to others' reactions to their behavior indicates a beginning ability to evaluate the self on the basis of others' reactions to them.

Gender Identity

An important part of one's sense of self is one's gender identity. By *gender identity* I mean an individual's personal experience of what it means to be a boy or girl, man or woman.[28] In this period, the child begins to evolve a sense of gender identity that grows in stages. First, children learn to give gender labels to boys or girls, men or women. This occurs at about age two. They then learn to associate gender labels with objects, activities, tasks, and roles. They develop a gender schema or organized body of knowledge of what it means to be a boy or girl. This occurs over a much longer time.

At two to two-and-a-half, a child proudly announces, "I am a boy," or "I am a girl." Children gradually learn that their gender is stable across time—they will always be a boy/man or girl/woman. They also learn gender is stable across situations—they are a girl whether they have short or long hair, wear pants or a dress, drive a truck or take care of a baby.[29] John Money says that by age four, children find changing their gender identity as difficult as it would be for an adult.[30]

Money states that gender differentiation results from an interaction of physical, psychological, and social forces. Physical influences include genes, which, in utero, trigger hormones that lead to the development of internal and external sexual characteristics. Societies and subcultures within societies pass on beliefs about what is appropriate for boys and girls.

From the day that the child's sex is known, now often before birth, parents and society shape the child's physical world in terms of colors, clothes, and toys, for example. Identification of the infant's sex shapes perceptions of the infant's behavior and appearance. Nevertheless, research indicates that the more familiar a person is with the child, the more the individual's characteristics shape the response to the child.[31] Thus, parents who interact with children every day show few consistent differences in the way they treat sons and daughters. The child's gender is related to responses to external events, such as school, parental divorce, and remarriage, but not to specific parental socialization practices.

Although they may not realize it, parents are more emotionally positive and more involved when children play with gender-appropriate toys.[32] This begins when children are about one year old but decreases by about age five.

Prior to eighteen months, boys and girls show no differences in behaviors like aggressiveness, toy play, large motor activity, and communications attempts, all of which exhibit gender differences at later ages.[33] Noting parental emotional responses to certain activities, toddlers learn the appropriate gender labels and begin organizing behavior in terms of them. Toddlers who learn the labels early begin to play with gender-appropriate toys early. Girls who pick up these labels early on are less aggressive as toddlers and more communicative with adults than are girls or boys who learn labels later. By age four, early and late labelers show similar behavior and choice of toys; however, early labelers are more aware of sexual stereotypes.

DEVELOPMENT OF SELF-REGULATION

Although children first show control by following the requests of others, they soon begin to inhibit their activities on their own volition.[34] For example, a toddler of fifteen or sixteen months may reach for an object, shake her head, and say, "No, no." Toddlers are most successful in avoiding forbidden activities when they direct their attention away from these objects or activities—looking elsewhere, playing with their hands, finding an acceptable substitute toy. A substantial number of two-year-olds can wait, alone, as long as 4 minutes before receiving permission to touch.[35]

At twenty-four to thirty-six months, the self is more firmly established.[36] Children are beginning to form internal standards and take pride in controlling their behavior. They show the capacity to comply with requests and to inhibit or delay activities. They can behave according to social expectations even when a parent is not physically present to monitor what is happening. The child now uses representational thinking and can remember sequences of action and can recall the mother's comments even when not looking at her. A two-year-old cannot wait or delay action well and is less flexible in adapting behavior to the social situation than is a three-year-old. Even though children understand routines and rules, any strong stimulus can tempt them to forbidden behavior—a two-year-old, for example, may run into the street to pursue a prized ball.

As children move toward greater control, their behavior shows increasing compliance with others' requests. Age also brings more sophisticated forms of noncompliance. Initially, toddlers rely on direct, often angry, defiance and passive noncompliance. These methods decrease somewhat with age as toddlers develop more skill in bargaining and negotiating. Despite these age changes, there is "modest stability" in children's general choice of behavior. Those children who used the most unskilled forms of resistance as toddlers use the most unskilled as five-year-olds. Those who used simple refusal and negotiating as toddlers are most likely to use bargaining at age five.[37]

Robert Emde and his co-workers conclude, "By 3 years of age, under normative conditions, we consider the child's self to be a moral self."[38] By *moral self* they mean the child has an internal set of rules as well as shame, pride, positive-affect sharing, and the beginnings of guilt. This moral self, they speculate, develops out of reciprocal relations with parents in the first year of life. Responsive caregivers appropriately regulate the child's feelings and establish daily routines that give infants a sense of how things happen and how people interact with each other. Gradually, these routines and forms of interaction are internalized as rules that govern and direct behavior. Children seem to internalize the presence of the parent and feel increased power and control. They talk about what "we" do and do not do. By age three, children have enough awareness of the rules that they can talk about ways of solving hypothetical "moral dilemmas" posed to them, such as how to get a Band-Aid for a hurt child when you have been forbidden to go into the bathroom.

In short, moral behavior develops earlier than many might believe and has its origins in very early emotional relationships with available caregivers who regulate the child's feelings appropriately. Thus, moral behavior derives primarily from emotional experiences.

Children's temperament also influences the development of self-regulation and moral behavior.[39] Boys and girls who are low in impulsivity and high in inhibitory control are more likely to internalize the rules, confess after wrongdoing, and make reparations. Girls with these characteristics are also likely to feel guilt and want to reestablish good relationships with the parent after wrongdoing. Girls who are temperamentally reactive also feel more guilt and concern about reestablishing good rapport, but the reactivity appears to make it harder for them to internalize the rules and regulate their behavior.

PARENT-CHILD RELATIONS

Toddlers can carry out more independent activities than infants can, so parents' relationships with them become more complex. In the first year of life, parents were primarily physical caregivers and playmates. Now, their role of physical caregiver decreases somewhat and they become authorities who give instructions for new activities and limit children's activities, in part so the children can survive their independent explorations. We are going to look at aspects of parent-child relations: (1) the continuing attachment relationship and (2) parents' role as authorities who intervene to regulate and guide toddlers' behavior.

Attachment

Attachment, as we discussed in Chapter 6, is the emotional tie between child and parent (or other caregiver) and is reflected in the child's wanting to be with the parent, seeking him or her out, and being upset at separation from that person. The quality of the child's attachment to the parent influences the capacity to relate to others, to play with objects, and even to move around physically in the environment. Jude Cassidy found that securely attached eighteen-month-olds have greater ability than their peers to maneuver physically in the world and, as a result, fall and stumble less.[40]

Several important ingredients in the caretaker's behavior solidify the attachment. First, the parent is available.[41] The mother's availability to the child, her readiness to respond to what the child does, creates an atmosphere that results in the child's enjoyment, curiosity, and greater exploration.

Second, the parent serves as a safe base that the child uses as a reference point in exploring the world. Toddlers note the emotional state of the parents as well as her or his words and gestures and pattern their behavior accordingly.[42] Third, synchronous relationships with toddlers allow parents maximum impact in giving information to the child. Children are more attentive to parents' concerns and wishes when they have experienced parents' respect for what they themselves are doing.[43]

INTERVIEW
with Claire Kopp

Claire B. Kopp is a professor of psychology at Claremont Graduate School. She has followed two samples of children and observed their development of self-regulation and self-control.

I think encouraging the development of self-control and self-regulation are major goals of parents in raising their children. What can they do or what are the best ways, in our experience, to help children develop these capacities.?

Parents help children learn self-control in different ways, depending on the age of the child. It's enormously important that early in the second year, parents include structure and routine in the child's day. Children learn from this structure and from the environment their parents create for them. A few parents go to one of two extremes—either no structure so the child runs wild or too much structure so the child is limited physically.

Early in the middle of the second year (fifteen months), children begin to understand daily routines, such as mealtime and bedtime. Although children are much more active at this age, their expressive language is still limited. They are also beginning to show signs of self-awareness. All of these factors have implications for what parents do.

In my view, the parent of a fifteen-month child should establish two or three important rules and focus on them. The parent can then give a great deal of positive reinforcement for following these rules and not make a fuss about other rules or behavior unless, of course, the child is doing something unsafe—hurting someone or destroying something. A parent of a fifteen-month-old might have such rules as, "You don't climb on a glass table," or "You don't run away from me in a parking lot, you hold my hand instead." Parents often have rules that protect the property of others. For example, "Don't go in your brother's room when he has asked you not to as it upsets him." "No's" are kept to a minimum. When a parent has forbidden an activity, he or she should try to move the child away from the temptation. So, at this age, parents have two or three rules, and they emphasize these rules by giving many rewards for following them.

I think eighteen-month-olds have their own agendas. Although they have temper tantrums, the tantrums are not extreme. I advise parents to handle such tantrums by distractions. Children of this age are easily distracted, and a parent can pick them up, sing to them, introduce a new toy, and so forth.

Children love movement. Parents must consider this love of movement when making the rules. Children should have an opportunity to be active. For many eighteen-month-olds, just pushing their own strollers is a great activity.

Two-year-olds are vulnerable children, and their parents are vulnerable too. Two-year-olds need to assert themselves, and they are negativistic. Although the child needs structure, that structure must be tempered by what is happening with the child on that particular day. Thus, parents need to be far more flexible with children of this age than with younger children.

Although parents never know what will set a two-year-old off, they are more effective as they become sensitive to the child's messages or signals. Clearly, safety rules and personal property rules remain no matter what, but parents can be flexible about routines. For example, a two-year-old may decide she has to wear a dress instead of overalls to day care. I don't think it is worth arguing with the child about this type of issue. We want to help the child to assume some responsibility. In choosing a dress, she is assuming responsibility for her behavior, so we should respect her choice.

With a two-year-old, on certain issues, like safety issues, a parent cannot be flexible and cannot give in. The parent must be firm and insist that the rule be followed. As a result, the child may lose emotional control. If the child has a tantrum, the child has a tantrum. A parent picks up the child and moves him or her to a safe spot. If that leads to six tantrums, the parent accepts that. When the parent is firm, the child gets the message.

I think parents become afraid of tantrums, particularly tantrums that occur in public. My advice is not to be afraid. The child will not die from a tantrum. It is most important that a parent exert control on safety issues. If it is not a safety issue, my advice is to be flexible.

As I have said already, there has to be structure in a child's life so the child can learn self-control. First, structure comes from the outside. Then structure comes from the inside. And children need the structure of rules. What is important is that something in the child's life is repeated every day or every other day. Then the child learns there is a routine. Organization comes not only from structure in what people do but also from structure in the child's inanimate world. For example, parents organize toys so they are not scattered all over the house. When Mom says, "Clean up," or when Dad says, "Time to put the toys away," they give children an important message about family values. It is important for children to learn that, in their family, things have a place. Thus, self-control is learned in structure in the inanimate world as well as in behavior and routines.

Although mothers are often inconsistent from day to day, parents should try for more consistency instead of less. It would take a robot to be perfectly consistent, so parents need not behave exactly the same way every time something comes up. They cannot be tied to a rigid, inflexible schedule, but they do have to see that there is organization in the child's life.

Somewhere between the ages of two and three, children begin to understand that there are rules. Parents can make it easier for children to adopt the rules. When cleaning up, for example, parents can say, "Do it," or they can make a game of it, saying, "Pick up all the red toys first" or, "Pick up all the trucks first." Parents can think of strategies to help the child get through the task so the rules are fun, not albatrosses.

At around two-and-one-half to three years old, the use of reasons becomes very, very important. The reasons need not be elaborate. When the child puts toys away, parents can say, "We put them away so you will know where they are tomorrow when you want your doll," or "We put the toys away so someone doesn't fall on them." In the best of situations, the rules come before the act. With safety issues, however, parents sometimes have to act first and give explanations later.

So, between ages two and three, it is most important for parents to make tasks more acceptable and more fun and to give reasons. Reasons are important because they provide clues for figuring out what to do in a new situation. In a year or two, the child may be able to reason independently, building on the clues parents have given.

This interview is continued in Chapter 8.

These first three qualities build a relationship of mutual understanding. In this state, a parent goes on to teach and guide children and reflects a fourth important quality—the ability to balance support and guidance with increasing independence for the child. The effective parent observes the child's level of interaction in a situation and stays, in a sense, "one step ahead." When the child confronts a new barrier, the parent steps in to give just the amount of help that enables the child to solve the problem and move on. Jutta Heckhausen terms this behavior "balancing the child's weakness" in order to stimulate a new level of skill.[44] This behavior is sometimes referred to as "scaffolding," as parental help provides the structure to compensate for the child's lack of skill with the task.

A final essential quality in parenting at this age is the parent's ability to match his or her behavior to the child's personality and particular needs. What is most helpful for one child is not necessarily best for another. For example, highly active toddlers will explore the environment most widely when parents give little stimulation or direction and let the child control the activity. Less active toddlers require just the opposite behavior and explore most widely when parents are more stimulating.[45]

Like the infant, the toddler is attached to both parents, but the parents' roles may differ. Mothers are primarily nurturers and caregivers. Fathers tend to take the role of playmates who teach children how to get along with others. Through physical play, infants and toddlers learn how to interpret others' emotional signals and how others respond to theirs so that social competence grows.[46] As children grow, mothers spend less time in caregiving, and their interactions with children become similar to those of fathers.

The amount of time fathers spend with children and their involvement in caregiving activities are not as important for toddler development as the qualitative aspects of the relationship.[47] Fathers who are sensitive to their children's needs, who are not bothered by the childish behavior of their children or their own lack of knowledge about parenting, and who encourage toddlers have children who are securely attached to them, have a positive mood, and persist at tasks. Thus, sensitive fathering, like sensitive mothering, greatly affects toddler development.

Children's developing behaviors are not the only source of change in the quality of the mother-child relationship. Mothers' reactions to the children's changes as well as events in the mothers' own lives produce changes in the attachment relationship. In one study, a large percentage of infants who changed from secure attachments at twelve months to anxious-resistant attachments at eighteen months had single mothers who were not involved with men and were not getting emotional support in mothering, or had been single mothers for the first six months of the infants' lives and then had married.[48] Such mothers may have had less energy for the parent-child bond. Those infants who changed from secure attachments at twelve months to anxious-avoidant attachments at eighteen months generally had mothers who were aggressive, suspicious, tense, and irritable. They disliked motherhood and showed little interest or delight in their developing child, though they were knowledgeable about child development and were effective caregivers.

Those infants who moved from anxious attachments at twelve months to secure attachments at eighteen months had mothers who initially lacked confidence, interest, or support. As the babies grew and the mothers gained experience and confidence, their relationships improved. Thus, we can see that a critical variable in the attachment relationship is the emotional involvement, interest, and delight the mother takes in the child. This diminishes when mothers lack confidence or interest.

When mothers perceive their six-month-old infant as difficult, they tend to persist in this view of the child into the toddler years.[49] Objective observers support the mother's impressions. Mothers and difficult children get into a vicious cycle in which children approach mild trouble—breaking a household rule or causing mild damage—about every 5 minutes. Mothers then react intensely even though the child has not actually carried out the act. Children then resist the mother's efforts at control, further irritating mothers. Easy or average toddlers are more responsive to mothers' efforts at control. Social support for mothers helps to counteract the effects of a difficult temperament in the child. This support increases the mother's feelings of self-esteem and protects against the feelings of helplessness that the difficult temperament can create.

Further, though both boys and girls who are insecurely attached to parents provoke problematic interactions, the two groups receive differential treatment. In one study, insecurely attached boys received little help or guidance from either mothers or fathers, but insecurely attached girls received more instructions and guidance from fathers, whose involvement compensated for the lack of involvement on the mothers' parts.[50] Insecurely attached girls were more likely to have avoidant attachments to mothers, and the girls' independence and lack of dependence may have been especially upsetting to mothers.

Parents' Role as Authorities

As the child's independence increases, the parents' behavior shifts. There is less physical contact, less caretaking, and more verbal guidance and verbal feedback as to what is correct. The parent serves as a mediator between the child and the environment. Parents find these tasks more difficult as children resist instructions and limits, and they report less satisfaction in parenting than do parents of infants.[51]

Parents can take preventive actions to head off conflicts before they arise.[52] Diverting children's attention from tempting objects and activities, they can suggest interesting substitutes. For example, in the grocery store, Dad might have his daughter pick out items, or Mom might make a game of identifying colors.

Parents generally introduce rules that dovetail with the toddlers' increasing abilities[53] (see Table 7-1). A detailed study of mothers' rules and toddlers' compliance reveals that the major rules at thirteen months center on safety issues—safety for the child, safety for other people (no hitting, kicking, or biting), and safety for possessions. At about eighteen months, the rules expand to include behavior during meals, requests to inhibit behavior and delay activity, and early self-care. At about twenty-four months, more is expected in terms of polite manners and helping with family chores (putting toys away). By thirty-six months, children are expected to do more self-care, like dressing.[54]

Parents do many things to encourage the child's compliance. They persuade, guide the child in what to do, and give feedback about difficulties. These verbal methods may succeed primarily because they make clear to the child what is wanted. Toddler negativism may occur because children do not understand requests.[55]

TABLE 7-1
SPECIFIC BEHAVIORAL STANDARDS, BY CATEGORY

Category	Category Items
Child safety	Not touching things that are dangerous. Not climbing on furniture. Not going into street.
Protection of personal property	Keeping away from prohibited objects. Not tearing up books. Not getting into prohibited drawers or rooms. Not coloring on walls or furniture.
Respect for others	Not taking toys away from other children. Not being too rough with other children.
Food and mealtime routines	Not playing with food. Not leaving table in the middle of meal. Not spilling drinks, juice.
Delay	Waiting when Mom is on the telephone. Not interrupting others' conversations. Waiting for a meal.
Manners	Saying "please." Saying "thank you."
Self-care	Dressing self. Asking to use the toilet. Washing up when requested. Brushing teeth when requested. Going to bed when requested.
Family routines	Helping with chores when requested. Putting toys away. Keeping room neat.

J. Heidi Gralinski and Claire B. Kopp, "Everyday Rules for Behavior: Mothers' Requests to Young Children," *Developmental Psychology* 29 (1993); 576. Copyright © 1993 American Psychological Association. Reprinted with permission.

Children's compliance for safety rules is high and increases with age. Overall compliance appears to increase up to age thirty months; after that, age changes consist in children's increasing ability to comply without help from the parent. Still, by age four, parents remind or guide about 40 percent of the time.

Noncompliance is best handled with the low-power techniques of reasoning and explanation—techniques that share the power with children. This sharing may have strong impact because it conveys essential respect for the child. Verbal and reasoning strategies may be especially useful in helping inhibited toddlers and preschoolers internalize rules, because these children are highly capable of inhibiting behavior.[56] With more temperamentally impulsive children, parents might use simple, structured directives and prohibitions to help children internalize the rules.

Defiance occurs most frequently when parents use high-power strategies like commands, threats, criticisms, and physical punishments to control children.[57]

INTERVIEW
with Judy Dunn

Judy Dunn is a professor at the Institute of Psychiatry in London.

What are the most important ways to help children have satisfying relationships with brothers and sisters?

It is reassuring for parents to learn how common it is for brothers and sisters not to get on. They fight a great deal. The main variable is the children's personality. This child is one way and that child is another, and they don't get along. They don't have any choice about living together, and so it's easy to see why they don't get on. It is such a "No holds barred" relationship. There are no inhibitions, and both boys and girls can be very aggressive.

It is reassuring for parents to know that fights occur not just in their family. No one really knows what goes on in other families, and so you think it is just in your own. But children can fight a lot and still end up with a close relationship.

When there is the birth of a new sibling, keep the level of attention and affection as high as possible for the firstborn. I think it's almost impossible to give too much attention to the first child at this time.

Also, keep their life as similar as possible [to the way it was before the arrival of the new baby]. Routine things matter a lot to little children. They like predictability. The mother structures their whole world, so that after a baby comes, they can be upset just by any changes Mother makes in their routine.

In middle childhood, there is a strong association between sibling fights and feelings that the other child is favored by the parent or parents. It is important to be aware how early and how sensitive children are to what goes on between parents and children. It is never too early for parents to think about the effects of what they are doing on the other child. So always be aware of how sensitive children are and avoid favoritism.

Children who have defiant outbursts often stay angry for a longer time than do most children. A two-year study of parents and toddler-sons' interactions shows how a subgroup of parents and children developed angry patterns of relating that lasted the entire period.[58] The boys resisted parents' directions, and, instead of making efforts to guide and teach sons, parents responded with anger that led to power struggles with the children, who continued to resist. Over time, parents began to express anger at the beginning of their attempts to control the boys—before the child resisted. The parental anger then triggered the child's resistance. By the age of three, boys in these consistently troubled families were more likely to have aggressive behavior problems than toddlers who did not have such families. Qualities of the child at one year did not predict the difficulties, though temperament could not be ruled out as a contributor.

When these children were one, the main predictors of parent-child difficulties in the toddler period were the families' economic, social, and psychological resources. Those families with the most resources had the fewest difficulties. Such resources appeared to afford parents the patience and energy for understanding.

THE JOYS OF PARENTING TODDLERS

"There is the excitement of baby talk becoming real words." MOTHER

"I enjoy the way she connects so well to everyone. She respects each person. She's outgoing, she likes people. She has a talk with each one and brings them a present. I also enjoy seeing her and her father together. To hear them talk together, to see her father so happy with her all the time is a great joy." MOTHER

"I enjoy that she directs me more than I could sense. Before, there was a 'Yes' or 'No' response, but now there is more back and forth. If I dress her, she shows me she wants to sit or stand—'Do it this way' is what she seems to say. Before, she was tired or not tired, hungry or not hungry, okay or not okay. Now there is much more variation." FATHER

"It is wonderful now, he comes into a room and sees me, and he runs across the room and yells, 'Daddy,' and leaps on me. I like that. Or we had company, and I came down the stairs and he started to say over and over my whole name—'Michael———Michael———.' I like that." FATHER

"He is kind of aggressive and wants what he wants; but a few weeks ago at a play group, there was another child who was looking for a particular piece for a toy he had, and he was crying because he could not find it. A woman said, 'Oh, I see you're upset because you can't find that. Maybe we can help you find it.' Meanwhile, Alexander heard the conversation and knew where the piece was and went and got it and gave it to the other boy, and I thought, 'Oh wonderful!'" MOTHER

"To see him put ideas together, to see him remember something that happened one time four months ago and tell us about it—I am sure all children do these things, but they continue to be the miracle of this evolving person and who he is; it's such a thrill. The four-month thing came up yesterday because we were talking about his old day-care person. In the summer we went to visit her, and I took her fresh-ground coffee. Yesterday I told him we were going to see her, and he said, 'Oh, I

Certainly, one cannot overestimate the amount of energy, time, and involvement needed to help children learn self-control. In one study, mothers of two-year-olds intervened every six to eight minutes to make a request or stop a behavior.[59] It is humbling for parents to realize that children most often comply with parental requests, and, in fact, attend more to parents' requests than parents do to children's requests.

Play and positive feelings increase children's compliance. Though the given studies were carried out with preschoolers, the results appear applicable to toddlers as well. When mothers played with children 10 to 15 minutes per day in a nondirective, responsive manner, following the child's lead; being a partner in the play, when possible; avoiding commands or questions—just being there—children's compliance in a laboratory task increased. To demonstrate that the positive feelings aroused in play were the important feature in the compliance, researchers induced a positive, happy mood, telling children to recall an event that made them feel good

"want to take her ground coffee.' It just came out of the blue, and that was four or so months ago. There's a real person who remembers things that are important and significant to him." MOTHER

"I've heard of this, and it's true; it's rediscovering the child in yourself. Sometimes, it's the joy that he and I hop around the couch like two frogs on our hands and knees. Or we're in the bathtub pretending we are submarines and alligators. Sometimes he likes to ride around on my shoulders, and I run and make noises like an airplane or a bird. And I am not just doing it for him, but we are doing it together, playing together." FATHER

"The joy comes from the things we do as a family, the three of us—going to see Santa Claus together or to see miniature trains and take a ride. Early in the morning we have a ritual. When he gets up early, he has a bottle of milk and gets in bed with us; the lights are out, and we are lying in bed, and he tells us his dreams and we watch the light outside and see the trees and see the sun come up. We do that in the morning, and it is a quiet joy." FATHER

"The things that children do, you know they understand, but they haven't got the words to say what they want, so they tell you in the other things they do. They let you know they understand. It is so exciting to see her grow, and say, 'Yes, Daddy.' At thirty-one months, they are so smart, they comprehend so much; but they cannot convey it in words. You see it in their actions." FATHER

"I was just blown away by the way he tries to help other children. From a very young age, he has done this. Now, when a little girl he sees every day cries, he takes her one toy after another, and says, 'This is? This is?' meaning 'Is this what you want?' until he gets her to stop crying by giving her something she wants. He's very people-oriented, very affectionate, and seems so secure." MOTHER

"Watching her grow, seeing her grow, seeing the different stages, I just take pleasure in everything she does now, because I know she will be on to a new stage soon." MOTHER

or excited.[60] When feeling positive, children complied in a fraction of the time and picked up twice as many blocks as did children encouraged to have a negative mood. Thus, it appears that playing with children brings benefits beyond the pleasures of the moment.

LARGER SOCIAL CONCERNS

Sibling Relationships

Growing up with brothers and sisters has long-lasting effects on children.[61] The relationships among siblings are emotional, intense, and affectionate but sometimes aggressive and full of conflict. By modeling activities for them, older siblings teach

Parents need to keep differences in mind as they interact with their children. This child shares her book with "Horsey," without thinking about whether it can have experiences the way she can.

younger ones. Sometimes they care for the youngsters and protect them; sometimes they fight with them.

How well siblings get along depends not only on the parent-child relationship but also on the children's gender and temperament. Because most firstborns have mixed feelings about new brothers and sisters, arguing is not uncommon. However, many positive features of sibling relationships exist.

Older siblings, three and four, can act as substitute attachment figures for their toddler siblings in the absence of the mother.[62] Even young toddlers show positive feelings toward their older siblings, miss them when they are gone, and try to comfort them when they are in difficulty. We now know that younger toddler siblings engage in more advanced behavior with their older siblings than was previously thought possible for children of this age. They play in more complicated and imaginative ways. They learn to stand up for their own rights and argue persuasively with their siblings, and so their social reasoning and ability to protect their own interests increase. They also become skilled in giving sympathy and support to others.[63] Toddlers are also capable of teasing older siblings in clever ways, such as getting mothers involved when the firstborn has violated a rule but not when they themselves have. They learn to pay careful attention to the feelings and intentions of others.

Most firstborn children under five show signs of upset after a sibling's birth.[64] Ninety-three percent of children in one study showed an increase in misbehavior —

refusing to follow rules and regular routines, being demanding when the mother was interacting with the baby. Over 50 percent of the children became more clinging and dependent. Many experienced changes in sleeping and toileting behavior. Most of these problems disappeared in eight or nine months. Firstborns often imitated the newborn's behavior right after the birth—wanting bottles and seeking to eat, toilet, and play like a newborn—but these behaviors began to decrease after the first month or so.[65]

Positive changes occur as well. Eighty-two percent of two- to four-year-old firstborns had positive feelings about being a big brother or sister one month before the birth, and 80 percent remained positive in the first year. They most enjoyed cuddling and smiling with the baby. They reported being upset by the baby's crying, which decreased in the first twelve months, and the infant's increasing interference with their toys and play.

Though upset at times, all firstborns reported helping with the baby, and 95 percent of mothers reported that they did. Most mothers (75 percent) reported that the two shared and played well by the end of the first year. The fact that 63 percent of firstborns wanted another sibling by the end of the first year suggests that overall it was a positive experience for them.

Many factors influence how firstborns will relate to the child. Children who are most likely to be upset at the birth of a sibling are those who are already irritable, sensitive, difficult to manage, and inclined to engage in many confrontations with their mothers. When mothers are unusually tired or depressed following the birth of the sibling, their firstborns tend to have negative reactions. When fathers have close relationships with firstborns, the latter tend to have less conflict with their mothers following the birth of the sibling, compared with those who have distant fathers.

Peers

Young toddlers from thirteen to twenty-four months can play with peers, taking turns and sharing. They develop a social competence that persists into the preschool years.[66] They can form stable friendships that persist for as long as a year. Between 50 and 70 percent of reciprocated friendships last at least a year, and 10 percent last two years. Further, these friendships are important emotional attachments. When children remained with the same group of friends or moved with their group of friends, their play remained reciprocal and interactive. When a change occurred without a friend or a friend moved, play became less interactive. Parents need to realize the depths of these relationships for some children.

Cultural and Social Differences

I have described how toddlers in the United States develop and form relationships with others. As such, I have emphasized the toddlers' growing independence, their drive to assert and accomplish their own goals, and their resistance to adult authority. Sometimes we assume this is the nature of toddlerhood.

Cross-cultural studies reveal, however, that in many cultures around the world, toddlers long to retain the status of infant with close physical contact with the mother. Social standards push them to be more separate from her but not from others in the extended family or community groups.[67] For example, in other cultures, newborns displace toddlers in their relationships with mothers, but toddlers are put in close contact with siblings, age mates, or fathers to continue the close emotional and physical connections toddlers continue to need.

A cross-cultural perspective may provide a fuller understanding of toddler development in U.S. culture. Toddlers do move off to investigate and explore the world, and they grow more inquisitive and self-assertive in conversations. Yet, they also focus on maintaining their shared mutual understandings with parents. They eagerly share their discoveries with parents, and they watch parents for signals and guidance for their behavior. As we have seen, they internalize parents' rules and respond more to parents' requests than vice versa. Toddlers move off but return to the secure emotional base that they want to share. Toddlers in this country might benefit from having more structured relationships with peers and adults to substitute for the loss of close contact with mothers.

TASKS AND CONCERNS OF PARENTS

Parenting tasks of this period expand to include new activities as well as greater refinements in previous caregiving behaviors. Parents are intensely involved in the following:

- Providing a safe, child-proofed environment (see Figure 4-1 on page 85)
- Being an available, responsive caregiver who serves as a safe base for the child's exploration of the world
- Facilitating what the child is doing without taking over
- Providing opportunities for exploration and for stimulating interactions with objects and people
- Setting appropriate limits to help the child gradually learn self-control
- Being a partner in the child's exploration—watching, listening to the child's observations, conversing, playing, and reading

Regarding problems, those strategists who focus on feelings suggest that parents increase the child's sense of selfhood and autonomy as they listen to the child's reactions and help him or her label them. Dreikurs and the behaviorists are most helpful in their counsel on establishing fair and firm limits and helping children conform their behavior to the limits. The problems of this period center on learning the basic routines of daily life—eating, sleeping, and toilet training, and relating to new siblings.

Eating

At about one year of age, children are likely to grab the spoon from the parent trying to feed them—they want to try to feed themselves. The exact age at which a child has the physical skill to get food in her mouth varies. All psychologists suggest patience and understanding in helping children to learn how to eat. Most eating problems during toddlerhood are related to the mechanics of eating—the child is still developing the skills needed to get food to the mouth without dropping or spilling it and the control needed to sit quietly at the table. All schools encourage independence in eating. Even a two-year-old can be told how to get his or her own drink of water in the bathroom or to get a piece of fruit from the kitchen table. The parent's work is reduced and the child's self-esteem grows.

Regarding conflicts, Thomas Gordon is more likely than other strategists to seek a solution that satisfies everyone's needs.[68] He gives the example of the toddler whose bottle leaked milk onto the rug. The mother solved the problem by putting water in the bottles that he sucked in the living room and milk in the bottles he drank elsewhere. Both mother and son were happy with the solution.

When a child begins to sit at the table and eat with the family, a few simple rules should be established. Gordon suggests that if a child breaks a rule, the parent should send an immediate I-message expressing displeasure and should use active listening to understand the child's response. If, for example, a child reaches over and takes food from the mother's plate, the mother can take the food back and give the child food from the serving bowl. There is no need for words. This simple, immediate, nonverbal I-message is adequate.

Rudolf Dreikurs says to include children in family meals as soon as they can feed themselves and can obey the rules established by the parents.[69] If they cannot feed themselves, they are fed before the family mealtimes so that their feeding does not disrupt family relationships. Dreikurs believes mealtimes are opportunities for the family to share conversation and humor; arguing is decreased by respecting children's preferences and giving small portions. But children must eat everything on their plates so that they will have a balanced diet. And they must behave well. No scolding, threats, or punishments are given. If rules are broken, children are sent from the table and will be permitted to join the family at dinner the next evening. If children do not come when called for dinner, their food is served cold. If children dawdle, their plate is picked up when the table is cleared, whether they have finished or not. Dreikurs pays attention to individual needs in making the rules, and children are expected to follow the rules without being reprimanded.

Behaviorists emphasize breaking the act of eating into small steps and giving reinforcement as each step is accomplished.[70] Thus, as a child learns to eat with a spoon or to hold his own glass, behaviorists recommend praise or other reward for attempts at independence, even if food is spilled or help is required. As the child's skill increases, parents reward complete success. Parents must be careful not to reinforce disapproved behavior. For example, if a child whines and cries for a cookie and then receives it, whining is rewarded. Parents can request that the child stop whining before he or she gets the cookie.

Sleeping

As noted in Chapter 6, most people in the United States do not engage in co-sleeping, and most believe children sleep best when they learn to fall asleep alone in their own beds, in a quiet, darkened room. When they awaken in the night briefly, as we all do, they can drop off to sleep again on their own.

Older infants, toddlers, and preschoolers often develop sleep routines that they cannot duplicate on their own. So when they wake up in the night and cannot go back to sleep, they cry, wanting comfort; or, if they are older, they crawl in their parents' bed for the rest of the night. Parents can change children's sleep associations, if they feel the change is important.

It is easier to institute change when parents imagine the difficulties they would have learning to sleep without a pillow. They might find it very difficult the first several nights, but gradually they would become used to sleeping without a pillow; they would drop off easily and not awaken completely in the night. The situation is the same for children when parents change their sleep routines. Children will be very uncomfortable in the beginning but will gradually learn new associations. Parents feel better about the change when they see themselves not as cruel and depriving.

Richard Ferber describes a gradual method for changing sleep routines.[71] He pays attention to the child's feelings and needs for security, at the same time setting limits in ways that shape the child's behavior. Parents should start his method only when they have the time and commitment to carry it out for several nights. Because it means that they will also go without sleep in the beginning, they should start on a weekend when not many stresses are present. First, parents must be sure children fall asleep alone in their rooms at night and at nap time without the presence of a parent. The main thrust of the program is to let the child cry for increasingly long periods before going in briefly to reassure the child he or she is not being abandoned. Parents can speak to the child for a minute or two and pat the child but must leave again within two to three minutes, while the child is still awake. Parents enter *not* to stop the crying or get the child to sleep, but only to reassure the child there is no abandonment. If the child continues to cry for 10 minutes, parents return, reassure the child again, and leave. If the child is still crying at the end of 15 minutes, parents repeat the intervention. After that, parents go in every 15 minutes if the child is still crying. Any awakenings in the middle of the night are treated in exactly the same way. The same procedure is followed at nap times, but a child who is still crying at the end of an hour is allowed to get up. On subsequent nights, 5 minutes is added to each interval so that the first entry on the second night occurs after 10 minutes of crying, the second after 15 minutes, and all other entries after 20 minutes. By the end of seven days, parents wait for 35 minutes of crying before making the first entry, 40 minutes for the second, and 45 minutes for still other occurrences. Nap time intervals are treated the same as the night ones for that day, with the child always allowed to get up after an hour of crying.

But suppose children don't stay in bed. Suppose they keep crawling out. Parents enter the room as soon as they suspect the child is out of bed. They put the child back in bed and say if the child does not stay in bed, the door will be closed. Parents do not threaten or spank the child. They offer support at the time of learning a new habit—perhaps reflecting the child's feelings of anger, frustration, and isolation. If the child gets up again, parents close the door and hold it closed for 1 minute. If the child is still up at the end of that minute, parents reenter, put the child back in bed and say the door will be closed for 2 minutes if the child gets up again. The third and subsequent times, the interval is extended to 5 minutes. Parents make clear to the child that the open door is under the child's control. The second night, the interval of door closing starts at 2 minutes and increases to 8 minutes.

Note that Ferber's approach takes account of the child's feelings and provides emotional support to the child at the time of change. It also uses behavioral principles to shape the child's behavior. Parents must be consistent in their use of this method and willing to lose their own sleep to help children learn what are generally accepted as healthy sleep habits. They also must have any daytime caregivers follow the same procedures at nap time.

Toilet Training

Most experts suggest that sometime between eighteen and twenty-four months children are ready to learn approved toileting behavior. Nathan Azrin and Richard Foxx suggest three guidelines for determining the child's readiness: bladder control (the ability to stay dry for several hours, to anticipate urination, and to urinate a significant amount at one time); physical readiness (the ability to get to the toilet alone and the dexterity to get pants down); and instructional readiness (the ability to understand an instruction and the ability to communicate a need).[72]

T. Berry Brazelton adds several other indicators of readiness; the child wants to imitate adult behaviors, like brushing teeth and eating neatly; knows when she has to go to the toilet and understands why it is desirable to wait until getting to an approved place; and is not highly negativistic.[73]

All methods of toilet training (1) take into account the child's physical readiness, (2) teach steps of the process through instruction or observation of others, (3) have parents remain calm and unperturbed by accidents, (4) say never give punishments for accidents. The methods differ in the use of material rewards and praise. Haim Ginott, Gordon, Dreikurs, and to some extent Brazelton recommend taking the accomplishments as indications of the child's natural capacities. The behaviorists and Azrin and Foxx use praise and rewards of candy or food, but they move in the direction of accepting the feat as a matter-of-fact event.

Parents are advised not to give undue attention to toilet training. Do not talk about it much or give much praise, because then the child can use the achievement to frustrate parents if he is angry. The child can also gain power over the parents by going to the toilet when parents do not want him to.

Azrin and Foxx, the authors of *Toilet Training in One Day,* describe the most complete approach to toilet training, incorporating insights from many different viewpoints. Their book presents one of the few suggestions for what should be done if the child has a temper tantrum during the process. The parent must wait until the child's resistance dies down and then proceed with the training in a calm tone, giving approval for all correct actions. Because the process of toileting is broken down into simple steps that bring rewards, children learn they are capable of doing what is asked. A couple of tantrums to test the parent's intentions are usually all that occur.

Brazelton has designed a method to help children train themselves when they are ready. Here, the parent plays a less active role and children become trained at their own pace. Children become accustomed to a potty chair easily and occasionally remind them, asking them if they need to use the potty. If children rebel or have accidents, parents put diapers on them and wait until they indicate that they are ready for training.

Note that even with the most successful techniques some parents will experience difficulty for reasons beyond their control. Recent research[74] reveals that a gene is strongly linked to primary enuresis or persistent bedwetting, in which children never achieve consistent nighttime dryness, and even after age seven are wetting the bed three or more times per week. Many other factors—physical, personality, and social—play a part in the child's ability to be trained.[75] A profile of a child at high risk for enuresis includes (1) occurrence of enuresis among parents or siblings, (2) a high level of motor activity and aggression, (3) poor adaptability to new situations, (4) low achievement motivation, (5) overdependent behavior, (6) a lack of negative reactions to wetness and urine control, and (7) prematurity.

Parents having trouble toilet training a child need to remember that this is a new experience for them and for the child. And they need to acknowledge that for reasons beyond the control of both children and parents, some children need more time than others to learn toilet habits.

Temper Tantrums

As parents of toddlers know, temper tantrums are common responses to parents' requests. With Goodenough's study on anger in mind, let us examine what Ginott, Gordon, Dreikurs, and the behaviorists suggest about parental management of children's temper tantrums. Ginott recommends accepting all angry feelings but directing children's behavior into acceptable channels. Parents can do this verbally by saying, "People are not for hitting; pillows are for hitting" or "Scribble on the paper, not on the wall." Neither parent nor child is permitted to hit. If children's tantrums are not ended by verbal statements, parents take action, even in public. Mothers have reported stopping the car until the fighting stopped in the back seat, or returning home if a child has a tantrum in a store.[76] These methods require time, but the mothers report success and say they felt better as a result of taking action.

Gordon suggests finding substitute activities to head off trouble. If no jumping is permitted on the sofa, parents can allow children to jump on pillows on the floor. Once anger surfaces, Gordon suggests that parents listen actively and provide feedback about the frustration and irritation the child feels—sometimes a child needs nothing more than acceptance of what he is feeling.

Gordon recommends mutual problem solving to find a solution agreeable to both parent and child. But when a compromise is not possible and a child is still upset, active listening may again be useful. He cites the example of a child who could not go swimming because he had a cold. When the child's mother commented that it was hard for him to wait until the next day, he calmed down.

Dreikurs recommends many of the techniques that Goodenough found were used by parents whose children had few tantrums. In establishing routines, Dreikurs suggests being flexible with children, concerned with their needs and interests, but firm in enforcing the routines.[77] When tantrums occur, parents are urged to ignore them and leave the room. Ignoring a child is appropriate in public as well as at home.

The behaviorists use a similar method of ignoring. John Krumboltz and Helen Krumboltz tell of a little boy who learned that if he cried and had a tantrum, his parents would pick him up instead of paying attention to the new baby.[78] When they realized that their actions were creating the tantrums, they agreed to ignore the outbursts. When the boy learned that he gained nothing by banging his head and demanding what he wanted, the tantrums stopped. The behaviorists insist that parents must be firm and consistent. Otherwise, tantrums will continue, and each time children will hold out longer because they have learned that they can win by outlasting the parents.

Strategists who emphasize communication of feelings to prevent tantrums suggest parental intervention by reflecting feelings. The parents of the boy who is jealous of a new baby might be advised to comment that if the boy wishes, he could be held like a baby; only after attending to feelings would Ginott, for example, take action. The behaviorists and Dreikurs, in contrast, focus on handling tantrums once they have occurred.

Stanley Turecki and Leslie Tonner, whose work with difficult children is described in greater detail in Chapter 8, draw a distinction between the *manipulative tantrum* and the *temperamental tantrum*.[79] Children who want their way use the tantrum to manipulate the parents into getting them what they want. In the case of a manipulative outburst, Turecki recommends firm refusal to give in to the tantrum. Distracting the child, ignoring the outburst, and sending children to their room are all techniques for handling that kind of tantrum.

In the more intense temperamental tantrum, children seem out of control. Some aspect of their temperament has been violated, and they are reacting to that. For example, the poorly adaptable child who is compelled suddenly to switch activities may have an outburst, or a child sensitive to material may do so when he or she has to wear a wool sweater. In these instances, Turecki advises a calm and sympathetic approach; parents can reflect the child's feelings of irritation or upset: "I know you don't like this, but it will be okay." Parents can then put their arms around the child, if permitted, or just be a physical presence near the child. No long discussion of what is upsetting the child takes place unless the child wants to talk. If the situation can be corrected, it should be. For example, if the wool sweater feels scratchy, let the child remove it and wear a soft sweatshirt. This is not giving in, but just correcting a mistake. All parents can do then is wait out the tantrum.

Throughout a display of the temperamental tantrum, parents convey the attitude that they will help the child deal with this situation. Though parents change their minds when good reasons are presented, they are generally consistent in waiting out the tantrum and insisting on behavior change when necessary. If parents believe that many of their toddler's tantrums are temperamental in nature, they should read the section on difficult children in Chapter 8 for further suggestions on ways of handling conflicts with toddlers.

Birth of a Sibling

Ginott tells parents that because no one likes to share center stage with another, a child is bound to feel some jealousy and hurt when his parents have another baby, no matter how well prepared he is for the event.[80] Preparation does help, however. Parents can say that soon there will be a new baby in the family and that a baby is both fun and a nuisance. They should express, and permit the child to express, negative as well as positive feelings. Before the baby arrives, parents can help the child to anticipate both the love and the feelings of being left out that he will experience. After the baby arrives, parents can watch for signs of jealousy, which they can reflect, acknowledging the older child's jealousy, resentment, and hostility. Ginott suggests special attention and "extra loving" for the older child during these times of stress.

Gordon recommends active listening so that the child can express fear that the parent likes the other child better, or anger at the intrusion. Active listening means listening to behavior as well as to words and realizing that when the child becomes irritable, aggressive, or immature, jealousy lies just under the surface. A parent can simply comment, "You are unhappy," "sad," or "lonely."

Dreikurs offers a thorough discussion of sibling rivalry.[81] He shows how children's responses to the new baby depend on both their own feelings at the time and on the characteristics of the new arrival. Dreikurs recommends accepting any verbal statements of hostility, any talk about wanting to get rid of the baby. The main way to help older children cope is by making them your partner in caring for the baby. Point out the older children's advantages, how big they are, how well they bring a diaper for the baby or tell a parent the baby is crying, how smart they are to figure out that the baby wants company. If possible, the father can spend more time with the older child. When the older child makes unreasonable demands for attention, parents should overlook these. Parents can also try to plan special treats for the older child while the baby is asleep. To minimize difficulties as children grow, parents are urged not to compare them.

The behaviorists suggest that when a new baby arrives, the older child can learn to do special tasks that will increase self-esteem. Robert Eimers and Robert Aitchison cite the case of a child who was always asking her parents if they loved her.[82] At first they answered, but as the question became repetitive, behaviorists advised them to ignore the question and to build the child's self-esteem by giving positive attention for what she did well. They began playing games with her and spending more time talking and reading to her. Because the child felt valued, she no longer needed to ask whether she was loved.

Dorothy Briggs says preventing all jealousy is like trying to eliminate the common cold, but parents can learn to identify the signs of jealousy and can act to reduce it.[83] Jealous children may accuse parents of not loving them or of giving siblings more attention. They may become irritable and fight with parents, deliberately breaking rules and wanting to be punished—even punishment is a form of attention. Parents help children handle their feelings when they provide opportunities for verbal and creative expression. One mother gave her daughter a doll to hit to express the anger the child felt toward a younger sister. Coloring, drawing, and molding clay can also help to express feelings. Briggs also suggests building the older child's self-esteem by teaching new skills that increase the child's competence.

Again, the strategists generally agree, although they focus on slightly different aspects of the problem. Ginott prepares the child for the birth. Gordon and Briggs elicit feelings through active listening. Briggs suggests ways to drain tension and, along with Dreikurs and the behaviorists, recommends building the child's self-esteem through attention and interest in positive behavior as well as through teaching new skills.

PARENTS' EXPERIENCES

Parents of toddlers are in Ellen Galinsky's authority stage (see Chapter 2), which lasts from the child's second to fourth or fifth year.[84] Dealing with their own feelings about having power, setting rules, and enforcing them, parents have to decide what is reasonable when children mobilize all their energy to oppose them and gain their way. In the nurturing stage, parents were primarily concerned with meeting babies' needs and coordinating their own with caregiving activities. Usually, the appropriate child-care behavior was clear—the baby had to be fed, changed, bathed, and put to bed. Although judgment was required in deciding about letting the child cry or timing sleep patterns, still the desired aim was clear.

In the authority stage, parents must develop clear rules and have the confidence not only to enforce them but also to deal with the tantrums that follow. Parents require self-assurance so they can act calmly and neutrally when they meet with opposition from their children. Many parents, bogged down in battle with their toddlers, find themselves doing and saying things they vowed they never would—the very words they hated to hear from their own parents when they were children. Parents are shaken and upset as their ideal images of themselves as parents collide with the reality of rearing children.

Parents' images of themselves undergo revision in light of the way they actually behave. Because it involves change, this can be a painful process. Parents must change either their ideal image or their behavior to come closer to living up to their own standards. Their images of children change as well. Parents discover that children are not always nice, loving, cooperative, and affectionate. Children can be extremely aggressive—breaking things, hitting parents, pulling their hair.

One father described how he coped with these feelings by revising the kind of parent he wanted to be and by finding new ways to relate to children so that he met the images he wanted to keep of himself as a parent:

> Stanley and his wife have one son, eighteen months old. Stanley is a doctor. "In my family, growing up, when someone got angry at someone, they'd stop loving them—which made me feel abandoned as a child.
>
> "When my son gets angry, the easiest thing for me to do would be the same—walk out and slam the door.
>
> "I tell him that even though I've said no, I still love him. I hold him while he's having a temper tantrum, and I tell him it's okay for him to be angry with me.
>
> "Being able to do this is recent, new, and learned, and it's hard work. In the past, I couldn't see beyond my own feelings. What I've now learned is that I have to see past them.
>
> "Another thing I've learned is that if I've gotten angry at my son or if I've done something that I feel I shouldn't have, I'm not the Loch Ness monster or the worst person in the world. I learned the reparability of a mistake."[85]

Parents must also deal with each other as authorities. It is wonderful if both parents agree on how and when to enforce rules. But this is frequently not the case. One parent is often stricter or less consistent; one may dislike any physical punishment, but the other may believe it is the only technique to handle serious rule breaking. Communicating with each other, finding ways to handle differences, is important for all parents. They may, for instance, agree to back each other up on all occasions. Other times, they may agree to discuss in private any serious misgivings they have about the other's discipline; then the original rule setter can revise the rule. Still other times, one parent may decide to let the other handle discipline completely. This is a less desirable solution because it means one parent is withdrawn from interaction with the child. Parents need to find ways to resolve differences so they can give each other the support they need in childrearing. Mutual support is the most important source of strength in parenting.

Single parents and employed parents must work with other authorities, such as day-care providers or relatives who provide major care, to develop consistent ways of handling discipline. Again, communicating with other caregivers helps provide consistent solutions to problems. When authorities do not agree, children become confused and are less able to meet expectations.

As parents become aware of their personal feelings about being authorities and learn to deal with them, they can put these misgivings aside and deal as neutrally with rule enforcement as possible. As with handling infancy, a range of preparation such as gaining information from books, groups, parenting courses, and other parents helps parents handle the demands of conflicting feelings in the authority stage.

MAIN POINTS

As their motor, cognitive, language, and social skills increase, toddlers

- develop a greater sense of self and independence
- take pleasure and delight in their new accomplishments
- express new emotions of pride, embarrassment, and shame
- refuse to do what parents want if it conflicts with their own goals
- gradually learn control of their behavior through internalizing rules and standards

As their independence grows, toddlers also develop closer relationships with others, and they

- become more physically affectionate with family, friends, and pets
- become more concerned about others
- are kinder and try to resolve angry interactions
- take delight in complying with some adult requests and meeting a standard of behavior
- are more likely to follow parents' requests than vice versa

As they develop a greater sense of individuality, toddlers develop a sense of gender identity that

- is proudly announced at about two to two-and-a-half years
- initially is based on parents' positive and negative emotional responses to gender-appropriate activities
- organizes activities so that boys manipulate objects and explore the world more and girls express feelings, ask for help, and give help more

Parents whose toddlers function well and have secure attachments

- are available, attentive, and sensitive to the child's individual needs
- grant the child as much independence as possible within safety limits

- provide models of kind, caring, controlled behavior
- talk with the child to explain reasons for what is done, to understand the child's view of what is happening, and to let the child express himself or herself
- play with the child to increase the child's positive mood and desire to cooperate in routines and activities

Parents regulate children's behavior effectively when they

- establish an atmosphere of mutual understanding
- act to prevent problems
- introduce rules that dovetail with the child's abilities
- focus on safety rules first
- use low-power techniques such as reasoning and explanation when noncompliance occurs
- work together so children get a set of consistent limits
- do not abuse their power

Problems discussed center on

- meeting physiological needs
- toilet training
- handling temper tantrums
- dealing with the birth of a sibling

Joys include the child's

- delight in increasing skills and personal achievements
- helping behaviors
- greater communicativeness

EXERCISES

1. Go to a toy store and spend $150 on toys for a toddler. Justify your choices and describe how they differ from the toys you would buy for a child in the first year of life.

2. Go to a playground and describe the play and language behavior of two toddlers for two 15-minute periods each, if possible. How verbal are they? Do they use many words or few? How much interaction is there with the caregiver? Does that person give the toddler much support or help? How assertive is the toddler? Compare the behavior of the two toddlers.

3. Investigate the nursery schools, day-care centers, and play groups available to toddlers. This might be done as a group project. If each student had a two-year-old, where would each want that child to be?

4. Interview parents of a toddler about the joys and stresses of rearing toddlers. You might want to interview a couple together about the joys and each person separately about their stresses. What worries do they have about their child? Where do they get support as they rear the child?

5. Survey other students on their parents' use of physical punishment. This can be done by breaking into small groups and tabulating information on the following topics: (a) Did your parents use physical punishments? (b) If so, which ones—spanking, hitting? (c) Was this punishment frequent (several times a month), occasional (a few times a year), or rare (can only recall one or two occasions in your life)? (d) For what misbehavior did your parents use physical punishment? (e) How do you recall feeling at the time of the punishment? (f) How do you feel now about it? (g) Would some other punishment have been more effective? (h) If so, what and why? (i) Do you now or do you intend to use physical punishment with your child or children? (j) Why or why not? Small groups can report to the class at large and entire class results on the topic can be tabulated.

ADDITIONAL READINGS

Brazelton, T. Berry. *Toddlers and Parents*. Rev. ed. New York: Dell, 1989.

Damon, William. *The Moral Child: Nurturing Children's Natural Moral Growth*. New York: Free Press, 1988.

Ferber, Richard. *Solve Your Child's Sleep Problems*. New York: Simon & Schuster, 1985.

Shatz, Marilyn. *A Toddler's Life*. New York: Oxford University Press, 1994.

THE PRESCHOOL YEARS

C H A P T E R   8

How does parenting change as children's skills and competence increase? Does parenting become easier as children talk more, take care of themselves more, and undertake more projects? How do parents support children's growing sense of self and self-control? How do parents help children relate to peers and others outside the home? Where do parents get support as they raise their preschoolers?

The preschool period, from three to five, is an exciting time. Children have control of their bodies and have learned a variety of motor skills. They can communicate verbally and have a sense of personal identity. Their capacities to think and reason grow. At this stage, they turn to the outside world to initiate activities. Preschoolers strive to obtain goals and savor the pleasure of accomplishments. They become little philosophers, questioning all that happens to others as well as to themselves.

PHYSICAL DEVELOPMENT

Although their rate of physical growth has slowed, preschoolers still grow 2½ to 3 inches taller and gain 3 to 5 pounds each year. By age five, they are about 42 inches tall and weigh 42 to 45 pounds.

Preschoolers' brains are active and primed for learning. Compared with an adult brain, the brain of a three-year-old has twice as many synapses (connections) among brain cells and is two and a half times more active, requiring more glucose and having more neurotransmitters (chemicals that facilitate the transmission of information from one cell to another).[1] Brain development helps the child control voluntary movements and increases alertness and memory, which in turn underlie observable advances in motor, cognitive, and personal-social functioning.

INTELLECTUAL DEVELOPMENT

Greater motor coordination enables the preschooler to interact with objects in the environment in more complex ways than were possible at a younger age. Increased

WHAT I WISH I HAD KNOWN ABOUT THE PRESCHOOL YEARS

"I wish I'd known how to react when they lied. You know kids lie, but it hurts me terribly. It was a very painful experience even though I know I did it." MOTHER

"I wish I had known how much frustration comes just because kids are kids and you have to be tolerant. They don't have the attention span for some things. They might want to do something with you, but they can only do it for about fifteen minutes. You have to go places prepared with all his things or with things to keep him entertained. In the car on a trip, we have a lot of things for him to do. When you plan ahead, you can still be spontaneous at times. You learn that if you are prepared, things really don't have to be a hassle." FATHER

"Everything. I wish I'd known more about communication, how to talk to your children, and the most effective way to help them grow with a strong ego, a good sense of self. We were raised with a lot of 'Do this and don't do that,' a lot of demanding and dictatorial things as opposed to trying to solicit participation in the process of decision making, trying to get in touch with your child's feelings so you really do understand how they feel about things. That's really hard to learn, and I don't know how you can learn it without the experience of actually having the child. But I'm continually learning how to understand her feelings about things." MOTHER

"I think it is incredible that we don't teach anything about being a parent. I have to learn it as I go along, because I want things to be different for them than they were for me growing up. I can't use my own experiences as a guide." FATHER

"I wish I had known how to handle them so they could be spontaneous and feel good about the things they did. How to be spontaneous with them is one of the hardest things for me." FATHER

"I wish I had known how to handle things like believing in Santa Claus, I didn't know whether to encourage it or not or when to tell her there was none. She learned gradually, I think, but she doesn't want to tell her little brother yet." MOTHER

attention span allows the child to pursue activities for a longer time, and increased memory enables her to recall more detailed sequences.

Thinking becomes more complex. Children can distinguish real events from imagined ones and from dreams and nightmares.[2] They have a greater interest in sociodramatic play in which they take on many different roles and learn from the process of acting out the behavior of other important people like parents and teachers.

Preschoolers' understanding of other people's behavior becomes more refined.[3] As toddlers, they took an interest in others' emotional reactions and used them to guide their behavior. But they had what is termed a *desire* psychology: They understood that other people had feelings and desires and assumed this is what governed behavior. Preschoolers' increased language and cognitive abilities enable them to develop more complex views of others' behavior. They learn that, in addition to desires, others have thoughts that often determine both feelings and actions. For example, children learn that when a parent believes they pushed a younger sibling by accident, his or her feelings and responses differ greatly from those of a parent who thinks they pushed the sibling on purpose. As they learn that beliefs or thoughts determine both feelings and actions, preschoolers develop a *belief-desire* psychology.

As their interest in the world and understanding of others grow, children show great excitement about all the mysteries waiting to be explored. David Elkind writes,

> As one youngster expressed it, "Mommy, why is there such a lot of things in the world if no one knows all these things?" Here the child expresses not only his awe of all there is to be known in the world but also his belief that everything exists for the purpose of being labeled and understood.
>
> In this connection, it is well to remember that to young children parents are all-wise, all-knowing, and all-powerful. The child assumes that every question can be answered and that parents have all the answers.[4]

In response to such questions as "Where was I before I was born?" Elkind suggests that, when possible, parents phrase their answers in terms of purpose or function. One can say that the rain falls so trees and flowers grow. Because most phenomena have a purpose, it is not dishonest to answer in these terms.

Although children have enormous curiosity, their concepts are more limited than those of adults, because children pay attention to only a small number of characteristics, usually observable features. They cannot organize objects into general categories, and they do not easily understand relational terms such as "darker" or "lighter," unless the objects being compared are very different.[5]

As parents interact with their children, they need to keep in mind that children's knowledge is incomplete. What is obvious and clear to parents as they look at an object or a series of events is not necessarily obvious to their preschool children. Thus, parents must be very specific in telling children how they see an object or event. Remember, too, that although children do not reason in the same logical way as adults, they can sometimes grasp the solution to a problem intuitively.

LANGUAGE DEVELOPMENT

During the preschool years, children's vocabularies continue to grow, and their use of language becomes more complex. The child of three puts three or more words together and has a vocabulary of about 900 words. By age five, the child possesses strikingly well-developed language skills and a vocabulary of more than 2,000 words. In their language, children progress from a preoccupation with their own wants and desires (in the two- to three-year period) to focusing on the self as differentiated from others (at three and four), to focusing on relations with other people (at four and five).[6]

EMOTIONAL DEVELOPMENT

Preschoolers' understanding and expression of feelings grow in breadth and complexity. Preschoolers become increasingly accurate in understanding the connections between feelings and the events and social interactions that produce them.

INTERVIEW
with Claire Kopp

(Continued from Chapter 7)

What can parents do to help children learn self-control and self-regulation in the preschool years? In Chapter 7, on Toddlerhood, we talked about the importance of parents' providing structure, simple rules, lots of rewards for following rules, and explanations for the rules. What can parents do when children are between three and five years of age?

Parents help children at ages three to four to develop strategies for doing things and strategies for emotional control. I think that it is around ages three-and-one-half to four that self-regulation and emotional control really come together. Society has rules for children's behavior and for their emotional outbursts and fears. We accept a child's fears and help the child to get control of the fears and learn to take responsibility for his or her behavior.

Of course, it is important for parents to expand the number of rules as children grow from two to four years old. As children are exposed to the larger social environment, more rules are appropriate for behavior with peers, with teachers, with parents, in stores, and in church. There may be a tendency to introduce many rules at one time, but parents are wise to introduce them gradually.

At this age, the issue of children's fantasy life comes up and whether or not these fantasies are lies. I do not think that four-year-olds lie with intent in the sense that an eight-year-old might lie. Rather, a four-year-old sometimes believes something happened when it did not. I do not think it is wise to argue with a child even though you have rules about not lying. The four-year-old fantasizes. Parents must accept that such fantasizing is his or her attempt to understand what is real and what isn't.

For example, a three-year-old boy was thrilled with a gift of several goldfish. Later, he came out of his room holding a dead goldfish, its head hanging down one side and its tail on the other. Clearly the spine was severed. When asked what happened, the child said, "Oh, a man came in the house with a knife and hurt the goldfish." Obviously, the child had inadvertently crushed the goldfish. Because he felt remorse, he made up the story. The parent could become upset about the "lying." It would be better to explain that something happened to the goldfish but that a man was probably not involved. Then drop the subject. Parents can allow children to differentiate what is right from what is wrong without giving them a sense of guilt or shame. Parents' major task is to help children see right from wrong.

Though they at first believe that feelings are temporary, by the end of the preschool period, they recognize that feelings can persist and are influenced by what one thinks.[7]

Children can accurately identify what triggers emotions, especially when there is a social cause for the feelings. In one study, preschoolers agreed 91 percent of the time with adults in giving reasons for other preschoolers' feelings as they occurred in the course of everyday activity.[8] Preschoolers were most accurate in understanding anger and distress and less accurate in regarding happy and sad reactions.

Parents accept children's imaginary experiences as part of growing up without worrying too much about "lied." These imaginary tales occur because the child can't always tell reality from fantasy. When parents do not make too much of the imaginary story, children see that the rules can bend a little.

I see the years between the ages of one and four as a dance between parent and child. In the early stage, the parent is the leading partner in the dance. In the years two-and-one-half to four, the child leads sometimes, and the parent leads sometimes. The parent is always there, though, and able to lead if need be. In general, the child is the leader.

Let us turn to what really hurts the development of self-regulation in children. We can distinguish within-parent and within-child factors. Let us start with the parents. Parents who do not understand child development or parents who are under stress because of unemployment or divorce may be too preoccupied to monitor children. Thus, they cannot step in and take "the lead" when necessary.

The development of self-regulation can be a problem for children who are developmentally delayed, who have language delays, or who have sensory disorders. Children with such delays sometimes have trouble deriving principles about the rules. They need help in seeing the way in which the rules go together, and they need more structure in terms of explanations.

Both parents and children contribute to misunderstanding of the rules. Even if only one member misunderstands, eventually the dyad suffers. Sometimes there is just a terrible mismatch between parent and child. I am talking about the temperament disparity Thomas and Chess describe (see Chapter 6). For example, a very, very active child and parents who find it very difficult to deal with the high activity level. I think the child is vulnerable here. The child needs constraints without severe limits. He or she needs a way to control that activity. If the parent finds it hard because of the temperament mismatch, difficulty can arise. There is no definitive research on the matter because it is hard to identify what the mismatch is.

Where does self-control come from? It comes from a desire to be part of a social order, a desire to have love and affection. Children do not follow rules because they think the rules are wonderful. Children are not like that. They want love and affection, and they see that by following the rules, they get love and positive reinforcement. I am concerned about children being in a situation where they are not rewarded for following rules, where they are not given reasons for rules, and where they do not get techniques or strategies that help them develop cognitive understanding of the rules.

Parents must find a way to strike a balance between structure and flexibility. The fortunate thing is that somehow or other, most parents seem to strike that balance.

Still, because differences exist between preschoolers' and adults' understanding of feelings, parents often do not understand their children's reactions. Preschoolers evaluate events by their outcome. If wrongdoers successfully achieve their ends, the preschooler assumes they feel good about that. The preschooler may know an act is wrong, but not necessarily feel wrong or bad for doing it.[9] Children of this age are particularly happy to evade punishment while still getting what they want.[10] Preschoolers, though, are highly sensitive to punishment, feeling angry or sad whether it is deserved or not.

The relationships among siblings are emotional, intense, affectionate — sometimes aggressive. How well siblings get along is partly determined by the parent-child relationship.

Preschoolers' most common form of emotional upset is crying, which accounts for 74 percent of the disruptions at home.[11] Anger represents about 23 percent of these incidents. Parent-child interactions are the main source (71 percent) of the upsets, with sibling conflicts accounting for only 13 percent and peer conflicts for 6 percent of the distress.

Parents' usual response to the distress is not to comfort but to give the child a practical, problem-solving response so that the child can deal with the situation. Children appreciate the help. When parents give directives, children tend to get angry. Parents' ways of responding to emotional distress are related to children's competence in nursery school. When parents encourage children to take action with problems, children are better able to plan and are more effective in social activities and other areas as well.

Children not only can express feelings but can hide them as well. By age three, children are already beginning to hide anger, disappointment, and guilt.[12] They not only hide their own wrongdoing but also mask feelings of disappointment when others are present. Girls are more likely to hide negative feelings and give full expression to positive ones.[13] Though they can hide feelings, it is hard for preschoolers to think of themselves as having two distinct emotions at the same time.[14]

They find it hard to understand that they can feel happy and sad all at once. Similarly, they feel if a person is nice, he is nice all the time. In the school years, they come to understand and accept the reality of feeling two emotions simultaneously.

Children's temperament influences their emotional reactions, the ease with which they can control them, and the forms in which they express these feelings.[15] Children who are emotionally intense and have heightened negative affect are more poorly controlled and less able to regulate the expression of their emotions. When angry or upset, they act out, often in aggressive ways. This behavior compounds their problem, because it generally does not lead to positive resolutions to the upsetting situation. Children who do not become overly aroused emotionally can regulate their feelings, talk over the situation, and find more adaptive solutions to the upset. Parents who encourage children to express their feelings of sadness and distress and teach them ways to deal with these feelings appropriately help children to express themselves and find solutions to upsetting events.

Anger

In the preschool years, angry outbursts last about as long as they did in the toddler years, but preschoolers get angry over different things.[16] While preschoolers continue to battle with authority figures over bedtime routines, eating and table manners, and control of anger, they also resent restrictions and punishments, and they become angry when they cannot accomplish what they want without help. In addition, children become increasingly frustrated and angry with playmates who take toys or who are unwilling to share. As children grow older, their outbursts feature less undirected physical energy and more organized activity directed toward getting what they want. The most competent children handle anger in direct ways that reduce further conflict and maintain social relationships. Boys express their feelings and take no action; girls assert themselves to obtain their wishes.[17]

Children continue to be sensitive to angry outbursts whether these occur with family members or strangers, and their reactions to anger affect their social relationships with others. Preschoolers from families with marital distress and resulting anger themselves become angry and noncompliant with parents and negative in their interactions with peers. These children show signs of stress: They produce high levels of stress-related hormones; play at a lower, less enthusiastic level with their friends; and, when their anger is aroused in these interactions, they have great difficulty dealing with it.[18]

Preschoolers who heard strangers arguing in the next room showed heightened arousal during anger episodes and increased verbal aggressiveness in play following the exposure to anger. Research found three emotional styles of responding to anger.[19] Concerned emotional responders (46 percent of children) showed negative feelings of upset during the episode and later said they felt sad and wanted to leave when they heard anger. Unresponsive children, who showed no emotional reaction, were only a small percentage of the group (15 percent). They were least likely to respond to aggressiveness in play with friends. Ambivalent responders (35 percent) showed both positive and negative feelings during the anger episode. They were upset, but later said they were happy during the episode. These children were most likely to become physically aggressive in play following the anger episode and were most responsive to aggressiveness in peers. Their behavior accounted for almost all the increased aggressiveness in play following the episode of anger. If these children had been able to handle their ambivalent feelings, they might have had no need to be aggressive.

Fear

Fears are a natural part of life as children grow up. In the early years of infancy, fears of noise, loss of support, and strangers are most evident, but these anxieties gradually fade. In the preschool years, children experience fears of animals, the dark, harm from imaginary creatures, and natural disasters like fires and storms. Anxiety and fear in response to unfamiliar people and strange situations may result from temperamental qualities. Some individuals demonstrate marked physiological excitability when confronted with the unfamiliar.[20] Such excitability is identified in infancy and manifests itself in inhibited, avoidant behavior that persists through the toddler and preschool years.[21] As the child becomes familiar with the person or place, fear of the unknown sometimes dissipates. Still, many inhibited children play less freely with peers at home and in alternative care settings. They have difficulty in taking turns and in engaging in fantasy play. As we saw in Chapter 2, by not rewarding the overreactivity and by providing structure for their child, parents can help the child overcome these reactions.

Realistic concerns about dangers like falling out of a tree and hurting oneself can motivate the child to be cautious when appropriate. Intense fears, however, can prevent the child from exploring the world and interacting with other people. Research suggests further that intense fears at this time have a long-term impact: Preschool boys who experienced intense fears of bodily harm were, as adults, anxious about sexuality, uninvolved with traditional masculine activities, and concerned with intellectual performance.[22]

Empathy

Children's ability to respond sensitively to others' needs increases as they grow. Preschoolers appear more able than toddlers to adopt the perspective of the other person and respond to him or her. Since preschoolers are better able to understand the sources of emotional reactions, their strategies for helping go more directly to the source of the problem. When another child is angry, they are likely to give some material thing to the child or share with him or her.[23] When another child is sad or distressed, they are more likely to do something positive for the child, playing with or comforting the child.

Sharing and giving with friends occurs most frequently in an atmosphere of comfort and optimism. Best friends continue to share when happy, appreciative responses follow. When sharing does not occur but the friend remains happy and smiling, the conflict does not escalate, and sharing is resumed.[24]

In the last chapter, we discussed the family characteristics associated with empathy. In the preschool years, other sources of learning become important as well. Children learn empathic behavior from television programs such as *Mister Rogers*.

They learn it from books and stories that have moral themes. Fairy tales, universal favorites of children, present models of kind, caring behavior that triumphs, often after many tribulations, over evil and cruelty.

DEVELOPMENT OF THE SELF

In early childhood, children continue to define themselves in terms of their physical characteristics and their actions. While they continue to use concrete descriptions, they are beginning to organize their self-perceptions and see themselves in more general though dichotomous terms such as good or bad, smart or dumb.[25] Most children continue to focus on their positive qualities and see themselves as "all good," but preschoolers who have experienced abuse are more likely than other children to consider themselves as bad.

Children at this age begin to compare themselves in the present with themselves in the past. As always, growing skills reinforce a positive self-concept. When they compare themselves with others, they do it to gain information on how to do something or to determine if they have received a fair share of a reward. They generally do not compare themselves to others to evaluate their performance.

In this period, children describe themselves in terms of skin color and facial features. Preschoolers can identify their own skin color, but African-American and Native-American preschoolers, like European-American children, choose the pictures showing European-American children as their preferred skin color. At the same time, however, these children have high self-esteem. Researchers speculate they are aware that white figures are preferred, feel good about themselves, and identify themselves with preferred status.[26]

Preschoolers have internalized standards by which they evaluate themselves and their achievements.[27] Still, as they approach tasks, they are optimistic.[28] They believe that when they want something, they will be able to achieve it, and they ignore any failures on their way. The reason is not cognitive immaturity, for they can pay attention to others' failures and make realistic predictions about their chances for success. But when success is important, they believe they will be able to exert whatever effort is necessary to achieve their ends. As we shall see in later chapters, such optimism is an aid to accomplishment rather than an obstacle to it.

Preschool children have established their own gender identity and know that this is an unchanging part of them even if their appearance or activities change.[29] During these years and well into the elementary school years, children learn what is associated with being a boy or girl. They learn first about their own gender and then about the other. Girls have a greater gender knowledge than do boys. Because children appear most prone to gender stereotyping while they are in the process of learning, the preschool years may show a peak in stereotyped activity.[30]

Even in these years, preschoolers will approve of themselves when they play with gender-appropriate toys and feel self-critical when they do not.[31] Standards frequently come from parents, but not always. When given a truck to play with, one little girl commented, "My mommy would want me to play with this, but I don't want to."[32] She apparently derived her standards outside the family. This illustrates clearly what two social scientists found in reviewing gender development: "Gender is not simply something that is imposed on children; at all points of development, children are actively constructing for themselves what it means to be female or male."[33]

In the preschool years, private speech directed to the self comes to function as a guide for the child.[34] Initially, private speech follows actions and is a response to what has occurred: "I made that tower," "I got my shoes and socks." Gradually, speech comes to precede the actions and helps the child plan appropriate behaviors: "I am going to get my shoes and socks," "I am going to get dressed." With increasing age, private speech changes from verbalizations to inner language and verbal thoughts.

DEVELOPMENT OF SELF-REGULATION

As their attention span and concentration increase and they use language to guide their behavior, preschoolers become capable of self-regulation.[35] They know the rules and can follow them, much of the time without reminders.[36] Though they may resist as much as in the past, resistance now takes new forms. Instead of crying and throwing temper tantrums, children use verbal means of refusing and negotiating compromises.[37] Parents who have used verbal requests to induce compliance and verbal feedback to modify inappropriate behavior have the most cooperative children at age five.

There are great individual differences, however, in the rate at which children gain control. In studies of preschool children, a group identified as "uncontrolled" children are spontaneous, impulsive, emotionally expressive, nonconforming, and exploring.[38] Qualities of undercontrol persist: Those three-year-olds described as undercontrolled in nursery school will often be classed as undercontrolled when they attend elementary school. Qualities of flexibility and adaptability do not appear as persistent as qualities of undercontrol.

SOCIAL DEVELOPMENT

Parent-Child Relationships

Throughout the growing years, the child's attachment to a parent serves "to protect children from danger, to facilitate their exploration of the environment, to play a role in regulating physical proximity, and to provide a sense of security and trust."[39] As children grow, verbal interaction replaces physical intervention as the means by which parents ensure safety and proximity and promote exploration.

Just as in earlier periods, sensitive, involved, flexible parenting promotes feelings of security in children. As in the past, shared play with parents brings enjoyment and opportunities for learning. But with children's increased understanding of others, wider spheres of interaction, and growing language skills, much of what children learn about parents' reliability and trustworthiness comes from observing parents' behavior with each other, siblings, and other relatives, as well as through conversations about the present and the past, and about what is approved and disapproved.[40] Feelings of security stem also from the ways parents negotiate conflicts with preschoolers—with their willingness to seek compromise and respect the child's autonomy while still providing limits that give security.

In this period, then, children's secure attachment to parents comes from a wide variety of behaviors. Because preschoolers have greater cognitive skills and thus can more accurately understand parents' behavior, their views of their parents are more realistic than those of toddlers and lead to greater predictability of parents' behavior.[41]

Four-year-olds tend to look at family interactions in ways that confirm the underlying dimensions that researchers propose. Four-year-olds' stories depict family interactions that focus on engagement/disengagement among family members, the amount of cooperation or conflict that exists, and the degree to which family members are equal or dominant. Their stories describe families' emotional tone as reassuring, rational, helpful, affectionate, gratifying, angry, aggressive, and punitive, showing that children focus on the very aspects of family life researchers find salient.[42]

Parents' behavior with children at earlier ages affects children's attachment and behavior in the preschool years. Securely attached infants whose mothers continue to be sensitive and responsive to them have no behavior problems in the preschool period.[43] Even if mothers had anxious attachment relations with infants, these children show no behavior problems if mothers become more respectful of their autonomy, more sensitive and responsive to their needs, and less intrusive. Children who had and continued to have anxious-avoidant attachments in infancy suffer many problems in the preschool years. They are dependent, noncompliant, hostile, impulsive, and withdrawn. Children with early and later anxious-resistant attachments lack confidence and assertiveness in their play, and they relate poorly to their peers.

Many factors, past and present, influence parents' behavior in their children's preschool years. First, there is the parents' own attachment relationships with their parents. Mothers who reported having secure attachments with their parents were warm, helpful, and supportive with their own preschoolers. These children, in turn, were securely attached to them and received all the benefits of that close relationship. Mothers who reported remote, detached relationships with their parents were cool, remote, and very directive with their own children. These children were insecurely attached to them, anxious, subdued, and suffering from behavior problems. A third group consisted of mothers who were also insecurely attached to their own parents but were preoccupied with these relationships. With their own children, these parents were confusing and controlling. They were sometimes warm and gentle, but then could be angry. Their children were negativistic and noncompliant.[44]

Mothers experiencing secure attachments reported as many negative events in their early lives as insecurely attached mothers did, but they seemed to interpret them differently. They focused on and valued what was positive in the relationship.

A second factor influencing parent-child relationships is the environment, characterized by the neighborhood, external danger, and living arrangements. Low-income mothers who are young and single, with little education and no supportive boyfriend, use more controlling techniques with their children, emphasizing obedience and safety.[45] Low-income mothers who feel they have the support of institutions such as a church or religion are able to be more child-centered in their discipline.

Third, parents' personal problems impinge on parent-child relationships, often in indirect ways. In one nonclinical sample of families, parents' depression was not directly related to children's problems.[46] When the depression leads to unhappy marriages, however, the unhappy marriages affect parent-child relationships. Depressed parents who are unhappily married are relatively less warm and less positive with their children, and the children are more aggressive and resistant with parents and other people as well. If depressed parents maintain happy marriages, they have more to give children, and their children function more effectively.

Alcoholic parents create a difficult family atmosphere of aggressiveness and hostility. One study shows the impact on three-year-old sons,[47] who begin to develop acting-out behaviors in this angry atmosphere. While the father's alcoholic behavior has serious impact on the family, it is primarily channeled to the child through the mother, who in this atmosphere often becomes less sensitive and responsive to children.

Highly significant research with preschoolers and their parents (see Chapter 3) reveals that when parents understand their own feelings and can coach their preschoolers on how to deal with anger and frustration, their children experience reduced physical and emotional stress.[48] They develop into elementary school students who, at age eight, have longer attention spans, better grades, and fewer behavior problems with friends, at home, and at school than do children with parents who do not coach them.

As we have seen, by "coaching," these researchers mean actively helping children figure out what they are feeling and what they can do to feel better. Researchers do not mean holding, cuddling, or sympathizing until the unpleasant feelings disappear. They mean what Thomas Gordon terms active listening, sending I-messages, and engaging in problem solving about the situation.[49] Coaching may be especially important at this age because children have increased capacity to control and regulate feelings if shown how to do this.

Sibling Relationships

In the preschool years, children have close, intense relationships with brothers and sisters. When preschoolers are older siblings, they often involve younger children in fantasy play, assigning them special roles that the younger ones are often happy to carry out. Preschoolers adapt their speech so that toddlers understand them better, speaking to them in short sentences, repeating phrases just as adults do. Preschoolers are helpful, soothing, and comforting, sometimes entertaining the younger ones by joining with them in physical activities—rolling around on the floor and jumping.[50] They are especially likely to be helpful and playful when they have affectionate relationships with their fathers.[51]

As in many close relationships, however, anger and frustration surface. In one Canadian study, 29 percent of the observed behavior between siblings was hostile.[52] Though the preschooler frustrates the younger child by taking advantage because of size, grabbing toys, or shoving, toddlers can be remarkably astute in irritating and distressing their older siblings. They know how to tease in subtle ways, taking a toy they know the older one prefers or taking apart the older one's play creations. As toddlers get older, they express their aggression more directly, in hitting, grabbing, and slapping. Aggressive disputes occur most often when mothers are intrusive and overcontrolling with children.[53] Sometimes one child in the interaction may be friendly and the other aggressive, but children learn to negotiate these differences.

Though many older siblings feel mothers favor younger siblings,[54] longitudinal studies of mothers' behavior with their two children at the same age—when each is one or two—reveal that mothers are quite consistent in the amount of affection and verbal responsiveness they direct to each child at that age.[55] Because their behavior toward the child changes as the child grows, one can see a difference in how they treat the two when they are different ages. Mothers are, however, less consistent in their ways of controlling different children at a given age, probably because they have learned from experience.

Peers

In the preschool period, children engage in more cooperative play with each other than when they were toddlers. Much of it continues to be reality-oriented, but they show an increase in fantasy play. As their sense of self becomes more secure and children have greater capability for symbolic representation, they are free to take on the roles of other people and pretend they are someone else. Boys' fantasy play involves using physical items as pretend objects—a stick becomes a sword. Girls are more verbal, with their fantasy play oriented toward play acting.[56]

As noted in Chapter 7, children form stable friendships in these years. Friends have as many fights as casual acquaintances, but they handle them differently.[57] Whereas casual acquaintances stand up for their rights until someone wins, friends tend to disengage and find an equal solution that gives each partner something. Friends can then continue to play with each other, whereas casual acquaintances drift away from each other after a fight.

Preschoolers like each other because they share the same activities and play together well. They want to enjoy themselves and have fun with minimum friction. Those who disrupt play and cause trouble are disliked by other children.[58] Observations of children's nursery school behavior indicate that the majority of interactions among children are friendly.[59] Children spend a high percentage of time (81 percent in this study) in friendly encounters that include asking, suggesting, and starting an activity with a smile or comment, saying, "Let's do . . ." Only 14 percent of interactions are demanding or aggressive, and 5 percent involve whining, begging, and crying. Even when others are domineering, many preschoolers are mature enough to either ignore the response or agree with the other child and thus avoid a conflict. Preschoolers enjoy a friendly atmosphere and tend to return the positive overtures of others. Children who reach out to others are sought as companions.

Even in early childhood, some children are more socially skilled than others. Social skill is related to being outgoing and able to regulate emotional responses in peer interactions.[60] Controlling one's anger and coping positively with other children's negative feelings is related to greater popularity and social competence, especially for boys. A difficult temperament and poor control of one's negative feelings in peer groups are related to aggressiveness and disruptive behavior.

Parental qualities associated with social competence include positive attachments that enable children to feel secure, trusting, and confident in social relationships, where they can further develop their skills.[61] When children are insecurely attached to parents, they come to view others as rejecting or neglectful. Further, they view social relationships as potentially rejecting, children tend to withdraw from peer interactions; when they view others as neglectful, they tend to be aggressive with peers.

When they monitor young children's social interactions and intervene to guide them, parents help their children succeed.[62] Parents who believe social skills are teachable are more likely to step in to teach their children how to join and play in groups. However, parents who believe social skills are inborn give little help to their children—they do not step in to guide children's behavior and to find solutions to problems.

As we saw earlier, parents' personal problems as well as marital conflict and poverty are associated with children's peer problems. Aggressive and disruptive behavior are most frequently reported for children who experience the additional stress of parents' difficulties.

CULTURAL INFLUENCES ON PARENTING

You may recall from Chapter 2 that Diana Baumrind identified three patterns of parenting preschoolers—authoritative, authoritarian, and permissive.[63] She found that competent, friendly, self-controlled children tended to come from authoritative families, where parents balanced acceptance with control. Parents who were authoritarian—high on control and low on acceptance—tended to have children who were self-reliant but unhappy. Permissive parents, high on acceptance and low on control, had the least self-reliant and controlled children.

These findings applied mainly to the middle-class European-American families in Baumrind's study. Among African-American parents of girls, the only major subgroup in Baumrind's study, authoritarian parenting did not have negative connotations but was related to girls' assertive, competent, outgoing behavior. Similar findings emerge in other ethnic groups. For example, in Chinese culture, strict adherence to standards and traditions without regard for individual preferences occurs in the context of family closeness and a strong desire for harmonious relationships among family members.[64] With a great concern and care for children, comes the expectation that they take their place in the social hierarchy, which emphasizes obedience to social and cultural traditions. In these groups, one does not find the problematic childhood behaviors associated with authoritarian child-rearing in the United States.

Research has revealed other noteworthy cultural differences in how parents communicate and teach children.[65] In the model emphasizing independence, parents most often use verbal instructions to influence their preschoolers, who are physically becoming more distant from them. Parents use verbal praise to encourage approved behavior; they also encourage preschoolers' verbal self-expression as a means of developing independent thought and curiosity. This verbal emphasis helps children in a culture where formal learning and schooling involve verbal instruction.

In groups stressing the interdependent model, parents rely on empathy and the close parent-child bond to instruct the growing child.[66] The parent gives little verbal instruction, because the child knows through empathy what the parent wants the child to do. Teaching in such groups often involves apprenticeship, in which the child stays close to the parent or other teacher, observes, and gradually takes on the behaviors of the teacher. Verbal interaction does not often occur; when it does, it usually consists of short directives to elicit a desired action. This tradition emphasizes respecting and following traditions, offering little encouragement or self-expression.

In the United States, one may well find a mixture of these two models in families. Parents may rely on empathy and the apprenticeship model to teach certain behaviors, such as kindness and sharing, but rely on verbal instruction to help children follow the rules and so forth.

TASKS AND CONCERNS OF PARENTS

Parenting tasks of earlier age periods continue and new behaviors are added. Parenting in this age period includes the following:

- Being a sensitive, responsive caregiver who provides feelings of security to the child
- Balancing acceptance of the child's individuality with control of his or her behavior
- Providing stimulating experiences with toys and people
- Helping children face challenges so they feel successful
- Serving as coach to foster the child's increasing competence in self-control and social relationships
- Helping the child to conform to rules outside the home
- Providing companionship and play

The preschool years can bring frustration for parents and children in many regards—eating, sleeping, night wetting. Problems at home can lead to trouble for the child in interactions with others. In this section, I emphasize behaviors at the extremes on the dimension of control: children's undercontrol in high activity level and aggressiveness, and their overcontrol and inhibition in dependence and fears.

Eating

Rare is the child who does not, at some time, experience some eating problems. Haim Ginott encourages parents to use the eating situation to provide children with choices.[67] By offering choices—between scrambled eggs and boiled eggs, between milk and orange juice, between hot and cold cereal—parents give the child less reason to refuse to eat. This approach gives children some power over their lives and encourages them to take responsibility for themselves. Ginott suggests that most food problems occur when a mother tries to get her child to eat more than the child needs to be well nourished. Provide a reasonable amount of healthy food, and the child has the responsibility to eat.

Gordon suggests that parents use active listening and mutual problem solving when dealing with eating problems.[68] Sometimes a child who demands a certain

THE JOYS OF PARENTING PRESCHOOL CHILDREN

"When she was four she was the only girl on an all-boy soccer team. Her mother thought she was signing her up for a coed team, but she was the only girl, and she enjoyed it and liked it even though she is not a natural athlete. She watched and learned and got good at it, and we got a lot of joy out of watching her." FATHER

"Well, every night we have a bedtime ritual of telling a story and singing to her. This is probably beyond the time she needs it, but we need it." MOTHER

"He's very inventive, and it's fun for both of us when he tells stories or figures out ways to communicate something he's learned or heard. When his mother had morning sickness, he heard the baby was in her tummy so he figured out the baby is making the morning sickness, pushing the food out." FATHER

"It's fun to get home in the evening; he comes running out and jumps up, which is really fun. It's a wonderful greeting." FATHER

"One of the delights that comes up is reading him stories, telling him the adventure of John Muir, at the four-year-old level. We were talking about places to go, and I said, 'Maybe we could go visit the home of John Muir.' He said, 'Oh, great, then I could go up there and have a cup of tea.' And I remembered I had told him a story about Muir's having tea in a blizzard, and he remembered that. He put that together, and it came out of nowhere. It knocked me over that he remembered that image." FATHER

"I enjoy her because I can talk to her; we have these wonderful conversations, and she can tell me about something that happened to her today at school that was really neat for her, and I just love to hear about it." MOTHER

"It's fun to hear him looking forward to doing things with us. He'll ask how many days until Saturday or Sunday because on those days I wait for him to get up before I have breakfast. Usually I'm up and gone before he gets up. He likes to come out and get up in my lap and share my breakfast, and it's a ritual. He looks forward to that and counts the days." FATHER

"She's really affectionate, always has been, but now out of nowhere, she'll tell you she loves you. She likes to do things with you, and when you give her special attention, one on one, she really likes it. We play games—Candy Land or Cinderella—or just one of us goes with her to the supermarket or to the park. We read stories every night and do some talking. Sometimes I put a record on and we dance." FATHER

food (for example, a piece of pie just before dinner) is really upset about something else. The request for food may be a request for attention or affection. If the parent senses this and can get the child to talk about it, what seemed like an unreasonable request may be forgotten as the child's real need is attended to. When a child refuses to eat necessary foods like vegetables, Gordon advises parent and child to sit down and figure out how the problem can be resolved. One little boy agreed that if his

"I miss this since the baby came, but we used to have special time together. We would go off and do things by ourselves. We would go driving in the car, go shopping, and have a lot of time to communicate, just the two of us. Four-and-a-half is a really wonderful, talkative, growing stage. She would talk about the stuff going on in her life, questions she has: 'Why does it rain?' We would sing songs she learns in school." MOTHER

"I like sharing in their joy and pride in what they do. I think it's fun to decorate the refrigerator with their work." MOTHER

"The time I like best with her is hanging out together, and she loves doing projects with me. She likes to help me with a project when I am working in the garage, and I'll show her how to use tools, and it's a special time with Dad." FATHER

"He's four, and he's so philosophical. He's always thinking about different things, and sometimes he'll tell me, and I am amazed. One day we were driving and he said, 'Can God see me riding here in the car?' Or one night at dinner, he was watching his little sister who's one, and he said, 'Do you think when she gets to be a big girl she'll remember what she did as a baby?' " MOTHER

"I like going for a walk with her, and we went skipping rocks at the reservoir. I was going to show her how to skip rocks because she had never seen that before. Of course, she wanted to try it, and I didn't think she was old enough to do it. I had found the best skipping rock; it was just perfect. I was going to hold her hand and do it with her. She said, 'No, I want to do it myself.' I thought, it is more important to just let it go. So I said, 'Here let me show you how.' So I showed her, and she said, 'No, I can do it.' She threw it and it skipped three times! The first time she ever threw one! She wanted to stay till she did it again, and we did a little; but it will be a while before she does that again, I think." FATHER

"I love it when they come and get in our bed with us and cuddle. As they get older, they do it less, but they still do." MOTHER

"It's fun watching preschoolers interact with other kids too when your friends come over with their children. It's fun to see how they respond to new kids or kids who don't come over that often. It's neat watching them get to know each other. They'll stand and look at each other for a few minutes. They don't have any of those built-in dislikes that grown-ups might have. They might be shy with each other because they don't know each other, but they don't dislike each other." FATHER

mother gave him vegetables that he liked he would be happy to eat them. Then they made a list of the child's favorite vegetables, and both felt the problem had been solved.

Rudolf Dreikurs, like Ginott, urges parents to be detached about children's eating.[69] Children are presented with healthy amounts of food at meals and permitted to eat what they like. At the end of dinner, the plate is removed, and no other food is served until the next meal. If the meal is dinner and the child must wait until morning, that is acceptable. In a few days children learn that all the food they get is served at mealtime and the problem is solved.

Dreikurs recognizes that taking food away is difficult for parents to do. Dreikurs says he is always surprised that parents who would not hesitate to spank a child recoil in horror at the idea of allowing the child to go to bed with hunger pangs. He believes that parents are more concerned about power than about food. They want the child to do as they say, and that control is what the child fights. When parents do not exert power, children eat.

The behaviorists recommend rewards to encourage good eating habits. When children have difficulty finishing their meals, parents tell them they can have dessert after they have finished what is on their plates. If children do not drop food on the floor or on themselves, they are given rewards to encourage neat eating habits. Several behaviorists advise parents to use praise. If a child is eating very little but is praised for that, eating becomes pleasurable. Praise and attention for eating will reward, and so increase, eating.

Eating is the child's responsibility. Gordon is active in modifying the situation so that the child will want to eat. Ginott and Dreikurs take a detached view. Behaviorists use praise and rewards. Both Gordon and Ginott, and Dreikurs to some extent, offer the child choices.

Sleeping

Many children in the preschool years develop nighttime fears about sleep. They are afraid to go to bed, afraid of monsters and eerie creatures who will come in the night. Offering a possible explanation for such fears, Richard Ferber says that as children get into bed and begin to relax, they have less control of their thoughts.[70] Their minds run free, and children may feel out of control. Even children who are confident and assertive in the daytime may experience night fears. Parents can practice active listening to understand the child's concerns. Ferber writes,

> So, your child does not need protection from monsters, she needs a better understanding of her own feelings and urges. She needs to know that nothing bad will happen if she soils, has a temper tantrum, or feels anger toward her brother or sister. At these times, she can be most reassured if she knows that you are in complete control yourself and of her and that you can and will protect her and keep her safe. If you can convince her that you will do this, then she will be able to relax. Your calm, firm, and loving assurance will do more to dispel goblins than will searches under the bed.[71]

Sometimes children will awake in the night crying and upset from scary dreams. If they have had a nightmare, they will be awake and can often tell parents about the dream. Though these dreams occur at night, they are related to conflicts, feelings, and stresses of the day. Nightmares are a part of growing up. They peak at about the time children enter school and again at ages nine through eleven. A child waking up from a nightmare is afraid and needs reassurance rather than logical arguments. A parent can remain with the child until he or she falls back to sleep, or perhaps can lie down with the child, but it is best not to make the latter practice a habit.

If nightmares occur frequently, parents can begin to examine what in the child's daylight hours is causing the trouble. There may be an adjustment to a new brother or sister, or a change to a new preschool group. Helping the child cope with stress during the day is the surest way to prevent nightmares.

It is important not to confuse nightmares with night terrors. In both cases the child awakes in the night, appearing very frightened. The causes for these two behaviors, however, differ. Nightmares are scary dreams that occur during light REM sleep, and they result in full awakening, often with the child's having some memory of the dream. The child will call and want comfort. Night terrors, however, occur during a partial awakening after a very deep state of sleep. Night terrors happen during the first few hours of sleep at night—about 1½ to 3 or 4 hours after the child goes to sleep—just as he is entering a light state of sleep. The child is not fully awake when he calls or cries. The cry may sound like a scream, and so the parents assume the child has had a nightmare. In this case, however, if a parent tries to hold the child, he pushes the parent away; comforting does not help. The child may drop back to sleep automatically and have no memory of the night terror the next day.

It is important to tell the difference between these two night occurrences, because the treatment is different for each. For nightmares, reassurance and comfort are the effective parental response. For night terrors, parents should not attempt to wake the child or offer comfort. Avoid interacting with the child unless she requests it, and let her fall back to sleep. If you believe it was a night terror, it is best not to make too much of it with the child, who may be frightened to hear how terrified and out of control she felt. Night terrors disappear as children get older.

Nighttime Wetting

Nighttime wetting is more common among boys than girls because the nervous system of boys matures more slowly. As we noted in Chapter 7, a genetic component is likely to be involved in primary or persistent enuresis in which the child has never gained control.[72] For this reason it is especially important to take an objective, nonblaming attitude toward enuresis and focus on how to deal with it. Gordon recommends I-messages and mutual problem solving; parents can present their reactions to the night wetting—saying that they don't like to get up and change sheets, that they don't like doing the extra laundry—and ask the child how he thinks he could help solve the problem. The child might volunteer not to drink liquids after dinner, go to the bathroom just before bed, and, if he wets the bed, wait until morning to have clean sheets.

Dreikurs suggests a detached attitude toward such undesirable habits as thumb sucking, nail biting, and night wetting. Parents must give encouragement yet remain unconcerned about the outcome. Scolding and punishment do not seem to help, and Dreikurs advises parents to turn the problem over to the child.

Behaviorists suggest that bed wetting can be controlled with rewards, a contracting system, and a learning program. Children may earn a gold star or a token for every dry night, and these can be exchanged for a privilege after so many are earned. At the time the contract goes into effect, however, parents must also encourage the child's overall responsibility, offering praise for other things done independently and making sure the child has age-appropriate chores that increase feelings of competence.

Various learning programs are available for dealing with bed wetting. Nathan Azrin and Victoria Besalel have developed a step-by-step program that actively involves the child. The child practices behavior that will enable him to become more sensitive to cues about bladder fullness and that links those cues with getting up and going to the bathroom. The procedure is described in their book, *A Parent's Guide to Bedwetting Control*.[73]

The methods just discussed rely on parents and children to work together to solve the problem. Two other strategies are possible—medication and a pad-and-buzzer system. The latter is a system that can be used in conjunction with the Azrin and Besalel technique. A special pad costing about $50 is placed under the child's sheet; as soon as it becomes wet, a buzzer goes off. This wakes the child, who then goes to the bathroom. This technique has proven effective for about 90 percent of children in one study.[74] Many parents, however, object to the method for several reasons. The buzzer wakes other people in the family. Parents have to get up and reset the buzzer when it goes off (sometimes more than once a night), so they lose sleep, especially if the method takes several weeks to train the child. The cost also discourages parents. Finally, children may become irritated with the buzzer and attempt to disconnect it. Nevertheless, parents may wish to try this before seeking any medication.

When bed wetting has proved resistant to other techniques and children suffer psychologically from it, parents may want to consult a pediatrician regarding medication to help the child control the problem.

Excessive Masturbation

For many years, parents discouraged masturbation, with threats that it would lead to insanity, illness, and other dire consequences. Physicians and mental health professionals now consider masturbation a natural occurrence that has no harmful physical effects. However, the ways in which parents handle their child's masturbation can help either prevent or produce harmful psychological effects.

Frances Ilg and Louise Ames describe two possible responses.[75] First, parents can punish the child and prohibit the activity. Second, they can ignore the masturbation. If it is excessive, parents can try to find out whether the child is unhappy or tense and can help the child deal with any underlying source of anxiety. If parents punish and criticize the child, the child may come to feel that he or she is evil for having sexual feelings. This can lead to difficulties at later ages, when the child may be unable to enjoy even approved sexual activity. In addition, children may feel so guilty that they cannot discuss any sexual activity or feelings with parents, even if they need help—for example, with infection or pregnancy.

Ginott is concerned only with prolonged masturbation because it prevents children from seeking pleasure in other ways. Children who masturbate excessively may be reluctant to seek friends or to play in the neighborhood. Like Ilg and Ames, Ginott recommends looking for possible sources of tension in the child's life and correcting them. When children feel loved and have opportunities to explore the world and achieve their goals, sexual self-stimulation will not be their main source of satisfaction.

Dreikurs believes that excessive masturbation results from not being part of a social group. If parents try to force children to stop masturbating, however, children may only become more resistant. Dreikurs recommends providing many opportunities for activities and feelings of competence.

Benjamin Spock says he has no moral objection to masturbation, but he does not want the child to masturbate in public view.[76] He advises what he terms gentle inhibition. Spock suggests that the parent should not frighten the child, but should say that masturbation is not polite or approved in general company. Masturbation should be done privately. Like other professionals, Spock believes that encouraging other activities is enough to end the problem.

Sibling Rivalry

In the last chapter, we examined problems that occur when a younger sibling is born. The older child feels jealousy and anger, as well as caring, warmth, and protectiveness. As children grow and become mobile and verbal, new kinds of problems arise.

In applying Ginott's principles to sibling rivalry, Adele Faber and Elaine Mazlish suggest that parents consider themselves negotiators in these situations.[77] They can recognize that each child's feelings are unique and justified and can accept the feelings without necessarily approving them. Parents need not feel they must settle the differences as long as neither child is in danger. A parent can always interrupt and say, "Hitting doesn't solve problems." If that fails to stop physical aggression, parents can step in and calmly separate the children.

Gordon advocates use of active listening. This enables children to express their feelings and grants them freedom to resolve differences. When children listen actively to each other, a climate is created in which children can work out their own problems. One mother whose children were four, six, and eight found that the children, including the four-year-old, devised rules that decreased fighting and name calling. The children were upset by verbal insults and decided they would try to send I-messages. If the situation became too heated, they would go to their rooms to cool off.

Dreikurs considers sibling rivalry in detail. He believes that parents can reduce the jealousy among children by making it clear to all that each child in the family is loved for his or her individual qualities and that it is not important whether one child does something better than another. Parents love each child. But a child's trust of that love can be diminished when parents use one sibling's behavior to humiliate another child—"Why can't you be more like Jimmy—he ate everything on his plate."

When siblings bicker or fight, Dreikurs recommends treating all children the same. They are all sent to their rooms if play becomes noisy. If one child complains about another, parents can react so that children feel a responsibility to live in peace. Parents can point out that a child who acts up today may only be trying to retaliate for an incident that happened yesterday. Misbehavior involves all children in the family, and they can learn to take care of each other. Cooperation can be fostered by taking children on family expeditions and having all the children play together. When they see that life is more fun when they cooperate and get along with each other, children learn to settle their differences.

Behaviorists also suggest that parents withdraw from the sibling fights but substitute rewards for cooperation as a way to increase positive interactions. Children will blossom when they hear praise for their good points. Once a fight breaks out, however, parents are encouraged to say as little as possible and to offer a reward for good behavior.

All these techniques are important, and parents must decide just which ones are most needed in a particular situation: helping children become aware of each other's feelings, increasing verbal communication, ignoring fights or administering punishments while making sure to reward positive interactions.

High Activity Levels

As the brain develops from birth to age three, a child's motor activity increases. From age three to nine, as the brain matures, the child's attention span increases, focusing improves, and motor activity decreases. The inability to inhibit motor behavior is, perhaps, the biggest single behavior problem in boys and often is identified as a problem in the preschool years. The child may always have been active, but when a great interest in activity continues after full learning is achieved in the toddler period and is accompanied by such other qualities as excessive restlessness, short attention span, and demanding behavior that permits no delay in gratification, problems arise. A child does not need to be classified as hyperactive to experience these problems. Children with high levels of activity still within the normal range are perceived negatively by preschool teachers, parents, and peers.[78] They are restless, fidgety, poorly controlled, and impulsive. They do not respond well to limits and are often seen as uncooperative and disobedient. With peers, they are outgoing and self-assertive, aggressive, competitive, and dominant.

These qualities persist, and children described in this way at ages three and four are viewed in similar ways at ages seven and seven and a half. This high activity level is also linked to poor performance on intellectual tests at age seven and a half.[79] Longitudinal data indicate that highly active preschool boys are likely to be competitive, sexually active men who lack intellectual interests.[80] High activity in girls was not as predictive of adult qualities.

Both mothers and fathers of highly active children possess qualities similar to those of their children.[81] They tend to be directive, intrusive, and rather authoritarian with children. They get into power struggles and competition with their children. Further, they appear hostile and unresponsive to the children's needs and interests. These qualities characterize mother-daughter, mother-son, father-daughter, and, to a lesser extent, father-son interactions. When fathers interact with highly active sons, they become more dramatic and seem to enjoy the challenge of their son's behavior, though they, too, get into power struggles.

Whether the behavior of highly active children produces these controlling qualities in parents or whether parents had these characteristics before the children became active is not known. Some evidence indicates that when hyperactive boys go on medication and their behavior changes, parents' behavior becomes less controlling.[82]

What can parents do? First, parents must get out of the vicious negative cycle that has been created. They must begin to spend some positive time with their children, enjoying them. Russell Barkley, an expert in this area, suggests that parents interrupt the cycle by spending at least 15 minutes per night doing what the child would like to do—playing a game, reading a story.[83] Parents are not to teach, direct, or criticize the child unless some extreme behavior occurs. Then, parents may use discipline as usual. This 15 minutes is to be a pleasant time in which the parent observes the child and plays with him or her as the child likes. Both parents do this each day.

At the same time, parents establish structure and daily routines in which the child takes an active role and puts to constructive use the high energy level that may otherwise be disruptive. The structure need not be rigid, but a general schedule of many daily activities will help a child. If, for example, the child has a simple breakfast that he or she can help fix — cereal, juice, toast — confidence and independence are encouraged, energy is consumed, and structure is accepted. The old saying "a place for everything and everything in its place" — especially toys and clothes — can be used to help a child participate in creating order in his or her life while using up excess energy. Parents can provide a chest or boxes for toys and child-height hooks and shelves for clothes.

Donald Meichenbaum and Joseph Goodman have found that impulsive children can be taught to guide their behavior and achieve greater control by using a form of self-instruction.[84] Parents show the child what they want done and at the same time talk about what they are doing. The child then acts and talks out loud to describe the actions — "First I take off my pajamas, then I hang them up, then I put on my shirt and pants." In a third step, the child can internalize these instructions and repeat the words silently. Since highly active boys like to be busy much of the time, fathers can be especially important figures in modeling this sequence of "say, then do" as they spend time with their active sons.

The behaviorists Robert Eimers and Robert Aitchison advise parents to be alert and consistent in providing rewards for positive behaviors.[85] Highly active children often feel rewarded by the attention they receive for misdeeds. "Try to catch the child being good," they suggest, and give rewards of praise and social approval. These seem to be more important than material rewards to active children.

Family rules should be simple, clear, and enforceable. When rules are broken, parents can use mild social disapproval delivered quickly. Each task the child is expected to perform should be broken down into simple easy steps that can be rewarded promptly.

To increase attention span, Eimers and Aitchison recommend helping children with puzzles and other games that require concentration. They urge parents to praise the child for completion of the task rather than for correctness. Children should have a place where they can play without distractions. Gradually, children can work at increasingly difficult games for longer periods of time.

Poorly coordinated active children benefit from opportunities to develop physical skills. Games that involve running, balancing, and gymnastic movements are helpful. Drawing and playing with Legos or other construction toys are activities that facilitate the development of fine motor coordination. Parents can stimulate interest by giving genuine praise for what the child does and with material rewards of food or other treats.

Because the highly active child is relatively difficult to live with and likely to get in trouble and receive social disapproval, parents must try to prevent the development of a poor self-concept — "I can't do anything right," "Nobody wants me around" — or a self-concept that reflects special privileges — "I am too much for anyone to handle," "I'm so active I don't have to go by the usual rules." Parents can sympathize that it is hard to have such a lot of energy without being able to control and enjoy it. When children harness their energy, they can accomplish a lot. The child who is rewarded for the things he or she does well and is given specific comments about behaviors that need changing can learn to deal with this high activity level. Because highly active children are sometimes aggressive, parents may also wish to consult the following section.

Aggression

Aggression has been defined as "an attitude of attack, as contrasted with passive withdrawal, which may or may not possess an element of hostility."[86] Aggressive behavior is of great concern to parents, and they are wise to deal with it promptly.[87] Other children do not like aggressive peers and reject them, so aggressive children have to deal with social as well as behavioral difficulties.

In handling aggressiveness, parents first want to do all they can to help children understand and regulate their feelings. Active listening, helping children identify what they are feeling under the anger—frustration, hurt, worry—is a start. Knowing the underlying problem that causes the aggression enables parents and children to arrive at effective solutions.

Parents can accept and discuss all aggressive feelings, but all strategists insist on firm limits for expressing anger physically. Ginott suggests such comments as "People are not for hitting; pillows are for hitting."[88] Gordon suggests I-messages such as "I cannot permit fighting because someone may get hurt."[89]

Dreikurs talks about the different meaning that aggression can have for children. One aggressive child may be motivated by a desire for attention, another may want power or revenge, a third may be feeling inadequate.[90] If parents can get the child to talk about how he or she is feeling, the parent and child can work together to resolve the difficulty. Dreikurs urges parents to focus on the purpose of the behavior, on what it will get the child (attention, power, revenge), not on the causes (jealousy, lack of confidence, or a feeling of being neglected).

The behaviorists have a variety of responses to aggressiveness. If children talk about fighting with peers, parents can remind them of the consequences of such fights. Children may then try to avoid those consequences. If fighting is occurring, parents can separate children and perhaps send them to separate rooms for a while. And parents can reward children when they play happily and cooperatively with other children.

At the same time that parents help children regulate aggressive feelings and control behavior, they find ways to promote the child's self-esteem. Pleasurable time spent with the child, positive emotional feedback that the child is important, and competence-building activities increase the child's self-esteem and decrease the likelihood of aggressive feelings.

Dependency

Though parents are usually more concerned about aggressiveness than social withdrawal, it too presents children with difficulties. It has less impact on parent-child relationships, however, and parents seem puzzled by it.[91] Ginott describes dependency in children as the result of overprotective parents. Such parents feed and dress the child and hover over the child long after other children are encouraged to take care of themselves. Overprotected children do not have a chance to grow and get to a sense of who they are and what they want. They have had little experience caring for themselves and so they are afraid to try. As a result, they continue to depend on the parent, who fosters dependency. A vicious cycle is set up, and parents need professional help if the dependency is too great.[92]

There is no hard-and-fast rule for determining whether parents encourage dependency. Do parents do things for the child that he or she could do alone? Do they rush to put on a sweater when the child could do it herself? Do they discourage the child from trying something new, like helping with the dishes, because they can do it faster?

It can be hard to know whether parents are appropriately careful or overprotective. Children mature at different rates, and there is no one age at which all children can do things independently. If other children are all doing more for themselves than the child in question, perhaps the parents are delaying the child's independence.

Such parents must try to figure out why they are protective and change their behavior accordingly. Do they do it to save time? Are they fearful that something might happen if the child acts alone? Is their fear realistic? Are they worried because what the child does is not perfect? Sometimes parents are overprotective because the child's dependence gives them a sense of importance. If a parent cannot determine the reason and such dependency continues, professional counseling is desirable.

To cope with the usual problems that children have in learning skills, Ginott recommends waiting patiently and making a calm comment that recognizes the difficulty — "It is hard to button your coat." Once such a comment is given, it makes no difference whether children succeed or fail. If they succeed, they know they have accomplished a difficult task, and if they fail, they know the parent understands that it was hard.

Gordon[93] states that when parents rely on solutions that draw on parental power to force children to conform, children in the early years become obedient, fearful, passive, and deny their own feelings. When adolescence comes and they feel they have more power, children frequently rebel with a vengeance, even though they are less mature than other children. When a family relies on mutual problem-solving techniques, children develop thinking skills and a sense of competence that carries over to other situations. With young children, parents may have to suggest many alternatives. But children can select acceptable answers, and gradually they learn to develop ideas.

Dreikurs[94] describes varying degrees of dependent behavior. At one extreme is the child who seeks attention by asking repeatedly for help with skills already learned. At the other is the child who has become so discouraged he or she has learned few skills and feels constantly inadequate and helpless. The remedy is "never do for a child what he can do for himself." The parent's effort does not serve the child, who is handicapped by the parent's attention, but instead serves the parent, who needs to demonstrate competence or is looking for meaning in his or her own life.

Behaviorists advocate reward for increasingly independent behaviors. Eimers and Aitchison[95] describe the case of Randy, three and a half, who was so tied to his mother that he refused to be out of her sight for more than a few minutes at a time. Initially, his mother had been pleased that Randy was so attached to her and liked being her little helper. She soon realized, however, that Randy was not at all interested in playing with other children. And her concern turned to worry when no amount of encouragement would get him away from her for more than a few minutes.

The mother handled the problem by rewarding her son for increasing his distance from her. At first she rewarded him with praise and social approval for staying in the next room for 5 minutes, then for 10 minutes. She gradually increased the amount of time and the distance he was away. Soon, she worked upstairs and he played downstairs. To get him out of the house and playing with others, she invited one child in to play and provided special food and games. She increased the number of children. One day, they invited him to play outside and he went along. At all stages, Randy's mother gave him praise, attention, and rewards. In time, he found that playing with friends was more fun than being with his mother, and the play itself was the reward.

Strategists agree about the cause of dependency — the parent's desire to be too involved in the child's activities. Ginott, Gordon, and Dreikurs all urge parents to stand back and let children take care of themselves. The behaviorists recommend rewarding independent behaviors until these become self-perpetuating. Parents who use this approach are active initially, but they soon stand back as the children become independent.

Children who are dependent and indecisive as preschoolers may continue on this path into elementary school.[96] Timid, tense boys have greater difficulty with intellectual problems. Anxious, inhibited girls have difficulties in interpersonal relations and may give in to others.

What can parents do to promote curiosity, creativity, and independence in their children? Give positive support of the child's exploratory behavior. Have and communicate confidence that what the child does or makes is valuable and worth attention, even if it is not perfect. Encourage the child's involvement in activities, and encourage the child to persist in an activity until he or she achieves the goal.

Fears

How can parents minimize the number of fears a child has? Some parents are sarcastic and critical, make fun of fears, or ridicule or punish children. These tactics do not decrease children's fear. Instead, they diminish self-esteem and make children more vulnerable. A model of confident, nonfearful behavior helps children handle fears. The model can be either a parent or another child who is not fearful. Learning nonfearful behavior occurs most easily in a happy atmosphere. An explanation of a frightening event — of a thunderstorm, for example — helps children understand what is happening and so helps to dispel their fears.

A newborn who is welcomed into a family that already includes a dog — even a Saint Bernard — will grow up unafraid of animals, which are an accepted part of the environment. If a child is afraid of animals, this fear can be overcome by exposing the child first to small, distant animals and gradually to closer, large animals. Visits to pet stores and later to a zoo can be fun and beneficial. Eventually, the child will be ready to play in a room where there is a small, friendly dog. And that experience will give the child a sense of control and confidence.

Many psychologists believe that children's greatest fear is fear of abandonment by parents. Parents should never threaten, even playfully, to leave the child. Parents are sometimes tempted, especially when out shopping, to tell the children that if they don't hurry they will be left behind. Ginott recommends against such statements because they "fan the flames" of the fantasy of being abandoned. If a parent must go away—for example, to the hospital or on a business trip—children should be prepared well in advance of the separation.

Doll play can be used very effectively to prepare a child for a parent's absence. Using dolls to take their roles, the child and the parent who is going away can enact the time of separation, the period of absence, and the parent's return. Tape-recorded messages from the parent for the child to listen to during the absence and pictures of the absent parent are also helpful.

The parent who makes careful preparation for even a short absence only to find that the child cries or is disconsolate anyway may find it wise to examine his or her feelings about being away from the child. Sometimes children seem to have built-in radar that makes them remarkably sensitive to even the unspoken feelings of those close to them. The child of an anxious parent may sense that anxiety and respond in kind.

Dreikurs considers separation anxiety the child's attempt to control the parent. He believes the best course is to ignore the fear. Parents must provide children with affection, love, and concern, but must not respond to fears. Because the fears often stem from feelings of helplessness, parents are encouraged to find opportunities for children to be more self-reliant and to win approval by cooperating with others.

Behaviorists handle separation fears and crying by finding ways of not reinforcing such behavior. They suggest that the mother should not stay home, because that rewards the crying. Parents should have a substitute caregiver they trust. Then they should leave and let the child settle down. To help the child adjust to baby-sitters, Wesley Becker recommends that the parents leave for brief periods at first, gradually staying away for longer periods.[97]

To reduce and eliminate fears, the behaviorists Eimers and Aitchison recommend that parents remain calm when the child is afraid and handle one specific fear at a time. Select a specific fear, like fear of dogs, to work on, even if the child has many. As one fear decreases, others may also, and a child can usually only deal with one problem at a time. Make gradual progress in small steps; do not arrange dramatic encounters with the feared object.[98]

Having the child observe other children, particularly friends, interacting with the feared object or situation also helps to reduce fears. Give praise and social approval for every approach to the feared object. Ignore statements about the fears, because that attention can be a reward. Instead, reward all positive statements the child makes that indicate an ability to handle the situation.

As children grow and perceive and experience more in life, they become aware of the many possible dangers that exist. Fears result from increasing awareness of such dangers. Mild fears and caution in new situations help children refrain from charging into potentially dangerous situations. When fears occur, as they do in the pre-school years, accept them as signs of the child's increasing maturity. Showing the child how to cope with fear and overcome it increases the child's competence and self-confidence.

The Difficult Child

Stanley Turecki, a New York psychiatrist, has developed a program for dealing with what he terms the "difficult child."[99] Alexander Thomas and Stella Chess have observed nine temperamental traits in young babies: activity level, distractibility, adaptability, negative mood, approach/withdrawal, intensity, regularity, sensory threshold, and persistence. On the basis of these traits they classified babies into three groups — easy babies (about 75 percent of the group), difficult babies (about 10 percent), and slow-to-adapt babies (about 15 percent). Other researchers, especially John Bates and his co-workers, have also identified infants with a difficult temperament.[100]

At the extreme, the difficult child is a highly active, distractible, intense child who finds it hard to adapt to change. This child generally has a negative mood and tends to withdraw from new situations. He or she tends to have a low-sensory threshold and to be bothered by stimuli other children would not notice. The difficult child often has an irregular schedule as well.

Though such a child is hard to raise, Turecki insists parents must accept that he or she is a normal child whose temperament creates the difficulty. Difficult children are not all alike. Some have few of the identifying characteristics; others have many in varying combinations. Although temperament is the problem, parents must nevertheless help the child live and function with it. In *The Difficult Child,* Turecki describes a program that combines sensitive, responsive, feeling-oriented techniques with behavioral modification procedures.

The first step in the program is a ten-day study period in which the parents familiarize themselves with their child's behavior and temperament and the link between the two. Parents make lists of the child's problem behaviors and the situations in which they occur, then they relate the child's problem behaviors to the child's temperamental traits. Having described the present situation in detail, parents work to regain adult authority in problem situations by changing their disciplinary techniques. Turecki has parents put their frustrations and irritations aside and adopt a neutral attitude that emphasizes thinking about the problem behavior episodes rather than simply expressing their feelings. Parents must first stand back and then react from a logical analysis that makes the child's behavior, not the child's or parent's mood or feelings, the focus of attention.

Parents question themselves when a problem arises: Is this behavior caused by temperament? Is it worth reacting to? Since parents of difficult children get into a vicious cycle with them, they tend to react to everything. Parents, however, must work together to arrive at the three or four behaviors they will focus on. When they see that a certain misbehavior is related to temperament, parents can openly label the behavior as a problem of temperament: "I know you are sensitive to the feel of certain clothes," "I know you don't always feel ready for bed at this time," "I know it's hard to listen and pay attention sometimes." Parents must then ask themselves whether it is worth intervening — Does it really matter whether the child wears the old or the new jeans? If an intervention is needed, Turecki prescribes many behavioral techniques: Intervene early; let the child cool off and calm down if necessary; prepare the child for changes; always get the child's attention when talking or giving directions. If punishment is needed, make it mild and quick.

A main thrust of Turecki's program is to help parents sympathize with the problems the difficult child experiences while still setting reasonable limits for the child.

Hostility is removed from disciplinary action, and both parents and child can focus on the behavior that needs controlling.

Turecki's approach helps parents understand their child and at the same time learn more effective ways to manage the child's behavior. Empathy with the child's problem produces not lack of discipline but more effective discipline. This program deals with all the common problems of difficult children and is unusual in addressing the needs of all family members—parents, child, and siblings.

PARENTS' EXPERIENCES

Parents feel stress as children resist routines, make demands, and invade parents' privacy.[101] Parents report greater stress when children are three than at the end of the first year of life. More important, as children get older, parents receive less outside support in coping with daily hassles, so overall life satisfaction decreases. Spouse, family members, and friends are major sources of support for parents, with mothers deriving more support from family, and fathers from friends. Still, those parents receiving the most support report the least stress.

Support helps parents be more effective. First, mothers who feel support are warmer, more understanding, and more willing to allow children independence in their activities.[102] Because more of mothers' needs are met, they can meet children's needs in positive ways. Also, mothers' greater well-being may color their views of their children and their feelings toward them. As noted in Chapter 3, when people are happy, they are more understanding and giving. When mothers have large social networks, children's cognitive and social development is advanced. Whether the large network itself exposes children to more experiences or whether mothers' sense of support enables them to promote development, we do not know.

Although these findings come from middle-class samples, similar results are obtained with lower-income families. Mothers who receive help with caring for children are less punitive in disciplining them—the greater the number of people who help, the more child-centered and less punitive the discipline.[103] Institutional support, like that from religious groups, also fosters a child-centered approach to parenting.[104]

All the evidence points to the importance of support for parents in every life circumstance. When children are older and parents are more experienced, the outside world offers less support. In fact, parents need more, and both they and their children benefit. With this outside help, parents feel better and children's development is enhanced.

MAIN POINTS

Preschoolers'

- increasing abilities enable them to explore the world more thoroughly
- expanding capacity to remember and think enables them to understand events and people more accurately

- greater language skills enable them to express their own points of view and learn from others
- more varied and advanced emotional reactions and understanding of emotions lead to greater self-control
- self-concept involves seeing themselves as active agents, having an unchanged sexual identity different from others in physical ways such as skin color, and being capable of evaluating their behavior by internal standards

Parenting in this period involves

- balancing acceptance of children and their individuality with control of their behavior
- giving reasons for rules in terms the child can understand
- looking for experiences that will expand the child's skills, such as contact with peers
- modeling controlled and sharing behaviors
- playing with children and sharing their enjoyment of life
- coaching children on how to handle their feelings and how to interact with others

In relationships with siblings, preschoolers

- are helpful and comforting but have hostile interactions about a third of the time
- tend to be aggressive when mothers are overcontrolling and intrusive
- tend to be prosocial when fathers are affectionate

In peer relationships, preschoolers

- want friendly interactions and dislike disruptive children
- learn social skills when parents coach them
- are warm and outgoing when they have secure attachments to parents and are withdrawn or aggressive when attachments are insecure

Parents in this stage

- must come to terms with their own emotional problems so they do not affect children's development
- are warmer and more giving when they have support from the community, relatives, and friendship networks

Problems discussed center on preschoolers'

- meeting physiological needs and getting control of bodily functions
- getting control of emotional reactions and behavior like fear and aggression

Joys include

- children's reasoning, increasing skills, and affection
- joint projects

EXERCISES

1. Interview parents (two couples) of preschoolers about their children's daily routines and their worries and pleasures regarding their children. What are the sources of stress and support for the parents? Are the stresses and supports similar in the two families?

2. In groups, recall early experiences of gender learning. (a) Did the teachings deal with activities, appearances, feelings? (b) Who was teaching you about gender-appropriate behavior—parents, sibling, peers, relatives, teachers? (c) Were you more likely to accept the teachings of adults or of peers? Make a group list of the kinds of experiences members had. (d) Are similar experiences occurring today?

3. In groups, recall early experiences with siblings. Was there much fighting? Did parents teach children how to get along? Did parents punish children for not getting along? What seems to make for the best relationships with siblings from group members' points of view? What roles do siblings play in your lives as you get older?

4. Watch Saturday morning television programs for children and decide how much time and what specific programs you, if you were parents, would permit your preschooler to watch. Justify your choices.

5. Interview three preschoolers about their joys in life. What do they like best to do? Do they get to do it as much as they want? How can parents make their lives happier? Are their requests reasonable? Do you think parents are aware of what makes their children happy?

ADDITIONAL READINGS

Eisenberg, Nancy. *The Caring Child.* Cambridge, MA: Harvard University Press, 1992.

Fraiberg, Selma. *The Magic Years.* New York: Scribner, 1959.

Galinsky, Ellen, and David, Judy. *The Preschool Years.* New York: Times Books, 1988.

Schacter, Robert, and McCauley, Carole Spearin. *When Your Child Is Afraid.* New York: Simon & Schuster, 1988.

Turecki, Stanley, and Tonner, Leslie. *The Difficult Child.* New York: Bantam, 1985.

THE ELEMENTARY
SCHOOL YEARS

C H A P T E R   9

The first day of school launches a child on a sea of opportunity to increase his or her competence. Additional stresses accompany the greater independence. How does a child manage in this expanded world away from the protection of the family? Parents' roles change dramatically as they encourage independence and continue to guide the child's behavior, but at the same time take on the task of interpreting the outside influences the child confronts. How do parents foster the child's development at school? How do they promote reliable habits and self-regulation? How do they help children deal with upsetting experiences and disappointments that lie beyond parental control?

The years from five to eleven are a time of expansion for children. They have learned the routines of living — eating, dressing, toileting — and can take care of many of their own needs. They can express themselves easily. Their world enlarges as they go off to school, meet new friends, and adjust to more demanding tasks. While they grow in competence, stress increases in their lives as well. Because they can now compare themselves to others and to external standards, they worry about their competence in many areas and feel vulnerable to embarrassment and feelings of inadequacy. Parents play a powerful role in helping children cope with these new demands.

PHYSICAL DEVELOPMENT

From ages five to ten, girls and boys have approximately the same height, weight, and general physical measurements. At five they are about 42 inches tall and weigh about 40 to 45 pounds. By age ten, they stand at about 52 inches and weigh about 75 to 80 pounds. In the elementary school years, children's coordination is well developed. They ride bikes, skate, swim, play team sports, draw, and play musical instruments. Nearly all the basic skills in the area of gross (running, skipping) and fine (cutting with scissors, drawing) motor coordination are laid down by age seven, and further development consists basically of refining these skills.

INTELLECTUAL DEVELOPMENT

Three major cognitive changes occur in the elementary school years.[1] First, children can reason generally. At about age seven, children become less focused on their own perceptions and more involved in the objective properties of what they observe. They can organize their perceptions and reason about a broader range of objects and situations. Because they also more easily adopt the other person's point of view, they can come to understand other people and their reactions better. At the end of this age period, around ten to twelve, thinking becomes more abstract and more closely resembles adults' ways of reasoning.

Second, children at this age can organize tasks and function more independently than before. They begin to be able to observe their own behavior and their thinking processes as well as set and pursue their own goals. Third, they acquire knowledge in an organized learning environment — school — that sets standards by which they and others evaluate their performance.

SCHOOL

School is a huge step forward in a child's life. The child learns new skills, meets new friends, and adjusts to a new group of adults who furnish new standards to meet. The school is a major force in both children's and parents' lives. In the next twelve years, children will spend almost as much time there as at home. Further, performance in school is not divorced from behavior in other areas of life. Children's success in school is related to such personal and social qualities as positive attachments to parents, the capacity for emotional regulation, and feelings of self-worth.

Characteristics of Parents and Home

As noted in Chapters 7 and 8, the amount of language spoken in the home, stimulating toys, and activities predict children's school achievement. Emotional qualities in the home are also related to school success. Children who have shared work and play activities with parents adjust more easily to school than do children who either resist or dominate parents.[2] When children have secure attachments to parents, they feel free to explore the world, and on all measures of cognitive functioning they are more advanced than children with insecure attachments.

Parents socialize their children for school. Their expectations regarding school achievement predict academic success more accurately than children's ability scores do. These expectations play a role from the start of school experience.[3] For example, one group of students in third and fifth grades, equal proportions of boys and girls, underestimated their abilities as measured by tests.[4] Basing their beliefs on their parents' views of them, they thought they were incompetent. Parents of such children inaccurately see them as less capable of academic success than they are; unfortunately, children see all too clearly their parents' assessments of their abilities. In school, such children attempt less challenging work, are less persistent, and as a result experience less success than do other children. Unfortunately, they avoid

WHAT I WISH I HAD KNOWN ABOUT THE ELEMENTARY SCHOOL YEARS

"I wish I'd known how much you need to be an advocate for your child with the school. When we grew up, our parents put us in public school and that was it. Then it was up to the teachers. Unless there was a discipline problem, parents did not get involved. Now, you have a lot more options, and the public schools aren't always great; so you realize how active you need to be in order to ensure a good education for your children.**"** MOTHER

"The main thing, I think, is how important temperament is. I knew about temperament, but I did not know how important it is to go with the child's temperament. My daughter was in one school that was very noncompetitive; that's a wonderful philosophy, but it wasn't right for her. She is very competitive, and in that atmosphere she did not do as well. So with the second child, we are going to be more careful to see that there is a good fit between her temperament and what she is doing.**"** FATHER

"I was surprised that even though the children are older, they take as much time as when they were younger; but you spend the time in different ways. I thought when they started school, I would have a little more time. Instead of giving them baths at night and rocking them, I supervise homework and argue about taking baths. Instead of taking them on Saturday to play in the park, I take them on a Brownie event. Knowing that things were going to take as much time would have made me less impatient in the beginning, and I would have planned better.**"** MOTHER

the very situations that would demonstrate their abilities. Conversely, when parents have positive expectations about children's achievement, children feel they have the ability and are more likely to do well because they are willing to work harder and persist until they meet the challenge.

Researchers have not determined how parents develop their expectations of children's abilities. Some have suggested that parents base it on initial school grades and school success.[5] If their child is retained in first grade, parents may alter their perceptions and consider the child incapable. Parents' definitions of success and how to achieve it relate, in part, to their ethnic backgrounds.[6] European-American parents tend to expect their children to achieve success through independent, self-assertive behavior. Because they believe that cognitive abilities, verbal skills, and creative abilities are important for success, they want teachers to focus on academic skills in the first grade. Children of such parents do well in school.

For some years, experts thought that the parents of minority students had lower aspirations for them, which in turn led to lower levels of achievement. Research shows, though, that African-American mothers and Hispanic-American mothers of elementary school children do greatly emphasize children's achievement.[7] They have high evaluations of their children's abilities and high expectations for their achievement in school. They want more homework, longer school days, and more competency testing than do European-American mothers.

"I learned that especially from five to eight, say, children are not as competent as they look. They really can't do a lot of things that on the surface you think they can. They have language, and they look like they're reasoning, and they look like their motor skills are okay. So you say, 'When you get up in the morning, I want you to make your cereal,' and they can't do it consistently. And so because we didn't know that with the first child, I think we made excessive demands on her, which led to her being a little harsher on herself. Now with the second one, if she can't tie her shoes by herself today, even though she could two weeks ago, we're more likely to say, 'Okay,' instead of, 'Well, you can tie your shoes; go ahead and do it.' If you give them a little help, it doesn't mean you are making babies of them; it means they have room to take it from there." FATHER

"I wish I'd known more about their abilities and work readiness. My daughter had some special needs in school. In preschool, she did well, although I could see there were immaturities in her drawings and writing, but she got lots of happy faces. I was misled by the positive comments they always wanted to make to her, and I thought she was doing better than she was. When she got to school, it came as quite a shock that she was having problems. With my son, I have been more on top, and I ask more questions about how he is really doing, because I want to get any special needs he has addressed. My advice to any parent is that, if at all possible, volunteer in your child's school. I gave up half a day's pay, and in my financial situation that was a real hardship. It is very, very important to keep a handle on not just what is happening educationally, but also who the peers are and what is going on." MOTHER

Parents who have immigrated to the United States from Asia and South America value cognitive skills but consider that noncognitive abilities like effort and self-management skills will lead to school success.[8] They want teachers to focus on how to do work neatly and carefully; they are uninterested in creative skills. If parents stress conformity and obedience excessively, though, their children do less well in school than do children whose parents stress independence and verbal skills.

In the United States, mothers see achievement as flowing from innate ability.[9] They see their job as supporting their children emotionally, and they put little pressure on them to achieve. In contrast, mothers in China and Japan feel that achievement flows from hard work and effort, and so they help children achieve the high standards they have set for them.

We have discussed the emotional qualities of the home and the types of parental support that lead to achievement. Family events like marital separation and divorce, parental abuse, and community violence, discussed in later chapters, all interfere with children's academic success.

Characteristics of Schools

Students' performance in school is maximized when teachers create a warm, supportive climate in the classroom, provide organization, and emphasize academic learning in focused lessons. Similarly, students perform best when their school is supportive and structured, promoting high expectations that they help children meet.[10] So, the characteristics of teachers and schools that promote learning resemble the family characteristics that increase learning.

Schools are structured so that girls' abilities are more valued than those of boys.[11] Girls tend to be less physical, more verbal, more responsive to auditory stimuli, and more able to concentrate on tasks as early as the preschool years. Though not all girls have these qualities, many do. Boys, on average, are more active and curious. They learn by doing, manipulating, seeing. They have greater difficulty concentrating. Given these gender differences, it is not surprising that boys are described as hyperactive three to five times more often than girls; boys are also more likely to have reading problems. Until schools are restructured, parents can expect boys to have more problems in school than do girls.

Though schools have traditionally favored learning through individual competition, research shows that cooperative learning in which students work as a group to learn material, may serve students better. In this approach, for example, a team member may learn a part of the material then teach it to other team members. Such cooperation results in children's learning as much as through individual work and competition; equally important, students like each other better as a result of the joint work.[12]

Characteristics of Students

Children who enter school with personal maturity adjust relatively easily. They can control their feelings, delay gratification, and respond in socially positive ways, which helps them profit from schooling.[13] Children who enter school with friends or who have a stable group of friends outside school also adjust relatively easily.[14]

Most children start school with positive beliefs about their abilities and capacities to learn. Children in first grade believe all children can learn and that all they need is effort — those who do best have worked the hardest.[15] As we saw earlier, some students respond to parents' inaccurate views and underestimate their own abilities, setting in motion a vicious cycle of disbelief in ability, less persistence and work, and poorer performance.

Helpless Feelings   Another group of students face difficulties in school. These children react strongly to any experience of failure or criticism.[16] When they fail a task or receive criticism, they feel bad, blame themselves, and see themselves as bad people who deserve punishment, even at young ages. They feel unworthy and inadequate, helpless to change the situation. Such children see failure as a sign they lack some innate quality. Because they believe that no amount of effort or hard work will lead to achievement, they abandon any attempts to improve. They avoid challenging tasks, and they give up at the first signs of difficulty. In contrast, those children who do persist see criticism or failure as signs to look for a different solution or ways to improve some aspect of their work. They feel good about what they have done and anticipate that others will appreciate their efforts as well.

Some training programs work to give helpless-feeling children new ways of looking at difficulties so they can surmount their helpless reactions and proceed with

Minority-group children learn what is distinctive about their culture and form a sense of identity.

learning.[17] Giving them strategies for goal-setting and interpreting failure in different ways, as well as encouraging these children to enjoy the process of learning rather than focusing on the achievements of learning, can reduce their feelings of helplessness. We shall talk about this further in a later section.

Culture   Children from different cultural backgrounds with different values may feel at a loss to achieve in what seems a strange environment.[18] They may be used to working in cooperative ways, focusing on the effects of objects on people, learning from traditions, obeying standards. The school atmosphere of competition, objective knowledge gained from reference books, and questioning teachers may require adjustment.

Despite the cultural differences, minority children share their mothers' enthusiasm for education. They enjoy school, feel good about themselves and their achievements, and expect to do well in the future. They work hard and are self-disciplined.[19]

While there are differences from the larger culture in minority students' level of achievement in the elementary years, these are minimal when social status is taken into account. Investigators do not understand why the high rates of failure and school dropout occur in the later years, when indicators at the fifth-grade level seem to predict future achievement for minority students. One speculation is that families may be so positive that they do not help children isolate those areas where they

INTERVIEW
with Barbara Keogh

Barbara K. Keogh is professor emeritus of educational psychology at the University of California at Los Angeles. Her research interests include the role of children's temperament in children's adjustment to school.

For many parents with children in the elementary school years, issues concerning school have a very great importance — how to get children ready for school on time, how to help them behave in school, how to get them to do schoolwork. You have done a great deal of research on children's temperament and school, and I think temperament plays a role in many children's adjustment.

It intrigued me when I started work in this area, a long time ago, that most of the work with temperament had been done with interactions in families, and yet when you think of the number of interactions that teachers have with children per hour, per day, in a classroom and add that up over the school year, temperament is an enormous potential influence.

When we began our research, we found that teachers have a very clear picture of what teachable children are like. One of the very important contributors to teachability is the stylistic variables or temperament variables that characterize children. Some children are easy to teach. They settle down better, they are not as active, they are not as intense, their mood is good, they adapt well, they like novelty, they are curious. All those things make teachers think, "Gee, I am a great teacher," when they have a whole classroom full of children with those characteristics.

So we are really operating on the assumption that children's experiences in school are influenced by individual variations in temperament. We have tried to document and understand the kind of impact these variations have on the teachers. We have used the concept of "goodness of fit" in a loose way.

I am convinced, and this is not a new idea, that teachers do not operate at random. They make decisions based on how they attribute the reasons for the behavior. They may think that active, distractible children are mischievous and need to be restricted and punished, and that children who are very slow to warm up or are withdrawn are lazy and uninterested. When we work with teachers and make them aware of temperamental characteristics, we get a very consistent response: "Oh, I never thought of that." Making teachers sensitive to temperament variations helps them reframe the child's behavior, and it makes the behavior much less upsetting to teachers.

need improvement. Inappropriate curriculum content seems a factor in lowering minority children's reading level and also may play a role in their later decrease in achievement.

The important point here is that minority elementary school students are as motivated and excited about learning as their peers in the majority culture are. So we have to look at the curriculum and teaching strategies that maximize students' abilities, because the present ones may interfere with learning.

It also carries planning implications. If you know a youngster is very distractible, very active, and very intense, then you can predict that every time you have a long wait in line, there's going to be a problem with him. It's predictable.

When teachers begin to think of the individual variations on a temperamental rather than motivational basis, they begin to manipulate the environment more effectively. Temperament helps teachers reframe the problem behavior so it is not viewed as purposeful. This is true for both temperamentally "difficult" and "slow to warm up" children.

Another example I like is that most of the youngsters in an elementary class are delighted by novelty. The teacher says, "Oh, we are going to have a wonderful surprise today. At ten o'clock the fire department is coming." Most of the kids are excited. There will be a few little "slow to warm up" youngsters who will say, "But at ten o'clock we are supposed to do our reading." They are upset because the usual routine is not followed. The teacher thinks, "What's the matter with that child? Why isn't he interested?" The child has a need for routine and a tendency to withdraw from newness or change. These children can profit from advance preparation. If they know a day in advance, they get a little forewarning.

Do you have any advice for parents as to how to help their children adjust to school?

Certainly parents have to be advocates for their child. That is absolutely necessary even if it means being confrontational, which is often not too productive. But certainly parents need to be aware when their child is unhappy at school, when their child is having problems, and address the problem with school people.

It has to be recognized that when we are working on a ratio of twenty-five youngsters to one teacher, there are going to be good matches and very poor matches in any class. In no sense does that demean the quality of the teacher or the nature of the child. But there are differences in style, and some styles match better than others.

One thing parents can do is to provide teachers with some recognition that their child might not be a good match for this classroom. It helps the teacher to know that the parents are aware of that. So they can direct their mutual efforts to modify the class so the demands are more reasonable, or they can give the child extra help in modifying his or her behavior so it is more compatible with what is going on in that class.

Do you feel most teachers are willing to change?

Yes, I do. We have worked with a lot of teachers in our research, and I think it helps them to think of ways that they can structure the situation so it is more compatible with the student without loss of educational goals. Yes, we have found teachers to be very open, and they were able to relate what we were saying to different children they have known: "Oh, yes, that's like Joey."

EMOTIONAL DEVELOPMENT

Elementary school children understand their feelings better than preschoolers do and realize that feelings depend, in part, on what led up to the event and how the event is interpreted.[20] For example, at ages six and seven, children are pleased with their success whether it comes from luck or effort. When they are nine and ten, children feel proud only if they believe their effort produced the success.

Children learn they can have opposite feelings about a person or event.[21] Memories of a previous interaction with a person can trigger one set of feelings while the current interaction triggers a different set. Not until about age ten do children realize they can feel both love and anger toward a person.

They also become increasingly skilled in understanding the difference between the appearance of emotions and the actual inner feeling of emotion.[22] They can talk about exactly how to hide feelings with words, but they have a much harder time changing facial expressions to hide their feelings.[23] Thus, a child's facial expression probably more accurately reflects his or her feelings than do the child's words.

Children are most likely to express their inner feelings when they are alone or with another when they believe that person will respond in a positive, understanding way.[24] Unfortunately, as children—particularly boys—grow older, they anticipate a less positive response from others, even from parents. Thus, older boys are much less likely to express their feelings than are girls or younger boys.

Children's ability to regulate their emotions appears related to temperamental qualities.[25] If emotional reactions are highly intense, children have difficulty modulating them and, as a result, become overwhelmed by them. If emotional intensity is in the mid-range, children can manage feelings better. Ability to regulate feelings at the age of four is related to early elementary school students' ability to sympathize with the plight of others and respond to them compassionately.

Common Feelings of Schoolchildren

Elementary school children reflect many common feelings, which parents must help them handle. Understanding the specific emotional tendencies of their children will help parents avoid misunderstandings and allow them to guide their children to emotional satisfaction and harmony in social settings.

Empathy   We have discussed the parental behaviors—nurturing, modeling, reasoning, and explaining the benefits of prosocial behavior—that create sympathy and helping behavior in children.

Because elementary school children's awareness of others' feelings have increased, they are better helpers and are more likely to offer social strategies rather than material ones to change distress when they see it in other people. When asked how to help distressed four- and five-year-olds, older children suggested giving verbal reassurance that the situation will pass, giving suggestions on how to solve the problem (such as advice on how to retrieve a lost object), or providing social activity to compensate for the unhappiness (having someone over to play, staying with a crying child).[26]

Children are most likely to help others when they feel happy, competent, and effective themselves. They are also most likely to help if they like the person and that person has helped them in the past. So, positive feelings about oneself and others lead to generosity at this age.[27]

Aggressiveness   Aggression decreases during this period. When it does occur, children usually express it verbally rather than physically.

Consistent individual differences emerge and are likely to persist over time. Further, aggressive children often have problems such as poor peer relations and difficulty in acquiring academic skills. From the toddler years, boys are more frequently aggressive than girls. This sex difference in aggression is seen in animal species and in cultures around the world. The reasons for it are complex. Because such differences appear early and consistently in so many cultures, they may well have a biological basis that is not specifically known at this time.

Gerald Patterson believes that family members train children to be aggressive by giving them inconsistent rewards for positive and negative behaviors.[28] Parents may laugh at mischievous defiance or allow children to escape rules or requests then children ignore them, refuse, yell, or use other coercive measures. Thus, children are more likely to refuse in the future because they know if they persist in refusing, parents will give in. At the same time, parents fail to train children for positive behaviors, so the children are aggressive and also socially unskilled.

Fearfulness   With age, children grow less fearful. Many of the fears of the preschool period — of animals, of the dark — decrease. Some specific ones remain, however — fear of snakes, of storms. These fears appear related to temperamental qualities involving general timidity. Up to age five, fears are equally prevalent in boys and girls, but beginning with the school-age years, sex differences increase. Fears and phobias are more prevalent in girls at all ages.

Loneliness   For a long time, social scientists thought that children could not experience loneliness prior to adolescence, when they became more separate from the family. Research, however, finds five- and six-year-old children have conceptions of loneliness as clear as those of adults.[29] They describe feelings of being sad and alone, having no one to play with. The remedy, they report, is to find a playmate. Older elementary school children give even more poignant descriptions of loneliness — "feeling unneeded," "like you're the only one on the moon," "always in the dark," "like you have no one that really likes you and you're all alone."

Extreme loneliness is related to lack of friends, shy and submissive behavior, and a tendency to attribute social failure to one's own internal inadequacies. Such loneliness, in turn, prevents the child from interacting with others and intensifies the problem.

Unhappiness   Parents and teachers described 10 to 12 percent of a representative sample of ten-year-olds as often appearing miserable, unhappy, tearful, or distressed.[30] The children themselves reported similar depressive feelings. Boys and girls were equally as likely to report such feelings.

Children around the world, regardless of sex or socioeconomic status, agree with each other on what is upsetting even more than the adults and children within the same culture do.[31] The loss of a parent is the most devastating occurrence, and the birth of a sibling the least upsetting. Parental fights are highly stressful. Children reveal their sensitivity in their distress at embarrassing situations — wetting their pants, being caught in a theft, being ridiculed in class. Although many students like school, it also causes them anxiety, frustration, and unhappiness, with many children worrying about grades, being retained, and making mistakes. Adults may be surprised at children's sensitivity to embarrassing situations and their concern about school. The data emphasize that children may have a perspective on life that may be quite different from that of their parents and often not immediately apparent to parents.

Daily journals of elementary school students in the United States reveal that boys are more likely to cite external situations and demands like school, chores, interruptions, and environmental factors as sources of stress.[32] Girls report disappointments with self and others and failure to live up to responsibilities as sources of stress in their lives.

Coping with Stress

In facing stress, children adapt in many ways. First, they use their own resources and the tools their parents give them. Second, they turn to trusted people for further support and guidance.

Strategies   When children ages six to twelve are asked how to handle stressful situations—like having a friend move away, going to the doctor's office for a shot, having a parent angry at them—their solutions generally attack the source of the problem to change the upsetting circumstances.[33] They are most likely to strike at the roots of the difficulty when the problem focuses on peers or school, where they feel they have more control.

Children tend to use distraction strategies to adjust to situations they cannot control, such as doctors' visits.[34] Children as young as five know that they can make themselves feel better if they get their mind off a problem or fear by turning to a fun activity. As children get older, they can distract themselves with mental fantasies or thinking of something fun to do.

Those children whose parents outwardly accept and comfort them tend to have a greater variety of strategies to use in confronting stressful situations. They rely on disengaging from situations in which they lack control.[35] Children also seek generally to buffer themselves from stress with enjoyable activities. Athletics, being at home with families, and special treats of food or surprises all help children feel good so they are better able to deal with stressors.[36]

Supportive People   When dealing with stressful or negative situations, children often seek out others to help them. Children "perceive mothers as being the best multipurpose social provider available, in contrast to friends and teachers, who are relatively specialized in their social value."[37] Friends provide companionship and emotional support second only to parents. Teachers provide information but little companionship. Fathers are excellent providers of information, but are generally less available for direct help. Figure 9-1 illustrates where children of different ages and ethnic groups seek support.[38] Until early adolescence, parents and extended family provide the primary sources of support. Extended family are more important for African-American and Hispanic-American children than for European Americans.

Parents play a powerful role in helping children cope with fears of tragic events and worries about school. Though parents cannot control the occurrence of these events, they can help children cope with them. Parents' interpretations of the events shape children's attitudes about difficulties and adversities. Recall Martin Seligman's views (described in Chapter 3) on the importance of teaching optimistic attitudes about life.[39] Optimistic attitudes motivate individuals to exert effort to get what they want.

FIGURE 9-1
CONVOYS OF SUPPORT

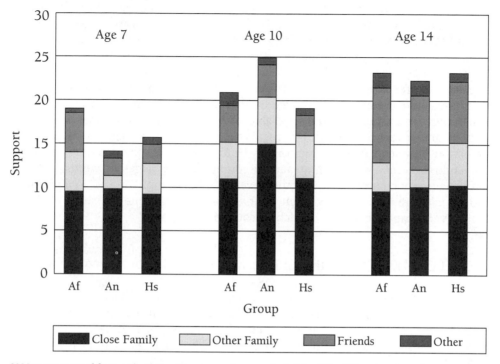

233Support received from each relationship category by age and ethnicity. (Af = African-American, An = Anglo/European-American, Hs = Hispanic-American.)

Mary J. Levitt, Nathalie Guacci-Franco, and Jerome L. Levitt, "Convoys of Social Support in Childhood and Early Adolescence: Structure and Function," *Developmental Psychology* 29 (1993), p. 815. Copyright © 1993 American Psychological Association. Reprinted with permission.

Seligman has documented the nature of pessimistic attitudes that lead to discouragement and withdrawal from challenging tasks. Pessimistic individuals consider difficulty a sign of a pervasive, permanent problem that is one's personal fault and is unchangeable. Pessimistic children see a poor math grade as the result of their own stupidity and inability to do math. They sometimes avoid studying because they are discouraged and feel they are no good at the subject.

As outlined in Chapter 3, parents can supply new interpretations of the problem. Perhaps the child did not study enough and that can be changed. If the child has a special difficulty with math, a tutor can be obtained. The teacher may have given a very hard exam or not allowed enough time. A child has no control over these factors but can deal with them by being overly prepared for the next test.

Parents can help their child to see that the outcome of any school or social event is determined by multiple causes, that the child never solely determines the events. Children must, however, work on those factors within their control. Parents can take the broad view over and over again to help children see that most situations can be improved with effort. Parents can also encourage children to use their time and energy selectively. When children have reached the maximum benefit of effort, parents can help them move on to other activities. For example, when a child feels rejected because she is not invited to a peer's birthday party, parents can suggest ways she might be a more outgoing friend. If new techniques do not work with that friend, the child needs to move on and make new friends to be happy. Parents should remain optimistic that children will either remedy a situation or find pleasure elsewhere.

Since children adapt their reasoning about difficulties from their parents' ways of reasoning, parents must be careful how they interpret events in their own lives. When they see a problem as unremediable and pervasive, they predispose their children to similar interpretations of events. When parents rely on derogatory criticism, no matter how accurate the criticism may be or how helpful the parent wants to be, the child becomes self-blaming and discouraged. The negative words — "You'll never have any common sense"; "You never learn anything. You just fool around"; "You don't care about anybody but yourself" — last a lifetime for some children, who never escape the impact of such discouraging messages.

DEVELOPMENT OF THE SELF

In elementary school, children become capable of integrating behaviors and forming a more balanced view of themselves that takes into account both positive and negative qualities.[40] They are no longer limited to thinking of themselves in extreme terms — instead of smart or dumb, they think of themselves as smart at some things and not so smart in others.

Children also begin to evaluate their behavior in comparison to their peers. In the early grades, comparisons may be overt and direct — "I can finish the work faster than you" — but as children grow older, comparisons become more subtle and indirect — "I have more friends than other girls in my class." With the ability to rank-order the performance of peers and compare it with their own, children become more vulnerable, because only the most competent ones will feel they are doing well, and many will feel they fall short.

Since children think of themselves in relatively general terms, they may let negative aspects of their behavior color their overall evaluations of themselves, or feelings of self-worth. Children over eight evaluate themselves in terms of four dimensions: (1) physical competence, (2) cognitive competence, (3) social competence with peers, and (4) overall feelings of self-worth.

Gender Roles

Psychologists used to think gender role development was largely completed in the preschool years. Studies of older children now reveal that a gender role develops over a long span of time and is never complete.[41] Stereotyped gender behavior peaks in the later preschool years, when children are rapidly acquiring gender knowledge. In the school years, children are more flexible in their preferences for activities, chores, and future careers, with girls being more flexible than boys. Children's tolerance of nonstereotypical activities in peers increases as well in the school years.

BOX 9-1
FOUR BASIC DIMENSIONS OF ETHNIC DIFFERENCES IN CHILDREN

1. An orientation toward group ties, interdependence, and sharing versus an orientation toward independence and competition
2. Active, achievement-oriented approach that changes a situation versus a passive fatalistic approach that insists on self-change to remedy the situation
3. Acceptance of, respect for, and belief in powerful authorities versus an egalitarian view that allows questioning of authority
4. Overtly expressive, spontaneous style versus an inhibited, formal style

Adapted from Mary Jane Rotheram-Borus and Jean S. Phinney, "Patterns of Social Expectations among Black and Mexican-American Children," *Child Development* 61 (1990): 543.

The most flexible and tolerant children come from families where parents and same-sex siblings are flexible in their activities. Same-sex peers also play an important role in promoting flexibility and tolerance.

Ethnic Identity

Children learn about their own ethnic identities in a process similar to that involved in gender identity.[42] First, children learn to identify their ethnic group (label themselves white, African American, Hispanic). This occurs in the preschool years for white and black children, and a little later on for other groups such as Asians. Children then learn what is distinctive about their own ethnic group. Children of all groups can do this by about age seven. Finally, again at about age seven, children learn ethnic consistency and constancy and realize they cannot change their ethnic identity.

In this period, minority group children learn what it means to be part of their culture. By age ten, they know their identity and prefer their own group. Mary Jane Rotheram-Borus and Jean Phinney suggest that children show ethnic differences on the four basic dimensions of behavior listed in Box 9-1.[43]

Though variations exist within groups, many studies find that Mexican-American children tend to be more group-oriented, eager to share and cooperate, and more adaptable to others' demands on them than either European- or African-American children. They rely on adult figures for advice and offer them great respect. If someone else is angry or aggressive toward them, be it child or adult, Mexican-American children feel sad and blame themselves. Compared with both European- and Mexican-American children, African-American children are more emotionally expressive, action-oriented, and assertive with peers. They too respect adults but, if scolded, apologize and do not feel bad about themselves. Little is known about how Asian-American children differ from the majority culture.

As they progress through elementary school, minority students become more attached to their cultural traditions, and the children with the highest self-esteem are most identified with their cultural behavior pattern, Still, some children identify with the majority culture. How this occurs and what it means for the child's well-being are not known.

Accuracy in Self-Perception

As children begin to compare themselves with other children, parents may want the comparisons to be accurate. However, evidence suggests that it is better to overrate your abilities and to see yourself more positively than objective tests or ratings might warrant. For example, children who overrate their abilities in school are more likely to respond to failure by getting help, finding out what they did wrong, and remedying the situation because it does not fit with their view of themselves.[44]

Albert Bandura, who has written on the importance of believing in one's own abilities to take effective action (self-efficacy), states that in hazardous situations, accuracy in self-perception of abilities is essential; for example, if you overestimate your ability to swim in heavy surf, you may not have a chance to correct the perception. In many nonhazardous situations, though, people prove more effective when they overrate their abilities.[45]

Life is full of problems; to overcome them, we have to persevere. People are most likely to persist when they believe in themselves. Optimistic views of the self, then, help people make the most of their talents. Young children appear naturally optimistic as they enter school and as they look ahead in life. Parents need to encourage and nurture this beneficial optimism.[46]

DEVELOPMENT OF SELF-REGULATION

To control behavior, children need to (1) monitor their own behavior, (2) compare their behavior with some standard or ideal, (3) then, when a discrepancy appears, modify their behavior to come as close to the standard as possible, and finally (4) develop new behaviors. In this area, we know the most about how children learn an internal standard with which they compare their behavior; we know the least about how they monitor themselves and how they go about modifying their behavior on their own, before the involvement of an adult.[47]

Children begin to learn simple family rules when they are about one year old. It is in the elementary school period, however, that they internalize family and social values — that is, make them part of their own internal system of thinking. Freud used the term *superego* to describe the internalized values that direct an individual's behavior. The child adopts the same-sex parent's values and beliefs, which then govern the child's conduct. Freud believed that the superego arouses pleasure or anxiety or guilt about possible actions, and these feelings permit or prevent the anticipated behavior.

Children can now distinguish between guilt (feeling you did something naughty, feeling very sorry, wanting to make amends, fearing others won't like you) and shame (feeling afraid of being laughed at, feeling embarrassed, wanting to run away).[48] Guilt comes when children feel they have broken a moral rule, whereas shame is related to both moral and social blunders.

By about the age of eight, children become more self-critical and their self-esteem is related to their ability to control verbal and physical aggression and other negative emotions. They feel ashamed when they violate a rule, and they take pride in being able to regulate their behavior and do what is approved. This is a good reason for parents' helping children to meet approved standards. Children do not feel good about themselves when they engage in behaviors they know others their age do not do.[49]

By the age of nine or ten, children can talk about how they use self-instructional plans to control anger, aggression, and other negative behavior to do what is correct. What works, though, varies with age. In one study, younger boys, age six or seven, were most able to delay behavior when they simply verbalized not doing the forbidden act. Older boys were more successful when they verbalized directing their attention elsewhere.

In describing why they follow household routines they do not like—brushing teeth, going to bed on time, doing chores—children between six and twelve initially focus on external rewards of approval or disapproval and the importance of following a rule. As they get older, they focus on more internal reasons—cleaning their room to find things more easily, going to bed to feel better the next day. So there is a progression from external reasons for self-control to internal ones.[50]

Children are most likely to develop a strong conscience when parents use low-power techniques of discipline and begin early to help children comply with the rules.[51] Early toddler compliance predicts conscience development six years later in elementary school years and supports Robert Emde's belief that moral development is based on early everyday disciplinary encounters between parent and child.

Boys and girls are equally concerned about issues of justice and fairness in interpersonal relations.[52] Lawrence Kohlberg describes three levels of moral reasoning.[53] At the earliest (premoral) level, individuals act to avoid punishments and gain pleasure or reward. They show little concern for the rights of others. At the second (conventional) level, individuals act to conform to the rules or regulations laid down by powerful authorities like parents or the law. At the most advanced (principled) level, individuals act to satisfy a set of internal standards of fairness and justice.

During the early elementary school years, until about age seven or eight, children reason at a premoral level and act to avoid punishments and gain rewards. By about age ten, conventional moral reasoning has developed, although premoral thinking still occurs. Very few children at this age display principled reasoning about moral problems. By the age of thirteen, a small percent rely on principled reasoning; conventional reasoning still prevails. Even at this age, however, many children still reason in terms of avoiding punishment and gaining rewards. Clearly, parents of elementary school children need to give praise and social recognition of approved acts and, at the very least, give punishments by ignoring disapproved acts.

SOCIAL DEVELOPMENT

In this period, children begin to spend more time away from home. While parents and home remain the center of life activities, friends begin to claim more of children's time.

Parent-Child Relationships

Parents spend half as much time with elementary school children and give them less physical affection, compared with preschoolers. Even so, parents enjoy parenting as much as in earlier years, and they report as much caring and regard for children as earlier.[54]

Parents' acceptance of, involvement in, and sensitivity to children's needs continue as major forces in helping children become responsible, competent, happy individuals. Parents are still the number one figures for schoolchildren, whose greatest fear is of losing their parents.

In these years parent-child relationships are related to both earlier and later behaviors.[55] Children who experienced positive attachments to parents in infancy and toddlerhood, versus those with insecure attachments, are more socially and personally competent at age ten. Individuals who had warm and affectionate relationships with parents at age five show strong psychological well-being at age forty-one; as adults, they are accomplished at work, feel less strain in their personal lives, and use many adaptive coping strategies. So, the quality of parent-child relationships have long-term impacts on later behaviors.

Because parents no longer have exclusive control of children, who spend several hours a day in school under the control of other adults, one can see changes in parent-child relationships. Specifically, parents tend to permit children to make decisions that the parents monitor, supervise, and approve. This coregulation or sharing of control with children serves as a bridge to the preadolescent and adolescent years when children will assume more control.[56]

Conflicts between parents and children center on children's interpersonal behavior with others (their fighting, teasing), children's personality characteristics (their irritability, stubbornness), and parents' regulating activities like TV watching, chores, bedtime, and curfews.[57] Parents tend to justify their point of view in terms of conventionality, practicality, and health issues. Children tend to listen to parents' rules that prevent harm and psychological damage to others. Children report that they have more conflicts with fathers than mothers. Rather than physical punishment, effective discipline involved removal of privileges.

In the elementary school period, mothers and fathers continue to relate to children in different ways.[58] Mothers take major responsibility for managing family tasks—scheduling homework and baths, for example. Mothers are both more directive with children and more positive in their reactions to them.

Fathers, though more generally neutral in affect, continue to engage in more physical play and give more affection to both boys and girls. When fathers have high-status jobs, they have less time to spend with their children, and so low job salience is related to men's playfulness and caregiving.[59] Men are most likely to be involved as fathers when mothers do not take on all the caregiving and managing, closing fathers out. Nevertheless, the more skillful the mothers are with children, the more skillful fathers become. Both parents are similar in being more demanding of boys than girls and more disapproving of boys' misbehavior.[60]

Though mothers and fathers have different roles, children see them as having many qualities in common.[61] Both parents are described as loving, happy, honest, responsible, self-confident individuals. Fathers are more interested in learning and creativity than mothers, and mothers are more concerned about others' feelings than fathers. Children describe themselves less positively than they describe their parents but still see many similarities with them. They are loving, happy, and interested in learning and creativity, but they are far below parents in self-confidence, co-operativeness, responsibility, and honesty. Children described "having good family relationships" as the most important family goal of mothers and themselves, but feel fathers' most valued goals are "educational/vocational."

When parents make demands on the child, social responsibility increases in boys, self-assertiveness in girls. Diana Baumrind suggests that parents actively encourage characteristics outside the usual gender stereotypes. Unless they exert a specific effort to encourage a broader range of characteristics, the natural tendencies for both mothers and fathers is to encourage assertiveness in boys and cooperation and a more dependent role in girls.[62]

Minority parents in this period intensify their efforts to socialize their children with regard to their racial or ethnic identity for several reasons. Children reason more logically and better understand parents' statements. In addition, they are more likely to have questions about ethnic identity because they spend increasing amounts of time away from the family in activities and with peers who may have different values. They may also experience prejudice or, at least, confusion at the different values other people hold.

Parents serve as a buffer between children and the larger society. As in so many areas, they interpret social experiences for their children and help them deal with them. To socialize children with regard to racial and ethnic issues, parents first teach children (1) their own cultural values, (2) the values of the majority culture, and (3) the realities of being a member of their own group in the majority culture and how people cope with the realities.[63] Successful socialization goes beyond this to teach pride in one's ethnic group and the importance of one's own self-development.

Box 9-2 shows the principal messages African-American parents use in socializing their children. We know more about the socialization process in this group than in any other minority sector, and studying African Americans might be instructive if other groups experience a similar process.[64] African-American parents think teaching about their racial identity is important, but not *the* most important information to pass on to children. To parents, being African American means children should learn how to deal with prejudice, feel pride and self-respect, learn the value of a good education, and recognize that their fair and moral behavior is not always reciprocated.

Many parents do not discuss ethnic issues with their children. In a national sample, over one-third of parents reported making no statements, and few of the two-thirds who reported making a statement touched on more than one area. Which parents are most likely to talk to their children? Older, married parents who live in racially mixed neighborhoods with a sizable white population are most likely to talk to children. Mothers are more likely to socialize children than are fathers. Parents living in the Northeast tend to discuss racial matters, perhaps because, as in mixed neighborhoods, there is more contact between the two races.

What do parents say to children? Only about 22 percent teach racial pride and a positive self-image, yet this is the area parents are most uniquely fitted to address. Both majority and minority children evaluate themselves the way others close to

◆
BOX 9-2
SOCIALIZATION MESSAGES
AFRICAN-AMERICAN PARENTS IMPART TO CHILDREN*

Message	% Parents
Achieving and working hard: *"Work hard and get a good education."*	22
Racial Pride: *"Be proud of being black."*	17
Themes of black heritage: *"Taught what happened in the past and how people coped."*	9
Focus on intergroup relations: *Summary category of many responses—accommodate whites,* *use collective action to help blacks*	9
Presence of racial restrictions and barriers: *"Blacks don't have the opportunities whites have."*	8
Good citizenship: *"Be honest, fair."*	7
Recognition and acceptance of racial background: *"Realize you are black."*	7
Fundamental equality of blacks and whites: *"Recognize all races as equal."*	6
Maintenance of a positive self-image: *"Instruct children to stay away from whites."*	5 3**

*Information from the National Survey of Black Americans, a representative national sample of 2,107 men and women. Statements tabulated from the answers to two questions: "In raising children, have you told them things to help them know what it is to be black?" and "What are the most important things you have said?"

**Remaining categories of 1 or 2 percent include a variety of responses having to do with emphasizing religious principles, discussing personal traits, and stressing general self-acceptance.

Michael C. Thornton, Linda M. Chatters, Robert Joseph Taylor, and Walter R. Allen, "Sociodemographic and Environmental Correlates of Racial Socialization by Black Parents," *Child Development* 61 (1990): 401–409.

them do; therefore, what parents convey strongly affects the children's self-esteem. Because a minority child may get inaccurate and negative messages from other children, the media, and authority figures like coaches or teachers, it is even more important for minority parents to encourage a positive self-image and racial pride. When parents emphasize awareness of social restrictions and barriers and at the same time encourage self-development and ethnic pride, children are happy, high in self-esteem, and successful in school.[65]

Sibling Relationships

The variety and intensity of feelings that marked sibling relationships in earlier years continue through elementary school.[66] Some children like to play with brothers and sisters, reporting they hardly ever fight. Others—almost equal in number—reported fighting all the time and rarely play together. One-third of children, when questioned, reported they would be happier without siblings. Despite all the criticisms, almost 75 percent of the group would like another sibling, perhaps because helpfulness and play occur more often than rivalry and hurt feelings.[67]

Sibling conflict has many causes, including temperamental factors.[68] When siblings are both highly active and emotionally intense, more negative behaviors occur between them. Maternal and paternal treatment of children is also related to the level of conflict between siblings. When mothers and fathers play favorites and respond to one child's needs but not the other's, conflict increases. Conversely, when parents meet all children's needs in responsive ways, positive interactions increase.[69] Finally, patterns of family functioning influence sibling interactions. When families discuss children's fights openly, accepting everyone's point of view and seeking mutually agreeable solutions, conflict decreases.[70]

Peers

In the elementary school years, children have more contact with peers, spending about 30 percent or more of their time with them in a wide variety of settings—school, sports, and interest groups with less adult supervision than before. Children are attracted to peers similar to themselves in interests and social behavior.[71] Relationships grow when children can express thoughts and feelings clearly and when interactions are positive. Friends negotiate so that both individuals' needs are met, and the relationship continues. Such experiences increase children's social competence as they learn to compromise and achieve solutions that balance individual and social goals.

When friends, compared with nonfriends, work on projects together, their interactions involve more smiles, laughter, and fun; even so, they stay task-focused and are more effective in their collaboration, perhaps because they know what to expect of each other.[72]

In these years children begin to compare their social behaviors with those of peers.[73] Some children are identified as popular and sought after as friends. These children are socially skilled and enter new activities or relationships in quiet ways, not drawing attention to themselves. Friendly, cooperative, sensitive to others' needs, and helpful, they rarely interfere with others' actions or plans.

Some children are rejected. This occurs mostly when they show aggressive behavior that disrupts the flow of activity or is verbally or physically hurtful to others. Rarely aware of their contribution to social difficulties, such children tend to blame others for their problems. A second group of children are rejected because of withdrawn behavior. Though peers do not notice this trait in the preschool years, in the school years they notice this deviant behavior and dislike it. Aware of rejection, withdrawn-rejected children feel incompetent and lonely.

Still another group comprise neglected children. They are neither accepted nor rejected, but overlooked. It is not clear why this happens, but these children do not appear to suffer the loneliness or dissatisfaction of withdrawn children.

Bullying is a new form of relationship that emerges in this age period.[74] The bully is an aggressive child with little control of aggressive impulses. He or she targets a single child or a small group and, though unprovoked, behaves aggressively toward the child. The bully pursues the victim and uses force in an unemotional way, divorced from conflict or disagreement. Victims are often anxious, insecure children who lack social skills and offer little resistance to the bully. Interestingly, victims often do not dislike bullies, as judged by their not naming them as disliked more often than they name other children. Bullying accounts for a significant amount of the aggression seen in peer groups in these years.

Although temperamental qualities such as emotional intensity or social inhibition may predispose children toward social difficulties, such relationships are not well understood at this time. It is clear that parents' beliefs and behavior are related to children's social competence.[75] When parents are warm and sensitive to children's feelings, child oriented, and authoritative using reasoning to induce cooperation, their children tend to be popular and skilled with peers. Because these parents believe social skills are learned, they coach children in how to express feelings and resolve problems. Aggressive-rejected children tend to come from homes where parents are either cold, harsh, and authoritarian or overly indulgent and permissive so children do not learn to control their own feelings. Less is known about the homes of withdrawn-rejected children, but researchers have suggested that the parents may be overly protective and controlling, so that children do not learn how to interact positively. Because parents of children with few social skills tend to believe that social competence is an inborn trait, they make less effort to teach children what they need to learn.

Children's social behaviors are related to other parental and home qualities as well. When one parent has a significant psychopathology, such as depression, or when the family faces stress from financial pressures or marital separation or divorce, children's social skills decrease.

Promoting social competence is important, because the ability to sustain friendships is related to later good adjustment, while early feelings of loneliness and rejection persist and are related to later adjustment difficulties.[76] Further, peer rejection in the early school years can influence a child's attitude about school and learning, thus introducing a multitude of problems.[77]

Although research on understanding and remedying peer rejection has emphasized the child's personal qualities and behavior, growing evidence indicates the peer group itself plays a role in children's acceptance or rejection.[78] Groups favor popular, friendly children and ignore any negative interactions they have but reject other children for similar behavior. Such groups also minimize the positive contributions of rejected children.

Additionally, peer groups favor children whose beliefs and behavior conform to approved patterns; they reject those who act different. Thus, children of ethnic groups with noticeably different appearance or behavior may be excluded because they do not engage in stereotypical behaviors.

TASKS AND CONCERNS OF PARENTS

Because elementary school children spend more time out of parents' direct care, parenting tasks include new activities as well as previous caregiving behaviors. In this age period, parenting tasks include the following:

- Being attentive, available, and responsive and modeling desired behavior
- Structuring the home environment so children meet school responsibilities
- Monitoring and guiding children's behavior from a distance
- Encouraging new skills, new activities, and growing interest in friends
- Participating in children's activities outside the home in supportive way (room parent, den leader)
- Serving as an interpreter of children's experiences in the larger social world
- Serving as children's advocate with authorities outside the home
- Sharing leisure activities and fun

As parents learn how to manage these tasks, they and their children face many concerns specific to this age. School is clearly a source of worry to children. Schoolwork is also a source of concern to parents, who pay great attention to promoting children's success in school. Other issues faced include isolation, aggression, lying and stealing, sibling rivalry, chores, and television watching.

Partnership of Families and Schools

In the past, people looked on the school as a separate entity that carried the primary responsibility for educating children. Parents played a secondary role—raising funds, volunteering in the school, and enriching the curriculum with their input and values. Recently, a partnership model of family and school relationships has been advanced.[79] Acknowledging the powerful impact of parents' involvement and encouragement on children's educational progress, the partnership model seeks to forge a strong link between parents and the schools. This model rests on six major kinds of involvement:

1. Parents are obligated to provide a home that allows children to (a) be healthy and attend school, (b) be calm and confident enough to pay attention in class and do their work, (c) receive encouragement to perform well, and (d) have home settings that support doing homework and educational projects. Schools can provide families with information on effective parenting and school-related issues; they may also provide supportive programs or workshops.

2. Schools are obligated to communicate and keep parents informed of school matters and students' progress and behavior. This involves notices of students' current performance, any difficulties that arise, and any noteworthy behaviors of students, as well as information on school programs,

THE JOYS OF PARENTING
ELEMENTARY SCHOOL CHILDREN

"I love watching them become little people who can take responsibility for chores, and also every now and then want to cook me dinner. Now they use the microwave; they can heat something up. They'll make tuna fish and raw vegetables." MOTHER

"It's really fun learning more about girls. She is a lot like her mother in her interests and her understanding of people. I wasn't a reader; I was out on my bike, and I really like that she is such a big reader and enjoys many of the books her mother had as a girl." FATHER

"This is the time when I can start instilling my values, why I do what I do, how people become homeless. When they were younger, you just had the rule, 'No play guns in the house,' and now you can talk about why you have the rule, and you are interacting on a whole new level." MOTHER

"He's nine, and for the last several months, maybe because I'm the Dad, he's come and said, 'Now there's this girl who's written me a note, what do I do?' Or, 'I have an interest here, how do I act?' I never heard any of this from my daughters. Then he says, 'What were you doing in the third grade? How would you deal with this when you were in the third grade?'" FATHER

"One of the joys is you are learning or relearning through your children, whether it's actual subject matter or reexperiencing things and seeing the way they handle something versus the way you did. It gives me insight into their independence that

school needs, and opportunities for parental involvement in projects. Parents must encourage students to bring these communications home. Effective communication also involves channels for parental input on programs.

3. Parents and other interested community members can volunteer in classrooms to promote children's educational progress. Schools can support this by arranging ways for working adults to participate in school programs. For instance, schools can vary program schedules and expand the kinds of participation possible for adults. For their part, families can find ways to contribute their special skills and knowledge to school programs — painting equipment, giving special lessons or presentations, introducing cultural practices of interest. Children can also find ways to meet school's needs by volunteering.

4. Teachers can help parents monitor and help children learn at home. Schools can make educational goals and curricula available, show parents how to assist their children, and even give joint assignments that parents and students carry out together. For example, parents can show children how to apply math skills in grocery shopping or purchasing a large appliance; students

they think of different solutions for things. There's always another way besides 'Mom's way." MOTHER

"Every night we have a talking time just before he goes to bed, either he and his Dad or he and I. He's a real deep thinker, and he likes to get advice or get a response, and he just needs that verbal connection. So a few years ago when he was five, he was talking about being afraid of death and that he might not be married and he might not have children and that would be the worst. I can hear parts of what he might hear at church or other places like school, and he takes it all very seriously; when it collides, he wants to know what the answer is. They are always things we don't know the answer to, either." MOTHER

"I enjoy the rituals we have developed. I don't know how it started, but every night we eat by candlelight. One lights the candles, and one turns down the dimmer, and it's a very nice touch after a day at work." MOTHER

"I can say as a father of two girls between five and ten that to be a father to girls is delightful. It's nice being looked on as a combination of God and Robert Redford. They have a little glow in their eyes when they look at Dad, and it's great. The younger one said, 'When I'm ticklish, you know why? Because I love you so much.'" FATHER

"He does well in school because he's willing to put in time on things. It is fun to work with him on projects. He wanted a Nintendo, and we said no because it is addictive and you spend too much time on it. He had a science fair project at school, and he decided to make up a questionnaire on how kids used their Nintendo, which he handed out to everyone. I helped him analyze the answers; and he proved the longer kids had it, the less they used it, and so it wasn't addictive. When his birthday came, we got it for him. He proved he was right." FATHER

may teach parents a history lesson they learned. In these and other ways, schools facilitate parents' education efforts.

5. Parents can participate in school organizations. Schools can encourage parents to join formal or informal groups that advise educators on school priorities, school improvement programs, and parents' and students' perceptions of problems in the school environment.

6. Finally, parents and schools can collaborate with the wider community to meet the needs of students and schools. This includes involving business organizations, local governmental agencies, and volunteer groups to form partnerships so that children's overall needs, such as outdoor exercise and play equipment, are met.

In the context of this school-family partnership, parents do many specific things at home to help children succeed at school. Parents can structure the home environment to promote school success. They can provide all the supplies needed, establish regular times and places for homework, and monitor homework. The parents of successful students also check homework for neatness and accuracy,

Most children have positive feelings toward little brothers and sisters, and at the end of a year, 62 percent say they want another brother or sister.

demonstrate the use of dictionaries and other resources, help with the homework as needed, and themselves read and study at home.[80]

Parents also serve as advocates for their children at school. In the course of their education most children confront academic or social difficulties requiring some form of parental intervention. A child may have a problem in learning a basic skill—reading, math, writing—or in paying attention or controlling overly social or aggressive behavior in class. In each case, parents would form a coalition with the teacher to find a solution. Sometimes, additional testing reveals a learning disability or a need for special instruction. Parents would then seek out additional professional help for the child.

Sometimes, a child has to work more consistently to complete assignments, pay attention, or control behavior. Having a daily or weekly contract that targets approved behaviors and the accompanying positive consequences can be helpful. For example, a student's school behavior is monitored in terms of completing homework, staying on task, and controlling classroom behavior during each period of the school day. If the student gets 75 percent positive checks in these three areas, then the student earns TV time. If target behaviors do not reflect realistic expectations for the child, the contract is unlikely to work.

On occasion, parents may believe that the teacher's and school's demands are unrealistic. Talking with the teacher, and perhaps the principal, to find a way to meet their needs in a more compatible way is useful. It is best for parents to resolve their differences with school authorities outside the child's presence and awareness, because witnessing parents' conflicts with teachers undermines the school's authority. At the same time, however, parents continue to pursue a solution to a real parent-teacher difference that affects the child's school progress.

The Isolated Child

If a child shows little interest in other people but has many activities that absorb his or her attention and seems happy, parents may not want to intervene. Activities, however, are sometimes used as substitutes for friends, and many children who do not have friends wish they did. There are two major reasons for not having friends, and they require somewhat different actions on the part of parents.

First, shy children who hesitate to reach out are uncertain what to say to other children, uncertain how to join in games, and worried about rejection. They are the neglected children mentioned previously. Other children do not dislike them, but rather overlook them. These children have to learn to be more friendly, outgoing, and confident with others. A second group of children are actively rejected. They often demand attention and are aggressive or disruptive with other children, wanting to direct the games and accusing others of being unfair to them. Underneath their outgoing, aggressive behavior, they may have the same feelings and worries as do shy children, but they handle them differently. They must learn to curb their aggressiveness, however, as well as learn friendly behaviors.

Helping shy children requires several actions, as seen in the example of a mother who used Haim Ginott's method. She discussed the problem with his teacher, who said she would involve him in more group activities.[81] The teacher also gave the mother a list of boys' names, so the mother could organize a group activity. After talking it over with her son, the mother started a bowling club. The club lasted only a week—at the first meeting, her son had the lowest score and refused to try again. A few days later, however, one of the boys invited him over to play, and a friendship began to grow.

As the mother observed her own and her son's behavior, she realized she had encouraged the boy to depend on her for companionship and had protected him from the rougher and more critical company of his older brother and father. She decided to give up her role as protector and to encourage a closer relationship between father and son. Thus, the mother modified her own behavior and at the same time increased the child's skills, just as a behaviorist would.

According to Thomas Gordon, the isolated child "owns" the problem with friends.[82] Parents can encourage these children to talk about this problem and can listen actively. As children talk about what is bothering them, they may find ways of solving their problems. But until then, or until the child asks for help, parents must accept isolation as the child's problem.

Rudolph Dreikurs also stresses the child's need to learn how to get along with other children and to accommodate his or her interests and activities to those of peers.[83] He believes that bashfulness and timidity may stem from overindulgence by parents. The child seeks attention and regard from others by doing nothing rather than by taking an active role. Parents can encourage positive interaction and ignore demands for attention. Although it may sound as if Dreikurs recommends doing very little, he does advise paying appropriate attention to children, playing games and working on projects with them, and encouraging them to participate in activities with other children.

More than other strategists, behaviorists have focused on ways of helping children make friends. Sherri Oden and Steven Asher have devised a system of coaching children in interpersonal skills.[84] They gave children verbal instructions about effective ways of interacting and provided opportunities to apply the rules in play sessions. Instructions covered four topics: (1) participating in group activities (getting started, paying attention to the game), (2) cooperating in play (sharing, taking turns), (3) communicating with the peer (talking or listening), and (4) validating and supporting the peer (giving attention and help). Benefits persisted, measurable a year later.

Parents can try to do this coaching as they observe their children's interactions with others. When parents comment later, in a calm way, on troubles that interfered with the child's having optimal fun and ask how such problems might have been avoided, they help to increase the child's social competence. The parents should not sound critical and interfering when making these remarks.

Philip Zimbardo and Shirley Radl offer many suggestions for the parent of the shy child. These measures focus on increasing the child's expressiveness (smiling, talking more), interactions with others (starting conversations), and opportunities for social contact.[85] All these actions are designed to increase self-esteem, confidence, and socially outgoing behavior. This behavior, along with coaching about group interactions, minimizes the likelihood of being bullied and enables the child to deal more effectively with bullies. Despite Gordon's and Dreikurs's belief that shyness is a child's problem, parents are advised to help their shy children develop social skills. Research suggests that shy behavior in the early grades persists into middle childhood. Because social competence is so important to children, being shy is related to feeling especially incompetent and lonely and to lacking feelings of self-worth; thus, these feelings persist along with the shyness.[85]

The Aggressive Child

Aggressiveness can take many forms. Children may physically hit or hurt others; they may be verbally assaultive, taunting, teasing, humiliating, threatening, or demanding. Many children are aggressive at home, at school, and with friends, but a sizable number are aggressive in only one setting.

When children show aggression at school, parents must sustain a detached attitude about tales of being picked on or discriminated against by peers. Parents must talk to teachers and principals to determine what really does happen at school. If children fail to see their part in provoking others' rejection, parents can go over events with them, after the children have cooled down, and present the other child's point of view. If children get in many fights at school or are very disruptive of others' play, a reward system can be set up with the teacher so that children earn privileges each day a positive report comes home. The teacher is involved and sends home a card with checks for all acceptable behavior in class, at recess, and at lunch. If children do not bring home the report at all, they lose TV or other privileges for that day. This procedure must be followed every day.

For the child who has developed many aggressive behaviors—hitting, yelling, teasing—and uses these negative behaviors in response to the parent's discipline, Gerald Patterson and his co-workers have developed an effective program parents can use.[87] Patterson describes the coercive, or forcing, process the child uses to try to get family members to do what he or she wants. To change these behaviors in the child, all family members must change. The program, developed at the Oregon Research Institute, involves an intake interview with the whole family. At this time, parents specify behaviors they wish to change. A trained team observes the family at home for two weeks to record and understand patterns of interaction in the family.

Parents then read either *Families*[88] or *Living with Children*,[89] books that introduce them to behavior modification techniques. After they pass a brief test on the ideas in the book, parents come in and pinpoint exactly the behaviors they wish to change. They are then trained in procedures for recording the behavior. In order to get an idea of exactly what is happening before interventions are made, parents record the occurrence of negative and positive behaviors before making any changes.

The parents and child draw up a contract. It is important that the child get points or tokens daily for behavior. For example, a child could accumulate 2 points for bed-making, 2 points for making a school lunch, 3 points for completing homework by a specific time, 2 points for picking up the bedroom, 1 point for brushing his teeth without being reminded. The child could use the points for an extra 30 minutes of TV watching (5 points), an extra story (2 points), an extra 30 minutes staying up in the evening (3 points). A child loses points for fighting with his siblings (2 points), or yelling at his parents (2 points). Parents deduct points without nagging, criticizing, or scolding. Each day, the points are added up and rewards given. Psychologists from the institute contact families at certain times to note their progress in changing their child's behavior.

The Oregon Research Institute treatment has the following effects: (1) significant and persistent changes in the child's behavior, (2) modest decrease in coercive behavior of all family members, (3) increased positive perception of the child by parents, (4) no further unconscious parental rewards for negative behavior, (5) more effective punishments, (6) a more active role by fathers in controlling children's behavior, and (7) mothers' perception of their whole family as happier.

Lying and Stealing

Ginott makes several basic points about lying.[90] First, lying may represent the child's basic hopes and fears and, in that sense, is an accurate statement of feelings although not an accurate statement of fact. This is particularly true of preschool children. When a parent knows a young child is lying, the parent can reflect the child's feelings: "You wish you owned a horse," or "You wish you were going to the zoo." Second, parents sometimes encourage lying about feelings. They punish a child who says she hates her sister or tells a relative she is ugly. The child learns it is best to lie about how she really feels. Parents are wiser to accept the child's feelings. They can also explain that polite refusal to comment is a way of being both kind and honest. There really are times when "if you can't say something nice, you shouldn't say anything at all."

Third, parents must avoid provoking a lie by asking an embarrassing question to which they already have the answer. For example, if a parent finds an overdue library book that the child has said he returned, the parent should not ask, "Did you return that book to the library?"

Dreikurs takes an understanding attitude toward lying and urges parents not to view it as a terrible act. If parents are not severe when children commit a misdeed, children will not be afraid and will not feel that they must always present themselves in the best possible light. When parents are truthful in their everyday lives, children are also likely to be truthful. When lying does occur, Dreikurs suggests parents remain unimpressed. Children may be lying to get attention or to win a power struggle and make the parents feel helpless.[91]

If a child lies and a parent does not know what to do, Dreikurs suggests that the parent think of what he or she should not do, and do anything else. The parent might point out how easy it is to fool a parent, and add that if the child needs to lie to feel important, the parent can take it. If this approach does not work, Dreikurs advises a game in which the parent demonstrates the importance of truthfulness in the family. In the game, all family members are free to say whatever they like, whether it is true or not. Mother may call a child for a meal that is not there or promise a movie but then say she did not mean it. A child may come to prefer the truth after such a game. When lying stems from a need to boost confidence, parents need to show approval and appreciation for positive behavior so that lying is not the only route to attention.

Like Dreikurs, the behaviorists urge parents to make telling the truth worthwhile. They illustrate how lying is rewarded in the following episode.[92] A young boy knocked over his mother's highly valued vase and broke it. Although he initially denied any knowledge about what had happened to the vase, a few days later he admitted he had broken it. His mother immediately restricted him to the house for the rest of the month, saying that would certainly teach him a lesson. From this incident, the boy learned he could avoid punishment if he lied and that if he told the truth he could get into trouble. The mother could have said that she was glad the boy had told the truth and asked him to contribute chore money to help pay for a new vase. If she had done that, her son would have learned that honesty is rewarded with respect and that he would have to help replace things he broke.

Like lying, stealing is not that uncommon among children. Ginott urges parents to remain calm and to insist that the child return the object or make restitution. If, as often happens, the child steals from the parent, the parent asks for return of the object or deducts the cost from the child's allowance. Children are expected to discuss their needs for money or possessions with parents. When stealing occurs, however, parents should not show anger, but instead express disappointment and hurt. As with lying, if parents know that a child has broken a rule, it is unwise to try to trap the child with questions like, "And where did you get this new whistle?" Once a parent has expressed frustration and upset, it is the child's responsibility to change his or her behavior.

Gordon recommends mutual problem solving, as in the following example. A father discovered that his five-year-old son was stealing loose change from the dresser. Father and son held a mutual problem-solving session. The father agreed to give the boy a small allowance, and the boy agreed to save for the special things he wanted. Dreikurs recommends taking a calm approach in which the child is not criticized or blamed, but helped to be honest.

Stealing results from a variety of motives. Often the child hopes "to put something over" on the adult and to get attention, power, or revenge. Often children do not know precisely why they steal. Calm insistence that articles be returned usually teaches the child not to steal again.

Sibling Rivalry

As children grow more skilled and competent in action and language, sibling rivalry takes on new dimensions with long-winded, teasing, or haranguing arguments. Parents can remember their own elementary school years, when they argued with siblings, and they may react to their children's fights and take sides on the basis of their feelings toward their own brothers and sisters. A mother using Ginott's system[93] could not help taking the side of her younger son against his brother, because she could recall how her older brother had dominated her. Her husband, however, remained detached. He reflected the anger between the two boys and suggested they go to their rooms and write down how the conflict started and what could be done to avoid similar arguments in the future.

Gordon's approach, of using mutual problem solving to eliminate the conflict, has research support. Mutual problem solving can eliminate conflicts between brothers and sisters. It also helps to strengthen relationships. When parents use Gordon's active listening and mutual problem-solving techniques, children receive equal amounts of attention and neither is favored.

Dreikurs believes that sibling rivalry occurs because children want attention from parents. When they realize that fighting doesn't work, they usually give it up. Dreikurs's unique contribution is his suggestion that when one child disrupts the family, all children should receive the same treatment. Charles, age eight, was a middle child between an achieving older brother and a well-behaved younger sister. He lied, stole, ruined furniture, and crayoned the walls. Dreikurs advised the mother to treat the children as a unit and make them all responsible for what Charles did.

The next time Charles crayoned on the walls, the mother asked all the children to clean the walls. Charles did not help, but he did not mark the walls again. He said it was no fun if the other children cleaned it up and his mother wasn't angry. When misbehavior no longer resulted in attention, the misbehavior stopped.

Behaviorists use rewards to promote acceptable behavior. In an illustrative incident, a mother offered her older son a trip to the store for an ice-cream cone if he could get along with his sister all afternoon.[94] When the children began quarreling, the mother reminded the boy of their agreement. He was unhappy, but he didn't say anything. The mother maintained the calm, detached attitude that Dreikurs recommends.

Chores

In every home, chores must be done. Children who help out contribute to the well-being of the whole family. Simultaneously, these responsibilities contribute to the psychological development of children—their competence and feelings of independence increase as they participate in activities that are necessary and useful to all. Children who help with family chores learn what is required to run a household, skills they will need as independent adults. When families share in planning and executing household tasks, they learn about each other's special strengths as workers, and they come to rely on each other. Thus, working together brings a special closeness not achieved in other activities.

Gordon recommends that when a parent needs help from a child, the parent should send I-messages that state the need clearly, and then parent and child should engage in mutual problem solving to decide exactly how the chores can be completed. Behaviorists establish a more formal system. They suggest listing all the jobs that need completing, parceling them out among family members, writing a formal contract, and posting a chart of everyone's jobs. It is difficult to establish a general timetable for including children in family chores. Dreikurs believes they can be included very early, as young as eighteen months to two years. Some families wait until children are older, between five and eight.

Television

"Television and other media occupy more time than any other activity except sleeping."[95] Infants react to what they see and hear on TV; toddlers attend to and imitate what they see. Viewing increases through the preschool years, so that by late childhood, children watch TV 3 to 4 hours a day. Viewing decreases in adolescence. Though television joins the family, school, and church as a major socializing influence, it is the only such influence that is primarily a commercial enterprise.

The exact impact of television depends on the characteristics of the viewer, the amount of viewing time, the general family and social circumstances, and, most importantly, the content of the programs. While educators have been concerned that television decreases cognitive skills and academic achievement, the effects of TV depend on the nature of the programs watched. When children watch educational programs, they can learn literacy and number skills and can increase their knowledge of science and history. Important for children in all income groups, educational programs especially serve children whose families have limited educational resources.

Television can also change social attitudes by breaking down social stereotypes and providing models of positive social actions. The day after Fonzie got a library card on *Happy Days,* the number of children applying for library cards increased fivefold.[96] Television, however, most often "presents a social world emphasizing violence, frightening events, and somewhat impersonal and casual sex."[97] Watching violent programs is consistently related to aggressive attitudes and behavior, and predicts antisocial behavior in adulthood. There is a bidirectional influence here, because measures of early aggressive behavior predict viewing violent programming. Since sexuality is not frequently discussed, it is not clear how television's presentation of sex as casual recreational activity affects children's developing sexual atti-

Television becomes an enriching family experience when parents and children watch quality programs together and then discuss the program.

tudes and behavior. One suspects such TV messages do have an impact, for they may fill the void resulting from lack of discussion.

The passive nature of TV watching concerns social scientists; however, it does require mental effort to understand and process programs. Still, watching TV appears to decrease creativity and to color the nature of daydreaming. Viewing educational programs is associated with positive themes in daydreams, and viewing aggressive programming with aggressive daydreams.

In general, little research has examined new technologies like computers and the Internet, but reviewers summarize their contributions as follows:

> The new technologies, like television itself, have been exploited to deliver entertainment of questionable taste and value at considerable cost to children and profit to the industry. The vast educational and prosocial potentials of the media have been touched, sampled, proved valuable, but not yet developed to even a fraction of that potential.[98]

Television viewing is inversely related to social background. Families with more education and more income watch less television, perhaps because they have income to pursue other activities.[99] When social status is controlled, European Americans watch less TV than do African Americans or Hispanic Americans. Hispanic Americans watch significant amounts, perhaps as a way to improve English and understand U.S. culture.

Television viewing needs to be considered in light of family and social contact. Children's viewing appears less related to the child's developmental/cognitive level or other personal qualities than to the family context and daily routines — how much parents watch, TV habits of older and younger siblings, preschool or attendance, mother's work schedule.[100] Families socialize young children's television use early on; by the age of three or four, a child's consistent patterns are established.

Television, in turn, affects family life. Studies found that when they are not watching TV, family members talk more to each other and engage in more stimulating activities.[101] When they are watching television, family members are in close physical proximity and are more relaxed. An interesting finding is that adolescents who watch TV with families report feeling better during time spent with their families than during time spent with their friends.

Heavy television viewing has negative effects. The more television adults watch, the worse they report they feel; yet they do not give up the habit. "One of the few consistent findings cited across many studies was that children who used television heavily, especially violent programming, had more difficulties in impulse control, task perseverance, and delay of gratification."[102] Further, heavy TV use deprives children of time they could be spending in more active pursuits like sports, studying, or interacting with other people.

How can parents get the educational benefits of television while minimizing the difficulties?[103] Parental example is the most significant way parents influence children's TV use. Parents provide a model of how to use television for education, discussion, and relaxation. In addition, children also view parents' TV choices so, from the beginning, the content of parents' selections influences their children. Second, parents can monitor the amount of time children watch and encourage educational programs. Third, parents can watch programs with their children and make TV viewing a social occasion by discussing the content of what they see.

Further, parents can take actions in the community. They can lobby to have television stations follow the guidelines of the Television Violence Act of 1990 and the Children's Educational Television Act of 1990. Finally, parents can lobby schools to teach critical viewing skills. Schools in Canada and Europe have organized media literacy training for all students, and some require students to pass a media literacy test.

Aimee Dorr and Beth Rabin suggest that, in addition to these direct interventions, parents organize the household and children's activities around other interests and pursuits.[104] They believe that emphasizing other activities may be a more successful way to curb TV use than regulating the amount of time children watch. They also recommend that parents become active socializers of their children, promoting a core of values that children internalize and rely on to counteract the messages that TV provides.

PARENTS' EXPERIENCES

Children's entrance into school marks a new stage in parenthood. Children spend more time away from their parents in school and with peers. They are absorbing new information and are exposed to new values. Ellen Galinsky describes this parental stage as the *interpretive stage*.[105] Parents share facts and information about the world, teach values, and guide children's behavior in certain directions. They decide how they will handle the child's greater independence and involvement with people who may not share similar values.

At this point, parents have a more realistic view of themselves as parents than before and a greater understanding of their children as individuals. Parents have been through the sleepless nights and crying of infancy, the temper tantrums of the toddler, and the instruction of their children in basic routines and habits. They have a sense of how they and their child will react in any given situation. Though some have a very negative view of themselves as parents, most have developed a sense of their strengths and difficulties and a confidence that, by and large, they and their children are okay. Children, however, leave the parents' control and enter a structured environment with rules and regulations. Children are evaluated in terms of their ability to control their behavior and learn skills that will help them as adults. For the first time, external standards and grades compare children with each other. Parents must deal with, and help their children deal with, these external evaluations, which may differ from those parents have formed at home.

For parents, bridging the gap between the way they treat their children and the way their children are treated by teachers, group leaders, and peers may be a constant struggle. Parents will develop strategies for dealing with teachers who may not see the child as they do, with doctors, and with principals. An attitude that stresses cooperation among adults seems most effective. When parents share their knowledge about their child, when they seek to understand the child's behavior that demands change, they can form a coalition with adults outside the home to produce a positive experience for their child.

In the process of explaining the world and people's behavior, parents refine their beliefs and values, discarding some and adding others. Children often prompt changes when they discover inconsistencies and hypocrisies in what parents say. If lying is bad, why do parents tell relatives they are busy when they are not? If parents care about the world and want to make it a safer place, why are they not doing something to make it safe? In the process of answering these questions, parents grow as well as children.

MAIN POINTS

Children's competence increases, and by the end of this period, they have

- acquired all the basic skills in gross and fine motor coordination
- developed more logical thinking abilities so that they can grasp the relations between objects
- learned greater understanding of their own and others' emotional reactions
- gained greater control of their aggressiveness and become less fearful
- learned to remedy situations they control and adjust to situations others control
- come to value themselves for their physical, intellectual, and social competence, developing an overall sense of self-worth

Schools

- are the main socializing force outside the family
- create stress in children's lives because children worry about making mistakes, being ridiculed, and failing

- promote learning when they provide a calm, controlled environment and teachers are gentle disciplinarians with high expectations for students
- often do not reward the values of ethnic groups that emphasize cooperation and sharing among its members
- are highly valued by many ethnic group members who wish their children to spend more time there, do more homework, and have more proficiency tests
- provide opportunities for social experiences

Regarding peers, children

- interact in an egalitarian, give-and-take fashion
- prefer those who are outgoing and supportive of other children
- interact more effectively when parents have been affectionate, warm, and accepting with them and less effectively when there is stress in the family

Parenting tasks in this period include

- monitoring and guiding children from a distance as children move into new activities on their own
- interacting in a warm, accepting, yet firm manner when children are present
- strengthening children's abilities to monitor their own behavior and develop new skills
- structuring the home environment so the child can meet school responsibilities
- serving as an advocate for the child in activities outside the home—for example, with schools, with sports teams, in organized activities
- providing opportunities for children to develop new skills and positive identities

Television

- benefits us by giving information, changing attitudes, and creating positive feelings
- can reinforce negative social stereotypes and takes time from growth-enhancing activities
- yields benefits when parents regulate and monitor its use

In Galinsky's interpretive stage, parents

- have achieved greater understanding of themselves as parents and of their children
- develop strategies for helping children cope with new authorities like teachers and coaches

Problems discussed center on

- helping children meet school responsibilities
- dealing with social problems such as social isolation
- changing rule-breaking behavior such as lying

Parents' joys include

- observing increasing motor, cognitive, and social skills in children
- reexperiencing their own childhood pleasure through their child's experience

EXERCISES

1. Break into small groups of four or five persons each. Take turns recalling (a) how your parents prepared you for school, (b) how you felt the first days you can remember, (c) what your early experiences were, (d) how confident or shaky you felt about your abilities. Then, identify ways parents and teachers could have helped more. Share your group's experiences with the class and come up with recommendations for parents and teachers.

2. In small groups, take turns recalling the pleasurable events you experienced during the years from five to ten. Then come up with a class list of twenty common pleasurable events for that period.

3. Take the list of twenty pleasurable events developed in Exercise 2 and rate each event on a scale of 1 to 7, with 1 being least pleasurable and 7 being most pleasurable, as you would have when you were a child of nine or ten. What are the most pleasurable events? How do parents contribute to them? (Recall from Chapter 3 that children six to fifteen saw friends as major sources of pleasure and parents as major sources of frustration.)

4. In small groups, recall the fears you had as a child from five to ten. How could parents or teachers have helped you cope with those fears?

5. Divide into small groups and discuss major activities that built sources of self-esteem in this period. Were these athletic activities? group activities like Scouts or Brownies? school activities? Come up with recommendations for parents as to the kinds of activities children find most confidence building.

ADDITIONAL READINGS

Armstrong, Thomas. *Awakening Your Child's Natural Genius.* Los Angeles: Jeremy T. Tarcher, 1991.

Blechman, Elaine A. *Solving Child Behavior Problems at Home and at School.* Champaign, IL: Research Press, 1985.

Damon, William. *The Moral Child.* New York: Free Press, 1988.

Dunn, Judy, *Sisters and Brothers.* Cambridge, MA: Harvard University Press, 1985.

Seligman, Martin E. P. *The Optimistic Child.* New York: Houghton Mifflin, 1995.

EARLY ADOLESCENCE: THE YEARS FROM ELEVEN TO FIFTEEN

C H A P T E R   10

Parents encounter many challenges during the time their children experience the physical and psychological changes that launch them into adulthood. Changes in physical form, in ways of thinking, in time spent away from parents, in school settings, and in the importance of peers all demand adaptation from both parents and teenagers. And in the midst of this change, parents must support early adolescents as they search for their own identity. How do parents maintain close relationships while teenagers are pulling away? How do minority parents help their teenagers deal with the specific problems minority youth confront while establishing their identity? How do parents grant autonomy while continuing to monitor their children's behavior? How do teenagers balance parents' demands with pressure from peers?

The early adolescent years of eleven to fifteen include many changes and transitions for children. Leaving the childhood years of stable growth, children experience all the stresses of rapid physical growth, a changing hormonal system, and physical development that results in sexual and reproductive maturity. Thinking matures as well; as a result, they may brood about situations and feelings in new ways. Most early adolescents enter the more demanding and less supportive environment of junior high school. Peer relations take on a new importance and provide both great pleasure and stress.

Throughout such change, early teenagers seek a stable sense of identity—who they are, what goals they will pursue. They question parents' authority and argue their own points of view. Parents have to find ways to encourage independence and self-esteem, helping children become more competent; yet parents must continue to monitor the teenagers' behavior and not permit so much freedom that children get into trouble they cannot handle. Though taxing for parents, this is an exciting time to watch children blossom as they take their first steps out of childhood into a new life.

**WHAT I WISH I HAD KNOWN
ABOUT EARLY ADOLESCENCE**

"They seem to get caught up in fads in junior high. They do certain things to the max to be part of the crowd. I wish I'd known how to handle that. At what point are these fads okay, because it's important to identify with your peer group, and at what point do you say no? If they are really dangerous, then it's easy; but with a lot of them, it's a gray area, and I wish I'd known what to do better." FATHER

"I wish I had realized that she needed more structure and control. Because she had always been a good student and done her work, I thought I could trust her to manage the school tasks without my checking. But she lost interest in school, and I learned only very gradually that I had to be more of a monitor with her work than I had been in the past." MOTHER

"I wish I had known more about mood swings. When the girls became thirteen, they each got moody for a while, and I stopped taking it personally. I just relaxed. The youngest one said, 'Do I have to go through that? Can't I just skip that?' Sure enough, when she became thirteen, she was moody too." MOTHER

"I wish I'd known how to help the boys get along a little better. They have real fights at times, and while they have a lot of fun together and help each other out, I wish I knew how to cut down on the fighting." FATHER

"I wish I knew what to expect. They are all so different, and they don't necessarily do what the books say. Sometimes, I'm waiting for a stage; now I'm waiting for adolescent rebellion, and there is none." MOTHER

"I wish I had known about their indecisiveness. He wants to do this; no, he doesn't. He gets pressure from peers and from what we think is right, and sometimes he goes back and forth. I am more patient about that now." MOTHER

"I wish I had known that if we had dealt with some behaviors when they were younger, we would not have had a problem from eleven to fourteen. He was always a little stubborn and hardheaded, wanting to do what he wanted. But right now, I wish we had done something about the stubbornness because it is a problem. He does not take responsibility, and it gets him into trouble at school. Looking back it has always been a problem, but we did not deal with it." MOTHER

PHYSICAL DEVELOPMENT

Adolescence begins with biological change. From five to ten, boys and girls have about the same height, weight, and general body configuration. The physical changes of puberty begin at about eight or nine and extend to the end of the second decade.[1] The brain triggers endocrine organs to release hormones that affect children's growth and secondary sexual characteristics (breasts, body and facial hair), resulting in reproductive maturity.

These changes take place over several years—for girls, from about age eight to seventeen, and for boys, on average, from eleven to twenty. Because the hormonal

258

CHAPTER 10
Early
Adolescence:
The Years from
Eleven to Fifteen

changes occur before any outward indications of puberty, parents do not know at first that puberty has begun. While the age at which the changes take place and the rapidity of the growth vary from child to child, the sequence of these changes remains consistent. Maturational timing also appears stable across ethnic groups with adequate nutrition.[2]

Sexual maturation accompanies the growth spurt. As mentioned, hormonal stimulation of the sex glands begins first in girls. Then at about age nine or ten, downy, light pubic hair appears and is most often the first sign of sexual maturity. Changes in the breasts occur at the same time. In the next year, the sex organs themselves grow—the uterus and vagina, the labia and clitoris. Pubic hair continues to grow and vaginal secretions appear. By the time *menarche* or menstruation begins at about age twelve and a half, the breast is well formed, and pubic and body hair are well developed. When girls first menstruate, they do not ovulate—send an egg to the uterus—with each period. Thus, conception is more difficult, though not impossible, in the period immediately following the onset of menstruation.

Boys' hormonal secretions of the sex glands first begin at about age eleven and a half, but the first visible sign of impending puberty is growth of the testes and the scrotum, the baglike structure that holds the testes. Pubic hair may appear as well. About a year later, as the physical growth spurt starts, the penis grows in size. Body and facial hair appear about two years after the pubic hair. Genetic factors determine how much body hair there will be.

Boys' voices change later in puberty. The larynx or Adam's apple grows significantly, and vocal cords double in length so the voice becomes lower. It takes many months, in some cases a year or two, for boys to regain control of their voices.

Psychological Reactions to Growth and Development

Physical qualities play an important role in how children evaluate themselves. Adolescents cite physical characteristics most often as those things they do not like about themselves. Areas of concern include skin problems, height, weight, and overall figure. Early adolescents are most dissatisfied with their bodies, whereas older adolescents feel better about their bodies, and college students best of all. With time, adolescents adjust to all the changes that have taken place and eventually feel good about themselves.

Menarche is an important milestone in a girl's life. Initially girls have feelings of ambivalence, confusion, and frustration at the inconvenience; these feelings are particularly strong in early-maturing girls and girls who are poorly prepared for the experience.[3] Girls who have begun to menstruate report less distress (less pain, less fluid retention, less negative emotion) than premenstrual girls anticipate. Expectations, however, are related to later experience. Those girls who anticipate distress generally experience it. When girls receive preparation for both the physical and psychological aspects of the experience, when they view menstruation as a normal part of life, they can accept it a positive experience.[4]

Ejaculation in boys usually comes within a year of the beginning of the growth spurt—at about age fourteen. At this point, boys are sterile, and it takes from one to three years before the ejaculate contains sperm. The first ejaculation may come

Changes in physical form, in ways of thinking, in time spent with peers and in school away from parents demand adaptation from parents and early adolescents.

260

CHAPTER 10
Early
Adolescence:
The Years from
Eleven to Fifteen

during masturbation or in dreams at night. Boys who have had no preparation for ejaculation may experience as much surprise and worry as girls who are unprepared for first menstruation. They may worry that they are sick or have some disease, because although they have had erections since birth, this is the first time that a substance has come from the penis. Thus, boys need as much preparation for this event as girls do for menstruation. Boys may also worry about breast changes that can take place in them at puberty. In all boys, the area around the nipple enlarges and the nipple is elevated. About 20 to 30 percent of boys have some breast enlargement at some point during adolescence.

The timing of the changes is important. Early-maturing girls have greater difficulties than later-maturing girls.[5] They experience more conflict with parents, perhaps because they want more freedom, and they are out of synch with the development of their age mates—both boys and girls—because their interests as well as bodies are more advanced. Early maturing girls sometimes get involved with older boys who encourage such involvement so that the girls' interest in school diminishes.[6] Early-maturing boys have an advantage because they develop the muscular strength and power valued in athletics. Unlike girls, they do not experience increased conflict with parents.

Pubertal changes at age ten to fourteen are associated with increases in family conflict.[7] Several factors may play a role in this increase. Hormonal changes leading to greater irritability and to negative emotionality may intensify conflict. Physical changes may result in critical comments from parents that, in turn, lead to arguing; they may also lead to changed expectations on the part of both parents and children. Children may assume that they are now mature and entitled to more freedom; parents may want to be restrictive now that teens are physically mature. We shall discuss these parent-child interactions later in the chapter.

Information and preparation about puberty and all the changes it brings help reduce anxiety and worry. Many parents, however, feel uncomfortable talking to their children on this subject. Children, too, feel uncomfortable asking questions. Over half of adolescents feel they cannot talk to their parents about sexual matters, and over half feel they do not get the information they want in sex education courses—either the teacher is too embarrassed or the information is not touched on.[8]

Adolescents do not know as much about sex as the mass media have suggested and parents may believe.[9] Sometimes they have fanciful notions—for example, if you do not want to get pregnant, you will not, no matter how often you have sex without contraceptives; you won't get pregnant if you have intercourse standing up. Even though parents may feel truly uncomfortable talking about sex, early adolescents need this information.

INTELLECTUAL DEVELOPMENT

Jean Piaget describes the years from twelve to fourteen as the period when adolescents begin to think like adults.[10] They enter the *formal operations period,* during which they come to think more abstractly than previously. Although children can reason logically when confronted with tangible objects and change during the period of concrete operations, Piaget believes they still cannot reason logically about verbal

propositions or hypothetical situations. In this period, adolescents can freely speculate and arrive at solutions without having the objects or people directly at hand.
They can analyze a problem in their heads. Further, they can enumerate all possible
combinations of events and take action to see what possibilities actually exist.

Their increased capacity for abstract thought enables adolescents to think about
their own thoughts. They become introspective, analyzing themselves and their reactions. They are also able to think about other people's reactions and anticipate
them. They think of the future, imagining what they might be doing as adults, what
might be happening in the world. They can think of ideal situations or ideal solutions and become impatient with the present because it does not meet the ideal they
have pictured. Their introspectiveness, concern about the future, idealism, and im-
patience with the present all affect parent-child relationships, as we shall see. Adolescents also begin to think more complexly about other people and their actions.
They see people more realistically and may cease to idolize their parents.

SCHOOL

Many early adolescents make transitions to middle or junior high school in this period.[11] These school settings do not meet the psychological needs of their students,
and academic achievement and interest in school decrease. Research shows increases in test anxiety and learned helplessness in response to failure. Both truancy
and dropping out increase.

Today's schools are larger than before and organized so that teachers know students less well, but they are also more demanding. Larger schools with less individual attention require a level of responsibility and self-direction that many early
adolescents do not have. As a result, students face what Jacquelynne Eccles calls a
"mismatch" between the developmental needs of early adolescents and the opportunities offered in the school environment.[12] The pressures from school affect girls
and boys of all ethnic groups in similar ways.

Parental involvement is a major determiner of positive or negative school outcome
in all ethnic groups and in economically disadvantaged conditions.[13] When parents
are involved and set positive expectations for children, early adolescents have more
positive views of their own abilities, become engaged in schoolwork and school activities, and have better attendance and grades.[14] Parents provide a context of beliefs
that shape the child's self-system that motivates action that has a positive outcome.

When parents fail to counteract students' natural discouragement with school
changes and stress, students develop negative beliefs about their own abilities and
self-worth, fail to attend and to do the work, and receive poor grades.[15] In even the
poorest and least advantaged economic situations, parents' involvement and optimism about children's abilities enable students to achieve academic competence.
Parents' actions help students to develop increased capacity for self-regulation,
which then leads to achievement.[16]

Boys who have academic difficulties because of aggressive, rule-breaking behavior in school are helped in similar ways.[17] Parents who monitor children's academic
work and effectively set rules and give children structure help adolescents become
engaged in the work and achieve greater success in school.

262

CHAPTER 10
Early
Adolescence:
The Years from
Eleven to Fifteen

EMOTIONAL DEVELOPMENT

Early adolescents describe their overall mood as favorable much of the time.[18] They are most active and interested in settings where they have control—with friends, away from home in parks, at the school lunchroom. They are least involved and motivated in adult-controlled activities—classrooms at school, church, jobs, school library. But even though they feel least involved in adult-controlled activities like classroom studying and working, these activities bring feelings of challenge and satisfaction, of being alive. Though teens do not seek out these activities, they feel good when they accomplish them. Teens most enjoy doing things with friends. Anything is more fun when done with a companion—shopping for school supplies, running an errand, studying.

Both parents and children agree that early adolescents experience significantly more negative life events in this age period than other times.[19] Early adolescents report that stress comes from conflicts with parents and siblings, with school authorities, and with friends. Though parents know of children's stress at school and with friends, they do not report parent-child conflicts as a source of stress to their children.

Part of the stress comes from early adolescents' ability to think about social situations in more complex ways.[20] They think about negative events for a longer time than before, brooding about what happened yesterday or worrying about what may happen tomorrow. Elementary school students who experience the same negative events do not continue to think or worry about them, so they feel less stress. Early adolescents' greater sensitivity to other people's feelings and to other points of view may also contribute to greater stress as they empathize with the feelings of all the participants.

In this period, too, adolescents experience heightened self-consciousness, worrying about how they appear to others. In one study, about a quarter of normal fourteen-year-olds reported feelings of being looked at, laughed at, or talked about.[21] David Elkind believes that the early adolescent "is continually constructing or reacting to an imaginary audience"[22] that also pressures the teen.

Despite all the physical, social, and psychological changes as well as the heightened sensitivity, two-thirds of early teens report low to medium stress. The one-third who report high levels appear to be dealing with additional stress from family events such as marital arguing and divorce.[23]

Depressed and negative moods also increase over the early adolescent years. While the increase seems slight for the majority of young teens, 10 to 20 percent of parents say their children have experienced some depressed mood—sad, unhappy feelings—in the last six months, and 20 to 40 percent of early adolescents report the same.[24] Depressed mood increases from ages thirteen to fifteen, peaks at about seventeen to eighteen, then drops to adult levels. Girls are more likely than boys to report depressed mood, particularly early-maturing girls. European-American and Asian-American teens report more depressive symptoms than do African-American and Hispanic-American teens, even when the level of stress is controlled. Gay and lesbian youth have a two- to threefold risk for suicide and most likely experience more depression.[25] In Chapter 15, we take up depression in greater detail.

Positive experiences can serve as a buffer against the effects of stress. Such experiences provide an "arena of comfort" in which early teens can escape stress, relax, and feel good.[26] When early adolescents from various ethnic backgrounds were asked about their sources of support, all pointed to the importance of close family relationships as the main support.27 As we saw in Figure 9-1, friends are very important as well.

DEVELOPMENT OF THE SELF

Because early adolescents now think more abstractly, they describe themselves in terms of more general traits.28 Though they may think of themselves as dumb because of poor grades and low creativity, they do not yet integrate this negative quality into their overall picture of themselves. The negative and positive qualities remain isolated as separate traits. This separation may serve as a psychological buffer so the negative traits from one sphere do not spill over and influence the overall view of the self.

In this period of change, adolescents begin to explore who they are, what they believe, what they want. They are in the process of forming what Erik Erikson calls a *sense of identity,* a sense of a differentiated and distinct self that is the real inner "me."29

The process of achieving a sense of identity occurs gradually over several years. Adolescents explore new experiences and ideas, form new friendships, and make a commitment to values, goals, and behavior. This can cause conflict and crisis as the choices get worked out. On the other hand, some adolescents choose traditional values without even considering for themselves what they want to do with their lives. They face no crisis or conflict, because they do not want to deal with issues. James Marcia terms commitment without exploration *identity foreclosure* to indicate that possibilities have been closed off prematurely.30

A different path is taken by adolescents who experience a *moratorium.* They experience a crisis about what they want to do. They have ideas they explore, but they have not yet made a commitment. So, a moratorium is exploration without commitment. Finally, some adolescents experience *identity diffusion* in which they can make no choices at all. They drift without direction.

One study found that adolescent boys who rank high in identity exploration come from families in which they can express their own opinions yet they receive support from parents even when they disagree with them.31 Boys are encouraged to be both independent and at the same time connected to family members. Adolescent girls who rate high in identity exploration come from families in which they are challenged and receive little support from parents who are contentious with each other. Girls may need this slightly abrasive atmosphere in order to pursue a heightened sense of individuality rather than follow the path of intensifying social relationships. However, these girls do have at least one parent with whom they felt connected.

Gender and Minority Issues

William Cross describes two aspects of identity or self-concept; *personal identity* (PI), which includes such factors as self-esteem and general personality traits, and *reference group orientation* (RGO), which includes group identity, group awareness, and group attitudes (see Figure 10-1).32 He discusses RGO primarily in terms of racial identity, to explain why people of the same ethnic group with equal commitments to

264

CHAPTER 10
Early
Adolescence:
The Years from
Eleven to Fifteen

FIGURE 10-1
SCHEMATIC OF TWO-FACTOR THEORY OF BLACK IDENTITY

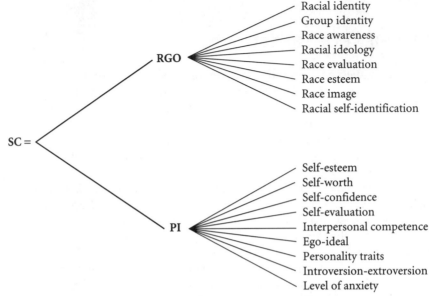

Note: Self-concept (SC) = personal identity (PI) + reference group orientation (RGO)

Reprinted by permission of Sage Publications, Inc. from *Children's Ethnic Socialization,* ed. Jean S. Phinney and Mary Jane Rotheram (Beverly Hills, CA: 1987), Figure 6.1, p. 122. Copyright © 1987 Sage Publications, Inc.

that group may have very different attitudes about ethnic identity—that is, their RGO is very different.

He states that RGO may be prominent in some groups and not in others—for example, some European-Americans think of themselves only as Americans whereas others have a strong ethnic identity as Italian-Americans or Irish-Americans. Cross shows the usefulness of these concepts in understanding gender identity. Two women might be similar with regard to self-esteem and self-worth, but one may have a strong RGO as a feminist and interpret much of her experience in the light of that group identity, while another woman might not.

In these early adolescent years, gender identity intensifies, with boys taking on a more masculine attitude and girls becoming more egalitarian regarding sex roles.[33] Although both sexes are aware of gender-appropriate activities, gender flexibility in terms of self-choices for activities and tolerance of others' gender choices continue to grow.[34]

Achieving a sense of identity is a more complicated task for minority than for majority youth. They have two cultures to explore, understand, and integrate in their quest for identity. They begin with a diffused view of their ethnic background. They talk to parents, family friends, and other adults about ethnic issues. They read books and share experiences with friends. They are aware of prejudice and think about its effects on their work and life goals. In the eighth grade, about a third of African-American students are actively involved in this exploration. By age fifteen, about half of minority students are actively exploring their cultural roots and traditions and an additional one-fourth have already achieved a sense of identity.[35]

Two difficulties arise.[36] First, many minority parents do not talk with their children about their cultural background, and they do not share their own experiences in the majority culture. Perhaps because they do not want to burden their children with experiences that no longer occur or perhaps because they are uncomfortable with issues of culture and race, many parents remain silent and offer no models. As such, children have to seek information elsewhere and cannot consciously pattern themselves after their parents.

Second, minority adolescents have to explore and integrate two cultures. Integrating one set of cultural traditions with the realities of everyday life is difficult enough. With two cultures that sometimes conflict with each other, the task becomes very complicated.

Which values does one select? Children and adolescents ideally should be permitted a bicultural identification that includes both cultures. Minority youth who combine, for example, the emphasis on cooperation and sharing found in many ethnic cultures with the assertive independence of the majority culture are effective in a wider range of situations than are those attached to just one set of values. Because peers or family may pressure the adolescent to adopt only the traditional cultural values, a bicultural orientation is not easy to achieve.

The process of achieving identity is even more difficult when the minority culture is devalued and adolescents experience negative stereotyping. Youth may then refuse to explore their ethnic roots and may seek a foreclosed identity. Evidence suggests that this happened more frequently among minority than majority adolescents.[37] Some adolescents internalize the negative images, feel deficient and worthless, and develop what Erikson calls a *negative identity*. Currently, more minority youth develop a positive cultural identity and feel high self-esteem than was true of adolescents in past years. A positive ethnic identity enables youth to replace tension and defensiveness with self-confidence about the future.

Self-Esteem

Measures of self-esteem over time reveal a drop in positive self-evaluations in early adolescence.[38] The physical changes, demands of school, and increased social comparisons threaten positive views of the self. Girls are more likely than boys to suffer from low self-esteem and early maturing. Further, girls are most likely to suffer losses in esteem they fail to recover as they move through adolescence.

Studies of self-esteem in minority youth have focused primarily on self-esteem in African-American teens.[39] The process of self-esteem formation is the same as with European-Americans, but there appears to be a stronger relationship between the support of others and self-esteem in African-Americans. The African-American family and community may play such a significant role because, in addition to presenting a positive self-concept to children, they filter out society's negative messages about African Americans.

Similarly, African-American students have higher self-esteem when they attend schools that provide positive social support for them. For example, they have higher self-esteem in racially segregated schools than in integrated schools. African Americans

266

CHAPTER 10
Early
Adolescence:
The Years from
Eleven to Fifteen

from single-parent families have lower self-esteem in integrated schools than do African Americans from two-parent families. The latter students more closely resemble other students in integrated schools and do not feel as different as students from single-parent families do. Clearly, we have a lot more to learn about the development of self-esteem in different groups and contextual factors that influence self-esteem in all children.

DEVELOPMENT OF SELF-REGULATION

Although early adolescence is a time of increasing physical and intellectual change, ways of handling impulses and degree of impulse control have nevertheless become characteristic features by this age period. Longitudinal studies of early adolescents that have followed them into adulthood through their thirties and forties find adult impulse control is well predicted from behavior during this period.[40]

Jack Block has looked at family characteristics associated with under- and overcontrol.[41] He found that poorly controlled men and women come from families who, in their early adolescent years, were unable to give children models of effective control. The parents were not able to put aside their own concerns and interests and provide the necessary consistency in discipline. They did not reward and punish children's behavior in a logical way that teaches children how to control themselves. Instead, they used discipline only when they themselves were extremely angry. The child, fearful and panicked by the rage, could not absorb the lesson and thus never received the teaching necessary to achieve good control of impulses.

Overcontrol in men seems to come from having authoritarian and highly controlling parents. The dominant mother who sets high standards and arouses guilt to punish the child for misdeeds is a powerful figure in establishing overcontrol. Fathers in these families withdraw from the parenting role and support their wives' domination. Together, the parents so overcontrol the son that he remains fearful of impulse expression, even of pleasure, as an adult. The average girl is so well controlled that Block found it difficult to isolate any one group of overcontrolled girls to study the qualities of the family.

Although enduring modes of impulse control appear by the early adolescent years, not every impulsive act forebodes a future life of impulsivity. Even the most responsible, dependable young teenager will engage in forbidden acts—partly to test the limits, partly to savor the experience, partly to impress friends. Such acts include drinking, smoking, driving the car without permission, and cutting school.

How to distinguish an isolated forbidden act from a more serious problem with impulse control is a skill parents must develop. This is discussed in a later section.

SOCIAL DEVELOPMENT

Parent-Child Relationships

In 1984, John Conger and Anne Petersen reviewed a wide body of research on parent-child relations and wrote the following comment that more recent research supports as well.

The single most important external influence in aiding or hindering the average adolescent (particularly the younger one) in the accomplishment of the developmental tasks of adolescence—at least in today's relatively isolated nuclear family—is his or her parents. The real question is not whether parental models are any longer important; rather, it is what kinds of parental models are necessary or appropriate in preparing contemporary adolescents to cope with the largely unpredictable world of tomorrow.[42]

While parents are important, young adolescents spend about half as much time with parents as they did in the elementary school years.[43] Parent and child are alone as often, but family group activities at home and with relatives decreases.

Parent-Child Conflict In the early adolescent years, any time together may well be spent in arguments. As noted earlier, parent-child conflicts increase and provide stress to children, though parents appear less aware of them.

This disparity between children's and parents' impressions exemplifies the divergent realities that can exist in families and that Reed Larsen and Maryse Richards consider as the source of difficulties at this age. They gave electronic pagers to parents and their children age nine to fifteen years and systematically beeped and asked them to write about their activities and feelings. After analyzing the data, Richards and Larson wrote, "Once we go inside family life we find that it is an illusion to talk about "the family," as though it were a single entity. The family is the meeting ground of multiple realities."[44] The authors believe that parents' and offsprings' inability to understand and deal with their different realities create problems for all family members.

In these researchers' Midwestern working and middle-class sample, fathers worked hard and viewed time at home as leisure. They brought home their work stress, which affected all family members. Mothers felt they should be able to create a harmonious home atmosphere; when frustrated, they sought pleasure in activities outside the home. Early adolescents, as noted, experience stress from many sources. When parents were available and responsive, negative feelings decreased.

Parents and children agree that the mundane, routine behaviors cause most conflicts. Schoolwork and grades become a more frequent topic as early adolescents move into junior high school. As they move into high school, chores become a focus and remain a major topic during later adolescence.[45]

Though they understand parents' insistence on following conventions, young adolescents simply do not agree with them. Early adolescents insist that many of these issues should be matters under their personal control. Though aware of their children's point of view, parents will not accept it as valid. Early adolescents do recognize that certain behaviors have important effects on other people; they, like parents, consider these moral issues that they will not challenge—for example, hitting others, not sharing.

Parents and children agree that most of the time conflicts end because children follow parents' wishes. In only 18 percent of conflicts do parents follow children's requests, and joint discussion and decisions settle just 13 percent of the disagreements. So although there are conflicts, children acquiesce.[46] The basic relationship between parents and children remains solid.

Mothers, however, bear the burden of the increasing disagreements,[47] perhaps because they are more involved than fathers in routine household management and

268

CHAPTER 10
Early
Adolescence:
The Years from
Eleven to Fifteen

INTERVIEW
with Anne Petersen

Anne C. Petersen is Senior Vice President at W. K. Kellogg Foundation in Battle Creek, Michigan. Her research interests center on adolescence; with John Janeway Conger, she is the author of Adolescence and Youth: Psychological Development in a Changing World.

What do parents of adolescents need to know?

The societal view of adolescents is negative. I collect cartoons, and they portray an extreme view of adolescents as having hormone attacks, being difficult, impossible.

This belief in our country that adolescents are difficult and want to be independent is one of the biggest pitfalls for parents. We know that, though adolescents want to be autonomous, they need parents. We know that young adolescents are argumentative, sometimes obnoxious. Parents throw in the towel and that is the worst thing they can do. Adolescents need to know that parental support is there. There have been historical changes in the family, increasing the possibility for kids to be independent with cars and to have more time away from home; all these changes have exacerbated the trend toward independence and separation. Too much freedom is detrimental to adolescents' development.

Parents need to know that when you ask adolescents, especially young adolescents, who is most important to them, they say the parents, even if the parents are reporting conflict. We find, then, that parents are less positive about their adolescents than their adolescents are about them. Adolescents' off-putting behavior—telling parents to get lost because the adolescents are mature—is not really the message they want to send. They are asking for a little more space; they are asking for help in becoming autonomous and interdependent rather than independent.

Research shows that conflicts are about little things, not big things. The conflicts are not about values, but largely about doing dishes, taking out the garbage. They are a way of relieving tensions. Parents ought to be a safe source for venting tensions. If they cease to be a safe source, then young adolescents are really lost; they have no one.

Parents sometimes believe that they need to be their child's buddy, but that's not true. They need to be parents. They need to provide unconditional love, firm guidelines, and strong expectations.

---

scheduling. It also may be that mothers are more emotionally reactive with adolescents, so both boys and girls argue with them more. When fathers are present as a third party in disagreements, boys are more respectful and mother-son relations improve. Father-adolescent relations are more open and interactive when mothers are not present as a third party.[48] Mothers seem to dominate the relationship, and fathers withdraw.

Physical development influences changes in social behavior.[49] As physical maturation occurs at puberty, both boys and girls report increasing conflicts with parents and feelings of distance from them. Girls report a decrease in calm discussions with fathers, and boys report less father-son cohesiveness. Hormonal changes may play a

Puberty and all the change that accompanies it is a difficult time for boys and girls, especially when they have to change schools. It seems to work slightly differently for boys than for girls. In general, boys seem less influenced by what is going on with parents, but basic support is pretty important. If parental support is not there, it is very bad for girls. Those girls who have a lot of family conflict or lack support are the ones who become the most depressed.

How would you say your own research has influenced the way you rear your children?

I think it has changed a lot of things. That my daughter rebelled was a big shock. I remember vividly the day she refused to do something. There was no door banging, but she said she would not do something I had just assumed she would do. I immediately had the stereotypic reaction, "'Oh my heavens, what is going on here?" All of a sudden I realized that this was what I had been talking about for a long time. Knowing all the data, why should I be surprised that my kid goes through this too?

It helped a lot to know what could be effective in dealing with this. We had a family conference. What she was saying was, "How about taking my needs into account?" She was upset that we just assumed she would be a part of some activity. It is enlightening to realize that we don't treat an adult, a colleague, or a friend like that. It makes sense to change your behavior toward young adolescents. Well, we worked it out. There are still occasional lapses of communication, and that's where the problems really are. Somebody assumes that somebody else is going to do something, and there is either a conflict of schedules or wishes. But at least saying, "Yes, you are right, you ought to have an increasing role in family decision making" and have a forum within which to do it made a lot of difference to her. She did not have to explode. She could put her two cents in.

When there is a good reason, we change our plans to meet her needs. It is important for us to show that we do not need to be controlling things, that we do respect her views, that she does have a voice. I am sure if you were to ask both our children, they would say they do not have as much say as they would like. That is because we still do believe that we are the parents and there are some things that we need to decide.

We believe that it is important to let them see how we are thinking about things and to understand decision-making processes. So, we talk in the family about money and about vacation plans, and we really try to include them—not just out of respect for them to increasingly become a part, but also to let them see how we think about things so they have the benefit of knowing how adults make decisions. That seems to work pretty well.

role in the rise of conflicts; increases in certain hormones have been found with increasing amounts of anger in boys and particularly girls in family disputes.[50]

When parents insist on retaining power and control and refuse to give children opportunities to share decision making, children become highly peer oriented.[51] They seem to seek egalitarian relationships and mutuality with peers because they are denied these experiences with parents. When parents monitor the behavior of early adolescents but permit them input in making decisions, the adolescents are better adjusted.

Parents may find themselves especially upset when their children argue with them, because it violates their expectations of compliance and communicativeness.

While the conflicts at this age do increase, children usually acquiesce to parent's requests, as we have seen. Only about 10 percent of families face serious relationship problems during adolescence, and these difficulties often preceded the age period.[52] The more usual arguing reflects not dysfunction but rather the many changes parents and children are undergoing.

Harmonious Parent-Child Relations   When parents use an authoritative style of parenting — being accepting, responding sensitively to needs while still maintaining reasonable limits — teens show effective, responsible behavior.[53] Sensitive acceptance and responsiveness promote self-esteem and social connectedness; firm standards promote self-control.

Nancy Darling and Laurence Steinberg distinguish between parenting style (for example, authoritative), which creates an emotional climate in the home, and specific parenting practices, or the day to day behaviors that influence children's behavior.[54] Grayson Holmbeck, Robert Paikoff, and Jeanne Brooks-Gunn consider the following parenting practices important in this age period:

1. Avoiding power-assertive and coercive or forcing practices
2. Having firm, consistent limits for children's behavior
3. Monitoring and supervising daily behavior to see limits are followed
4. Being warm and accepting of children
5. Using calm reasoning to gain the child's cooperation in a generally democratic family setting
6. Encouraging curiosity, empathy, connectedness to others, and individuality[55]

Parents must also give children needed information on such topics as sexuality, alcohol, drugs, and a healthy lifestyle. They must present not only facts but also their values in these areas for, as we shall see in the next chapter, teens respond to parents' values when expressed. They do not, however, sometimes understand how important certain values are unless parents express them verbally. If parents do not feel comfortable giving information on such topics as sexuality or drugs, they need to direct their children to doctors or adolescent health clinics that do provide such services.

Though the parenting practices just listed apply to most other age periods, they are particularly important in early adolescence. Parents must also be flexible and willing to modify their practices, as their child receives growing responsibility for decision making. Recall that in Chapter 9 we talked about parents' monitoring children from a distance. As they move into early adolescence, children receive even greater opportunities for decision making under parents' decreasing supervision. The art lies in knowing when to keep control of children's behavior and when to relinquish it.

Parents also serve as models and sources of information for minority adolescents exploring their ethnic culture and sense of identity. James Comer states that the entire African-American community has to act together

> to help each child establish a personal and group identity . . . that allows each young person to feel, "I am an individual, an Afro-American with a tradition of sacrifice, struggle, and excellence; and it is my job to restore and carry on the tradition for my own sake, for the good of the Afro-American community, and for the good of America."[56]

BOX 10-1

**METHODS TO ENHANCE IDENTITY FORMATION OF ETHNIC
MINORITY YOUTH**

1. Methods should be proposed to keep minority youth in school and academically oriented, since lack of education increases the risk of poverty and disadvantage.
2. Efforts are required to heighten health consciousness, because poor health interferes with identity processes. The physical health of many minority youth lags behind that of majority youth.
3. Importance of social networks should be affirmed. As they socialize children, churches and extended families are important resources for minority families.
4. Methods should be proposed to support parents as cultural transmitters. Many ethnic-group parents do not discuss their distinctive values and experiences, and such parents must receive support as they begin to do this.
5. Proposals are needed to offer a media-focused, cultural emphasis that affirms positive group identity for all youth to combat negative stereotyping.
6. Methods are needed to promote teaching of native languages and cultures, particularly for American Indians at risk for losing their cultural heritage. Creativity is required to encourage biculturalism while preserving cultural traditions.
7. Programs are required for the special training of teachers so that they will be sensitive to cultural traditions, communicative patterns, and sometimes the language of minority students.
8. Child-rearing support by way of teaching parenting skills is required to promote parents' sense of ethnic pride and enhance the home-school partnership.
9. Improved training is required for mental health workers serving ethnic minority populations.

Adapted from Margaret Beale Spencer and Carol Markstrom-Adams, "Identity Processes among Racial and Ethnic Minority Children in America," *Child Development* 61 (1990): 305–306.

These are appropriate feelings for all children to have about their ethnic tradition. Margaret Spencer and Carol Markstrom-Adams make nine recommendations, listed in Box 10-1, to promote positive identity formation of minority youth.[57]

Parents must not hurry their children through the early adolescent period. Sometimes, children will retreat a bit when they need time to think or to deal with a conflict. Elkind has described the stress children experience when parents press them to grow up and take on adult characteristics. In *The Hurried Child*, he writes that parents who experience extreme pressure in their own lives want their children to grow up quickly, eliminating that source of stress.[58] Children are pressured to achieve, to take on more chores and responsibilities, without too much participation on the parents' part. The push to turn children quickly into adults can be very detrimental at this age, because many early adolescents seem to like the greater freedom but cannot handle it yet. Elkind regrets this pressure on children, because it robs them of the childhood they need to grow, learn, and develop fully.

272

CHAPTER 10
Early
Adolescence:
The Years from
Eleven to Fifteen

THE JOYS OF PARENTING EARLY ADOLESCENTS

"Seeing him care for younger children and babies is a great pleasure. He's a great nurturer with small children. He has endless patience." MOTHER

"He is a talented athlete, and his soccer team got to a championship game. He scored the winning goal, and when he took off with the ball down the field, I was very proud of him. It was a unique feeling of being proud that someone I had helped to create was doing that. He had felt a lot of pressure in the game, so to see how incredibly pleased he was gave me great joy." FATHER

"I enjoy the fact that she is very independent and makes up her own mind about things. She is not caught up in fads or with cliques, and I can trust her not to follow other people's ideas. The down side of that is that she resists some of my ideas as well." MOTHER

"I enjoy her sense of humor. She jokes about everyday events, and I laugh a lot around her." MOTHER

"I like that he does things I did, like play the trumpet. He started at the same age I did and since he took it up, it has rekindled my interest and I started practicing again. This last weekend, we played together. He also brings new interests too. Because he like sailing I have started that and really like it." FATHER

"She is in that dreamy preteen state where she writes things. She wrote a poem about the difference between being alone and loneliness. She has a real appreciation of time on her own and how nice being alone can be. I like that because I had that at her age." MOTHER

"It's nice just being able to help them, feeling good because they are being helped out and benefited." FATHER

Though parent and adolescent alike may have intense emotional interactions around these issues, each is preoccupied as well with his or her own life events. When a family member develops psychological symptoms as a result of these events and daily hassles in the home increase, then other family members are affected. When family members can deal with their individual problems without developing symptoms or becoming overly stressed, then other family members are not drawn in and upset. It is not the occurrence of a major life event that disrupts the family; it is how the individual involved copes with it. Both parents and children respond to the distress they see in those close to them.[59]

Some researchers have suggested that adolescents are most reactive to fathers' symptoms. Mothers in general express negative feelings such as anxiety and depression more, so children may be more accustomed to their upset and become alarmed only when fathers reveal marked distress. However, when mothers show major

"It's nice to see her being able to analyze situations with friends or with her teachers and come to conclusions. She said about one of her teachers, "Well, she gets excited and she never follows through with what she says, so you know you don't have to take her seriously." MOTHER

"I really enjoy being in the scouts with the boys. Once a month we go on a camping weekend, and I really look forward to that." FATHER

"I was so impressed and pleased that after the earthquake, he and a friend decided to go door to door and offer to sell drawings they made of Teenage Mutant Ninja Turtles. He raised $150 that he gave for earthquake relief. I was very proud that he thought this up all by himself." FATHER

"I was very happy one day when I found this note she left on my desk. It said, 'Hello!!! Have a happy day! Don't worry about home, everyone's fine! Do your work the very best you can. But most important, have a fruitful life!!!' I saved that note because it made me feel so good." MOTHER

"He enjoys life. He has a sense of humor. He's like a butterfly enjoying everything; eventually he'll settle in." MOTHER

"He's very sensitive, and his cousins two years older than he is ask his advice about boys. They may not take it, but they ask him even though he's younger." FATHER

"It's very rewarding to see them in their school activities. My daughter sings in the school chorus, and I enjoy that, and my son is in school plays." FATHER

"I am very pleased that she is less moody now than she used to be. We used to refer to her lows as 'Puddles of Frustration,' but she has got past that now." MOTHER

"Well, they have their friends over, and we have Ping-Pong, pool, cards, and we stressed having these things available. I enjoy playing all these games with them." FATHER

symptoms of depression, and parent-child relationships are disrupted, then poor grades and behavioral problems at school follow.[60]

So, though intense conflicts center on everyday life activities and teens tend to draw away from parents, all family members still want the best for each other and react negatively when another family member is distressed.

Happy family times are important, because they provide a reservoir of good feeling that sustains all family members through times of conflict and crisis. Family life focuses so heavily on routine chores that it is mainly when the family leaves home for an outing that members can be together to share fun. Happy experiences, however, need not be limited to excursions. Family card games, mealtime rituals, and watching certain TV programs together can provide a sense of sharing and solidarity that adolescents report as highly meaningful to them. Making time for fun and games in a busy schedule may save time in the long run as conflicts and arguing decrease.

274

CHAPTER 10
Early
Adolescence:
The Years from
Eleven to Fifteen

Sibling Relationships

As in previous age periods, young adolescents show a great deal of ambivalence toward siblings. Ninety-seven percent of a large group of teens say they sometimes, or usually, do like their brothers and sisters, and only 3 percent say they do not like them. However, they rank brothers and sisters as one of their biggest problems, more of a problem than parents or peers.[61]

What do siblings do that is so upsetting? Primarily, they invade the early adolescent's privacy. They go into their rooms, take their possessions, try to be part of their activities. A second major complaint is that younger brothers and sisters get privileges older ones did not get at that age. Adolescents feel their brothers and sisters are getting away with something. Teasing is a third source of complaint. Sometimes teasing is not meant to be cruel, but it is a way of having a kind of conversation. A fourth reason for resentment is that parents favor another child. Sometimes early teens feel that older siblings get more respect and trust, and younger ones get more attention. Sibling conflict may be fueled by tensions from other areas. For example, if a teen has had a hard day with teachers and a fight with friends, she cannot come home and yell at her parents, but she can yell at a bratty brother or sister who made a face at her.[62]

Siblings can become close during these years for the same reasons that peers are close — they can understand the emotional ups and downs, the problems that early adolescents are feeling, in ways that parents may not. They may become allies in asking parents for privileges or rule changes. Sibling relationships usually improve as older siblings become more independent and no longer compete for parental attention or resources.

Peers

Young adolescents report fewer close friends than elementary school children do, but they gain more support from these relationships than younger children do (see Figure 9-1 in the last chapter).[63] Friends have equal status, and they often understand what the other is experiencing in ways parents cannot.

In these years, children form cliques, small groups of five to nine members who choose each other as friends.[64] The most common activities are hanging out, talking, walking around school, talking on the phone, watching TV, and playing physical games. Girls spend more time than boys talking and shopping, and boys more time than girls playing contact sports. Group activities serve several purposes: They provide sociability and a sense of belonging, promote exploration of the self and achievements, and provide opportunities for learning and instruction. Hanging around and talking promote closer social relationships, whereas competitive games promote achievements and greater understanding of the self. Both kinds of activities contribute to psychological growth and give children the kinds of experiences they need to form a stable sense of identity.

In the beginning of early adolescence, teens spend most of their time in same-sex groups.[65] Girls spend only about an hour a week in the presence of a boy, and boys spend even less time in the presence of a girl. However, in the seventh and eighth grades, children spend four to six hours a week thinking about the opposite sex, but only about an average of one-half to one-and-one-third hours actually with them. As teens move through high school, they spend more time with the opposite sex.

Parents worry that their children will rely on peers for advice and guidance. But, as in earlier years, children usually pick friends who are like themselves and reflect their parents' values. Parents can relax a little when they read this conclusion of psychologists: "Although the influence of peer groups and friendships increases across adolescence, parents retain their primary influence over major decisions regarding life values, goals, and future decisions."[66]

TASKS AND CONCERNS OF PARENTS

Parents' tasks expand as they become not only caregivers and interpreters of the social world but also models for an increasing number of behaviors in the world outside the home. Parenting tasks include the following:

- Continuing to be the single most important influence in the child's life
- Being sensitive to the child's needs and open to discussion of the child's viewpoint
- Modeling self-controlled, responsible daily behavior in all areas of life and in discussions with children
- Monitoring children's activities and behavior
- Communicating information and values on important but difficult-to-discuss topics like sexuality, substance use, and discrimination
- Making time, being available for conversation when the child is ready to talk
- Giving children more decision-making power
- Providing support as children undergo many physical changes and social challenges, so home is an understanding place
- Sharing pleasurable time

In earlier chapters, we focused on routine behaviors like eating and sleeping. It seems strange to consider them again with early adolescents, yet problems in eating and sleeping occur in the adolescent years and require attention.

Eating

With changes brought by physical maturation and increases in peer sociability, eating patterns may change in adolescence. Parents grow concerned that teenagers do not get the proper nutrition necessary for healthy growth. Parents, of course, have no control over what children eat when they are not at home; they do, however, control the food purchased and served in the home.

Using behavioral techniques, parents can encourage healthy eating habits. Having regular family meals consisting of well-balanced foods can be difficult when family members have so many different activities. But eating together is an important social as well as nutritional event, and well worth the effort required to cook a meal and get everyone together for it. When good food is served well, teenagers will

276

CHAPTER 10
Early
Adolescence:
The Years from
Eleven to Fifteen

most likely eat even if they have been snacking beforehand. Though it is easier to get people together for dinner during the week, large breakfasts or brunches may be most feasible on weekends. At the same time that parents provide and eat healthy foods, they can occasionally discuss the importance of healthy diets.

Sleeping

The average eleven- to fifteen-year-old needs between 9 and 10 hours of sleep every night, says Richard Ferber, head of the Children's Hospital Sleep Disorder Clinic.[67] Most, however, get only about 8 hours of sleep, so they are often sleep deprived and forced to make up for lost sleep on weekends. To get the best night's sleep possible, even early adolescents need a pleasant bedtime routine and time to unwind.

Adolescents, too, can have sleep problems. Late sleeping can occur when they stay up late on weekends and sleep until noon or one o'clock the next day. Then they also have a late sleep phase during the week when they most need to be alert and have to adjust back to their regular schedule.

Teenagers also sometimes have night terrors and partial awakening in which they may yell and scream, thrash about, and even get up and walk. Although there is no magic age to determine whether awakening is a problem, the general rule is that beyond seven, the awakenings are psychological in origin. Psychological difficulties may not be severe, but they do require attention. The child may be under special stress or have few outlets for emotional expression and so may be discharging feelings in that way. Parents can talk to children, listen to feelings, and suggest actions to remedy stress. The parents can also try to be sure that the child gets sufficient sleep, because these awakenings tend to occur when the child is tired.

Temper Tantrums

During periods of typical moodiness, early adolescents often lose their tempers and go storming off. Though parents can no longer practice time out with adolescents, they can do active listening.

Haim Ginott gives the example of a thirteen-year old girl who wanted to play the violin in the kitchen while her mother cooked dinner.[68] The mother repeated the rule, "No practicing in the kitchen at 6:00." The girl left the kitchen, but when her sister began practicing the piano, she ran screaming to her mother, demanding to know why the sister could practice and she couldn't. Her mother replied that she knew why. The next day the girl was furious because she felt her mother was not giving her answers. She wrote her a note, expressing her rage. Her mother wrote back and repeated the household rule—no violin playing in the kitchen between 5 and 7 P.M. The mother accepted her daughter's feelings but repeated the rule.

Thomas Gordon describes the family in which the thirteen-year-old was used to getting her way. Her parents were trying to solve the problem at hand when she charged out of the room and ran off in tears. Instead of consoling or ignoring her, her father ran to the bedroom door and sent an I-message about how upset both parents were that she would not try to find a solution in which they all could win. He made strong statements: "I'm darned angry at you right now. Here we bring up something that is bothering your mother and me and you run away. That really feels like you don't give a darn about our needs. I don't like that. I think it's unfair. We want this problem solved now. We don't want you to lose, but we sure are not going to be the ones to lose while you win. I think we can find a solution so we'll both win, but we can't for sure unless you come back to talk."[69] Her father did not give in to the tantrum but expressed his views strongly.

Don Dinkmeyer and Gary McKay use Rudolf Dreikurs's approach.[70] Adolescents, they say, can use their emotions to try to have their own way. Crying and shouting invite parents to retreat or to get into a battle that either obscures the issue or makes them feel sorry for the child. Crying and shouting can be used to obtain attention, power, and revenge or to display inadequacy. Dinkmeyer and McKay recommend that parents let adolescents be responsible for their emotions. Parents may listen, try to understand or to help find a solution, but basically the feelings belong to the teen, and the parents remain detached. Thus, when a daughter has a tantrum, her father can go for a walk.

The behaviorists Robert Eimers and Robert Aitchison recommend techniques very similar to those of Ginott and Gordon.[71] When a teen explodes, they advise parents to be good listeners; don't blame but state your own feelings. Deal with specific behaviors and not character traits, and praise the child for communicating.

All experts advise parents not to give in, but to listen to the child's feelings and express their own. In general, parents need to maintain a detached attitude toward this child's intense feelings and an interested attitude toward working to find a solution to what is causing the child's problem.

Dirty Room

Ginott says a child's room is a private place.[72] Parents should maintain distance and let the child does as he or she pleases about dirt. If the room becomes too smelly or unsanitary, however, then we assume he would advise the parent to take action.

Gordon[73] and Eimers and Aitchison[74] recommend problem solving and contracting to reach an agreement acceptable to parents and teenager alike. Gordon describes a situation in which mother and daughter discussed what to do about the daughter's dirty room. She did not mind it, but her mother did, so they arrived at an agreement. The daughter liked to cook and agreed to cook two evenings a week in exchange for her mother's cleaning her room.

Eimers and Aitchison describe a contracting session between a boy and his parents so that each could get what was wanted. The boy wanted certain privileges about going out, freedom to wear longer hair, and freedom to be alone in his room when he chose to be. Parents wanted him to stop using profanity and to help around the house, including cleaning his room. They made an agreement by which both the boy and his parents could achieve their goals.

Dinkmeyer and McKay describe an approach based on Dreikurs's strategy.[75] The daughter's room stays as she likes it until it offends her mother. When the mother becomes concerned because of the smell and disarray, a new limit is set: The daughter has to clean the room before she leaves the house that day.

All approaches involve a form of problem solving, contracting, or negotiating. The child's privacy is respected up to the point it infringes on parents' sensitivities, and then parents and teenager negotiate a new solution.

278

CHAPTER 10
Early
Adolescence:
The Years from
Eleven to Fifteen

The Noncommunicative Early Adolescent

Noncommunication is a common problem for parents, though the child does not see it this way. Parents complain that children come home, go to their rooms, and shut the door. When they emerge for meals or snacks, they say little, answering any question with only a word or two. They don't talk about what they are doing, thinking, or feeling. Children don't seem unhappy, but parents feel they don't know them anymore. Parents may feel hurt when children say little to them but talk for hours on the phone to their friends.

Parents can, however, interact with children to promote conversation. Dinkmeyer and McKay advise three strategies: (1) comment on nonverbal behavior, (2) ask for comments, and (3) be a model of conversing.[76] For example, parents can try commenting on facial expressions or body language: "Looks like you had a good day today," or "You look happy." Teens may not follow up with any comments, but parents have made an effort.

Parents can ask for comments, saying, "How's school going" or "What are you and Jenny doing tonight?" If the child answers with one word or two, parents should drop the conversation and wait for another time. Parents can remain good models of communication, however, talking about their day, their friends, their plans.

Once teens begin to talk, parents can listen and communicate their feelings. If parents jump in with criticism, judgments of the child or others, blame, or sarcasm, children clam up. Reflecting the teenagers' feelings helps teens to continue to talk. If teens talk about problems they are trying to work out and want to discuss them, parents can encourage them to list options, explore the advantages of each, and then act.

There are many "don'ts" to the process of encouraging conversation. Don't force the child to reveal her feelings. Don't give advice once the teen has begun to talk. Don't rush to find the solution. Don't hurry to answer questions; delaying an answer can stimulate thinking. Adele Faber and Elaine Mazlish give the example of a girl who asked her mother, "Why don't we ever go to any place good on vacation like Bermuda or Florida?" The mother answered, "Why don't we?"

The girl replied, "I know, I know. Because it's too expensive. . . . Well, at least can we go to the zoo?"[77]

Faber and Mazlish describe useful techniques when teens begin to talk about discouragement or frustration. They suggest showing respect for the child's struggle with comments like "That can be hard," It's not easy," or "Sometimes it helps when . . ." then giving a piece of information: "It helps when you're rushed to concentrate on the most important item." Teens are free to use the information or not. Parents have to watch their tone of voice or the information can sound like advice.

Faber and Mazlish also present interesting alternative responses to saying "no." Since teens are very sensitive to control and may not like to ask if they hear a lot of "no's" in response, having other ways to respond is useful and will encourage greater talkativeness. Suppose a teen wants his mother to take him to the store at 5:30 while she is cooking dinner. Instead of giving a flat "no," she can say, "I'll take you after dinner." If she is completely unable to do it, she can say, "I'd like to be able to help you out, but I have to get dinner on the table and get to that meeting at 7:00." A parent can leave out the "no" and just give information. For example, if a teen asks for an extra, expensive piece of clothing, the parent can say, "The budget just won't take it this month." If there are ways the teen can get the item, the parent can pass that information on: "If you want that as a birthday present at the end of the month, that would be fine."

All strategies recommend fostering self-esteem and autonomy by focusing on the positive things teens do. When children feel good about themselves, they talk more. Dinkmeyer and McKay describe how parents use encouragement to foster self-esteem at times of frustration. Encouragement focuses on effort, improvement, and interest and is reflected in phrases like "You really worked hard on that" or "I can see a lot of progress" or "You were really a big help to your brother in cleaning his room." Though using all these different strategies does not guarantee a talkative teenager in the home, it does increase the likelihood of conversation.

Forbidden Acts

A major task for parents is to learn when to take firm action about impulsive acts and when to be understanding. If problems occur with drinking or violating a major rule more than once or twice and seem to be developing into a serious problem, parents can take several actions. Dinkmeyer and McKay state that parents must change their attitudes toward the teen and the abusive behavior. It's pointless to criticize or to blame the teen or themselves. Alcohol and other substances are available for use when teens are discouraged or frustrated. Rather than blaming, the focus must be on finding resources for meeting the problem. Since low self-esteem and lack of confidence often underlie such behavior, communicating respect for the child and looking for resources initiate positive movements. It is wise to seek family counseling at least for an evaluation of the problem. Sometimes parents have a tendency to want to deny a problem, and more objective observers may be able to see the extent of any problem that exists.

The Isolated Child

Adolescence brings a special poignancy to the problem of the isolated child, because children want to have satisfactions with peers. Peer acceptance involves both a cognitive understanding of others and oneself and appropriate peer behavior.[78] When children have difficulties—either being too inhibited or too aggressive—problems may exist in how they view people as well as how they behave. Aggressive children, for example, are quick to see others' negative behavior as intentional and therefore worthy of retaliation.[79] Part of the way to help such children is to encourage them to examine their interpretations of others' behavior and use more benign views of others' intentions. When they view negative behavior as accidental, aggressive children cease to be so aggressive. Similarly, shy, inhibited children should be encouraged to review their positive traits and identify the positive contributions they can make to social activities. Peer acceptance requires outgoing behavior that shows respect for others and oneself by listening to others, being open and friendly, having a positive attitude, initiating interactions, and avoiding aggressive, negative behaviors.[80]

Shirley Radl and Philip Zimbardo (a psychologist who has studied shyness in all age groups and has established a Shyness Clinic at Stanford) make several suggestions specifically geared for the adolescent years of twelve to seventeen.[81] Because

280

CHAPTER 10
Early
Adolescence:
The Years from
Eleven to Fifteen

Parents model appropriate behaviors for teenager — exercising, not smoking, not drinking excessively.

appearance is so important in the early and late adolescent years, Zimbardo and Radl suggest working from the outside in, concentrating first on appearance so that teenagers look as good as possible from their point of view. Skin problems should be attended to immediately. Parents must consult a dermatologist if skin problems cause any distress for teens. Weight, too, can be a problem. They recommend first seeing a pediatrician who can discuss weight and put the child on a diet. Parents then should have suitable foods available and serve as models of good eating patterns. Teeth sometimes need attention. Because many children and adults now wear braces, they aren't the source of embarrassment they once were.

Grooming and clothes also aid appearance. Most early adolescents will take lengthy showers and shampoo their hair daily. When it comes to clothing, parents should allow the teen to follow the current fashion as far as the budget allows. When clothes are more expensive than parents can afford, possible solutions include buying, for example, one or two pairs of expensive pants rather than four or five cheaper ones. Or teens can earn money to make up the difference between what the parents can afford and what the clothes cost.

At home, parents can do all the things that increase children's sense of security and self-worth. Respecting privacy, treating the child with respect, keeping lines of communication open, giving responsibility, giving appropriate praise, not prying into the child's thoughts and feelings, and having rules and structure—these all contribute to a sense of security that enables the child to reach out to others in these sensitive years.

School Problems

Experts are divided on the handling of school problems. Some give all the responsibility to the early adolescent to handle the problem; others encourage the parent to take an active role.

Ginott cites the example of a thirteen-year-old boy who brought home a note from the teacher about his poor behavior.[82] His mother said, "You must have felt terrible to have to bring home a note like that." He agreed he did. His mother wrote the school that she was sure he would handle the problem. (In the past she would have yelled and screamed.) The next day, she met with the principal, but her son had already begun to improve his behavior.

Gordon, as well as Dinkmeyer and McKay, considers that the child has the problem, an issue he or she must deal with. A parent can be a model of effective work habits and can be interested in the child's feelings about school, but essentially schoolwork is up to the child.

Not so with the behaviorists. Eimers and Aitchison describe recommendations to help an eleven-year-old boy who was failing school.[83] Testing revealed he was bright and had no special learning problem. He just misbehaved in class and did not do homework. Eimers and Aitchison described the problem as the boy's not getting sufficient rewards for doing work. Parents found a suitable work place in the dining room, and the boy was given a choice of rewards for spending specified amounts of time on his homework. Initially, the amount of time he put in was brief, but gradually it was increased so that he could obtain the reward.

But as the boy's homework improved, his classroom behavior still required changing. He was given points for working predetermined amounts of time at his desk. When he clowned in class, he was put in time-out for a brief period. The teacher also praised the boy for on-task behavior. We can see here that parents and teachers can do many things to change school behavior—organizing the environment, giving praise and rewards for appropriate behavior, and punishing for inappropriate behavior.

282

CHAPTER 10
Early
Adolescence:
The Years from
Eleven to Fifteen

Research suggests that parents should take an active role in dealing with school problems. Given the age of early adolescents, mutual problem-solving sessions and sending strong I-statements of concern might be appropriate tactics. If this does not lead to an effective plan for change, then parents can try the behavioral system. If children fall behind in school because they aren't doing the work, they can find it very hard to catch up when they finally decide to take action. For this reason, the more active approach of the behaviorists has merit.

PARENTS' EXPERIENCES

Many parents report that they do not feel ready to have teenage children. The childhood years have gone so fast, it seems too soon to have a daughter with a mature figure and sons with bulging muscles and low voices. Parents also find their children's sexual maturity disconcerting. They are surprised to see sons with *Playboy* magazines and hear girls talking about the sexual attractiveness of boys.

Their adolescents' mood swings and desires for greater freedom throw parents back to some of the same conflicts of the early toddler and preschool years. The elementary school years were stable because parents could talk and reason with children, but now they are back to dealing with screaming, crying, moody creatures who sometimes act younger but at the same time want more freedom. Parents may have felt they themselves have grown and matured as parents, able to handle crises, only to find themselves back at square one, yelling and feeling uncontrolled with their children.

Though difficult to give up images, parents must do so. Children are no longer children; they are physically and sexually mature. They are not psychologically mature, however, so they still need the guidance parents can give. Parents often have to give up images of themselves as the perfect parent of an adolescent. They all recall their own adolescence, the ways their parents handled them, and in many cases they want to improve on that. Sometimes they find they are not doing as well as they want and have to step back and see where they are going off the track.

As they mature, early adolescents gain the physical glow and psychological vitality that comes from feeling the world is a magical place. At the same time, parents are marching to or through middle age. Parents often do not feel vibrant and alert, and it is hard to live with offspring who may present such a physical contrast to how parents themselves feel. Further, the world is opening up to adolescents just as parents may feel it is weighing them down. Parents have heavy work responsibilities, often duties of taking care of aging parents as well as growing children. Parents feel they have little time and money at their own disposal, yet they live with young people who seem to have a great deal of both.

Thus, parents have to be careful not to let resentment of the freedom and excitement of their teenagers get in the way of being effective parents. As parents develop reasonable expectations of the amount of freedom and responsibilities their children are to have, they must be careful not to overrestrict or overcriticize out of envy.

Ellen Galinsky calls this the *interdependent stage* of parenting to highlight the greater freedom and control children have.[84] Parents have several years to work through these issues before their children are launched. When parents can become more separate from their children, be available to help them grow yet not stifle them in the process, then parents' and children's relationships take on a new dimension and richness.

MAIN POINTS

In early adolescence, sexual development

- begins and takes years to complete
- triggers psychological reactions in young people
- is related to increases in family conflicts

Early adolescents

- begin to think more abstractly and analyze themselves and other people
- find the transition to junior high difficult because the school environment is a mismatch with early adolescent needs
- worry about conflicts with parents, friends, and school authorities
- experience stress when many changes occur at the same time
- are more involved than previously in peer relationships and cliques

Sense of identity

- depends on exploring a variety of alternatives and making a commitment to values, goals, and behavior
- can be foreclosed if you make a commitment without exploring their options
- is not achieved when early adolescents experience a moratorium and explore without making a commitment
- is achieved in a complicated way by youth of different ethnic groups who must integrate two cultures and deal with prejudice

Peers

- are sought as primary attachment figures when parents are uninterested and give little guidance
- are sought for different kinds of relationships by boys and girls—with girls wanting to talk and express their feelings and boys wanting to engage in group activities with little self-revelation

In this period, parents

- continue to be the single most important influence in aiding or hindering the adolescents' development
- provide role models of ethical, principled behavior and provide accurate information on topics such as sexual behavior and substance use/abuse
- monitor children's activities and behavior

284

CHAPTER 10
Early
Adolescence:
The Years from
Eleven to Fifteen

- give more decision-making power to adolescents
- add to children's stress when they cannot deal with problems in their own lives

Problems discussed center on

- maintaining regular routines at times of change
- controlling emotional reactions and dealing with social difficulties
- failures in communication

Joys include

- observing accomplishments in physical, artistic, and intellectual endeavors
- feeling good because the parent has helped the child in a specific way
- observing child's capacity to take responsibility for self
- emotional closeness

EXERCISES

1. See videos of three movies such *Boyz N the Hood, To Sleep with Anger, Avalon,* or *Parenthood.* Compare parenthood in the majority culture with that in different ethnic groups. What are the roles of grandparents and parents in each culture? How do adults socialize the young to be part of the culture?

2. In small groups, take a survey of students' school experience in the years when they were eleven to fifteen. What size was the school and what grades were included? Have each student rate that school experience from 1, very dissatisfied, to 7, very satisfied. Tabulate the average ratings for each kind of school setting and note whether students were happier when older students were included.

3. Break into small groups and have students list the kinds of experiences that increased their self-esteem in early adolescent years. With input from the whole class, write suggestions for parents who want to increase the self-esteem of their early teenagers.

4. Divide into pairs. In the first exercise, have one partner take the role of a parent who wants to talk to his or her early adolescent about appropriate sexual behavior for the teenager, while the partner takes the role of the teen who wants more freedom. Then reverse roles, and have the second "parent" try to convey values about appropriate uses of substances in adolescent years to the second "teen." Have each student practice active listening and sending I-messages.

5. Have students discuss the importance of peers in their early adolescent years. Did they experience peer pressure? Were parents willing for them to spend time with their friends? What do they think are reasonable rules with regard to time spent with peers? At what age do they think dating should begin? Why that age?

ADDITIONAL READINGS

Csikszentmihalyi, Mihaly, and Larson, Reed. *Being Adolescent.* New York: Basic Books, 1984.

Dinkmeyer, Don, and McKay, Gary D. *STEP/TEEN Systematic Training for Effective Parenting of Teens.* Circle Pines, MN: American Guidance Service, 1983.

Elkind, David. *The Hurried Child.* Reading, MA: Addison-Wesley, 1981.

Gordon, Sol, and Gordon, Judith. *Raising a Child Conservatively in a Sexually Permissive World.* Rev. ed. New York: Simon & Schuster, 1983.

Larson, Reed, and Richards, Maryse H. *Divergent Realities: The Emotional Lives of Mothers, Fathers, and Adolescents.* New York: Basic Books, 1994.

Steinberg, Laurence, and Steinberg, Wendy. *Crossing Paths: How Your Child's Adolescence Triggers Your Own Crisis.* New York: Simon & Schuster, 1994.

LATE ADOLESCENCE: THE YEARS FROM FIFTEEN TO NINETEEN

C H A P T E R 11

How do late adolescents use their parents and families as a secure base when they venture farther away from home in activities, schooling, and jobs? How do late adolescents use their new ways of thinking and reasoning to deal with the powerful challenges of greater freedom? How do they stay safe when so many risks abound? In this chapter, we look at how parents give information and support to benefit their children while they themselves are changing.

Late adolescents have matured physically and sexually. They have adjusted to bodies with new silhouettes and new capacities. They have adapted to their new ways of thinking and grown accustomed to the idea of a world that does not exist in an ideal state, that has imperfections. They have become used to their moods and more moderate in their self-criticisms.

Having accommodated themselves to these many changes, late adolescents are ready to look to the future. They begin to envision careers, future lifestyles. They spend increasing amounts of time away from home and away from parents. Sexual relationships become important to them; they make choices about sexual activity, deciding how far to go and with whom. At the same time, they balance pleasure with work at school or in jobs.

Parents, too, are in a process of adjusting to their children's many changes. As adolescents make choices, parents stand by to provide information and to help if problems develop. Parents in this stage sense their child's impending departure from home and what life may be like for them as mature adults.

PHYSICAL DEVELOPMENT

As the physical changes of maturation near completion, adolescents must integrate them. They must learn to practice healthy behaviors, such as eating a good diet, exercising, and avoiding risky behaviors such as smoking, drinking, using illegal substances, and engaging in high-risk sexual activity. Psychosocial factors are intimately related to physical health: The leading causes of death in these years, accounting for 75 percent of deaths among adolescents, are accidents, suicide, and homicide—all potentially preventable.[1]

Health Concerns

In the high school years, girls rate their physical health as less good than that of boys their age and less good than that of girls ten to fourteen.[2] Evidence suggests they are accurate in their assessments. High school girls exercise less and diet more. The incidence of acute conditions is higher in adolescence than in any other age period except toddlerhood.[3] Illness and accident restricts adolescents' activity about nine days a year. Girls are more likely to make physicians' visits and be hospitalized, primarily because of reproductive health needs. While boys give themselves a better health rating than girls do, boys are twice as likely to die because they are more often involved in motor vehicle accidents.

A socioeconomically mixed group of 1,400 teens rated their health concerns as follows: acne, obesity, menstruation, headaches, sexuality, sexually transmitted diseases, substance use, "nervousness," and dental problems.[4] Concerns are similar in samples of European Americans, African Americans, and Hispanic Americans. In large measure, these are the same concerns that adults have for teens' health.

Although adolescents have more acute conditions than do children or adults, they seek care for them less often.[5] When asked why they did not get needed medical care, 40 percent of girls and 27 percent of boys said they did not want to tell their parents. An additional 20 to 25 percent of each sex said they did not have the time to get care. These two reasons account for a larger percentage than the third of boys and girls who said they had no insurance or the cost was too much.[6]

Boys and girls have concerns about engaging in high-risk behaviors. Because these behaviors are the main source of mortality for teens, such concerns are realistic. Figure 11-1 presents questionnaire date gathered from 3,000 high school students in 1996 and 1997.[7] More worrisome figures about alcohol use indicate that in a large-scale study of high school seniors in the class of 1992, one out of three boys and one out of five girls indicated that they had consumed five or more drinks in a row in the past two weeks.[8] Dangerous in and of itself, such behavior is also related to both injuries and deaths from motor vehicle accidents.

Adolescents also correctly consider mood problems as health concerns. As noted, depressive symptoms increase in these years (we consider depression in detail in Chapter 15). Suicide increases in these years and is the second leading cause of death among European-American boys.[9] While rates of suicide among African-American boys have been much lower, recent statistics indicate that their rates are rising at a rapid pace and may soon equal the rates of European-American boys.[10]

High-risk behaviors are related to current mood and life experiences. For example, girls who have depressive symptoms are twice as likely as those with no or few depressive symptoms to smoke, drink, or take drugs, and three times as likely to have eating disorders.[11] Girls who have been physically or sexually abused or forced to have sex on dates are at risk in the same ways.

288

CHAPTER 11
Late
Adolescence:
The Years
from Fifteen
to Nineteen

FIGURE 11-1

RISKY BEHAVIORS: SMOKING, DRINKING, USING DRUGS; OLDER GIRLS AND
BOYS REPORT SIMILAR RATES

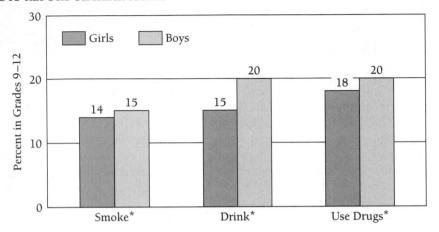

*Smoke = Smoked several cigarettes or a pack or more in the past week
Drink = Drink at least once a month or once a week
Use Drugs = Used illegal drugs in the past month

Cathy Schoen et al., *The Commonwealth Fund Survey of the Health of Adolescent Girls* (New York: Commonwealth
Fund, 1997), p. 25. Reprinted with permission from The Commonwealth Fund.

Parenting behaviors also affect adolescent engagement in high-risk behaviors.
Parental support and monitoring are related to avoidance of high-risk behaviors.
Positive family experiences also promote health.[12] In a study of early adolescents, a
parenting style termed *the energized family* promoted the positive health practices of
good nutrition, exercise, dental care, and nonsmoking. The energized family used
reasoning, granted children autonomy, and did not use punishment. These parental
practices still predicted children's health when parents' health behaviors were controlled. We shall discuss parenting effects further in a later section.

Adolescent Sexual Activity

Before they become sexual with a partner, adolescents engage in self-stimulating
sexual activities like fantasizing and masturbation. These may occur separately or
together—fantasies are used by half the teens who masturbate. Masturbation,
which often begins between age twelve and fourteen for boys and girls, is the most
common form of orgasm in both sexes in the adolescent years.[13]

Heterosexual activity usually proceeds from kissing to petting above the waist, to
petting below the waist, and then to intercourse.[14] Figures vary for the exact percentages of adolescents experiencing sexual intercourse. The most recent figures indicate
that in 1993, about 50 percent of high school seniors had engaged in intercourse.[15]

Boys are more sexually active than are girls. In one study, almost 30 percent of
boys reported intercourse by age 16, but only 13 percent of girls.[16] At age 18, the
comparable figures are 64 percent of boys and 44 percent of girls. Ethnic groups

TABLE 11-1
REASONS TO HAVE OR WAIT FOR INTERCOURSE

Reasons to Have Intercourse	
Girls	**Boys**
Peer Pressure (34%)	Peer Pressure (26%)
Pressure from boys (17%)	Curiosity (16%)
Curiosity (14%)	Everyone does it (10%)
Everyone does it (14%)	Sexual gratification (10%)

Reasons to Wait
Danger of sexually transmitted diseases (65%)
Danger of pregnancy (62%)
Fear of discovery by parents (50%)
Fear of having reputation with friends ruined (29%)

Adapted from Herant Katchadourian, "Sexuality," in *At the Threshold: The Developing Adolescent,* ed. S. Shirley Feldman and Glen R. Elliott (Cambridge, MA: Harvard University Press, 1990), p. 344.

vary. African-American boys and girls tend to be more advanced than European Americans and Hispanic Americans. For example, by age 17, 92 percent of African-American boys report intercourse, while only 50 percent of Hispanic Americans and 43 percent of European Americans make similar reports. By age 17, 40 percent of African-American girls report having had intercourse, compared with 25 percent of European-American and 24 percent of Hispanic-American girls. Table 11-1 describes reasons for waiting or not waiting to have intercourse.

Among sexually active teenagers, intercourse may occur infrequently and with a limited number of partners.[17] According to one survey, most teens had intercourse again with the first partner, but the relationships were not long-lived. The typical teen had zero to one partner with whom they had sex, usually less than a couple of times a month. About two-thirds of adolescents in one study experienced their first intercourse in the homes of parents or friends. Their partners were most often people they knew well—a steady date or close friend.

Many mothers underestimate their teens' sexual activity.[18] Older mothers who have good relationships with teens, who are strongly opposed to their having sexual relations, and who do not talk to them about sex are most likely to underestimate their teens' sexual behavior. Though very responsive to perceived parental values, teens often misperceive the strength of the mother's disapproval of sexual activity, in part because they share little conversation about sex.

It is important for parents to recognize that children need to hear parents' personal views expressed, that they do not automatically know what matters to parents. When they do know, many are willing to conform. Half of adolescents who do not have sexual relations say that the main reason they do not is that they fear their parents would find out about it.

290

CHAPTER 11
Late
Adolescence:
The Years
from Fifteen
to Nineteen

WHAT I WISH I HAD KNOWN ABOUT LATE ADOLESCENCE

"I wish that I had got my children involved in more family activities. When they were mostly through adolescence, I heard a talk by a child psychiatrist who said that often when teenagers say they don't want to do something with the family, at times you have to insist because they do go along and enjoy the event. I wish I had known that sooner, because I accepted their first 'No,' when I perhaps should have pushed more." MOTHER

"This may begin earlier, but it goes through adolescence. I had always heard they look for their own independence, their own things to participate in, but until you really experience it with your own, it's hard to deal with it. When you read about independence, it sounds like it's carefully planned out. When it actually happens, all of a sudden they want to do something that they have never done before and which you firmly believe they have no idea how to do. It can be driving for the first time or suddenly announcing they want to go somewhere with friends. I knew it was going to happen, but exactly how to handle it myself and handle it with them so they got a chance to do something new without it being dangerous has been a challenge to me." FATHER

"I wish that I had known that I had to listen more to them in order to understand what they were experiencing. I sort of assumed that I knew what adolescence was about from my own experience, but things had a different meaning to them. What was important to me was not that important to them, and I wish I had realized that in the beginning." MOTHER

"I wish I knew how to raise children in adolescence when you have traditional values and many of the people around you do not. It's very hard to do here in California compared to the South, where we came from. There, everyone reinforces the same values, and it is a lot easier for parents." MOTHER

"I wish I had known to be more attentive, to really listen, because kids have a lot of worthwhile things to say and you come to find out they hold a lot of your viewpoints." FATHER

"I wish I had known it was important to spend time with the children individually. We did things as a family, but the children are so different, and I think I would have understood them better if I had spent time with them alone." MOTHER

When asked to define sexual health, high school students give a range of answers—"feeling comfortable with your own body and all of its good strange feelings," "being caring, honest, responsible, respectful, and proud of yourself," "not getting knocked up because you were using protection."[19] Poor sexual health is described as sexual activities that are physically or emotionally harmful or exploitive. Adolescents see sexual health as a way of having a happier, richer life, and they look to parents to help them achieve positive sexual health.

Though sexual health involves contraceptive use, rates of use are very low in the early adolescent years—23 percent of girls under fifteen used contraceptives within the month of first intercourse but 42 percent delayed use for the first year. In contrast, among older adolescent girls, 50 percent used contraception at first intercourse.[20] Forty-eight percent of boys between ages 12 and 14 used condoms at first intercourse, compared with 60 percent of those 15 to 19 years old.[21]

The condom is the most popular birth control method reported by unmarried teen girls, of all ethnic groups, when they first have sex.[22] Hispanic-American teenagers are less likely than other groups to use contraceptives, perhaps because many are recent immigrants who have language difficulties, limited access to health care, and a cultural tradition of not preventing pregnancy.

Sexual health also involves protection against sexually transmitted diseases (STDs), a major risk for adolescents because of early age of intercourse and a lack of regular contraceptive use. Next to homosexual men and prostitutes, adolescent girls have the highest rates for any age group of gonorrhea, cytomegalovirus, and pelvic inflammatory disease. And now they face the added specter of AIDS (acquired immunodeficiency disease syndrome).[23]

Because of the disease's long incubation period, the precise risk that AIDS presents to teenagers is not known. Many people coming down with it in their twenties presumably contracted it as teenagers. However, adolescents may be at high risk, because the number of teen cases is increasing and because teens often do not use contraceptives. Unprotected sex with drug-using individuals is a major form of transmission in the heterosexual population. Further, teens are more susceptible than adults to all STDs, so they may be more vulnerable to AIDS as well.[24]

INTELLECTUAL DEVELOPMENT

Late adolescents' thinking advances and becomes more abstract than before. Teenagers can keep in mind several dimensions of a problem and do not focus on just one. They think of possibilities and generate more options for action and evaluate more facts. They think in relative rather than absolute terms. Compared with younger children, they can take a more understanding view of people and issues. They can stand back and take a look at their own thought processes.[25]

Though revealed in laboratory research studies, adolescent abstract reasoning capacities may not be seen in the decisions adolescents make in their everyday lives. For example, driver training improves the knowledge and driving skills of sixteen- to eighteen-year-olds, but increased knowledge and skill have not reduced the number of teenage driving accidents. So, teenagers have knowledge but do not necessarily have the maturity to put it to use in day-to-day actions. Using abstract thought depends on social and emotional factors as well.[26]

Karen Bartsch focuses on another factor that affects children's and adolescents' knowledge and thinking: their individual theories about the material at hand.[27] From early years, children develop ideas and "theories" about the way things are. Some of these theories are inaccurate and interfere with their learning new material; that is, they reject new material when it does not agree with their preexisting theories.

Increasing knowledge is not accomplished by just feeding new facts into a receptive learner. First, one must dispel inaccurate theories and then present new facts when the person is receptive and ready to absorb the information. For example, as

292

CHAPTER 11
Late
Adolescence:
The Years
from Fifteen
to Nineteen

long as some teenagers hold the false belief that they can get pregnant only if they want a child or if they make love standing up, as some believe, they will not take in contraceptive information because they believe it is not relevant to them. It does not fit with their idea of how one gets pregnant. In discussing factual information with teens, parents are wise to get the teen's beliefs or underlying assumptions out in the open first before presenting new facts.

Adolescents become more abstract when they think about themselves as well as about more objective matters.[28] They are able to see that individual qualities that might be contradictory can fall under a more general category, and thus become more understandable. For example, an early teenager may describe herself as having several contradictory mood states in changing succession—mad, sad, happy, irritable, loving—and ignore the contradictions because she cannot understand them. The late adolescent may subsume the contradictory moods under the self-description of "moody" and cease to be puzzled by them.

In addition, adolescents accept greater differentiation in their behaviors. For example, they do not expect to relate to friends, parents, and teachers in the same way. Boys more easily move from one role to another, but girls appear to expect themselves to be more consistent across many roles.

SCHOOL

The transition to high school brings problems similar to those experienced in the transition to junior high school.[29] High schools are still larger and more impersonal than junior high schools. The increased bureaucratic structure reduces interactions between students and teachers; it also reduces opportunities to really get to know each other so students can use teachers as mentors.

In adolescence, peers play a more important role in scholastic achievements than they have in earlier years.[30] Because young teens want to gain peer acceptance, they are vulnerable to their friends' views of them. If new friends devalue academic achievement, adolescents may shift away from academic pursuits to concentrate on social activities or sports.

Parents' practices affect students' achievement. Students who describe their parents as authoritative perform well in school and are actively engaged in school activities. Students who report their parents as authoritarian or permissive have the lowest grades.[31]

Students' achievement is related also to how they feel about themselves and their abilities. Underachievement in high school, defined as getting grades significantly below what would be expected on the basis of students' ability tests, occurs in all socioeconomic and ethnic groups.[32] In one study, underachieving boys and girls shared a set of qualities. Compared with students of the same ability who achieved grades appropriate to their ability, underachievers had lower opinions of their abilities, lower feelings of competence, less involvement in academic and extracurricular activities, lower educational and occupational aspirations, and more involvement in heterosexual relationships. Additionally, underachieving girls had fewer friends and less family support for their occupational desires and tended to be the youngest children.

When followed up thirteen years later, underachievers were less likely to have completed college, more likely to have frequent job changes, and more likely to divorce. The behavioral theme that characterizes these students is "lack of persistence." Those underachievers who had self-esteem and higher educational and occupational aspirations tended to catch up with their abilities and achieve more after high school.

Some students find school so frustrating and unsatisfying that they drop out. Dropouts usually have a long history of school problems, and many have repeated grades. Though most are of average intelligence, they are two years behind in reading and arithmetic achievement by the seventh grade, and most of their grades are below average. Further, they appear to have difficulties in many areas. For example, 90 percent of future dropouts are lower-status adolescents who feel they do not fit in with middle-class adolescents socially as well as academically.[33]

Family characteristics associated with dropping out include lack of understanding and acceptance of the adolescent, poor communication, and a generally unhappy home atmosphere. These families have weaker ties with friends and are generally less stable than families of students who graduate from high school, who tend to come from the same kinds of homes as high-achieving boys—homes where parents share recreation with children and are understanding and accepting of teens. These families are more stable and more involved in a network of friends with whom they share mutual support and reciprocity.

Students who drop out share certain psychological characteristics. They are less happy, less confident, less sure of themselves and where they are going than are students who finish school. Frustrated at school, they see leaving it as the only solution. They are rebellious and angry at others, wanting to resist adult authority. When parents stress to (such children) the importance of staying in school, dropping out is less likely.

What are the results of dropping out? The main negative consequences are fear of unemployment and actual higher rates of unemployment. If they can get work, however, high school dropouts do not, compared with high school graduates, have worse, unsatisfying jobs. They can be good employees.[34]

To prevent dropping out, school interventions must occur early in students' careers so that their frustration and low self-esteem do not accumulate. Students do not drop out at the first hint of trouble; they usually have had difficulties for a long time and see little hope of reversing the process. Early interventions can enable them in some small measure to experience success and pleasure at school.

WORKING

Studies show that youth employment has increased in the United States from the 1950s through the 1980s; even so, official reports may underestimate the number of working adolescents.[35] Official figures indicate that about 60 percent of high school sophomores and 75 percent of seniors report current or recent jobs. In a national survey, only 7 percent of seniors stated they had never worked. Most who work are employed in retail sales, food service, and general unskilled work.

294

CHAPTER 11
Late
Adolescence:
The Years
from Fifteen
to Nineteen

Adolescents derive decided benefits from work. They gain understanding of other people. They come to understand the dynamics underlying conflicts among co-workers, between supervisors and workers, and between workers and customers. In addition, working students feel more self-reliant and independent following employment.[36]

Working causes few changes in the relationships between parents and adolescents. Parents tend to control the money students earn and determine the amount they save. Working girls feel more distant from their families, whereas working boys tend to talk about problems with fathers. Work also causes few changes in peer relationships. Employed students spend as much time with friends as do nonworking students; they keep their friends and show no tendency to substitute co-workers for friends.

There appear to be costs to adolescents' working, however. First, they show less interest in and enjoyment of school. This attitude seems to follow getting a job, because those who seek jobs do not dislike school before starting to work. Second, adolescents show effects from stress in the job itself.[37] Stresses on the jobs include poor work environment (heat, noise, dirt, time pressures), meaningless tasks that are routine and boring, conflict with other roles (interfering with school activities), domineering supervisors, impersonal organizations, and low wages. When job stress scores are related to measures of physical or psychological distress, we find that adolescents with high-stress jobs are more likely than others to skip school and to use alcohol, cigarettes, and marijuana more. Thus, a stressful job puts strain on the adaptational reserves of adolescents just as it does on adults. So, the value of a job for adolescents depends in part on the nature of the work. If the job is stressful, the teenager may be well advised to wait for a less stressful job.

Ellen Greenberger and Laurence Steinberg, who conducted a large study of teenage work experience, are concerned that the current pattern of adolescent employment—spending many hours in unrewarding work—not only creates the stress just detailed but also prevents adolescents from developing fully as individuals.[38] Teenagers who work many hours do not have leisure to explore and develop interests, do not have solitude to think about their lives and fantasize about the future, and do not have time for deepening friendships with peers. Both the cynicism that develops from poor work experience and the results of alcohol and drug use are costly effects of adolescent work. The researchers' guidelines for teen work are discussed in a later section.

What is the parent's role in helping a child find enjoyable work? First, the parent who works provides a model. We know that a high percentage of sons follow in their fathers' professional footsteps. A son may be most likely to enter the father's occupation if it is one the child observes while growing up—if, for example, the father is a veterinarian or has a small business. Studies show a relationship between the example of a father who is happy and satisfied in his work and a son's occupational adjustment and success in adulthood.[39] Girls, too, model their work commitments on their mothers' examples.[40] Daughters of working women are more likely to plan to work when they are married than are girls whose mothers do not work. To serve as a work model, however, the parent does not need to have a job. If a mother or father has stimulating interests, such as hobbies and community activities, children can follow the example of a disciplined and accomplished person. Fathers who do not earn much money or achieve high status can still be excellent models because of their interests and their commitment to what they enjoy.

EMOTIONAL DEVELOPMENT

Describing the overall mood changes of 1,400 Chicago students who wore pagers for a week, researchers write,

> "Is there a pattern in the ways in which things go wrong? The most frequent scenarios seem to involve becoming overwhelmed. Again and again, adolescents are overpowered by situations: the demands of school, the intransigence of a parent, high expectations they impose on themselves. The result is anxiety, worry, agitation, panic, anger, and fear."[41]

The opposite of feeling overwhelmed is feeling bored and uninterested in what is happening. This is most likely to occur when teens feel others are in control of what is happening — for example, at school. Boredom comes, too, when adolescents lack worthwhile goals that challenge them.

As in the early adolescent years, teens enjoy friends, sports, hobbies, and art. These activities and experiences make them feel alive. A definite pattern appears in enjoyable activities. First, such activities require concentration on some aspect of the environment. Teens have to learn rules of interaction, whether for music or football. Next, as they learn an activity and really participate in it, they get feedback about their performance and can improve. As they continue with the activity, teenagers feel less self-conscious and experience a feeling of self-transcendence. There is great involvement in the activity itself and a feeling of effortlessness. To achieve these positive feelings, there has to be a good match between the teen's skills and the activity's challenges.

Teens' feelings about themselves and their lives tend to remain the same from early to late adolescence.[42] Those who were happy in the first year of high school are happy as juniors. They show more stability in their feelings about friends and school, however, than they do in their feelings about family and solitude, which change. Feelings about family improve — 52 percent say they are happier with family as juniors, 12 percent say less happy, and 36 percent report no change. This greater happiness appears to derive from late adolescents' broader perspective. They interpret experiences in a new light and as a result become more accepting both of family and of solitude.

Stressful life events include family loss such as the death of a parent; relationship loss such as the loss of boyfriend or girlfriend; physical problems such as having acne, needing to wear glasses or braces, or being overweight; and school problems such as failing one or more subjects or going to a new school.[43] The more stresses a middle-class teen experiences, the more likely he or she is to develop problems like depression, alcohol use, or delinquent acting out. Family support helps girls under high stress avoid difficulties. For boys under stress, the support of friends rather than family helps to reduce problem behaviors to a slight degree.

Inner-city youth who experience stress cope best with negative life events when they have high self-esteem and are socially expressive with peers.[44] While they may report more anxiety than do teens with low stress, these adolescents get good grades and relate well to others despite the stress in their lives.

Adolescents who reported many negative events not only felt depressed but experienced poor physical health as well following the event. Hormonal changes may also play a role in depressed mode or aggressiveness.[45] The experience of positive

296

CHAPTER 11
Late
Adolescence:
The Years
from Fifteen
to Nineteen

events, however, can serve as protection against the effects of negative events when they do occur.

A sense of self-efficacy or belief in one's abilities to take decisive action plays a more important role in adolescence than before. Teens make many choices, some of which will have long-term implications.[46] Beliefs in their abilities to face challenges improve adolescents' emotional well-being and protect against depression at this vulnerable time. Thus, belief in one's abilities plus support from parents and peers are major deterrents to low mood. (We shall discuss depressive symptoms in greater detail in Chapter 15.)

DEVELOPMENT OF THE SELF

Though later adolescents think of themselves in terms of general psychological qualities, they cannot yet form an integrated picture of themselves incorporating contradictory aspects of their peers.[47] They often refer to the many "me's"—the self with parents, the self with a set of friends, the self with a boyfriend. They reflect on their behavior and continue to be self-conscious about their appearance and behavior. Seeing their behavior shift by circumstance intensifies concern about "the real me." They feel they express their true selves when they discuss their inner thoughts, feelings, reactions to events; they express "false" selves when they put on an act and say what they do not mean. Teens report they act falsely (1) to make a good impression, (2) to experiment with different selves, and (3) to avoid others' low opinions of them. When they believe they have parents' support, adolescents can voice their opinions and express their true selves. The higher the level of support, the more adolescents can express themselves. They continue to see themselves as having contradictory qualities—like being intelligent and an airhead—without finding unifying themes to explain their behavior.

As adolescents continue to define their own identities, they do this, in part, by means of the activities they engage in and by thinking about themselves and life. Table 11-2 describes their goals in life.

Differences in gender identity appear mainly in the content of the identity, not in the process by which identity is formed. In the past, boys' identity has been linked with independence and achievement at work, and girls' identity linked with close relationships with others. Boys have been socialized to get ahead, and girls to get along.[48] These traits are expressed in their self-descriptions. Boys see themselves as more daring, rebellious, and playful in life than girls and, at the same time, more logical, curious, and calm. Girls see themselves as more attuned to people than boys are—more sympathetic, social, considerate, and affectionate—and more emotionally reactive—more worrisome, more easily upset, more needing of approval.[49]

Adolescent girls are socialized both to have close relationships with others and to succeed at work. Like minority youth, they may have a more difficult time as they attempt to integrate their identities in a greater number of roles—wife, mother, worker—whereas boys focus on their work roles.[50]

In adolescence, a small percentage of teens identify themselves as gay, lesbian, or bisexual.[51] For boys, the mean age of awareness of same-gender attraction is thirteen, with self-description as "homosexual" occurring between fourteen and twenty-one.

TABLE 11-2
WHAT ADOLESCENTS WANT MOST IN LIFE

To be loved	41%
To be healthy	38%
To do the kind of work you really like	29%
To be successful in your work	25%
To be rich	22%
To be married	13%
To do something worthwhile for the world	9%

Jane Norman and Myron Harris, *The Private Life of the American Teenager* (New York: Rawson Wade, 1981), p. 289.

For lesbians, the average age of awareness is sixteen, with self-description occurring around twenty-one years of age.

Society's negative view of homosexuality and lesbianism creates pressure and self-doubt in adolescents attracted to same-sex partners. Adolescents reported strong negative reactions from parents (43 percent) and friends (41 percent) on revealing their same-sex preference. They reported discrimination by peers (37 percent), verbal abuse (55 percent), and physical assault (30 percent).[52]

Because such discrimination and rejection create additional psychological problems, it is not surprising that gay adolescents are two to three times more likely to attempt suicide than are other adolescents and may make up as much as 30 percent of completed suicides.[53]

In spite of prejudice, homosexual and lesbian adolescents can evolve a positive self-concept of themselves as lovable, respectable, competent individuals. As with ethnic minority youth, support from family and others may be especially critical in forming a positive self-concept and combating the social disapproval they may encounter.

DEVELOPMENT OF SELF-REGULATION

Because of new capacities for abstract thought and the ability to see more options, adolescents are capable of higher levels of moral reasoning. They have internalized the rules. At the same time they are better able to understand others' points of view so they are able to reason in a more sympathetic way, emphasizing general reciprocity between people.[54]

A major task of this age period is to engage in healthy behaviors and avoid high-risk activities such as smoking, drinking, drugs, and early sexual intercourse. Parents' support and monitoring contribute to teens' development of internal restraint or the internalization of standards that, in turn, guide their behavior onto positive paths.[55] In the next section we deal in detail with the parents' role. Here, we shall focus on adolescents' qualities that enable them to pursue healthy activities.

Adolescents' positive orientation to school and their intolerance of harmful behaviors such as physical aggression, stealing, and property damage predict avoidance

298

CHAPTER 11
Late
Adolescence:
The Years
from Fifteen
to Nineteen

I N T E R V I E W
with Susan Harter

Susan Harter is a professor of psychology at the University of Denver and has carried out extensive studies on self-esteem. This interview is continued from Chapter 2.

Self-esteem seems very important because it gives the person a kind of confidence to try many new activities.

One of the things that I began to fret about was that we had spent a lot of government money examining what feeds into self-esteem. I bolted upright one day and said to myself, "What if self-esteem doesn't do anything? What if it doesn't have any ramifications for everyday lives and happiness? We know what creates it, but if it does not really impact our lives, who cares?"

So, this is how we got interested in depression. We looked at the dimensions of depression, and mood is the most cardinal aspect of depression. To make a long story short, self-esteem has powerful implications for mood. The correlation between how much you like yourself as a person and your self-reported mood on a scale from cheerful to depressed is typically about .80.

Low self-esteem is invariably accompanied by depressive affect. We have extended these findings in developing a model that helps us understand suicidal thinking in teenagers. We included Beck's concept of hopelessness and have measured specific hopelessnesses corresponding to the support and self-concept domains. We ask, "How hopeless are you about getting peer support, parent support, about ever looking the way you want in terms of appearance?" "How hopeless are you about your scholastic ability?" There are various separate domains.

The worst consequences occur if you feel inadequate in an area in which support is important and feel hopeless about ever turning that area around. Moreover, if you don't have support and feel there is nothing you can ever do to get that support, this feeds into a depression composite of low self-esteem, low mood plus general hopelessness. Thus, the worst case scenario is the feeling that I am not getting support from people whose approval is important, I am not feeling confident in areas in which success is valued, I am hopeless about ever turning things around, I don't like myself as a person, I feel depressed, and my future looks bleak. That, in turn, causes kids to think of suicide as a solution to their problems, as an escape from painful self-perceptions leading to depression.

of problem behaviors such as drinking, drugs, and precocious sexual intercourse for both boys and girls in three different ethnic groups.[56] Low self-esteem, low expectations of success, and having friends who model problem behaviors all predict adolescents' engagement in these disapproved behaviors.

Other individual qualities predicting drug use include a large time commitment to part-time work, higher income, and more evening recreational time.[57] Drug use tends to be lower among those with religious commitments. And drug use shifts in

There is another scenario that may also lead to suicidal thinking—namely, the teen who has done extremely well in all these areas. Then they experience their first failure, for example, scholastically (they get their first B), athletically (they feel they are responsible for a key loss), or socially (they don't get invited to a major party). As a result, they consider suicide as a solution to their humiliation. These teens seem so puzzling, but we think that conditional support plays a role here. We saw kids whose support scores were reasonable, but when we interviewed them, they would say, "Well, my parent only cares about me if I make the varsity team or if I get all As" or whatever the formula is for that family. So conditionality of support is important.

Another aspect about suicide is the co-occurrence of symptoms. People have talked about internalizers and externalizers as though you are one or the other. Most people have both qualities. When you look at measures of internalizing and externalizing symptoms, a correlation is about .65. Typically, you don't have a separate group of internalizing people who only engage in behaviors directed against the self. In clinical samples, it is often difficult to predict whether problem adolescents will act out against themselves or take it out on someone else. It may depend on the specific circumstances. Is the other person actually there when the adolescent is distressed or is the adolescent alone? Is there a weapon available? These factors partially determine whether one acts against the self or against the others.

That leads to another point. We asked teenagers who reported depressed affect, Which specific emotions comprise depression for you? We all suspect it is sadness of some kind but are there other feelings that are part of the depressive experience? Eighty percent of adolescents tell us it is sadness plus *anger*. Who is the target of that anger—are they angry at themselves (the classic view of depression), or are they angry at someone else? We found that the majority of teens are angry at someone else. They have not yet internalized the anger against themselves. They will tell you, "Yeah, I am really, really sad, and I am angry at my mom. She got divorced and isn't paying attention to me or she is on my case."

Typically, adolescents view the causes of depression to be actions of others against the self. Other people have rejected them or are in conflict with them or aren't treating them the way they want to be treated. A few of them will admit they are angry at themselves, but most anger is directed at others.

I think it is important to point out that the reason people are spending so much energy and money on studying self-esteem is that low self-esteem has so many consequences such as depressed mood, lack of energy to get up and do age-appropriate tasks, be productive, and, for some, thoughts of suicide. Most parents want their children to be happy, and self-esteem is an important pathway to happiness and the ability to function in today's world.

response to information on the risks of given drugs. A significant number of adolescents give up drugs such as marijuana and cocaine as more accurate information on their harmful effects becomes available.

While parents and social scientists have long worried about the negative influence of peers, less attention is paid to the positive influence of a high-achieving, competent friend who may shift a teen's behavior in a more positive direction. In the next section, we shall examine peer relationships more closely.

300

CHAPTER 11
Late
Adolescence:
The Years
from Fifteen
to Nineteen

SOCIAL DEVELOPMENT

Parent-Child Relationships

As teenagers progress through the high school years, they spend less time with their families, dropping from 25 percent of their time in their first year in high school to 15 percent in the senior year. Much less than 15 percent is spent exclusively with parents.[58]

Although parents see less of their adolescents, the dimensions of parenting that predict competence in the preschool years continue to predict adolescent competence reflected in self-reliant, independent behavior and in the capacity for meaningful relationships with others. Diana Baumrind followed her sample from the preschool years through adolescence and identified three major components of parenting in the adolescent years—parental *commitment* along with the balance between *demandingness* (establishing rules, monitoring compliance, and enforcing rules), and *responsiveness* (being supportive of the child and paying attention to the child's needs and interests).[59] How parents relate to children during adolescence is more important in determining adolescent competence than are earlier parenting techniques.

Parenting Styles   Baumrind describes six different parenting patterns and relates them to the child's drug use. *Authoritative* parents have strong commitments to children and balance demands with responsiveness to children's needs: "Unlike any other pattern, authoritative upbringing *consistently* generated competence and deterred problem behavior in both boys and girls, at *all* stages."[60] *Democratic* parents who have strong commitment to children and are highly responsive to their needs are only average in demandingness. Their children are highly competent as well, but are freer to explore drugs.

Nonauthoritarian-Directive parents who are high on conventional control and value conformity have children with the least drug use, but this is accomplished by strict obedience to rules so that children are conforming and dependent on adult approval. *Authoritarian-Directive* parents are even more restrictive and less supportive and have less competent children. Parents of both types are moderately committed to their children.

Unengaged parents are neither demanding nor responsive, nor are they committed to children. They either actively reject or neglect parenting responsibilities. Free of adult authority, children from these families have little direction and so are described as immature. These adolescents have had problems dating back to the preschool years, and they lack competence in many areas of adolescent functioning. The *Good Enough* parent is about average on the different dimensions, and their children are about average in competence.

Although Baumrind's sample was relatively small, primarily white, and middle class, her family classifications applied equally to a large, ethnically diverse sample of 4,100 adolescents between the ages of fourteen and eighteen who were followed for two years.[61] Regardless of the adolescent's sex and socioeconomic or ethnic background, authoritative parenting was related to adolescent self-confidence, competency, self-reliance, avoidance of delinquent activity, and general good mood. In

European-American and Hispanic-American families, authoritative parenting was also related to school achievement, but African-American and Asian-American students did not show increased school performance. In no cases were adolescents from nonauthoritative homes better off than those reared in authoritative families.

Authoritative parenting is also related to adolescent personality and peer group membership in European-American students who seek out crowds that reinforce academic achievement and school involvement. These students receive the same message about values and behavior from parents and peers.

Among minority youth, no relationship exists between authoritative parenting and peer group membership. This appears to result from ethnic minority members' not having equal access to all peer groups. For example, an Asian American may be excluded from the "jocks" or the "druggies," and an African American may be excluded from the "brains" (see the section on peers for a discussion of such groups).

Authoritative parenting exerts an even greater influence when the teenager's friends' parents also rely on authoritative parenting. Friends tend to be more competent, and such peers help to maintain high levels of adjustment.

Neglectful or unengaged parenting is consistently associated with low competence, psychological distress, and acting out. Adolescents from indulgent and authoritarian homes fall somewhere between those from authoritative and neglectful homes.

Studies of adolescents who avoid high-risk behavior such as cigarette smoking, drinking, or drugs indicate that parental support—in the form of affection, interest in the child, praise, encouragement—and parental monitoring of behavior are the two family factors most clearly related to nondrinking and nonproblematic behaviors.[62]

In considering the concept of parental control, Brian Barber makes an important distinction between two kinds of control: psychological and behavioral.[63] He defines psychological control as parents' intruding on and controlling the child's thoughts and feelings and manipulating the child's behavior through guilt or withdrawal of love. Psychological control deprives the adolescent of a sense of autonomy and is related to depressive and internalizing problems. On the other hand, while low psychological control promotes adolescent development, low behavioral control—poor monitoring and supervising—leads to externalizing problems, as children receive no guidance and get into high-risk activity.

Clearly, parenting practices significantly predict adolescents' behavior. Recent work suggests further that parents' individual personality characteristics are also predictive.[64] In a study of adolescent boys' behavior, a measure of fathers' self-restraint and self-control in early adolescence predicted academic achievement, personal competence, conflict resolution skills, and good morale four years later. Conversely, fathers' low self-restraint predicted adolescent drinking and drug use, poor peer relations, low grades, multiple sexual partners, and symptoms of depression. Fathers' self-restraint was predictive, even controlling, for sons' self-restraint in early adolescence.

So, in looking at all the evidence regarding healthy functioning in these years, we can conclude that adolescents need positive role models of restraint and they need both emotional support and guidelines for behavior that parents monitor and supervise. Authoritative parenting serves as a buffer even when teens have friends who urge them toward drug use or lowered standards of schoolwork.[65]

302

CHAPTER 11
Late
Adolescence:
The Years
from Fifteen
to Nineteen

Late teens may spend more time in their bedrooms than in any other setting in the home. Parents are expected to respect the teen's privacy, including phone conversations, mail, and personal effects, but they are also expected to include them in leisure activities and family events.

Serving as Consultants   A parent serves as a reliable resource and consultant for children in areas of importance not only by providing factual information and values, as described in Chapter 10, but also by helping teens develop the confidence to carry out effective behaviors. I can illustrate this in the area of sexual behavior. In addition to giving information about reproduction and the consequences of early sexual activity, parents promote the postponement of sexual activity by encouraging teens to have interests and activities that absorb their time and attention and give them great satisfaction.[66]

Parents also help adolescents develop the social skills to withstand pressure for sexual activity and to insist on safe-sex practices when they are sexually active. Further, parents provide supervision and, as far as possible, do not permit teens to be in situations that can lead to spontaneous sexual activity. For example, since first intercourse most often happens at home, parents should not go away for the weekend and leave teenagers alone at home.[67]

In addition, parents can serve as consultants when teenagers want to enter the world of work. Ellen Greenberger and Laurence Steinberg suggest parents play an active role in discussing the pros and cons of work in the light of the child's needs and other demands on the child's time.[68] If work is an option, then parents can help teens decide the kind of job that would meet their needs—how many hours, how far from home, the exact time of day for working, ways to handle the money and then monitor the child's work experience after the job has started to be sure it is not too stressful and does not have negative effects on schoolwork, friendships, and social behavior like drinking. If it does, then parents can discuss changing the job or the hours.

The ways that parents can help teenagers make long-term vocational plans resemble the ways they help them make choices about sexual activity. Parents can provide factual information about expanding fields and possible careers, about the personal qualities and interests needed to do various kinds of work, and about how teenagers can get more information and test their interests. Parents can also provide information about possible occupations based on their observation of children's skills and interests.

Parents also can help children develop the interpersonal skills and the self-confidence that will enable them to pursue vocational goals. They can talk about how to prepare for interviews and how to present abilities; at times of failure and frustration, they can offer encouragement and suggest alternative actions. As children make choices, however, parents must stand back and keep silent.

Parents also serve as consultants to help their teens relate to the larger community. Because the larger society may fail to validate the identity minority youth are achieving, minority parents play an especially important role in this process. Parents can provide information and relate their own experiences to illustrate how to cope with discrimination and prejudice. This may be done differently with boys and girls depending on the experiences of the particular ethnic group. Research suggests, for example, that African-American parents focus on racial barriers in rearing sons but emphasize racial pride in rearing daughters, perhaps because boys experience greater hostility from the majority culture.[69]

While parents present information, positive models, and encouragement, they are also involved in resolving conflicts. In the previous chapter, we saw that conflicts between parents and adolescents center most frequently on mundane issues like chores and school grades. Later adolescents understand that some activities are done because they benefit the whole family. Although conflicts about everyday issues continue, late teens accept and respect their parents' conventional views on situations and thus please their parents. Teens do not necessarily give in, but parents are more likely to grant their requests now, perhaps because teens seem to understand their reasoning.[70]

When adolescents struggle less over power with their parents, they become more self-governing and independent without giving up warm family relationships. Parents and adolescents then form a partnership directed toward establishing such autonomy.[71] When attachment is secure, parents and teens can regulate emotional responses and engage in problem-solving behaviors with relatively little anger and frustration.[72] With secure attachments, both parents and teens can discuss differences and arrive at compromises. Anger appears to motivate securely attached family members to overcome differences and restore harmony. When the attachment is secure, a balance exists between the needs of the individual and the needs of the relationship.

When attachment relationships are insecure, one partner may try to dominate the other, refusing to listen or to compromise. Anger in these relationships serves to create greater distance. When separation occurs in the context of family misunderstandings

304

CHAPTER 11
Late
Adolescence:
The Years
from Fifteen
to Nineteen

and emotional distance from parents, teens report loneliness and feelings of dejection.[73] When issues of power are settled, about half the respondents in a large survey report positive relationships with parents, which they want to continue as they move through later adolescence.[74]

Childhood behavioral problems intensify the usual problems of adolescence. If parents have been overprotective or neglecting, children will have difficulty making and carrying out independent decisions. If teenagers have never had satisfying friendships with important emotional interchanges, they will be poorly prepared to handle the difficulties of achieving peer acceptance, and they may acquiesce easily to peer pressure. When control of impulses and physical activity has always been hard, teenagers will find it hard to cope with the excessive push to action that many feel during these years.

David Elkind has pointed out that adolescents may try to pay parents back for treatment they felt was unfair when they were younger.[75] As young people achieve an increasing capacity to earn their own money, physical equality with parents, and freedom to drive and do things for themselves, many feel that they have, at least, somewhat equal footing with parents. If they have felt mistreated, now they are capable of redressing the imbalance between what parents have demanded and what they have given. Nevertheless, most teenagers *do* want good relationships, and family ties can be strengthened during these years.

Sibling Relationships

Sibling relationships improve in later adolescence, compared with those same relationships in the elementary school years and early adolescence.[76] Relationships become more egalitarian and less intense. Egalitarian relationships may occur in the context of either support or growing distance.

The standing in the family constellation partly determines the perception of the relationship. Older adolescent siblings are less likely to dominate younger siblings than before, but they also report less companionship and affection than younger siblings want. Younger siblings look up to older ones and report less conflict than older siblings report. Even though adolescents and other family members spend less time together, the attachment among siblings remains moderately strong.

Peers

Peers play many important roles in the psychological development of adolescents. As in previous age periods, they provide opportunities for developing social skills, but they also provide support and understanding in the process of separating from parents. In Japan and the Soviet Union, adolescents spend 2 or 3 hours per week with peers.[77] In the United States, in a typical week, high school students spend twice as much time as peers (29 percent) as with parents (13 percent).[78]

In the adolescent years, other changes in peer relationships take place as well.[79] First, peer interactions are generally unsupervised by adults. Second, they are more likely to include larger numbers of peers who form crowds. Finally, peers gravitate to members of the opposite sex.

In adolescence, friendships become more intimate.[80] In addition to joint activities, friendships involve more self-disclosure, expression of feelings, and support for friends as needed. Friends are expected to tell each other their honest opinions and to express satisfactions and dissatisfactions with the other person. Friends also have to learn to resolve conflicts as they arise. So, friendships promote the development of social skills that, in turn, enrich friendships. Intimacy in friendships is related to adolescents' sociability, self-esteem, and overall interpersonal competence.

Adolescents feel quite loyal to their friends—in continuing friendships despite parental disapproval and in not revealing details of the relationships to others. Although overall 56 percent would report that a friend was considering suicide, far fewer (17–20 percent) would break a confidence about drugs and alcohol, and almost none (6 percent) would tell if a friend was shoplifting.[81]

Peer groups that form in adolescence are larger than the cliques of the early adolescent years. Bradford Brown refers to these as *crowds*.[82] As noted in Chapter 10, cliques form out of mutual choice. Crowds, though, are based on judgments of personal characteristics, and a person must be invited to join. Through time we have seen slight shifts in the kinds of crowds, but generally studies find groups of "jocks" (athletes), "brains," popular kids, "druggies" or delinquents, and "nerds."

A recent study, conducted over a year's time, describes peer groups formed on the basis of members' feeling upset and distressed.[83] Individual adolescents seek out peers with similar levels of distress. Boys tend to be influenced by the mood of peers, growing more similar to the mood of the group; girls tend to maintain their own personal level of distress. Though feeling distressed does not prevent teens from having friends, it does shape the kind of friends they will have.

As noted earlier, peers also impact adolescent engagement in high-risk behaviors. A peer who engages in such behavior may serve as a model; on the other hand, high achievers also serve as models. Parents' behavior indirectly influences the kinds of group friendships adolescent children form.[84] Members of four groups—"brains," popular crowd, "jocks," and "druggies"—described their parents' child-rearing practices. When parents stress achievement and monitor children closely, children tend to get high grades and belong to the "brains" group. When parents fail to monitor and do not encourage joint decision making, children tend to become part of the popular crowd and/or may be exposed to the drug crowd. Peer group norms are most likely to reinforce those behaviors that parenting strategies have encouraged.

Different ethnic groups were more likely to belong to certain groups. European-American students tended to be part of the popular crowd or the druggies. Asian Americans were more likely to belong to the "brains," and African Americans were more likely to belong to the "jocks."

Dating

Dating serves many important functions in adolescence. It is a way to learn how to relate to people of the opposite sex; it provides a structure for meeting people, exploring compatibility, and terminating a relationship with a minimum of embarrassment. Finally, dating gives practice in developing feelings of trust and enjoyment with the opposite sex. Because there are almost no studies of same-sex dating, we shall discuss heterosexual dating here.

Although the sexual revolution has brought many changes, the concerns of adolescents who date remain much the same as those of their parents. "Will he like

306

CHAPTER 11
Late
Adolescence:
The Years
from Fifteen
to Nineteen

me?" "Will she go out with me?" "What do I say on a date?" Girls still wait for boys to call, and almost two-thirds of a national sample of girls say they have never asked a boy out. Boys rather enjoy being asked out, and only 13 percent said it would "turn them off."[85]

What qualities do boys and girls seek in each other? Over 90 percent of girls ages sixteen to twenty-one said the important qualities in boys are good personality, kindness, good manners, and a sense of humor. Over 70 percent said compassion, good looks, and charm are important. The least popular qualities are heavy drinking, inability to communicate, drug use, and profanity, followed by indecisiveness, being a "super jock," and not being affectionate. Boys said they are initially attracted by a good figure and good looks, but for them, too, the most important qualities are personality and a good sense of humor — then beauty, intelligence, and psychological warmth. So even though boys place an initial emphasis on physical qualities, they are basically seeking the same qualities in girls that girls seek in them.[86]

Most girls begin dating at about fourteen and boys between fourteen and fifteen. By their senior year in high school, about half of adolescents date more than once a week, and one-third between two and three times a week. It is widely held that boys are oriented toward sexual activity more than girls are. But even though adolescent boys desire physical intimacy early in the dating relationship, they want increasing affection and intimacy as the relationship progresses, just as girls do.[87]

About one-quarter of boys and one-third of girls say they are going steady. Going steady occurs most frequently among older adolescents sixteen to eighteen; 30 percent of boys and 40 percent of girls of this age say they are going steady. Over half the adolescents say they have been in love, with girls reporting this more frequently than boys. The intensity of these feelings and the pain that comes when the relationship ends rival anything any adult feels in such a situation. Some love relationships of adolescence develop into more committed relationships, but frequently the feelings fade.[88]

Adolescents who have definite educational and vocational plans and who wish for marriages like those of their parents go steady less often and report being in love less often during adolescence than the norm. When girls have high self-esteem, they date more often but go steady less often. Those who are most likely to be going steady do not want marriages like their parents have. In general, involvement in dating too early and too intensely may block opportunities for same-sex relationships or more casual opposite-sex relationships that develop the capacity for intimacy and closeness at later ages.

Adolescents believe that the quality of the relationship between people, the way they treat each other, is the most important factor in making the decision about sexual activity. About three-quarters of adolescents today believe it is all right for people to have sex before marriage if they love each other, and about two-thirds believe that what two people want to do sexually is moral if they both want to do it and it doesn't hurt anyone.[89]

TASKS AND CONCERNS OF PARENTS

In this age period, parents remain caregivers but also grant their teens greater autonomy. Parenting tasks include these:

- Continuing their commitment to children by monitoring and enforcing rules while supporting and accepting their individuality
- Being an available, responsive caregiver
- Serving as a model of responsible behavior
- Communicating information and values in an atmosphere of open discussion
- Serving as a consultant to children as they make important decisions
- Allowing children to separate in an atmosphere of acceptance
- Sharing enjoyable times together

The problems encountered during adolescence relate to physical and intellectual functioning, social behavior, and family interactions. Among the most prevalent and difficult are those associated with family, school, friends, and social behavior—shyness, dress, sexual activity, and limit setting that involves curfew and the use of alcohol and drugs.

Eating Problems

As physical growth stabilizes during the adolescent years, most teenagers attain a desirable weight and maintain it with only occasional departures corrected with diet. A minority of adolescents, however, develop problems in eating that result in obesity (gross overweight), *anorexia nervosa* (severe underweight), or *bulimia nervosa* (binge eating following by self-induced vomiting or purging with laxatives). In contrast to obesity and anorexia, which are observable because they change physical appearance, bulimia may be difficult to detect, because the bulimic frequently maintains average weight.

These three eating problems are not entirely distinct from each other. About 50 percent of anorexics are also bulimics. Anorexics and bulimics may, at one point, have been obese or become obese as they grow older. It is difficult to know the exact numbers of adolescents suffering from these eating disorders. Though anorexia and bulimia are rare, they do appear to be increasing in the population. These two disorders are more commonly seen in girls than boys, most probably because physical attractiveness, defined as thinness, is so valued for girls in U.S. society.

Although the three eating problems have different outcomes in terms of physical appearance, they share several features in common. Each condition may be caused by a variety of factors: hereditary factors play a role in weight gain; physical factors such as metabolism or feedback control mechanisms may be related to anorexia nervosa; family patterns of eating and interacting influence eating behavior. Though physical and biological factors play a role, psychological and social factors are thought to be the main contributors to these disorders.

Many kinds of psychological factors predispose individuals to gain or lose excessive weight. In the case of obesity, families may equate love with food; adolescents may then use food to buffer them in times of disappointment. In the case of all three eating disorders, problems in identity formation may underlie the behavior. Teenagers who have found it difficult to establish separate identities for themselves as worthwhile, valued individuals may overeat, starve, or purge themselves. Anorexics often

308

CHAPTER 11
Late
Adolescence:
The Years
from Fifteen
to Nineteen

 THE JOYS OF PARENTING LATE ADOLESCENTS

"I think it's really fun to watch them grow up and mature. It's fun to see them discover things about themselves and their lives. The older ones have boyfriends, and I'm seeing them interact with the boyfriends." MOTHER

"Sometimes the kids have friends over, and they all start to talk about things. It's nice to see them get along with their siblings as well as their friends. It gives you a good feeling to see them enjoying themselves." FATHER

"I felt very pleased when my son at sixteen could get a summer job in the city and commute and be responsible for getting there and doing a good job." MOTHER

"I like it when they sit around and reminisce about the things they or the family have done in the past. They all sit around the table and talk about an outing or a trip we took, saying 'Remember this?' It's always interesting what they remember. This last summer we took a long sight-seeing trip, and what stands out in their minds about it is funny. They remember Filene's basement in Boston or a chicken ranch where we stopped to see friends. One father took the Scouts on a ski trip. They got stuck in the snow on the highway for hours, and the car almost slid off the road. He said, 'Never again.' I said, 'Don't you realize that because of those things, the boys will probably remember that trip forever? You have given them wonderful memories.'" MOTHER

"I really enjoy her happiness. She always sees the positive side to a situation. Things might bother her from time to time, but she has a good perspective on things." FATHER

"I really like to see them taking responsibility. Yesterday they had a school holiday, and I was donating some time at an open house fundraiser. They got all dressed up and came along and helped too. The older one coaches a soccer team of four-year-olds, and the younger is a patrol leader in the Scouts, so they both have responsibility for children. They complain sometimes that it's hard to get the little kids' attention to show them things, but I think they like it." MOTHER

have outstanding successes in many areas but still do not feel competent and independent even though others believe they are. Underlying concerns about sexuality and interactions with opposite-sex peers can spur eating problems that prevent appropriate dating and sexual behavior because appearance is so deviant.

Eating problems in turn create difficulties. People with eating disorders often feel self-conscious, depressed, and discouraged about their pattern of eating. Bulimics often fear being discovered in their purging while anorexics fear their weight loss will be noted. (Most adolescents, in fact, feel others are critical of them for their eating behaviors.) Not only do psychological problems result, but serious medical conditions can follow as well. Bulimia can lead to metabolic changes, electrolyte imbalances, ulcers, and bowel problems. Severe overweight can result in heart and blood

"I enjoy that she is following in the family tradition of rowing. I rowed in college, and my brothers did, my father and grandfather did, and she saw a city team and signed up. She does it all on her own and has made a nice group of friends through it." FATHER

"I can't believe that she has had her first boyfriend and it worked out so well. They met at a competition; and he lives some distance away, so they talk on the phone. He has a friend who lives here, and he comes for a visit sometime and does lots of things with the family. We all like him, and it is nice for her to have a boyfriend like that." MOTHER

"The joys are seeing them go from a totally disorganized state to a partially motivated, organized state. You can see their adult characteristics emerging." FATHER

"I enjoy seeing my daughter develop musical ability, seeing her progression from beginning flute to an accomplished player who performs, and seeing how much pleasure she takes in her accomplishment." MOTHER

"It really gives me a lot of pleasure to see the two of them help each other. They seem to have respect for each other. She is the brain and helps him with school, and he helps her too at times." FATHER

"I enjoy his maturity. He's so responsible. He tests us, but when we're firm, he accepts that. I'm real proud of him because he looks at the consequences of what he does." FATHER

"I enjoy his honesty and the relationship he has with his friends. He is real open with his feelings, and his friends look up to him. He's a leader." MOTHER

"He's not prejudiced. His best friends are of different ethnic groups. People trust him and like him because he's real concerned about people." FATHER

"I feel really pleased about the way the boys get along together. There is rivalry, but there is a lot of love. The older one takes the younger one under his wing, and the younger one looks up to him." FATHER

pressure problems and diabetes. Anorexia can result in electrolyte imbalances, malnutrition, cessation of menstruation, and even death in 5 to 15 percent of cases.

Parents whose children develop these problems need first to consult physicians for medical confirmation of the problem and for help in planning treatment. Parents play a role in modifying their child's eating behavior by having appropriate foods at home and establishing regular mealtimes that are enjoyable occasions for all family members. Parents are also advised to seek psychological counseling for children with these difficulties. In some instances, family counseling that includes all members of the family is the treatment of choice. Salvador Minuchin and his associates,[90] for example, report very good treatment results for anorexics when they and their families are seen together. In some cases, individual or group therapy may be

310

CHAPTER 11
Late
Adolescence:
The Years
from Fifteen
to Nineteen

useful. Individual therapy is most helpful in getting at conflicts that underlie the eating disorder. Group therapy can enable adolescents to share their feelings about the psychological factors that cause and follow the eating disorder. Adolescents often acquire strong feelings of support for themselves in these groups. Parents also help children with their eating problems when they act to increase their children's self-esteem and self-confidence.

Dress and Physical Appearance

In matters of dress and physical appearance, all strategists agree that the choices belong to the teenager except under special circumstances. Accepting such an approach is not easy for many parents. One father wanted his children to dress to please his peer group, not theirs. When he thought about the problem, he realized that his children were individuals who were also trying to please their peer group. He accepted their desire to be like their friends and said no more about the issue.

Special circumstances will permit parents a greater say in the matter. For example, if teenagers are going to attend a function made up of parents' friends, then they can ask young people to dress in a way acceptable to that group. If they feel they cannot, parents might ask them to stay home. When adolescents see that what they do has a specific effect on the parents, they often will change, as seen in an example cited by Thomas Gordon. The father, a school principal, felt his son's long hair jeopardized his job in a conservative city. When he explained the tangible effect of his son's appearance on him, the boy cut his hair.

Alcohol and Drugs

Because parents serve as consultants to their children on such topics as substance abuse, they must have accurate knowledge so they can present valid and reliable information and form realistic assessments of their adolescent's behavior. Table 11-3 presents the percentage of adolescents who use different substances. Percentages have dropped gradually since 1980 when use was at its peak. For example, in 1980, 60 percent of teenagers had used marijuana, 16 percent had used cocaine, 15 percent had used sedatives, and 15 percent had taken tranquilizers. There is a growing concern, however, that LSD use, which decreased in the 1980s, is on the rise again.[91]

The most frequently used substances, alcohol and cigarettes, serve as an introduction to other drugs.[92] Parents often think that marijuana is the "gateway drug," but in fact, the substances parents use most often provide adolescents' introduction to substance use. Following teens' drug use for ten years, investigators found a five-stage model of drug use most useful in understanding behavior. In stage 1, adolescents use no drugs; in stage 2, they consume beer or wine; in stage 3, they use cigarettes and/or hard liquor; in stage 4, they use marijuana; and in stage 5, they use other illicit drugs.

As indicators of how adolescents develop problems with alcohol and drugs, two longitudinal studies provide information on the antecedents and implications of substance use and abuse in the high school years.[93] Both samples were followed

TABLE 11-3
DRUG USE OF ADOLESCENT HIGH SCHOOL SENIORS: 1992

Percentage Who Ever Used the Following:	
Alcohol	88
Cigarettes	62
Marijuana	33
Inhalants	17
Stimulants	14
LSD	9
Cocaine	6
Other Opiates	6
Sedatives	6
Tranquilizers	6
Crack Cocaine	3
Heroin	1

The World Almanac and Book of Facts, 1994, ed. Robert Famighetti (Mahwah, NJ: Funk and Wagnalls, 1993), p. 692.

from the preschool years, with careful assessment of both parents and children. Children's substance use was determined in interviews in the 1980s.

Though the investigators categorized substance use slightly differently, both found that the most serious use of alcohol and drugs in their samples was related to serious psychological problems both in adolescence and in early and middle childhood. In both studies, adolescents with the most serious alcohol and drug use lack general competence, have poor impulse control, and experience emotional distress. In Diana Baumrind's study, these problems date back to preschool years; and in Jonathan Shedler and Jack Block's study, frequent users have different personality characteristics from experimenters and abstainers as early as age seven, when they relate poorly to other children and feel generally insecure.

Both studies found that adolescents who experiment casually with drugs do not have serious psychological problems and, in fact, are competent, outgoing adolescents. These studies find, too, that many abstainers are anxious, conforming individuals who are fearful of taking risks. Baumrind divided abstainers into two groups—risk-avoidant nonusers and rational nonusers who justify their choice for realistic reasons—"I don't like my mood changed chemically." Risk-avoidant nonusers are less explorative, less resilient, and less competent than are rational nonusers, who are more socially and intellectually confident.

Several family variables are identified as antecedents. Baumrind found that adolescent substance use parallels parent use. Abstainers come from families where parents do not use substances, and abusers come from families where parents abuse

312

CHAPTER 11
Late
Adolescence:
The Years
from Fifteen
to Nineteen

TABLE 11-4
RESOURCES FROM WHOM ADOLESCENTS
WOULD SEEK HELP FOR SUBSTANCE ABUSE

	Early Adolescents (Age 12–14)	Middle Adolescents (Age 15–18)
Friends and Other Adults	24%	31%
Parents, Friends, and Other Adults	22%	24%
Parents and Other Adults	15%	9%
Other Adults Only	11%	11%
Friends Only	11%	11%
No One	11%	8%
Parents and Friends	3%	4%
Parents Only	3%	2%

Adapted from Michael Windle et al., "Adolescent Perceptions of Help-Seeking Resources for Substance Abuse," *Child Development* 62 (1991): 183. With permission from Society for Research in Child Development.

substances. Adolescents with the lowest substance use come from Nonauthoritarian-Directive and Authoritative homes (recall Baumrind's descriptions of these parenting patterns), and the abusers from Unengaged families, where they lack direction and encouragement. Findings from the Shedler and Block study reinforce the view that abusers come from disorganized, unprotective families. Abstainers, as in Baumrind's study, come from homes where parents exert control over children, but these homes are not as supportive and encouraging as those of nonusers in the Baumrind sample.

The agreement in the findings of the two studies is noteworthy. Both indicate casual or experimental use occurs in the context of competent, outgoing social behavior in adolescents. The most serious use of substances is associated with lack of competence and psychological problems dating back to early and middle childhood. Shedler and Block point out the importance of recognizing the long-standing nature of the substance abuser's problems and the need for extensive help if the problem is to be dealt with.

When teens develop an alcohol or drug problem, where do they go for help? As shown in Table 11-4, a New York State sample of 27,000 teens, age twelve to eighteen years, described whom they would seek out if they had a problem.[94] Regardless of age, gender, or ethnic background, the majority of teens would seek out someone other than parents. Other adults appear as a resource in the four most frequently selected sources of help. While "parents only" are the least sought-after resource, adults, including parents, are the most common resources. Social isolates, about 10 percent of the sample, would seek help from no one, and an additional 10 percent rely on friends only, so only about 20 percent of the sample would not involve an adult in getting help for their problem.

Ethnic differences in help-seeking behavior indicate that African Americans and Hispanic Americans are overrepresented in the social isolate category. Both these ethnic groups are, however, more likely than European Americans to involve other adults as sources of help, so they appear to rely more on the extended family or community. Gender differences reveal that boys are more likely than girls to be in the social isolate group and seek help from no one.

Children do not often tell parents they are using drugs, and many parents overlook indicators of possible drug use because the idea is painful to them. They ignore their children's grade changes, lack of energy, lack of interest in usual activities, changes in friends, and changes in aggressive behavior. They engage in what Beth Polson and Miller Newton term *parent denial,* refusing to look at the problem and pretending it is not there.[95] Parents find many excuses for their teen's altered behavior, and most teens who are using drugs are happy to accept the excuses put forth by parents.

Newton's experience with his son provides an illuminating example. Newton served as the executive director of the state association of alcohol treatment in Florida, and his wife was a supervising counselor at a treatment agency. Both parents were knowledgeable about the use of at least one drug. Their two older children, nineteen and twenty, were both happy and competent people. The first time their fifteen-year-old son Mark came home drunk, the family rallied around him, gave him information about alcoholism in the family, and began to monitor his behavior more closely. He was a bright, curious boy with many interests and a passion for healthy living, so the family was unprepared for the next drunk episode two months later. Mark was violent and threatening with his father and brother. At that time he admitted he was using some pot as well.

Close family supervision followed, and Mark was allowed to go only certain places and had to be home at certain times. His parents said that if there were recurrences, Mark would go into a treatment program. When a fight erupted a few months later, the parents found evidence of much drug use. Mark entered a residential treatment program and has been free of drugs for four years.

In their book *Not My Kid: A Parent's Guide to Kids and Drugs,* Polson and Newton outline actions parents can take to promote a healthy, drug-free adolescence.[96] They insist that how families live day by day is the most important factor. Parents need to be involved family members who know what their children are doing and who their friends are. Then they must make clear to adolescents that theirs is a drug-free family in which there is (1) no use of illegal drugs or misuse of any legal drugs or prescriptions, (2) no routine use of alcohol by parents, (3) no intoxication by adults, (4) no alcohol use by underage children, and (5) no use of drugs to lose weight, sleep, relax, or wake up. Every family member agrees to this contract. If a child is found to be using drugs, parents call the parents of all the child's friends to discuss ways of promoting organized student activities.

If a child tries drugs, the family contract is repeated. If the behavior continues, the child is taken to some additional form of counseling that deals with the child and the family. Since family members can help drug-oriented children, family counseling is important in addition to any individual therapy prescribed. As in many other areas, the family joins with other families to provide support and actions to promote a healthier, safer adolescence.

CHAPTER 11
Late
Adolescence:
The Years
from Fifteen
to Nineteen

School Problems

Teenagers cut classes; they ignore homework assignments; they fail to complete courses; they pick courses that will not prepare them for what they say they want to do; they drop out of school. All strategists advise parents to move cautiously. Schoolwork and college and vocational choices are areas in which children make choices. Parents, however, can be helpful consultants. They can place responsibility on children, question the source of the problem, seek remedies, and support children's coping techniques by reminding them of earlier successes. They can also communicate their feelings about the seriousness of the situation and the importance of dealing with it. This approach takes more time than does criticism or advice on how to improve.

When adolescents are achieving below their ability levels, studies have found two general approaches helpful.[97] The behavioral technique of regularly monitoring schoolwork by means of a progress report and giving positive consequences like privileges and rewards helps students raise their performance level. A second strategy is a comprehensive approach to increase teens' study skills, their academic skills (by means of tutoring), and their social skills so they feel more at ease at school. Parents' involvement and use of consequences is also key to such a program. Addressing academic problems alone through tutoring or private therapy has not been as helpful as multifaceted approaches.

Fitzhugh Dodson cites an example of how parents can serve as consultants in helping children with courses of study. He received the following letter:

> My son is sixteen and he just despises the academic aspects of school (and 90 percent of it is academic). The only things he likes are wood shop, metal shop, auto mechanics, and P.E. He does poorly in all of his academic subjects. But he is very good with his hands. He loves to take his car apart and work on it, and he's terrific when it comes to fixing our TV set or tinkering with radios or CBs. But college is coming up soon, and I don't know what to do.[98]

Dodson advises getting information on community colleges or trade schools nearby as the son seems to be suited for a skilled trade. Show the young man the variety of skilled trades and how to get training in one that appeals to him. Dodson concludes with this comment: "Some parents have a snobbish resistance to the idea of their son or daughter learning a skilled trade instead of going to an academic college. I think this is a mistake. Better a good auto mechanic, happy at his job, than an unhappy and inept teacher or insurance salesman.[99]

Curfews

Once children have friends, they want to stay out at night. When adolescents come home after the agreed-on time, parents worry. Haim Ginott[100] and Gordon[101] both recommend expressing the fear and worry that underlie the anger parents often show when children are late. One parent who had been following Ginott varied the curfew with the occasion and encouraged her daughter to call if she were to be late. The mother told the girl that she would like a worry-free evening; the girl accepted her parent's concern and called.

John Krumboltz and Helen Krumboltz describe an active way to handle late-ness.[102] Parents can set an alarm clock for 15 minutes after the curfew. If the child is home, then he or she turns off the alarm before it goes off. If the child is still out, the alarm alerts the parents. Dodson, using behavioral principles, suggests over-looking lateness of 15 or 20 minutes. He says if children come home 45 minutes or an hour late, parents are entitled to make a ruckus.

Dorothy Briggs cites a more unusual curfew problem.[103] A teenager asked her mother to come downstairs five minutes after she came home from a dance with her boyfriend and insist that she come to bed. When the mother asked why, the daugh-ter said the boy liked to "make out," and she was not interested. The mother came down as instructed and delivered her message. As she went upstairs, she heard her daughter whisper, "She's a drag, isn't she?" Briggs explains that the daughter needed a scapegoat, so that her denial seemed not to be what she wanted but what she was forced to do. Briggs advises parents to help children be assertive, clear about what they want, and able to communicate their own wishes in a gentle but firm way. Ex-press your concern about the child's welfare. Adjust curfews if they are unreason-able. If lateness is habitual, this should be discussed in a family session.

Choice of Friends

By the time children reach their teens, they are aware of the qualities their parents value in people. They are also, more than ever before in their lives, subject to pres-sures from their peers. And they experience for the first time the strong and unfa-miliar stirrings of sexual feelings. Small wonder, then, that teens—pushed and pulled by these many influences—often seem to pick friends parents find less than desirable.

Sometimes they are wiser and more discerning than parents are. The quiet girl who dresses in dull colors turns out, on closer acquaintance, to be bright, gentle, and interesting. The very tall, fidgety boy with all those freckles and a strange laugh, parents learn after a few weeks, is good with cars and even better with pets—and not afraid to express his affection for animals or people, or food.

But what should parents do when a teenager loses her good sense over a Leonardo DiCaprio look-alike who is inconsiderate and insensitive, or when an adolescent son can suddenly think and talk about nothing but what the parent sees as an empty-headed cheerleader?

All the strategies discussed in this book agree that parents should not intervene directly to forbid or end a relationship. Instead, they should do what behaviorists call "letting the behavior run its course." The child's choice is respected, and the child respects the parents' feelings. The strategies differ on how parents should ex-press their reservations. The possibilities include waiting to comment, refusing to encourage or facilitate the relationship, and arranging situations in which the child can see the problem as the parents do.

When teens pick same-sex friends with different values, parents may worry that their children will be led into situations they cannot handle—heavy drinking, speeding in cars, cutting school. Parents should first examine their own reactions. Is the friend really likely to create trouble for their child? Or are they objecting to less important characteristics, such as appearance and manners? If the friend really is a

CHAPTER 11
Late
Adolescence:
The Years
from Fifteen
to Nineteen

problem, does the child have some underlying conflict or need that attracts him or her to such a friend? Does the child feel insecure and seek out a daredevil to mask the insecurity? If so, it is best for parents to deal with the underlying problem and try to find ways of bolstering confidence.

If parents object because the friend has a terrible driving record, cuts school frequently, or is failing courses, they need to sit down and share their concerns with their teenager. They should respect the child's right to have this friend, but they must point out the possible consequences to their child. If not pressured, the child will be able to understand what they are saying and may begin to spend less time with the friend. If the two continue to spend time together, it is possible that the friend may change. It is also possible that, as the parents get to know the friend, they may begin to understand why their child values this friendship. If the friendship continues and trouble does result for the child or seems about to occur, the parents may want to take action to end the relationship by forbidding it. This is difficult to enforce if the teen is determined to see the friend. In some situations, however, this firm action may be what the child wants.

Ginott tells of a situation in which parents gave their teenager freedom of choice yet exerted influence by raising questions for her to consider. Their eighteen-year-old daughter felt she had met the boy of her dreams. Her mother worried that she was being swept away in a world of fantasy and physical attraction and that was not asking practical questions about how compatible they might be in a permanent relationship. The mother, however, did not raise these issues while her daughter was up in the clouds. Empathizing with her daughter's feelings, she waited for the best time to suggest realistic considerations.

Shirley Gould cites the example of a boy in his late teens who became interested in a girl his parents disapproved of. Gould advises being pleasant to the girl, but says the parents do not need to lend the car for dates nor entertain her in their home.[104]

In another example, described by Krumboltz and Krumboltz, a couple found that their sixteen-year-old daughter was serious about an older boy they disliked, and they feared an early marriage would occur.[105] They disliked the boy and were worried because their daughter wanted to go steady. Instead of forbidding the relationship, they invited the boy to eat all weekday dinners with them and to spend time on weekends going on family excursions. The parents came to like certain qualities in the boy, but after three months their daughter ended the relationship and started dating other boys.

Sexual Behavior

Parents can provide as much information as they feel comfortable with and then refer teenagers to physicians or other professionals who can answer questions. Parents can also discuss their values. Experts disagree on whether the parent should go with the adolescent to get contraceptive devices. Dodson recommends this active approach, but Ginott does not. In light of Baumrind's comments and the deadly risk of AIDS, parents might want to take an active role.

One million teenage girls get pregnant each year. In *Not My Daughter*, Katherine Oettinger discusses teenage pregnancy and how to handle it.[106] Parents and daughter must consider the circumstances, the maturity of the partners, and the emotional and financial supports available. Professionals emphasize that once a teenage girl is pregnant, there are no simple, easy alternatives. Everyone must communicate feelings openly, consider all the alternatives, and keep a clear focus on handling the problem without making accusations or placing blame. In making plans for the future, everyone needs to keep in mind the adolescent's continuing education. When adolescents continue in school, they improve future opportunities.

An increasing number of teenagers also face sexually transmitted diseases. Ginott describes the case of a mother who was horrified when confronted with the possibility that her daughter might have gonorrhea. The mother did not blame or criticize the child, however. She remained calm and talked about what they would do—see the doctor, get the diagnosis, and obtain treatment if necessary. Of primary importance from any perspective is dealing with the infection. Then the girl must decide whether and how she will protect herself in the future. If this is a divisive issue for family members, then family counseling is in order.

Delinquency or Responsibility?

As teenagers become more independent, they want more privileges but often also fewer responsibilities. The average teenager does not hesitate to ask to use the family car, but is also likely to have a disorderly room and no interest in washing the dinner dishes. More and more teenagers are going beyond the kinds of behavior our parents may have thought inappropriate when we were in our teens—like staying out late and having a beer after bowling—and are drinking or using drugs, or both. And many leave home at an age when that can still be considered running away.

All the strategists discussed in this book agree on some principles for coping with the problems that result from the growing independence of teenagers. Parents need to grant freedom of choice, particularly in clothes, entertainment, and friends. They must also set limits by stating their views and what they want and insisting that those limits and values be incorporated in solutions. Communication and sensitivity continue to be essential ingredients in the relationships between parents and children.

Conflicts arise around work. Ginott gives the example of a woman whose son was offered a job as art director of a camp. Though she thought it was an ideal job for him, he was reluctant to take it. She had a hard time not urging him to take the job, but she realized that he had to make his own choice, that her task was to observe silently from the sidelines unless he asked for her opinion.

Gould tells of a nineteen-year-old who wanted to stay at college during the summer and earn money there, although his parents wanted him to work in the family business. They felt he owed it to them to do that, because they had been paying his college expenses and providing spending money. After discussing the matter with Gould, the parents decided to give their son his college expenses and a limited amount of spending money, with no strings attached. The boy learned that he could not have everything he wanted from his parents, but he was free to spend his time as he pleased. His respect for his parents and himself grew as he became more independent and relied less on his parents.

Often the needs of parent and child conflict. Ginott tells of the problem one mother had with her teenage daughter, who charged an expensive dress to the mother's account. The daughter was excited and pleased with the choice, but the

318

CHAPTER 11
Late
Adolescence:
The Years
from Fifteen
to Nineteen

mother was upset at the expense. She calmly insisted that the girl take the dress back. The mother reflected the daughter's feelings about not wanting to return the dress but was firm, and the girl took it back. In this case Gordon might have problem solved the situation to see if there were some way the daughter could have earned the money for the dress so that she could have kept it but the mother would not have paid for it.

Gordon cites many examples in which problem solving is used to meet the needs of all family members. For instance, he tells of a situation that occurred in his own family. When his daughter was fifteen, she told her parents she wanted to spend Easter vacation at a beach with friends her own age. Her parents were afraid of what might go on during an unsupervised vacation with boys and liquor, but their daughter discounted their worries. Through active listening, they discovered she wanted (1) to spend the vacation with a particular friend, (2) to be near a beach so she could have a tan when she returned to school, and (3) possibly to meet boys. She suggested that her parents take her and the girlfriend to an area where the parents could enjoy golf, and she and her friends could go to the beach each day. Because the parents had not had a vacation, they were delighted—and everyone had a good time. Note that parents do not automatically go along with a child's request when they think it could involve danger. Instead, parents and children all work together to find an acceptable alternative.

Briggs makes a unique suggestion. She advises talking to children who are about to be teenagers, as well as to their brothers and sisters, about the difficulties of adolescence. With advance coaching, siblings may be more understanding and less provocative and teasing with teenagers. The adolescents are forewarned and not so surprised when they have mood swings and feel a need to explode or to go off by themselves.

Role playing can help teenagers rehearse new and possibly fearful situations. Krumboltz and Krumboltz tell of a father who helped his adolescent daughter prepare for pressure from her friends to smoke marijuana. She did not want to, nor did she want to seem square. The father took the role of pressuring friend. The daughter stood her ground and came up with answers that suited her.

Many parents are afraid that if fighting escalates in the family, teenagers will run away. Both Gordon and Krumboltz and Krumboltz give examples of how such problems can be handled. Gordon tells of a family in which two teenagers, both using drugs, ran away from home after months of fighting with their parents about friends, cutting school, and drug use.[107] The parents had tried psychiatric counseling for one boy and psychiatric hospitalization for the other after a drug overdose. The teens found that being independent at fourteen and sixteen was extremely difficult, and before long they returned home. The parents began to use Gordon's parent effectiveness principles. Although they were awkward in active listening, they tried expressing feelings, and gradually the family atmosphere changed. Initially, laughter and teasing followed the active listening, but parents continued to tell the children their reactions to what was going on. Though I-messages were difficult to send, gradually all the family members learned to state their feelings and concerns clearly. The mother felt the problems of the two older children could have been avoided if she and her husband had learned these skills earlier.

Krumboltz and Krumboltz cite the case of Frank, a sixteen-year-old boy who had been a quiet but somewhat surly teenager. He ran away with a friend, leaving no explanation or address. Three weeks later the police found the two boys working in another city and contacted their parents. After conferring with the police, the high school principal, and a swimming coach of the boy's team, Frank's parents decided to let Frank stay where he was. The police kept an eye on the boys but did not talk with them. A week later, Frank returned home and his parents welcomed him warmly. He said he realized he needed an education to get a decent job and had decided to finish school. The cooperation of the police, who watched out for the boys' welfare but did not interfere, enabled the parents to let the boy's behavior run its course.

ToughLove   ToughLove is an organization started by parents to help themselves and other parents cope with rebellious, out-of-control adolescents. Parents form support groups with other parents and develop communication with agencies and individuals to promote community responses to truancy, drug abuse, running away, and vandalism. Parents seek real consequences for this behavior so adolescents will learn to avoid the disapproved behaviors.

The founders of ToughLove, Phyllis and David York, are professional people who had difficulty with their impulsive, acting-out adolescents.[108] They found it hard to set firm, fair limits that they could enforce. Meeting and talking with other parents gave them feelings of support as they set limits and carried them out. In fact, when parents in the group find limit-setting difficult, other parents will meet with the family or the teenager and back up the rules. Others offer to go to court hearings or other official meetings. By providing many sets of adults to help parents help children, the group becomes a community effort to establish and maintain a safe environment for all children.

The founders of ToughLove see the roots of the problem as cultural and social. Too much emphasis, they believe, is placed on psychological explanations for impulsive behavior, with too little awareness of all the social changes that have occurred since the 1960s. These changes encourage freedom and less responsibility for teenagers. With all these freedoms granted to children, we have not valued enough the firm, fair limits that they need for healthy growth. Parents alone, however, are not always able to establish limits, especially in the middle of a crisis situation. ToughLove helps parents by giving them the support they need to provide limits and reasonable guidelines for adolescents.

Many parents may believe the general principles discussed in this chapter are fine as long as serious acting out is not involved. But they think that when teenagers break the law and get in serious trouble, other approaches—including severe punishment—are required. Research suggests, however, that the techniques discussed here are equally valuable with delinquent teenagers. When asked about advice for parents of delinquent adolescents, one convict said, "The job of a parent is not to be a cop, preacher, judge, or even a perfect parent; but that of a loving, concerned guide, to provide direction that will allow your kids to be whole, stable, mature adults."

YOUTH CHARTERS

Parents often feel overwhelmed by cultural forces that do not support their efforts to rear children well. For example, the media bombard teens with messages about

320

CHAPTER 11
Late
Adolescence:
The Years
from Fifteen
to Nineteen

sexuality that do not conform to families' values. William Damon has developed a program he calls "Youth Charters" to combat cultural forces that make rearing children more difficult.[109]

Parents can initiate this program to organize teachers, clergy, police, and all who care about children to develop community practices and standards that promote children's healthy development. Parents' child-rearing efforts serve as a bridge to connect children to community activities at school, with peers, and in the neighborhood. But communities have to be organized to support parents' goals.

In his book *The Youth Charter: How Communities Can Work Together to Raise Standards for All Our Children,* Damon outlines a way of organizing concerned adults so they identify children's specific needs and work together to find ways to meet them. Standards and expectations are drawn up for children and for the community so that parents and concerned citizens and youth can control members' drinking, vandalism, and early pregnancy, and build a community more supportive of children and families.

He illustrates the program with youth charters developed in Wellesley, Massachusetts.

> "Beneath the sense of isolation that has divided our communities, we all share a deep well of concern for the younger generation. If we can find a way to tap into that well, child rearing can become the secure and fulfilling joy that it should be, rather than the risky and nerve-wracking challenge that it has become for too many parents.[110]

PARENTS' EXPERIENCES

As their new identities form, teenagers need confirmation from parents and society at large that these identities are valued. Such confirmation comes from respectful treatment, but it also comes from work and activities that reinforce the teenagers' feelings of competence. At the very time when changes are rapid and children's needs are great, many parents experience mid-life crises. Men may be dissatisfied with their occupational achievements and style of life. As children leave home, women have more time; they may wish they had broader horizons. Both husbands and wives may have gnawing feelings that life has not given them what they want and perhaps never will. On the other hand, many parents find that their children's growing independence leaves them free to explore possibilities in their own lives — to travel, take new jobs, develop new interests. Parents, then, may have varying reactions to their teenagers, who are young and ready to embark on all kinds of adventures. If unhappy in their own lives, parents may envy their children's increasing freedom. If parents feel a corresponding freedom and sense of choice in their own lives, they may be especially understanding of their adolescents' dilemmas. Parents' reactions to their teenagers' behavior stimulates their own personal growth. George Vaillant writes,

> In his discovery of his adolescent children, the adult remembers, rediscovers, and often defensively reworks parts of himself. Like the character disorder and infant, the adolescent has the capacity to get under our skin, rekindle old flames, and to stimulate parents

in parts of their innermost selves that they had forgotten existed. These fresh identifications act as catalysts for change within adult personalities and allow for further growth.[111]

Parents can be a great strength to each other as they rear teenagers. Single parents can find a friend or friends who supply the support given by a second parent. Parents balance each other; when one is weary and tired, the other takes over. Combining two parents' views of a situation often results in a more accurate, reliable picture. For example, a parent who always encourages independence may overlook possible dangers for a teenage son. When independence is tempered by the other parent's more cautious view, more realistic guidelines for the adolescent emerge. Parents may also gain a greater understanding of each other in the process—a clearer view of each other's strengths and a greater respect for each other's judgment. Parents become closer as they share doubts about their decisions, doubts about how teenagers will handle more freedom, and worries about what may be happening to children when they are late coming home at night. There are also the joys to share—vicarious enjoyment of special dances or parties; the thrills of achievements that come after long hours of work on the adolescent's part; the warm delight that comes when teenagers show kindness and thoughtfulness to others or good judgment when parents thought they could not look beyond tomorrow. All these experiences bring parents closer and enrich their lives together, as they feel they have contributed to the child's growth and development.

Laurence Steinberg followed 204 families for three years to understand how parents react and adapt to the changes and turmoil of their children's adolescence.[112] He found six aspects of a child's adolescent behavior that trigger parents' emotional reactions: puberty and the physical changes themselves, maturing sexuality, dating, increasing independence, child's emotional detachment, and the child's increasing de-idealization of the parent.

Parents with the following risk factors were most likely to experience difficulty: (1) being the same sex as the child making the transition; (2) being divorced or remarried, especially for women; (3) having fewer sources of satisfaction outside the parental role; and (4) having a negative cognitive set about adolescence. Protective factors that ease parents' adjustments to adolescence include having satisfying work and interests and a happy marriage. The positive supports buffer parents, so at times of difficulty with children, they have other sources of satisfaction and self-esteem.

Steinberg found that about 40 percent of parents experience difficulty. He terms them *decliners* because their well-being, life satisfaction, and self-image decrease, and they experience nervousness, depressions, and physical ailments. About 20 percent of the parents, *thrivers,* report greater well-being, self-esteem, and life satisfaction. They enjoy their children and relish greater freedom for themselves. About 40 percent of the sample, *survivors,* respond to their children, but children's changes do not affect them personally.

Based on his research, Steinberg makes the following suggestions for handling this stage of family development: (1) make sure you have genuine and satisfying interests outside of being a parent; (2) don't disengage from your child emotionally; (3) try to adopt a positive outlook about what adolescence is and how your child is

322

CHAPTER 11
Late
Adolescence:
The Years
from Fifteen
to Nineteen

changing; (4) don't be afraid to discuss what you are feeling with your mate, your friends, or, if need be, a professional counselor.

MAIN POINTS

In this period, late adolescents

- reach sexual maturity
- engage in sexual activity, and many have their first experience of sexual intercourse
- think more abstractly and can generate more options and possibilities
- get excited at school when permitted active participation in discussing or organizing experiments
- are stable in their feelings about friends and school but become more positive in their feelings about their parents
- are likely to become depressed or develop problems such as alcohol abuse if stress is high

Work experience

- is gained by a sizable number who benefit from understanding people better, feeling more self-reliant, and earning money
- can create stress for teens who have demanding jobs and domineering supervisors and expose them to poor habits such as alcohol and drug use
- seems to result in decreased interest in school and takes away from time to explore and develop interests and plans for the future

When late adolescents consider themselves, they

- describe themselves in psychological terms and through introspection begin to see patterns to their behavior
- need positive support from family and community
- reveal gender differences in their self-descriptions, with boys seeing themselves as both more daring, logical, and calm than girls, and girls seeing themselves as more attuned to people and more emotionally reactive than boys

Peers

- are major sources of support and pleasure in life and are sought out in times of trouble; teens are loyal to friends
- begin dating at about age fourteen and go steady more frequently in the sixteen- to eighteen-year-old period
- seek personal characteristics of good humor and responsibility in opposite-sex relationships, though boys do place an initial emphasis on good looks

- usually seek only one sexual partner at a time and are only very rarely sexual adventurers with each other

Parents

- continue their commitment to children by monitoring, supervising, and enforcing rules, yet at the same time supporting and accepting children's individuality
- serve as consultants and provide factual information on topics of importance to teens
- share more power in decision making with teens so they can be more self-governing in the context of warm family relationships and so teens can separate with a sense of well-being

Parents' reactions to their children's growth

- stimulate their own growth, as parents often rediscover and rework feelings and conflicts from their childhoods
- often stimulate parents to find new possibilities in their own lives
- may bring parents closer to each other

Problems discussed center on

- eating problems
- substance use/abuse
- dating and friendship issues
- school problems
- failure to take responsibility for sexual behavior
- delinquent behaviors

Joys include

- observing increasing social maturity and closeness with friends
- enjoying greater personal freedom
- seeing altruistic behavior
- watching adult traits emerge

EXERCISES

1. Break into small groups; discuss how parents can help their teenagers resist peer pressure to have sexual relations before they are ready.
2. Interview parents about their experience during adolescence: Did they grow up in a city or smaller town? How much freedom were they allowed? What were the rules for them? What were the stresses for adolescents at that

CHAPTER 11
Late
Adolescence:
The Years
from Fifteen
to Nineteen

time? Whom did they go to for support? How did their parents discipline them? Return to class and break into small groups; discuss the ways that parents' experiences differ from those of adolescents of today and report to the class on four major differences.

3. In small groups, describe the most effective discipline techniques parents used with you and write ten suggestions for parents of adolescents.

4. Turn in three ways you reduced stress as an adolescent; compile a class list of 10 ways to reduce stress at that age.

5. In small groups discuss ways adolescent boys and girls can share experiences to they can come to understand how life experiences can differ and what the stresses are for each gender. Share ideas with the whole class.

ADDITIONAL READINGS

Greenberger, Ellen, and Steinberg, Laurence. *When Teenagers Work*. New York: Basic Books, 1986.

Riera Michael. *Uncommon Sense for Parents with Teenagers*. Berkeley, CA: Celestial Arts, 1995.

Steinberg, Laurence, and Levine, Ann. *You and Your Adolescent*. New York: HarperCollins, 1990.

Steinberg, Laurence, with Steinberg, Wendy. *Crossing Paths: How Your Child's Adolescence Triggers Your Own Crisis*. New York: Simon & Schuster, 1994.

Wolf, Anthony E. *Get Out of My Life but First Could You Drive Me and Cheryl to the Mall?* New York: Noonday Press, 1991.

PARENTING AND WORKING

CHAPTER 12

Combining working and parenting has been a major challenge for men and women in the 1990s. The majority of mothers work from the time their children are infants, and more fathers than ever before are involved in child care. How do parents solve the common problems that arise in integrating work and family lives? How do they find child care that promotes children's development? How do they adjust routines to enhance the quality of time they spend with children? How do they adapt to their many responsibilities and maintain a sense of well-being?

This chapter examines the impact of working on parents, on their parenting, and on their children. In Chapter 1, Urie Bronfenbrenner described parents' work as part of the exosystem that exerts a major influence on children's development.[1] Though children do not participate directly in parents' work settings, what parents experience there affects their behavior at home, their relationships with their children, and, as a result, children's development.

Our understanding of the relationship between parents' work and family lives is limited for many reasons. First, parental work is not a unitary phenomenon but a multifaceted experience that varies in many ways for parents—number of hours worked, level of satisfaction, amount of stress. So, conclusions regarding parenting and work have to be generalized cautiously because they may not apply to everyone. Second, the relationship between parents' work and family life has been a focus of research for only about twenty-five years, so we do not have an agreed-on body of research findings. Third, the findings we do have are subject to modification as society and work itself change.

To arrive at the best understanding of research in the area of working and parenting, I shall emphasize patterns and trends from several studies and examine findings to identify the underlying family processes that account for the results.

IMPACT OF WORK ON PARENTS AND FAMILIES

Social Status

Whether one or two parents are employed, parents' work shapes family life in many ways. Parents' job classification — professional, business, skilled or unskilled labor — is the main determiner of the family's social status. The family's social status, in turn, influences its social attitudes and child-rearing practices. Middle-class parents value self-reliance and independence in children. To encourage these qualities, such parents tend to explain what they want to their children to motivate them to do what is necessary on their own. Working-class parents value obedience and conformity in children and tend to use power-assertive techniques to force compliance. They use physical punishment more than do middle-class parents; they refuse to give explanations, simply stating, "Because I said so." They are less interested in explanations, saying, "Do it now."[2]

Social status also determines the effects of mothers' employment. In a broad range of middle-class children, followed from age one through adolescence, mothers' work status per se had little effect on children's development.[3] The children of employed and unemployed mothers were equivalent on cognitive, academic, social-emotional, and behavioral development. The quality of the homes and parent-child relationships, regardless of mothers' work status, determined children's growth.

In lower-status African-American families, however, mothers' employment is related to children's language and achievement.[4] In another study, children of single working mothers had higher self-esteem, greater academic achievement and academic self-esteem, and they reported greater family cohesiveness than children whose mothers received aid to dependent children. In families with fewer resources, added income may be the main factor, but it may also be the influence of an achieving parent that contributes to the difference.

Work Patterns

Besides job classification, the pattern of parents' work influences family life. Later in the chapter, we shall discuss in detail how family life changes when mothers work, but here simply note that if and when mothers go to work determines who will care for young children, how involved fathers will be in the caregiving and household activities, how many household responsibilities children will share, and whether children care for themselves at older ages.

Fathers' pattern of work influences many aspects of family life. When fathers are absent because of work in remote areas or because they work unusual shifts, mothers engage in fewer community and social activities — they see fewer friends and participate in fewer organized activities. Mothers then lose support from the social network that nurtures them and, in turn, are less playful and stimulating with their children.[5] So, when fathers do not participate in family life, it is less social and stimulating.

Compared with nonworking mothers, working mothers are less likely to visit neighbors, and their children participate less in neighborhood activities.[6] Working conditions also influence the ways mothers divide household responsibilities. When mothers work long hours, have higher incomes, and hold more prestigious jobs, they perform less housework and are less likely to do traditionally feminine housework chores.[7] Women with high-status jobs may have enough influence with husbands so the men will share the housework. Mothers' work characteristics do not, however, determine parent-child activities or mothers' monitoring activities.

Psychological Benefits

In addition to providing income for basic support and forming a pattern of family life, work also brings many psychological benefits in terms of advancing parents' social, cognitive, and emotional development.[8] Work helps parents develop a sense of competence and self-esteem. Mothers who worked as volunteers in Head Start programs, for example, became more confident and motivated to go on in school. One of the benefits of this child-centered program has been to empower the parents who have worked there.[9]

Work often helps parents develop interpersonal skills that they then use at home. Workers in a manufacturing plant described how they used democratic work practices in solving problems at home. One man told how he started holding team meetings with his family: "After all, a family is kind of a team."[10] A mother commented to a psychologist, "Well, my daughter was having trouble going to sleep so I decided to handle the problem like we would at work. I asked her what she thought would solve the problem, and she said 'Reading two stories to me.' I did that, and she went to sleep. That cured the problem."[11]

Work also offers a range of friendships and supports. When asked to describe how she handled stress at home, one mother said, "I go to work. At work we are like a family. Friends listen to me, and we have fun even though there is a lot of work."[12] Supervisors also offer support and help at times of trouble. When a father was severely ill, the supervisor organized co-workers to donate vacation hours so he could keep his benefits as long as possible.

Economic Hardships and Job Stress

Work provides material resources for daily life, and nothing is more stressful to families than job demotions, layoffs, or firings. We saw in Chapter 1 that poverty sets in motion a train of psychological events that decrease parents' effectiveness with children and increase children's problem behaviors.

Parenting difficulties occur even under milder conditions of economic hardship. In contemporary society, layoffs, demotions, and economic strain in paying bills lead to a pattern similar to that found when parents live in poverty.[13] When parents experience economic hardship, they become more irritable and more easily frustrated. Their psychological tension has a direct impact on parenting and on their children. They do not communicate with children as openly or share power as much as in less stressful times; this tension can affect children's schoolwork and behavior. When economic conditions improve, parenting skills improve, as does children's behavior.

Economic strain also has an indirect effect on children's behavior. When parents are upset and frustrated, they argue with each other and give each other less support, so parenting declines because parents are not working together.[14] When fathers remain supportive of mothers during economic hardship, mothers' parenting skills do not decrease at all.[15] While social support from outside the family helps to reduce parents' low moods, it is support from the other parent that maintains parenting effectiveness.

An increase in minor work stresses such as work overload and arguments with co-workers also diminishes parents' morale. One study examined couples' diaries concerning work stress and home activities. The study revealed that fathers with work overload are less active and less communicative at home.[16] Mothers compensate and do the household chores, but fathers are less likely to reciprocate if mothers have work overload.

When parents have interpersonal conflicts with a supervisor or co-workers, they tend to argue more than before with a spouse about home responsibilities. Work disputes are more detrimental to family life than is work overload because the resulting marital arguments create stress and depression in parents. Parents in this study argued only with spouses after a work dispute, not with children. Men tend to take stress from home and have subsequent arguments at work, but women are less likely to do so.[17]

Work can be a positive force for psychological growth and, at the same time, present tensions and general strain to whoever participates. In the next section, we examine the ways that family life changes when both parents are employed.

WHEN PARENTS WORK

Approximately 55 percent of mothers with children younger than one year old are in the workforce. The percentage of working mothers increases with children's age: 66 percent of the mothers of preschoolers, 75 percent of mothers of school-age children, and 77 percent of mothers of adolescents are employed outside the home.[18] Thus, the majority of families today are dual-earner families (in which both parents have paid employment). Families employ several strategies to adapt to parents' employment and maintain marital satisfaction and family morale.

Parenting Strategies

Adults use many strategies to make the most of their time so they can meet both work and family responsibilities. It is difficult to make sweeping statements about parenting strategies as the choice depends on the composition of the family and its educational and socioeconomic level. The general principles are (1) that the work load at home is shared—with a spouse if one is present, and with children if they are old enough—and (2) that available time is focused on the top priority—meeting children's needs.

Sharing the Workload   In 1960, fathers put in 1 hour of work at home for every 4 hours worked by mothers. In 1996, women spent about 3.7 hours per day on household chores, and men spent about 3 hours per day.[19] Men, however, worked an average of 48 hours per week at a full-time job; mothers worked 42. So women do about 55 percent of the housework, and men work longer hours at a job. Today, there is a second shift for both men and women who work, though women may feel it more keenly because they tend to take primary responsibility for seeing children's needs are met.

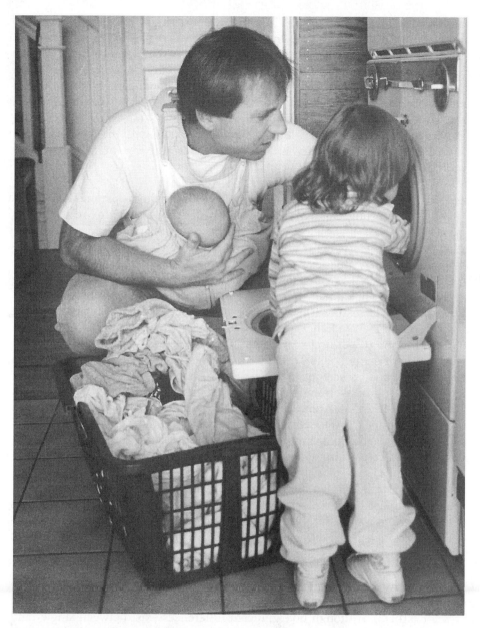

Young children learn that laundry is a family job, not a mommy job.

Fathers' participation in home activities enables children to see that both parents can have jobs and care for children. It also accounts for one of the most consistent findings about children in dual-earner families—that they have less traditional views of the appropriate roles for men and women than do children in single-earner families.[20]

Although fathers in dual-earner families participate more than fathers in single-earner families, mothers in both families still do significantly more child care and household activities than do fathers. In a study reported in 1986, employed mothers spent about 44 hours per week in household work and child care, compared with 30 hours spent by their husbands.[21] Differences between mothers and fathers were most pronounced during the week; they spent about equal amounts of time in these activities on weekends. While fathers in single- and dual-earner families spend the same amount of time, they spend it differently. In dual-earner families, fathers do more child care and have more solo time with children.[22] In single-earner families, fathers do more leisure activities and spend more time with the child in family activities. When fathers are caregivers, they manage routine care in much the same way mothers do.[23]

Focusing on Children's Needs   A major strategy for employed parents is to focus their energy on meeting children's needs, especially their needs for relationships with parents.

Fathers who engage in much child care when children are little, maintain strong involvements in daily activities with children across the childhood years and into adolescence.[24] Such fathers play more games and share educational activities during the week, spending equal time with sons and daughters. The children of involved fathers are more socially mature at age 6 and more academically successful at age 7, than are children of uninvolved fathers.

Employed mothers working more than 20 hours a week spend less time with their infants and preschoolers than do nonemployed mothers. Mothers with a higher education compensate for time at work by spending more time with children in the evenings and on weekends. Children appear to become willing partners in this arrangement. They sleep more during the day-care hours and remain awake and play for longer periods in the evening. In single-earner families, evening time is reserved for fathers, but in dual-earner families, mothers use this time to relate to children, giving them verbal stimulation. While fathers are "crowded out" in these early family interactions, they have their own time alone with the child and, in fact, spend more time with children than do fathers in single-earner families.[25]

Although employed mothers of infants spend less time with them, these mothers are as sensitive and responsive as nonemployed mothers.[26] Mothers who are satisfied with their work and feel they get support are more responsive with their toddlers than are unemployed mothers, giving more guidance and using lower power-assertive techniques.[27]

Once children reach school age, mothers spend more time in single activities[28] with children than fathers do (90 minutes per week for mothers compared with 60 minutes for fathers). Although no significant differences exist between single- and dual-earner fathers in the amount of time spent with children, they allot the time differently. Dual-earner fathers spend 60 minutes per week with sons and 60 with daughters. Single-earner fathers spend 90 minutes per week with sons and 30 with daughters. Researchers speculate that daughters of working mothers may do well in part because they have more time with fathers. (See the interview with Susan McHale.)

Time with children fluctuates seasonally for some mothers, with nonemployed and seasonally employed mothers spending more time in activities with children in the summer than in the winter.[29] Mothers who are employed the same number of hours throughout the year do not show this seasonal variation. Parenting of seasonally employed mothers becomes more traditional in the summer, as they have more involvement with children at that time than do fathers. Parenting becomes more egalitarian when mothers return to work.

Maintaining mother-child activities is important because such activities may buffer the child against possible negative effects from maternal absence.[30] When mothers with full-time employment or an increase in work hours maintain their time in shared activities with their children, the children show no decrease in social and cognitive functioning compared with children whose mothers are at home. When mothers' hours of employment decrease and activities shared with the children increase, the children's functioning improves; if activities do not increase when work hours decrease, there is no improvement.

In the early adolescent years, the overall amount of time children spend with parents does not differ in single- and dual-earner families, but again, the difference is in *how* the time is spent. Full-time employed mothers spend more time doing homework with children and less time in leisure activities.[31] Children of mothers employed part-time report more time spent playing sports with parents.

Monitoring A major task of parenting is monitoring and supervising children's activities. Although working parents are often not home after school, they can monitor what school-aged children do and make certain children are engaged in approved activities. Studies have found that parents in dual-earner families monitor as carefully as parents in single-earner families.[32] This is important because less well-monitored boys have lower school grades and less skill in school-related activities, regardless of whether mothers are employed. Studies have not found girls' behavior as clearly related as boys' behavior to monitoring.

In a recent study of after-school experiences and social adjustment of early adolescent boys and girls, Gregory Pettit found that parents' careful monitoring of their early adolescents was related to a lack of externalizing problems such as disobeying and fighting.[33] Careful monitoring counterbalanced the effects of living in an unsafe neighborhood and having a lot of unsupervised activities with peers, two other predictors of externalizing problems.

As children progress through adolescence, parents' lack of monitoring is associated with both boys' and girls' engaging in disapproved activities such as drinking.[34]

Encouraging Family Cooperation in Household Work Although women usually retain primary responsibility for household management, men's participation in traditionally female household chores serves as a positive example for boys and girls, who do less stereotyping when fathers do such chores.[35] Further, children who participate routinely in chores that benefit the family tend to show concern for others' welfare.[36]

Though women may have traditionally borne the major responsibility for meeting the household needs, they are shifting the responsibility to the family as a whole. Jacqueline Goodnow and Jennifer Bowes's interviews with parents and children concerning the distribution of household work reveal that the meanings people attach to particular jobs (men's/women's work, Dad's/Mom's responsibility), the feelings they have about the jobs (like/dislike, competence/incompetence), and underlying principles of fairness shape how families distribute work.[37]

INTERVIEW
with Susan McHale

Susan McHale is an associate professor of human development at Pennsylvania State University and co-director of the Pennsylvania State University Family Relations Project.

From your experience in studying dual-earner families, what kinds of things make it easiest for parents when both work?

We look at how the whole family system changes when mothers work, and we found very interesting changes in how fathers relate to children between nine and twelve years old when their wives are employed. We collect a measure of "exclusive" or dyadic time—how much time the father spends alone with the child doing some fun activity like attending a concert or school activity. In single-earner families, fathers spend about 90 minutes a week with boys in "exclusive" (dyadic) activities and about 30 minutes with girls, so there is quite a sex distinction in these families. In dual-earner families, fathers spend equal amounts of "exclusive" time with boys and girls—about 60 minutes per week—so mother's working may enhance the relationship between *father* and daughter and decrease involvement between father and son.

We do not get any straightforward sex differences in the effects of mother's working—that is, boys do not necessarily do less well—unless these are mediated by some other process. For example, we have just finished a paper on parental monitoring of children's activities. To collect data on monitoring, we telephone both the parent and the child and ask specific questions about what has happened that day: Did the child do his homework? Did he have a special success at school that day? Our measure of monitoring is the discrepancy between the children's report and the parent's report. (We presume the children are right.) We thought

Several recommendations emerge from the discussion with families. First, a problem-solving approach that focuses on the specific question of "Who does this particular job?" is useful. Couples who successfully achieve a balance in household tasks avoid getting caught in old definitions of work (men's versus women's jobs). Instead, they concentrate on how to achieve household goals in an effective and efficient way.

Second, families must negotiate chores in an atmosphere of fairness, respect, and open-mindedness. People's preferences are respected and considered in assigning chores. Principles of fairness operate. Families naturally divide household chores into two categories: (1) self-care (making one's bed, picking up clothes or toys) and (2) family care (setting the table, taking out garbage). Most families assign self-care responsibilities to children as the children become able to do them. Doing self-care chores gives children feelings of independence and competence because they can care for themselves. As family chores are shifted among family members, children receive their share to promote feelings of being important participants in family life.

With a changing society expressing such varying opinions about family members' household responsibilities, families often feel dissatisfied with what they are doing

that monitoring might be related to children's adjustment. We do find that in families where the child is less well monitored, boys are a little bit more at risk for problems in conduct and school achievement. This is independent of who does the monitoring; as long as you have at least one parent who is a good monitor, you do not get these effects.

When we look at what helps families function well when parents work, we find one factor is the agreement between *values and attitudes* on the one hand and the *actual roles* family members assume in daily life. This finding applies to adults and children. I am talking about sex-role attitudes. When parents have young children, we found the incongruencies between sex-role attitudes and behavior are related to problems in the marital relation. Specifically, when husbands and wives have traditional sex-role attitudes but the organization of daily life is egalitarian, couples were much more likely to fight, to have lower scores on a measure of love, and to find the relationship less satisfying.

When we looked at children's involvement in household chores, we found additional evidence of the importance of congruence between attitudes and family roles. For example, the more chores boys in dual-earner families perform, the better their adjustment; the reverse was true for boys in single-earner families, however. The mediating factor seems to be the father's sex-role attitudes. In single-earner families, fathers are more traditional and less involved in tasks themselves. Therefore, when sons do a lot of housework, their behavior is out of concordance with their fathers' values. In both kinds of families, dual and single earners, boys whose roles are incongruent with their fathers' values feel less competent and more stressed, and they report less positive relationships with their parents.

The congruence between values and beliefs and the kinds of family roles children and adults assume is what predicts better adjustment. Whether you can change people's attitudes and beliefs or whether it is easier to change family roles is hard to say. Part of the problem is that the work demands in dual-earner families require that family roles change before people feel really comfortable with that.

and want to alter their patterns. Box 12-1 contains suggestions for successfully negotiating dissatisfactions and moving on to a new style of handling such responsibilities. This process has three key components: (1) maintain underlying respect and caring for other family members' needs, seeing changes as ways of giving to people who matter to one another; (2) stay flexible — reassign, reduce, or eliminate jobs; and (3) focus on the positive benefits for all family members of pulling together and contributing to family life.

Marital Relationship

In general, the marital relationship is not related to the work status of the mother.[38] A positive relationship is more likely when mothers are well educated, want to work, and have part-time jobs. Marital dissatisfaction is more likely when one or both parents resent the mother's employment, when the family is working class, or when mothers and fathers have traditional views of men's and women's roles but must perform nontraditional behaviors. When men do more child care than they want, they tend to report dissatisfaction and less love for their wife.

◆

BOX 12-1
MOVING TO NEW PATTERNS OF HOUSEHOLD WORK

1. *Take a look at what bothers you.* Ask yourself why you are doing this chore. What specifically bothers you about the chore? What is the worst part of the chore for you?

2. *List the alternatives.* Jobs can be changed in many ways—eliminated, reassigned to someone else in the family, reduced (e.g., iron only some things but not everything), moved outside the family.

3. *Look carefully at the way you frame the problem and at the way you talk and negotiate.* Explain what you want, stick to the point in discussing the problem, and frame the issues in terms of practicality, logic, or benefits to all family members. Avoid name calling.

4. *Be prepared for difficulties.* The greatest difficulty is dealing with family members' having different standards for completing chores. Children often do not want to do chores because of criticism. Focus on the effort each person puts in and do not insist on perfect completion.

5. *Remember that there is more than one way to express caring and affection in a family.* Men and women have to give up old beliefs that caring must be shown by being a "good provider" or a "good homemaker." Caring for a family is more than doing housework.

6. *Keep in mind the gains as well as the costs.* Although all family members give up time to do household chores, everyone gains. All family members gain in doing chores and contributing to family functioning. They gain self-respect, skills, and the primary benefit of greater closeness to other family members.

Jacqueline J. Goodnow and Jennifer M. Bowes, *Men, Women and Household Work* (Melbourne, Australia: Oxford University Press, 1994), pp. 197–201.

Recall from Chapter 5 that one of the biggest predictors of how a couple manages the transition to parenthood is the similarity of their views about sharing the workload. When couples have different ideologies, they tend to have more marital conflict. As Susan McHale commented in her interview, couples experience difficulty when their family roles change before they feel comfortable with changes.

Satisfaction and Morale

There is no simple relationship between mothers' employment status and either men's or women's psychological morale.[39] A great deal depends on whether couples want the mother to work or whether they have anxiety or misgivings about her employment.

When mothers want to work, when they feel that their children do not suffer from their working, and when they have husbands' support, they feel increased satisfaction with themselves and with life.[40] Even if they work when they would prefer to be at home, they do not experience depression or decreased well-being, provided they think that what they are doing is important for the family. Women who want to work but who stay at home for fear of adverse effects on the child become depressed.[41] Further, their children do not function as well as those whose mothers are satisfied with their choice. Academic and social performance of kindergartners was related to mothers' satisfaction with their work status.[42] Children of mothers who stayed at home when they wanted to work or thought they should work had lower levels of performance than did their peers whose mothers either worked and enjoyed it or stayed home and enjoyed that.

Men have high self-esteem and morale when wives work provided that these men have nontraditional attitudes about working. When men have traditional beliefs that wives' working reflects negatively on their ability as a provider, then they show decreased morale.[43] Like mothers, fathers also experience a drop in morale when they are concerned about child-care and children's adjustment to mothers' working.[44]

Although parents experience satisfaction in working, they also feel conflict and role strain—stress in the way they perform in their various roles. A 1993 national study reveals that mothers and fathers feel equal amounts of conflict in balancing work and family commitments. About 20 percent of men and women report a lot of conflict, and an additional 40 percent report some conflict. Men experience about the same level of conflict regardless of whether their wives are employed.[45] In addition, men of all socioeconomic levels experience similar amounts of conflict, so this is not a phenomenon restricted to "yuppie" fathers.

In combining working and parenting, both parents may feel role strain. A study of parents of preschoolers revealed that fathers were most likely to experience role strain if they (1) were highly committed to work but not satisfied with their job performance, (2) felt they were not living up to their own standards in being a husband or father, and (3) felt they got little support from their wives in meeting their responsibilities to children.[46]

The sources of mothers' role strain were similar: (1) being highly involved in work activities but dissatisfied with their job, (2) feeling dissatisfied with the level of support from husband and neighbors in meeting all their responsibilities, and (3) feeling they were not living up to their standards of being a wife. Women with high role strain feel tension in meeting all the demands on them.

In addition to role strain, mothers develop anxiety when they feel they have no chance to make things work out satisfactorily, and depression may accompany the anxiety when mothers feel really committed to parenting and are putting their energy into it, but things are not working out.

On the basis of interviews conducted throughout a large U.S. corporation, Arlie Hochschild believes that many parents feel more comfortable at work and seek longer hours there because of the stress from family demands that they feel they cannot meet.[47] Even when companies offer family leave, few parents take it. Hochschild believes parents need to instigate a "time movement" that would support having less time at work and more time with families. Other studies show that men benefit from support from wives, and women benefit from a broad array of support from husbands, neighbors, and co-workers.[48]

For parents, one potential source of strain is their children's nonparental caregivers. Now we shall consider the impact, both positive and negative, of nonparental care on families.

IMPACT OF NONPARENTAL CARE ON CHILDREN

As we look at the effects of nonparental care at different ages, we should keep clearly in mind Michael Lamb's comment on the effects of nonparental care:

> Although it seldom receives the amount of attention it deserves, there is clear evidence that the quality of children's interactions and relationships with their parents and family members and the quality of care children receive at home continue to be the most important sources of influence on the development of young children, even when they receive substantial amounts of care outside the home.[49]

In evaluating research, we must keep in mind first that a selection process related to mothers' education, personality, and interests determines who, in fact, chooses to return to work once children are born.[50] Second, maternal employment is not a unitary phenomenon, and its meaning in a child's life depends on (1) the child's characteristics (age, sex, temperament), (2) family characteristics (education and socioeconomic level, father's involvement in the home, mother's satisfaction with working), (3) work characteristics (number of hours mother works, level of her stress at work), and, perhaps most important, (4) the nature of the child's substitute care. Because researchers cannot control all these factors, we have to interpret findings from several studies and draw our own conclusions. In discussing the research, we shall focus on children's socioemotional and cognitive functioning.

Infancy and Early Childhood

Quality of care is a major determiner of the effects of nonparental child care on children.

Quality of Care   There are two kinds of indices of quality of care—process measures and structural measures.[51] Process measures examine appropriate caregiving for children—that is, appropriate activities in a safe, stimulating setting. Structural measures look at the amount of teacher or caregiver training/experience, appropriate group sizes, and staff turnover. These two kinds of measures are usually correlated. The adult-child ratio and the extent of teacher training are thought to be the best structural measures of quality in day care centers; in family day care, group size, safety, and caregiver appropriateness are the best measures. Caregivers' salaries are good measures of caregiver stability; when salaries are high, caregivers stay.

Children who enter high-quality day care in the first year develop many positive social qualities seen later in preschool and elementary school: They are well-controlled, popular, and considerate of peers in preschool; socially competent and able to focus and stay on task in kindergarten. In grade school, they are outgoing, affectionate, nonhostile children who perform well in school.[52] In Europe, high-quality care in the first year is associated with cognitive and social maturity through childhood and into early adolescence.[53] So, while children may be at risk for insecure attachment and noncompliance when mothers return to work for extended hours in the first year, there appears to be no risk and many benefits if they go into high-quality day care.

What is high-quality care? The National Academy of Sciences Panel on Child Care Policy uses six criteria to describe quality care:[54]

1. Minimum child-staff ratios varying according to the child's age — 1:4 for infants to 1:7 for preschoolers

2. Caregiver training that includes courses in child development

3. Organized activities programs that are varied enough to permit choice on the child's part

4. Structured space so that activities and groups of children of different ages are separated

5. For family day care, a moderate range of ages of children

6. For day-care centers, maximum group sizes ranging from 6 to 8 for infants and 16 to 20 for preschoolers

In high-quality day care settings, children build secure attachments to teachers and develop the many positive social qualities associated with early secure attachment to parents.[55] Clearly, secure attachment to a teacher requires the same qualities in the teacher as those that promote attachment to parents. This adult must be an available, stable, sensitive, responsive caregiver who provides stimulating activities and monitors the child's behavior to increase self-regulation. The child uses this figure as a safe base for exploring the world, just as he or she uses the secure attachment with the mother or father. In the child's first thirty months, it is important for the teacher to remain the same; otherwise, the child-teacher relationship becomes unstable. After thirty months, however, the teacher can change and the child-teacher relationship still remain stable.[56]

Secure teacher attachment in the first year has a powerful impact on a child's development. It is teacher attachment and day care qualities, not family socialization practices, that predict later childhood competence for children entering day care in the first year.[57] For children entering day care at later ages, it is the family socialization in the first year and the child's characteristics that predict later qualities.

There are, of course, confounding factors. Highly motivated, stable parents seek out high-quality care for children.[58] Those infants who go into low-quality care often have parents who are less organized and use less appropriate socialization practices. A vicious cycle may develop for the infant in low-quality care. Highly stressed families give less attention to the child, and the child goes into a day care setting that offers few adults with whom to interact and little to do. These children have less contact with adults and receive less stimulation both at home and in day care than do children of motivated parents. Thus, they have cumulative risks for problems in development.

Some have expressed concern that early and extensive nonparental care can have negative effects. Lamb writes that one of the most consistent findings has been that early entrance into nonparental care "fosters excessive assertiveness, aggression, and noncompliance in some children for reasons that are not well understood."[59] This appears in part related to poor relationships with caregivers. Children who have high-quality care with stable caregivers are not more aggressive.

Jay Belsky reviewed research from several studies and found that the rates of insecure maternal attachments are higher (36 to 43 percent) for infants with extensive early and poorer quality day care than for infants cared for by a parent (23 to 29 percent).[60] On reanalyzing the data, Lamb and co-workers similarly found a slightly higher rate of insecure attachments for those already at risk, for example because of insensitive maternal behavior.[61] The exact reasons for this finding are unknown but may well relate to qualities of the caregiver.

Early and continuing programs that stimulate cognitive development, like the Abecedarian intervention program, promote intellectual growth during the school years as well.[62] Such programs have reduced grade retention and the need for special programs in the first three years of elementary school. These programs stimulate intellectual growth in children from economically disadvantaged families. However, even controlling for effects of social class and family background, high-quality care in infancy is related to academic performance and verbal skills at age eleven.

Lower Quality of Care   Most of the research on the effects of day care focuses on high-quality programs. Yet, authors of several recent surveys estimate that many children experience poor-quality care. Lower quality can have harmful effects depending on the age of entrance and the amount of time spent at a facility, as well as the child's individual characteristics.[63]

Social scientists debate the significance of the findings of negative behaviors associated with early, extensive nonparental care in the first year of life. Alison Clarke-Stewart suggests that such findings may be artifacts of the measurement process.[64] Jay Belsky is highly concerned with what he considers to be a nation of young children at risk because an increasing number are experiencing poor-quality care in the early years of life, which puts them at risk for later social and cognitive difficulties.[65] Both Clarke-Stewart and Belsky agree that the solution is to provide more high-quality care for children.

Later Childhood Adolescence

The association between early, extensive nonparental care in the first year of life and negative behavior continues in the elementary school years. Extensive care in the first year of life is related to hitting, kicking, and conflictful interactions in the first three years of elementary school.[66] Contemporaneous after-school day care that is not high quality is also related to being rated as noncompliant by teachers and less well liked by peers.[67] As in the early years, quality after-school care is related to effective functioning.[68]

Although some samples of young children in self-care, or latchkey children, function better than those in poor-quality day care, lack of supervision and monitoring of early adolescents is related to increased use of alcohol, cigarettes, and marijuana.[69] Eighth-graders in self-care for more than 11 hours a week—whether from dual- or single-earner families, from high- or low-income families, with good or poor grades, or active or nonactive in sports—were more likely than those not in self-care to use these substances. Self-care leads to feelings of greater autonomy and puts early teens at risk of being influenced by peers who are substance abusers.

In adolescence, however, maternal employment is also associated with self-confidence and independence. The benefits are more pronounced for girls who obtain good grades and think of careers for themselves, most likely because their mothers serve as role models of competence.[70]

Boys of employed mothers may not do as well in school, but that has not been a consistent finding in more recent research.[71] Because fathers' involvement in the home is found to stimulate cognitive performance, it may be that fathers' increasing participation has reduced that problem.

Sex Differences

In several studies, boys were found to be more vulnerable than girls when their mothers work during the boys' early childhood. It is not clear whether boys require more attention, nurturance, and supervision; whether they are more sensitive to deficiencies in child-care settings; or whether they make more demands on parents who are stressed from working, have less patience with them, and see them more negatively.

Lois Hoffman concludes that boys may have a more difficult time in dual-earner families, and girls more problems in single-earner families.[72] In single-earner families, girls are more at risk for insecure attachments, their behavior is viewed more negatively by mothers, they have less time with fathers, and they receive less encouragement for independence. So, girls profit from the changes in dual-earner families, but boys may not. It is possible, however, to combine the best of both forms of family life so boys and girls get an optimal balance of nurturance, attention, supervision, and independence.

SELECTING DAY CARE

Parents seek child care in many places. Recent data concerning child care for children under five reveal that 28 percent are cared for by a nonrelative at home or in another home; 24 percent are in a day care or nursery school; 15 percent are cared for by the father; 9 percent, by the mother at her work; 21 percent, by another relative; and 1 percent, in some other form of care.[73]

The most important factor in selecting day care, particularly for a child in the first year, is the quality of the caregiver. For toddlers and preschoolers as well, having a secure attachment with a sensitive caregiver promotes social competence.

Once parents have a reliable, sensitive caregiver, they want to focus on the opportunities available for the child to socialize with others and to be involved in stimulating activities.[74] The child's needs will depend somewhat on his or her age and temperament.

Types of Day Care

Each form of care has certain advantages and possible drawbacks. Care by parents and relatives has the advantage that children know these people and have special ties to them. Although parental care is usually considered high quality, a parent may be sleeping after working a shift or may be doing child care with other children. Thus, parental care can be of variable quality.[75]

Substitute care at home is expensive but requires the child to adjust only to the new person; everything else in the environment remains the same. This form of care

I N T E R V I E W
with Jay Belsky

Jay Belsky is a professor of human development at Pennsylvania State University in College Park. He is the initiator and director of the Pennsylvania Infant and Family Development Project, an ongoing study of 250 firstborn children whose parents were enrolled for study when the mothers were pregnant in 1981. He has done systematic research on the effects of day care.

What advice would you give to parents in the first two years about day care?

For working parents I say again and again that nothing matters as much as the person who cares for your baby. All too often parents don't look "under the hood" of the child-care situation. They walk in, the walls are painted nicely, the toys are bright, the lunches are nutritious. Especially with a baby, once the minimal safety standards are met, what matters more than anything else psychologically is to find out about this person who'll care for the baby. So, who is this person, and what is his or her capacity to give individualized care? Because babies need individualized care, this issue matters above all else.

The second thing to consider is whether the caregiver and parent can talk together easily. Each person spends less than full time with the baby. The time factor is not necessarily handicapping them, but it can if information is not being communicated back and forth. So the trick then is, "If the caregiver gets to know my baby during the day, what can she tell me in the afternoon, and if I have the baby in the evening and the morning, what can I tell her when I drop the baby off?" There has to be an effective two-way flow of information.

The third thing to consider in selecting care is that the arrangement has to last a decent interval of time. That doesn't mean that you must take the child to the same center for a year's time; it means that the same *person,* or *persons,* takes care of him or her for a year or so. If you find a great person who treats the child as an individual and communicates well with the parent but stays for only a few months, you are not buying yourself a lot. In a baby's life, changing caregivers more than once a year will be stressful. If a baby goes through three or four changes in a year, it may not matter what kind of caregiver he or she gets. Even though the caregivers may get to know the child, the child won't know them. Each has to know the other.

has the advantage of being available when the child is sick. As children get older, home care is often supplemented with nursery school attendance or other group activities so the child can be with peers.

Family day care — that is, care in the home of another family with other children — is cheaper than home care and has some advantages. A family day care setting provides a more varied environment for children in the toddler years than does a day care center.[76] In family day care, children can engage in many of the same activities they would if they were at home with their mother or father.

Because there are fewer children, family day care is sometimes more flexible than a center in meeting children's individual needs. Family day care homes are licensed;

For dual-career couples, quality time with their children is extremely important. Dorothy Briggs defines a genuine encounter as "focused attention (on the child) . . . attention with a special intensity born of direct, personal involvement . . . being intimately open to the particular, unique qualities of your child."

some are part of a larger umbrella organization that supplies toys and training to home caregivers. Day caregivers who are part of such a network can give higher-quality care than can untrained caregivers. Guidelines for making a choice of a family day-care home are similar to those for choosing a day care program. Parents should make one visit with the child and one visit alone when gathering information to help them choose a child-care provider.

Day care centers provide care for children from infancy, and may provide after-school care for children in the elementary grades. In most states, such centers must meet specific standards intended to ensure the health and safety of the children. The parent whose child goes to a day care center is sure of having child care available every day—at some centers from 7 A.M. until 7 P.M. Many centers have credentialed personnel who have been trained to work with children, and many centers have play equipment and supplies not found in most home-care situations. All centers provide opportunities for contact with same-age children.

When children start elementary school, they receive care there for 3–6 hours per day and require special provision only before or after school and on vacations. Approximately 2–10 million children ages six to eleven are unsupervised after school.[77] Approximately 11 percent of children ages eight to ten and 38 percent of children ages eleven to twelve are in self-care.[78] Financial pressures and lack of available care encourage parents to permit children to come home and care for themselves. Edward Zigler and Mary Lang cite four possible dangers to this system: (1) Children alone may feel bad and rejected; (2) accidents or mistreatment may befall these children when alone; (3) children may not develop appropriate skills when unsupervised, such as not becoming responsible for schoolwork and other chores; and (4) children may engage in disapproved behavior like delinquent acting out or premature sexual activity.[79]

Although problems can arise with this arrangement, some children describe benefits such as increased independence, responsibility, and time to think and to develop hobbies. In part, some children flourish because of their personalities or the living situation. Some children entertain themselves well, and others have friends or activities in the neighborhood so they are not really alone. A recurrent theme in children's accounts of successful latchkey experiences is that parents and children have good relationships with one another. These children feel that their parents are supportive, and their parents encourage phone contact and activities during their absence.[80]

Availability and Affordability of Day Care

We have described the kinds of care possible, but how available and affordable are they? The average cost of quality full-time care for a child prior to school age is approximately $3,000 per year. Infant and toddler care can cost close to $5,000 per year. In certain geographical areas, the costs are higher.[81] Child care takes about 10 percent of an average family's budget but about 22–25 percent of a poor family's income.[82]

Families receive little governmental support in arranging child care. A tax credit of $2,400 does not cover the full cost of the care and helps primarily middle- and upper-middle-class families. Single parents and lower-income parents do not pay sufficient taxes to get a large benefit from the credit. Though federal subsidies provide some block support for child-care expenses of poorer families, only about 10–15 percent of those eligible receive such benefits.

Experts disagree about the availability of care. Most agree, however, that shortages in service exist for infants and school-age children. As noted, between 2 and 10 million children ages six to eleven are unsupervised at home before and after school. Further, service is limited for children at certain times of the day—early mornings, early and late evenings—and at times of a child's illness.

Even when care is available, the quality of care is uneven. Approximately 70 percent of day care homes are unlicensed. Many day care centers have rapid turnovers of staff and too few staff for the ages and number of children attending.[83] Chapter 16 takes up the question of how to provide affordable and quality child care.

PARENTING TASKS WHEN PARENTS WORK

As discussed in previous chapters, the main tasks of parenting are forming and maintaining close emotional relationships with children and modifying children's behaviors so they can function in a competent manner. Here we focus on how working parents can accomplish these tasks.

Returning to Work

Both monetary and psychological factors play a role in a mother's decision to return to work after a birth. In a four-state study, high- and low-income women were more likely to return to work than were middle-income women. Women who felt that working was important to their self-image and women who earned a large share of the family income typically returned to work. Complications in pregnancy and birth and in the child's health, as well as poor performance at work, were factors in women's deciding not to return to work.[84]

Among those who do return, a subsample remain unsure about the effects of their work on the child. Although they are sensitive and responsible caregivers, their anxiety leads to their being intrusive and out of sync in their interactions with their child.[85]

With regard to returning to work, Stanley Greenspan, Clinical Professor of Psychiatry, Science, and Pediatrics at George Washington University, says there is no best *time,* but there is a best *process* for returning to work.[86] Ideally, the mother should have a prolonged time to get to know her baby and form an intimate relationship with the child. But mothers must sometimes return to work sooner than they would like. This means finding a suitable caregiver.

After a caregiver is selected, the child is eased gradually into the relationship with the person, first going for short visits, then for longer ones. When mothers actually return to work, it is best if mother and caregivers can overlap by 30 minutes so each can catch up on what has happened during the day or the preceding night. When mothers are optimistic about caregivers, babies often are, too.

Coping with Separation Anxieties

Separation anxiety is not experienced solely by children. Working parents—both mothers and fathers—often feel guilt about leaving children with a caregiver, and separation anxiety is as traumatic for them as it is for young children.

In the first year of the baby's life, mothers' anxiety about separation from the infant, particularly separation related to employment, changes with time.[87] Educated, older career women have strong feelings of anxiety about separation from their infant for the baby's first two months, seeing the child as vulnerable and in need of nurturance. In the course of the first year, such anxiety decreases, most rapidly in those women who want to return to work. Among women who do not want to return but do so, anxiety about their ability to balance work and family needs increases, but this anxiety, too, fades with time. Women who continue to stay home as their infant grows continue to have strong concerns about their ability to be both mothers and workers, and no doubt these concerns keep them at home.

Anxiety about balancing home and work commitments is a distinguishing feature of those mothers who have secure attachments with their infants, regardless of whether they work.[88] This anxiety again may be what keeps mothers at home, but even employed mothers who had strong concerns in this area have infants with secure attachments to them. It is possible that the anxiety motivates employed mothers to find the best nonmaternal care. When mothers cannot come to terms with their anxiety, they may become intrusive and overcontrolling with their infants, thus contributing to an insecure mother-infant attachment.[89]

A parent who believes that it is reasonable for him or her to work and that doing so does not deprive the child of anything essential can handle crying or pouting at separation calmly. The child's feelings are recognized and accepted—he or she is entitled to feel disappointed that the parent will not be available for several hours.

When they return from work, parents must deal with children's eagerness for their attention—to tell them the day's events, to play with them. Parents are advised to develop a routine for themselves and their children so children know when they will receive attention and parents have a chance to organize themselves for family activities. Parents may talk first and then cook dinner, or they may prefer to rest first and then talk while preparing dinner. Depending on children's and parents' particular needs, any number of arrangements are possible.

Maintaining Ties to Children

When both parents are at work all day, parents and children want to keep in touch during these hours of separation. When the child is old enough to use the phone, a regular call at a time convenient for both provides contact and gives them a chance to share news. Some parents leave messages where the child will find them. Others send postcards, to the delight of the child who doesn't receive much mail. Families find a tape cassette useful. The imaginative parent can use time during lunch hour or after the children are in bed to tape a "letter" or a story. Older children can use the tape recorder to tell parents about important events at school and to leave messages if they are going to be away when the parents get home.

Working parents find it helpful to meet with children's teachers at the beginning of each school year to describe their work schedules and clarify how each parent would like to be involved in school projects. Communicating the interest and willingness of both parents to help is sufficient to prompt the teacher to include them.

Parents can strengthen ties with children by including them in their work lives whenever possible, just as parents participate in school events and observe classes. The child who visits the parent's office, shop, or factory and even helps there on a vacation day learns a little about what the parent does all day and something about a particular vocation.

Spending Quality Time   The parent who works spends less time with children than the parent who is home and available to the children all day. Further, the working parent must, during nonworking hours, manage to do chores and errands and eat and sleep and play. Time is precious. And the *quality* of the time shared by parent and child matters.

Dorothy Briggs's definition of a genuine encounter provides a good definition of *quality time:* "focused attention [on the child] . . . attention with special intensity born of direct, personal involvement . . . being intimately open to the particular, unique qualities of your child."[90] Having a genuine encounter means being "all there" with the child. The quality of the relationships, not the nature of the specific activity, is the crucial factor.

Genuine encounters differ according to the age of the child. In infancy, quality time might consist of active play with the baby. In the toddler years, it might involve watch-

---

BOX 12-2
SUGGESTIONS FOR QUALITY TIME WITH CHILDREN

1. Spend time one on one with each child. Develop a ritual done with just that child and enjoy that special time together.
2. Hug even when your children are big. Both mothers and fathers can give hugs or other forms of physical affection, in ways that are meaningful to boys and girls of any age. However, parents should be sensitive to children's feelings and give physical affection when children will appreciate it.
3. Reconnect when returning from work by joining in what children are doing. If they are doing homework, ask a specific question about it or about some activity that occurred at school. Specific questions elicit more information than "What did you do today?"
4. Join a parent-child program like Scouts or Voyagers (formerly known as Indian Guides and Indian Princesses).
5. Take children to work and show them what you do, specifically.
6. Take children on business trips or special excursions, if possible.
7. Include children in household chores.

Adapted from James A. Levine and Todd L. Pittinsky, *Working Fathers: Strategies for Balancing Work and Family* (Reading, MA: Addison-Wesley, 1997), pp. 172–179.

---

ing as the child explores an area and waiting for the child to bring back the latest discovery. In the preschool years, it might mean arranging a special experience—a trip to a dairy farm—or getting a puppy or kitten and taking the time to show the preschooler how to play with and care for the animal. In the elementary school years, it might include helping the child create a work area and a routine for schoolwork, going on excursions with a group, and listening as the child practices a musical instrument. In the adolescent years, it might involve listening to long discussions on the merits of different kinds of jeans or the advantages of a particular kind of sports equipment.

We think less often of shared experiences doing household work as quality time. Yet, in the course of working together, parents and children learn about each other's special strengths and weaknesses as they can in no other situation. The teenager who keeps her room a mess may reveal unexpected competence as she devises shortcuts while working in the yard with her mother. Working together also provides time for conversations that might otherwise never occur.

Quality time also includes attention focused on the needs of the child even when that child is not present—planning some special event for a son or thinking about the wisdom of getting a daughter into a sport. Although no direct interaction with the child occurs, this time is devoted to actions that convey to the child that he or she is special and worthy of attention. Helping to paint playground equipment demonstrates that the child's activities are important and worthy of support. (See Box 12-2 for further suggestions regarding quality time.)

How is quality time related to quantity of time? Quality time is time spent with children when parents have the energy and interest to focus on the children. Other concerns and worries must be put aside, and that may be difficult when so much must be done. The parent who makes an effort to arrange quality time will have a special relationship with the child regardless of the parent's work status.

Setting Appropriate Limits　In all families, reasonable limits are required for children. Ellen Greenberger and Wendy Goldberg find that having high investment in work does not mean parents must drastically change their standards for behavior or their disciplinary methods.[91] In fact, parents can have high investments in both areas; and when this is the case for mothers, they are most likely to rely on authoritative disciplinary techniques that have been found to be successful with children of all ages. Parents using these techniques tend to view their children's behavior positively and see them as having few behavior problems.

It is, of course, important to set and enforce appropriate limits and monitor behavior, as described in Chapter 4. Parents may be inclined to indulge children to compensate for being gone all day, but the working parent needs to remember that chores are not an imposition but a shared responsibility in the home.

Parents who permit immature and emotional behavior are also being indulgent. Working parents sometimes feel children are justified in being angry at their absence. When a four-year-old has a temper tantrum because both parents are leaving the house and he cannot go, the parents are sometimes apologetic and comforting, giving the child the impression that a tantrum is a realistic response.

Alternatively, parents may find that when they both work outside the home, they demand too much from children. They may ask them to do chores that are too difficult, such as caring for younger children when they themselves are just able to care for themselves. They may ask energetic children to be quiet while a parent sleeps in the daytime so he or she can work at night. As parents set limits and establish structure, they must check their expectations of children: can the child do the task? If so, is the amount of work or responsibility so great that the child is robbed of childhood pleasures? Often, children can do far more than we expect. However, if children begin to develop behavior problems, parents can decide to change the responsibilities.

THE CARE OF BOTH PARTNERS

In the excitement and busyness of working, parents forget that the family started with the primacy of the couple. Further, the satisfaction that the couple have with each other and their ways of doing things make solutions effective. The continuance of a strong, loving bond between parents is a primary factor in the success of combining working and parenting.

Further, more than anything else in the world, children want the family to stay together. To do this, parents need a strong relationship. Their relationship, however, usually gets put aside during child rearing, especially in the earliest years.

James Levine and Todd Pittinsky suggest that parents make a weekly date to do something without the children.[92] If money is a problem, set aside some special time at home—rent a video, have a special dinner. Baby-sitting, an expensive item, can be exchanged in baby-sitting cooperatives. The date should be exclusive time with the spouse to reconnect and share what is happening. Parents can organize daily rituals that give them special time together—reading the paper together, sitting close to each other while listening to music, talking after dinner, or just being physically close together watching TV. Telephone calls during the day also help parents stay connected.

Working parents who take care of themselves can take better care of their children and each other. Couples who exercise regularly, eat a balanced diet, and make sure they have private time for thinking and pursuing interests are less likely to be tense and tired and more likely to enjoy their job and family. Gloria Norris and JoAnn Miller suggest the following ways for parents to be good to themselves:[93]

1. Keep up friendships—exercising with a friend several times a week is ideal.

2. Develop ways of easing the transition from office to home—walk the last block or two, take a quick shower before dinner, rest for ten minutes after arriving home.

3. Learn personal signs of stress and do not ignore them; get rest and spend time relaxing.

4. Discover the most stressful times of the day and find ways of relieving tension; a different morning or evening routine can reduce stress.

5. Develop a quick tension reliever, like yoga exercises, deep breathing, or meditation.

The life of the working parent is challenging and demanding. But most working parents find the challenges worth the efforts required, as work makes life richer and more exciting for the whole family.

MAIN POINTS

Work

- influences social values in child rearing and the social life and status of families
- develops adults' skills and provides many supports
- creates stress that disrupts parenting skills

When parents work, adaptation strategies include

- sharing workloads
- focusing time on children
- supervising carefully
- developing family cooperation in household work

Nonparental care of children

- in the first year can promote positive qualities when infants can form positive attachments to consistent, sensitive caregivers

- in early childhood promotes competence when children have secure attachments to sensitive teachers who provide stimulating activities and monitor them
- in the elementary school years and adolescence is associated with social and intellectual competence if children are supervised
- may be more problematic for boys than girls
- can have a negative impact if it is of low quality

Of the various forms of day care,

- at-home care provides a specific caregiver in familiar surroundings
- family day care involves smaller numbers of children in a homelike atmosphere that can provide more individualized attention at a lower cost than can at-home care
- day care centers have trained personnel, the greatest variety of educational and play equipment, and reliable care that provides contact with children of the same age
- self-care can have positive and negative consequences

Effectively combining working and parenting requires parents to find time

- for quality relationships with children
- for the marriage relationship
- to attend to their own individualized needs

EXERCISES

1. Break into small groups and discuss the research finding that the effect of mothers' working seems to depend on the sex of the child. (See the comments of Susan McHale in the interview early in this chapter.) Discuss the finding that boys may experience more negative effects because they need more monitoring. How can parents take action to optimize effects for both boys and girls?

2. Imagine you had a child under age five—infant, toddler, or preschooler. Investigate day care available in the community for a child of that age. You might form groups to investigate care for a child of a particular age, with each student visiting at least one center to get information and summarize impressions. One group might investigate family day care in the area and compare the quality and the cost of care with that available in a center.

3. Design an ideal day care program for infants or toddlers, specifying the number of caregivers, their qualities, the physical facilities, and the daily routine.

4. Imagine what your family and work life will be like in ten years. Write diary entries for a day during the week and for a day on the weekend about your life at home and at work.

5. Write a short paper containing advice you could give to a parent of the same sex as you who feels frustrated and pressured trying to incorporate an infant and the care of the infant into his or her work life.

ADDITIONAL READINGS

Booth, Alan, ed. *Child Care in the 1990s: Trends and Consequences.* Hillsdale, NJ: Erlbaum, 1992.

Goodnow, Jacqueline J., and Bowes, Jennifer M. *Men, Women and Household Work.* Melbourne, Australia: Oxford University Press, 1994.

Hayes, Cheryl D., Palmer, John L., and Zaslow, Martha J., eds. *Who Cares for America's Children?* Washington, DC: National Academy Press, 1990.

Hochschild, Arlie. *The Time Bind: When Work Becomes Home and Home Becomes Work.* New York: Holt, 1997.

Levine, James A., and Pittinsky, Todd L. *Working Fathers: New Strategies for Balancing Work and Family.* Reading, MA: Addison-Wesley, 1997.

SINGLE PARENTING AND STEPPARENTING

C H A P T E R 13

Biologically speaking, it takes two parents to create a new life. In U.S. society, family has traditionally meant a mother and father and their biological children. But now, more children are born to single mothers, and a sizable number of children experience divorce of their parents with subsequent remarriage. How does life change for children in single-parent households? How does life change when parents remarry? How can parents help children cope with all these changes?

In 1995, 69 percent of children lived with two parents, one of whom may have been a stepparent; 26 percent lived in households headed by women; and 5 percent lived in households headed by men. Most single women raising children are divorced or separated from husbands, but a sizable number are never-married mothers. In 1993, the most recent year for which we have statistics, approximately 30 percent of babies were born to unmarried mothers.[1]

It is estimated that 50 percent of all children will experience divorce of their parents and spend an average of five years in a single-parent family. About 75 percent of mothers and 80 percent of fathers remarry, so a sizable number of these children will go on to live in stepfamilies. Many may experience a second divorce, as approximately 50 percent of these marriages end as well.[2] This chapter describes the challenges both parents and children face as they experience these changes.

THE HETEROGENEITY OF SINGLE-PARENT FAMILIES

Both numbers and proportions of single-parent families have increased in all Western countries and in all ethnic groups in the United States. African-American families have a somewhat higher rate of single-parent families than do other groups; this does not appear to be the result of increased sexual activity among young women, but rather of the fact that birthrates have remained the same in this group while rates of marriage have dropped. Thus, more children are born to unmarried mothers.[3]

Single-parent families not only have grown from 9 percent of families in 1960 to 31 percent of families in 1995, but also have become more diverse in form.[4] In 1970, 73 percent of children in single-parent families lived with a separated or divorced parent, 20 percent with a widowed parent, and only 7 percent with a never-married parent. In 1990, 31 percent lived with a never-married parent, 62 percent with a separated/divorced parent, and only 7 percent with a widowed parent. And, as we shall see, never-married parents have a variety of lifestyles.

Because the child's experience depends on the specific conditions in his or her family, it is difficult to generalize about the effects of being reared in a single-parent family. Many studies suggest, however, that children in single-parent families are at greater risk for developing emotional and academic problems.[5] This should not be surprising, as it is more difficult for one parent to provide as much nurturance, monitoring, and supervision as two parents, who have the additional benefits of greater resources and support from each other.

A major reason for the difficulties of single-parent families may be the increased rate of poverty. In 1993, the average income of female householders with children under age eighteen was $13,472; for two-parent families, $45,548; and for male householders, $22,348.[6] Half of all single parents are poor, and "no other major demographic group is so poor and stays poor for so long."[7] As we noted in Chapters 1 and 12, economic hardship and poverty bring stress, which decreases parents' abilities to be nurturant and effective in setting limits.

However, economic factors are not the only difficulties. Studies of single mothers committed to raising their children alone have found that these women report more stress than do mothers in two-parent families, even when families are matched on education, income, and area of residence.[8] The single mothers had to work longer hours and were more worried about finances than were their married counterparts. The greatest difference between these two groups of mothers, however, was that single mothers had fewer social and emotional supports when their children were young. And it was precisely this kind of support that predicted optimal parent-child interactions in both single- and two-parent families. When single mothers had social-emotional support, their children's behavior was similar to that of children in two-parent families. Stressful life events such as poverty, which occurs more frequently in single-parent families, reduced overall parent effectiveness. Mobilizing both economic and social-emotional resources can help single-parent families function as effectively as two-parent families.

MARITAL OR PARTNER CONFLICT AND DIVORCE

We have seen in several earlier chapters (e.g., 1, 2 and 5) that the quality of the marital relationship affects the parenting behaviors of mothers and fathers. Marital satisfaction and marital intimacy are positive supports that contribute to parents' sense of well-being, their confidence, and their skills as parents.

But unresolved conflicts affect children in two ways. First, unresolved anger directly affects children's physiological and social functioning in negative ways, as noted in Chapter 3. Second, marital conflict affects children indirectly by impairing parents' skills and behavior with children. When parents are unhappy with each other, they experience anger, sadness, and guilt and frequently express these emotions in the family, becoming negative and intrusive with children.[9]

In a negative family atmosphere, children develop behavior problems. Children from high-conflict homes are at risk for developing (1) externalizing problems such as increased aggressiveness, noncompliance, and unacceptable conduct; (2) internalizing problems such as depression, anxiety, and social withdrawal; (3) problems in school such as poor grades; and (4) an angry, negative view of themselves and the world.[10] These problems persist, and in adolescence, both boys and girls who experienced parental disagreements in the preschool years are poorly controlled and interpersonally less skilled.[11] Boys also show difficulties in intellectual functioning. So, boys whose parents later divorce are already impulsive and poorly controlled ten years before the divorce.[12]

There is growing evidence that young children who witness extensive partner conflict and violence are at risk for neurobiological changes in brain structure that, in turn, affect later neurological development.[13] The nature of the violent arguing—its frequency and intensity—determine how the brain will internalize the experience. If the child is terrified, the brain may be in a constant state of hyperarousal that will make it difficult for the child to absorb cognitive stimulation and information, and cognitive growth may be delayed.

Again, the keys to minimizing the impact of conflict on children are to resolve the conflicts in mutually agreeable ways and to remove any feelings of self-blame the child may have about the conflict. However, when parents cannot resolve their conflicts, they often seek a divorce. Mavis Hetherington,[14] who has carried out longitudinal studies of intact, divorced, and remarried families, describes four considerations that underlie all her research: (1) Divorce is not a single event, but an event that triggers many changes for children and parents over time; (2) changes associated with marital transitions have to be viewed as changes in the entire family system; (3) the entire social milieu—peer group, neighborhood, school, friendship network—will influence an individual's response to the transition; and (4) there is great diversity in the ways children and parents respond to marital transitions. Most studies of families in transition focus on white middle-class families, and we do not know how widely we can generalize these findings.

Financial and Legal Issues

Hetherington and Kathleen Camara emphasize that divorce is a parental solution to parental problems.[15] Children often view divorce as the cause of all their problems. For both parent and child, however, divorce brings many related stresses with it. Financial problems arise; there is no way two families can live as cheaply as one. Often, mothers must go to work or increase their hours at work, so children may see not only much less of their father, who is no longer living with them, but less of their mother, who must work more. Reduced income means many families must move, so the child has a new neighborhood, new school, and new friends to deal with. As resources grow more limited, parents may become more irritable, discouraged, and impatient with children.

As the divorce rate has risen, society has begun to accommodate the needs of divorcing families. The legal system has changed, making it easier for both parents to continue to be involved in the care of children. With joint legal custody, mothers and fathers, though divorced, continue to make decisions about children, with each parent taking an equal part. Some have joint physical custody, in which children spend significant amounts of time with both parents. When parents have difficulty coming to agreement about custody issues, many states now provide court mediation services. Professional counselors help parents explore children's and parents' needs and reach agreement on reasonable living arrangements.

Further, laws have been passed to make it easier for single mothers to obtain child support payments decreed by the court. This is imperative because, as noted, mothers who are single heads of household have incomes far below those of other family units.

Telling Children about Divorce

When a couple decide to divorce, it is best if both parents together tell the children about the divorce before one parent leaves the home. Judith Wallerstein suggests wording like this: "We married fully hoping and expecting to love each other forever, but we have discovered that one (or both) of us is unhappy. One (or both) does not love the other anymore. We fight with each other. The divorce is going to stop the fighting and restore peace."[16]

Parents present the decision as a rational, sad one:

The goal is to present the child with models of parents who admit they made a serious mistake, tried to rectify the mistake, and are now embarking on a moral, socially acceptable remedy. The parents are responsible people who remain committed to the family and to the children even though they have decided to go their separate ways.[17]

When parents express their sadness at the solution, then children have permission to mourn without hiding their feelings from adults.

It is also important to express reluctance at the solution because children need to hear that parents know how upsetting this will be for them: "Put simply, parents should tell the children they are sorry for all the hurt they are causing."[18]

There are many things divorcing parents should *not* say. First, they should not burden their children with their own negative views of each other. Second, they should not blame the other parent for all the problems. Third, they should not ask children to take sides — children usually need and want to be loyal to both parents. Parents may be surprised at the loyalty that children feel to both parents, to the marriage, and to the family. Even when one parent has abused the other or the children, children often want the abusive parent present in the family. Even when children are willing to accept a parent's absence, they often do not want anything negative said about him or her.

Wallerstein comments on how little support most children get as they go through the initial turmoil of divorce. Often, no one talks to them, no one listens to them talk about their feelings or answers their questions, and few relatives give added help and support. Children frequently are left on their own to manage as best they can.

To keep communication going, each parent should permit children to express their feelings and should guide the children into acceptable forms of behavior that remedy what can be changed. Parents need to hear that children may be angry at them or the other parent. Using active listening and sending I-messages are appropriate ways to keep channels of communication open.

Children's Reactions to Divorce

Emotional reactions to divorce, common to children of all ages, include sadness, fear, depression, anger, confusion, and sometimes relief; the predominant emotions vary with the child's age and require somewhat different reactions from parents.[19] In the preschool years, children often feel abandoned and overwhelmed by the events. They worry that they may have caused the divorce. Although they usually try hard to handle their feelings with denial, they need parents who will talk to them and explain what is happening, not once but many times. Children may regress, begin wetting the bed, have temper tantrums, and develop fears. Parents can help most by providing emotional support. Outside interventions are not as useful as interventions by parents. Parents are urged to (1) communicate with the child about the divorce and the new adjustments, explaining in simple language the reasons for each change that occurs, and (2) reduce the child's suffering, where possible, by giving reassurance that the child's needs will be met and by doing concrete things such as arranging visits with the absent parent.

Preschool children are often protected initially by their ability to deny what is happening. Five- to seven-year-olds are vulnerable because they understand more but do not have the maturity to cope with what they see and hear. The most outstanding reaction of a child this age is sadness and grief. The child is not yet old enough or independent enough to arrange activities that will bring pleasure and some relief from the worry. The divorce dominates the thoughts of a child this age. One little girl, whose parents had just divorced, was asked what she would like if she could have just three wishes. Her reply: "First, that my daddy would come home. Second, that my parents would get back together. And third, that they would never, ever divorce again."[20]

Fear is another frequent response. Children worry that no one will love them or care for them. Their world has fallen apart and is no longer safe. Many children feel that only a father can maintain discipline in the family.

Children ages nine and older may find outside intervention useful, and several weeks of counseling may help them sort out their feelings about the divorce, custody, and visitation. Counseling provides a neutral third party to validate the child's feelings. When children are depressed, angry, and worried, it is reassuring for them to hear a professional person say, "Yes, this is a very difficult time, and it is understandable that you feel upset and sad." Children can then accept their feelings more easily.

In helping older children handle divorce, parents need to keep in mind that these children may feel responsible—they may believe they have done something that has brought about the divorce or that they could have fixed the marital difficulties. Parents need to say clearly and often, when opportunities occur, that the divorce was *not* caused by the children, but it *was* caused by difficulties between the parents. In addition, parents need to remember that children worry about them and how they are doing. It is not always possible to confine grief and distress to times when the children are not there, but parents can help children by trying to wait until they are alone to express sadness or anger.

The children of a divorcing or divorced couple need, perhaps more than anything else, to be able to talk with their parents about what is happening. Parents can encourage children to ask questions and to express their feelings. And they should respond to questions with clear statements. Children need to know what the practical arrangements for their lives are—where they will be living and with whom. And they need to know that their parents continue to care about their welfare and about their feelings.

Thus far, we have described the reactions of children who regret their parents' divorce. But some children, about 10 percent, feel relieved at their parents' divorce.[21] Often, they are older children who have witnessed violence or severe psychological suffering on the part of a parent or other family member. These children feel that dissolution of the marriage is the best solution, and progressing from a conflict-ridden home to a more stable environment with one parent helps these children's overall level of adjustment and functioning.

From a follow-up of children fifteen years after the divorce, Wallerstein and Blakeslee conclude that it is very difficult to determine the long-term adjustment of the child from the child's reactions at the time of the divorce.[22] Some children who seemed to have had very strong, disorganizing reactions were, nevertheless, doing well many years later while others who seemed to have made a good initial adjustment had long-standing problems.

Parents' Reactions to Divorce

Parents' reactions to divorce are many and varied, but almost all are intense. They often suffer many symptoms—headaches, rapid heartbeat, fatigue, dizziness.[23] Their moods and behavior change at the time of the divorce, and these mood changes may be one of the most upsetting aspects of the divorce process for their children. Each parent may respond differently at different times, and both may show similar behavior only when they are angry with each other. Children are helpless in the face of their parents' extreme moods. One parent may be sad, depressed, and lacking in energy; the other may be busy, agitated, and preoccupied with his or her concerns. Both often lack self-esteem and seek out people or experiences to make them feel good again.

Divorced men and women both start dating again, though men date in larger numbers and older women tend to remain isolated and alone. Heterosexual relationships now become a source of anxiety and tension. Women wonder how to respond to sexual advances, and men worry about sexual performance. Nevertheless, new intimate relationships after divorce tend to boost parents' self-esteem.

Parents must deal with the intense feelings that arise during the divorce process, even if those feelings were not there in the beginning. They feel sad at the end of their marriage, even if the dissolution was necessary. They feel pain as the divorce becomes real—material possessions are divided, money is dispersed, and custody and visiting rights are arranged. Anger keeps the relationship alive for a time, but gradually, detachment and distance mean the marital relationship is truly ended. The loss is real.

Long-term emotional reactions to the divorce are diverse. Seventy-five percent of divorced custodial mothers report that at the end of two years, they feel happier than they did in the last year of the marriage. Many of these women go on to develop independent lives and careers that increase their self-esteem. Some divorced women, however, report depression, loneliness, and health problems six to eleven years after the divorce. Still, they do not have as many problems as nondivorced women in high-conflict marriages, who are more depressed and anxious and have more physical problems.[24]

Factors Affecting Adjustment to Divorce

Several factors influence how well a family adapts to divorce:[25] (1) the amount of conflict among family members, (2) the availability of both parents to their children, (3) the nature of the relationship changes in the family, (4) the responsibilities family members take, and (5) the defensibility of the divorce from the child's point of view.[26]

Moving from a household with two parents always in conflict to a stable household with one parent can lead to better adjustment for children.[27] Parents often continue the fighting when they live separately, however, and this is harmful to children; boys tend to react with undercontrolled and girls with overcontrolled behaviors.[28] It is possible that the increased conflict children witness during divorce, not the divorce itself, leads to their poorer adjustment. Increased conflicts can also occur between parents and children in a one-parent household in which the second parent is not available as a buffering agent. In addition, a parent may find the child a convenient target for feelings aroused by the other parent. In the midst of this raging conflict, the child feels very alone. Minimizing the fighting in all arenas aids everyone's adjustment.

Parents can help insulate their children from the conflict that accompanies a divorce. Box 12-1 lists some behavior characteristics of parents who work to protect their children from the parents' own conflicts.

When children have continuing relationships with both parents, they are more likely to adjust well following the divorce process.[29] It is impossible to predict how fathers, who are usually the ones to move out of the home, will respond after the divorce. Some previously devoted fathers find not living with their children so painful that they withdraw and see less of the children. Other fathers, previously uninvolved, discover that caring for children alone on visits deepens their attachment, and so they increase their contact with their children. Fathers are more likely to maintain relationships with their sons than their daughters. In fact, many mothers relinquish custody of older sons to fathers because they feel sons need a male role model.

Not only do children need relationships with both parents, but they also need to be able to relate to each separately as a parent.[30] Recently divorced parents often find it difficult to direct their energy to parenting. Thus, at this time of great need in the first year following divorce, when they actually need *more* attention, children receive less attention from their parents. Frequently, children's behavior goes unmonitored, and rules are not enforced. The parent outside the home often becomes highly indulgent and permissive with children; seeing so little of them, he or she hates to spend precious time in discipline. But children function most effectively

◆

BOX 13-1
OUT OF HARM'S WAY:
PROTECTING CHILDREN FROM PARENTAL CONFLICT

Children can continue to grow and thrive even through a divorce if their parents in-sulate them from intense or prolonged hostilities. Parents who accomplish this share some important qualities:

1. They make it clear that they value their child's relationship and time both with them *and* with the other parent.
2. They work out a fair and practical time-sharing schedule, either temporary or long-term, as soon as possible.
3. Once that agreement is reached, they make every effort to live up to its terms.
4. They tell each other in advance about necessary changes in plans.
5. They are reasonably flexible in "trading off" to accommodate the other parent's needs.
6. They prepare the child, in a positive way, for each upcoming stay with the other parent.
7. They *do not* conduct adult business when they meet to transfer the child.
8. They refrain from using the child as a confidant, messenger, bill collector, or spy.
9. They listen caringly but encourage their child to work out problems with the other parent directly.
10. They work on their problems with each other in private.

Robert Adler, *Sharing the Children* (New York: Adler & Adler, 1988). Used with permission of the author.

when both parents take time to monitor their behavior and enforce the usual rules, as in the past.

In the family with two households and both parents working, the need is greater for children to take on more responsibilities.[31] When demands are not excessive and are tailored to the abilities of children, then children may feel pleased with their contribution to the family and the new competence they are developing. When the demands are too great, however—when they are given too much responsibility for caring for younger children or doing chores—then children become resentful, feel-ing they are being robbed of their childhood. Realistic demands for responsibility can help children grow in this situation.

Children seem better able to cope with divorce and its aftermath when the di-vorce is a carefully thought-out, reasonable response to a specific problem.[32] When the problem improves after the divorce, children are better able to accept it. They are less able to deal with divorce that is an impulsive act, that may have had little to do with the marriage but was related to other problems in the parents' life. For ex-ample, one woman divorced her husband following the death of her mother. She later regretted the decision but could not undo what had hurt four people.

Protective Factors for Children

Protective factors for children as they adjust to the divorce include qualities of the child, supportive aspects of the family system, and external social supports.[33] The child's age, sex, and intelligence serve as protection. Intelligence can help children cope with all the stress. Younger children appear less affected than elementary school children or early adolescents at the time of the divorce or remarriage. Because they are becoming increasingly independent of the family, late adolescents seem less affected than younger children. Boys appear to suffer more difficulties at the time of the divorce, and girls appear to have more problems at the time of the mother's remarriage.

The child's temperament also influences the process of divorce. An easy, adaptable temperament helps. Because children with a difficult temperament are more sensitive to change and less adaptable to it, they can become a focal point for parental anger. In part, they elicit the anger with their reactive behavior; in part, they provide a convenient target for parental anger that may belong elsewhere.

For difficult children, the more stress they experience, the more problems they have. For easy children, the relationship is different. With moderate amounts of stress, easy children actually develop increased coping skills and become more competent than when stress is either low or high.

We have already touched on some forms of family interaction that are protective — reduced conflict between the parents, structure and organization in daily life, and reasonable assignment of responsibilities within the family. Mothers must be especially firm and fair in establishing limits with boys, as their tendency is to develop a vicious repetitive cycle of complaining and fighting.

Researchers point to siblings and grandparents as potential supports.[34] When family life is harmonious after divorce, then sibling relationships resemble those in intact families.[35] When there is conflict between parents, siblings fight, with the greatest difficulty occurring between older brothers and younger sisters.

Grandparents can support grandchildren directly with time, attention, and special outings and privileges that help ease the pain of the divorce. As one girl said, "If it weren't for my grandparents, I don't think I could have made it past sixteen."[36]

Grandparents provide support indirectly by helping one of the parents. In fact, returning to live in the home of one's parents is a solution many young parents choose when they do not have the resources to be on their own. Grandparents can be loving, stable baby-sitters who enrich children's lives in ways that no one else can. The mother can work and carry on a social life, knowing that her child is well cared for in her absence. And this arrangement usually reduces living expenses. When the mother and grandparents agree on child-rearing techniques and the mother is respected in the household as a mature adult, this solution may be attractive.

Such an arrangement, however, can reflect the neurotic needs of both the mother and the grandparents — and, when this is the case, it is likely to create additional problems for the child. If the grandmother was a protective mother who refused to allow the daughter to become independent, that relationship may continue. The daughter may have tried to escape into a marriage that did not last. If the daughter returns to her parents' home, she may have to start again to develop her independence. She will have to establish new supports that will enable her to become more independent and to continue her growth as an individual.

School is a major source of support for children. Authoritative, kindly teachers and peer friendships give pleasure and a sense of esteem to children. Educational and athletic accomplishments contribute to feelings of competence that stimulate resilience.

Some of the protective factors lie beyond a parent's control—age, sex, and temperament of the child—but many lie within it—setting aside anger, establishing structure, monitoring behavior, and seeking out external supports for children.

Family Changes over Time

Previous sections have discussed children's and parents' reactions to divorce and factors affecting their adjustment to this major life change. In this section, we examine how these factors affect interaction among family members over time.

Right after a divorce, *custodial mothers* are under pressure because of all the changes occurring in their lives.[37] Many of these parents become more negative with their children than they were earlier, particularly with boys, and less involved in monitoring their behavior; a small group of these mothers, however, become too lenient and permissive. In response, both boys and girls become more anxious, demanding, aggressive, and noncompliant with peers and adults. As time passes, however, custodial mothers adjust and become more nurturant and more consistent in behavior management. Girls' behavior improves, and mother-daughter relationships often are very close. Relationships with boys improve somewhat, but many boys continue to have some behavior problems.

Custodial fathers initially complain of feeling overwhelmed, angry, confused, and isolated, but after two years, they report better adjustment, perhaps because they generally have greater financial resources and better support or because they typically get custody of older children.[38]

After the divorce, *noncustodial fathers* tend to become either permissive and indulgent or disengaged. They are less likely to be disciplinarians and more likely to play the role of recreational companion than are custodial mothers.[39] Many times, however, noncustodial fathers do not stay involved. One study reported that two years after the divorce, 25 percent of children had not seen their fathers in the past year; eleven years after the divorce, the number had risen to 50 percent.[40] More recent work indicates, however, that three-and-a-half years after the divorce, two-thirds of adolescents still have contact with their fathers, even if only at holidays and summer vacation.[41] Fathers are most likely to stay involved when they feel they play an important role in their children's lives and their long-term development.

Noncustodial mothers of adolescents are more likely to stay involved than noncustodial fathers. Mothers are more active and involved with and supportive of children than are fathers, who often continue their role of recreational companion.[42]

Children's Behavior over Time

Children's behavior problems do improve over the first two years, but boys continue to have some difficulties six to eleven years after the divorce. Beginning at age ten, girls, especially early maturing girls, show behavior problems as well. Both boys and girls are less competent in school, more defiant and noncompliant with rules, and more negative in mood—anxious, depressed, sometimes suicidal—compared with children of nondivorced parents.[43]

Early adolescents' rule breaking and resistance to custodial parents' authority may result from the early autonomy and independence many experienced during the family adjustment period immediately after the divorce. They have been joint decision makers with their custodial parents, and parents have been less insistent and demanding that children meet family rules. Therefore, they feel entitled to pursue their own ends.[44]

In intact families, parents exert more constraint on early adolescents. They insist that the teens do chores and follow the rules. These parents monitor carefully; there are more arguments and less harmony in intact families than in divorced families. Divorced custodial mothers, however, become careful monitors in midadolescence, especially with daughters. So, at a time when parents in intact families are disengaging and trusting children's judgment in midadolescence (age fifteen), divorced mothers are often becoming more authoritative.[45]

Children in divorced families resist custodial mothers' authority; these mothers are more successful and the children have fewer problems when another adult (such as a grandparent, *not* a stepparent) lives in the home and reinforces the mother's authority.[46]

Feeling caught between divorced parents who are in conflict intensifies adolescents' anxiety, depression, and poor adjustment.[47] Even when parents have high conflict with each other, adolescents can do well, provided parents do not put them in the middle. The feeling of being caught between parents contributes to these children's problems.

Again, we find great diversity in children's adjustment.[48] Although many children of divorce show aggressive and insecure behaviors in adolescence, others are caring, competent teenagers who cooperate with divorced parents and make significant contributions to family functioning. Still others are caring, responsible teenagers whose autonomy and maturity are accompanied by feelings of depression and low self-esteem. They appear to worry that they will be unable to meet the demands placed on them.

Regardless of family type and sex of the child, when parents are warm and positive, monitor children carefully, and don't behave negatively toward them—in brief, when they use authoritative parenting—their children are most likely to develop social and cognitive competence. When parents view their children negatively and use authoritarian/conflictual parenting, children often externalize their problems and perform poorly in school. Positive parental qualities are also related to the quality of sibling relationships, which, in turn, contribute to children's competence.

Those children who have the most difficulty with externalizing behaviors do not have a single caring adult in their lives. Their parents are neglectful, disengaged, and authoritarian, and the children cannot find support outside the family.

Paul Amato and Brian Keith reviewed ninety-two studies to determine the degree of difficulty children of divorce experience.[49] They concluded that divorce is associated with increased risk for problems in cognitive and social competence. But recent, better-controlled studies reveal that the differences between children of divorce and children in intact families are small and that there is much overlap in the functioning of the two groups.

Amato and Keith examined three possible sources of the increased difficulties: parental loss, economic deprivation, and family conflict. Parental loss is a significant contributor to problems. Children who lose a parent through death experience difficulties similar to those of children whose parents divorce, shown by lower levels of well-being, poorer academic achievement, and conduct problems, compared with children in intact families; however, they do score significantly higher on these dimensions than do children in divorced families. Further, when custodial parents remarry, the children's behavior and functioning generally do not improve. Finally, involvement of the noncustodial parent brings only modest improvement. So, although parental loss is an important factor, it is not the only cause of difficulties in children of divorce.

Similar findings occur with economic disadvantage. When studies control for income, children of divorce still appear to have more problems than do children in intact families, and when parents remarry and income increases, children's behavior problems continue.

The third factor, family conflict, appears to be the main contributor to children's difficulties. Children in high-conflict, intact marriages have greater difficulties in self-esteem and adjustment than do children in divorced families in which such conflict is reduced. Level of family conflict and family conflict resolution styles are more powerful predictors of children's overall adjustment status than is family status (intact, divorced, or remarried). Further, longitudinal studies indicate that as time passes after the divorce and, presumably, the conflict, the child's adjustment improved (except when a developmental stage such as adolescence increases problems for all families). Finally, when postdivorce conflict is low, children function more effectively. Thus, living in conflict—whether in an intact or a divorced family—appears to be the most powerful contributor to children's adjustment problems.

We now find that the effects of divorce do not necessarily end with childhood.[50] Young adults whose parents divorced when they were children have lower educational attainment than adults from intact families, earn less money, are more likely to have a child out of wedlock, are more likely to get divorced, and are more likely to be alienated from one parent. Again, there is diversity of outcome. Most adult children of divorce function well within the normal range of most measures of adjustment. The only exception is in having poor relations with the father. In the section on parenting tasks at the end of the chapter, I present general guidelines for parenting at times of marital transitions.

NEVER-MARRIED PARENTS

Never-married parents, the fastest-growing group of single parents, are a varied group. If they are living in committed relationships with the other biological parent or another adult of the opposite sex, they may share many of the problems of divorced parents. These relationships tend to be less stable than marriages, and parents and children may experience all the stresses of a married family that undergoes divorce.[51]

Some never-married parents are living in committed relationships with same-sex partners, rearing children conceived either in a previous marriage or by means of artificial insemination. These relationships sometimes dissolve, and again, parents and children undergo the stresses of divorce.[52]

Research on lesbian and gay parents has initially concentrated on their effectiveness as parents, in order to counteract judicial challenges to custody and visitation issues. Findings indicate that gay and lesbian parents are as competent as heterosexual parents and their children function as well with peers as do children of heterosexual parents. Children of lesbian parents show no special problems with self-concept, emotional adjustment, or sexual identity.[53] Thus, there is great similarity in the children from lesbian and heterosexual families. Because these findings appear clear, researchers are now turning to the study of the diversity of lifestyles within gay and lesbian families to identify the factors that help families function well enough even though they face all the usual contemporary life issues along with the stress of having a family lifestyle opposed by some in the majority culture.

Many never-married mothers have deliberately chosen to have a child alone. They may have planned the pregnancy or decided to continue the pregnancy once they learned of it. Although many such mothers are young and poor, the percentage of educated business and professional women who have chosen to have a child without marriage increased from 3 percent in 1980 to 8 percent in 1990.[54] These women are older and have achieved occupational stability. Perhaps fearing they will not marry in time to have children, they elect to have a child alone. They have financial and psychological resources that the young, particularly adolescent, mothers do not have.

Still other never-married parents have chosen to adopt, often an older child. These parents have been found to be emotionally more mature and less easily frustrated than their peers.[55]

Fathers

As noted, never-married parents rearing children alone have all the problems of divorced mothers and fathers—many demands, the necessity for building a support system and having to build a parenting coalition with a person one never married. In the past, less attention has been paid to never-married fathers; books are written for mothers. Yet, many studies detail how fathers contribute positively to children's growth and the effects of their absence on children. This concerted effort is directed at involving never-married fathers as active parents to their offspring.

James Levine, the founder of the Fatherhood Project in 1981 at the Bank Street College of Education in New York, has written extensively on the advantages for children and fathers of fathers' increased involvement regardless of whether fathers are married to mothers.[56] He identifies three lessons he has learned over the years.

The first important ingredient in successfully involving fathers is the expectation that fathers want to be involved and can be effective parents with preparation and help. Second, single fathers need a support network that guides their behavior. Third, women play a key role in supporting men as fathers.

Figure 13-1 describes the "on-ramps" that facilitate men's connections with their children and families. Such on-ramps come from those in the community who interact with fathers—at the hospital, at doctors' visits, at schools. Levine writes,

> Our model does not absolve any man from primary responsibility; indeed, it holds that all fathers—whether unmarried, married, or divorced—are responsible for establishing and maintaining connection to their children. But it broadens that responsibility so it is also shared appropriately by all those in the community who, in their everyday work, have

FIGURE 13-1
CONNECTION—A SHARED RESPONSIBILITY

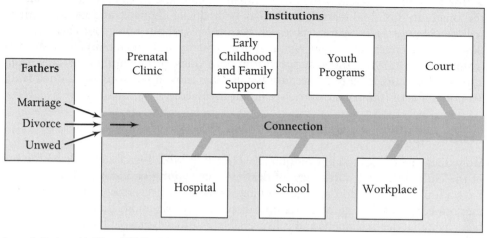

James A. Levine with Edward W. Pitt, *New Expectations: Community Strategies for Responsible Fatherhood* (New York: Families and Work Institute, 1995), p. 41. Reprinted with permission from the author.

the opportunity and the capacity to build—or influence the building of—the on-ramps to connection.[57]

As Levine mentioned in his interview in Chapter 5, the context of interactions with fathers can help involve them. One example is the Hospital Paternity Establishment Program in West Virginia, which has increased the number of unwed fathers who establish paternity from 600 per year to 3,000 per year. Recall that new expectations emphasize that new fathers need education about establishing paternity, and they need to be approached in terms of the benefits to the father and the child rather than to the state. Hospital staff were educated to involve fathers when they visited the newborns. Fathers then met with professionals such as a child psychologist, who could explain the psychological importance of the father to the child; a doctor, who could explain the medical importance; and a lawyer, who could discuss the legal benefits to the child of having a father who is known. "Public education is the key," says Gary Kreps, who designed the program. "We need to start educating both moms and dads about the importance of fathers. And we need to educate teachers, counselors, coaches, the clergy, parents, and anybody who works with kids. And we need to educate our politicians."[58]

WHEN A PARENT DIES

According to Earl Grollman,

> One of the greatest crises in the life of a child is the death of a parent. Never again will the world be as secure a place as it was before. The familiar design of family life is completely disrupted. The child suffers not only the loss of the parent, but is deprived of the attention he needs at a time when he craves that extra reassurance that he is cared for.[59]

Many of the changes in the family that occur at the time of divorce occur in the family that experiences the death of a parent. The whole family must come to terms with a profound loss that brings with it many changes. One parent assumes all the responsibility for child rearing, there may be financial changes, and certainly, there will be changes as one parent takes on both roles without relief. But there are important differences, too. A surviving spouse usually has greater financial support from insurance. Sympathetic support from both sides of the family is usually available. And conflict is reduced because the death is most often seen as no one's fault. Still, it is a very traumatic experience for all involved.

Telling Children

How does one tell a child a parent has died? Exactly what is said depends on the age of the child and the family's view of death.[60] Very young children (below age five) have a limited conception of death and may consider it a reversible condition — one dies but comes back to life at a later time. Between ages six and eight or nine, children recognize that death happens and is irreversible, but they believe it happens mainly to other people. Because logical thinking is not yet established, children may associate unrelated events with death. For example, one boy had heard that Abraham Lincoln was shot to death. When told of his grandfather's death, the boy asked "Who shot him?" As children move into the preadolescent years, they begin to understand death about as well as adults do.

In giving explanations about death, parents should be truthful and should phrase the information in a way that makes sense to the child. The child's questions will indicate the need for more information, which the parent can then give.

Because each situation is unique and needs to be handled with sensitivity, it is impossible to determine exactly what a parent should say. Grollman lists explanations to avoid. If they do not believe it themselves, parents should not describe heaven and tell the child that the dead parent is happy for eternity. A child will sense the discrepancy between what a parent says and how the parent feels and will become more confused. It is also unwise to say that a parent has gone on a long journey, because the child may focus on the return or feel angry at being abandoned. One child, told that his mother had gone on a journey, cursed every time he heard her name, until he was told she had died and was shown her grave. When he understood his mother's absence, the boy was sad but no longer felt abandoned or rejected by her. It is unwise as well to say that the parent died "because God loves good people and wants them in heaven." If goodness is rewarded with death, the child may shun good behavior or assume that those who live long lives are, in some undetectable way, bad. Finally, when death is equated with sleep, some children begin to fear sleep and are unwilling to go to bed.

Dealing with Children's Reactions

Once the information about a parent's death is given, how will the child experience the grief? John Bowlby describes three phases similar to those experienced by adults: (1) protest when the child cannot accept the death and tries to regain the parent,

(2) pain and despair as the child gradually accepts the death, and (3) acceptance and hope that life goes on.61

Experts agree that, after the child has been told of the parent's death, the child should be included in as much of the funeral and formal mourning process as seems comfortable to parent and child. Experts also agree, that unless children protest, they should view the body to understand that the parent is truly gone. This is not a rigid rule, however, and if either parent or child feels upset, or if the body of the dead parent has been disfigured by disease or injury, then this is not wise. During the mourning period surrounding the funeral and burial, family members may be surprised when young children, although devastated with grief, scamper away to play, only to cry bitter tears an hour later. Parents should not hold back their own tears, and they should not discourage children from crying. Tears are a healthy release of emotion, and many books on grief and mourning recognize the healing quality of tears. Also, parents should not encourage children to "Be brave!" or "Be a little man!" Rather, they should say realistically, "Yes, this is a hard time for you. Life is very sad now." Such statements acknowledge grief without minimizing it. Parents, however, should not insist on a display of grief.

Grollman listed a variety of children's reactions to death; many adults have similar responses.62

1. *Denial:* "I dreamt it! Mommy is coming home tomorrow." The child cannot accept the death because it is too painful.

2. *Anxiety expressed in bodily symptoms:* The child develops symptoms the dead parent had or symptoms expressing tension and sadness — "I can't eat" or "I have stomach pains."

3. *Hostile reactions:* Why did Mommy leave me like this?" These reactions may be very upsetting to the surviving parent.

4. *Guilt:* "Daddy died because I didn't wash the dishes right. I killed him."

5. *Anger:* The child shows anger at such people as doctors, nurses, or the surviving parent, who did not do what they should have to save the parent.

6. *Panic:* "Who will love me now?" The child anticipates being abandoned by the remaining parent through death or remarriage.

7. *Replacement:* The child looks for a family member or friend who will move in and take the parent's place.

8. *Taking on mannerism or habits of the deceased parent:* The child tries to be like the dead person in interests, activities, and personal traits, as a way of replacing the person who died.

9. *Idealization:* "No one can say anything against Mommy. She was wonderful."

Healthy mourning may include some or all of these reactions. Mourning becomes unhealthy when such reactions persist many months after the death and interfere with a return to satisfying activities. It is important to note that some children and adults may react so strongly during the grieving period that they hallucinate about the dead person. This is one of the few situations in life in which hallucinations can occur in the course of a healthy adaptation to a crisis.

A frequent reaction in a situation like this, and one that has to be handled carefully, is guilt. Young children in particular often assume they are personally responsible for what happened even though they are in no way involved. The surviving parent must be very alert to pick up on statements suggesting guilt and should introduce the possibility that the child feels guilt, even if the child has not mentioned it. For example, a parent might say, "Sometimes when a person dies, those close to her wonder if something they did was related to the death. I sometimes think, 'Would things have been different if I had called the doctor sooner?' But I know everything was done that could be done. Do you ever wonder or have thoughts like that?"

Thomas Gordon gives the example of a mother who actively listened as her three-year-old asked such painful questions as, "When is Daddy coming home?" and "Where did they put him?"[63] One night, two months after the father's death, the boy awoke and began sobbing that his daddy was dead. As the mother reflected his upset, the boy was able to talk about how much he missed his father and wanted him back. The mother thought that after this expression of feeling, her son seemed less anxious about the death. This three-and-a-half-year-old child asked many questions that were hard for the mother to answer. But she responded as well as she could, without criticism or complaint.

When parents understand and accept their child's feelings and respond with empathy and love, they help the child move through the grief process. As memories of the parent are recalled and relived, the death gradually becomes real. At times, the child may want to express unbearable pain or anger by striking at pillows or engaging in some physical activity. This can be encouraged. The child's individual reaction to death always should be respected. Grollman sums up the most helpful parental responses:

> Demonstrate in word and touch how much he [the child] is truly loved. A stable and emotionally mature adult who accepts the fact of death with courage and wisdom will bring the truth to the youngster that the business of life is life. Emotional energy formerly directed toward the absent person must now be directed toward the living. This does not mean wiping out the memories of the deceased. Even in death, the absent member can and should remain a constructive force in family life and be remembered in love without constant bitterness or morbidity.[64]

REMARRIAGE

As many as 35 percent of children, 54 percent of women, and 60 percent of men live in second marriages.[65] Remarriage provides many benefits to parents. First, it provides emotional closeness, intimacy, and sexual satisfaction to parents. In caring relationships, parents feel greater self-esteem, contentment, and happiness. Second, parents have someone with whom they can share both the financial and caregiving responsibilities. Wallerstein and Blakeslee find that many parents do not repeat the mistakes of the first marriage.[66] Though remarried parents report feelings of stress and depression related to the many demands they experience, the marriages still are as happy as those in nondivorced families, perhaps because the couple are more pragmatic in their expectations and in seeking solutions to problems.[67]

We know most about remarried families that consist of the custodial mother, her children, and the stepfather, who may or may not have children. There are fewer studies of stepmothers. Few studies focus on marriages of single mothers with children even though these have many characteristics of stepfamilies.

Challenges of Stepfamilies

Stepparenting is more demanding than parenting in intact families for several reasons.[68] First, a stepparent does not have long-standing emotional bonds with the children to help all of them overcome feelings of frustration and stress that occur during the changes the family undergoes.

Second, stepfamilies include more people than does a nuclear family, and all have different needs and interests to consider. There are husbands and wives, their biological children, ex-spouses, stepbrothers and stepsisters, half-brothers and half-sisters, and stepgrandparents. Parents have the multiple tasks of solidifying and maintaining marital ties while sustaining relationships with their biological children and promoting positive sibling relationships.

Third, members of blended families may have deep feelings of jealousy and ambivalence. Because so many more people are involved and the newly married parents want to devote time to their relationship, stepparents may have less time to give to individual children. Children may feel that the new marriage is depriving them of the parent. Parents must accept those feelings as realistic—there is less time for each child. Conversely, the parents may feel that the children are intruding on the marriage.

Fourth, both parents and children are haunted by the earlier marriage. Stepparents may feel insecure as they live with children who are constant proof that the spouse loved another person. Further, the biological parent usually continues to have contact with the former spouse because of the children.

Fifth, former spouses may use the children and their needs to attack the biological parent and the stepparent. One father and stepmother reported that the mother never bought the children clothes, and when the father did this in addition to making the monthly child support payment, the mother would not launder them. Conversely, one mother reported that the father and stepmothers, rather than providing money for clothes for the children, instead bought the children fancy clothes that were appropriate for the lifestyle of the father and stepmother, but not for the children's needs at school and play.

Sixth, there are no clear guidelines for being a stepparent. There are few enough for biological parents, but the role of stepparent remains even more vague. The stepparent must create his role according to his or her individual personality, the ages and sexes of the children, and their living arrangements.

Stepparents who are forewarned about the problems of stepparenting and who think and talk in advance about how to cope with these problems can find their new roles rewarding and exciting.

Family Changes over Time

Just as parents' behavior changes after a divorce, *remarried custodial mothers'* behavior changes as well at the time of the remarriage.[69] These mothers become more

INTERVIEW
with Emily Visher and John Visher

Emily Visher is a clinical psychologist and John Visher is a psychiatrist. They are founders of the Stepfamily Association and authors of such books as Stepfamilies: Myths and Realities *and* Old Loyalties, New Ties: Therapeutic Strategies with Stepfamilies.

You have worked with stepparents and stepfamilies for many years, so I want to talk to you about what you feel are the important things for parents to do in order to ease the difficulties that can arise in stepfamilies.

E. Visher: We talk about a parenting coalition that is the coalition between all the adults in the child's life. For example, you see, there could be three or four parenting adults—if both parents have remarried, there will be four. If those adults can somehow develop a working relationship around raising the children, the loyalty conflicts of the children will be much less. The adults will get a lot out of it, too, because there is less tension, and better relationships develop between stepparent and stepchild.

We chose the word *coalition* because it means a temporary alliance of separate entities for accomplishing a task. The households and couples are separate, and it is a temporary alliance between all the adults. The task they are working on together is raising the children.

Families can flounder on the basis of the stepparent's trying to be a parent, and the children saying basically, "I've got a mother or a father." We have moderated panels of teenagers in stepfamilies, and we always ask them, "What do you want your stepparents to be? What is their role?" I don't think we have ever heard anyone say anything other than "a friend." The difficulty is that, by "friend," they mean something very different. They don't mean a pal; it's closer than that.

They are able to talk to the stepparent in a meaningful way that is different from the way they would talk to a parent. They are freer to talk to a stepparent because they are not so involved. One teenager on a panel said she wanted her stepfather to be her friend, and then later she said, "I love my stepfather, and I've never told him." She's saying she wants a friend, but she has very deep feelings for him. He was in the back of the room and heard her.

It is important to take a role that is satisfying to the adult and to the child, and that may be different for children living in the same household and for children in different households. The relationship is different depending on the age of the child—a six-year-old needs something different from a sixteen-year-old. For the young child, the stepparent may well become a parent.

J. Visher: The only power the stepparent has as a parent is delegated from the remarried parent.

E. Visher: The adults need to be supportive of one another. Together they need to decide what the house rules are, and the parent of the children takes care of enforcing the rules until a relationship is set up.

J. Visher: Another major tip is to develop realistic expectations about what it is going to take to make everything work. So many people feel they have failed after a few weeks or months, that the remarriage has faltered because things are chaotic. It takes four or five years for things to settle down and for people really to get satisfaction out of the whole family relationship.

One of the keys is for people to inform themselves by reading or talking to other people who also are in stepfamilies. They learn that making the stepfamily work takes time and you shouldn't expect close family relationships quickly.

The most common pattern now is for children to move back and forth and feel part of two households. If all the adults form a parenting coalition, then children are most likely to feel they belong in both places.

Working out the parenting coalition so that it is at least civil makes an enormous difference to everybody. The children can go through the remarriage smoothly if there is not constant warfare. Sometimes parents who divorce or separate are tied together in bonds of anger. The anger can reflect an inadequate separation between the biological parents. They keep together by fighting.

E. Visher: Truman Capote said, "It's easy to lose a good friend, but it's hard to lose a good enemy." The anger ties you together. Hostility eats you up and you are not free to go on.

J. Visher: Most people don't understand how much damage they are doing to themselves and to the children. Sometimes people say, "How can I work with that S.O.B. when I couldn't even stay married to him?" We say maybe you can split off the part that does not want to be married to him and share the parenting experience.

E. Visher: What the children need from that parent is different from what the spouse needed.

What can you do to decrease the hostility?

J. Visher: One thing is to trade assurances between the households that you are not trying to take the child away from them or trying to get the child to like you better. Often, in a single-parent household, the parent is afraid of further loss, afraid that the ex-spouse and his or her new spouse will encourage the child to stay there and the child will want to because it is a more attractive place or there is more money. This fear fuels the anger and makes the parent cling to the child more and try to influence the child to turn against the other parent.

E. Visher: So we think that sometimes the anger is not leftover from the former marriage, but has to do with the fear that builds up between the two households, the fear of more loss. The other household becomes a threat, and the ex-spouses become like enemies rather than like people trying to raise a child. The parents are afraid of each other, and they are not aware that the anger substitutes for fear. If they are more aware of it, they can deal with it.

Also important is the guilt the remarried parent feels. He or she feels guilty that the children have been unhappy through the death or divorce and then the remarriage. That parent has a real investment in its being a big, happy family right away. Yet they have difficulty setting limits for the children who live there or visit there. The stepparent goes up the wall.

Sometimes they feel that to form a good couple relationship and make that primary is a betrayal of their relationship with their child. The parent-child relationship is different from the relationship with the spouse.

J. Visher: There may be an unusually strong bond between parent and child; perhaps it has lasted for many years, and the new spouse is a rival. It becomes a power struggle between spouse and child for the loyalty of the biological parent. The child is sometimes suddenly out of a job as confidant.

E. Visher: I don't think people realize the change for the children, that now they have to share. One mother described that she and her daughter had lived together for five years.

continued

INTERVIEW with Emily Visher and John Visher *continued*

When she came home from work, she talked to her daughter. Now that she is remarried, she talks to her husband. That one little thing is not so little, as the daughter has to share her mother.

If people are aware of the losses for the children in the new structure, they can acknowledge those changes with the children and do things differently—sit down with the children alone and talk. When children sense their feelings are accepted, they will talk about them. One stepmother commented to her stepson that when the father talked to the son, she felt left out, and she wondered if he felt left out when the father talked to her. He agreed he did, and they talked about it. There was not a lot they could change, but after they had the talk, they got along better.

J. Visher: We hope that as people are more informed, they will be able to deal more effectively with the situation.

negative and less controlling, and there is much conflict between mother and children, particularly with daughters. If children are eight or younger when parents remarry, improvements occur with time. When children are nine or older, there are slight improvements, but monitoring and control stabilize at lower levels than in intact families. Regardless of the child's age at remarriage, conflicts increase in early adolescence and relationships are more conflictual than in intact families. Even in midadolescence, children remain more distant from their custodial, remarried mothers.

When children live with *custodial fathers* and *stepmothers,* it is again girls who have greater difficulty.[70] Frequent contact with their biological mothers seems to increase the difficulty, but this unusual finding may be the result of biological mothers' having special problems that argued against their having custody. However, the longer girls live in such families, the more positive the relationship grows between the daughter and the stepmother.

There are no differences in how biological parents parent their own children in nondivorced and remarried families. Regardless of family status, mothers and fathers are warmer, more supportive, and closer to their biological children than to their stepchildren, and their children are more often closer to them.[71]

No matter what the age of a child at a parent's remarriage, *stepfathers* initially feel less close to their stepchildren than to their biological children, and they do not monitor behavior as well as fathers do in intact families. When children are relatively young at the time of the remarriage, stepfathers may be able to build relationships with stepchildren by taking on the role of a warm and supportive figure and foregoing the role of disciplinarian until a relationship is established. Preadolescent boys may settle down in a relationship with a stepfather, but preadolescent girls usually resist stepfathers' overtures and direct angry, negative behavior to the custodial mother.[72]

When children are early adolescents at the time of the remarriage, there appears to be little adaptation to the new family over a two-year period.[73] Children are negative and resistant even when stepfathers attempt to spend time with them and establish a relationship. As a result, stepfathers remain disengaged, critical, and distanced from the day-to-day monitoring of children. The negative behavior of the children shapes stepparents' behavior more than stepparents shape children's behavior. When, however, stepparents can be authoritative parenting figures—warm, positive, appropriate in monitoring—then children's adjustment improves. With adolescents, stepparents fare better when they are authoritative from the start.

Adolescents at the time of the remarriage are often resistant, withdrawn, and unwilling to become involved with stepparents. They frequently retreat from the families and establish strong relationships with families of friends. At the same time, they become more argumentative with the biological parents, both the custodial and noncustodial parent. Their emotional attachment to the parent is shown in a negative rather than a positive way. As noted, adolescents feel closer to noncustodial mothers than to noncustodial fathers.[74]

In stepfamilies, marital happiness has a different relation to children's behavior than it has in intact families.[75] In nondivorced families, marital happiness is related to children's competent functioning and positive relationships with parents. In stepfamilies, marital happiness is related to children's negativistic and resistant behavior with parents. Girls may be especially resentful of the loss of the close relationship with the custodial mothers. Boys, having less to lose, may settle more easily into a relationship with a stepfather. Nevertheless, adolescent daughters respond positively to the satisfying marital relationship, perhaps because it serves as a protective buffer to an inappropriate relationship between stepfather and stepdaughter.

Relationships with siblings are less positive and more negative in remarried families than in nondivorced families.[76] Sibling relationships in divorced families fall between these two groups and do not differ significantly from either of them. Although girls tend to be warmer and more empathetic than boys, they are almost equally aggressive. As siblings become adolescents, they become more separated from each other. Interestingly, relationships with their stepsiblings appear less negative than relationships with their own siblings.

Children's Behavior over Time

Children's adjustment in stepfamilies varies. There are often initial declines in cognitive and social competence after the remarriage, but when boys are young and stepparents are warm and authoritative, problem behaviors improve, and boys in these stepfamilies have levels of adjustment similar to those of boys in nondivorced families. Young girls continue to have more acting-out and defiant behavior problems than do girls in intact or divorced families.[77]

Most gender differences in adjustment disappear at early adolescence, when both boys and girls have more problems. At all ages, children in remarried families, like children in divorced families, have poorer school performance, problems in social responsibility, and more rule-breaking behaviors than do children in intact families. Parenting by the same-sex parent, whether custodial or noncustodial, is positively related to the child's adjustment.[78]

Although some children in remarried families have adjustment problems, the majority do well. Between two-thirds and three-quarters score within the average range on assessment instruments. Though this falls below the comparable figure of 90 percent for children of nondivorced parents, it indicates that most children in remarried families are doing well.[79]

As with children of divorced families, children of remarried families are at a disadvantage in early adulthood.[80] Compared with children of nondivorced parents, they are more likely to leave home at an early age, less likely to continue in school, and more likely to leave home as a result of conflict. As adults, they feel they can rely less on their families. Still, there is diversity of response, and many of these children feel close and supported in stepfamilies.

Many of the difficulties stepfamilies encounter can be avoided or lessened if they are foreseen and prepared for. Box 13-2 lists eight steps that stepfamilies can take to strengthen their ties.

NEW RELATIONSHIPS

Everything written about stepparenting attests to its complexity, its intensity, and its challenge. We do not often enough emphasize the rewards. Brenda Maddox sums up the strengths of the stepfamily and the joys of participating in it:

> There are a few plain truths about stepparenthood that I learned writing this book [*The Half Parent*]. I was blind not to have recognized them when I got married. Stepfamilies can be happy, even happier than families in which there has never been more than one mother or father but it takes more work. The tensions of the stepfamily are special and real. A stepparent cannot be the same as a real parent. There are no new Mommies and new Daddies. Yet there are compensations for the strains. My own particular reward has been to help two young people who are nothing like me to be more like themselves and to watch the bond grow between the two sets of children. Stepfamilies in general do have positive advantages. When a stranger has to be taken into the family circle, when children have a parent who lives somewhere else, the family has an extra dimension. There is not that claustrophobia that led the anthropologist Dr. Edmund Leach to describe the ordinary family "with its narrow privacy and tawdry secrets" as "the source of all our discontents." The stepfamily is open and tough. It is not a bad place to live for those who can accept the uncomfortable fact that many of the tensions between stepparents and stepchildren will be inevitable as long as spouses are replaceable and parents are not.[81]

Though life in stepfamilies can be tough, adults can take special pleasure in seeing children biologically unrelated to them flourish and grow and in taking part in that growth. Such close and warm and sometimes conflictual relationships can serve as examples that people do not need to be either biologically related or romantically connected to produce profound and positive effects on each other's lives. For a happy family, both biological parents and stepparents need to feel comfortable with themselves and free of inflexible views of the other parents, so all can help children become "more like themselves." When adults relate to their own or other people's children in this way, there is no distinction between a biological parent and a stepparent.

◆
BOX 13-2
EIGHT-STEP PROGRAM FOR
STRENGTHENING TIES IN STEPFAMILIES

Step 1: Nurturing the Couple's Relationships

a. Plan something you like away from home once a week.

b. Arrange 20 minutes of relaxed time alone each day.

c. Talk together about the running of the household at least 30 minutes each week.

Step 2: Finding Personal Space and Time

a. Create a special "private" place for parents and for each child who lives or visits there.

b. Take at least 2 hours a week to engage in personally enriching activities—reading, TV, hobby, sports.

Step 3: Nourishing Family Relationships

a. Share with one another every day something each family member appreciates about one another—perhaps at dinner or in less formal settings.

b. When presenting what is appreciated, avoid discussing negative feelings or problems.

Step 4: Maintaining Close Parent-Child Relationships

a. Have parent and child do something fun together for at least 20 minutes once or twice a week.

b. Provide these times no matter what, and do not make them dependent on good behavior.

Step 5: Developing Stepparent-Stepchild Relationships

a. Do something fun together 15 or 20 minutes a week—if a child visits only occasionally, make this a longer time.

b. Accept a child's refusal, and offer to do something at a later time.

Step 6: Building Family Trust

a. Schedule a family event once a month, and give each member a chance to choose what to do.

b. Begin special traditions in the remarried family.

c. Do not always schedule events when nonresident children are there, because resident children may believe they are less important.

Step 7: Strengthening Stepfamily Ties with Regular Family Meetings

Step 8: Working with the Child's Other Household

a. Give adults in the other household positive feedback once a month.

b. Give positive message without expectation of reciprocation.

Adapted from Emily Visher, "The Stepping Ahead Program," in *Stepfamilies Stepping Ahead,* ed. Mala Burt (Baltimore: Stepfamilies Press, 1989), pp. 57–89. Used with permission from the Stepfamily Association of America.

PARENTING TASKS AT TIMES OF MARITAL TRANSITIONS

Several suggestions for parents emerge from research on divorced, single-parent households and on remarried families. First, they should maintain positive emotional relationships with children. Even if there is pronounced conflict between parents, relationships between parents and children can be satisfying if parents make a special effort to keep them out of the conflict. Parents need to make time for the open communication of feelings, for asking and answering questions, and for sharing enjoyable activities. These same rules apply to relationships with stepchildren.

Second, parents must learn effective ways of resolving conflicts, regardless of who is involved. Box 13-1 listed suggestions for minimizing harm from conflict between parents; Chapter 3 discusses effective ways of dealing with anger between parents and children. According to Amato, the most important thing society can do to promote safe and secure environments for children is to encourage parents to learn ways to resolve conflicts within marriages and to settle disputes if they get divorced so children are not put in the middle.[82] It is children's feelings of self-blame, whether parents are married or divorced, that contribute to children's poor adjustment to life.

Third, parents should rely on authoritative parenting techniques, which include warmth, positivity, and consistent monitoring of children. These techniques are related to children's competence regardless of children's sex, age, or family status. Parents can form parenting alliances with biological parents and parenting coalitions in remarried families so all adults in children's lives provide consistent, fair rules and children's behavior is carefully and consistently monitored.

Fourth, parents need to model and encourage positive relationships with all family members—siblings, grandparents, and all the relatives involved in stepfamilies. Box 13-2 gave many suggestions for stepfamilies.

Fifth, parents need to help children seek positive experiences in their own social milieu—with friends, relatives, schoolmates, and teachers. These supports help children cope in time of change.

Finally, parents need to recall that at times of marital transition, they need to do all the things that are beneficial in nondivorced families, but they need to do more of them to buffer children from the stress of change. It is harder to do these things when parents themselves are under stress.

Still, parents promote children's growth and competence in all times of change when they foster close, positive emotional relationships with children and monitor their behavior carefully to ensure that it falls within appropriate limits.

MAIN POINTS

Society has begun to accommodate the needs of divorcing families by

- making it easier for both parents to stay involved with the children
- providing court mediation services to help families make decisions in the child's best interests
- making it easier for mothers to get financial support from ex-husbands

In reacting to divorce, children

- of preschool age feel overwhelmed, abandoned, and worried that they caused the divorce, and they need parents' support and acceptance of their feelings
- ages five to seven are vulnerable and try to deny intense feelings of sadness and grief, but divorce dominates their thoughts, and they need to talk about feelings
- ages nine and older may feel responsible for helping parents and may get benefit from counseling

Parents' emotional reactions to divorce

- are intense and include many of the feelings children experience—anger, sadness, anxiety, and depression
- can interfere with their providing care and support for children

Factors affecting adjustment to divorce include the

- amount of conflict among family members
- availability of both parents to children
- defensibility of divorce from the child's point of view

Factors that protect children at time of divorce include

- a child's age, sex, intelligence, and temperament
- manageable amounts of stress and appropriate support from grandparents and other relatives
- a child's getting positive feelings from his or her own achievements

Children's behavior

- becomes more problematic at the time of divorce but improves as time passes
- is less carefully monitored in single-parent homes in early adolescence
- improves when parents resolve their anger and use authoritative parenting

Parents' role in helping children cope with a parent's death is to

- include children as active participants in the funeral/memorial
- offer children many opportunities to express their feelings
- accept children's feelings as they go through stages of grief
- provide a model of an adult who grieves but who goes on with life

When parents remarry, they

- experience many emotional benefits such as closeness, intimacy, and sexual satisfaction
- do not necessarily report the mistakes of the first marriage
- experience stress as they integrate everyone into a new family with few guidelines

When parents remarry, children

- differ in their reactions, with girls having more difficulty in adjusting to parents' remarriage than do boys
- show initial declines in social and cognitive competence
- show improvements in behavior, following an initial decline, when parenting figures are warm and authoritative

Parenting tasks at times of marital transition include

- maintaining positive emotional relationships with children
- learning effective conflict resolutions skills
- relying on authoritative parenting strategies
- modeling positive relationships with the extended family
- encouraging children to have positive experiences in their own social world

EXERCISES

1. Suppose your friend's parents divorced when he or she was a small child, and now your friend fears intimacy and commitment. What could you do to help him or her be less fearful? What advice could you offer your friend to lessen such fears? In a class discussion, share your ideas of how to advise the friend.

2. Imagine that your married brother, sister, or friend came to you and said he or she was getting a divorce and wanted help in making arrangements so his or her eight-year-old daughter and six-year-old son would experience the fewest negative effects. What guidelines would you give your relative or friend?

3. Pair off with a classmate, preferably of the same sex. Imagine one of you is eight and the other fifteen years old. You have just learned that one of your parents has married your partner's parent; you are now stepbrothers or step-sisters. How would you feel now that you are going to be living intimately with each other—perhaps sharing a room, having your time with your biological partner reduced so the parent can spend time with this stranger, having the amount of money available to you dependent on the needs of these new people? Would being older or younger make a difference in the reactions? Describe what your parents could do to ease the adjustment process.

4. Attend divorce court for a morning and summarize the cases presented there. What issues do parents argue about? What issues about children arise? Describe whether you agree with the judge's ruling, and state why.

5. Write a script for what a mother and stepfather might say to the mother's two children (ages nine and thirteen) and the stepfather's two children (ages six and nine), who visit every other weekend, about their expectations of how they hope the children will get along and how the parents will handle arguments as they arise. What rules can parents set for children of these ages? What will the stepfather's role be?

ADDITIONAL READINGS

Adler, Robert E. *Sharing the Children.* Bethesda, MD: Adler & Adler, 1988.

Booth, Alan, and Dunn, Judy, eds. *Stepfamilies: Who Benefits? Who Does Not?* Hillsdale, NJ: Erlbaum, 1994.

Cummings, E. Mark, and Davies, Patrick. *Children and Marital Conflict: The Impact of Family Disputes and Resolution.* New York: Guilford Press, 1994.

Visher, Emily B., and Visher, John S. *Stepfamilies: Myths and Realities.* New York: Carol, 1993.

Wallerstein, Judith S., and Blakeslee, Sandra. *Second Chances.* New York: Ticknor & Fields, 1989.

PARENTING IN TIMES OF TRAUMA

C H A P T E R 14

When traumatic events occur, parents face enormous challenges. What reactions can parents expect from children? What can parents do to help children cope? Which children are most likely to suffer long-term effects from traumatic events? What can parents do to protect children from violence and enable them to feel secure in a world that is sometimes unsafe?

This chapter focuses in greatest detail on three forms of violence children may experience: sexual abuse, physical abuse, and violence in the community. We look at definitions and the incidence and prevalence of such behaviors, ways children react to such experiences, and ways to help them deal with their experiences. We also focus on how parents can help children take actions to minimize their risk of violent encounters.

VIOLENCE AGAINST CHILDREN

The discussion of violence is divided into three areas for clearer comprehension. However, David Finkelhor and Jennifer Dziuba-Leatherman[1] caution that fragmenting the study of violence against children into separate areas has prevented social scientists from recognizing and developing a field of general victimology of children to "highlight more clearly the true vulnerability of children to victimization, the overlap and co-occurrence of different types of victimization, and the common risk factors and effects."[2]

Children are more prone to victimization than are adults. Throughout childhood, they are more often subject to family violence, and adults report beating them harder than they beat spouses. Children are also at greater risk for sexual abuse. Teenagers are more subject than adults to all the crimes reported by adults, and both children and teenagers also experience forms of assault that adults do not—such as sibling assault.

378

FIGURE 14-1
TYPOLOGY OF CHILD VICTIMIZATION

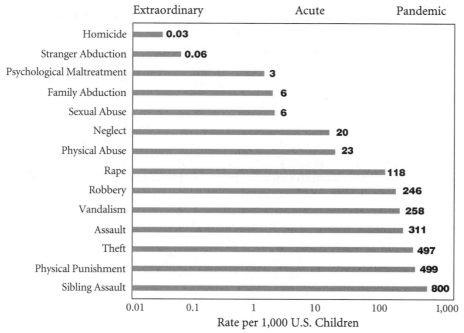

David Finkelhor and Jennifer Dziuba-Leatherman, "Victimization of Children," *American Psychologist* 49 (1994): 176. © 1994 American Psychological Association. Used with permission.

Figure 14-1 shows the rates per 1,000 children for various kinds of violence and serves to highlight the many dangers with which children live. Finkelhor and Dziuba-Leatherman group forms of victimization into three categories: (1) the *pandemic* (frequent events affecting most children, such as sibling fights); (2) the *acute* (events that affect a small but significant percentage of children — for example, neglect and sexual and physical abuse); and (3) the *extraordinary* (events like kidnapping or homicide). The most frequent events, experienced by five to eight of every ten children, are fighting with a sibling, receiving physical punishment (usually by parents), and being the victim of theft. These events are rarely studied, but they should be, because so many children experience them and report fears about them.

Children are more at risk for violence than are adults for several reasons. First, children are more dependent on others for care. The concept of neglect, for example, has no meaning in regard to independent adults. Second, children are small and less cognitively mature and cannot easily protect themselves from older children and adults. Third, children have less choice about their surroundings and associates than do adults. They have to live at home and have to go to school, so they are forced into contact with abusive people. They cannot leave.

It may be not only unwise but also difficult to separate the various kinds of abuse, because there is considerable co-occurrence of the different types. In one sample, all 70 children experienced more than one form of abuse; in another, 90 percent of 160 children experienced more than one form.[3] Maltreatment of a single kind may be quite rare in reality.

Over time, research in these areas has become more sophisticated, with samples better controlled, several different measures of children's functioning used, and more longitudinal studies carried out. There is concerted effort to delineate the specific effects of abuse separately from the effects of low socioeconomic status or accumulated stress from negative life events. Even so, more controls are needed. Children are often described as either abused or not abused. They are not described in terms of the severity or frequency of abuse or by the closeness of their relationship with the perpetrator. These factors make a difference.[4] As such, researchers are exerting an increasingly greater effort to control them. As we get more information on these topics, our understanding of the effects of abuse and violence will become more refined.

A major conclusion from the more sophisticated studies of both physical and sexual abuse is that there is no one path, no one set of risk factors, and no definite set of characteristics that qualify as "the effects" of abuse.[5] Jay Belsky wrote in 1993, "All too sadly, there are many pathways to child abuse and neglect."[6] And, we can add, there are many effects triggered by the abuse. Later, we shall examine a model that describes the many factors that lead to abuse and violence and their potential consequences. First, let us look at the criteria of violence.

Distinguishing the Levels of Abuse

In 1994, approximately three million children were reported to Children's Protective Services (CPS) for suspected abuse. About a third—one million cases—were substantiated.[7] Of this million, 54 percent were cases of neglect, many of which may have been associated with poverty. About one-quarter involved physical abuse; 11 percent were primarily sexual abuse, 3 percent were emotional neglect, and 6 percent were outside of these categories.

Population surveys result in higher figures.[8] A Gallup poll of a representative sample of one thousand American families reported in 1995 found that 5 percent of children met the criteria of physical abuse, and approximately 2 percent met the criteria for sexual abuse. These are ten to sixteen times higher than the rates reported to official agencies.

The criteria for establishing abuse must be specified. For example, because Finkelhor and Dziuba-Leatherman consider spanking as physically violent, they categorized far more children as victimized than does Gallup's poll which defined physical abuse as being hit with an object (reported for only 5 percent of the children).

Robert Emery and Lisa Laumann-Billings believe it might be useful to distinguish between family *maltreatment,* characterized by minimal physical, sexual, or psychological harm, and family *violence,* characterized by serious physical injury, sexual exploitation, or psychological trauma.[9] This distinction is made not to minimize the physical and psychological effects of maltreatment but to separate cases that need supportive services from those that require serious coercive intervention, like the removal of the child from the home. At present, so many of the resources go into investigating cases and making sure violence exists that little remains for the larger number of families in which maltreatment is the problem. At present, these families

381

An Ecological/
Transactional
Model of
Community
Violence
and Child
Maltreatment

receive little treatment, guidance, or support to help them learn to manage aggressive feelings more appropriately.

Experiencing and Witnessing Violence

So far in this chapter we have focused most heavily on the effects of experiencing violence. Yet, as we shall see in discussing community violence, more children witness violence than experience it, and those who witness suffer also and require services.

In looking at forms of family violence, then, we must keep in mind that those who witness violence to another family member suffer as well. In the last chapter, we saw the physical and physiological consequences of witnessing marital arguments and conflicts.[10] One suspects that similar suffering and physical changes occur when children witness a parent's abuse at the hands of a spouse or a sibling's abuse at the hands of a parent. So, children and siblings should be considered victimized and in need of services when a spouse or another child in the family is abused.

AN ECOLOGICAL/TRANSACTIONAL MODEL OF COMMUNITY VIOLENCE AND CHILD MALTREATMENT

Dante Cicchetti and Michael Lynch propose a model of how community violence and child maltreatment affect children's development.[11] Although this model was not applied to sexual abuse, it is relevant in that area. This transactional/ecological model describes how the child's characteristics and the characteristics of the caregiver and the environment interact to shape the child's development. Risk factors for development are those events or people that increase the possibility of a negative outcome; protective factors serve to buffer children from the impact of negative events and promote a positive outcome.

Risk factors can be divided into two groups: (1) transient or fluctuating factors and (2) enduring or ongoing factors. An enduring risk factor for child maltreatment might be a parent's history of being abused, and a transient risk factor might be a parent's loss of a job. An enduring protective factor might be a child's easygoing temperament, and a transient protective factor might be a sudden improvement in the family's financial status. When risk factors outweigh protective ones, child maltreatment will likely occur.

Using Bronfenbrenner's ecological model of development described in Chapter 1, we can envision child maltreatment and community violence at several levels. At the macrosystem level, cultural beliefs promote violence and abuse. For example, as a society, we believe in spanking, in the acceptability of force to settle disagreements, in the importance of sexual gratification for potency or manliness, and in children as the property of adults who think they can do what they want with children. All these beliefs at the macrosystemic level contribute to a climate that encourages violence toward and maltreatment of children.

At the exosystemic level are the social structures that influence children's development. Because young children are no longer primarily in the care of female biological relatives they have more exposure to male figures who are not related to them and who may view them as sexual objects. The economic structure is such that many families with children live in poverty, a risk factor for both community violence and child maltreatment. Community structures sometimes lack the supports that enable parents to be more nurturant and caring with children, such as good schools that provide after-school recreational programs for children, easy availability of immunization programs and other preventive health services, and parenting programs. Neighborhoods with a high degree of social isolation among residents are at greater risk for child maltreatment. In some instances, supports may be there, but maltreating parents move so often that they do not get connected to support systems.

Factors at the community level can interact with factors at the family level. For example, a neighborhood characterized by unemployment and drug addiction may have more shootings and more violence than a less-stressed community; these disruptions, in turn, can increase the frustration of an unemployed father, who then becomes more physically punishing with a son. Unemployed parents cannot move out of the neighborhood and have to deal with the ongoing frustration that interferes with their parenting.

Children experience violence at the microsystemic level—in daily interactions with siblings, parents, peers, and teachers. Both parents and children bring their individual characteristics to these interactions. Parents who maltreat children, compared with those who do not, are more likely to have experienced abuse in their own childhood. Still, the majority of adults who have been abused do not abuse their children. Abusive parents tend to form unstable, conflictful adult-adult relationships,[12] and they interact with children in many negative ways besides the actual abuse. They are less satisfied with their children and use more disciplinary techniques than do nonmaltreating parents. They want their children to be independent but insist that they meet unrealistically high standards. Abusive parents quite often reverse roles and expect children to act as the parents' caregivers.

Children's individual characteristics also can influence the likelihood of abuse. There is the child's sex; in several studies, boys were found to be more likely to experience physical abuse,[13] and girls more likely to experience sexual abuse.[14] The child's age is a factor; the median age for sexual abuse is about eight,[15] but approximately one-third of sexually abused children are under six.[16] Physical abuse peaks between the ages of three and eight. Although children appear to be less at risk after age eight, recent data show that adolescents are subject to significant abuse as well.[17] This finding may be a function of more careful reporting of adolescent injuries. Children who are physically abused may be noncompliant and difficult to care for, but this behavior most likely results from rather than causes negative caregiving.

A final level of analysis is ontogenic—the development that occurs within the individual. Cicchetti and Lynch identify five areas that may be problematic for children following the abuse: the attachment relationship with the parent, regulation of emotion, self-concept, peer relationships, and adaptation to school and learning.

Children who have been either physically or sexually abused by parents may develop an insecure attachment to that parent and internalize a negative internal working model of relationships. Abuse suggests to children that they are basically unlovable, unacceptable, and unworthy of being cared for, and so they internalize a working model in which they are unworthy and the other person is undependable

383

An Ecological/
Transactional
Model of
Community
Violence
and Child
Maltreatment

and unavailable. These working models are carried over into other relationships, and unless intervention occurs, they create lifelong problems in relating to others. Violence experienced in the community might have no demonstrable effect on children's attachment to parents, though it could serve to strengthen it if parents are seen as especially supportive.

As a result of abuse and violence, children may be unable to regulate their own emotions. Their feelings of anxiety, anger, or sadness may overwhelm them. Or they may handle the emotions by blunting them and feeling little. If their caregivers are not reliable figures who can help them process the feelings or, in fact, are the *cause* of the feelings, then children have an added burden: They have very intense feelings and little external help in coping with them. Some studies suggest that, in addition, abused children have fewer words for feelings than nonabused children and are less skilled in identifying the feelings of others.

Children who experience both physical and sexual abuse tend to have negative attitudes about themselves. When they are older, they see themselves as less competent and less worthy than their peers. Their self-descriptions contain mostly negative terms.

In view of their insecure attachments, their difficulties in regulating their feelings, and their negative self-perceptions, it is not surprising that many abused children have problems with peer relationships. They are more likely than nonabused children to be aggressive with their peers and less positive and caring in interactions. Even more sadly, children who are in special need of positive peer relations because of a negative family atmosphere may have the greatest difficulty forming them. Finally, their capacity for learning and for adjusting to school may be compromised, because these children cannot regulate their feelings and are quick to feel frustrated with tasks and with peers.

The model developed by Cicchetti and Lynch describes risk factors that exist at the cultural, societal, and familial levels and the many ways that abuse may affect an individual's development in several areas. This model also has implications for interventions. First, there are interventions at the microsystemic level, with the individual and the family—helping them deal with the situation, the feelings that arise from it, and the problems that ensue.

Then there are interventions at the exosystemic level—helping parents and children reach out to social agencies and social structures such as schools and community organizations to get support to enable the family to cope. Community and state agencies offer a variety of programs to train parents in anger management, stress reduction, and effective disciplinary techniques. Comprehensive programs seek to preserve the family by meeting its many needs for such services as financial and household management, job-finding help, and alcohol abuse treatment. They provide broad-based services while the family stabilizes and becomes involved in a network of agencies that can continue to meet these needs.[18] These services reduce the need for social agencies to provide out-of-home living arrangements for abused children.

Community agencies also identify high-risk parents who, because of their own characteristics (for example, substance abuse) or characteristics of their children (physical injuries or conditions that make care very difficult), are in need of special services to prevent possible abuse.[19] These agencies provide, often in the home, training and modeling in appropriate caregiving and help parents adopt effective problem-solving skills.

Finally, there are interventions at the macrosystemic level—changing the societal views of violence and sexuality that permit victimization of children. Although this is a complicated process, giving all parents training in effective caregiving and child-rearing strategies makes abuse less likely.[20] Requiring parent training as part of a junior high or high school education not only provides needed skills but also sends a strong social message about the importance of parenting skills. Abuse of children affects the entire society, because we must live and interact with those who are hurt by it and, additionally, must provide services to deal with the hurt.

Currently, there is only limited research on the most effective forms of intervention. But all levels of intervention appear necessary to help children and prevent the recurrence of abuse.[21]

DEALING WITH ABUSE AND VIOLENCE

As noted in Chapter 1, children in U.S. society are at increased risk for a variety of traumatic experiences. Among them are sexual abuse, physical abuse, and community violence. Because all have the potential to cause lasting physical and/or psychological harm, parents must handle such situations with care.

Sexual Child Abuse

The National Center on Child Abuse and Neglect defines child sexual abuse as

> contacts or interactions between a child and an adult when the child is being used for the sexual stimulation of the perpetrator or another person. Sexual abuse may also be committed by a person under the age of 18 when the person is either significantly older than the abuse victim or when the perpetrator is in a position of power or control over another child.[22]

Abusive experiences can range from intercourse to touching to viewing an exhibitionist. Abuse can occur within the family (incest or intrafamilial) or outside the family (extrafamilial). Abuse need not involve an adult; it can occur when one child is significantly older (usually defined as five or more years) or has power over another child. Although much of the research on abuse has focused on girls, we are increasingly aware of abuse perpetrated on boys.

Prevalence　Determining the incidence and prevalence of sexual abuse in childhood is extremely difficult, as the acts are disapproved and most are not reported. In a sample of 1,800 college students, one-third of both men and women reported experiencing sexual abuse in childhood. Only half of the women and a tenth of the men had reported the incident to an adult. Estimates are that one in four girls and one in six boys has experienced some form of sexual abuse by age eighteen.[23]

Diana Russell interviewed a random sample of San Francisco women concerning childhood sexual abuse.[24] Her definition of abuse was narrower than that of the National Commission, including only actual sexual contact and not exhibitionism. She found that by the age of eighteen, 16 percent of women had been abused by a family member and 31 percent by a person outside the family. When both categories of abuse are combined, 38 percent of 930 women reported at least one experience of abuse by age eighteen and 28 percent by age fourteen. Only 2 percent of intrafamilial abuse and 6 percent of extrafamilial abuse were ever reported to police.

In intrafamilial abuse, 38 percent of the abusers were members of the nuclear family (parents or siblings). The most frequent other relatives were uncles, male first cousins, and grandfathers. Of extrafamilial abusers, only 15 percent were strangers; 42 percent were acquaintances and 43 percent were friends of the victim or family.

Karen Meiselman describes the family at high risk for incest as having one or more of the following components: (1) an alcoholic and violent father; (2) a mother who is away from home, physically ill, depressed, or passive; (3) an older daughter who has had the responsibility of a mother; (4) parents who have failed to establish a satisfying sexual relationship; (5) fathers and daughters who spend much time alone with each other; (6) any condition, such as psychosis or below-average intelligence, that reduces an individual's capacity for self-control; (7) previous incest in a parent's family; and (8) a romantic attachment with unusual amount of physical affection between adult and child.[25]

Consequences The impact of sexual abuse depends very much on the child and the specific circumstances of the abuse—the nature, duration, and frequency of the physical contact and the identity of the perpetrator. Further, it is difficult to disentangle the effects of the family conflict prior to the abuse, the abuse itself, and the events around the disclosure of the abuse. A broad review of studies[26] suggests that sexual abuse likely to produce the greater number of symptoms involves (1) a close relationship with the perpetrator; (2) sexual acts of oral, anal, or vaginal penetration; (3) frequent occurrences; (4) a long duration; and (5) lack of maternal support at the time of disclosure. These separate aspects of abuse, however, are related to one another. A close family member often has greater opportunity for frequent contact with the victim over a long period of time.

Sexually abused children report many different symptoms following the abuse, and no one symptom characterizes the majority of sexually abused children.[27] The most frequently reported symptoms are fears, nightmares, sexualized behaviors (sexualized play with dolls or toys, putting things in the vagina or anus, public or inappropriate masturbation) that suggest sexual stimulation from adults or peers, depression, aggression, withdrawal, school problems, poor self-esteem, acting-out, regression of behavior, and symptoms of posttraumatic stress (reliving the experience, dread of dire consequences to the victim). These symptoms generally follow the patterns of difficulties that Cicchetti and Lynch proposed in their transactional/ecological model of maltreatment: difficulties in attachment, regulation of emotion, self-concept, peer relationships, and school performance. Although there is no clear-cut evidence of insecure attachment relationships, the symptoms reported reflect all the other difficulties in development.

Preschoolers most often report fears, nightmares, sexualized behaviors, withdrawal, and aggressive and uncontrolled behavior. School-age children report all these symptoms, as well as school problems, hyperactivity, and regressive behaviors. Adolescents most often report depression, suicidal acting out, anger, running away, and antisocial behavior. Depression is the most commonly reported symptom in adults who have been sexually abused.

I N T E R V I E W
with Jill Waterman

Jill Waterman is an adjunct professor of psychology at the University of California in Los Angeles. She has coauthored Sexual Abuse of Young Children: Evaluation and Treatment *and* Behind the Playground Wall: Sexual Abuse in Preschools.

Parents worry that their children may be sexually abused. Do you think there is a greater risk for children or is the increase in reports of child abuse a function of greater sensitivity to the problem?

I think the increase in the number of reports is due to the awareness of the problem and breaking the taboos about telling. There is more support for children who do tell.

Some parents fear sending their children to preschool because of the possibility of abuse there. Is this a valid concern?

For preschoolers, the likelihood of being abused in day care, including preschool, is less than the risk of being abused at home. Currently, 5.5 children per 10,000 are abused at day care, whereas 8.9 per 10,000 are abused at home. To reduce the risk at preschool, parents need to be sure that (1) they are welcome at the school at any time (there should be no time when they are barred from the school); (2) the school is an open environment where all personnel are easily observed (avoid schools with isolated areas or classrooms); (3) they can observe and feel confident about the way the adults in the school interact with children.

In the past, girls were more at risk for abuse than boys. Now, however, at the preschool level, the risk is about equal for boys and girls. Boys' experiences were underreported, perhaps because boys worried about being victims or being seen as wimpy, but now there is an increase in reporting of boys being abused. Still, in the latency and adolescent years, more girls than boys are abused.

There is more awareness now that women may also be molesters. When women are molesters, they are more likely to be part of a team with a man rather than be a solo molester—an aunt and an uncle, for example. Still the great majority of molesters are males.

There is a real increase in those identified as juvenile offenders or older children who molest other children. In almost all cases, they are repeating abuse done to them by adults.

How can a parent minimize the likelihood that the child will be abused?

First, teach children that their bodies are their own and no one has the right to touch them. Children have a right to stop whoever does touch or tries to touch their bodies. Second, teach children the concept of private parts of the body—that area that is covered by a bathing suit—and teach the concept of good touch and bad touch. When parents are comfortable with affection and have children who feel comfortable with giving and receiving affection, then children have a sense of what feels good and is good touch. Those children are more likely to identify bad touches quickly. Third, help children identify an adult they can go to if bad touching occurs. Teach them which adults can help—teachers, principals, group leaders. Role-play with them how they would tell someone.

Whom are children most likely to tell about abuse?

Whether the abuse is inside or outside the home, the child is most likely to tell the mother. An adolescent may tell a friend who then tells her mother who then reports. Most molesters never admit what they have done. Often, there is no way to prove it because much abuse does not involve penile intercourse. Touching and oral sex may leave no evidence at all.

In the event a child does not tell a parent, what are signs by which a parent might tell whether a child has been sexually abused?

In most cases, there are no blatant behavioral indicators of sexual abuse. Rarely, the child may have genital bruising or bleeding. If the child begins sexual play with other children repeatedly, I would be concerned. If a child becomes preoccupied by masturbation to the extent of preferring to masturbate rather than interact with family or other children, I would also be concerned. More commonly, a sexually abused child may shows signs of distress that could be due to a variety of causes, not just abuse. Some of these distress signs are nightmares, sudden fears, withdrawal, or depression. However, these signs would alert a parent only to distress in a child, not necessarily sexual abuse.

If a child has been abused, how can parents act to minimize the impact of the event on the child?

The most important factor is how the parents respond. When parents believe the child and act to protect the child from the molester and get therapy and help for the child, then the child is best able to handle what has happened. When parents do not believe the child or support the perpetrator, the child does least well. This may seem counter to what you would expect, but mothers are more likely to believe a daughter if she is reporting the biological father than if she reports a stepfather. The explanation may be that the mothers have a greater stake in a relationship with a boyfriend or stepfather—it is a newer relationship—than with the biological father and are therefore more likely to support the newer man in their life.

A mother may not support her daughter because she has been abused herself and has not yet resolved that issue in her mind. To support her daughter, she would have to face what has happened to herself as well. Or the mother may have blocked from her mind the experience of her own abuse with only occasional flashbacks. Since these trigger a lot of internal conflict, she needs to deny her child's abuse.

The worst outcomes for abused children occur when a close family member has abused the child so the child has difficulty developing trust in other relationships. There is mixed evidence concerning how much the severity (frequency, length of time, types of acts) of the abuse affects the outcome for the child. Sometimes, the severity seems to have great impact, sometimes not. Still, the response of the parents is the most important determiner.

Research shows that sexual abuse of a child is a family trauma and has a major impact on parents. In a study of children abused outside the home, many couples found it difficult to have sex in the first nine months. The parents got images of the child in a sexual situation and could not continue. A small but significant number of couples developed alcohol and drug problems, and a significant number of parents reported they were depressed. They had a decreased trust in all societal institutions—the law, religions, schools, police, media. They lost their belief in a fair, just world.

continued

Interview with Jill Waterman   *continued*

In another follow-up study we did of children, 46 percent of abused children had scores in the clinical range on behavior problem checklists at the time of the disclosure. Five years later, only 17 percent had scores in that range. Remember, though, that only 2½ percent of a representative sample score in that range. All the abused children received treatment, but many still experienced internal distress several years later. These children are more likely to have symptoms of anxiety and somatic concerns than acting-out, aggressive problems.

What kinds of therapy are most helpful for children who have been abused?

Well, everyone in the family needs some form of individual therapy. Each member needs someone to talk to, to explain what the experience is like for them and to express their feelings. Groups are helpful for children of all ages, even for little children. Linda Damon of the San Fernando Valley Child Guidance Clinic developed parallel groups for mothers and children in therapy. Some therapists work with the mothers on a series of topics, and other therapists work with the children on the same topics. The therapists talk to the mothers about what to expect from the children on that week's topic. For example, on the topic that it is okay to say "No," the therapists tell mothers that this week they might expect the children to say a lot of no's. Moms, instead of getting angry at them, should help children see the situations in which it is appropriate to say "No" and those in which, like going to bed, you have to do it anyhow.

Groups for all children over age four have the advantage of reducing children's feelings of being weird. They don't feel like "damaged goods," because they see other children who have gone through the same thing and are doing well. So the group helps to take the stigma away from being abused.

Family therapy has a place down the road, I think, only when the perpetrator admits what he has done and the family has made a decision to stay together. Then you really need family therapy.

How long does it take for the child to come to terms with the abuse?

It depends on what happened as well as the age of the child. Some people argue that if the child is really young, he or she does not truly understand the meaning of the events and is less likely to experience negative outcomes. The research data are mixed about the age at which children are most or least affected. As children get older — in midlatency — they may feel they are responsible for what happened, that it is their fault. Adolescents may feel guilty as well. Treatment helps them to deal with these feelings.

Between a third and a half of children who have been sexually abused report no symptoms initially.[28] These may be the children who experienced the least damaging abuse or received the most supportive response at the time of disclosure, and they may be the most resilient children. It is possible, however, that they have suppressed their feelings and may experience difficulties later. Evidence from longitudinal work suggests that between 10 and 24 percent of children report an increasing number of symptoms over a two-year period. In most cases, though, symptoms decrease over an eighteen-month period, with fears, nightmares, and anxiety disappearing first and anger and aggressiveness with peers and siblings tending to remain longer. Follow-up from one to five years later reveals that a small percentage of children — 6 to 19 percent — were abused again. This is lower than the reabuse rate for physical abuse and neglect.

Four mechanisms are believed to account for the variety of symptoms sexually abused children experience:[29] (1) traumatic sexualization (the child's learning inappropriate sexual responses as well as faulty beliefs and ideas about sexual behavior), (2) betrayal, (3) stigmatization, and (4) powerlessness.

"Traumatic sexualization is the process by which a child's sexuality is shaped in developmentally inappropriate and interpersonally dysfunctional ways."[30] A child is taught sexually inappropriate responses through rewards of attention and affection, or a child's anatomy is fetishized, or pain and fear are associated with sexual activity. A child too young to understand the sexual implications of the activity may be less traumatized.

Children may experience the pain of betrayal, the feeling that someone they trusted or depended on has harmed them. Feelings of betrayal may come from the abuse itself or from the way the family responds to the abuse. When the adult is a trusted family member, or when a family member knows about the abuse but does not act to protect the child, the child feels betrayed. The family's response to disclosure can also trigger a sense of betrayal. If the focus of concern is on the perpetrator or on the consequences to other family members, or if the child is blamed or rejected, then the abused child may feel betrayed.

Children also feel powerless and helpless when someone has completely disregarded their feelings and forced them to perform or experience unwanted acts. If the child is threatened or feels trapped, or is not believed or supported at the time of disclosure, then the child experiences powerlessness. If the child can act to end the abuse and is supported, these feelings decrease.

When a child is stigmatized for the sexual activity, the experience of abuse then may become part of the child's self-image. Sometimes, the abuser blames the child or makes the child feel shameful for the activity. Others in the family or community may blame the child or feel the child is now "damaged goods" because he or she has had such experiences. Keeping the abuse a secret may heighten the child's sense of shame. When a child learns that abuse happens to other children and that the children are not at fault, he or she may feel less stigmatized.

Traumatic sexualization can account for the increased sexualized behavior some children show. Stigmatization may account for depression and poor self-esteem. Powerlessness can be related to fears, feelings of dread, and a sense of imminent disaster; and feelings of betrayal may account for the anger, aggressiveness, and antisocial acting out that abused children display.

An agreed-on finding is that the family plays a powerful role in helping the child deal with the effects of abuse.[31] Family support, particularly from the mother, is the key to the child's improvement. When mothers believe the child and take action to protect him or her, the child has the fewest symptoms over time. Conversely, a maltreating, dysfunctional family, unable to focus on the needs of the child, no doubt contributes to the impact of the abuse.

Court involvement may slow a child's recovery.[32] If the child has to make numerous court appearances, if the legal process extends over time, and if the child is afraid of the perpetrator, then negative effects and symptoms of the abuse may be prolonged. If cases are settled quickly and if the child has to testify only once and can testify by closed-circuit television, then risks to his or her recovery are reduced.

Recent studies of school-age children and adolescents suggest that abuse may push their development along distinctive pathways that can create additional problems for such children.[33] Sexual abuse in childhood may result in reduced learning and in poorer social competence at school, in poorer overall academic performance, and in school avoidance. These behaviors have profound consequences for later occupational success. Similarly, problems with a negative self-image and self-concept can lead to a broad spectrum of problems for these children in schoolwork and with peers.

Responses   We have looked at the prevalence of sexual abuse and its effects on children. What should be done when abuse has occurred and has been reported? First, the security of the child should immediately be arranged. Second, the child should have the opportunity to vent with a therapist feelings of anger, fear, guilt, and shame about the act. Although some children may initially resist, the experienced therapist can encourage the child to talk and can offer reassurances that help the child deal with the feelings created by abuse. Play therapy can also help the child deal with feelings of betrayal and powerlessness. In play, the child regains feelings of personal power and confidence. Support of these feelings helps the child rebuild trust. The child learns to control his or her world again, and healing and growth proceed.[34]

Groups for children help them to deal with the experience of abuse, and participation in such a group may do even more than a therapist can to help children talk about and handle what has occurred and what they are feeling. For example, when a young girl hears that others have had a similar experience, when she realizes that she has not been singled out for some inexplicable reason, it may be easier for her to accept her own victimization.

Family therapy helps all members cope with their reactions to the abuse. Parents and siblings may have strong feelings of sadness, anger, and guilt. They, too, need help in coming to terms with what has happened.

Physical Child Abuse

There is no commonly agreed-on definition of physical child abuse. In defining an act as physically abusive, consideration is given to the nature of the act, its intensity and frequency, its impact on the victim, the intent of the perpetrator, and community standards. Some acts are so clearly abusive that everyone would label them as such — for example, physical discipline that resulted in a broken bone or severe injury — and some acts are clearly not abusive — for example, talking to a child calmly and respectfully about a misdeed. But between the two extremes, abuse becomes a matter of interpretation. Some define abuse as any physical act that the recipient does not want; others extreme yelling and pushing; others, any spanking; still others, any spanking that results in a bruise or injury. Robert Emery suggests that the same standards of violence that apply to acts between strangers in public be used to define violence in the home with family members.[35]

The question arises of whether or not violence toward children is a single continuum varying from no physical punishment at the low end through varying degrees of abuse to homicide at the high end.[36] If one believes in a single continuum, one would search for mechanisms that underlie all aspects of violence. Another theory is that physical punishment, mild abuse, severe abuse, and homicide represent different categories of behavior. The search then is for mechanisms that underlie each category and that may differ from category to category. Evidence from the Second National Family Violence Survey supports a distinction between physical punishment and severe abuse, as the predictors are somewhat different.[37]

Prevalence   Depending on their source, statistics on abuse vary. In 1985, a national probability sample was surveyed by telephone. Of the 6,002 households contacted, 3,232 included a child under eighteen. The caregivers for 60 percent of children reported that they used physical punishment and minor violence (pushing, grabbing, shoving, and slapping) with children. The caregivers for 10 percent of children reported one or more instances of physical abuse or severe violence consisting of kicking, biting, hitting with a fist or object, or burning.[38]

These were self-reports of punishment and abuse. In 1994, three million agency reports of suspected child abuse were made.[39] The number of reports of abuse to social agencies falls far below the self-report rate of 10 percent. Had caregivers for 10 percent of all children been reported as abusers, the number of reports would have been about 6 million. It is estimated that between 1,200 and 5,000 children die from abuse each year.[40]

Precipitating Factors   Certain characteristics of parent, child, and living setting that are related to physical abuse have been identified. In the National Family Violence Survey, female caregivers most frequently reported physical punishment and minor violence, but there were no sex differences in reported physical abuse or severe violence.[41] Younger parents with many children were more likely than others to be abusive. Although abuse occurs at all socioeconomic levels, it was most frequently reported when fathers were unemployed or underemployed and when families lived below the poverty line. Abusive parents also were more likely to report drug use. For example, state agencies reported in a survey that substance abuse was the major issue in 68 percent of child protection cases being followed.[42]

Other studies have shown that 30 percent of parents who have been abused abuse children, but still, the majority who experience abuse do not repeat it.[43] Abusive parents, compared with nonabusive parents, are more likely to form families in which spousal abuse and domestic violence occur.[44] More demanding and more negative with children, these parents are more likely to view child rearing as a burden. They believe in strict, firm, physical discipline. Although in the past there has been mention of an "abusive personality," research has not identified one. A maltreating individual is associated with being especially reactive to negative events and with having low self-esteem, poor impulse control, and impaired capacity for empathy.

Characteristics of the child include those mentioned earlier: age — most are between three and eight years of age with an increasing number of teenagers who are reported to be abused—and sex—with boys being more often physically abused.[45] Any negative qualities of abused children prior to the abuse are thought to result from parents' generally negative child-rearing behaviors.

Abused parents who do not abuse their children have higher IQs, greater emotional stability, and less anxiety and depression than do abused parents who abuse their children. They are also more likely to have a supportive partner.[46]

Glenn Wolfner and Richard Gelles, who have studied family violence extensively, believe that violence to children is the result of parents' predispositions to violence in combination with stressful life conditions.[47] The potential for violence is present in everyone in varying degrees as a result of social learning. Those individuals who have learned to respond to stress with violence are those most likely to abuse children when they experience stressors like job loss or financial problems.

Children's Reactions   Children react to physical abuse in many ways. As we saw in discussing Cicchetti and Lynch's transactional/ecological model, five main areas of development are affected: attachment relationships, regulation of emotion, self-concept, peer relationships, and school adjustment.[48]

When children are maltreated in infancy and early childhood, they often develop insecure or disorganized/disoriented attachments. In one study, 80 percent of maltreated infants were classified as disorganized/disoriented in their attachments to mother, compared with 20 percent of nonmaltreated infants. Further, these disorganized attachments are stable, as 90 percent of these infants are classified in the same way a year later. When children are between ages seven and thirteen at the time of abuse, about 30 percent report confused patterns of relationships to their mother, so age appears to reduce the impact on this attachment.

Abused children's internal working models of relationships based on experiences with abusive parents may generalize to other relationships, leading these children to have negative views of how others will treat them and how reliable and predictable others are. Thus, not surprisingly, abused children often have problems with peers. Some abused children are fearful and insecure with peers, often withdrawing from or avoiding them. Others are physically and verbally aggressive and find it difficult to be positive and considerate.

Children's ability to regulate their feelings affects all aspects of their functioning. Abused children have difficulty controlling their emotions, in part because these emotions are so intense. The children are likely to feel chronic stress, anxiety, depression, and helplessness. They tend to be inflexible and inappropriate in expressing their feelings. They also have difficulty in communicating their feelings verbally and in identifying the feelings of others. They lack the cognitive control of feelings that children their age usually have. Emotional dysregulation is related to peer difficulties as well, because peers find it hard to be with children who lack control of their feelings.

In view of their poor attachment relationships and intense amounts of uncontrolled feelings, it is not surprising that abused children often have unrealistic self-concepts. When young, they may inflate their sense of competence, feeling overly confident, but as they get older, they describe themselves as less able than and less accepted by others.

Emery states that it is not clear whether the many symptoms come from the abuse itself or from family interactions leading up to the abuse.[49] He notes (as described in Chapter 3) that angry episodes, even those not involving the child, distress the child. Children's distress motivates them to get involved in parental conflicts in order to end them. Because their misbehavior distracts parents from their quarrels, children are likely to repeat misbehavior to stop conflicts even if by doing so they become victims themselves.

Despite the abuse they experience, a sizable number of maltreated children develop competence and caring and are resilient and resourceful in surmounting problems. The most competent and well-functioning children are those who have developed ego control, ego resilience, and self-esteem.[50] The capacity for a more reserved, controlled, and rational way of interacting with others predicts overall competence in maltreated children. This factor does not predict competence in nonmaltreated children, perhaps because control is not as central to competence in nonmaltreated children.

Interventions   Just as with child sexual abuse, there are two forms of intervention for physical abuse: (1) providing security and safety for the child and (2) getting psychological services. There is some indication that, at least with spousal abuse, having the perpetrator arrested prevents recurrence more effectively than mediating the dispute informally or having the perpetrator leave the property for 48 hours. In child abuse cases, children deserve at least as much physical protection as they would get if a stranger attacked them. Gelles believes some parents are so abusive on a single occasion that family reunification should never be considered.[51]

Physically abused children need the same form of therapy as sexually abused children. They need the opportunity to vent and understand their intense feelings, to learn to express them appropriately, and to control them when they are very intense. They need help forming positive, trusting relationships with both adults and peers, and they need help in developing the self-esteem that will enable them to explore their world actively.

Interventions are also directed toward the abusing parent. When appropriate, perpetrators are referred to abuse treatment programs. They are taught parenting skills and other ways to manage their anger. Sometimes, home visitors are sent into the home to teach and monitor parenting skills. In a sense, these interventions help provide the community resources that parents had earlier failed to or been unable to access.

Other Forms of Personal Abuse

Physical neglect is defined as failing to provide responsible care, proper support, education, and medical care required for well-being. In one large study, it was the most often reported form of abuse, and in Figure 14 1, it has about the same rate of occurrence as physical abuse.[52] It is less often studied, however, so we know less about it. Neglect includes inadequate supervision and abandonment. Although it is related to living in poverty, most poor people adequately care for their children. Parental drug addiction often plays a role in neglect. Children who suffer neglect have been found to be socially withdrawn and aggressive, to suffer intellectual deficits, and to be at risk for delinquent behavior.

Emotional abuse includes terrorizing, exploiting, and missocializing children.[53] Defined as acts of omission or commission that damage the behavioral, cognitive, affective, and physical functioning of the child, it is hard to prove. Emotional abuse is associated with a child's withdrawal, loss of self-esteem, aggressiveness, and failure to trust others.

Moral-legal-educational maltreatment involves failure to help the child develop appropriate social and moral values. Behaviors include such acts as exposing the child to illegal drugs or giving them to the child, involving the child in illegal activity, or failing to intervene when the child is involved in such activity.

Because the majority of abused children experience more than one form of abuse, pure subtypes of abuse rarely exist, but some differences among parents who commit different types are beginning to be identified.[54] For example, physically abusive parents may be more likely to have insecure adult attachments to their own parents in which they dismiss or deny painful experiences and so are less likely to appreciate their own child's pain. Neglectful parents appear to have insecure adult attachments in which they are preoccupied with feelings and are less available to monitor and care for children.

Community Violence

We have seen that in any form, exposure to unresolved anger and aggression harms children, whether they witness it or experience it. Children do not meet aggression only in their personal lives. Our society has become increasingly violent, with many children exposed to traumatic events. Although a large proportion of violence occurs in lower socioeconomic areas, people face violence in restaurants, schools, and middle-class communities. No child is immune to the effects of community violence. Even if it does not touch a child personally, he or she may be acquainted with someone who has had a family member die or experience harm.

Prevalence   Children are more likely to witness violence than to experience it. In a study in a low-income, moderately violent neighborhood in Washington, D.C., 19 percent of children in grades one and two had been physically threatened, chased, mugged, or shot, and 61 percent had witnessed such acts as muggings, stabbings, and illegal drug use, not once but several times per year.[55] By grades five and six, 32 percent of children had been victims, and 72 percent had witnessed violence.

When questioned, older children reported that none of the victimizations took place at home, but 48 percent occurred near home; 55 percent took place at or near school. Most of the violence the children witnessed took place near home. Although it usually occurred outside the home, children knew about two-thirds of the perpetrators; only about a third were strangers to them.

Parents report that their children experience or witness less violence than the children report. However, children may not tell parents all they see. Anecdotal reports suggest that parents may discourage children from talking about the violence they see.[56] This is unfortunate in that it prevents children from dealing with their feelings and parents from helping their children cope with the violence.

Effects   Exposure to community violence by itself does not predict personal problems and school difficulties. Even in combination with many other stressors, such as low income, many family moves, and the father's absence, it does not predict difficulty.[57] To have a negative effect, community violence must impact family life.

When this violence erodes the safety and stability of the child's home, such as when drug dealing and guns are in the home, then the child is affected. Thus, the child experiences community violence at the level of the microsystem—in day-to-day interactions with his or her parents. When parents can somehow prevent the stressors from disrupting the stability of the home and not allow the violence in the community to influence parent-child relationships, children can then function successfully.

John Richters and Pedro Martinez write,

> It seems reasonable to assume that family stability and safety are ultimately the products of choices made by children's caretakers about how they will cope with and/or react to the circumstances within which they find themselves. We have much to learn about how, why, and in what ways such choices are made, but in advance of those answers it seems self-evident that these are factors over which caretakers have and must exercise control.[58]

Children exposed to community violence develop many of the symptoms of children who have been physically or sexually abused. They have difficulty sleeping, remembering, and concentrating, and they exhibit anxious attachment to parents (not wanting them to leave), aggressive play, severe limitation of activities and exploration, and regressive behavior.[59] Lenore Terr describes the denial and numbing children use to block out frightening reality.[60] Children also experience feelings of grief and loss when a significant loved one dies as a result of violence.

All these reactions make it hard for children to develop intellectually and socially. They come to expect violence, and develop a sense of fatalism about their lives, a feeling that they have no future. They believe that planning is not important because they could be crippled or killed before their plans are fulfilled.

Even in adverse circumstances, a significant number of children function well at school and appear to have few behavior problems. Such children are active individuals who seek to surmount obstacles. The main agent for helping them is their family and the stability it provides.[61] A second source of help is their own internal sense that life can improve, that they can influence what happens to them and make life better in the future.[62] Children who live in difficult circumstances but still maintain positive expectations of the future are more successful later on. But again, it is most likely the immediate family members who help children build positive expectations about the future.

James Garbarino and his colleagues summarize the parents' role and its dangers:

> If parents, or other significant caregivers, can sustain a strong attachment to their children, can maintain a positive sense of self, and can have access to basic resources, children will manage, although it may be at great cost to the psychic and physical welfare of those parents, who may be "used up" caring for their children.[63]

Coping Resources   Several factors influence how children cope with the experience of violence.[64] Intelligence, self-confidence, self-esteem, sociability, easygoing attitude, affectionateness, and good nature all increase children's coping ability. Such children demand little, yet they relate positively and happily to others and tend to receive support. Environmental factors include the presence of at least one stable emotional relationship with a caregiver who serves as a model of coping, as well as social relationships outside the family with relatives and family friends. The community can give support in many ways—friends, neighbors, teachers, and members of religious groups can provide support and encourage the competence of parents and children.

The school is a major refuge for children who confront difficult experiences. After the family, the school is the most important social institution in children's lives. Many resilient children find school activities to be a source of self-esteem and competence. They make friends with and get support from schoolmates and from teachers who take an interest in them.

In *Children in Danger,* Garbarino and his associates describe the schools as a major unit of intervention to counteract the community violence in children's lives. He outlines a school-based intervention program in which teachers form close emotional attachments with students to promote their development. The researchers believe that these relationships serve as the basis for learning in all areas. Teachers and programs provide structure and control for these children, who adopt the values, behavior, and attitudes of a significant other person.

In Garbarino's plan, day care centers can be included in programs to reach children below school age. An attachment teacher is assigned to every six or seven students, and a consistent substitute attachment and subgroup are assigned to each child. Children have an unvarying placement in small groups. Formal teaching programs stimulate the child's curiosity and level of development.

The organized school environment, with familiar teachers and programs, provides security and predictability in a changing world. Teachers are specially trained to work with these children, taking courses in child development and in understanding children's reactions to stress, violence, and loss. Teachers remain available to students who exhibit fluctuating or changing emotions and help the children deal with them.

Therapy can help children cope with their emotional reactions to trauma.[65] All major personality shifts resulting from trauma require treatment. Such personality changes occur in almost all physically and sexually abused children, as well as those who experience some form of trauma.

Parents should arrange psychiatric treatment for a child as soon after a trauma as possible. If several children are involved, participants can be seen in a minimarathon group session with a highly trained professional. When each member shares his or her experiences, the possibility of anyone's denying the situation (and thus prolonging traumatization) is lessened. Schools serve as the familiar setting appropriate for such group sessions. If a family has been traumatized, then it can be treated as a unit. However, family therapy is not recommended when a parent has physically or sexually abused a child, because the child is not really free to express the anger he or she feels in the presence of the abuser.

Behavioral therapy is useful for children who have developed fears as a result of the trauma. Deconditioning is useful as an addition to individual treatment designed to deal with the emotional reactions, but behavioral therapy by itself is limited.

A person should begin treatment as soon as possible after the trauma. However, treatment is useful any time a person recognizes that he or she is suffering the effects of a trauma, even if therapy cannot reverse all the effects of the experience.

Parents want to know what to do to prevent violence and trauma in their children's lives. Nothing can completely prevent violence, but children who receive support are most likely to recover from the experience.

Common Themes in Abuse and Violence

Several general themes emerge in the study of abuse and violence. First, no one set of circumstances leads inevitably to abuse; rather, many risk factors increase the likelihood of abuse and violence and increase the traumatic effects on children.

Second, children respond in many ways to trauma, and several different kinds of trauma lead to similar problems in children. For example, all forms of abuse are associated with difficulties in emotional control, in relationships with adults and peers, in self-concept, and in school adjustment. Further, problems are similar to those seen in children when their parents lose their jobs or suffer from prolonged unemployment, get divorced, or remarry and blend families. Sexualized behavior seems to be the one form of reaction that is most frequently linked with sexual abuse.

A question arises of whether abuse and violence contribute significant difficulties beyond those related to low income or negative life stress. A recent study statistically disentangled the contributions of these factors — physical abuse, low income, and life stress events.[66] Indeed, physical abuse made a significant contribution to children's behavior problems beyond that related to economic disadvantage and stress as a result of negative life events.

Physical abuse was associated with additional problems in relationships with peers, and peer problems occurred after physical abuse regardless of the sex, socioeconomic status, or stress level of the abused person. The abusive experience in the family appears to lead to distortions in how people relate to each other and what is required to get along. As noted earlier, this is especially sad because children then lose a major source of support in coping with other problems. Other stressors such as low income and negative life events produce few changes in self-perceptions or behavior problems unless they are unusually severe.

Therefore, other difficulties in life appear to produce less marked changes in children's moods and behaviors. Abuse and violence damage children's trust in their peers and decrease their capacity for positive relationships, thus removing an important resource for such children.

In all these difficult situations, the family remains the main source of support for children. Agencies and therapies can help, but it is individuals who are close and have a sense of the child's individuality who are truly helpful. If parents cannot do this, other relatives or family friends, teachers, or day care workers can step in.

PREVENTION OF VIOLENCE

From October 1, 1997, to April 1, 1998, four dramatic school-based shootings by adolescents claimed the lives of eleven students and a teacher. For a brief time, Americans focused on the amount of violence that children experience or witness.[67] In a chapter concerning the neurobiological effects of experiencing and witnessing trauma, Bruce Perry writes,

> The ultimate solution to the problems of violence, whether from the remorseless predator or the reactive, impulsive youth, is primary prevention. Our society is creating violent children and youth at a rate far faster than we could ever treat, rehabilitate, or even lock them away. No single intervention strategy will solve these heterogeneous problems. No

set of intervention strategies will solve these transgenerational problems. In order to solve the problems of violence, we need to transform our culture.[68]

Where can we start? Katherine Christoffel describes the necessity of viewing violence in the form of firearm injuries and deaths as a public health problem rather than a criminal one.[69] Once we do that, the main goal becomes decreasing injuries, and we can search for a variety of strategies to do this.

By describing how we reduced motor vehicle injury deaths, she illustrates how we might reduce violence. In the late 1960s, motor vehicle injury deaths were redefined as a public health problem, and a variety of actions were taken to decrease them. Car manufacturers improved the safety of cars, passenger restraints were developed, road construction improved, and changes in the driving laws to increase penalties for alcohol intake and failure to use seat belts were passed. The number of deaths dropped from 55,000 in 1968 to 45,000 per year in 1990, though the number of cars and drivers had increased.

Using a public health model, one can make the public aware of the risk we all face from firearms. While deaths from motor vehicles are dropping, deaths from firearms are rising. In 1992, 37,776 U.S. citizens of all ages died of firearms. Some have estimated that by the year 2000, deaths from firearms will exceed deaths from motor vehicle injuries, but preliminary analysis of 1994 data indicate this may already have happened.

Strategies

Understanding the lethality of guns and their risk to the general population, the public can shift the focus from crime, law enforcement, and civil liberties to a focus on prevention and reducing injuries and deaths from firearms. The emphasis becomes having handgun-free homes and neighborhoods, restricting handgun sales and ownership, and developing other self- and home-protection devices. For example, we can emphasize the safe storage of guns and ammunition in locked and separated areas, and states can pass laws making owners responsible for others' use of their guns.

While we have taken some action to regulate people who buy guns, we have paid little attention to gun manufacturers and distributors. Licenses to distribute handguns are cheap and can be obtained through the mail. In 1990, there were more firearm licensees than gas stations in the United States. Many of these distributors, unknown to local officials, operate out of their homes. Thus, their compliance with existing laws may be minimal, and could no doubt be improved if all distributors were known.

Another form of prevention is to encourage health professionals to advise and counsel all families on the danger of handguns and the need to have them locked away. They can track the number of injuries and deaths from handguns carefully and educate the public on the importance of reforms to control handgun use and storage.

We can also work to change the content of the media.[70] Research indicates that media violence contributes to violent behavior in three ways: (1) It increases aggressive behavior and willingness to use violence, (2) it desensitizes viewers so that they accept violence as a normal part of life, and (3) it creates a belief in a "mean world syndrome" that makes people more fearful of a world they see as dangerous.

John Murray suggests that families need to act in three ways to counteract media violence. First, they need to change their behavior at home. So that children can become informed consumers of TV fare, parents need to watch TV with children and talk about what they see. Parents and children can learn from each other in these discussions.

Second, parents can lobby for the inclusion of media literacy courses, so, again, children learn critical viewing habits. Third, parents can begin to lobby the government and industries to make children's TV less violent. For example, they may lobby for stricter viewer discretion warnings at the beginning of programs of concern. They might also lobby the industry to reduce the amount of time allocated to violent programs during prime time. There are encouraging signs that the chairman of the Federal Communications Commission is ready to make changes. These are just a few of the actions that parents can pursue as they seek to make the world a safer place for children.

THE CHALLENGE MODEL

Therapy can help children deal with the effects of certain traumatic events and troubled family situations. Some therapists have become concerned, however, that certain forms of intervention so emphasize the pain and damaging effects of these difficulties that children and adults believe they are doomed to emotionally impoverished lives as a result of the trauma.

Steven Wolin and Sybil Wolin term this the *damage model* of human development, in that it focuses on the harmful effects produced by traumas; therapy in this model can only help individuals understand the damage and how it occurred. Drawing on clinical insights and on the research of such people as Ruth Smith and Emmy Werner (see the interview with Emmy Werner in Chapter 3), Wolin and Wolin have developed a challenge model of development.[71] Although adversity brings stress, harm, and vulnerability to the individual, Wolin and Wolin believe it also stimulates the person to branch out, to take measures to protect him- or herself and find other sources of strength that promote development. So, the individual experiences pain but develops resiliencies that can limit the pain and promote accomplishment and satisfaction.

In their book *The Resilient Self,* Wolin and Wolin identify seven resiliencies that help individuals rebound in the face of difficult circumstances:

1. *Insight* — developing the habit of asking tough questions and giving honest answers

2. *Independence* — drawing boundaries between oneself and one's troubled parents; keeping emotional distance while satisfying the demands of one's conscience

3. *Relationships* — building intimate and fulfilling ties to other people that balance a mature regard for one's own needs with empathy and the capacity to give to someone else

4. *Initiative* — taking charge of problems; exerting control; acquiring a taste for stretching and testing oneself in demanding tasks

Children cope best with community disasters when family members are supportive.

5. *Creativity*—imposing order, beauty, and purpose on the chaos of one's troubling experiences and painful feelings
6. *Humor*—finding the comic in the tragic
7. *Morality*—developing an informed conscience that extends one's wish for a good personal life to all of humankind[72]

Their book describes the many ways resiliencies grow in childhood, adolescence, and adulthood and offers an optimistic approach that encourages survivors of traumas and difficult childhood experiences to review their lives in terms of the strengths they have developed. As a result, people experience pride in their ability to overcome hardships and confidence in their capacity to make further changes as needed. In focusing on pain and the sources of pain in the past, the damage model tends to discourage individuals because the past cannot be changed and the pain undone. The challenge model asserts that life can be satisfying and productive even with the scars of the past.

KEEPING CHILDREN SAFE

As children spend more time away from parents and home, going to and from school or to friends' homes, parents become concerned about their safety. They want to help children be independent and safe in the world, yet they do not want to frighten them and make them afraid of strangers and new experiences. Grace

Hechinger, an educational consultant, has interviewed police officials, school safety officials, individuals involved in neighborhood safety programs, and victims of crime and assaults.[73] From this research, she has organized information to help parents prepare their children to be safe as they spend more time on their own.

Fostering children's awareness of danger, sense of caution, and preparedness for unsafe situations does not mean making children live in fear. Children can learn that even though most people in the world are good and helpful and most situations are safe, some people and experiences are not, and everyone must learn to protect him- or herself from dangers that arise. It is helpful if parents can put this knowledge in perspective for children. Life has always involved danger of some sort, and many objects or experiences that are positive also have dangerous aspects. Cars are useful—they get us to work, to stores, to hospitals—but they can be dangerous if they hit us while we are crossing the street. The answer lies not in eliminating cars, because before we had cars, there were dangers from horses and horse-drawn vehicles. The solution is to take precautions to minimize dangers and enjoy the benefits.

Families need to develop a set of instructions in the event of certain dangerous situations, to be discussed and revised as necessary. A one-time discussion is not enough; periodically, parents must review instructions with children. Children can learn these safety rules gradually—for example, when and where they may go alone or what they should do if bothered by someone on the street or in a store, even when parents are nearby. Learning safety rules can become as natural to children as learning to brush their teeth. The emphasis in teaching is that children are learning skills to deal with the environment, to make them competent and independent.

Although parents worry that talk of possible fearful events will damage the child, the risks that come with ignorance are much greater. Parents can begin with simple discussions of traffic safety—where, when, and how to cross the street. They can move from that topic to others of importance for the child. Television may start a discussion. Hechinger suggests a game: "What If?" Parents ask a variety of questions and give children chances to develop solutions to difficult situations. Parents should not be upset if their children's initial answers are impractical, because children can learn more reasonable responses. Box 14-1 gives some sample "what if" questions.

Parents should have clear safety rules on (1) behavior for a fire at home, (2) traffic behavior, whether on foot or on a bicycle, (3) boundaries within which the child can come and go freely and outside of which an adult or parent must be present, (4) behavior in public with strangers, (5) behavior at home if strangers telephone or come to the house, (6) behavior when the child is a victim or witness of muggings by peers or adults, and (7) behavior when sexual misconduct occurs.

If children are victimized—a bike is stolen, their money is taken, a stranger approaches them—parents' reactions can help speed the healing process. When parents listen to children's reactions and help children take constructive action, such as notifying the police, they help children cope. When parents' responses are exaggerated ("This is horrible!") or detached ("I cannot deal with this"), children get no help in coping with their feelings. If they cannot talk about how they feel, they will find it difficult to work out their feelings. Active listening and simple I-messages ("If that happened to me, I'd be really upset") give children a chance to say what the experience meant to them. Sometimes, children need to describe the event several times. Each time, more details emerge, as do more feelings. Gradually, after the incident,

---

BOX 14-1
SOME "WHAT IF" QUESTIONS FOR YOUNG CHILDREN

Parents ask children what they would do if the following situations arose. If children give the wrong answers, parents can calmly tell them more practical alternative responses. What if:

1. We are separated in a shopping center, in the movies, at the beach?
2. You are lost in a department store, in the park, at a parade?
3. A stranger offered you candy or presents to leave the playground?
4. A stranger wanted you to get into his car?
5. A stranger started fussing with your clothing?
6. Your friends wanted to play with matches?
7. Someone you did not know asked your name and phone number?

Grace Hechinger, *How to Raise a Street-Smart Child* (New York: Ballantine Books, 1984), p. 59.

---

children will regain their self-confidence. If a child's eating, sleeping, or play habits change or if marked changes in schoolwork or personality continue for some time, professional help should be sought.

An important step in promoting children's safety is working with people in the community. Developing community awareness and programs gives everyone a positive feeling of working together, which does much to banish fear. Promoting public safety programs with school and police officials and organizing block-watch programs to help children in the neighborhood are useful steps. In block-parent programs, one house in the neighborhood is designated as a house where children may come if they need help or reassurance when no one is home.

Family members grow stronger when they face problems and work together to deal with them. Sense of community is strengthened when families and agencies cooperate to make the environment safe for children.

MAIN POINTS

Victimization

- can be classified as pandemic, acute, or extraordinary
- is more common for children than for adults
- occurs mainly because children are more dependent on adults, are less able to protect themselves, and have less control of associates and surroundings

An ecological/transactional model of violence and child maltreatment

- focuses on risk and protective factors
- describes characteristics of child, parent, and environment that increase risk of violence

- describes violence at several ecological levels: the macrosystem, the exosystem, and the microsystem
- emphasizes that factors at different levels interact to increase the likelihood of violence
- describes the effects of violence in five areas of a child's behavior: attachment relationships, regulation of emotions, self-concept, peer relationships, and school adjustment
- has implications for types of intervention

Sexual child abuse

- is estimated to be experienced by one in four girls and one in six boys by the age of eighteen
- affects children in different ways depending on the specific act, its duration, its frequency, and its perpetrator
- appears most traumatic when it involves someone close who frequently engages in forceful sexual acts of penetration over a long time period and when mothers provide little support
- results in behavior changes such as changes in sexualized behavior, in emotional regulation, in attachment relations, in self-concept, in relations with peers, and in school adjustment
- does not always produce symptoms; about one-third to one-half of children show no symptoms at the time they are studied, because abuse has been suspected
- victims require protection from the abuser
- victims can profit from individual, group, and family therapy

Physical child abuse

- is difficult to define precisely
- results from a variety of factors, including characteristics of the parents, the family, and the environment
- is learned in the context of the family
- results in a wide variety of symptoms relating to self-concept, emotional control, relations with peers and adults, and adjustment in school
- victims can be resourceful and surmount problems
- requires therapy for victim, perpetrator, and family
- may be so severe on a single occasion that the child should not live with the person again

Community violence

- affects all children but most particularly those in lower socioeconomic areas
- is more often witnessed than experienced
- has a negative impact when it erodes the safety and stability of family life
- results in many symptoms that hinder children's development

• requires interventions at the community level to decrease the violence and provide support for children who experience such violence
• victims can be helped with individual, group, and family therapy

The challenge model

• focuses on strengths people develop to cope with negative family experiences or other traumas
• identifies seven resiliencies: insight, independence, relationships, initiative, creativity, humor, and morality
• presents an optimistic view of people's capacity to create satisfying lives despite the scars of painful experiences

Keeping children safe

• requires that parents teach children about potential dangers and ways to minimize them
• requires that parents teach children coping techniques for dangerous situations
• means that parents and society as a whole have to work to provide a safer community for everyone

EXERCISES

1. Imagine that a close friend told you that her four-year-old had just showed her how a male relative of twenty-five had touched her genitals. The daughter said he told her it was a secret between them, but she decided to tell her mother because they do not keep secrets from each other. How would you advise your friend to help her daughter after she has reported the event to authorities? What would you advise her to do to help herself?

2. Divide into groups of four and work as a unit. Describe the general information you would choose to include in an eight-session parenting course for men and women who have physically abused their children. Share your group's results with the entire class. What elements were chosen by only one or two groups? Combine the best information from all groups and come up with one eight-session program. If possible, compare it with a program offered in your area by Parental Stress or another such agency.

3. Divide into groups of four and work as a unit. Describe a parenting program for adolescent mothers and fathers to prevent physical child abuse. Is it identical to the program designed for those who have already committed abuse? In what ways does it differ?

4. Imagine that you had unlimited money to go into a low-income housing project in a high-crime area. What kinds of programs would you devise to help children cope with the violence they witness around them?

5. Think about what you most feared as a young child. What would you tell a nine-year-old brother or sister who was afraid of being kidnapped on the street? Of experiencing an earthquake or hurricane or flood? Of being shot?

ADDITIONAL READINGS

Adams, Caren, and Fay, Jennifer. *Helping Your Child Recover from Sexual Abuse.* Seattle: University of Washington Press, 1992.

Garbarino, James, Dubrow, Nancy, Kostelny, Kathleen, and Pardo, Carole. *Children in Danger.* San Francisco: Jossey-Bass, 1992.

Kraizer, Sherryll. *The Safe Child Book.* New York: Fireside, 1996.

Melton, Gary B., and Barry, Frank D., eds. *Protecting Children from Abuse and Neglect.* New York: Guilford Press, 1994.

Statman, Paula. *On the Safe Side.* New York: HarperCollins, 1995.

PARENTING CHILDREN WITH SPECIAL NEEDS

C H A P T E R   15

How do parents respond to the challenge of nurturing and providing guidance to children with special needs? How do children's needs shape parents' behaviors? Are there common threads in what parents do in these special situations? Where do parents get support for themselves?

In this chapter, we look at parenting behaviors when children are premature, are adopted, have physical illnesses, are depressed, have attention deficit/hyperactivity disorder, have learning disabilities, live in poverty, or have special talents and gifts. Though this chapter does not include all children who require special consideration, it does focus on children within the main categories of special needs. We look at what their needs are and how parents can meet them so children can develop to their full potential.

ADOPTED CHILDREN

Adoption is defined as taking a child into a family through legal means and raising the child as one's own.[1] It is not known exactly how many children are adopted each year, as the government does not keep statistics on this.

It is estimated that about 60 percent of adoptions are by relatives, such as step-parents and grandparents.[2] Also, about 30,000 to 40,000 infants are adopted each year in the United States, and about 14,000 older children and special-needs children. Approximately 2 to 4 percent of children in the United States are adopted.[3]

As a result of better contraception, availability of abortion, and unmarried mothers' keeping babies, there are fewer healthy European-American babies available than before, at a time when many want to adopt.[4] Thus, many couples seek babies in such countries as Korea, Colombia, Peru, China, and Rumania. Further, adoptive parents are no longer required to meet traditional standards for families such as having two parents, having a comfortable income, and being young. Homosexual parents are adopting infants as well. In short, adoption is more complex now than in the past.

Transition to Parenthood

Having a child by adoption affects the transition to parenthood in several ways. Most parents seek to create a family by means of adoption when they cannot have biological children. Infertility or genetic problems leading to child death are major reasons for adopting. Though a small group adopt because they want a child of a certain sex or because of belief in the importance of adoption, parents usually come to adoption with feelings of loss and inadequacy because they cannot produce biological children. As they prepare for parenthood, usually a happy time for couples, they must deal with their feelings of guilt, inadequacy, loss, and sadness before they adopt. Professionals believe couples must acknowledge and accept such feelings before adoption so they do not use it to deny the feelings of loss.

When a couple decide to adopt, they can approach an agency to begin proceedings. Unlike a pregnancy, there is no definite nine-month period in which to prepare for parenthood. Parents may have to wait months or years, never knowing if or when a child may come. They are often so worried about whether they are going to get a child that they cannot go through the process of planning to be parents. They do not think about the kind of parent they want to be or wonder about their competence until the question of having a baby is settled. When that occurs, the baby is already there and parents must cope with all the adjustments of new parenthood at once. The image making that frequently occurs in a leisurely way during pregnancy occurs rapidly while the family members make many other adjustments and add stress to the initial parenting experience.

Although babies ideally come to the adoptive home from the hospital, this may not occur. Infants may arrive from foreign countries, weak and tired, unfamiliar with the language and culture. Or babies may arrive sad at losing foster parents who have cared for them while their biological parents were making decisions about adoption. Older children may have already experienced several different households and so come with feelings of insecurity, frustration, and anger.

If the adoptive parents worry that the biological parents or court will remove the child from them, they may be reluctant to become completely attached to their child. Also, adoptive parents may not get the support from relatives and friends that biological parents get, because some adults in our society feel adoption is a second-best way to have a child. Instead of rejoicing family and friends, adoptive parents may face a series of questions—"Where did you get the child?" "Who are the biological parents?" "How do you feel about taking care of another person's child?"

Fortunately, adoptive parents have buffers. Such parents tend to be older, with all the advantages of older parents described in Chapter 5.[5] They are more settled in their work, have greater financial resources, have been married longer, and have developed more effective coping skills than younger parents. Although they often have experienced much frustration because of fertility problems, they come to parenthood with a great appreciation for the opportunity to be parents.

Studies following adoptive parents and their children find that difficulties in the transition do not affect the attachment to the babies, and their babies do as well at ages one and two as do children of biological parents.[6] Adoptive parents themselves report better coping with the many demands of children and greater satisfactions in the role of parent than do nonadoptive parents.

Parenting the Adopted Child

As attachment grows between parents and children and parents' confidence in their parenting skills increase, they steel themselves for the day their child will ask questions and need to be told he or she is adopted. Before deciding exactly what to say, parents need to understand their own feelings about being adoptive parents. If they feel comfortable about adoption and believe they are true parents because they nourish and protect their child, helping him or her grow, then they convey a sense of confidence and security about the adoption process to the child. When parents feel secure, they neither overemphasize the fact of adoption nor hide it. They can explain the different ways to form a family. Telling the child he or she is adopted makes it clear to everyone that the family is not linked together by biology as most families are. Parents must accept that their child has links to two families—to them and to biological parents.

The general advice is to tell children sometime in the toddler and preschool years.[7] Research finds that psychological adjustment of the child is not related to variations in time of being told within this period. Adoption, however, is not something you explain once or twice when the child is young and then forget about. Recent research evidence suggests that most preschoolers are unlikely to understand what adoption is even when parents have explained it to them and they refer to themselves as adopted.[8] Preschoolers confuse adoption and birth, making no distinction between the two ways of having children. By the age of six, most children can understand that there are two paths to parenthood—birth and adoption—and they understand that adoption makes the child a permanent member of the family.

Just as in most other areas of knowledge, children's conceptions of adoption broaden at ages eight to eleven. Children begin to understand that adoption is not the usual way families grow. They become more aware that their biological parents exist somewhere, and many children become concerned that their biological parents may return and take them away from their adoptive families. By the end of this period, children return to a belief in the permanence of adoption even though it is not until early or middle adolescence that they understand it as a legal process.

Young children think adoption occurs because adoptive parents have strong needs to love and care for children, providing them a good home. In elementary school, between age eight and eleven, children recognize that parents adopt children for additional reasons such as infertility, family-planning needs, and the welfare of children. Very young children do not wonder why they needed to be removed from their biological parents. With increasing age, children distinguish financial reasons, parental death, and their biological parents' immaturity as reasons for adoption.

In the school years, children may become confused as to where their loyalties lie—to the family they live with or to their biological parents.[9] They become more aware of reciprocity in relationships and focus more carefully on the reasons biological parents relinquished them.

Parents need to realize that the child's growing ambivalence about being adopted is normal, not a sign of pathology or poor parenting. The ambivalence indicates grief at the loss of the biological family, relatives such as grandparents and siblings. Also, the ambivalence may reflect self-consciousness at the stigma and loss of status attached to being adopted.

◆

BOX 15-1
HOW CHILDREN EXPLAIN ADOPTION

One couple had five children, all of whom were adopted from different biological parents. Because they moved, the adoptive parents got their information about the biological parents from different agencies that gave varying amounts of detail. When the children asked why their mothers gave them up, the mother did not know what to say. She had information on only two situations and wanted to treat all the children alike. She decided to turn the question back to the children.

"I don't know why your mothers didn't keep you, but maybe each of you can think of some good reasons."

Mrs. Bartlett was taken aback by the offhand way in which the children pondered what was to her a solemn matter. From each child a spontaneous explanation came forth.

"I bet they were killed in an auto accident," said the ten-year-old auto buff.

"Mine had too many babies already," announced the eight-year-old, jealous of her younger brother.

"That's silly. My mother and father just weren't married," retorted the practical thirteen-year-old.

"I don't think they had enough to eat," said the hungry six-year-old.

"Well I know for sure my mother thought I was too ugly to keep," the self-deprecating fifteen-year-old declared.

The rejection of her children by their birth mother seemed to Mrs. Bartlett a tough and everlasting injury from which her adopted children would forever suffer. She had vowed to cushion them as much as she could from the hurtful consequences. As her children described their trials by rejection, Mrs. Bartlett's solicitude dissolved into amused appreciation as she listened to each of them mirror their own self-absorbed individuality. They seemed less concerned by the rejection than she was by the concept of it.

From Linda Cannon Burgess, *The Art of Adoption* (New York: Norton, 1981), p. 102.

The challenge for adoptive parents during this period is to create a caregiving environment that supports their children's growing curiosity regarding their origins, reinforces a positive view of their heritage, maintains open communication about adoption issues, and supports their children's efforts to "work through" or cope with the grief associated with adoption-related loss.[10]

When children become teenagers, their questions about adoption may focus on identity issues. "What was my biological family like?" "What are my roots in this world?" "Who am I really?" "How am I like my biological parents?" As sexual interest increases in adolescence, children's interest in their own conception and birth may also increase. They fantasize about their biological parents—usually as either inferior or superior beings. Though the fantasies start in earlier childhood, perhaps with ideas of being an abandoned member of royalty, in adolescence the fantasies become more specific and tied to real possibilities—being the product of a rape or an affair with a married man. Adolescent girls may worry that they are going to follow in their biological mother's path and conceive a child who will be put up for adoption. Girls and boys may wonder whether they have inherited an overly sexual nature that they cannot control.

As we can see, the fact of adoption can color all feelings and changes in adolescence. Just as biological parents have to try to understand and listen, send active I-messages, and set limits, adoptive parents must act similarly. It is especially stressful when adolescents lash out on a sensitive area like adoption. Parents' best protection and soundest guide is self-confidence in their own parenting skills and the wisdom to know when to listen and when to set limits. When teenagers carry on too long about the problems of having adoptive parents, such parents have to set limits with firm I-messages of discomfort at what is said. They can always be willing to talk when such statements stop.

As adopted children get older, parents may face the possibility at some point that their children will want to seek out their biological parents. Many do this not because they are unhappy with their adoptive parents, but because they want a greater sense of their genetic history and an understanding of their social roots inherited from the biological parents. They want to understand their biological connections in the world. Adoptive parents cope best when they can sympathize with their children's desires, when they see the search as a reflection of the child's basic need for as complete a sense of identity as possible. Parents have the greatest difficulty coping when they see the search as a reflection on their adequacy as parents. Sometimes parents discourage the search for fear children will learn unpleasant facts. But in many instances actual knowledge, even of an unpleasant sort, is more welcome than the unknown or imagined.

The Psychological Adjustment of Adopted Children

There is evidence that adopted children are overrepresented in samples of psychiatric inpatient and outpatient groups. Although adopted children form 2 percent of the general population, they represent 5 percent of the population of psychiatric outpatients and 10 to 15 percent of inpatients.[11] Between 6 and 9 percent of adopted schoolchildren show psychological, educational, neurological, or perceptual problems. While the risk of these problems is clearly greater for adopted children than others, the vast majority of such children do not suffer these difficulties.

Analysts have suggested several causes for these statistics. First, adoptive parents may tend to refer more quickly for problems because they are sensitized to the possibility of problems and because they are more used to working with social service professionals. They also may find psychological difficulties a greater threat to family unity and want help earlier.[12] Other factors perhaps accounting for increased problems are genetic predispositions of biological parents and biological vulnerability from prenatal and immediate postnatal environments.[13]

When adopted children have psychological problems, they are more at risk for aggressive, oppositional, and defiant behaviors such as lying and stealing.[14] They also have a higher rate of learning disorders, but about the same rate of internalizing problems, such as anxiety.

In nonclinical samples of adopted children, research has found little difference between infants, toddlers, and preschoolers of adoptive and nonadoptive parents.[15] Studies of elementary school children have found some differences. For example, elementary school teachers rate adopted children as less emotionally, socially, and academically mature than their peers. These differences decrease in adolescence.

Age then appears to be a factor in adjustment. The problems of adopted children do not emerge until their awareness of the meaning of adoption and feelings of loss associated with it grow. Some researchers believe that the feelings of loss, not the adoption itself, trigger adjustment problems.[16] Problems of adjustment increase when parents either overemphasize or ignore the meaning of adoption. An "open, nondefensive, 'acknowledgment of differences' approach to adoption issues is more conducive to healthy adjustment among family members"[17] than either insisting on difference or ignoring it. Just as with biological children and their parents, parental satisfactions with adoptive parenthood and warm acceptance of the child as an individual are associated with positive outcome of adoption.

Adoption of Special-Needs Children

With the greater demands for adoption, children who would not have been adopted in the past are currently being adopted. These include children older than four, those with physical or psychological problems, those with developmental disabilities or serious medical conditions, and those in foster care. The rate of adoptive disruptions or return of the child has also risen. This occurs in 10–20 percent of children with special needs.

Despite all the problems, the outcome in these adoptions is generally positive.[18] For example, adoptive parents of developmentally disabled children report less stress in family and child functioning than do biological parents of such children.

Parents of special-needs children must accomplish five tasks: (1) integrate the child into the family, (2) become attached and help the child through the grieving process, (3) develop realistic expectations of the child, (4) deal with behavior problems, and (5) draw on family supports and services.[19]

Parents most likely to adopt special-needs children are those who in the past would not have been approved for adoption—namely, older, single, gay or lesbian, disabled or poorer adults. Research indicates these adoptive parents experience great satisfaction in their roles as parents and have good placement outcomes.[20] In addition, they have no increased risk of disruptions. Children adopted by single parents do as well as those adopted by young couples, even though single parents tend to adopt the more difficult children. We should make such conclusions with caution, however, because no longitudinal studies have been done as yet.

Though no one has studied children adopted by gay and lesbian parents, current studies show that nonadopted children raised with gay and lesbian parents develop as other children and show no special problems (see Chapter 5).[21]

Transracial Adoptions

In the United States in the 1970s, concerns grew about children adopted by parents not of their ethnic background. African Americans and American Indians were most concerned about this issue; thus, such adoptions were discouraged in this country for a time.[22] Currently, agencies encourage adoption within the child's ethnic group but prefer a transracial adoption to no adoption.

Research indicates no overall negative effects of transracial adoptions in this country on adopted children and their families.[23] African-American children adopted by European-American parents report as adolescents and adults that they feel close to their families. They consider race an issue outside the family but not inside it. Parents, too, are pleased with transracial adoptions—84 percent would recommend it to others.[24]

International transracial adoptions, however, are growing because of the unavailability of infants for adoption in the United States. Parents choosing this form of adoption may face particular problems, because children may have suffered from early inadequate care and from culture shock in coming to a country with a different language and strange customs. If they come from war zones, they may also have suffered traumatic experiences. Nevertheless, research indicates that children adjust to their new families and do well.[25]

Adjustment is easier when children have contact with others of their ethnic background. Adoptive parents must make special efforts to see that adopted children from different races and ethnic groups have opportunities to relate to people of the same racial and ethnic background and to become knowledgeable about that group's culture. When possible, parents should live in neighborhoods where people of these ethnic groups also live, so their children will have access to adult models of that culture and to have children of that culture as their friends. Parents can attend churches and attend social events relating to that culture as well.

Parents need also to sensitize themselves to the kind of prejudice their children may meet in situations at school and in the community, so they can help them deal with it. By seeking guidance from friends of that culture, they may find useful solutions for their children.

Open Adoptions

Open adoptions have been increasing. These are adoptions in which birth parents, usually the birth mother, maintain contact with the adopted child. The amount and kind of contact is negotiated between adoptive and birth parents with the clear understanding that the adoptive parents are the legal guardians of the child. The birth parent often plays the role of an aunt or uncle.

Because the child knows the birth parents, there are no secrets or mysteries about them or the adoption.[26] They can know why they were adopted, what their biological roots are, what their biological parents are like.

Birth parents sometimes take an active role in choosing the adoptive parents and maintain an ongoing relationship that varies in closeness. They, too, experience fewer mysteries. They know how the child is growing and developing. They know how the child spends birthdays and holidays, how the child is like them and how not. It is sometimes easier for birth mothers to move on with their lives when they maintain contact with their child. For adoptive parents, the mystery of what the child might find if he or she looks for biological parents is solved.

The limited research on open adoptions suggests that the birth mothers show better adjustment after placement than do birth mothers who do not maintain contact.[27] Adoptive parents also seem to feel better because they are less fearful of losing their children; they seem to have a better understanding of birth parents and can communicate more with the child about adoption. As rated by adoptive parents, children in open adoptions appear to have fewer problems than do other adopted children.

Many states are beginning to set up clearinghouse agencies where adopted children and biological parents who have no knowledge of one another can register if they are interested in contact with the other person; in this way both parties can be sure the other wishes to meet. Currently, groups are run for biological parents and adopted children who meet so they can discuss their feelings and deal with them.

Though the process of parenting usually involves biological parents and child, it need not. Like stepfamilies, adoptive families are a testament to the human capacity to form strong, caring bonds that last a lifetime, even though children are not biologically related.

PREMATURE CHILDREN

Approximately 2–9 percent of children require specialized care in neonatal intensive care units. The majority are born prematurely, weighing less than 5 pounds.[28] The term *premature* covers a wide variety of newborns—from the child born three months early in need of intensive care to the thirty-five-week gestation child who weighs 5 pounds and can go home within a few days. Premature babies are divided into two groups—low birth weight babies, who weigh between 3 pounds, 5 ounces and 5 pounds, 8 ounces, and very low birth weight babies, who weigh less than 3 pounds, 5 ounces. Babies in the first category do very well, with 95 percent surviving and 90 percent showing no scars from their prematurity. Babies in the second category are being successfully treated as well, with the vast majority surviving and 75 percent with no scars from prematurity. Even when problems do arise, they are mild and include such things as nearsightedness and learning disabilities. A minority of these children have serious impairments such as cerebral palsy or mental retardation.[29]

This section is written about parents with very low birth weight babies who require extensive care. It covers the grieving process, the bonding process, and relating to the child when he or she comes home from the hospital.

Most often, the reasons for prematurity are unknown. Certain factors, however, place women at risk for premature delivery: (1) the mother's own prematurity or having already given birth to a premature child; (2) poor medical or nutritional care, (3) the age of the mother (under sixteen or over forty); (4) the weight of the mother prior to pregnancy (under 100 pounds); (5) the mother's having given birth less than one year before the present pregnancy; (6) the mother's having a high-stress career that involved physical labor, standing, or nervous tension; and (7) the mother's cigarette smoking. Robert Creasy of the University of California at San Francisco states that the single most important factor is the mother's own obstetrical history—if she has given birth to one premature child, her risk of a second is about 40 percent.[30]

Infants' need for care depends on how premature they are and whether they experience complications. In general, the smaller the baby, the more problems he or she will encounter.

Transition to Parenthood

Parents with a premature newborn, or "preemie" as these infants are often called, face many problems.[31] They must cope with their own worries about the child's health and survival. They must deal with a host of professionals—nurses, doctors of many kinds, technicians. They must deal with their feelings of guilt, responsibility, loss, and anger. They must find new ways to attach to a child whom they cannot cuddle, rock, and nurse at the onset. They must handle the anxieties they may feel about being able to meet all the needs of this newborn. When they take their baby home, they must deal with uncertainties about his or her future development.

Following the sudden, unexpected birth, the parents' first concern is for the survival of their child. This concern persists or comes and goes as crises occur. As long as the baby's survival is at stake, it is difficult for parents to focus on other issues. They can only wait and support each other.

Once survival seems probable, the parents must come to terms with the fact they have not had the birth process or the child they anticipated. As noted in earlier chapters, during pregnancy parents build images of their baby-to-be and of themselves as parents. Now they must accept that they have not had the healthy, full-term baby they looked forward to. If the baby has a few complications and weighs enough to go home in a few days, this process may be a short one, as the reality has not been too different from that expected. However, if the baby has a very low birth weight and must stay in the hospital for two months undergoing many procedures, then the birth and baby are very different. Parents must become aware of feelings of guilt. They may wonder what they did to cause the prematurity. They may review past events, wondering whether there was too much physical exertion, sexual activity, or emotional stress that may have triggered the labor. The mother may have underlying feelings of inadequacy—everyone else can produce a healthy child but she cannot. Parents may feel angry at the unexpected loss, cheated of what everyone else has experienced. When parents do not deal with their disappointment, they are less active in the care of the infant.[32] They stay aloof. Yet continuing interaction with the child, seeing the child's health stabilize and the child grow, also helps disappointment decrease.

Parents need to talk to each other, discuss their feelings, and accept what each other feels. There is no right or wrong way to feel, and feelings change. Being able to express how one feels and listening carefully to how the other person feels are important skills at this time. Parents need not feel the same way, but knowing that one's partner understands and accepts one's own feelings is a source of support.

Because the preemie may be very sick, in an incubator or a warming bed, hooked up to elaborate equipment with several tubes and wires, parents cannot pick up and hold or cuddle their child. The child may not look like a baby, resembling more the fetus in the womb, with downy hair, transparent skin that quickly changes color, and little fat. So the baby is physically inaccessible and lacks the appealing babyish qualities of a rounded, pink body. As the baby begins to recover, is safe and able to come home, parents begin to believe the baby will be theirs and bond to it.

Robin Henig and Anne Fletcher discuss in detail how parents bond to the preemie.[33] They recommend that parents photograph their child so that if the child has to be transferred to another hospital, they at least have a picture. Parents should visit the intensive care nursery as soon after birth as possible. If the baby is in another hospital, the father may start visiting alone while the mother remains in the hospital. Some fathers feel close to their preemie children because they began the bonding process with the child. Parents should touch their preemie as soon as possible. The extremities are not as sensitive as the trunk, so parents can start by stroking an arm or leg. Even if they can only reach through a window and stroke a little, it is important to do this if the baby accepts the stroking. Research indicates the preemies who are touched 20 minutes a day beyond routine care fare better physically. They gain weight better, have less apnea (breathing stoppages), and score better on tests of development in later years than do preemies who don't receive this attention.

These authors also suggest talking to the child. Combined with touching, talking enables the premature baby to incorporate stimulation from two senses. Because the baby is already familiar with parents' voices from pregnancy, these voices may be soothing as they are associated with pleasant times. When parents are not there, they can leave a tape with their voices singing lullabies or reciting rhymes for the nurse to play occasionally.

Parents are wise to take over as much of the care of their premature newborn as possible and start as soon as the child is out of danger. Doing routine care cements the bond between parent and child and helps parents feel more like parents. Some hospitals have arranged rooming-in for babies and mothers before they go home. When mothers have the opportunity to be completely responsible for care while still being able to ask questions, their skills and self-confidence increase.

Premature infants' motor behavior, visual and auditory behavior, and spontaneous motility all increase with age to a significant degree during the period from thirty-two conceptual weeks to full term.[34] During this period of development, premature babies also express individual differences in their behavior that are stable, just as full-term babies do. Mothers and fathers of preemies show the same sex differences in relating to infants that the parents of full-terms show. Mothers are more active, nurturant caregivers and fathers will engage in play and stimulation when appropriate.[35]

Parenting the Premature Child

When preemies go home from the hospital, they are often less alert, less responsive, and less active than are term babies.[36] Many of their mothers, too, are less active and responsive to babies than are mothers of term babies. When babies have experienced many neonatal complications, however, mothers tend to be more involved in caregiving. They provide more stimulation, hold the child more, direct the child's attention more.

Over time, preterm babies come to resemble term babies in their development, but mothers of preterm babies may use different strategies to achieve these ends. For example, they may hold children more to encourage mutual gaze and responsiveness. Research shows they treat their babies in response to their needs. At twelve to eighteen months, preterm babies have equally secure attachments to parents despite all the early differences in parent-infant interactions.[37]

INTERVIEW
with Anneliese Korner

Anneliese F. Korner is a professor of psychiatry and the behavioral sciences research at Stanford University School of Medicine. She has studied infant development for the last thirty years and in the last seven has collected data and developed a test, the Neurobehavioral Assessment of the Preterm Infant. This test assesses a premature baby's progress in the early weeks of life.

You have done research with infants, particularly premature infants, for many years. What would you say are the important things for parents to do that will be helpful for their premature child?

To hang in there! One of the things that many, many studies have shown, not mine because I do not follow the infants beyond the hospital, is that when preemies go home, they usually are not as rewarding to parents, in the sense that they get easily disorganized with too much stimulation, and they are not as responsive as full-term babies. Particularly if a mother has already had a full-term baby, she will find that the preemie whom she is bringing home, who may have been very sick, may not give her the rewards that a full-term would. Sometimes parents begin to feel rejected, and a vicious cycle is set up. The less the baby responds, the more the mother tries; she overstimulates the child further, and the baby turns away even more. It takes sometimes as much as five to eight months for a baby to become more responsive; by that time many parents have become rather discouraged. It is exactly at that time when they really should be responding to the baby. One can't blame them because they have had this history of trying so hard and not getting anywhere and feeling discouraged. Kathy Barnard, for example, has said this is when parents need help. They are turned off, unrewarded, and the baby really needs them at that age, so parents need encouragement to get reinvolved.

What qualities do you think help parents to cope well with premature children?

Well, one thing that is helpful in the first few months is for parents to understand the behavioral cues of the child. For example, it is better not to feed the child when the baby is in

The fact that preterm infants grow and develop skills is heartening to parents. In most premature children, there are few signs of disabilities in mental development or expressive or receptive language development at age two and just slightly poorer motor skills than those of full-term children.[38] When intervention programs have helped the mothers become sensitive to their babies' needs, there are no cognitive differences between preterm and full-term babies at age four.[39] In one particular study, these children will be followed into school, and it will be important to see whether the intervention program, carried out at birth with the mothers, continues to have an effect. Preterm babies whose mothers did not have such help did not catch up with full-term babies and at age four remained slightly below in overall cognitive level, though they may catch up later.

Looking at preterm infants' cognitive development over time and the supports that facilitate it emphasizes the very powerful role that the mother's attitude has on the baby's growth. Mark Greenberg and Keith Crnic found that the attitudes moth-

deep sleep. It would be better not to interrupt the baby's deep sleep but let him gradually wake up to feed. Respond to what the baby is conveying as much as possible because the baby can in some ways convey his needs. This is true of full-term babies also.

Are many preemies irritable for some period?

That depends. When a baby is irritable and cries, that is actually an achievement, because the younger babies cannot muster the strength to cry. When a baby cries lustily, that's a good sign. But it is true that preemies have been described as more restless and more irritable, and that can test any mother's patience. The important thing to know is what state the baby is in. Before the parents take the baby home, someone needs to explain that and there isn't always someone available. Have you ever seen a baby in REM sleep? They grimace a lot, they open and close their eyes a lot, their eyes dart all over the place. It has happened that, not knowing the state of the baby, people think the baby is convulsing. This is a total misreading. Someone needs to explain the infant's state to parents. Some hospitals have rooms for patients and before they go home, parents learn to take care of the baby for a day or two under the supervision of nurses. That is a wonderful luxury that few hospitals have.

Can a parent spoil a child with a lot of picking up?

Certainly not in the early months. In the early months, the parents are a shield for the baby, and certainly if the baby is very uncomfortable, restless, or is crying, the idea of picking him up also gives him the feeling of being able to have an effect on people. He's not spinning his wheels; he's trying to communicate, and he is successful. One hears less about spoiling babies these days.

One of the most important things for a relationship is to enjoy each other. It is infinitely more important than pushing a child to achieve. In other words, there is so much richness in the parent's responding with joy to what a baby does and in the normal give-and-take that is part of the early relationships that the interchange is a rich source of stimulation and gratification for both participants. A mother is an infinitely complicated stimulus for a baby . Enjoying the child, being reciprocal, just being there, is what it is all about.

ers of full-term babies had about themselves, their babies, and their husbands were only moderately related to their babies' growth; but in the preterm sample, mothers' attitudes were very strongly related to the baby's progress.[40] When mothers in this sample felt that their role was important and that they were doing a good job, when they felt positively about the baby, their husband, and life in general, their babies developed well.

It is important for parents of premature babies to understand their strong and important role and the child's capacity for healthy growth, for our culture seems to hold subtle negative beliefs about preterms. A study of prematurity stereotyping found that labeling a child "premature" brings a host of negative perceptions.[41] When mothers were told an unfamiliar six-month-old baby was premature, they were more likely to rate the child as smaller, less cute, and less likable, even when the child was actually full-term. In brief interactions, they touched the child less and offered a more immature toy for play. What is startling is that the babies' behavior changed with these women, and they became less active. College students watching videos of the interactions could tell immediately whether the child was described as full-term or preterm.

This negative view of premature babies may not affect the parents directly, because they are influenced by their daily contact with the child. Such stereotypes, however, may influence friends and relatives of the parents, who in turn affect the parents. In one study, although mothers of both full-term and preterm infants had equivalent support from relatives and friends, the effect of such support differed in the two groups.[42] Mothers of full-term infants were more sensitive in their caregiving when they had a closely knit support group. Mothers of preterm infants were less sensitive caretakers when surrounded with such a network. Possibly, the distress that relatives and friends feel over the unexpected prematurity is conveyed to mothers frequently and serves to disrupt their mothering. Another study on the support provided to mothers as they make the transition to home care indicates that mothers who do well tend to adopt and nurture an optimistic attitude about the long-term outcome for the child. Professional support that discusses possible difficulties and coping strategies is at times disruptive for these mothers, although such help is useful to women who feel under stress with their infants.[43]

As the child grows and develops in the first year, parents must remember the child's age is not measured from the actual birthday. If the preemie was born on July 7, eight weeks premature, he or she is not the same age as a full-term baby born on that date. Because the last two months of development that would have occurred in the womb took place after birth for the preemie, the child is always about two months behind full-term children born on the same date and two months must always be deducted from the chronological age to get the child's true age. It is important for parents to keep this fact in mind when looking at developmental milestones in the first year. Preemie babies are expected to be slower to sit, crawl, stand, and verbalize, depending on the number of weeks of prematurity. By age two or three, however, these differences are not so important.

Because preemie babies start life with special problems, their parents often become overprotective. Parental overprotectiveness is not unusual in the first several months as the child grows and becomes stronger. If overprotectiveness persists after the first year or exceeds what the pediatrician considers reasonable, however, parents have developed a problem. They may be so fearful, as a result of their initial worries about the child's survival, that they are not permitting the child opportunities for exploration, independence, or contact with children. Overprotectiveness can cover anger, too. All children can be demanding and irritable, and all parents at one time or another have had fleeting feelings of anger at the demands made on them. When they cannot accept this anger, they sometimes cover it with a layer of overprotectiveness to demonstrate how much they love and care for the child.

Because overprotectiveness, as noted, robs the child of opportunities for growth, parents must learn to grit their teeth and let their initially vulnerable babies take a few tumbles and some hurts. Giving children freedom to grow also gives parents free time to spend with each other. Sometimes they may choose to get a baby-sitter and go out. This is important. As we have discussed in Chapter 5, parents must make time to nourish the marital relationship if they are to develop a close, satisfying family life.

Having a preemie baby is stressful. Parents' feelings are intense, and they have much to do. Knowing that most babies grow and develop with few scars from their early entry into the world can be reassuring. Through the difficult experience, parents may gain a greater confidence in their abilities to cope and a special closeness may grow among the family members who have shared the crisis and grown from it.

CHILDREN WHO ARE PHYSICALLY ILL

One of the hardest tasks in life is caring for children when they are physically ill, particularly when the illness is serious. The work itself is not the problem, but rather seeing a child in pain or discomfort and not being able to remove the pain. Fortunately, most parents' experience with such tasks is confined to a broken bone or occasional bouts of flu, colds, and infectious diseases like mumps or chicken pox. A significant number of children, however — 5 to 20 percent, depending on the exact definition — are considered to have a chronic physical illness or handicap that lasts for months or years, involves some decrease in functioning, and may or may not result in an early death. The most common forms of such illnesses in children under eighteen include asthma (2 percent), epilepsy (1 percent), cardiac conditions (0.5 percent), orthopedic illness (0.5 percent), and diabetes mellitus (0.1 percent).[44]

Parents must cope not only with episodes of acute illness but also with the problems that result when a child has a chronic physical problem that affects the daily regimen of all family members as well as the sick person. In this section, I present information about children's conceptions of their bodies and the nature of illness and cure, as such ideas influence response to treatment. Parents may incorrectly assume that children understand much more about their bodies than they do; in fact, patient explanations and repetitions of the causes and factors involved in physical illness are usually required. Then, I describe parenting techniques in the case of acute and chronic conditions.

Children's Conceptions of Their Bodies and Illness

Children's earliest conceptions of themselves are in terms of their physical characteristics — their sex, their eye and hair color. As in other areas of thinking about the world, however, children's understanding of their bodies is initially rudimentary. From about age four to eight, concepts are vague and few in number. Between age eight and ten, there is a leap in the complexity and accuracy of ideas concerning the contents and functioning of the body, and by age eleven to thirteen, conceptions are fairly accurate.

Preschool and early elementary school students refer to parts of the body they see or feel — their eyes, nose, skin, bones.[45] They tend to see the body as a large cavity filled with food, bones, and blood. At early ages, they see all parts of the body as equally important to life, and the loss of any part — for example, a tooth — may be considered a major trauma. As they get a little older, children view as most important those parts they see or feel most directly — their hearts, eyes, legs.

Young children get their ideas about the body from colloquial expressions.[46] For example, nerves make you nervous or mad, or keep you from being a coward. Ideas come, too, from cultural or religious sayings—one child thought humans are made of dirt and return to dirt when they die. Children also get ideas from their physical sensations; they describe bones where they feel them. Finally, they base their ideas about the importance of body parts on the amount of time and attention given to them. For example, one girl thought hair was the most important part of the body.

With increasing age, children's concepts of their body become more accurate and detailed. Still, their notions of how the body works remain rudimentary, even in early adolescence. Though young children understand air is important to life, it is not until about age fifteen that they understand the role lungs play in breathing. One thirteen-year-old thought lungs were in the throat—one was for breathing and one for eating. Early on, children have a clear idea of where the heart is, and 50 percent of four-year-olds know it is essential to life. Though seen as related to circulation, the heart is primarily seen as the organ of feeling and affect. The doctor listens to your heart to be sure you are happy; the heart makes you dream. Sometimes religious thoughts are considered physical explanations—the heart is where God lives. Even young children know the brain is for thinking, but it is not until they are older that they link it with control of other bodily functions like movement. Although eating and elimination are both important aspects of life, children know more about elimination than digestion, perhaps because as a culture we put so much emphasis on cleanliness.[47]

Since it is not until age twelve or thirteen that accurate ideas about the body develop, parents and health professionals must not overestimate children's understanding of their bodies and what is happening to them at times of illness. Parents should explore with children all their ideas about their physical functioning, because truths and half-truths are often joined happily together in their minds.

Just as children's ideas about their bodies develop, so their conceptions of illness expand with development.[48] In the early years, children think of an illness in terms of a single symptom caused by a vague event. They can, however, understand that they can catch a cold from someone else or get a scraped knee from an accident.[49] In these early years, children sometimes describe illness as the result of an immoral act—you are bad and get punished. Parents must be aware of this tendency and seek to reassure their young child, who may wonder frantically what he or she has done to deserve this illness. Young children see cure as an instantaneous process; once the medicine has gone down, the person is well.

As children move into the elementary school years (age seven to ten), they think illness consists of several symptoms that include reference to external parts and some internal organs. Illnesses are caused by germs, dirt, and—still—bad behavior. Direct contact with germs causes illness. The cure comes from surface contact with the curing agent, whether it be ointment, person, or activity. The child feels more in control because illness can be avoided if you stay away from direct contact with the invading agent.

Children age eight to ten see the person's physical condition as playing a role in causing the disease. The external germs invade the body, and the body is receptive to them. External agents are seen as sources of cure, but children believe that in many cases the body heals itself. For example, no one takes medicine for measles, and they go away. Children assume other illnesses follow this same pattern.

In Piaget's stage of formal operations (age twelve or older), children think in more abstract terms. They understand there are more causes of illness—internal organs malfunction, for example. There are as many sources of illness as there are parts of the body that malfunction, and there are many kinds of cures. In the most advanced stage, adolescents view psychological factors as important influences on bodily functioning.

As we have seen, changing conceptions of illness give children a greater sense of control over what is happening to them. In the early years, children may feel especially vulnerable because they believe even distant events like the sun can cause an illness, and there is little they can do about that. As they grow more mature, they realize that external agents must have direct contact with the body and produce some physical change. Attention centers on cures as well as ways to prevent illness by avoiding contact with germs.

As children grow older, their definitions of illness become more objective.[50] At first, they rely on subjective feelings—"I don't feel good." Then they define illness in terms of observable symptoms. Parents have an important role to play in helping younger children understand and integrate the experience of poor health so they do not feel so vulnerable.

Routine Medical and Dental Visits

Because children do not conceive of their bodies or medical procedures the same way adults do, routine events can have special significance. In preparing children for visits to the doctor and dentist, honest answers are most helpful. When children are old enough to have a sense of time, it is wise to start a short time in advance by saying that an appointment has been made for a regular checkup. If the child asks about shots or painful procedures, the parent gives information as honestly as possible. If a parent knows a shot will be given and the child says he or she does not want one because of the pain, a parent can agree that it is painful for a very brief period, but the pain is worth it because the shot prevents illness that might be much worse. A tone of voice that accepts the fear as natural, but the shot as a necessity to be safe against other disease, helps keep the situation calm. When a child learns at the doctor's office that a shot is to be given, Lee Salk recommends that a parent say, "You are going to get an injection, and it is probably going to hurt; if you want to cry, that's all right, because when something hurts, it may make you cry."[51] If the child cries, the parent can respond sympathetically, "Yes, I know, it hurts—that's why you're crying." If the child doesn't cry, a parent can comment on the child's bravery. This technique is useful for any hospital procedure, too.

Behaviorists recommend that parents associate medical visits with pleasurable events. Thus, having routine visits with no illness and only occasional shots helps the child become comfortable in the medical setting. Doctors and dentists often give a reward at the end of the visit—a balloon, a plastic toy—to link pleasure with the visit. Parents can also arrange a special treat after the visit.

Acute Illness

Acute illnesses are time-limited medical problems that may require a few days or up to a few months for recovery. Although severe acute illnesses can lead to chronic problems, usually the child returns to his or her previous level of functioning. In the course of acute illness, four problems besides fear emerge: (1) ensuring that the doctor's orders on medicine and rest at home are followed, (2) filling the time so that children do no become too bored, (3) handling the child's immature behavior, which often crops up in the face of stress, and (4) minimizing the aftereffects of an illness. Hospitalization, which an acute illness may require, is covered in a later section.

When children are ill, accepting the child's feelings, handling his or her fears openly, and being supportive but not indulgent are tactics that prevent temporary problems from becoming long lasting.

Arthur Parmelee believes acute illnesses like colds and stomach or bowel upsets can be beneficial to development because they help children learn the difference between physical and emotional distress and they give opportunities for empathy and caregiving.[52] As the average child under five has between four and nine acute illnesses a year, and the average family of four has about twenty, children experience their own illnesses and witness those of others fairly frequently.

Chronic Physical Illness

The term *chronic illness* refers to many different physical conditions or illnesses. In all conditions, however, individuals must adjust to some long-term symptoms or problems that limit behavior or functioning to some degree and may have more psychiatric problems than those with severe handicaps. The mildly handicapped child can still engage in many, but not quite all, previous activities, and this sense of being "not quite like everyone else but able to be with everybody else" may be more frustrating and irritating than having definite limitations that remove the child from that setting.

Depending on the age of the child, chronic illness may be particularly upsetting. Boys around eight to ten and adolescent girls may have the greatest difficulty in adjusting to physical limitations. At this age, boys are concerned about their physical prowess, their ability to run and compete with other boys. Adolescent girls are concerned with physical attractiveness.

Parents help their children to cope in many ways. To determine what leads to successful coping, Jerome Schulman conducted interviews with children who had a serious illness and with their parents. He summarizes his impressions of important factors as follows:

1. Parents and children who cope well "are living by affirming life." They live one day at a time, take events as they come, and try to get some happiness each day.

2. Parents and children both have developed good self-concepts. They accept themselves as "satisfying human beings" and maintain self-esteem. This quality may not always have been there, but people do develop it in adverse circumstances.

3. Ability to avoid a sense of guilt about the illness enables patients and parents to adjust to the illness. "Few can explain how their feelings of guilt disappeared," but it ceased to be an influence.

4. Religion is important to some families, but not all, and when it is important, it is of nonsectarian, nondogmatic kind.

5. Mutual support between husband and wife results in open acknowledgment and praise of each other's strengths with an absence of blame.

6. Emotional and practical support of relatives and friends provides a network of help for the family.

7. A major feature of the interviews is the openness and honesty that all family members show to each other and to relatives and friends.

8. Parents separate the illness from the child. They believe the sick child should be treated as nearly as possible like a healthy child, even if the child is dying. They have chores within their capacities, go to school, receive discipline like other children.[53]

Going to the Hospital

Occasionally, an acute or chronic illness requires hospitalization. Preparation reduces anxiety, and that reduction helps healing. When hospitalizations are scheduled in advance, children can sometimes tour the ward and meet the nurses ahead of time. This reassures children about the place.

In preparing children for the hospital, parents can use the guidelines researchers have developed to direct adults in time of emergency.[54] They recommend a message in simple words that tell (1) what is happening, (2) why it is happening, and (3) what the person is to do. Incorporating these guidelines, a parent might say, "We are going to the hospital so the doctor can fix your foot (or whatever area is involved). You need this operation because your foot is not growing in the proper way (explain whatever the reason is) and the surgery will correct that. You will be there for a short time, and I shall be with you almost all the time you are there." A parent might want to repeat this statement—often the child cannot take it all in the first time—and then answer any questions. The parent's confidence and calmness will be a large factor in helping the child accept the procedures.

Along with reassurance that everything is expected to go well, the essential ingredient in helping the child face the experience is honesty about what is happening. One need not describe a procedure or the aftereffect in great detail, but if a child asks about pain or bleeding, a parent can say, "That may happen, but there are ways of taking care of it if it does." A child may have many questions, and all should be answered.

Parents' presence and participation in hospital care help reassure the child. Further, parents can help interpret and explain what is happening in the hospital and get feedback from the child about his or her understanding, for, as noted earlier, children think of illness and cure differently from adults. Having parents available to explain devices like intravenous tubes, catheters, and nose tubes helps children cope better. Parents' providing physical care for the child as well as supplying helpful information not only eases the strain of the entire experience but also can increase the child's confidence that his or her parents are there when they are needed.

Illness: A Family Affair

Perhaps the most important issue in a family with a chronically ill child is the emotional tone of the family members as they relate to each other and cope with all that has to be done. While the burden of extra work can strongly influence emotional tone, the work need not determine it. When families recognize that how they relate to each other emotionally is more important than anything else, then they can take steps to have as positive an atmosphere as possible.

Siblings are often forgotten as individuals who bear part of the burden when a child is ill, and a recent study on their adjustment illustrates how important emotional tone is.[55] Children with disabled siblings were compared with children who had healthy siblings in terms of extra work load and psychological well-being. Children with disabled brothers and sisters had more caregiving activities and spent more time doing them. They rated disabled siblings positively, however, and enjoyed their contact with them more than did children with healthy siblings. Girls did tend to feel more angry at disabled siblings at times, and both boys and girls felt they had more negative relationships with their mother.

Children with disabled siblings had more complaints of subjective distress. While their scores generally fell in the normal range on mood tests, they reported more anxiety; girls reported more depression, and boys felt less competent. The number of complaints was related to the mother's negativity, however, not to the amount of caregiving. Mothers perhaps were more short-tempered because of the many responsibilities and had less time for their healthy children. So chronic illness affects each person in subtle ways. In this study there were no ratings with regard to fathers in the family, so their role was not known. We do know that maintaining as optimistic and happy a tone as possible is helpful for everyone. Reaching out for support from other family members and friends often gives the extra caring that helps everyone in the family.

DEPRESSED CHILDREN

In the last fifteen years, mental health professionals have focused on depression in children. It used to be thought that young children could not be depressed. According to this reasoning, their thinking was not mature enough to produce negative self-evaluations and feelings of hopelessness much before early adolescence. Now we are aware that much younger children — five, six, and older — can be depressed and in need of treatment. Because depression is best treated in its early stages and because it can affect so many areas of life, this section describes what depression is, what seem to be the causes, and what parents can do about it. We shall focus first on the early years and then adolescence.

Depression varies along a spectrum. At the one end are depressed moods — feeling down, unhappy over an upsetting event like failing a test or fighting with a friend.[56] The feelings may last a brief or extended time. (We discussed them in the chapters on early and late adolescence.)

At the most serious end of the spectrum is clinical depression. The essential features of depression are depressed mood and loss of interest or pleasure in usual pursuits. The depressed person may feel blue, down in the dumps, hopeless, or helpless in dealing with the mood. Disturbances in sleep, eating, and activity patterns may or may not accompany the depressed mood. Sometimes people awake early in the morning and cannot return to sleep. Their appetite decreases (some may eat compulsively and gain weight). Their energy level drops, and they move more slowly and accomplish less than formerly. Sometimes depression is accompanied by loss of concentration and poor memory, so school performance may drop. Because they feel less interested and withdraw, depressed children may have fewer friends. These are the main markers of depression.[57]

Estimates of clinical depression range from 1 to 4 percent for children and 1 to 15 percent for adolescents.[58] The lifetime prevalence estimate for major depression for adolescents is 15 to 20 percent, a rate comparable to adults, indicating that adult depression may begin in adolescence. Before puberty, boys and girls are equally likely to be depressed; after puberty, girls' rate doubles.

In some cases, depression is a normal response to a loss—death of a parent, divorce of the parents, loss of an important pet, moving to a new location. Children may show signs of depression off and on for months following the event, depending on the severity of the loss. But gradually the depression will lift. Early adolescent years are times of mood changes, and many boys and girls find themselves blue. These moods are temporary and do not involve the global retreat from other people and decline in schoolwork that depression does.

Depression can be seen early in life. Infants and toddlers who lose or are deprived of a maternal caregiving figure become sad, uninterested in things, quiet, and inactive. They may fail to grow and develop if deprived for an extended period, as in a hospital or orphanage. At about the age of four or five, when language and thought are more advanced, a specific diagnosis of depressive disorder can be made. A small number of children have depressed moods that alternate with periods of hypomanic behavior—high energy, overactivity, high productivity, aggressiveness.

In childhood, and to a greater extent in adolescence, depression can be accompanied by angry, rebellious, acting-out behavior that masks the underlying condition. Some children who are serious discipline problems in school and become involved in drugs, alcohol, and risk-taking behavior are depressed. They lack self-esteem and feel helpless about themselves and helpless to change.[59]

Causes

Many factors are thought to cause depressive states, including biological factors. For example, a family history of depression in parents and close relatives indicates greater susceptibility to the disorder.[60]

As reviewed in earlier chapters, children of depressed mothers are at risk for difficulties in several areas:[61] for avoidant or distressed behavior as infants, for out-of-control and dysregulated behavior as toddlers, for self-critical and self-blaming feelings as they become older, and for overly sensitive responses with peers. Though these reactions may be the forerunners of a childhood depression related to biological predisposition, they are certainly related to interactions with depressed mothers.

Life events also contribute to depression. Loss of loved ones through death, divorce, or separations; family stresses that result in neglect, abuse, or rejection of the child; academic pressure on the child to perform in school; and emotional deficits in the family so the child does not learn to identify and express feelings in a healthy way are all possible factors contributing to depression.[62]

Nevertheless, no one kind of circumstance produces depression. Some depressed children come from disorganized families that have experienced multiple stresses.

Some depressed children lack friends and do poorly in school, but other depressed children are highly successful and seem to have many friends and enjoy much success.

Suicide

As a result of any combination of factors, children can become depressed and develop the hopeless feeling that they are confronted with an unresolvable problem that will continue. They blame themselves as incompetent, inadequate, and unworthy in some way.[63]

Prior to puberty, suicide attempts are rare, but after puberty, the rate of suicide attempts skyrockets. An estimated 90,000 adolescents attempt suicide each year, and approximately 6,000 kill themselves.[64] Suicide is the third leading cause of death in teenagers and sometimes ties for second place. More girls than boys attempt suicide, but more boys actually die. Further, 24 percent of high school students report they have thought seriously of suicide, 19 percent made a plan, and about 9 percent attempted suicide.[65]

Susan Harter and her co-workers have isolated the significant factors they believe account for the suicidal ideation seen in some adolescents.[66] They believe when adolescents feel incompetent in areas important to them and to others, as well as feel lack of support from important others like parents and friends, then they will feel hopeless. Hopelessness leads to a "depression" composite consisting of low self-esteem, general hopelessness, and depressed mood. Depression then leads to suicidal ideation.

Harter writes,

> There are powerful implications for *prevention* as well as *intervention*. For example, our findings suggest that intervening at the front end of the model, by influencing self-concept and social support, will have the biggest impact, since it is here that the chain of causal influences appears to begin. Thus, we can intervene to improve self-esteem, by helping the individual to become more competent in areas in which he/she has aspirations, or by aiding the individual to discount the importance of domains in which high levels of success are unlikely. Self-esteem can also be improved by intervening to provide more opportunities for support and approval from significant others. Such interventions should not only enhance the individual's self-esteem, but prevent the more insidious cycles that involve hopelessness, depression, and associated suicidal thoughts and gestures that may serve as the ultimate path of escape.[67]

Many signs can alert parents to the possibility of depression in their child. Depressed mood—feeling sad, hopeless, helpless—is a main indicator, as is loss of pleasure and interest in usual activities. Other signs include disturbance in eating and sleeping, lack of energy, and falling grades because of poor concentration. Talking to children often reveals the extent of their depressed mood, because children can be verbal about their feelings. When parents notice these signs, they should seek qualified professional help.

At the present time, there are no definitive studies on the best form of help for depression.[68] However, family therapies and therapies aimed at helping the child change the negative self-evaluations are useful. Medications are sometimes used as well. Recently, medications have become more effective, but we have few long-term studies of them. If parents are uncertain whether their concerns about their child

427

Children
Who Have
Attention
Deficit/
Hyperactivity
Disorder

are justified, they can always consult a therapist by themselves to determine the severity of the depression and the need to bring the child in.

Once help has been obtained for the child and the family, parents can listen and accept all the child's feelings about being depressed. Many parents, eager to see their children feel better, try to argue the child out of the depression, pointing out all the reasons the child should not be depressed—these are the best years of their lives; children should enjoy them. Trying to argue someone out of depression, however, can make the individual even more depressed. He or she believes the other person is right: "I must be really weird for feeling this way."

Some parents minimize the importance of talk about suicide, saying those who talk about it don't do it, they must want attention. Never consider such talk only an attention getter. Even attention getting can be fatal, as those attempting to get attention sometimes kill themselves by mistake.

In addition to getting professional help, parents can help depressed children in several ways. First, they can help children with negative thinking by encouraging optimistic thinking, as outlined in Chapter 3. Parents can encourage problem solving when difficulties arise and express confidence that children will find acceptable solutions to problems. Programs that help prevent depressive symptoms in at-risk children rely on teaching children to view difficulties as temporary problems they can actively manage. Children's symptoms decrease when they feel competent to handle whatever conflicts or problems arise. In *The Optimistic Child*,[69] Martin Seligman describes how parents can carry out such a program.

Parents can also follow Harter's suggestions to boost the child's self-esteem and enjoyment in life. Arranging pleasurable outings with a parent or the whole family or arranging a special treat can help. Parents need not expect an overwhelmingly positive response, but it is worth carrying through even in the face of protest. I have noted many times that pleasurable activities bring family members closer together. If teenagers are not interested in any special activity, they may well be open to conversation with parents on all manner of things, provided parents are available and forgo advice, criticism, or guidance. Just sitting and listening to the adolescent, reflecting love in their interests in what is said, are positive steps parents can take during treatment.

CHILDREN WHO HAVE ATTENTION DEFICIT/HYPERACTIVITY DISORDER

Children with attention deficit/hyperactivity disorder can show a wide range of behaviors. One group of children is inattentive. They are easily distracted, do not seem to listen or finish tasks, do not concentrate on tasks or stick to play. Another group of children is impulsive. They act before thinking, calling out in class, not waiting turns at activities, needing a lot of supervision to prevent rule breaking and disruptive behavior. Still other children are hyperactive; they are in constant motion, restless, fidgety, overly talkative.

The terms for this group of behaviors have shifted over the years, but in 1994 the American Psychiatric Association termed the syndrome attention deficit/hyperactivity disorder (ADHD) and referred to two parallel symptom lists.[70] One emphasizes inattention, distractibility, and disorganization, and the other emphasizes hyperactivity and impulsivity. A child can have a diagnosis of ADHD, predominantly inattentive type; ADHD, predominantly hyperactive/impulsive type; or ADHD, combined type.

Problems with ADHD begin early in life and are present by age seven. The new diagnostic criteria require that the behaviors must exist for six months, because many children in stressful situations have similar symptoms. The new definition requires that symptoms be pervasive — that is, be present in at least two settings such as home and school — and result in clear impairments in functioning at school, at home, or with friends. It is easy to see that when children have ADHD, they are at risk for having several other problems. Inattentive children find it hard to complete schoolwork and thus fall behind in school. When they are disruptive, noncompliant, and hyperactive, they are at risk for rejection by peers, teachers, and other adults. As a result of the difficulties, ADHD children sometimes develop low self-esteem and depressed mood.

Approximately 5 to 10 percent of children are diagnosed with the problem, with boys being five to nine times more likely than girls to receive such a diagnosis. In a Canadian study, 9 percent of boys and 2 percent of girls were diagnosed with the problem, but the recent definition requiring ADHD in two or more settings would likely decrease that number. The present estimate is that 1 to 7 percent of children might be classified as ADHD by the 1994 definition. Originally, children were thought to outgrow these problems, but recent follow-up studies suggest that many of the children continue to have problems in adolescence, and for some, the behavior continues into adulthood.[71]

Researchers have raised several questions about the diagnosis as it now exists. It is not clear why ADHD behaviors need to be present in two situations for a diagnosis of the disorder, as many children show the behaviors in only one setting, such as school, and still suffer significant impairment. More important, there are subgroups of children with the same diagnosis but different behaviors that have different courses of development and most likely different causes.[72] For example, Table 15-1 shows two subgroups Stephen Hinshaw has described: attention deficit disorder without hyperactivity (ADD/WO) and attention deficit disorder with hyperactivity (ADD/H).

Children with ADD/H come from families in which there is a history of ADHD and problems with rule-breaking behavior. They develop oppositional and aggressive behavior, suffer peer rejection, and are often suspended from school. Because of the aggressiveness and rule breaking, they are at risk for later difficulties. Children with ADD/WO come from families with a history of learning disabilities and internalizing symptoms like anxiety and withdrawal from situations. They are inattentive, daydreamy children who are more likely to be neglected in social situations than rejected. They have a higher than normal rate of learning disabilities. Much less is known about their subsequent development.

Causes

Several factors are identified as possible causes of ADHD — neurological, environmental, genetic, and psychosocial.[73] There is recent evidence for a specific genetic cause for a small number of children. In addition, we know that ADHD runs in families, suggesting a possible genetic contribution.

429

Children
Who Have
Attention
Deficit/
Hyperactivity
Disorder

TABLE 15-1
DIFFERENCES BETWEEN ATTENTION DEFICIT DISORDER WITHOUT
HYPERACTIVITY (ADD/WO) AND ATTENTION DEFICIT DISORDER
WITH HYPERACTIVITY (ADD/H)

Feature	ADD/WO	ADD/H
Family history of psychopathology	Internalizing-spectrum disorders; learning disabilities	Antisocial-spectrum disorders and ADHD
Symptomatology	Distinct pattern of attention problems (sluggish, daydreaming; some evidence for internalizing problems)	Oppositional and aggressive behaviors
Peer problems	Social isolation, peer neglect	Active peer rejection
Academic achievement	Some evidence for higher rates of learning disabilities	Higher rates of school suspension and special education
Neuropsychological deficits	Suggestion of slow automatization, similar to children with learning disabilities.	Mixed evidence for frontal/prefrontal deficits
Course	Few extant data	Risk for antisocial outcomes and negative course; disinhibitory behaviors are predictors
Treatment response	Tend to respond to lower stimulant dosages	Tend to respond to moderate stimulant dosages

Stephen P. Hinshaw, *Attention Deficits and Hyperactivity in Children* (Thousand Oaks, CA: Sage, 1994), p. 72. Copyright © 1994 Sage Publications, Inc. Reprinted with permission.

Other factors may also be involved. For example, there may be some immaturity in neurological maturation of the brain so that these children are slower to develop the structure and brain organization to control certain behaviors. Birth complications may play a role as well. Environmental toxins and neurological damage account for only a very small fraction of cases.

Psychological factors are associated with ADHD also. Recent studies suggest that early caregiving behaviors play a role in increasing or decreasing activity level.[74] The relationship is complicated. Maternal stimulation that increases exploration and competence in less active toddlers decreases exploration in highly active toddlers. When mothers try physically and verbally to direct and guide highly active toddlers, the toddlers resist and become less active and less competent. What is helpful to other children interferes with the behavior of highly active children.

In a longitudinal study of children from birth to age six, Deborah Jacobvitz and L. Alan Sroufe found that when mothers are intrusive with their infants, interacting with them without regard for the babies' needs, and when mothers are overstimulating with their preschoolers, their children are more likely than others to be labeled

ADHD in kindergarten.[75] Jacobvitz and Sroufe speculate that when mothers are intrusive and too stimulating, children experience sudden, unpredictable state changes that are hard for them to learn to regulate. Rather than soothing the child and getting him or her into a regulated state, intrusive mothers overexcite the child, who cannot then learn to self-regulate.

Hyperactive boys' interactions with mothers, with fathers, and with both parents remain intense as they get older.[76] Hyperactive boys offer clear examples of difficult children. During discussions with parents, these boys resist attempts to control their behavior, and they are more negative with their parents, particularly their mothers. Mothers of hyperactive boys, in turn, are seen as more demanding of them. Boys, however, are more expressive and emotionally warmer with their mothers than with their fathers. Boys with average activity levels showed similar patterns of behavior toward their parents, but their behaviors were less extreme.

Psychological changes occur as a result of ADHD too. Parents can become very frustrated with children who are inattentive and noncompliant. When children resist, parents yell and threaten yet use punishment inconsistently. Parents begin to fight with each other, and the family comes to resemble the families of aggressive children described by Gerald Patterson in Chapter 9. When children's behavior changes under medication, parents' behavior changes as well.

Strategies

There are many strategies for dealing with ADHD syndrome. Parents, teachers, and authority figures can modify their behavior and increase the likelihood that children will comply. Reasonable goals, effective rewards, and consistent negative consequences help to promote more attentive, controlled behavior on the child's part. Second, adults can focus on dealing with academic problems that may increase a high activity level in the child. They can establish reasonable and achievable learning goals and reward achievements. As children achieve academic success, inattention and poor performance decrease. When these methods do not bring the problems under control, parents may consider certain medications that help children focus their attention so that distractibility and impulsivity decrease. Different medications are available, but all have side effects. Teachers and parents report significant improvement in attention and ability to concentrate with these medications.[77] Further, when children take them, their social behavior improves, and they are not so disruptive, silly, and inappropriate. In fact, they resemble other children their age in social behavior.[78]

In dealing with overly active children, parents can first take several actions to spend more positive, rewarding time with them. This tactic reverses the vicious cycle put into motion in which the child is noncompliant and parents are frustrated. Parents would begin by spending 15 to 20 minutes per evening playing with the child (see Box 15-2). Parents learn to pay attention when the child is compliant. They also learn to give rewards when the child is not bothering them (see Box 15-3). As a result of these actions, children will receive more positive attention and begin to get a sense of their good qualities.

Second, parents use all the techniques described in Chapter 4 to modify the child's behavior in the direction of greater control. Depending on the age of the

431

Children
Who Have
Attention
Deficit/
Hyperactivity
Disorder

BOX 15-2
SPENDING ENJOYABLE TIME WITH HIGHLY ACTIVE CHILDREN

To reverse the vicious circle that can develop between parents and highly active children, parents are to spend free play time with that child daily in an activity of the child's choice. Choose 15 or 20 minutes in the afternoon or evening and tell the child you want to spend special time with him or her in an activity of the child's choosing. If other children in the family want special time, they can receive 15 or 20 minutes at another time; they are not allowed to participate in this child's time.

1. The child selects what he or she wants; you are not to help with the decision or to criticize it as long as the activity is within the bounds of generally approved activities.
2. In the beginning, say very little about the child's behavior and simply observe what is happening. Then enter into the activity by describing what the child does. "I see you are coloring (drawing, building with blocks, playing with trucks). You are using the red crayon . . ." Pretend you are a narrator describing what is happening.
3. Relax and enjoy the session. Do not ask questions or give suggestions. Do not criticize, label, judge, or make fun of what the child does.
4. Give no orders and make corrections of behavior only if large matters of discipline are involved (breaking items, hitting parent).
5. If the child begins to act up (yells, acts silly), ignore the child and pay attention to another positive event that is occurring—the child's actual production. If the behavior becomes more difficult, leave the room.

Adapted from Russell A. Barkley, *Hyperactive Children* (New York: Guilford Press, 1981), p. 307.

---

child, suggestions for the difficult child in Chapter 8 and the aggressive child in Chapter 9 are appropriate.

Third, parents find ways to build the child's self-esteem. They find areas of strength in the child and explore ways to help him or her get pleasure and satisfaction from them. For example, if the child is very athletic, sports of different kinds may channel the energy. If the child is creative, parents can support an artistic activity like music or writing.

Parents also address other areas of special concern. For example, many ADHD children lack friends. In a recent review article, Barbara Henker and Carol Whalen state that the extent of the interpersonal problems ADHD children experience has become clear only in the last decade.[79] These children are rejected in many social settings because of their disruptive, inappropriate actions. Parents can help children develop the social skills of sharing, turn taking, and cooperative play. Suggestions for the isolated child in Chapters 9 and 10 are useful for ADHD children.

Parents can forget labels and concentrate on all those techniques for dealing directly with the child's disapproved behavior. In the course of doing this, parents can

◆
╔══╗

BOX 15-3
PAYING ATTENTION WHEN YOUR CHILD
IS NOT BEING DEMANDING

There will be many times when you are on the telephone, having visitors, cooking dinner, or driving a car and you cannot pay direct attention to the child. Many children act up at precisely this time—when you are busy—to gain your attention.

When you are engaged in activities and the child is behaving well, stop the activity and go compliment the child. Tell him or her that you really like having the time to do your work without interruption—e.g., "I like it when you play quietly because then I can talk on the phone more easily. Thank you." "It's easier to drive when there is quiet, and I appreciate that."

In the beginning, do this every 5 to 8 minutes, and gradually increase the time between compliments. Eventually the child will go 45 minutes or an hour without disturbing you. Parents may object to interrupting their activity to talk to the child, but remember that if the child were misbehaving, you would also have to stop and talk to him or her.

If you have more than one child, pay attention to the one who is not bothering you and ignore the others.

Adapted from Russell A. Barkley, *Hyperactive Children* (New York: Guilford Press, 1981), p. 321.

╚══╝

become closer to their children and form more rewarding relationships as they work together to solve the problem.

CHILDREN WITH LEARNING DISABILITIES

Sometimes a child may do well in several school subjects but perform far below his overall ability in one or two special areas. Or a child may have so much difficulty with subjects like reading and writing that all school work is affected, even though she seems to understand math or history. When this happens, parents should have the child tested for physical problems, like poor eyesight and poor hearing. If these are ruled out as causes of the child's problems, the parents need to consider the possibility of a learning disability.

In 1989, the National Joint Committee on Learning Disabilities gave the following definition of *learning disabilities:*

Learning disabilities is a general term that refers to a heterogeneous group of disorders manifested by significant difficulties in the acquisition and use of listening, speaking, reading, writing, reasoning or mathematical abilities. These disorders are intrinsic to the individual, presumed to be due to central nervous system dysfunction and may occur across the life span. Problems in self-regulatory behaviors, social perception and social interaction may exist with learning disabilities but do not by themselves constitute a learning disability. Although learning disabilities may occur concomitantly with other handicapping conditions (for example, sensory impairment, mental retardation, serious emotional disturbance) or with extrinsic influences (such as cultural differences, insufficient or inappropriate instruction), they are not the result of those conditions or influences.[80]

Byron Rourke, who has conducted research on children with learning disabilities for over twenty years, emphasizes the importance of identifying reliable subtypes of learning disabled children by means of neuropsychological tests.[81] He believes that problems in central processing can result in vastly different kinds of disabilities and, as a result, different problems in school.

He has identified three basic subtypes of disabilities.[82] First, children with disorders of linguistic functioning find it difficult to read and spell, and their attention to and memory for auditory verbal material is impaired. They have lowered verbal output. The children are usually identified early because they have difficulty reading, and so they get help. Many of these children have no psychological problems, and those that exist are partly related to stress created by others' expectations that they should perform better than they do.

The second group of children have disorders in nonverbal functioning. They read, spell, and express themselves verbally very well. They have great difficulty, however, with visual/spatial/organizational skills. They do poorly in arithmetic and in novel problem-solving situations. They have difficulty with reasoning and organizational skills. Because they read and spell well, they are frequently identified later in their school years and do not get remedial help to deal with their academic problems that often surface later when they have trouble with reading comprehension, science, and math.

Their basic problems with problem solving and reasoning in new situations lead to difficulties in social situations. They do not read nonverbal cues well and so sometimes do not understand what others are communicating. They also find it hard to process a large number of cues in a social situation, so they sometimes feel anxious and withdrawn. The psychological problems children in this group experience may stem from the same neuropsychological deficits in central processing abilities that lead to academic problems.

A third group of children have difficulties with output in all spheres of material. They find it difficult to organize all aspects of behavioral expression—verbal and written. These children often act out in their early school years. They may continue to have these problems or develop additional problems with anxiety and social withdrawal as they get older.

Rourke recommends strongly that parents get information on the child's specific intellectual assets and deficits so a professional can help plan a didactic program to address the deficits. He is particularly concerned about the child with nonverbal learning disabilities because this child is often overlooked and fails to get help that is so necessary to overcome the deficits.

Parents must observe when, where, and how children have difficulties and help children find strategies to deal with them. Parents encourage children to anticipate difficulties so they can make plans for dealing with these problems; parents also encourage them to generalize successful strategies to new situations. In all endeavors, parents seek specific information—about the specific difficulties, about their exact impact on academic work, and about detailed ways to manage them. While many learning disabled children have no psychological problems, some do, and these can be addressed with appropriate psychological help.

I N T E R V I E W
with Carol Whalen

Carol K. Whalen is a professor and chair of the Department of Psychology and Social Behavior at the University of California at Irvine. With Barbara Henker, she is the editor of Hyperactive Children: The Social Ecology of Identification and Treatment.

You have done research on hyperactive children for many years. What do you think are the most important things for parents to do with regard to hyperactive children?

Well, the issue of medication comes up right away, and that is always a big problem for parents. It is hard. Some parents are totally antimedication from the beginning—it is a closed book before it ever got open. I don't think that is a very useful position. On the other hand, we have seen parents who say, "Oh, good! Is that the problem? Medication will solve it." They conscientiously go through a systematic assessment, but sometimes any effort to address other problems, like being behind in school, get lost because we now have the diagnosis and the treatment. Medication should not be the first resort, but not the last either. It should not be ruled out as one of the possibilities.

I would suggest to parents that before they go to the physician for diagnosis they arrange to have the teacher rate the child's behavior at school. Schools usually have such forms, and most teachers are very willing to do this for the child's treatment. The diagnosis used to be based on the physician's tests and observations, but now the value of teachers' ratings in making the diagnosis is more widely recognized. Parents can go to the physician's office prepared with them and be assertive in insisting that they be included as important information.

When the doctors are trying to figure out the effectiveness of medication and the proper dose, it is very helpful to have ratings on the child's behavior before and after the medication. When the ratings are done by the teacher who does not know whether the child is or is not taking the medicine, then you have some objective information on the effectiveness of the pills. It is important to repeat such a procedure about once a year, because sometimes a child is put on medication, which is assessed as helping him, and it might just continue on and on for years. You don't really know whether or not it is continuing to help him or in what ways some things might be better without medication.

If medication is effective, it is important for parents not to attribute all the positive outcome to the medicine. When things are getting better, a parent may be tempted to say, "Oh, your medication is working." It is better to avoid that kind of statement. I like the idea of explaining to the child that medication is like a pair of glasses. It will help you see and learn to read, but it does not do the seeing and reading for you. It is a help. We have seen children who think of the medication as the "spelling" pill or their "good behavior" pill, a magic pill idea. The medication may have a negative effect if the child attributes all the successful outcome to the pill rather than to the things he is learning to do and the competencies he is developing.

Related to this, parents should avoid saying, "I can't stand the way you are acting. Are you sure you took your pill?" Over the weeks and years, the underlying message is, "I'm not counting on you or expecting you to do the right thing." That is telling the child there is an external source of control rather than an internal self-control.

A second thing parents need to consider is what J. McV. Hunt called the problem of the child-environment match. Hyperactive children might be more extreme on this dimension or that dimension, such as having trouble concentrating or being impulsive or highly active. But these are behaviors parents are used to coping with; the problem is the extent, it's being over and over, day to day, setting to setting. Sometimes some environmental changes really do have remarkable effects. In some schools, it may be a matter of changing the classroom environment or changing to a different classroom that is structured in a different way. Just exploring those possibilities, parents can be really creative if they have the notion of finding the right niche or the right match between the child's disposition and the environmental setting. I think that's a basic part of good parenting. There is more of a burden on parents with difficult children to work harder to optimize this match and to be more creative.

Parents must remember another thing. This is a chronic condition, rather than a problem of diagnosing an illness and then taking a pill and getting better. We are really talking about a lifestyle, whether it is temperament or personality. We are talking about a long-term situation that you must adjust to and plan for.

We stress the cognitive-behavioral aspect of managing and guiding the behavior. When hyperactive children learn to control their behavior, they can be more productive and may feel better about themselves. They do not get in trouble as much and also they feel a sense of mastery that they should have, because this is a normal part of childhood but one that they have missed so often.

There are all the other effects of failure in the classroom—school gets to be unpleasant, peers start to make fun of them, and they are chosen last to be on teams. I think the problems they have with peers have been underplayed because people have been so concerned, for good reason, with the school problems. Many of these children are not making it with peers even though they may seem dominant and in charge. These children often do not have friends, except perhaps younger ones, and it may not get better as they mature. Medication itself will not solve these problems.

With parents, there is the whole search for what went wrong. Most parents start out blaming themselves. There is such a need to figure out what caused the problems, and they often conclude that they are at fault—which is rarely the case. Sometimes even the diagnosis of hyperactivity, and certainly the prescription for medication, is a positive event for parents because they think, "Oh, it wasn't my fault. The child was born with it." That can be an adaptive shift or transition as long as the parent does not also begin to feel, "Well, I didn't cause it and so there is nothing I can do about it."

Like all parents, those with hyperactive children have to be careful that they do not try too hard to protect their children from negative experiences or from situations they assume the child cannot handle. When they do, they can really circumscribe their child's learning. It is a matter of fine-tuning what you will encourage and what you will limit, and it is a process that all parents go through to one extent or another.

Causes

We do not know how many children are affected with these problems or what causes them, but several possible causes have been suggested: (1) a genetic component, since learning disabilities tend to run in families and boys are affected most frequently; (2) prenatal, birth, and postnatal factors like prematurity, low birth weight, or poor oxygen supply during labor; (3) general immaturity or developmental lag; and (4) environmental factors like poor nutrition. Learning disabilities are not caused by low intelligence—children at all levels of intellectual ability have learning disabilities. Einstein and Edison were both thought to have learning problems, yet both were geniuses.

Diane McGuinness, a neuropsychologist, believes that teachers and parents use the term too quickly to refer to children who are simply slower to learn reading, writing, and math.[83] She believes that just as there are great individual differences in athletic and artistic abilities, there are great individual differences in the ease with which children master academic skills. Yet the schools make no provision for these individual differences. Children are expected to keep pace with their age mates; if they do not, they are labeled "learning disabled" and sent to special classes. She points out that no one talks about athletic or artistic disabilities; we expect and accept them as normal. So, differences in rates of learning must be accepted as normal.

McGuinness believes sex differences in abilities in part account for some learning disabilities. Boys and girls learn in different ways, and these sex differences in learning predispose them to difficulties in certain areas. From infancy girls are skilled in verbal expression. They rely on verbal communication to learn, whereas boys learn about the world through direct action with objects. Their interaction with the physical world helps them develop the ability to visualize movement in space. When children come to the school experience, girls are more skilled in processing words and reading, and boys are later more skilled in higher mathematics. It is boys who are most frequently identified as having *dyslexia* (difficulty in reading) because they have poorly developed auditory and language skills. Girls do less well in higher math and are thought to have a math phobia.

McGuinness believes schools need to develop innovative programs that group children according to skill level rather than chronological age. Children work to learn the material or blocks of information, then go forward at their own pace. She also believes there are better ways to teach basic subjects like reading and math.

New methods are just beginning to be used. It will be some time before they are available to all children. In the meantime, parents must get help for the disability and the accompanying behavioral problems, such as hyperactivity, poor attention span, and inability to delay actions.

Strategies

Here we focus on how parents can help children cope with the behavioral problems and with parents' psychological reactions that accompany learning disabilities. Parents should consult teachers, educational therapists, or specialists in learning disabilities. Two outstanding books are available for parents—*Learning Disabilities: A Family Affair* by Betty Osman,[84] an educational therapist, and *No Easy Answers: The*

Learning Disabled Child at Home and at School by Sally Smith,[85] an educational psychologist who focuses on educational intervention. She is the founder and director of the Lab School in Washington, D.C.

Osman discusses parents' initial reactions of attempted denial, anger, guilt, and depression. In their disappointment, parents sometimes blame the child, but more often parents blame themselves. They sometimes feel guilty that they did not recognize the problem sooner. Parents need to accept not only their own feelings, but also the feelings and reactions of the child's siblings. Brothers and sisters tend to resent the time and attention that go to the learning disabled child.

After accepting their own mixed feelings, parents must explain to the child as clearly and honestly as possible what the problem is. We all have difficulties that we must learn to manage—a learning disability is one such difficulty. Children often realize, far sooner than their parents, that they have difficulty learning some kinds of material. They may ignore the problem, focusing instead on the things they do well. They may lose books, forget assignments, or tell parents that they have no homework.

Parents can help a learning disabled child in several ways. First, they can show love and attention, regardless of the level of schoolwork. They can value the child's feelings and encourage the expression of the frustration and anger felt at the extra effort required to do the work other children do easily. Anger at parents and teachers for setting firm limits and giving reminders of work is also felt and should be expressed as well.

Second, organizing the environment and establishing regular routines help such children to function more effectively. Box 15-4 contains suggestions for parents who want to structure the environment. Behavioral techniques described in Chapter 8 for the highly active child are also effective.

Third, parents can help by serving as a resource for the child, taking a more active role to show a child how to do a task. Osman says parents may have to show a child how to structure a book report or work a math problem the first time the task is assigned. The next time the child can do it alone. Help with homework must not become a routine, however. Equally important, parents can engage children in many games that will strengthen intellectual skills and help integrate motor and perceptual behavior.

Fourth, disciplinary techniques that anticipate and prevent problems from arising are useful. For example, if a child is easily excited, careful scheduling of events and monitoring of the amount of incoming stimuli, even in the home, can reduce emotional outbursts. If a parent sees a child building up a lot of irritation or frustration at a sibling, separation before a blowup is helpful.

Fifth, parents can help children build social skills. The experience of being a slow learner in one or more areas does little for one's self-esteem or feelings of confidence with peers. This is particularly true during the elementary school years, when it is so important to the child to be liked by everyone else. And so, learning disabled children may become loners. Parents can help by arranging brief get-togethers with other children, for an hour or two. These will give the child valuable experiences that contribute to confidence. Parents also help by encouraging the child to develop a special skill that will bring recognition in the group.

Parents must be careful neither to overindulge nor to overprotect a learning disabled child. If parents feel guilty, they must deal with their own feelings so that they can be truly helpful to the child. Otherwise they may rob the child of the opportunity to develop competence and confidence.

◆

BOX 15-4
ORGANIZING THE ENVIRONMENT FOR
LEARNING DISABLED CHILDREN

1. Hang a bulletin board in each child's room and in a central family area, like the kitchen, so schedules, chores, and reminders for important events can be posted.
2. Get in the habit of posting signs on mirrors, the refrigerator door, and the front door to remind children of special events or chores.
3. Have children leave messages of whereabouts or telephone calls in one place so each family member can check there.
4. Have the key to the house on a heavy string or bright ribbon that is hard to lose, and get a special hook in the child's room for it.
5. Identify all clothing with name tags so children can easily find lost items at school or friends' homes.
6. Write names and addresses on all notebooks and other possessions like eyeglass cases or backpacks in the event they are lost; keep identification in wallet or purse if carried.
7. Have bedroom furnished with plenty of cabinets or shelves for storage; have dividers in drawers to keep clothes separated.
8. Have a specific desk or study area for each child where the child can take books, notebooks, and papers immediately on returning home and where all schoolwork can be done. It reduces the number of places you have to search for papers and books.
9. Try to organize a daily family routine, a regular time for getting up, eating meals, leaving the home, and returning. Such a regular schedule helps to compensate for poor memory.

Adapted from Betty B. Osman, *Learning Disabilities: A Family Affair* (New York: Random House, 1979), p. 59.

CHILDREN WHO ARE POOR

In Chapter 1, I described the high rate of poverty among children in the United States. About one in five children live below the poverty level, and another one in five live in families whose income is not more than twice the poverty level.[86] As poverty among children has become a more stable aspect of U.S. society, researchers have been able to study its effects on children's development. In this section, we examine measures of poverty, who is poor, the effects of poverty on children's development, the pathways by which poverty exerts its influence, and ways to address the problems associated with poverty.

Measures of Poverty

The most common measure of poverty is the official federal index of poverty developed in the 1960s and based on pretax, cash income, and the number of people in the family.[87] The index is determined by the estimated cost of food multiplied by 3, as food was found in surveys to absorb about one-third of the family income. For example, the 1995 poverty threshold for a single person was $7929, and for a family of four (two adults and two children), $15,455.[88]

The National Research Council has strongly recommended revising the index to take account of such factors as geographic variations in costs of living, family benefits of food stamps and medicaid, and how far below the poverty threshold a person falls.[89] Revision is likely, as a result of the Welfare Reform Act of 1996. This law, called the Personal Responsibility and Work Opportunity Reconciliation Act, returns to states the responsibility for dealing with the problems of those who lack adequate income. Each state will have its own definition. At present, most research concerning those in poverty relies on the federal poverty index.

In addition to the poverty index, a measure of duration of poverty yields important information for understanding the effects of poverty.[90] While one-third of all children in the United States will be poor for least one year before they reach age eighteen, two-thirds of those who are poor spend less than five years in poverty. Fifteen percent of poor children, however, are poor for more than ten years of childhood, and these children experience the most severe poverty, because their family cash income is half that required to exceed the poverty index.

A measure of neighborhood poverty is significant as well, because it conveys information on services available to children and families. High-poverty neighborhoods are those with more than 40 percent of residents living in poverty. Such residents are less likely to have good health care, schools, parks, community organizations, and informal social support.[91] Neighborhoods with fewer than 20 percent of residents living in poverty are considered low-poverty neighborhoods.[92]

Who Are the Poor?

Children, particularly the youngest, are the poorest individuals in the United States. In 1960, about 27 percent of children under 18 were poor.[93] That figure dropped to a low of 14 percent in 1969. Then, the rate began to rise slowly, with a sharp increase between 1979 and 1984, resulting in 22 percent of children being poor in 1984. The figure dropped briefly, but has remained at about this level for a decade. In 1995, the rate of poverty for children under 6 was even higher—at 24 percent.

Not only are more children poor, but the disparity between the incomes of those children in families with the lowest and highest incomes has increased.[94] Between 1973 and 1990, the adjusted mean cash income for children in families with the lowest fifth of income dropped 30 percent, while the mean cash income for children in families with the highest fifth of income rose 13 percent. The disparity has increased in the last eight years as more income has become concentrated in the wealthiest families.

Rates of poverty are higher for children in certain ethnic groups.[95] As noted in Chapter 1, in 1994 43 percent of African-American and 41 percent of Hispanic-American children were living in poverty, compared with 16 percent for European-American children. Studies on the persistence of poverty have to be carried out over many years; those reported in the 1980s focused primarily on comparisons between African-American and European-American children. Ninety percent of persistently poor children are African American.

African-American children are also more likely to live in poor neighborhoods. From 1980 to 1990, the percentage of African-American children living in such areas increased from 37 to 45 percent. In contrast, about two-thirds of European-American poor children live in neighborhoods with low poverty rates.

Rates of poverty vary according to family structure, with children in single-parent families more likely to be poor than those in two-parent families.[96] Still, in one study, almost half the years children spent in poverty were when they were living with two parents. While African-American children are more likely to be living in single-parent families and are thus more at risk for poverty, living in two-parent families does not protect these children against higher rates of poverty. In one study, European-American children in two-parent families averaged six months in poverty, while African-American children in two-parent families averaged three years. In another study, European-American children spending their entire childhoods in single-parent families had the same rate of poverty as African-American children in two-parent families.[97]

Many factors influence rates of poverty. Declines in the number of children per family and increases in parental education generally decrease poverty.[98] Vonnie McLoyd points to three factors that push more children into poverty: decreases in the number of skilled jobs that can support families, increases in the number of single-parent families, and reductions in government benefits to families.[99]

Effects of Poverty on Children's and Adolescents' Development

Jeanne Brooks-Gunn and Greg Duncan describe the effects of poverty on various aspects of children's functioning.[100]

Birth Outcomes and Physical Health   Low birth weight (born at less than 2500 grams) and infant mortality are almost twice as common among poor infants as among nonpoor infants. Further, growth stunting (being less than fifth percentile in height for age), often considered a measure of nutritional status, is twice as common in poor children as nonpoor. Lead poisoning, often related to many physical and cognitive impairments, is 3.5 times more common among poor children than among nonpoor. It is not surprising that poor children are less often characterized as having excellent health than are nonpoor children, and more often described as having fair or poor health.

Cognitive Development and School Achievement   Table 15-2 reveals poor children are more likely to experience cognitive delays and learning disabilities than are nonpoor children. The poorer the child, the more the delay. The poorest children, who live below half the poverty level of income, score between 6 and 13 points below poor children who live at 1.5 to 2 times the poverty income level on such measures as IQ, verbal ability, and achievement. These differences appear on children's ability measure as early as age two and persist into the elementary school years. These differences persist even when mothers' age, marital status, education, and ethnicity are controlled.

TABLE 15-2

SELECTED POPULATION-BASED INDICATORS OF WELL-BEING FOR POOR AND NONPOOR CHILDREN IN THE UNITED STATES

Indicator	Percentage of Poor Children (unless noted)	Percentage of Nonpoor Children (unless noted)	Ratio of Poor to Nonpoor Children
Cognitive Outcomes			
Developmental delay (includes both limited and long-term developmental deficits) (0 to 17 years)	5.0	3.8	1.3
Learning disability (defined as having exceptional difficulty in learning to read, write, and do arithmetic) (3 to 17 years)	8.3	6.1	1.4
School Achievement Outcomes (5 to 17 years)			
Grade repetition (reported to have ever repeated a grade)	28.8	14.1	2.0
Ever expelled or suspended	11.9	6.1	2.0
High school dropout (percentage 16- to 24-year-olds who were not in school or did not finish high school in 1994)	21.0	9.6	2.2
Emotional or Behavioral Outcomes (3 to 17 years unless noted)			
Parent reports child has ever had an emotional or behavioral problem that lasted three months or more	16.4	12.7	1.3
Parent reports child ever being treated for an emotional problem or behavioral problem	2.5	4.5	0.6
Parent reports child has experienced one or more of a list of typical child behavioral problems in the last three months (5 to 17 years)	57.4	57.3	1.0
Other			
Female teens who had an out-of-wedlock birth	11.0	3.6	3.1
Economically inactive at age 24 (not employed or in school)	15.9	8.3	1.9
Experienced hunger (food insufficiency) at least once in past year	15.9	1.6	9.9
Reported cases of child abuse and neglect	5.4	0.8	6.8
Violent crimes (experienced by poor families and nonpoor families)	5.4	2.6	2.1
Afraid to go out (percentage of family heads in poor and nonpoor families who report they are afraid to go out in their neighborhood)	19.5	8.7	2.2

Note: This list of child outcomes reflects findings from large, nationally representative surveys that collect data on child outcomes and family income. While most data come from the 1988 National Health Interview Survey Child Health Supplement, data from other nationally representative surveys are included. The rates presented are from simple cross-tabulations. In most cases, the data do not reflect factors that might be important to child outcomes other than poverty status at the time of data collection. The ratios reflect rounding.

Jeanne Brooks-Gunn and Greg J. Duncan, "The Effects of Poverty on Children," *Future of Children* 7 (2): 58–59. Reprinted with permission of the David and Lucille Packard Foundation.

Poor children are twice as likely as nonpoor to repeat a school grade and to drop out of school. After controlling for relevant variables, the effects of low income per se on the school attainment are small unless low income occurred in the first five years.

Duration and timing of poverty influence its effects on children's functioning. Those children who live in poverty thirteen years or longer have significantly lower scores on cognitive measures than those who experience short-term poverty in the year of the study. Poverty in the first five years of life is negatively associated with high school graduation, whereas poverty in the adolescent years is not.

Emotional and Behavioral Development   Poverty is less clearly related to emotional outcomes than to physical and cognitive development. Parents of poor and nonpoor children report the same number of behavioral problems, but nonpoor children are almost twice as likely to get treatment for them (see Table 15-2). Persistent poverty, however, is related to emotional problems such as dependency, anxiety, and feelings of unhappiness. Current poverty is related to such behaviors as hyperactivity and peer problems. These differences are found even when mothers' age, education, and mental status are controlled.

In addition to differences in health and cognitive skills, poor children are more likely to experience hunger, abuse, and neglect. They are more likely to experience violent crimes and to be afraid to go out in their neighborhoods. As teens, they are more likely to bear a child out of wedlock.

Pathways Accounting for the Effects of Poverty

Brooks-Gunn and Duncan identify five ways that poverty may influence children's development—health, home environment, style of parental interactions with children, parents' mental health, and neighborhood characteristics.[101]

Although health status itself is, in part, a consequence of poverty, it can influence subsequent development. Low birth weight is associated with increases in learning disabilities, grade retention, and school dropout; lead poisoning is associated with reduced IQ and reduced scores on cognitive measures.

The home environment of poor families provides less stimulation and fewer opportunities for learning; because they are unsafe, neighborhoods often do not permit exploration or play outside. The HOME scale, a measure of household resources, toys, and reading materials, differentiates the homes of children with lower and higher family incomes. The lack of stimulation available in poor homes appears to account for up to half the effect of poverty on the IQs of five-year-old children.

Harsh parental interactions with children are more characteristic in poor families; poor mothers, for instance, spank children more often than do nonpoor mothers. The increases in children's emotional problems and poor school achievement may be related to such harsh practices. These findings have occurred in smaller studies, and a larger study has found only weak relationships between ineffective parenting and poverty status.

When parents are poor, they are more likely to be irritable and depressed and less able to control the expression of these feelings. Poor control of parents' feelings is directly related to increased conflict with children and indirectly related to difficult relationships. Parents with emotional problems are less stimulating with their children, and they use less effective parenting practices.

Family income affects children's development through area of residence. Poor children are more likely to live in neighborhoods with poor schools and fewer parks, playgrounds, and community activities.

Brooks-Gunn and Duncan refute the argument that the problems of the poor result from parents' genetic endowment or their work ethic. They report that siblings reared in the same family with the same parental attitudes can differ in the age and duration of poverty in their lives and thus serve to control for the effects of parental characteristics on poverty. That sibling differences in income were related to siblings' years of completed schooling suggests that income does matter even when genes and work ethic are controlled.

Ways to Intervene

Two general kinds of programs exist for poor children and their families.[102] First are cash transfer programs that directly give poor families money through programs such as Aid to Families with Dependent Children (AFDC) or Earned Income Tax Credit (EITC), which gives low wage earners a refundable credit against their income tax.

Second are programs that provide services, such as food stamps and subsidized lunches, housing supplements, health care, and early childhood education. Food stamps and AFDC, available to all who have a certain level of income, are termed *entitlement programs*. Other programs, such as Head Start and housing supplements, are available to only a portion of those who are eligible.

It is beyond the scope of this section to review the effectiveness of the variety of programs available. A 1997 issue of *The Future of Children* focuses on the causes and effects of poverty and contains detailed analyses of interventions to deal with the problems. Summarizing the journal's findings, Eugene Lewit, Donna Terman, and Richard Behrman write,

> Contrary to much current rhetoric claiming that public programs for children do not work well, the evidence presented in this journal issue suggests that existing policies do alleviate hardships for a number of families with children and that it is possible to identify specific programs that produce important benefits for children.[103]

Clearly, the United States has markedly reduced poverty among those over 65. In 1960, 35 percent of those over 65 were poor; in 1995, the comparable figure was 11 percent.[104] This low figure has existed for a decade and is half the poverty rate of children. If it is important to provide adequate income and living for those who are fully developed, how much more important is it to provide adequate life experiences for those in the process of development?

CHILDREN WHO ARE GIFTED OR TALENTED

Parents often think how delightful it would be to have talented children. How enjoyable to sit back and see them excel in some activity—what a joy to see the talent unfold and the child express creativity! It is a pleasure to see, but this pleasure is accompanied by hard work of many years' duration, sacrifice on the part of the child and the family, and gradual attainment of outstanding skill. As we shall see, the process is much the same as the process parents use in overcoming special difficulties.

In this section we look at the process of developing world-class abilities in the areas of athletics, artistic activities, and intellectual pursuits. We describe the parenting behaviors that contribute to success. We then look at the parenting behaviors useful in promoting success in general.

A University of Chicago team of researchers studied 120 young men and women who had achieved international levels of performance in their special areas, which included swimming and tennis in the athletic area, piano and sculpture in the artistic area, and neurology and mathematics in the intellectual area.[105] They interviewed the individuals, their parents, and in many cases their teachers and coaches to understand the process by which they earned success. Talent development, the researchers found, requires at least twelve to fifteen years of commitment. It can be divided into three stages—early, middle, and late years—with family and teachers providing essential support. Few of the outstanding individuals are identified as special in the beginning. It is the combination of individual commitment, family support, and outstanding instruction that lead to accomplishment.

In the early years, the parents are influential in introducing the child to the talent area, though they do not select the exact activity. Parents may be athletic, musical, or artistic, but the exact sport, instrument, or medium is the child's choice. Initially, the activity is one of enjoyment and fun and is pursued for pleasure. Parents select an early teacher who primarily works well with children and teaches basic skills. The teacher is easily available in the neighborhood, and the relationship between teacher and child is a comfortable one in which the child gets much positive feedback. Parents monitor progress. If a teacher does not seem to work out, they get another one. Parents also schedule daily practice of about an hour and make sure the child has prepared for lessons. They are supportive and encouraging, often helping solve difficulties though they may not be experts in the field. Most important, parents emphasize the ethic of hard work and doing one's best. They model this trait in their own lives as well as talk about it. Gifted children are quick learners who easily absorb instruction and enjoy success at the activity.

In the middle years, after children have achieved initial success in the area and made good progress with their initial teachers, parents begin to search for more skilled instruction and find an expert or special tutor to teach the child. This person usually lives some distance from the student and has a reputation for developing talent in that area. Children often have to demonstrate sufficient skill to be taken on as a student. These teachers are perfectionists who demand the highest level of performance from the child and expect superior accomplishment. It is unlikely that a child could start with this kind of instruction because of the demand placed on the child. At this time, children are expected to spend 3 to 5 hours a day at the activity, mastering and refining all the techniques.

Parents play an active role in this process. Financial expenses and time commitments increase. There is more driving, not only to lessons, but to competitions as well. The whole family's schedule changes to adapt to the child's training routine, and the child becomes identified as special within the family. Parents' responsibilities for monitoring the child's progress decrease as the teacher takes on this role, but parents do continue to see that practice schedules are maintained.

In the middle years, children make an increasing commitment to the activity. They begin to think of themselves as swimmers or pianists. Motivation becomes internal in that children strive to achieve their best. With the help of their teachers or coaches, they begin to set goals for themselves and to take pleasure in achieving them. They begin to enjoy the competitions and measuring their skills against others'.

In the later years, children make a complete commitment to the activity and plan ways to reach the highest level of achievement in their fields. They work on perfecting the fine points of their skills and going beyond that to fashion their own style in carrying out the activity. At this point, they receive instruction from master teachers who accept only a few students. Gifted students now play a greater role in planning their own career with the advice of the teacher, who often makes contacts in the field at large for them.

Such students commit almost all their waking hours to the activity. Relationships center on the activity, with major support coming from other students with whom they also compete. The parents' main role now is to provide financial resources and emotional support as needed. The student's motivation is completely internal. Public recitals and competitions serve as measures of achievement on the road to outstanding success.

Benjamin Bloom and his co-workers believe it is difficult to identify outstanding achievers early, because what one does and learns at eleven or twelve is so different from what one learns and does ten years later:

> The outstanding young student of mathematics or science (or music, art, tennis, or swimming) is a far cry from becoming an outstanding mathematician, neurologist, pianist, and so forth. And being good as a young student in the field is only in a small part related to the later development. In between is a long process of development requiring enormous motivation, much support from family, the best teachers and role models possible, much time, and a singleness of purpose and dedication that is relatively rare in the United States at present.[106]

Researchers following talented teens from the beginning of their high school careers to the last two years confirm Bloom's findings.[107] Adolescents nominated as highly talented in athletics, art, music, mathematics, or science were given beepers and asked to record what they were doing, what they were thinking about, and how they were feeling at random times of the day and evening. Self-reports of activities, thoughts, and feelings reveal that talented teenagers have complex personality characteristics. They are able both to concentrate heightened attention on their specific interests and to remain open to a broad range of activities and new challenges. Because they enjoy their interests so much in the present, they are highly motivated to pursue them, and they look ahead to attaining future goals.

Cultivating their abilities takes time away from hanging out and socializing with friends. Talented teens are also more cautious about getting involved with opposite-sex peers. Instead, they focus their time on studying and pursuing their interests, and their contacts with peers center on these goal-oriented activities. It is not surprising then that their moods are more serious than those of other teens.

Families are highly supportive and encouraging. Teens spend much time with their families and feel close to them. Parents support teens' goals and relieve them of routine chores so they have more time for their pursuits, and teens use the freedom to develop their abilities. Positive family relationships and a positive emotional atmosphere at home make it unnecessary for teens to worry about parental conflicts or other family difficulties that can drain energy away from the teens' own activities.

Schools unfortunately do not consistently provide the kinds of interactions that stimulate talented students. Talented adolescents need teachers who have passionate interests in their areas and convey the excitement and value of the work, yet at the same time can connect with the individual student, know his or her interests, and be aware of exactly what the student needs to develop further. The relationship between teacher and student is very personal, but they focus on developing specific skills and abilities. Schools emphasize their role of conveying information, so there is less time for the more personal relationship.

Studies of talented and world-class achievers emphasize that if talent goes unrecognized, it is unlikely to develop on its own. Enormous long-term effort on the part of many people goes into its gradual development. Identifying gifted minority students may require going beyond the usual test measures of intellectual ability.[108] Because minority youth often have limited access to the kinds of experiences leading to success on standardized tests, other means are sometimes used. A combination of test scores, teacher nominations, and interviews with students has led to identification of gifted minority students who go on to achieve in high school and college. Peer nominations of creativity have also been successful in identifying gifted minority students. A novel approach has involved community nominations of giftedness, based on the child's performance in community activities. Longitudinal follow-up has not yet evaluated this form of identification.

Special considerations may be necessary to promote giftedness in minority groups as their families may not have the finances and time to give to students though they may be very supportive of them. Schools and communities have to step in and serve as sponsors for these students.

The study of gifted individuals yields principles that apply to developing talent at any level. Parents and early teachers respond to the child's interest in an area and teachers give basic instruction. Children receive much support and external rewards of praise in the beginning. As children continue, though, they become more internally motivated, more interested in developing their talent to the highest degree, competing with others, learning techniques of their discipline and then going beyond them. Finally, they impose their own style, plan their own career advances, and receive support and inspiration from others in their field.

Parents are early models of interest and enjoyment in a general field as well as models of hard work and achievement. In daily life, interacting with children, parents can be on the alert for special interests and skills and can encourage children to engage in these activities.

Parental Support

We have noted in earlier chapters what parents can do to provide optimal development of intellectual and other abilities. In infancy and toddler years, children's cognitive growth flourishes when parents are responsive, affectionate, and interested in the children but not restrictive of them. When the home is organized and there are regular routines along with opportunities for variety in play, intellectual growth is enhanced.[109] When parents are encouraging and give children a sense that they can accomplish tasks, children are more willing to try and more likely to meet with success.

When children are young and primarily under parents' influence, parents have greater control of what opportunities their children have for learning and success. Special abilities can be encouraged and developed at the child's own rate. When children move into the school system, however, parents may have to become active advocates to ensure that their children get the best educational experience for them. Just as parents of children with special disabilities must push for special classes or arrangements that meet their children's needs, so must parents of children with special gifts. The school system is not necessarily organized to meet the needs of a gifted child. So, for example, if a child reads well before entering kindergarten, consultation with the school can provide a plan for meeting this child's needs for academic stimulation. He or she may go to the first grade for reading or may be put into a combination kindergarten–first-grade class where he or she can easily join first-graders for certain subjects. Specific arrangements must be made for each child, because public schools usually have no classes for gifted and talented children before third grade.

Providing a broad array of activities in the early elementary school years enables children to find those interests and pursuits of greatest enjoyment to them. Parents can then seek out further activities in that area of special interest. Initially, parental support and encouragement are important; as children grow, their own motivation enables them to plan further development.

Parents not only help by providing activities of possible interest, but they also provide structure and discipline as children wish to learn more. They show children how to set up practice times and stick to them, how to seek out more information, how to solve problems as they arise. They model what they want their children to do in terms of striving for achievement. As parents do all these things, they provide the nurturing soil for all gifts to grow to mature expression.

Bloom and his co-workers emphasize the positive features of talent development. They believe all individuals have within them the potential for talented performance in some area and that some combination of home, school, and community enables individuals to manifest their talent. They wish to identify that combination of circumstances that promote talent so potential does not go undeveloped. Their study subjects report few regrets about pursuing excellence. Individuals realized they gave up certain activities to pursue achievement and endured a great deal of frustration, but their interest in the field and their enjoyment of the activity outweighed negative features.

Many parents would question the wisdom of pushing children to make such demands on themselves. All know of some outstanding performer who sacrificed happiness and emotional well-being to achieve, and parents are reluctant to encourage their children to strive for outstanding levels of achievement. Certainly many creative, intelligent, gifted people enjoy the challenge of learning and are happy. If children seek out such activities and pursue them when opportunities are offered, parents can offer support. Parents, teachers, and coaches need not encourage children to go beyond certain limits in the pursuit of excellence. If children persistently and consistently voice doubts about what they are doing, if they push themselves with little joy in the activity, then parents and coaches may suggest a rest, a change in activities, and/or an opportunity for counseling if temporary discouragement becomes depression.

COMMON THREADS

In this chapter, we have looked at children with special needs. Certain adaptive parenting behaviors are common to all special situations; indeed, these parenting behaviors are those already described as helpful to children in general. Parents' underlying positive regard for the child—seeing the child as important, competent, and special in his or her own way—is an essential ingredient in dealing with special needs. Though children may have difficulty in a certain area—a learning difficulty or overactivity—they are still competent in many ways, and the competence must be emphasized so that the disability remains in proper perspective. The positive emotional tie between parent and child remains stable.

In dealing with difficulties or gifts, structured, organized routines and periods of practice help. Parents provide these and monitor children's adherence to them. Parents also become advocates for their child, relating to professionals and other adults such as teachers in the larger community to obtain the best possible care, the best possible education, or the most appropriate instruction, for the child. The focus is always on providing for the child's particular strengths or traits needing improvement in a cooperative venture in which parents and other adults work together to foster growth.

So we can see that just as parenting under usual circumstances involves maintaining positive emotional ties and providing structure and organization, so these two parenting tasks matter to children with special needs. Under usual circumstances, getting support from the larger community network and working with other adults is useful; with children who have special needs, it is essential. These needs force parents to relate more closely to other professionals and institutions in getting help for their children. As they do this, parents often form support groups of their own to address the problems of their children. These groups serve important functions. Parents who have been through similar difficult experiences understand each other and can offer support and advice in ways that are invaluable and impossible for professionals to duplicate. Cooperative ventures in meeting children's needs provide feelings of great satisfaction on everyone's part.

MAIN POINTS

Children with special needs include

- premature children, who represent approximately 10 percent of new births
- adopted children, who number about five million, half of whom are under eighteen
- children with chronic illness, who number between 5 and 20 percent of children, depending on the exact definition
- depressed children, whose exact number are unknown, but 400,000 teenagers attempt suicide each year
- hyperactive children, who number between 1 and 7 percent of children, with far more boys than girls diagnosed as having ADHD
- learning disabled children, whose exact numbers are not known
- talented and gifted children, whose exact numbers are not known

Premature babies

- fall into two groups — low birth weight babies (between 3 pounds, 5 ounces and 5 pounds, 8 ounces) and very low birth weight babies (under 3 pounds, 5 ounces)
- in most cases have a good outlook for long-term development

Parents of premature babies face several problems:

- dealing with their own anxieties about the baby's immediate and long-term future
- dealing with doctors, nurses, other hospital personnel
- learning to care for the child, who may need more than the usual amount of care
- dealing with negative stereotyping and attitudes of close friends and family

Preemies' emotional reactivity involves

- greater irritability
- being quicker to become overstimulated by parents
- being less interactive with parents

With adopted children, the transition to parenting includes

- realizing that the infant can arrive with a history — previous placement in a foster home or in an institution in another country, special physical problems
- little advance notice of the baby's arrival
- recognizing that one may not have usual supports given to new parents of biological children — parties, help, leave from work

Adoptive parents are usually advised that

- they should tell the child about adoption by age five
- explanations about adoption will have to be given several times, and child's questions may change with age
- parents' active listening helps children express their feelings about adoption so parents can give help
- adopted children are more likely to have adjustment problems in school years, but the majority of adopted children do not have such problems
- adopted children of different ethnic and racial backgrounds need opportunities to relate to people of the same background and to become knowledgeable about that group's culture

Open adoptions

- remove many of the mysteries for children and birth parents
- may have the drawback of keeping everyone's feelings about the adoption heightened

Children's conceptions of illness

- initially are of a single symptom caused by a vague event such as being bad
- change with age, giving children a greater sense of control as they grow older
- are influenced by subjective feelings of distress—one is sick because one doesn't feel good

Acute illness

- is difficult for children to understand, so they require repeated explanations
- decreases a child's level of functioning
- increases a child's desire for attention, affection, and entertainment
- can help children learn differences between physical and psychological distress
- of other family members gives children an opportunity to be empathic caregivers

Children with chronic physical illness cope best when they

- have a positive self-concept
- live in an atmosphere of honesty and openness with the support of parents and relatives
- are allowed to live as much like healthy children as possible

Children who are depressed suffer

- feelings of self-criticism and self-blame
- loss of interest in pleasures and usual activities
- feelings of helplessness and hopelessness

Suicide

- results in 6,000 adolescent deaths per year
- is the third leading cause of death among teenagers and sometimes ties for second place
- is attempted more frequently by girls and completed more frequently by boys

When children are depressed, parents' tasks are

- to get professional help for the child
- to cooperate with the recommendations of professionals and, if not satisfied with them, seek further professional advice
- to act to boost the child's self-esteem
- to increase, where possible, enjoyable activities for the child
- to help the child see difficulties as temporary and manageable

Children with ADHD have some of the following characteristics:

- are easily distracted
- act before they think

- need a lot of supervision
- have difficulty organizing activities or tasks
- seem to need to be the center of others' attention
- often have poor grades because of inattention
- are sometimes disliked by peers and teachers, because such children do not follow rules or wait turns
- have low self-esteem and are sometimes depressed

Help for children with ADHD consists of

- cognitive/behavioral methods of behavior control, which should be tried first
- medication when behavioral controls are not sufficient
- building their social skills
- activities to increase their self-esteem

Children with learning disabilities

- may perform below overall ability in one or two areas
- may have deficits in basic learning skills, such as reading, that affect all work
- may have trouble in an area because of individual differences in ability, not because of a special problem

Parents help children with learning disabilities by

- accepting and loving the child regardless of ability level
- using disciplinary techniques that anticipate and prevent problems
- helping children build social skills
- helping children put their disability in perspective

Poor Children

- are more likely to have birth complications, cognitive delays, and learning disabilities than nonpoor children
- are more likely to experience neglect and abuse
- lack income that affects development through health care, home environment, and neighborhood qualities
- benefit from government programs

The three stages of talent development are

- the early stage of introducing the child to the activity, having the child enjoy the activity, and teaching basic skills
- the middle stage of getting more-skilled instruction for child and establishing intense practice routine and involvement in task
- the later stage, when child makes a complete commitment to the activity and can give her or his own imprint or style to the activity

Common threads to all these areas include

- parents' positive regard, acceptance, and support of the child's individuality
- establishing organized structure and routine in daily life so the child can most easily learn and practice
- working with professionals in the community to get the best help for the child

EXERCISES

1. Divide into small groups and discuss questions concerning depressed teenagers. How can parents and friends help depressed teenagers? Are there sex differences in the ways depression is expressed so that depressed girls tend to feel self-critical, self-blaming, and low in self-esteem while depressed boys feel angry, are impulsive, and lack self control? Each subgroup can come up with suggestions for parents and friends as ways to help. How much overlap is there from group to group?

2. Break into small groups and discuss how you would feel if you had some chronic condition like diabetes, severe asthma, or allergies that limited your activities and imposed extra burdens of care on you. How could parents help children cope most effectively with such problems?

3. Break into small groups and discuss how you think having outstanding talent would change your life. Has it? Would you like all these changes? What are the costs as well as the benefits of such achievement?

4. Visit the pediatric section of a hospital and write a summary of your impressions of the children there, how they are spending their time, who is with them, and how they seem to be managing. Interview nurses about what seems to help children cope most effectively.

5. Visit a learning resource class at an elementary school and summarize your impressions of how the children seem to feel about being there and what programs are available to them.

ADDITIONAL READINGS

Bloom, Benjamin S., ed. *Developing Talent in Young People.* New York: Ballantine, 1985.

Jason, Janine, and Van Der Meer, Antonia. *Parenting Your Premature Baby.* New York: Holt, 1989.

Seligman, Martin E. P. *The Optimistic Child.* New York: Houghton Mifflin, 1995.

Smith, Sally L. N. *No Easy Answers: The Learning Disabled Child at Home and at School.* Rev. ed. New York: Bantam, 1995.

Taylor, John F. *Helping Your Hyperactive/ADD Child.* Rev. ed. Rocklin, CA: Prima, 1990.

SUPPORTS FOR PARENTS AND CHILDREN

C H A P T E R   16

Supports for parents and children make parenting easier and more effective. What support is available for parents in the United States? What family rituals and traditions help foster the child's sense of belonging? What individuals within and outside the extended family contribute to a child's development and a parent's sense of well-being? What community resources are currently available and what kinds of programs are proposed to help children develop and to assist parents with their task?

In looking at different aspects of parenting—understanding children's needs, forming relationships with them, setting limits, responding to problem behaviors, stimulating positive growth—we have focused on what parents can do to accomplish these formidable tasks. The parent-child relationship is nested in a social context that can hinder or help parents as they strive to achieve their child-rearing goals. Urie Bronfenbrenner's ecological model of development emphasizes the many ways the environment affects family life, and he suggests the kinds of supports most useful to families.[1] In Chapter 1, I described the mesosystem as the level at which parents interact with other adults who also care for children—teachers, school authorities, day care givers, coaches. Ongoing exchange of information, mutual accommodation, and respect among all caregivers provide support for parents and children. At the exosystemic level, parents' work can establish patterns of behavior that enable parents to be more effective. At the macrosystemic level, society can establish public policies and programs that support not only parents and children but all caregivers, teachers, and institutions that foster children's growth. In this chapter, we examine all three types of supports.

SOCIAL SUPPORTS

Social supports are those people, activities, organizations, and environmental resources that provide emotional, instrumental, and informational benefits to children and parents. *Emotional benefits* include feeling cared for, valued, encouraged, understood, and validated as a person. *Instrumental benefits* include help with certain tasks

453

454

like housework and specific aid like money or child care. *Informational benefits* include advice about child care, referral to resources, and specific guidance about tasks.[2]

Children and adults have different roles and activities in life; nevertheless, the same general categories of support are useful to both. Supports are divided into those within the family and those outside the family. Further, we can talk about *people* who are supports (relatives, nonrelatives like neighbors and friends), *activities* that are supports (hobbies, recreations), and *organizations* (work, churches, government). Finally, we talk about the *environment,* a composite of people, activities, and organizations that are supportive, such as neighborhoods.

What will be most supportive to individuals may vary with the age and the stage of life experience. For example, as we shall see, activities with adult relatives are most supportive to young children, but adult nonrelatives may be most supportive to adolescents as they move away from the family. Single mothers who work may get the most support from nonrelatives in the workplace; nonemployed single mothers may get the most support from relatives.[3]

We like to think that *all* parents and children have equal access to social supports and that only personal initiative and effort are required to get support. Yet, research suggests that this is not so. There are constraints on access to social supports. People who have education, employment, income, and congenial neighborhoods receive more supports than those who do not.[4] Approximately 40–50 percent of nonrelative support is affected by these variables. More than any other variable, education determines the number of social contacts a person has and the depth and breadth of the social support network. Education appears to increase confidence and skills in social interaction as well as to enhance opportunities for meeting new people.[5] Income provides money for activities and for a stable lifestyle in a safe neighborhood. When people live in lower socioeconomic areas that are not safe, they socialize with neighbors less often. Thus, schooling, income, and neighborhood are interacting factors that influence the amount and kind of support people get.

Though these social constraints exist, people are "biologically wired" for social relationships and seek others out.[6] But the development of their social networks is influenced by cultural, ethnic, socioeconomic, and gender-related factors.[7] Middle-class families have larger social networks than do working-class families, primarily because the former include many nonfamily members with whom they engage in many social and leisure activities.[8] Working-class families' social networks are smaller, more family oriented, and centered on activities that are practical and child related.

Regardless of culture or class, two-parent families have larger social networks than do single-parent families.[9] Married mothers have slightly larger networks than do married fathers, and both groups have larger networks than do single mothers, primarily because married parents are involved with more relatives. It is not known whether this is due to a single mother's having less access to a spouse's relatives or less time in which to engage in activities with relatives. Though single mothers have fewer people in their networks, they rely more heavily on those they consider to form their primary networks. Through community programs, single mothers can be encouraged to enlarge their support networks.

A comparison of the social networks of ethnic and nonethnic whites and African-American mothers in two-parent and single-parent families revealed that ethnic white women have larger family and friend networks than do nonethnic white or

African-American mothers.[10] There are few differences between nonethnic white and African-American mothers except that the latter are less likely to have friends outside the neighborhood.

Regardless of number, supportive social ties operate generally to improve children's social-emotional functioning[11] and their academic work,[12] and to increase parents' self-confidence and well-being and to enhance their perceptions of their children.[13] Next, we examine in more detail the different kinds of supports available.

SUPPORTS WITHIN THE FAMILY

The family environment is the most immediate source of support for both children and parents. This support comes from people within the family and from family rituals.

Supportive Family Members

Potential support within the family comes from siblings, grandparents, and other relatives.

Siblings　Positive relationships can develop between siblings. The older sibling may be a model for the younger one, stimulating more advanced play and verbalization and increasing the younger child's empathy and understanding of others. The younger child gives the older one a chance to be a protective caregiver. So, parents have allies in siblings.

Emmy Werner and Ruth Smith point to the strong role siblings play in helping children overcome the effects of family instability and turmoil.[14] Many of the resilient adults in their study mentioned sibling relationships as an important positive feature of their childhood years. The emotional closeness and shared activities with siblings helped compensate for other difficulties.

Even in well-ordered families, close sibling relationships begun in childhood are maintained and valued in middle and old age even when there is little contact. Sibling relationships appear to gain their power by giving people a sense of intimacy, closeness, and security: "Contact with siblings in late adulthood provides not necessarily deep intimacy, but a sense of belonging, security, attachment to a family."[15]

Grandparents　In U.S. society, many grandparents function as the primary caregivers for children, with all the responsibilities and tasks of parents. Here, however, we shall focus on them as supports to parents. As psychologists turn their attention to important people outside the child's nuclear family, they focus attention on grandparents, who exert influence in direct and indirect ways.[16] They influence grandchildren directly when they serve as caregivers, playmates, and family historians who pass on information that solidifies a sense of generational continuity. They are a direct influence when they act as mentors to their grandchildren and when they negotiate between parent and child. They influence grandchildren indirectly when they provide both psychological and material support to parents, who then have more resources for parenting.

Because minority families are more often extended ones, more information on the role of grandparents in such families is available than for other families. For example, in 1984, 31 percent of African-American children lived in extended families with one or both parents.[17] The extended family often includes one or both grandparents. Grandmothers help families nurture and care for children in a less structured, more spontaneous way than is possible when only two generations are present. The grandparents' role depends on whether one or both parents live in the home. For example, grandmothers are less involved in parenting when both parents are present.[18]

Contacts between grandparents and grandchildren vary depending on the age, health, and proximity of grandparents.[19] Grandparents typically see their grandchildren once or a few times a month. Although a few studies suggest that only a small percentage of grandparents enjoy close, satisfying relationships with their grandchildren, many other studies indicate that young adults generally feel close to grandparents (averaging 4 on a 5-point scale of emotional closeness) and that "the grandchild/grandparent bond continues with surprising strength into adulthood."[20]

Geographic proximity is the most important predictor of the nature of the relationship.[21] When grandparents live close by, contact naturally increases. When grandparents are young and healthy enough to share activities, grandchildren feel close because of the shared fun. But at the same time, when grandparents are older and in less good health, grandchildren feel close because they can help them.

When grandchildren are very young, they look to grandparents as sources of treats and gifts. When grandchildren are in elementary school, they look to grandparents to share fun and activities with them, and in early adolescence, they also share a variety of activities with them. Grandchildren often see grandparents as more patient and understanding than parents, and contemporary grandparents try to live up to this expectation.[22] They seek to be "supportive" to grandchildren—being their advocates, mediators, and sources of support, rather than being intrusive, critical, overprotective, and "old-fashioned." As noted in Chapter 13, a grandparent can become particularly close at times of family change and serve as confidant and advocate for the child who may become lost in the chaos of events.

Other Relatives   Other relatives include aunts, uncles, cousins, and in-laws. Support from these relatives appears especially helpful to parents in their parenting role. Relatives baby-sit, give advice, provide financial help, and offer emotional support. Such support increases parents' positive view of their children and of themselves as parents. As noted, such support is also related to children's improved school performance.[23]

While relatives can be sources of support, they can also add stress when their comments to parents are negative and critical. Still, parents do better with relatives' support.[24] Single mothers appear less likely to have the support of relatives but can increase such support when they feel more confident and reach out for help.[25]

For children, extended family members are like grandparents who convey a sense that the child is special, important, and capable. Joint activities with relatives—such as washing cars or gardening—has predicted better performance in school. Outings with adult male relatives (but not with nonrelative adults) were especially helpful for boys living in single-mother homes.[26]

Family rituals, such as dinners and holiday celebrations, give members feelings
of security.

Family Rituals

Steven Wolin and Linda Bennett describe the positive force of family rituals in
everyday life and in the long-term development of children.[27] They divide rituals
into three categories: (1) *family celebrations* (Thanksgiving, Christmas), (2) *family
traditions* (vacations, birthday activities), and (3) *patterned family interactions* (dinner, bedtime). They believe these rituals provide a sense of rhythm and continuity
to life that increases children's feelings of security and their capacity to communicate with adults.

Rituals provide stability by ensuring predictability in family life — no matter
what else happens, the family eats dinner together, decorates the Christmas tree,
and serves special meals on birthdays. Rituals also provide stability by linking the
present family with the past and the future. Families carry on certain traditions from
grandparents, and children grow up planning to carry out the same activities with
their children.

INTERVIEW
with Steven Wolin

Steven Wolin is a professor of clinical psychiatry at George Washington University and a researcher at the Center for Family Research. He has published several articles on the importance of rituals and, with his wife, the psychologist Sybil Wolin, co-authored The Resilient Self.

I have read about your belief in the importance of rituals in family life and their protective value when families experience chronic problems. How did you get on to the importance of rituals?

I am a psychiatrist, and I have a long-standing interest in research on families. I was studying alcoholism back in 1980, examining interactions in marriages in which one partner was an alcoholic. I was mainly interested in ways family life was destroyed by alcohol and was, at that time, what I now call "a damage model" thinker.

I got a grant from the Institute on Alcohol Abuse and Alcoholism to study the transmission of alcoholism across generations. I decided to use family rituals as the variable for study. I have always been interested in culture as a powerful factor in family life with family members expressing their shared beliefs through their rituals. I learned a lot about rituals from anthropology and hired a young anthropologist, Linda Bennett, who became my coinvestigator. I had the hypothesis that those families whose regular rituals were destroyed by alcohol would have a greater likelihood of transmitting alcoholism to their children.

We compared those families who had two generations of alcoholics (transmitters) with families who only had a parent who was an alcoholic (nontransmitters). The severity of the alcoholic parent was the same in both kinds of families in terms of years of drinking, hospitalizations, etc. We then systematically compared the most important rituals in these two kinds of families. We looked at holiday celebrations, traditions (like family vacations or visits to extended family members), and routines (like dinnertime rituals, greeting rituals, parties). Sure enough, we demonstrated that when alcoholism destroyed the family rituals, then transmission of alcoholism to a child occurred more frequently.

At this point, I became more interested in those families that did *not* transmit alcoholism and, for the first time in my life, asked a strength-based question: "How did you do this thing that succeeded? How did you prevent transmission from occurring?" And families were in fact doing something very deliberate. Nontransmitters were protecting their cherished, nonalcoholic rituals. For example, they made certain that Christmas was protected from the alcohol abuse of a parent. They determined that certain of their routines persisted in the face of trouble, and they kept their healthy holidays alive. Nontransmitter families actually were working to keep their families healthy, in spite of the chronic illness process of the alcoholism.

The second project focused on couples from this type of troubled background. How did they negotiate the construction of rituals of the new generation? Since they come from such troubled families, we know that many of the rituals of the family were destroyed or taken over by the alcohol or substance abuse. How do they decide what is the family of heritage in the new generation?

We selected a group of sixty-eight couples, all of whom had one alcoholic parent. The couples were around thirty years of age and often had young children themselves. We did extensive interviews regarding the ritual process in the couple as well as the rituals in each of the families they had come from. Coders did not know whether the adult children became alcoholics themselves. In half the couples, alcoholism was transmitted to the second generation, and in half not. Sure enough, once again a clear pattern emerged. When rituals were protected in the family of origin and carefully selected in the present generation, alcoholism was not passed on to the children. Couples used a process we came to call deliberateness — the careful planning and carrying out of plans for ritual maintenance and rejection.

I became more interested in the notion that individuals acted in a resilient way to prevent themselves from repeating the past even if they are at risk. When you look at the children-of-alcoholics literature, it is not all so bleak. Sometimes, people worry a lot and are afraid they are going to repeat the past. In fact, they often do not. Most children of alcoholics do not become alcoholics.

We are now describing resilience in general, and the ways individuals and couples remain strong in the face of an at-risk past situation. We did a third project that looked at little children; we examined families in which there was an alcoholic parent or grandparent in the previous generation and the adult children who may or may not have gotten into trouble. We looked at their children. Those couples who acted most deliberately, who used this careful planning and carrying out of plans, and who were most conscious and aware of what the task was in the new generation, did the best, and their children did the best. They are grandchildren of alcoholics, and they are often doing well. Like Emmy Werner's sample of resilient children, they have mastered the problems of the previous generation.

What helps couples act in a deliberate way?

They practice healthy styles of communication. They are aware of the task in front of them. A lot of couples talk about knowing exactly what to do in the new generation because it is exactly the opposite of what happened when they were kids. Healthy families will have flexibility; they can be chaotic for a while without damaging a child. But the family that is fragmented and has problems really needs healthy rituals.

Would you say the dinner rituals are most important?

We studied dinner and holiday rituals because they are so different. We found dinner rituals disappear first in the alcoholic family. We felt that holiday rituals were the most important because when they went, the family seemed to be in the most trouble. Those families who could not carry out Thanksgiving and Christmas had their identity as a family destroyed by the alcohol. Perhaps mother was so drunk she could not come down for dinner or she lit the tree on fire or there was no money left for gifts. Although holidays are less frequent, they have positive importance and are the more highly valued rituals because everyone in the culture celebrates them. Family traditions like birthdays are more individual; the family defines itself by the way it does the tradition — how much importance it gives to birthdays or vacations.

Our current work is taking kids who are partially resilient and strengthening those clusters of strength in them. We want to focus on their strengths and apply the strengths to the areas that are not so strong. For example, if a child happens to use initiative and becomes a good problem solver, but has poor peer relationships, then the child has to learn to apply those same skills to relationship building that he uses to solve problems.

Similarly, children have to learn to do things differently from their parents. They have to see that what their parents did is not necessarily what they have to do. By recruiting "parent substitutes," children can help themselves have new kinds of relationships so they avoid the past. They will see the various hurdles in front of them as challenges and use initiative to continue to work at their problems.

The drama and excitement of rituals and traditions encourage communication among family members. Family members are more affectionate and more involved with one another at celebrations and holidays. In addition, rituals reduce the gap between parents and children, because everyone engages in the rituals as equals—everyone in the family hits the piñata at a birthday, everyone gets stuffed at Thanksgiving.

Children who grow up in alcoholic families that nevertheless maintain their family celebrations and rituals are less likely to become alcoholics themselves than are children who grow up with an equally alcoholic parent who does not maintain traditions. The rituals serve as protective, positive forces at times of stress, giving children added feelings of security and closeness to others.

SUPPORT OUTSIDE THE FAMILY

Support outside the family includes neighbors, friends, and co-workers, as well as such organizations as churches, community groups, and the government.

People outside the Family

A variety of individuals serve as supports to children and to parents. Often, supportive individuals for children, like teachers, support parents as well, conveying information and guidelines on caring for children. Parents' supports indirectly affect children when they help parents feel better about themselves and encourage a more positive view of the children.

Teachers   Most of us can recall a teacher who played a positive role in our school years. The teacher may have identified a special talent or skill and encouraged its development or directed us to an area of study that proved important or motivated us to achieve our very best.

Systematic research also has identified teachers as major sources of support to both children and parents. Werner and Smith write,

> During adolescence, a caring teacher was an important protective factor for boys and girls who succeeded against the odds. This teacher served not only as an academic instructor but also as a confidant and an important role model with whom a student could identify.[29]

Even teachers of very young children have a lasting positive impact on children. Innovative research documented the long-term impact of an acknowledged effective first-grade teacher.[30] Not only were the achievement scores of her students higher in first and second grades, but their achievement as adults (twenty-five years later) was rated much higher than that of students from other classes involved in the study. Statistical analysis revealed that the teacher's influence was stronger than any other background factor—including father's occupation, family economic situation, and number of children—in predicting the adult status of her students. Pupils described the attention, kindness, and confidence she gave to them. "Her secret of success was summarized by one of her colleagues this way: 'How did she teach? With a lot of love!' "[31]

School organization and atmosphere have a positive impact on children, too. Schools that serve as protective factors against the development of delinquency have structured classrooms, emphasize homework, preparation, and competence, and encourage students to take responsibility for their behavior.[32]

Other Nonrelatives This group includes neighbors, co-workers, and community residents. Parents and children are most likely to reach out to neighbors when neighborhoods are safe. Neighbors can and do provide many of the benefits of relatives for families who have little support from relatives. They baby-sit, give advice, and lend or provide material resources. Mothers who work are especially likely to reach out to co-workers as additional sources of support.

While children get more support from adult relatives, adolescents appear to get support from nonrelatives. Male adolescents who interact with adult nonrelatives generally perform better in school than do other boys.[33]

Parenting Programs outside the Family

Organizations and agencies provide formal and informal support for parents and children. Of special interest here are programs for parents at various stages of the parenting process.

Because family members often are not readily available for advice, parents may seek support from other parents. They form or join parenting groups often organized around a particular theme—parents of infants and toddlers, parents of adolescents, parents of hyperactive children, parents of children with learning disabilities—or continue parent groups begun during pregnancy.

Carolyn Cowan and Philip Cowan found that parenting groups for mothers and fathers, beginning in the last trimester of the pregnancy, provide ongoing support for parents as they create new families.[34] In their study, six groups of four couples each met for six months. Couples discussed the stresses of adjusting to parenthood and found reassurance in learning that others have similar problems. The parents discussed what reduces stress and what produces well-being and closeness between parents. In following the families over a five-year period, the Cowans found that all the couples who were in the parenting groups were still together when the child was three years old, whereas 15 percent of couples who had not been in groups were divorced. When children were five years old, the divorce rate was the same for the two groups of parents.

Impressed that the six-month groups had an effect for three years, the Cowans have begun a new intervention study offering such groups at the time of the child's entrance into elementary school. They hope to increase parents' coping skills and their satisfaction in their marriages.

Organized parenting programs are available to parents as well. These usually last from six to twelve weeks and consists of 2-hour sessions geared toward giving parents new skills and new approaches to parenting. Thomas Gordon has organized Parent Effectiveness Training (P.E.T.) sessions lasting from three to six months. A meta-analysis of twenty-six studies reveals that P.E.T. has a significant effect on parents' knowledge of the course material and a small-to-moderate effect on parenting attitudes and behavior toward children and on children's self-esteem.[35]

A review of twenty-one studies of Rudolf Dreikurs's method (discussed in Chapters 3 and 4) and the STEP (Systematic Training for Effective Parenting) program reveals that parents' attitudes change.[36] They are less strict and less intrusive with children than before; they listen more and encourage children more; they are more supportive and trusting of the child. There is slight evidence that children's behavior improved as well.

Studies of parent behavioral training indicate that such training has its greatest success in decreasing problem behaviors such as bed-wetting, bedtime fears, infant crying, and noncompliant behavior.[37] Parents learn specific management skills. Active modeling and parents' role-playing increase the effects of parents' training.

Gerald Patterson and Carla Narrett point out that the benefits of behavioral training for parents are greatest with young, defiant children and are limited with older, more severely disturbed adolescents.[38] Even when defiant children improve at home, the benefits of the training do not always generalize to the school setting, where children continue to have difficulty. Patterson and Narrett consider children's behavioral change to be the most important marker for parent effectiveness. Parents report overall improvement at home even when the child's specific behavior has not changed.

The parenting courses just described can last from six weeks to several months. A recent study found, however, that even a brief intervention with parents can be useful for both parents and infants.[39] First-time parents attending childbirth classes were routinely assigned to one of two groups. During pregnancy, one group received four sessions of behavioral training in helping their newborn develop healthy sleep patterns. The control group had equal discussion time with instructors but no behavioral training. When infants were six to nine weeks old, investigators collected six measures of sleep patterns over several weeks. Infants of trained parents had longer sleep episodes, fewer night awakenings, and fewer night feedings. Trained parents experienced less difficulty with their babies and felt more competent and confident in managing babies' sleep patterns. In contrast, nontrained parents reported a greater number of hassles in caring for their infants.

In a detailed review, Philip Cowan, Douglas Powell, and Carolyn Cowan categorize parenting programs in terms of whether they focus on the child, the parent, or the parent-child relationship.[40] Parenting programs, however, are often difficult to classify, because they can effect more behaviors than the one in question. For example, teaching parents how to improve the child's behavior includes teaching parents new behaviors that, in turn, can affect the parent-child relationship. Indeed, this seems to have happened in the study just described. Parents who established healthy sleep patterns for infants had fewer hassles with babies and felt more competent in caring for them.

Cowan, Powell, and Cowan point out that interventions can be targeted for families at high risk for problems—such as those with adolescent mothers or aggressive children—and for families at low risk for problems, such as the general population.

These researchers cite several examples of programs designed to help parents manage their responses to normative transitions like becoming parents or to help parents dealing with children's special problems such as aggressiveness or attention deficit-hyperactivity disorder.

Some of these programs include interventions at home, at school, and on the playground. Programs designed to improve the child's behavior have had greater ef-

Providing quality programs for young children strengthens families.

fects when time is devoted to improving parents' abilities to work together. Improving parents' communication and problem-solving skills increase parents' satisfaction with the program and their effectiveness with their children.

As these researchers point out, many of the programs available for families are not well validated. Those with the most evidence to support them have been developed at university and research centers and are not widely available to the public. Further, there remain many unanswered questions about parenting interventions. Is work with parents essential or can changes in children trigger changes in parents? Is it important which parent participates and changes? What are the important ingredients for change?

Further, though millions of children experience cognitive, social, and emotional difficulties, the political forces in the United States are reducing programs for children and parents. Cowan, Power, and Cowan write, "It is clear that many parents need more assistance than is currently available. The question is whether we as a society are willing to devote energy and resources toward the creation of comprehensive programs for families all along the continuum from low risk to high distress."[41] Box 16.1 presents The Parents' Bill of Rights, developed by Sylvia Hewlett and Cornel West to illustrate and promote the many ways in which society can give parents necessary support in rearing children.

Workplace Supports

As noted in Chapter 12, workplaces can ease the pressures of parenting.[42] First, they can make it possible for parents to spend time with their children in the early years of children's lives. Extended parental leave at birth or adoption of a child can help parents bond with the child and provide sensitive caregiving that enhances the child's development. Providing day care at work in the early years of childhood relieves parents' worries about the care children are receiving while they are at work. Flexible work schedules permit parents to be at home during the time children are there. More companies are making these kinds of programmatic changes to help parents coordinate work and family life.

While programs are important to parents, a family-friendly work climate is equally important to workers.[43] When supervisors sympathize with the needs of parents, there is less spillover of work tension to the home. Bronfenbrenner and Peter Neville suggest that companies establish a family resources office or specialist.[44] Such an office or individual would serve as an advocate for parents and children in family-work issues. They would collect information on family services in the community and on child development and parenting concerns. They would provide referrals for services as needed and promote work practices that reduce stress of parents. Studies indicate that when parents feel that their employer is sympathetic to their needs, they are happier, more stable employees as well as better parents.

Governmental Supports

Edward Zigler and Mary Lang emphasize that governmental supports are not available for all U.S. families, as they are in Europe and many parts of the world. All families in Canada, for example, receive a family allowance based on the number of children under eighteen in the family. France provides many services for parents. For example, a young-child allowance begins in the fifth month of pregnancy and lasts for nine months. An additional tax-free allowance is available when a family has subsequent children, provided the mother gets prenatal care and the infant gets regular medical care. Low-income families receive additional aid. France also provides low-cost day care for infants and toddlers. Child care givers are trained and licensed and included in the social security system.[45]

In the United States, one must be sick, handicapped, or poor to qualify for the services available through local, state, and federal agencies. David Hamburg describes the variety of programs available for children and parents in *Today's Children*.[46]

BOX 16-1
A PARENTS' BILL OF RIGHTS*

I. Time for Children

A. Paid Parenting Leave—24 weeks that either parent can use in the child's first six years
B. Family-Friendly Workplaces—tax incentives for companies offering flexible hours and home-based work
C. A Safety Net—income support for poor parents with children under six; teen mothers would live with experienced mothers

II. Economic Security

A. Living Wages—$7.00 per hour minimum wage and subsidies for low-wage workers
B. Job Opportunities—programs that improve job skills
C. Tax Relief—eliminating payroll taxes for parents; extended child care credit
D. Help with Housing—mortgage subsidies; rent vouchers

III. Pro-Family Electoral System

A. Incentives to Vote
B. Parents' Voting in Behalf of Children

IV. Pro-Family Legal Structure

A. Stronger Marriage—tougher standards for marriage and greater obstacles to divorce
B. Support for Fathers—paternity leave; generous visiting for noncustodial parent
C. Adoption Assistance—benefits to people adopting children

V. Supportive External Environment

A. Violence-Free and Drug-Free Neighborhoods
B. Quality Schooling; Extended School Day and Year
C. Child Care and Family Health Coverage
D. Responsible Media
E. Organized Voice—creation of organization to promote parents' interest

VI. Honor and Dignity

A. Index of Parental Well-Being—measure reflecting parents' wages, time for children, affordable housing, and health care
B. National Parents' Day
C. Parent Privileges—education for parent who cares for child; reduced costs for certain family activities

*From Sylvia Ann Hewlett and Cornel West, *The War Against Parents,* Boston: Houghton Mifflin, 1998, pp. 230–258.

Initially, many programs are available in conjunction with the health care system. Some private and public hospitals, for example, offer prenatal care, supplementary nutrition for women and children, and home visits by nurses to demonstrate well-baby care and healthy parenting practices. Nurses can identify high-risk parents who need more services because of either a baby's medical condition or other difficulties in the family.

States provide for single mothers and families who demonstrate financial need. The amounts may vary from state to state, but even in the most generous states, a family receives less than the amount considered adequate to exceed the poverty level.

Several intervention programs have targeted infancy. For example, federally funded Parent Child Development Centers involved the family from the birth of the child to age three. This program (1) provided information for parents on home management and child-rearing techniques; (2) offered preschool education for children; (3) connected families with services for health care, nutrition, and employment; and (4) provided an array of services for low-income families of different ethnic backgrounds. Assessments of children and parents over an eight-year period showed that children in the program were more advanced in intellectual and social behavior and that parents and children were more positive toward each other, more affectionate, and better able to work out problems. This program ended because of lack of funds.

Federal funds support early childhood education for low-income children through the Head Start program. However, because funds are limited, only a small percentage of children eligible for the program can participate. As children approach adolescence, government programs exist for discouraging early pregnancies and increasing school attendance and academic performance.

Summarizing the programs necessary to promote children's healthy growth, David Hamburg writes,

> The approach taken here has been to recommend fostering early interventions that offer support similar to that of the traditional family. The pivotal institutions are schools, churches, community organizations, the media, and the health-care systems. A developmental sequence of interventions starts with prenatal care and goes to preventive pediatric care, parent education, social supports for young families, high-quality child care, preschool education, a constructive transition to elementary school, a reformulated middle school. Beyond that lies the possibility of further growth in high school in the transition to work and to higher education, drawing on the principles elucidated here.[47]

Hamburg believes that coordinated health- and growth-fostering programs might well be cheaper to finance than all the programs geared to problems once they have occurred. For example, universal prenatal care likely would cost less than variable care for compromised babies, who require expensive neonatal care and prolonged programs of compensatory care.

Zigler's comprehensive plan for child care in the country illustrates the kind of coordinated program Hamburg envisions. Zigler's plan could be implemented in modules or as separate programs, depending on the needs and resources of the individual community. Zigler, the first director of the Office of Child Development and the chief of the Children's Bureau from 1970 to 1972, outlines seven basic principles for child care in the United States.[48]

1. *All* children must have access to high-quality child care when needed.

2. The caregiver is the single most important determinant of the quality of the child care — caregivers must have adequate training and supervision so they perceive and attend to the child's needs.

3. Child care must meet the child's needs in all areas of development — health, nutrition, education — so children's physical, social, emotional, and intellectual growth flourishes.

4. Child care should be well integrated with other social systems such as health and education and must involve parents as active participants.

5. Child care programs must offer options to the great variety of children and families in society, and parents should play a role in evaluating different programs.

6. Quality child care requires a permanent commitment of resources to children and families.

7. A child-care system must be responsive to larger social demands as these change — for example, the child-care system must support healthy growth that permits individuals to contribute to society.

Because the school system is a permanent part of the social fabric and schools are dispersed throughout communities, Zigler centers his program in local schools. As a result, communities can be sensitive to local preferences, and parents need not go far to get services. All proposed programs are optional for parents; no one is required to participate.

Zigler proposes that after-school and vacation care for the many unsupervised children ages six to eleven be available at school sites. Parents would pay, on a sliding scale, for the hiring of additional personnel, who would use the school facilities before and after regular school hours. A second proposed program at the school site would provide year-round, all-day care for preschoolers from three to five years of age. This program would promote all aspects of the child's development. Parents again would pay a sliding-scale fee, and local private and public agencies could contribute to its funding.

As Zigler suggests, schools could serve as a central network for neighborhood family day care providers who care for infants and toddlers in that area. Schools would provide caregiver training and supervision and make the providers part of the larger community network. Schools would also serve as a resource and referral system directing parents to needed community services and could be the sites of such services as well. Further, schools would provide a base for outreach services to parents, beginning in the last trimester of pregnancy. Parent education and screening programs would ensure that parents and children get the care they require.

Like Hamburg, Zigler argues that it might be cheaper to provide preventive services than to pay for problems that develop when families do not have the supports they need. He has outlined funding for such services.

Community Programs

Many existing programs serve as examples of what communities can do to provide support to parents and children. Norman Rice, writing as mayor of Seattle, summarizes in Box 16-2 what a city supportive of families and children looks like. Local

---

◆
BOX 16-2
FAMILY-FRIENDLY CITY

What would a family-supportive city look like? Every city can set a vision that is truly family-focused: a city where neighborhoods would feel and be safe, and everyone would have access to open space, dynamic community centers, and a wide array of cultural, artistic, and recreational activities; a place where people could easily use public transportation and could work and play in environments that supported a mix of individual and family needs. The workplace would be flexible and family friendly. People would be able to find housing they could afford, and building and land-use codes would encourage development with families in mind.

In this community, all people would share responsibility for protecting the natural environment, and business involvement in human development would be consistent and supportive. All families would have others who visited and supported them in their efforts to grow and thrive. When family members needed additional help, affordable health care and social services would be readily available.

School and city facilities would be open for community use after school and on weekends. Taking into account the many ways people learn, schools would support the development of every learner. Everyone would have the opportunity to learn skills for entering and returning to the job market. All families would have access to high-quality early childhood development programs, child care, and elder care, as necessary.

In this thriving community, all segments of the population—people of every age, both genders, all levels of ability, and every sexual orientation, race, and cultural background—would participate fully in the decision-making process and would work together to build a caring community.

Norman B. Rice, "Local Initiatives in Support of Families," in *Putting Families First,* ed. Sharon L. Kagan and Bernice Weissbourd (San Francisco: Jossey-Bass, 1994), pp. 324–325. Copyright © 1994 Jossey-Bass Publishers, Inc. Reprinted with permission of the publisher.

---

government serves as the catalyst to build coalitions of government agencies, private organizations, and individuals who live in the neighborhoods where services are provided.[49] These partnerships of government and private resources address issues of the most immediate interest to residents, such as schools, parks, day care services, and programs for adolescents. Where possible, high-quality community programs are supported. When this is not feasible, city government targets specific problems and pilots innovative programs to meet needs.

In a 1993 report, the U.S. Advisory Board on Child Abuse and Neglect proposed a neighborhood-based program to prevent child abuse and neglect.[50] Community programs are especially important in this area, because socially isolated, unstable neighborhoods offering little support to families are at high risk for increased incidence of child abuse and neglect. The board's proposals focus on ways to provide physically safe and socially supportive neighborhoods in which "people care about, watch, and support each other's families."[51]

To strengthen neighborhoods, residents must become involved in positive actions to improve the quality of life in their area.[52] Several principal guidelines are used in organizing services. Comprehensive community services such as medical care, education, and employment become geographically accessible to area residents. Neighborhood-based programs coordinate services that focus on the needs of recipients not providers. One-stop locations, referrals, and follow-up are organized to meet recipients' needs. Neighborhood residents and organizations participate at all levels of decision making and eventually may come to control the services. Many benefits accrue to residents in the course of planning and implementing services, and the neighborhood or community becomes closer and more effective in dealing with problems.

In general, these programs work best when individuals begin with a single issue of concern and then go on to other issues. For example, Irene Johnson, a mother living in a low-cost housing project in Chicago, was concerned about the safety of her children in the project because of gangs, drug dealing, and gambling.[53] With the help of her friends and social workers, Johnson formed the LeClaire Residents Committee and researched ways to manage the housing project more effectively. The group selected resident management, in which tenants form corporations to run the projects. After several years, the Housing Authority agreed to a trial of such management. Tenants took courses to learn how to perform all the services required, and the annual funds for running the project were turned over to residents.

Tenants organized a neighborhood watch, hired a security firm, and met with police to explore ways to decrease violence and crime. Crime dropped 50 percent in the project. Residents began to organize new services like a laundry and convenience store on the premises. As a result, tenants' income and skills level rose, their children enjoyed a safer environment, and their hopes for the future improved.

Roger Weissberg and Mark Greenberg review school and community programs designed (1) to enhance children's competence in all areas of functioning and (2) to prevent the development of problems.[54] Like parenting programs, these can be targeted for low-risk or high-risk groups or for all families. Programs are designed to improve several aspects of functioning—health, school performance, and social and psychological functioning.

Community programs target children from birth through the adolescent years. They include a wide variety of services such as home-visiting programs (see Chapter 6), which involve parents actively, and school-based programs, which work primarily with children and may never involve parents.

These programs are most effective when implemented for several years and include many forms of intervention by a multidisciplinary team. For example, in Baltimore, Johns Hopkins Medical Center worked with the school system to provide a school-based reproductive health service to an inner-city junior high school and senior high school. The university provided a nurse and a social worker to give sex education presentations once each semester; they were also available two and half hours a day in a school health suite, providing individual counseling, reproductive health care, and education.

The staff also trained supervised students to be peer leaders in discussion groups. In the first two years of the program, students' knowledge and use of contraceptives improved: Fewer than 20 percent of girls had unprotected sex, compared with 44 to 49 percent in schools without the program. After 28 months of the program, the pregnancy rate dropped 30 percent, whereas it increased 57 percent in comparison schools. For those in the program three years, the initiation of sexual activity was postponed seven months.

Other programs have targeted several areas of functioning. New Haven school district set up a comprehensive program to decrease high-risk behaviors such as drug use, teen pregnancy, AIDS, delinquency, and school failure. They believed that poor social skills underlay all these behaviors.

Administrators set up a multifaceted program extending from kindergarten through twelfth grade. In the early years, students learned self-monitoring, problem solving, and communication skills. They also learned about taking responsibility for healthy behaviors. As students got older, educational and recreational activities at school and in the community reinforced what they were learning at school. The Extended Day Academy was established; it included after-school clubs, health services, and an adventure club.

Evaluations of the program indicate improvements in students' social skills, with decreases in acting-out behaviors. Students felt safer at school and in the neighborhood and more positive about future prospects. Decreases in adolescent high-risk behaviors were not found after five years in the program; however, one may need such interventions for longer periods to decrease such behavior.

Church Support

In their study of resilient children who overcame the difficulties of growing up in troubled families, Werner and Smith point to the importance of faith:

> A potent protective factor among high-risk individuals who grew into successful adulthood was a faith that life made sense, that the odds could be overcome. This faith was tied to active involvement in church activities, whether Buddhist, Catholic, mainstream Protestant, or fundamentalist.[55]

When parents attend church themselves, it is easy to incorporate the children in that religious life. If parents have no religious affiliation, they may wonder what to do.

One such father of a young child wrote to Joan Beck, author of *Effective Parenting,* to ask for her advice.[56] He could not pretend a belief he did not have in God, but he wanted his daughter to have the freedom to make her own decision as she matured.

Beck suggested that each family must find its own answer. Parents have three options: (1) ignore the whole question, (2) send children for religious instruction without parents' participation, or (3) develop an inquiring attitude about religion that can be shared with children as they grow.

Church attendance is relatively low; it has been increasingly easy to raise a child without religious instruction. Such children, however, may then have many questions that remain unanswered: Who is God? What happens when we die? Will God punish me? As such children see the involvement of grandparents and of other families with religion, and as they encounter religious references in the media, they may feel a void in their own experiences. This void may be intensified if they lack a source of comfort or solace when a painful loss occurs.

Sending a child for religious instruction without parental participation, however, seems hypocritical. The most reasonable alternative for some parents is to develop an individual belief system that they share with children as they grow. Parents can explore different conceptions of God, convey to children what they accept and do not accept in each conception, and discuss the meanings of rituals and symbols and the reasons others may find them important. In investigating the ideas of different churches, parents may discover a group they can join wholeheartedly, rediscover the religion of their parents, or find they want to join a group devoted to social action rather than worship. The process of searching for an agreed-on source of spiritual or secular meaning can enrich the entire family.

In fostering children's faith, parents have a natural ally in children themselves. Robert Coles reviewed his interactions and interviews with children concerning crises in their lives and their moral and political views of life. He concluded that the area he ignored for too many years of his professional life was children's intense engagement in religious concerns—the meaning of life, the purpose of their individual lives, their goodness and/or badness, and their duties and obligations to themselves, to their families, and to others.[57]

Seeking to understand their spiritual lives, Coles interviewed children around the world about their conceptions of God and the meaning of God in their lives. His book *The Spiritual Life of Children* summarizes numerous poignant interviews and conversations with children, individually and in groups. Religious concerns are not dry intellectual matters to many children, but emotionally intense concerns strongly integrated into their personalities and understanding of themselves and life. Coles states,

> I began to realize that psychologically God can take almost any shape for children. He can be a friend or a potential enemy; an admirer or a critic; an ally or an interference; a source of encouragement or a source of anxiety, fear, or even panic. . . . Often, children whose sternly Christian, Jewish, or Moslem parents don't hesitate to threaten them with the most severe of religious strictures (and thus who do likewise with respect to themselves) can construct in their thoughts or dreams a God who is exemplary yet lenient, forgiving, encouraging, capable of confessing a moment's weakness or exhaustion now and then.[58]

Like Werner and Smith, Coles finds that religious beliefs give children a feeling of security that life is predictable and understandable—God knows and understands and controls all. In conversations with God, children experience an emotional closeness—God is "a companion who won't leave."[59] God provides strength and help as needed, though how and when are often difficult questions. With benefits come obligations of moral behavior in interactions with others. Children's conception of God sometimes adds security to life by providing fallible parents with a backup expert who helps them. "God is my parents' parent and mine too,"[60] stated one girl.

Church programs help both parents and children. Many churches offer general parenting classes and classes in teaching values. Churches also provide recreational and family activities that bring pleasure and feelings of belongingness and security to all family members.

A Catholic church leadership project in Harlem illustrates the powerful support church activities can provide for adolescent boys.[61] Several decades ago, the church selected fourteen boys on the basis of academic and personal potential for participation in a two-year program. The boys attended cultural events, listened to speakers, and went on weekend retreats that combined fun and discussion of serious

INTERVIEW
with Andrew Billingsley

Andrew Billingsley is a professor in the Department of Family Studies at the University of Maryland. He is the author of many books, including Black Families in White America, The Evolution of Black Families, *and* Climbing Jacob's Ladder: The Enduring Legacy of African-American Families.

You have talked about the strengths in people's lives, particularly the church, so I wanted to talk to you in more detail about that. What role do you see the church playing in people's lives?

The church is a major community support, particularly in African-American communities. The churches are increasingly developing programs that support and help young people. Not all churches have embraced this mission. In a large-scale study, about a third of all churches were not involved in supportive programs, a third were moderately involved, and a third were actively involved in elaborate programs for people from cradle to the grave.

In Washington, D.C., an enlightened minister, the Reverend Henry C. Gregor III, came to the men in the church and said, "We have to develop a program to rescue the young boys in our community. Many are in danger of losing their way. They are vulnerable, and there are many snares waiting for them. You men are strong. You must lend some of your strength to these boys." Now, there is a program at the church involving young boys from nine to fifteen. They are at church every afternoon, getting a snack, tutoring. These men stay in touch with the boys' parents, their teachers. They organize activities for them; they focus on the kids to help them get what they need to do well. There is a saying that it takes a whole village to raise a child. A child needs more than parents to grow up well; the child needs community support.

The church can be an agent of reform. On its 100th anniversary, The Friendship Baptist Church in Columbus, Georgia, decided to do a survey to identify community needs. The survey identified needs for day-long affordable child care and for an after-school program for older children. First, it organized a high-quality child-care program for parents in the neighborhood so they did not have to go far to get good care for their children. Professional teachers give intellectually stimulating material and spiritually enriching lessons. The church also established an after-school program that involved children from six to thirteen in constructive activities, including lessons on African-American history and culture.

issues. Though the program designers hoped to recruit some boys for the priesthood, almost all married, some became fathers, and only one became a priest. In large part, they are professional men.

In looking back at what they gained from the experience, the men made such comments as "My whole life I owe to it. It made me realize my self-worth. Growing up where I did, you never saw the outside world for what it was. I learned that you can be successful by giving it your all." "It was taking this bunch of energy and this bunch of mouth and channeling it into something positive. It helped me stand up and formulate some thoughts in an intelligent way." This project is now open to boys and girls.

For example, Robert Smalls was a slave who worked on a Confederate warship during the Civil War. In the middle of the night, after the captain and the crew left the ship, Smalls and the other slaves took it over. The next day, dressed correctly, standing on the deck, he and the other slaves sailed the ship out of Charleston harbor, giving all the correct signals so that no one realized who they were. They stopped to pick up their families and then sailed to freedom past Fort Sumter. So then you say to youth, "What do you want to be? These people achieved against great odds. Now, what do you want? What are you going to be?"

The church takes a positive approach to people and says, "You might have made a lot of mistakes, but God loves you." When the church gets into action, it says, "We love you too, and we will help you accomplish what you can." The church can have dramatic results.

I was visiting the oldest continuous black church in America. Scholars think that it is in Philadelphia, but the oldest is the First African Baptist Church in Savannah, founded in 1773 and still functioning. There, about ten teenage boys told me a story. In April of 1993, a bunch of black teenagers got into a fight at the high school. No weapons or blood, just pushing and shoving. The school was integrated, but the fight was only among blacks. The school had an overwhelming need to punish violence. The boys were arrested and taken to court. The school had decided there would be zero tolerance for violence, and the boys were sentenced to thirty days in jail. Now if the boys missed ten days of classes, the school required they repeat the entire grade. The judge and the school were not aware of the long-term consequences of these actions for the boys. They would be out of school and could get into trouble.

A minister, the Reverend Thurman Tillman, went into action and talked to the judge. The boys had no previous trouble and all were passing their classes, so the judge agreed to take another look at the cases. After one week in jail, the boys were assigned to the minister, and he supervised their community activities and reported back to the judge every few days as to how they were doing. At first, the school would not accept them back, so the minister organized a school so they could keep up with their grade. He got them special T-shirts, and overall the boys became more responsible citizens. Last April, at the end of probation, the minister took them all for a treat. Six of the boys have now graduated from high school. The schools need to be more sensitive and the legal system needs to be more flexible instead of just sending these teenagers away. If left to their own devices, the boys may not have done it right. But the church stepped in.

The church holds out hope and can be an affirming experience for people who don't get that elsewhere. Little children sing, "I am a promise, I am a possibility, I can be anything God wants me to be."

THE POWER OF A SINGLE INDIVIDUAL

All the programs mentioned outside the family have involved large organizations. It seems fitting to conclude a discussion of supports with an example of what a single person with a clear goal can accomplish when she gathers community resources to provide support for children and parents.

Barbara Barlow, a pediatric surgeon at Harlem Hospital in New York, became concerned at the growing number of preventable injuries she was treating. Children fell from open windows, were hit by automobiles while playing in the street, or were victims of violence.[62]

In 1988, she started Harlem Hospital's Injury Prevention Program (IPP) with a grant from the Robert Wood Johnson Foundation. With a staff of three, she worked to rebuild playgrounds and parks in the community, because there were no safe places for children to play. She photographed all the parks and playgrounds and took the information to the Parks Department and the Board of Education. The Parks Department has since made nearly all the parks in the area safe. Private funding was sought for playgrounds, and at the suggestion of teachers and students, two new playgrounds have been built and six more planned.

The IPP has expanded to include activities that foster children's competence. An in-hospital art program, begun so patients could express their feelings about illness and hospitalization, has expanded. Children have exhibited and sold their work, with half the profits going to the children and half to the art program. The IPP also sponsors a dance program, baseball teams, a soccer team, and a greening program in which children can grow flowers and vegetables.

Major injuries to children in Harlem have decreased by 37 percent, motor vehicle accidents have decreased by 50 percent, and fewer children fall from windows. In addition, the young dancers, athletes, artists, and gardeners have developed skills they would not have had without the programs.

The increase in violent injuries to children has led Barlow to start the Anti-Violence Project, which contains several specific programs for (1) teaching children how to stay safe, (2) helping children deal with violence after they experience it, and (3) teaching children, their parents, and educators conflict resolution techniques and other ways to avoid violence.

Funding for these programs comes from individuals, corporations, foundations, and fees from Barlow's speaking engagements. She concludes, "You have to give to get in this world, and we give a lot. We put in lots of hard work, but it's immensely satisfying. There is no such thing as not being able to make things better. In any community, every individual can make a tremendous difference if they truly care, if they look around to see what needs to be done."[63]

MAIN POINTS

Social supports

- provide emotional, instrumental, and informational benefits to children and parents
- are divided into people, activities, organizations, and environments
- vary with the individual's age and life stage
- are constrained by socioeconomic, cultural, ethnic, and gender-related factors

Supportive family members

- include siblings, grandparents, aunts, uncles, and cousins
- increase feelings of closeness and belonging
- serve as companions in activities
- can help carry out parenting activities and nourish and protect children
- teach children new skills

Family rituals

- provide stability by ensuring predictability in family life
- encourage communication among family members
- link family members with the past and the future
- serve as a protective factor in times of difficulty

Teachers and nonrelatives

- serve as models and mentors to children
- provide encouragement for children
- encourage responsibility and competence in children

Parenting programs

- can provide support groups for parents
- teach specific skills to parents
- enable parents to reduce children's behavioral difficulties
- reduce the stress of parenting
- increase parents' self-confidence and feelings of competence

Workplace supports for parents

- enable parents to spend more time with children
- can provide quality care for children
- help parents integrate the demands of work and family life

Government and community programs supportive of parents

- are available only for parents with some special difficulty
- often have too limited funding to help all who are eligible
- can be operated in conjunction with the health care and educational systems
- may be cheaper when funded to prevent rather than treat problems
- can, according to Zigler, be operated through schools and provide quality care for children of all ages

Churches

- help children make sense of life and provide them with a sense of security
- provide emotional closeness with a special figure who focuses attention on the children
- offer guidelines for daily conduct and can provide programs that help children develop competence

Individuals

- can mobilize resources to support parents and children
- can make an enormous difference in the lives of children and parents

EXERCISES

1. List activities, people, and organizations that provided you with positive support when you were growing up. Looking back, what do you think were the factors that gave your parents support when they were raising you?

2. Describe family traditions in your family of origin. What feelings did these traditions create in family members? How will you incorporate these traditions in your own family?

3. Think about the positive supports your school provided for you and your parents. Were there teachers who gave you special encouragement? Did you develop any lifelong interests at that time?

4. Investigate the supports a large company in your area provides its employees. Do they have on-site day care? Flex time? Family-leave policies?

5. Investigate the services your community provides for parents and children. Does it offer parenting programs? Recreational programs? Summer day programs for children? Joint parent-child activities? How friendly is your community to families and young children?

ADDITIONAL READINGS

Coles, Robert. *The Spiritual Life of Children*. Boston: Houghton Mifflin, 1990.

Hamburg, David A. *Today's Children*. New York: Times Books, 1992.

Werner, Emmy E., and Smith, Ruth S. *Overcoming the Odds*. Ithaca, NY: Cornell University Press, 1992.

Wolin, Steven J., and Wolin, Sybil. *The Resilient Self*. New York: Villard, 1993.

Zigler, Edward F., and Lang, Mary E. *Child Care Choices*. New York: Free Press, 1991.

NOTES

Preface

1. David Gutmann, "Parenthood: A Key to the Comparative Study of the Life Cycle," in *Life Span Developmental Psychology: Normative Life Crises,* ed. Nancy Daton and Leon H. Ginsberg (New York: Academic Press, 1975), p. 170.
2. Arthur T. Jersild et al., *Joys and Problems of Child Rearing* (New York: Bureau of Publications, Teachers College, Columbia University, 1949), p. 1.
3. Ibid., p. 122.

Chapter 1

1. U.S. Bureau of the Census, *Statistical Abstract of the United States: 1996,* 116th ed. (Washington, DC: U.S. Government Printing Office, 1996).
2. William Morris, ed., *The American Heritage Dictionary of the English Language* (Boston: American Heritage Publishing and Houghton Mifflin, 1969), p. 952.
3. David Blankenhorn, "Introduction," in *Rebuilding the Nest,* ed. David Blankenhorn, Steven Bayme, and Jean Bethke Elshtain (Milwaukee, WI: Family Service of America, 1990), pp. xi–xv; Lynn Okagaki and Diana Johnson Divecha, "Development of Parental Beliefs," in *Parenting: An Ecological Perspective,* ed. Tom Luster and Lynn Okagaki (Hillsdale, NJ: Erlbaum, 1993), pp. 35–67.
4. Ellen Goodman, "Why Jaycee Is Parentless," *San Francisco Chronicle,* September 16, 1997, p. A21.
5. Morris, *American Heritage Dictionary,* p. 1043.
6. Jay Belsky, "The Determinants of Parenting: A Process Model," *Child Development* 55 (1984): 83–96.

7. Urie Bronfenbrenner and Pamela A. Morris, "The Ecology of Developmental Processes," in *Handbook of Child Psychology,* ed. in chief William Damon and vol. ed. Richard Lerner, vol. 1: *Theoretical Models of Human Development,* 5th ed. (New York: Wiley, 1997), pp. 996, 1015.
8. Mary Jane Gandour, "Activity Level as a Dimension of Temperament in Toddlers: Its Relevance for the Organismic Specificity Hypothesis," *Child Development* 60 (1989): 1092–1098.
9. Belsky, "Determinants of Parenting."
10. Carolyn Pape Cowan and Philip A. Cowan, *When Partners Become Parents* (New York: Basic Books, 1992).
11. John D. Coie et al., "The Science of Prevention: A Conceptual Framework and Some Directives for a National Research Program" *American Psychologist* 48 (1993): 1013–1022.
12. Mark Mellman, Edward Lazarus, and Allan Rivlin, "Family Time, Family Values," in *Rebuilding the Nest,* ed. Blankenhorn, Bayme, and Elshtain, pp. 73–92.
13. Lois Wladis Hoffman and Jean Danby, "The Values of Children in the United States: A New Approach to the Study of Fertility," *Journal of Marriage and the Family* 41 (1979): 583–596.
14. Bronfenbrenner and Morris, "The Ecology of Developmental Processes," p. 1015.
15. *People Weekly,* November 10, 1997.
16. Hoffman and Danby, "Values of Children."
17. U.S. Bureau of the Census, *Statistical Abstract of the United States: 1996.*
18. John Newson and Elizabeth Newson, "Cultural Aspects of Child Rearing in the English-Speaking World," in *The Integration of a Child into a Social World,* ed. Martin M. P.

NOTES

Richards (London: Cambridge University Press, 1974), pp. 53–82.

19. Herbert Ginsburg and Sylvia Opper, *Piaget's Theory of Intellectual Development* (Englewood Cliffs, NJ: Prentice-Hall, 1969).

20. David C. Rowe, *The Limits of Family Influence* (New York: Guilford Press, 1994).

21. Ross D. Parke and Raymond Buriel, "Socialization in the Family: Ethnic and Ecological Perspectives," in *Handbook of Child Psychology,* ed. in chief William Damon and vol. ed. Nancy Eisenberg, vol. 3: *Social, Emotional, and Personality Development,* 5th ed. (New York: Wiley, 1997), pp. 463–552.

22. Barbara J. Tinsley and Nancy B. Lees, "Health Promotion for Parents," in *Handbook of Parenting,* ed. Marc H. Bornstein, vol. 4: *Applied and Practical Parenting* (Mahwah, NJ: Erlbaum, 1995), pp. 187–204.

23. Wendy Haight and Katherine Sachs, "The Portrayal of Negative Emotions during Mother-Child Pretend Play," in *Exploring Young Children's Concepts of Self and Other through Conversation,* New Directions for Child Development, ed. Linda J. Sperry and Patricia A. Smiley, no. 69 (San Francisco: Jossey-Bass, 1995), pp. 33–46.

24. Betty Hart and Todd R. Risley, *Meaningful Differences in the Everyday Experience of Young American Children* (Baltimore: Paul H. Brookes, 1995).

25. Belsky, "Determinants of Parenting."

26. Coie et al., "Science of Prevention."

27. Sandra Scarr, "Developmental Theories for the 1990s: Development and Individual Differences," *Child Development* 63 (1992): 3.

28. Diana Baumrind, "The Average Expectable Environment Is Not Good Enough," *Child Development* 64 (1993): 1299–1317.

29. Jacquelyne Faye Jackson, "Human Behavioral Genetics, Scarr's Theory, and Her Views on Interventions: A Critical Review and Commentary on Their Implications for African American Children," *Child Development* 64 (1993): 1318–1332.

30. Jerome Kagan, Doreen Arcus, and Nancy Snidman, "The Idea of Temperament: Where Do We Go from Here?" in *Nature and Nurture and Psychology,* ed. Robert Plomin and Gerald E. McClearn (Washington, DC: American Psychological Association, 1993), pp. 197–210.

31. G. R. Patterson and D. M. Capaldi, "Antisocial Parents: Unskilled and Vulnerable," in *Family Transitions,* ed. Philip A. Cowan and Mavis Hetherington (Hillsdale, NJ: Erlbaum, 1991), pp. 195–218.

32. L. Alan Sroufe, Byron Egeland, and Terri Kreutzer, "The Fate of Early Experience Following Developmental Change: Longitudinal Approaches to Individual Adaptation in Childhood," *Child Development* 61 (1990): 1363–1373.

33. Mike Allen, "Conservatives Lobby for Parental Rights," *New York Times,* January 15, 1996.

34. Lizette Alvarez, "After Death of 6-Year-Old Girl, Report Shows System's Collapse," *New York Times,* April 9, 1996.

35. Ibid.

36. Ibid.

37. Douglas J. Besharov, "How to Save Children" *New York Times,* January 13, 1996.

38. Richard Wexler, "Beware the Pitfalls of Foster Care," *New York Times,* January 21, 1996.

39. Robin Meredith, "Parents Convicted for a Youth's Misconduct," *New York Times,* May 10, 1996.

40. Urie Bronfenbrenner, *The Ecology of Human Development: Experiments by Nature and Design* (Cambridge, MA: Harvard University Press, 1979); Urie Bronfenbrenner, "Ecology of the Family as a Context for Human Development," *Developmental Psychology* 22 (1986): 723–742.

41. Parke and Buriel, "Socialization in the Family."

42. Ibid., p. 496.

43. Coie et al., "Science of Prevention."

44. Arnold J. Sameroff, "Models of Developmental Risk," in *Handbook of Infant Mental Health,* ed. Charles H. Zeanah, Jr. (New York: Guilford, 1993), p. 8.

45. Steve Farkas et al., *Kids These Days: What Americans Really Think about the Next Generation* (New York: Public Agenda, 1997).

46. James Rainey and Dan Morrison, "Boy's Grim Life May be Key to Attack on Baby," *San Francisco Chronicle,* April 28, 1996; Lori Olszewski, "Charges Suspended against Boy in Baby Beating Case," *San Francisco Chronicle,* July 13, 1996.

47. Edward Epstein and Michael Taylor, "How Law Treats Violent Kids: Big Change since 1971 Alba Case," *San Francisco Chronicle,* May 6, 1996.

48. Farkas et al., *Kids These Days.*

49. Urie Bronfenbrenner and Peter R. Neville, "America's Children and Families: An International Perspective," in *Putting Families First,* ed. Sharon L. Kagan and Bernice Weissbourd (San Francisco: Jossey-Bass, 1994), pp. 3–27.

50. "Rich Nation, Poor Children," *New York Times,* August 15, 1995.

51. Farkas et al., *Kids These Days.*

52. Elizabeth Gleick, "The Children's Crusade," *Time,* June 3, 1996.

53. Judith Rich Harris, "Where Is the Child's Environment?" A Group Socialization Theory of Development," *Psychological Review* 102 (1995): 458–489.

54. Jay Belsky and John Kelly, *The Transition to Parenthood* (New York: Delacorte Press, 1994), p. 23.

55. Bronfenbrenner and Morris, "Ecology of Developmental Processes."

56. Jay Belsky, Elliot Robins, and Wendy Gamble, "The Determinants of Parental Competence: Toward a Contextual Theory," in *Beyond the Dyad,* ed. Michael Lewis (New York: Plenum, 1984), pp. 251–280.

57. U.S. Bureau of the Census, *Statistical Abstract of the United States: 1996.*

58. Ibid.

59. Ibid.

60. Ibid.

61. Ibid.

62. Ibid.

63. Algea O. Harrison et al., "Family Ecologies of Ethnic Minority Children," *Child Development* 61 (1990): 347–362.

64. Diana Baumrind, "Subcultural Variations in Values Defining Social Competence," Society for Research in Child Development, *Papers Presented at Western Regional Conference,* April 1976, p. 26.

65. Jeannie Gutierrez and Arnold Sameroff, "Determinants of Complexity in Mexican-American and Anglo-American Mothers' Conceptions of Child Development," *Child Development* 61 (1990): 384–394.

66. U.S. Bureau of the Census, *Statistical Abstract of the United States: 1996.*

67. Ibid.

68. Vonnie C. McLoyd, "The Impact of Economic Hardship on Black Families and Children: Psychological Distress, Parenting, and Socioemotional Development," *Child Development* 61 (1990: 311–346.

69. U.S. Bureau of the Census, *Statistical Abstract of the United States: 1996.*

70. McLoyd, "Impact of Economic Hardship on Black Families and Children."

71. Rand D. Conger et al., "A Family Process Model of Economic Hardship and Adjustment of Early Adolescent Boys," *Child Development* 63 (1992): 526–541.

72. Katherine Kaufer Christoffel, "Firearm Injuries Affecting U.S. Children and Adolescents," in *Children in a Violent Society,* ed. Joy D. Osofsky (New York: Guilford, 1997), pp. 42–71.

73. Ibid.

74. Ibid.

75. Joseph A. Califano, Jr., "It's Drugs, Stupid," *The New York Times Magazine,* January 29, 1995.

76. Linda C. Mayes, "Substance Abuse and Parenting," in *Handbook of Parenting,* ed. Bornstein, vol. 4, pp. 101–125.

77. Ibid.

78. Ibid.

79. Ibid.

80. Arlene Skolnick, *Embattled Paradise: The American Family in an Age of Uncertainty* (New York: Basic Books, 1991).

81. David A. Hamburg, *Today's Children* (New York: Times Books, 1992), p. 328.

Chapter 2

1. Erik H. Erikson, *Childhood and Society,* 2d ed. (New York: Norton, 1963).

2. Erik H. Erikson, "Human Strength and the Cycle of Generations," in *Insight and Responsibility,* ed. Erik Erikson (New York: Norton, 1964), pp. 109–157.

3. Lynn Okagaki and Diana Johnson Divecha, "Development of Parental Beliefs," in *Parenting: An Ecological Perspective,* ed. Tom Luster and Lynn Okagaki (Hillsdale, NJ: Erlbaum, 1993) pp. 35–67.

4. Barbara J. Tinsley and Nancy B. Lees, "Health Promotion for Parents," in *Handbook of Parenting,* ed. Marc H. Bornstein, vol. 4: *Applied and Practical Parenting* (Mahwah, NJ: Erlbaum, 1995), pp. 187–204.

5. Ibid.

6. Tinsley and Lees, "Health Promotion for Parents"; Nancy Eisenberg and Bridget Murphy, "Parenting and Children's Moral Development," in *Handbook of Parenting,* ed. Bornstein, vol. 4, pp. 227–257; Patricia Chamberlain and Gerald R. Patterson, "Discipline and Child Compliance," in *Handbook of Parenting,* ed. Bornstein vol. 4, pp. 205–225; Gary W. Ladd and Karen D. LeSieur, "Parents and Children's Peer Relationships," in *Handbook of Parenting,* ed. Bornstein, vol. 4, pp. 377–409.

7. Nancy Eisenberg, "Introduction," in *Handbook of Child Psychology,* ed. in chief William Damon and vol. ed. Nancy Eisenberg, vol. 3: *Social, Emotional, and Personality Development,* 5th ed. (New York: Wiley, 1997), pp. 1–24.

8. Ibid.

9. Rima Shore, *Rethinking the Brain* (New York: Families and Work Institute, 1997).

10. Ibid., p. 15.

NOTES

11. William Greenough, "We Can't Focus Just on Ages Zero to Three," *American Psychological Association Monitor,* November 1997, p. 19.

12. Bruce D. Perry, "Incubated in Terror: Neurodevelopmental Factors in the 'Cycle of Violence,'" in *Children in a Violent Society,* ed. Joy D. Osofsky (New York: Guilford, 1997), pp. 125–126.

13. Diana Baumrind, "The Development of Instrumental Competence through Socialization," in *Minnesota Symposta on Child Psychology,* ed. Ann D. Pick, vol. 7 (Minneapolis: University of Minnesota Press, 1973), pp. 3–46.

14. Luis M. Laosa, "Maternal Teaching Strategies in Chicano and Anglo American Families: The Influence of Culture and Education on Maternal Behavior," *Child Development,* 61 (1990): 429–433.

15. Eisenberg, "Introduction."

16. Barbara Rogoff, "Cognition as a Collaborative Process," in *Handbook of Child Psychology,* ed. in chief William Damon and vol. ed. Deanna Kuhn and Robert S. Siegler, vol. 2: *Cognition, Perception, and Language,* 5th ed. (New York: Wiley, 1997), pp. 679–744.

17. Tinsley and Lees, "Health Promotion for Parents."

18. Esther Thelen, "Motor Development: A New Synthesis," *American Psychologist* 50 (1995): 79–95.

19. Ibid.

20. Ibid.

21. Ibid., p. 94.

22. Jean Piaget and Barbel Inhelder, *The Psychology of the Child* (New York: Basic Books, 1969); Herbert Ginsburg and Sylvia Opper, *Piaget's Theory of Intellectual Development* (Englewood Cliffs, NJ: Prentice-Hall, 1969).

23. John M. Belmont, "Cognitive Strategies and Strategic Learning," *American Psychologist* 44 (1989): 142–148; Laboratory of Comparative Human Cognition, "Culture and Cognitive Development," in *Handbook of Child Psychology,* ed. William Kessen, vol. 1: *History, Theory, and Methods,* (New York: Wiley, 1982), pp. 295–356; James V. Wertsch and Peeter Tulviste, "L. S. Vygotsky and Contemporary Developmental Psychology," *Developmental Psychology* 28 (1992): 548–557.

24. Robert J. Sternberg and Wendy M. Williams, "Parenting toward Cognitive Competence," in *Handbook of Parenting,* ed. Bornstein, vol. 4, pp. 259–275.

25. Daniel Goleman, *Emotional Intelligence* (New York: Basic Books, 1995).

26. Pamela M. Cole, Margaret K. Michel, and Lawrence O'Donnell Teti, "The Development of Emotion Regulation and Dysregulation: A Clinical Perspective," in *The Development of Emotion Regulation,* ed. Nathan A. Fox, Monographs of the Society for Research in Child Development 59, serial no. 240 (1994), p. 76.

27. Ross A. Thompson, "Emotion Regulation: A Theme in Search of Definition," in *The Deveopment of Emotion Regulation,* ed. Fox, pp. 25–52.

28. Robert N. Emde et al., "The Moral Self of Infancy: Affective Core and Procedural Knowledge," *Developmental Review* 11 (1991): 251–270.

29. Tiffany Field, "The Effects of Mother's Physical and Emotional Unavailability on Emotion Regulation," in *The Development of Emotion Regulation,* ed. Fox, pp. 208–227.

30. Myron A. Hofer, "Hidden Regulators in Attachment, Separation, and Loss," in *The Development of Emotion Regulation,* ed. Fox, pp. 208–227.

31. Thompson, "Emotion Regulation."

32. Ibid.

33. Goleman, *Emotional Intelligence;* Allan N. Schore, *Affect Regulation and the Origin of the Self* (Hillsdale, NJ: Erlbaum, 1994).

34. Susan Harter, "Causes, Correlates, and the Functional Role of Global Self-Worth: A Life-Span Perspective," in *Competence Considered,* ed. J. Kolligian and Robert Sternberg (New Haven, CN: Yale University Press, 1990), pp. 67–97.

35. Ibid.

36. Susan Harter, "Visions of Self: Beyond the Me in the Mirror," university lecture, University of Denver, 1990.

37. Ladd and LeSieur, "Parents and Children's Peer Relationships."

38. Ross D. Parke and Raymond Buriel, "Socialization in the Family: Ethnic and Ecological Perspectives," in *Handbook of Child Psychology,* ed. Damon and Eisenberg, vol. 3, pp. 463–552.

39. Eisenberg and Murphy, "Parenting and Children's Moral Development."

40. James Q. Wilson, *The Moral Sense* (New York: Free Press, 1993), p. 226.

41. Eisenberg and Murphy, "Parenting and Children's Moral Development."

42. Nancy Eisenberg and Richard Fabes, "Prosocial Development," in *Handbook of Child Psychology,* ed. Damon and Eisenberg, vol. 3, pp. 701–770.

43. Eisenberg and Murphy, "Parenting and Children's Moral Development."

44. Ibid.

45. Baumrind, "The Development of Instrumental Competence."

46. Ann V. McGillicuddy-De Lisi and Irving E. Sigel, "Parental Beliefs," in *Handbook of Parenting,* ed. Marc H. Bornstein, vol. 3: *Status and Social Conditions of Parenting* (Mahwah, NJ: Erlbaum, 1995), pp. 333–358.

47. Jacqueline J. Goodnow and W. Andrew Collins, *Development According to Parents* (Hillsdale, NJ: Erlbaum, 1990).

48. Okagaki and Divecha, "Development of Parental Beliefs."

49. Sara Harkness and Charles Super, "Culture and Parenting," in *Handbook of Parenting,* ed. Marc H. Bornstein, vol. 2: *Biology and Ecology of Parenting* (Mahwah, NJ: Erlbaum, 1995), pp. 211–234.

50. Patricia M. Greenfield and Lalita K. Suzuki, "Culture and Human Development: Implications for Parenting Education, Pediatrics, and Mental Health," in *Handbook of Child Psychology,* ed. in chief William Damon and vol. ed. Irving E. Sigel and K. Ann Renninger, vol. 4: *Child Psychology in Practice,* 5th ed. (New York: Wiley, 1997), pp. 1059–1109.

51. Jean L. Briggs, "Mazes of Meaning: How a Child and a Culture Create Each Other," in *Interpretive Approaches to Socialization,* ed. William A. Corsaro and Peggy J. Miller, New Directions for Child Development, no. 58 (San Francisco: Jossey Bass, 1992), p. 25.

52. James Youniss, "Rearing Children for Society," in *Beliefs about Parenting: Origins and Developmental Implications,* ed. Judith G. Smetana, New Directions for Child Development, no. 66 (San Francisco: Jossey-Bass, 1994), pp. 37–50.

53. Parke and Buriel, "Socialization in the Family."

54. Greenfield and Suzuki, "Culture and Human Development."

55. Erika Hoff-Ginsberg and Twila Tardif, "Socioeconomic Status and Parenting," in *Handbook of Parenting,* ed. Bornstein, vol. 2, pp. 161–188.

56. Melvin L. Kohn, *Class and Conformity: A Study of Values* (Homewood, IL: Dorsey, 1969).

57. Betty Hart and Todd R. Risley, *Meaningful Differences in the Everyday Experiences of Young American Children* (Baltimore: Paul H. Brookes, 1995).

58. Joan E. Grusec, Paul Hastings, and Norma Mammone, "Parenting Cognitions and Relationship Schemes," in *Beliefs about Parenting,* ed. Smetana, pp. 5–19.

59. Jacqueline J. Goodnow, "Parents' Knowledge and Expectations," in *Handbook of Parenting,* ed. Bornstein, vol. 3, pp. 305–332.

60. Okagaki and Divecha, "Development of Parental Beliefs."

61. Goodnow, "Parents' Knowledge and Expectations."

62. McGillicuddy-DeLisi and Sigel, "Parental Beliefs," p. 350.

63. Goodnow, "Parents' Knowledge and Expectations."

64. Ibid.

65. Ellen Galinsky, *Between Generations: The Six Stages of Parenthood* (New York: Times Books, 1981).

66. Ibid. p. 317.

Chapter 3

1. Haim G. Ginott, *Between Parent and Child* (New York: Avon Books, 1969); Haim G. Ginott, *Between Parent and Teenager* (New York: Avon Books, 1971); Adele Faber and Elaine Mazlish, *Liberated Parents/Liberated Children* (New York: Avon Books, 1975); Adele Faber and Elaine Mazlish, *How to Talk So Kids Will Listen and Listen So Kids Will Talk* (New York: Rawson Wade, 1980).

2. Thomas Gordon, *P.E.T.: Parent Effectiveness Training* (New York: New American Library, 1975); Thomas Gordon with Judith G. Sands, *P.E.T. in Action* (New York: Bantam Books, 1978); Thomas Gordon, *Teaching Children Self-Discipline* (New York: Random House, 1989).

3. Dorothy C. Briggs, *Your Child's Self-Esteem* (Garden City, NY: Doubleday, 1970).

4. Rudolf Dreikurs, *The Challenge of Parenthood,* rev. ed. (New York: Hawthorn, 1958); Rudolf Dreikurs with Vicki Soltz, *Children: The Challenge* (New York: Hawthorn, 1964).

5. Gerald R. Patterson, *Families: Applications of Social Learning to Family Life,* rev. ed. (Champaign, IL: Research Press, 1975); Gerald R. Patterson, *Living with Children,* rev. ed. (Champaign, IL: Research Press, 1976); Wesley C. Becker, *Parents Are Teachers* (Champaign, IL: Research Press, 1971); Robert Eimers and Robert Aitchison, *Effective Parents/Responsible Children* (New York: McGraw Hill, 1977); John D. Krumboltz and Helen B. Krumboltz, *Changing Children's Behavior* (Englewood Cliffs, NJ: Prentice-Hall, 1972).

6. Briggs, *Your Child's Self-Esteem,* pp. 61–62.

7. Ibid., p. 64

8. Jay D. Schaneveldt, Marguerite Fryer, and Renee Ostler, "Concepts of 'Badness' and 'Goodness' of Parents as Perceived by Nursery School Children," *The Family Coordinator* 19 (1970): 98–103.

9. John R. Weisz, "Autonomy, Control and Other Reasons Why 'Mom Is the Greatest'" A Content Analysis of Children's Mother's Day Letters," *Child Development* 51 (1980): 801–807.

10. Eleanor E. Maccoby and John A. Martin, "Socialization in the Context of the Family: Parent-Child Interaction," in *Handbook of Child Psychology,* ed. Paul H. Mussen and E. Mavis Hetherington, vol. 4: *Socialization, Personality, and Social Development,* 4th ed. (New York: Wiley, 1983), pp. 1–101.

11. John A. Clausen, Paul H. Mussen, and Joseph Kuypers, "Involvement, Warmth, and Parent-Child Resemblance in Three Generations," in *Present and Past in Middle Life,* ed. Dorothy H. Eichorn et al. (New York: Academic Press, 1981), pp. 299–319.

12. J. Kirk Felsman and George E. Vaillant, "Resilient Children as Adults," in *The Invulnerable Child,* ed. E. James Anthony and Bertram J. Cohler (New York: Guilford Press, 1987), p. 298.

13. Charles R. Carlson and John C. Masters, "Inoculation by Emotion: Effects of Positive Emotional States on Children's Reactions to Social Comparison," *Developmental Psychology* 22 (1986): 760–765.

14. Jane B. Brooks and Doris M. Elliott, "Prediction of Psychological Adjustment at Age Thirty from Leisure Time Activities and Satisfactions in Childhood," *Human Development* 14 (1971): 61–71.

15. Mona El-Sheikh, E. Mark Cummings, and Virginia Goetsch, "Coping with Adults' Angry Behavior: Behavioral, Physiological, and Verbal Responses in Preschoolers," *Developmental Psychology* 25 (1989): 490–498.

16. John M. Gottman and Lynn F. Katz, "Effects of Marital Discord on Young Children's Peer Interaction and Health," *Developmental Psychology* 25 (1989): 373–381.

17. E. Mark Cummings, "Coping with Background Anger in Early Childhood," *Child Development* 58 (1987): 976–984.

18. Jennifer S. Cummings et al., "Children's Responses to Adult Behavior as a Function of Marital Distress and History of Interparent Hostility," *Child Development* 60 (1989): 1035–1043.

19. John H. Grych and Frank D. Fincham, "Children's Appraisals of Marital Conflict: Initial Investigation of the Cognitive-Contextual Framework," *Child Development* 64 (1993): 215–230.

20. Katherine Covell and Brenda Miles, "Children's Beliefs about Strategies to Reduce Parental Anger," *Child Development* 63 (1992): 381–390.

21. E. Mark Cummings et al., "Resolution and Children's Responses to Interadult Anger," *Developmental Psychology* 27 (1991): 462–470.

22. Katherine Covell and Rona Abramovitch, "Understanding Emotion in the Family: Children's and Parents' Attributions of Happiness, Sadness, and Anger," *Child Development* 57 (1987): 985–991.

23. Keith Crnic and Marcela Acevedo, "Everyday Stresses and Parenting," in *Handbook of Parenting,* ed. Marc H. Bornstein, vol. 4: *Applied and Practical Parenting* (Mahwah, NJ: Erlbaum, 1995), pp. 277–297; Theodore Dix, "The Affective Organization of Parenting: Adaptive and Maladaptive Processes," *Psychological Bulletin* 110 (1991): 3–25.

24. Ernest N. Jouriles, Christopher M. Murphy, and K. Daniel O'Leary, "Effects of Maternal Mood on Mother-Son Interaction Patterns," *Journal of Abnormal Child Psychology* 17 (1989): 513–525.

25. John U. Zussman, "Situational Determinants of Parenting Behavior: Effects of Competing Cognitive Activity," *Child Development* 51 (1980): 772–780.

26. Keith A. Crnic and Mark T. Greenberg, "Minor Parenting Stresses with Young Children," *Child Development* 61 (1990): 1628–1637.

27. Crnic and Acevedo, "Everyday Stresses and Parenting"; Jay Belsky, Keith Crnic, and Sharon Woodworth, "Personality and Parenting: Exploring the Mediating Role of Transient Mood and Daily Hassles," *Journal of Personality* 63 (1995): 905–929.

28. Dix, "The Affective Organization of Parenting."

29. Ibid., p. 4.

30. Mark Mellman, Edward Lazarus, and Allan Rivlin, "Family Time, Family Values," in *Rebuilding the Nest,* ed. David Blankenhorn, Steven Bayme, and Jean Bethke Elshtain (Milwaukee, WI: Family Service of America, 1990), pp. 73–92.

31. Ginott, *Between Parent and Child,* pp. 39–40.

32. Gordon with Sands, *P.E.T. in Action,* p. 47.

33. Judy Dunn, Jane Brown, and Lynn Beardsall, "Family Talk about Feeling States and Children's Later Understanding of Others' Emotions," *Developmental Psychology* 27 (1991): 448–455.

34. Faber and Mazlish, *Liberated Parents/Liberated Children.*

35. John M. Gottman, Lynn Fainsilber Katz, and Carole Hooven, "Parental Meta-Emotion Philosophy and the Emotional Life of Families: Theoretical Models and Preliminary Data," *Journal of Family Psychology* 10 (1996): 243–268.

36. John Gottman with Joan DeClaire, *The Heart of Parenting* (New York: Simon & Schuster, 1997).

37. Gordon, *Teaching Children Self-Discipline.*
38. Dreikurs with Soltz, *Children,* p. 108.
39. Gail D. Heyman, Carol S. Dweck, and Kathleen M. Cain, "Young Children's Vulnerability to Self-Blame and Helplessness: Relationship to Beliefs about Goodness," *Child Development* 63 (1992): 401–415; Martin E. P. Seligman, *Learned Optimism* (New York: Pocket Books, 1990).
40. Seligman, *Learned Optimism.*
41. Ibid., pp. 221–222.
42. Ibid., p. 222.
43. Dreikurs with Soltz, *Children.*
44. Ibid., p. 39.
45. Brooks and Elliott, "Prediction of Psychological Adjustment."
46. Mellman, Lazarus, and Rivlin, "Family Time, Family Values."
47. Carolyn Pape Cowan and Philip A. Cowan, *When Partners Become Parents* (New York: Basic Books, 1992).
48. Joseph Procaccini and Mark Kiefaber, *Parent Burnout* (New York: New American Library, 1984), p. 41.
49. Rex L. Forehand, Page B. Walley, and William M. Furey, "Prevention in the Home: Parent and Family," in *Prevention of Problems in Childhood: Psychological Research and Application,* ed. Michael C. Roberts and Lizette Peterson (New York: Wiley, 1984), pp. 342–368.
50. Crnic and Acevedo, "Everyday Stresses and Parenting."
51. Ibid.
52. Nancy Samalin with Catherine Whitney, *Love and Anger: The Parental Dilemma* (New York: Penguin Books, 1992).
53. Jane Nelson, *Positive Discipline* (New York: Ballantine Books, 1981).
54. Dreikurs with Soltz, *Children,* pp. 55–56.
55. Arthur T. Jersild et al., *Joys and Problems of Child Rearing* (New York: Bureau of Publications, Teachers College, Columbia University, 1949), pp. 1–2
56. Ibid., p. 122.

Chapter 4

1. Patricia Chamberlain and Gerald R. Patterson, "Discipline and Child Compliance in Parenting," in *Handbook of Parenting,* ed. Marc H. Bornstein, vol. 4: *Applied and Practical Parenting* (Mahwah, NJ: Erlbaum, 1995), pp. 205–225.
2. Eleanor E. Maccoby and John A. Martin, "Socialization in the Context of the Family: Parent-Child Interaction," in *Handbook of Child Psychology,* eds. Paul H. Mussen and E. Mavis Hetherington, vol. 4: *Socialization, Personality and Social Development,* 4th ed. (New York: Wiley, 1983), pp. 1–101.
3. Daphne Blunt Bugental and Jacqueline J. Goodnow, "Socialization Processes," in *Handbook of Child Psychology,* ed. in chief William Damon and vol. ed. Nancy Eisenberg, vol. 3: *Social, Emotional, and Personality Development,* 5th ed. (New York: Wiley, 1997), pp. 389–462.
4. Diana Baumrind, "The Discipline Controversy Revisited," *Family Relations* 45 (1996); 405–414.
5. Joan E. Grusec and Jacqueline J. Goodnow, "Impact of Parental Discipline Methods on the Child's Internalization of Values: A Reconceptualization of Current Points of View," *Developmental Psychology* 30 (1994): 4–19.
6. Maccoby and Martin, "Socialization in the Context of the Family," p. 65.
7. George Holden, "Avoiding Conflicts: Mothers as Tacticians in the Supermarket," *Child Development* 54 (1983): 233–240.
8. Mary Jane Gandour, "Activity Level as a Dimension of Temperament in Toddlers: Its Relevance for the Organismic Specificity Hypothesis," *Child Development* 60 (1989): 1092–1098.
9. Eleanor Maccoby, "Socialization and Developmental Changes," *Child Development* 55 (1984): 317–328.
10. Rudolf Dreikurs with Vicki Soltz, *Children: The Challenge* (New York: Hawthorn, 1964).
11. Thomas Gordon, *P.E.T.: Parent Effectiveness Training* (New York: New American Library, 1975).
12. Robert Eimers and Robert Aitchison, *Effective Parents/Responsible Children* (New York: McGraw-Hill, 1977).
13. Haim G. Ginott, *Between Parent and Child* (New York: Avon Books, 1969).
14. Larry P. Nucci and Elliot Turiel, "Social Interactions and the Development of Social Concepts in Preschool Children," *Child Development* 49 (1978): 400–407.
15. Gordon, *P.E.T.*
16. Eimers and Aitchison, *Effective Parents/Responsible Children.*
17. Dreikurs with Soltz, *Children.*
18. Ginott, *Between Parent and Child.*
19. "How Americans Raise Their Children," *Brown University Child and Adolescent Behavior Letter,* December 1993, p. 5.
20. Diana Baumrind, "The Development of Instrumental Competence through Socialization," in *Minnesota Symposia on Child Psychology,* vol. 7, ed. Ann D. Pick (Minneapolis: University of Minnesota Press, 1973), pp. 3–46.

21. Glenn D. Wolfner and Richard J. Gelles, "A Profile of Violence toward Children: A National Study," *Child Abuse and Neglect* 17 (1993): 199–214.

22. Ray Guarendi with David Eich, *Back to the Family* (New York: Simon & Schuster, 1991).

23. Thomas F. Catron and John C. Masters, "Mothers' and Children's Conceptualizations of Corporal Punishment," *Child Development* 64 (1993): 1815–1828.

24. Baumrind, "The Discipline Controversy Revisited," p. 413.

25. Chamberlain and Patterson, "Discipline and Child Compliance in Parenting."

26. Ibid.

27. Rosemary S. L. Mills and Kenneth H. Rubin, "Parental Beliefs about Problematic Social Behaviors in Early Childhood," *Child Development* 61 (1990): 138–151.

28. Ann V. McGillicuddy-De Lisi, "Parental Beliefs within the Family Context: Development of a Research Program," in *Methods of Family Research: Biographies of Research Projects*, ed. Irving E. Sigel and Gene H. Brody, vol. 1: *Normal Families*, (Hillsdale, NJ: Erlbaum, 1990), pp. 53–85.

29. Grazyna Kochanska, "Maternal Beliefs as Long-Term Predictors of Mother-Child Interactions and Report," *Child Development* 61 (1990): 1934–1943.

30. Jane Loevinger, "Patterns of Parenthood as Theories of Learning," *Journal of Abnormal and Social Psychology* 59 (1959): 148–150.

31. Ibid., p. 150.

32. Arnold Gesell and Frances L. Ilg, *The Child from Five to Ten* (New York: Harper & Row, 1946), p. 308.

Chapter 5

1. Lois Wladis Hoffman and Jean Denby Manis, "The Value of Children in the United States: A New Approach to the Study of Fertility," *Journal of Marriage and the Family* 41 (1979): 583–596.

2. Ibid.

3. Gerald Y. Michaels, "Motivational Factors in the Decision and Timing of Pregnancy," in *The Transition to Parenthood*, ed. Gerald Y. Michaels and Wendy A. Goldberg (New York: Cambridge University Press, 1988), pp. 23–61.

4. Michaels, "Motivational Factors"; Ross D. Parke and Raymond Buriel, "Socialization in the Family: Ethnic and Ecological Perspectives," in *Handbook of Child Psychology*, ed. in chief William Damon and vol. ed. Nancy Eisenberg, vol. 3: *Social, Emotional, and Personality Development*, 5th ed. (New York: Wiley, 1997), pp. 463–552.

5. Michaels, "Motivational Factors."

6. Ibid.

7. Carolyn Pape Cowan and Philip A. Cowan, *When Partners Become Parents* (New York: Basic Books, 1992); Pamela Daniels and Kathy Weingarten, *Sooner or Later: The Timing of Parenthood in Adult Lives* (New York: Norton, 1983).

8. Cowan and Cowan, *When Partners Become Parents*, p. 32.

9. Ibid.

10. U.S. Bureau of the Census, *Statistical Abstract of the United States: 1996*, 116th ed. (Washington, DC: Government Printing Office, 1996).

11. Ibid.

12. Melissa Ludtke, *On Our Own: Unmarried Motherhood in America* (New York: Random House, 1997).

13. Ibid.

14. Marsha Weinraub and Marcy B. Gringlas, "Single Parenthood," in *Handbook of Parenting*, ed. Marc H. Bornstein, vol. 3: *Status and Social Conditions of Parenting* (Mahwah, NJ: Erlbaum, 1995), pp. 65–87.

15. Ludtke, *On Our Own*.

16. Jane Mattes, *Single Mothers by Choice*, 2d ed. (New York: Times Books, 1997).

17. Marilyn Fabe and Norma Wikler, *Up Against the Clock* (New York: Random House, 1979).

18. Weinraub and Gringlas, "Single Parenthood."

19. Daniels and Weingarten, *Sooner or Later*.

20. Henry P. David, "Developmental Effects of Compulsory Pregnancy," *Child, Youth, and Family Services Quarterly*, Spring 1992.

21. Tamar Nordenberg, "Overcoming Infertility," *FDA [Federal Drug Administration] Consumer*, January–February, 1997.

22. Robert R. Franklin and Dorothy Kay Brockman, *In Pursuit of Fertility*, 2d ed. (New York: Holt, 1995).

23. Carol Harkness, *The Infertility Book*, 2d ed. (Berkeley, CA: Celestial Arts, 1992).

24. Franklin and Brockman, *In Pursuit of Fertility*.

25. Lisa Belkin, "Pregnant with Complications," *The New York Times Magazine*, October 26, 1997.

26. Franklin and Brockman, *In Pursuit of Fertility*.

27. Belkin, "Pregnant with Complications."

28. Ibid.

29. Harkness, *Infertility Book.*

30. Ibid.

31. Franklin and Brockman, *In Pursuit of Fertility.*

32. Ibid.

33. Ibid., p. 253.

34. Harkness, *Infertility Book,* p. 323.

35. Ibid., p. 327.

36. Daniels and Weingarten, *Sooner or Later.*

37. U.S. Bureau of the Census, *Statistical Abstract of the United States: 1996.*

38. Andrew Yarrow, *Latecomers: Children of Parents over 35* (New York: Free Press, 1991).

39. Ibid.

40. Frank F. Furstenberg, J. Brooks-Gunn, and S. Philip Morgan, *Adolescent Mothers in Later Life* (Cambridge: Cambridge University Press, 1990), pp. 145–146.

41. U.S. Bureau of the Census, *Statistical Abstract of the United States: 1996.*

42. Wendy Baldwin, "The Consequences of Early Childbearing: A Perspective," *Journal of Research on Adolescence* 3 (1993): 349–352.

43. Ibid.

44. Christine A. Bachrach, Clifford C. Clogg, and Karen Carver, "Outcomes of Early Childbearing: Summary of a Conference." *Journal of Research on Adolescence* 3 (1993): 337–348.

45. Ibid.

46. James McCarthy and Janet Hardy, "Age at First Birth and Birth Outcomes." *Journal of Research on Adolescence* 3 (1993): 373–392.

47. Ibid.

48. Nan Marie Astone, "Are Adolescent Mothers Just Single Mothers?" *Journal of Research on Adolescence* 3 (1993): 353–371.

49. Ibid.

50. Joy D. Osofsky, Della M. Hann, and Claire Peebles, "Adolescent Parenthood: Risks and Opportunities for Mothers and Infants," in *Handbook of Infant Mental Health,* ed. Charles H. Zeanah, Jr. (New York: Guilford Press, 1993), pp. 106–119.

51. Ibid.

52. Jeanne Brooks-Gunn and P. Lindsay Chase-Lansdale, "Adolescent Parenthood," in *Handbook of Parenting,* ed. Bornstein, vol. 3, pp. 113–149.

53. Osofsky, Hann, and Peebles, "Adolescent Parenthood."

54. Brooks-Gunn and Chase-Lansdale, "Adolescent Parenthood."

55. Osofsky, Hann, and Peebles, "Adolescent Parenthood."

56. Brooks-Gunn and Chase-Lansdale, "Adolescent Parenthood."

57. Osofsky, Hann, and Peebles, "Adolescent Parenthood."

58. Judith Musick, "The Special Role of Parenting in the Context of Poverty: The Case of Adolescent Motherhood," in *Threats to Optimal Development: Integrating Biological, Psychological and Social Risk Factors,* ed. Charles A. Nelson (Hillsdale, NJ: Erlbaum, 1994), pp. 179–216.

59. Brooks-Gunn and Chase-Lansdale, "Adolescent Parenthood."

60. Ibid.

61. Ibid.

62. Furstenberg, Brooks-Gunn, and Morgan, *Adolescent Mothers in Later Life.*

63. Ibid.

64. Osofsky, Hann, and Peebles, "Adolescent Parenthood."

65. Ibid., p. 116.

66. Parke and Buriel, "Socialization in the Family."

67. Ibid.

68. Al Santoli, "They Turn Young Men with Children into Fathers," *Parade Magazine,* May 29, 1994.

69. Ibid., p. 19.

70. Jean E. Veevers, "Voluntarily Childless Wives: An Exploratory Study," *Mental Health Digest* 5 (1973): 8–11.

71. Victor J. Callan, "The Personal and Marital Adjustment of Mothers and of Voluntarily and Involuntarily Childless Wives," *Journal of Marriage and the Family* 49 (1987): 847–856.

72. Christoph N. Heinicke, "Determinants of the Transition to Parenting," in *Handbook of Parenting,* ed. Bornstein, vol. 3, pp. 277–303.

73. Eleanor E. Maccoby and John A. Martin, "Socialization in the Context of the Family: Parent-Child Interaction," in *Handbook of Child Psychology,* ed. Paul H. Mussen and E. Mavis Hetherington, vol. 4: *Socialization, Personality, and Social Development,* 4th ed. (New York: Wiley, 1983), pp. 1–101.

74. Jude Cassidy, "Emotion Regulation: Influences of Attachment Relationship," in *The Development of Emotion Regulation,* ed. Nathan A. Fox, Monographs of the Society for Research in Child Development 59, serial no. 240 (1994): 228–249.

75. Ibid.

76. Heinicke, "Determinants of the Transition to Parenting."

77. Ross D. Parke and Barbara J. Tinsley, "Family Interaction in Infancy," in *Handbook of Infant Development,* 2d ed., ed. Joy Doniger Osofsky (New York: Wiley, 1987), pp. 579–641.

78. E. Mark Cummings and Patrick Davies, *Children and Marital Conflict: The Impact of Family Disputes and Resolution* (New York: Guilford Press, 1994).

79. Gretchen Owens et al., "The Prototype Hypothesis and the Origins of Attachment Working Models: Adult Relationships with Parents and Romantic Partners," in *Caregiving, Cultural, and Cognitive Perspectives in Secure-Base Behavior and Working Models,* ed. Everett Waters et al., Monographs of the Society for Research in Child Development 60, serial no. 244 (1995): 216–233.

80. Cowan and Cowan, *When Partners Become Parents.*

81. Jay Belsky and John Kelly, *The Transition to Parenthood* (New York: Delacorte Press, 1994).

82. Cowan and Cowan, *When Partners Become Parents;* Belsky and Kelly, *Transition to Parenthood.*

83. Ellen Galinsky, *Between Generations: The Six Stages of Parenthood* (New York: Times Books, 1981).

84. Myra Leifer, "Psychological Changes Accompanying Pregnancy and Motherhood," *Genetic Psychology Monographs* 95 (1997): 55–96.

85. Cowan and Cowan, *When Partners Become Parents.*

86. Belsky and Kelly, *The Transition to Parenthood.*

87. Cowan and Cowan, *When Partners Become Parents.*

Chapter 6

1. Peter H. Wolff, *The Causes, Controls, and Organization of Behavior in the Neonate* (New York: International Universities Press, 1966).

2. Tiffany Field, "The Effects of Mother's Physical and Emotional Unavailability on Emotion Regulation," in *The Development of Emotion Regulation: Biological and Behavioral Considerations,* ed. Nathan A. Fox, Monographs of the Society for Research in Child Development 59, serial no. 240 (1994): 208–227.

3. Judith A. Schickedanz et al., *Understanding Children,* 2d ed. (Mountain View, CA: Mayfield, 1993).

4. Ibid.

5. Yvonne Brackbill et al., "Arousal Level in Neonates and Preschool Children under Continuous Stimulation," *Journal of Experimental Child Psychology* 4 (1966): 178–188.

6. Rudolph Schaffer, *Mothering* (Cambridge, MA: Harvard University Press, 1977).

7. Schickedanz et al., *Understanding Children.*

8. Abraham Sagi and Martin Hoffman, "Empathic Distress in the Newborn," *Developmental Psychology* 12 (1976): 175–176; Andrew Meltzoff and M. Keith Moore, "Imitations of Facial and Manual Gestures by Human Neonates," *Science* 198 (1977): 75–78.

9. William S. Condon and Louis W. Sander, "Neonate Movement Is Synchronized with Adult Speech: Interactional Participation and Language Acquisition," *Science* 183 (1974): 99–101.

10. Aidan Macfarlane, *The Psychology of Childbirth* (Cambridge, MA: Harvard University Press, 1977), pp. 82–83.

11. Mary K. Rothbart and John E. Bates, "Temperament," in *Handbook of Child Psychology,* ed. in chief William Damon and vol. ed. Nancy Eisenberg, vol. 3: *Social, Emotional, and Personality Development,* 5th ed. (New York: Wiley, 1997), p. 109.

12. Anneliese F. Korner, "Individual Differences at Birth: Implications for Early Experience and Later Development," *American Journal of Orthopsychiatry* 41 (1971): 608–619.

13. Rudolph Schaffer and Peggy E. Emerson, *The Development of Social Attachments in Infancy,* Monographs of the Society for Research in Child Development 29, whole no. 94 (1964).

14. Rothbart and Bates, "Temperament."

15. Anneliese F. Korner et al., "The Relation between Neonatal and Later Activity and Temperament," *Child Development* 56 (1985): 38–42.

16. Rothbart and Bates, "Temperament."

17. Carl E. Schwartz, Nancy Snidman, and Jerome Kagan, "Early Childhood Temperament as a Determinant of Externalizing Behavior," *Development and Psychopathology* 8 (1996): 527–537; Jerome Kagan, Doreen Arcus, and Nancy Snidman, "The Idea of Temperament: Where Do We Go from Here?" in *Nature and Nurture and Psychology,* ed. Robert Plomin and Gerald E. McClearn (Washington, DC: American Psychological Association, 1993), pp. 197–210.

18. John E. Bates, Christine A. Maslin, and Karen H. Frankel, "Attachment Security, Mother-Child Interaction and Temperament as Predictors of Behavior Problem Ratings at Age Three Years," in *Growing Points of Attachment Theory and Research,* ed. Inge Bretherton and Everett Waters, Monographs of the Society for Research in Child Development 50, serial no. 109 (1985): 167–193.

19. Ann Sanson and Mary K. Rothbart, "Child Temperament and Parenting," in *Handbook of Parenting*, ed. Marc H. Bornstein, vol. 4: *Applied and Practical Parenting* (Mahwah, NJ: Erlbaum, 1995), pp. 299–321.

20. Avshalom Caspi and Phil A. Silva, "Temperamental Qualities at Age Three Predict Personality Traits in Young Adulthood: Longitudinal Evidence from a Birth Cohort," *Child Development* 66 (1995): 486–498.

21. Sanson and Rothbart, "Child Temperament and Parenting."

22. Kagan, Arcus, and Snidman, "The Idea of Temperament."

23. Sanson and Rothbart, "Child Temperament and Parenting."

24. Ibid.

25. Kagan, Arcus, and Snidman, "The Idea of Temperament."

26. Sybil Escalona, *The Roots of Individuality: Normal Patterns of Development in Infancy* (Chicago: Aldine, 1968).

27. Patricia M. Greenfield and Lalita K. Suzuki, "Culture and Human Development: Implications for Parenting, Education, Pediatrics, and Mental Health," in *Handbook of Child Psychology*, ed. in chief William Damon and vol. ed. Irving E. Sigel and K. Ann Renninger, vol. 4: *Child Psychology in Practice*, 5th ed. (New York: Wiley, 1997), pp. 1059–1109.

28. Marc H. Bornstein, "Parenting Infants," in *Handbook of Parenting*, ed. Marc H. Bornstein, vol. 1: *Children and Parenting* (Mahwah, NJ: Erlbaum, 1995), pp. 3–39.

29. Gwen E. Gustafson, "Effects of the Ability to Locomote on Infants' Social and Exploratory Behaviors: An Experimental Study," *Developmental Psychology* 20 (1984): 397–405.

30. Jean Piaget and Barbel Inhelder, *The Psychology of the Child* (New York: Basic Books, 1969); Herbert Ginsburg and Sylvia Opper, *Piaget's Theory of Intellectual Development* (Englewood Cliffs, NJ: Prentice-Hall, 1969).

31. James V. Wertsch and Peeter Tulviste, "L. S. Vygotsky and Contemporary Developmental Psychology," *Developmental Psychology* 28 (1992): 548–557.

32. Robert McCall, *Exploratory Manipulation and Play in the Human Infant*, Monographs of the Society for Research in Child Development 39, whole no. 155 (1974).

33. Lois Bloom, "Language Acquisition in Its Developmental Context," in *Handbook of Child Psychology*, ed. in chief William Damon and vol. ed. Deanna Kuhn and Robert S.

Siegler, vol. 2: *Cognition, Perception, and Language*, 5th ed. (New York: Wiley, 1997), pp. 309–370.

34. R. V. Tonkova-Yampol'skaya, "Development of Speech Intonation in Infants during the First Two Years of Life," in *Studies of Child Language Development*, ed. Charles A. Ferguson and Dan Isaac Slobin (New York: Holt, Rinehart & Winston, 1973), pp. 128–138.

35. Bloom, "Language Acquisition."

36. Carol Zander Malatesta and Jeannette M. Haviland, "Learning Display Rules: The Socialization of Emotion Expression in Infancy," *Child Development* 53 (1982): 991–1003.

37. Ibid.

38. Jeannette M. Haviland and Mary Lelwica, "The Induced-Affect Response: 10-Week-Old Infants' Responses to Three Emotion Expressions." *Developmental Psychology* 23 (1987): 97–104.

39. Carol Z. Malatesta et al., "Emotion Socialization and Expression Development in Preterm and Full Term Infants," *Child Development* 57 (1986): 316–330.

40. Geraldine Dawson, David Hessl, and Karin Frey, "Social Influences on Early Developing Biological and Behavioral Systems Related to Risk for Affective Disorder," *Development and Psychopathology* 6 (1994): 759–779.

41. Eleanor J. Gibson and Richard D. Walk, "The Visual Cliff," *Scientific American* 202 (April, 1960): 64–71.

42. Robin Hornick, Nancy Risenhoover, and Megan Gunnar, "The Effects of Maternal Positive, Neutral, and Negative Affect Communication on Infant Responses to New Toys," *Child Development* 58 (1987): 936–944.

43. Rima Shore, *Rethinking the Brain* (New York: Families and Work Institute, 1997).

44. Marshall H. Klaus and John H. Kennell, *Maternal-Infant Bonding* (St. Louis, MO: Mosby, 1976).

45. Michael Rutter, "Continuities and Discontinuities from Infancy," in *Handbook of Infant Development*, ed. Joy Donziger Osofsky, 2d ed. (New York: Wiley, 1987), pp. 1256–1297.

46. Field, "The Effects of Mother's Physical and Emotional Unavailability on Emotion Regulation."

47. Saul A. Schanberg and Tiffany M. Field, "Sensory Deprivation Stress and Supplemental Stimulation in the Tar Pup and Preterm Neonate," *Child Development* 58 (1987): 1432–1447.

48. Elizabeth Anisfeld et al., "Does Infant Carrying Promote Attachment? An Experimental

Study of the Effects of Increased Physical Contact on the Development of Attachment," *Child Development* 61 (1990): 1617–1627.

49. Field, "The Effects of Mother's Physical and Emotional Unavailability on Emotion Regulations."

50. Tiffany Martini-Field and Susan M. Widmayer, "Motherhood," in *Handbook of Developmental Psychology,* ed. Benjamin G. Wolman (Englewood Cliffs, NJ: Prentice-Hall, 1982), pp. 681–701.

51. Karlen Lyons-Ruth and Charles H. Zeanah, Jr., "The Family Context in Infant Mental Health: I. Affective Development in the Primary Caregiving Relationship," in *Handbook of Infant Mental Health,* ed. Charles H. Zeanah, Jr. (New York: Guilford Press, 1993), pp. 14–37.

52. Robert Emde and James F. Sorce, "The Rewards of Infancy: Emotional Availability and Maternal Referencing," in *Frontiers of Infant Psychiatry,* ed. Justin D. Call, Eleanor Galenson, and Robert L. Tyson (New York: Basic Books, 1983), pp. 17–30; Louis W. Sander, "Polarity, Paradox and the Organizing Process in Development," in *Frontiers of Infant Psychiatry,* ed. Call, Galenson, and Tyson, pp. 333–346.

53. Field, "The Effects of Mother's Physical and Emotional Unavailability on Emotion Regulations."

54. Lyons-Ruth and Zeanah, "Family Context."

55. Alicia F. Lieberman, Donna R. Weston, and Jerie H. Paul, "Preventive Intervention and Outcome with Anxiously Attached Dyads," *Child Development* 62 (1991): 199–209.

56. Lyons-Ruth and Zeanah, "Family Context."

57. Karlen Lyons-Ruth et al., "Infants at Social Risk: Maternal Depression and Family Support Services as Moderators of Infant Development and Security of Attachment," *Child Development* 61 (1990): 85–98.

58. Joy D. Osofsky, Della M. Hann, and Claire Peebles, "Adolescent Parenthood: Risks and Opportunities for Mothers and Infants," in *Handbook of Infant Mental Health,* ed. Zeanah, pp. 106–119; Joy D. Osofsky, "Risk and Preventive Factors for Teenage Mothers and Their Infants," *Newsletter of the Society for Research in Child Development,* Winter 1990.

59. Lyons-Ruth et al., "Infants at Social Risk."

60. Ross A. Thompson, "Early Sociopersonality Development," in *Handbook of Child Psychology,* ed. Damon and Eisenberg, vol. 3, 104: pp. 25–104.

61. Ibid.

62. Ibid.

63. Ibid.

64. Nathan A. Fox, Nancy L. Kimmerly, and William D. Schafer, "Attachment to Mother/ Attachment to Father: A Meta-Analysis," *Child Development* 62 (1991): 210–225.

65. Susan Golombok and Robyn Fivush, *Gender Development* (New York: Cambridge University Press, 1994).

66. Ibid.

67. Jay Belsky, Bonnie Gilstrap, and Michael Rovine, "The Pennsylvania Infant and Family Development Project I: Stability and Change in Mother-Infant and Father-Infant Interaction in a Family Setting at One, Three and Nine Months," *Child Development* 55 (1984): 692–705.

68. Ibid.

69. Thompson, "Early Sociopersonality Development."

70. Jay Belsky et al., "Instability of Infant-Parent Attachment Security," *Developmental Psychology* 32 (1996): 921–924.

71. Anisfeld et al. "Does Infant Carrying Promote Attachment?"

72. Kathryn E. Barnard, Colleen E. Morisset, and Susan Spieker, "Preventive Interventions: Enhancing Parent-Infant Relationships," in *Handbook of Infant Mental Health,* Zeanah, pp. 386–401.

73. Ibid.

74. Lyons-Ruth et al., "Infants at Social Risk."

75. Barnard, Morisset, and Spieker, "Preventive Interventions"; Samuel J. Meisels, Margo Dichtemiller, and Fong-ruey Liaw, "A Multidimensional Analysis of Early Childhood Intervention Programs," in *Handbook of Infant Mental Health,* ed. Zeanah, pp. 361–385.

76. Thompson, "Early Sociopersonality Development."

77. Thomas G. R. Bower, *A Primer of Infant Development* (San Francisco: Freeman, 1977).

78. Thompson, "Early Sociopersonality Development."

79. Martha F. Erickson, L. Alan Sroufe, and Byron Egeland, "The Relationship between Quality of Attachment and Behavior Problems in Preschool in a High Risk Sample," in *Growing Points of Attachment Theory and Research,* ed. Bretherton and Waters, pp. 147–166.

80. Susan Harter, "The Development of Self-Representations," in *Handbook of Child Psychology,* ed. Damon and Eisenberg, vol. 3, pp. 553–617.

81. Claire B. Kopp, "Antecedents of Self-Regulation: A Developmental Perspective,"

Developmental Psychology 18 (1982): 199–214.

82. Donelda J. Stayton, Robert Hogan, and Mary D. Salter Ainsworth, "Infant Obedience and Maternal Behavior: The Origins of Socialization Reconsidered," *Child Development* 42 (1971): 1057–1069.

83. Jeanne Brooks and Michael Lewis, "Infants' Responses to Strangers: Midget, Adult and Child," *Child Development* 47 (1976): 323–332.

84. Jacqueline M. T. Becker, "A Learning Analysis of the Development of Peer-Oriented Behavior in Nine-Month-Old Infants," *Developmental Psychology* 13 (1977): 481–491.

85. Bornstein, "Parenting Infants."

86. Gilda A. Morelli et al., "Cultural Variations in Infants' Sleeping Arrangements: Questions of Independence," *Developmental Psychology* 28 (1992): 604–613.

87. Ibid.

88. Ibid.

89. Richard Ferber, *Solve Your Child's Sleep Problems* (New York: Simon & Schuster, 1985).

90. Marc Weissbluth, *Crybabies* (New York: Arbor House, 1984).

91. Ibid.

92. Sylvia M. Bell and Mary D. Salter Ainsworth, "Infant Crying and Maternal Responsiveness," *Child Development* 43 (1972): 1171–1190.

93. Judy Dunn, *Distress and Comfort* (Cambridge, MA: Harvard University Press, 1977), p. 23.

94. Urs A. Hunziker and Ronald G. Barr, "Increased Carrying Reduces Crying: A Randomized Controlled Trial," *Pediatrics* 77 (1986): 641–647.

95. William A. H. Sammons, *The Self-Calmed Baby* (Boston: Little, Brown, 1989).

96. Weissbluth, *Crybabies,* p. 13.

97. Ibid.

98. Ibid.

99. Thomas Gordon with Judith Gordon Sands, *P.E.T. in Action* (New York: Bantam Books, 1976).

100. Rudolf Dreikurs with Vicki Soltz, *Children: The Challenge* (New York: Hawthorn, 1964), p. 40.

101. John D. Krumboltz and Helen B. Krumboltz, *Changing Children's Behavior* (Englewood Cliffs, NJ: Prentice-Hall, 1972).

102. Ellen Galinsky, *Between Generations: The Six Stages of Parenthood* (New York: Times Books, 1981).

103. Roberta Plutzik and Maria Laghi, *The Private Life of Parents* (New York: Everest House, 1983).

104. Marshall Klaus and John Kennell, *Maternal-Infant Bonding* (St. Louis, MO: Mosby, 1976).

Chapter 7

1. Jean Piaget and Barbel Inhelder, *The Psychology of the Child* (New York: Basic Books, 1969); Herbert Ginsburg and Sylvia Opper, *Piaget's Theory of Intellectual Development* (Englewood Cliffs, NJ: Prentice-Hall, 1969).

2. Barbara Rogoff, "Cognition as a Collaborative Process," in *Handbook of Child Psychology,* ed. in chief William Damon and vol. ed. Deanna Kuhn and Robert S. Siegler, vol. 2: *Cognition, Perception, and Language,* 5th ed. (New York: Wiley, 1997), pp. 679–744.

3. Robert Bradley et al., "Home Environment and Cognitive Development in the First Three Years of Life: A Collaborative Study Involving Six Sites and Three Ethnic Groups in North America," *Developmental Psychology* 25 (1989): 217–235.

4. Lois Bloom, "Language Acquisition in Its Developmental Context," in *Handbook of Child Psychology,* ed. Damon, Kuhn, and Siegler, vol. 2, pp. 309–370.

5. Ibid.

6. Ibid.

7. Inge Bretherton et al., "Learning to Talk about Emotions: A Functionalist Perspective," *Child Development* 57 (1986): 529–548.

8. Ibid.

9. Bloom, "Language Acquisition."

10. Richard Elardo, Robert Bradley, and Betty M. Caldwell, "A Longitudinal Study of the Relations of Infants' Home Environments to Language Development at Age Three," *Child Development* 48 (1977): 595–603.

11. Celeste Pappas Jones and Lauren B. Adamson, "Language Use in Mother-Child and Mother-Child-Sibling Interactions," *Child Development* 58 (1987): 356–366.

12. Betty Hart and Todd R. Risley, *Meaningful Differences in the Everyday Experience of Young American Children* (Baltimore: Brookes, 1995).

13. Michael Lewis, "The Emergence of Emotions," in *Handbook of Emotions,* ed. Michael Lewis and Jeanette M. Haviland (New York: Guilford Press, 1993), pp. 223–235.

14. Deborah Stipek, Susan Recchia, and Susan McClintic, *Self-Evaluation in Young Children,* Monographs of the Society for Research in Child Development 57, serial no. 226 (1992).

15. Deborah J. Stipek, J. Heidi Granliski and Claire B. Kopp, "Self-Concept Development

in the Toddler Years," *Developmental Psychology* 26 (1990): 972–977; Pamela M. Cole, Karen Caplovitz-Barrett, and Carolyn Zahn-Waxler, "Emotion Displays in Two-Year-Olds during Mishaps," *Child Development* 63 (1992): 314–324.

16. Michael Lewis, Steven M. Alessandri, and Margaret W. Sullivan, "Differences in Shame and Pride as a Function of Children's Gender and Task Difficulty," *Child Development* 63 (1992): 630–638.

17. Marion Radke-Yarrow et al., "Learning Concern for Others," *Developmental Psychology* 8 (1973): 240–260; Herbert Wray, *Emotions in the Lives of Young Children,* Department of Health, Education, and Welfare Publication no. 78-644 (Rockville, MD: 1978).

18. Carolyn Zahn-Waxler et al., "Development of Concern for Others," *Developmental Psychology* 28 (1992): 126–136.

19. E. Mark Cummings, Ronald J. Ianotti, and Carolyn Zahn-Waxler, "Influence of Conflict between Adults on the Emotions and Aggression of Young Children, "*Developmental Psychology* 21 (1985): 495–507.

20. Carolyn Saarni, Donna L. Mumme, and Joseph J. Campos, "Emotional Development: Action, Communication, and Understanding," in *Handbook of Child Psychology,* ed. in chief William Damon and vol. ed. Nancy Eisenberg, vol. 3: *Social, Emotional, and Personality Development,* 5th ed. (New York: Wiley, 1997), pp. 237–309.

21. Florence L. Goodenough, *Anger in Young Children* (Minneapolis: University of Minnesota Press, 1931).

22. Ibid.

23. Harriet L. Rheingold, Kay V. Cook, and Vicki Kolowitz, "Commands Cultivate the Behavioral Pleasure of Two-Year-Old Children," *Developmental Psychology* 23 (1987): 146–151.

24. Claire B. Kopp, "Regulation of Distress and Negative Emotions: A Developmental View," *Developmental Psychology* 25 (1989): 343–354.

25. Ibid.

26. Ibid.

27. Susan Harter, "The Development of Self-Representations," in *Handbook of Child Psychology,* ed. Damon and Eisenberg, vol. 3, pp. 553–617.

28. Susan Golombok and Robyn Fivush, *Gender Development* (New York: Cambridge University Press, (1994).

29. Kay Bussey and Albert Bandura, "Self-Regulatory Mechanisms Governing Gender Development," *Child Development* 63 (1992): 1236–1250.

30. John Money, "Human Hermaphroditism" in *Human Sexuality in Four Perspectives,* ed. Frank A. Beach (Baltimore: Johns Hopkins University Press, 1976), pp. 62–86.

31. Beverly I. Fagot, "Parenting Boys and Girls," in *Handbook of Parenting,* ed. Marc H. Bornstein, vol. 1: *Children and Parenting* (Mahwah, NJ: Erlbaum, 1995), pp. 163–183.

32. Ibid.

33. Ibid.

34. Claire B. Kopp, "Antecedents of Self-Regulation: A Developmental Perspective," *Developmental Psychology* 18 (1982): 199–214.

35. Brian E. Vaughn et al., "Process Analyses of the Behavior of Very Young Children in Delay Tasks," *Developmental Psychology* 22 (1986): 752–759.

36. Kopp, "Antecedents of Self-Regulation."

37. Leon Kuczynski and Grazyna Kochanska, "Development of Children's Noncompliance Strategies from Toddlerhood to Age 5," *Developmental Psychology* 25 (1990): 398–408.

38. Robert N. Emde et al., "The Moral Self of Infancy: Affective Core and Procedural Knowledge," *Developmental Review* 11 (1991): 251.

39. Grazyna Kochanska et al., "Maternal Reports of Conscience Development and Temperament in Young Children," *Child Development* 65 (1994): 852–868.

40. Jude Cassidy, "The Ability to Negotiate the Environment: An Aspect of Infant Competence as Related to Quality of Attachment," *Child Development* 57 (1986): 331–337.

41. Robert N. Emde and James F. Sorce, "The Rewards of Infancy: Emotional Availability and Referencing," in *Frontiers of Infant Psychiatry,* ed. Justin D. Call, Eleanor Galenson, and Robert L. Tyson (New York: Basic Books, 1983), pp. 17–30.

42. Tedra A. Walden and Tamra A. Ogan, "The Development of Social Referencing," *Child Development* 59 (1988): 1230–1240.

43. Lorraine Rocissano, Arietta Slade, and Victoria Lynch, "Dyadic Synchrony and Toddler Compliance," *Developmental Psychology* 23 (1987): 698–704.

44. Jutta Heckhausen, "Balancing for Weaknesses and Challenging Developmental Potential: A Longitudinal Study of Mother-Infant Dyads in Apprenticeship Interactions," *Developmental Psychology* 23 (1987): 762–770.

45. Mary Jane Gandour, "Activity Level as a Dimension of Temperament in Toddlers: Its Relevance for the Organismic Specificity

Hypotheses," *Child Development* 60 (1989): 1092–1098.

46. Lisa J. Bridges, James P. Connell, and Jay Belsky, "Similarities and Differences in Infant-Mother and Infant-Father Interaction in the Strange Situation: A Component Process Analysis," *Developmental Psychology* 24 (1988): 92–100.

47. M. Ann Easterbrooks and Wendy A. Goldberg, "Toddler Development in the Family: Impact of Father Involvement and Parenting Characteristics," *Child Development* 55 (1982): 841–864.

48. Byron Egeland and Ellen A. Farber, "Infant-Mother Attachment: Factors Related to Its Development and Changes over Time," *Child Development* 55 (1984): 753–771.

49. Carolyn L. Lee and John E. Bates, "Mother-Child Interaction at Age Two Years and Perceived Difficulty Temperament," *Child Development* 56 (1985): 1314–1325.

50. Beverly I. Fagot and Kate Kavanagh, "Parenting during the Second Year: Effects of Children's Age, Sex, and Attachment Classification," *Child Development* 64 (1993): 258–271.

51. Fagot and Kavanagh, "Parenting during the Second Year"; Keith A. Crnic and Cathryn L. Booth, "Mothers' and Fathers' Perceptions of Daily Hassles of Parenting across Early Childhood," *Journal of Marriage and the Family* 53 (1991): 1042–1050.

52. George Holden, "Avoiding Conflicts: Mothers as Tacticians in the Supermarket," *Child Development* 54 (1983): 233–240; Thomas G. Power and M. Lynne Chapieski, "Childrearing and Impulsive Control in Toddlers: A Naturalistic Investigation," *Developmental Psychology* 22 (1986): 271–275; George W. Holden and Meredith J. West, "Proximate Regulation by Mothers: A Demonstration of How Differing Styles Affect Young Children's Behavior," *Child Development* 60 (1989): 61–69.

53. J. Heidi Gralinski and Claire B. Kopp, "Everyday Rules for Behavior: Mothers' Requests to Young Children," *Developmental Psychology* 29 (1993): 573–584.

54. Ibid.

55. Sandra R. Kaler and Claire B. Kopp, "Compliance and Comprehension in Very Young Toddlers," *Child Development* 61 (1991): 1997–2003.

56. Grazyna Kochanska et al., "Inhibitory Control in Young Children and Its Role in Emerging Internalization," *Child Development* 67 (1996): 490–507.

57. Eleanor E. Maccoby and John A. Martin, "Socialization in the Context of the Family: Parent-Child Interaction," in *Handbook of Child Psychology*, ed. Paul H. Mussen and E. Mavis Hetherington, vol. 4: *Socialization, Personality, and Social Development*, 4th ed. (New York: Wiley, 1983), pp.1–101.

58. Jay Belsky, Sharon Woodworth, and Keith Crnic, "Troubled Family Interaction during Toddlerhood," *Development and Psychopathology* 8 (1996): 477–495.

59. Cheryl Minton, Jerome Kagan, and Janet A. Levine, "Maternal Control and Obedience in the Two-Year-Old," *Child Development* 42 (1971): 1873–1894.

60. Keng-Ling Lay, Everett Waters, and Kathryn A. Park, "Maternal Responsiveness and Child Compliance: The Role of Mood as Mediator," *Child Development* 60 (1989): 1405–1411.

61. Judy Dunn, *Sisters and Brothers* (Cambridge, MA: Harvard University Press, 1985).

62. Robert B. Steward, "Sibling Attachment Relationships: Child Infant Interactions in the Strange Situation," *Developmental Psychology* 19 (1983): 192–199.

63. Judy Dunn and Penny Munn, "Becoming a Family Member: Family Conflict and the Development of Social Understanding in the Second Year," *Child Development* 56 (1985): 480–492; Judy Dunn and Penny Munn, "Development of Justification in Disputes with Mother and Siblings," *Developmental Psychology* 23 (1987): 791–798.

64. Dunn, *Sisters and Brothers*.

65. Robert B. Steward et al., "The Firstborn's Adjustment to the Birth of a Sibling: A Longitudinal Assessment," *Child Development* 58 (1987): 341–355.

66. Carollee Howes, *Peer Interaction of Young Children*, Monographs of the Society for Research in Child Development 53, serial no. 217 (1987).

67. Patricia M. Greenfield and Lalita K. Suzuki, "Culture and Human Development: Applications for Parenting, Education, Pediatrics, and Mental Health," in *Handbook of Child Psychology*, ed. in chief William Damon and vol. ed. Irving E. Sigel and K. Ann Renninger, vol. 4: *Child Psychology in Practice*, 5th ed. (New York: Wiley, 1997), pp. 1059–1109.

68. Thomas Gordon with Judith Gordon Sands, *P.E.T. in Action* (New York: Bantam, 1978).

69. Rudolf Dreikurs with Vicki Soltz, *Children: The Challenge* (New York: Hawthorn, 1964).

70. John D. Krumboltz and Helen B. Krumboltz, *Changing Children's Behavior* (Englewood Cliffs, NJ: Prentice-Hall, 1972).

71. Richard Ferber, *Solve Your Child's Sleep Problems* (New York: Simon & Schuster, 1985).

72. Nathan H. Azrin and Richard M. Foxx, *Toilet Training in Less Than a Day* (New York: Pocket Books, 1974).

73. T. Berry Brazelton, *Doctor and Child* (New York: Dell, 1978).

74. Daniel Goleman, "Gene Link Found to Bed-Wetting Proving Problem Isn't Emotional," *New York Times*, July 1, 1995.

75. Mordecai Kaffman and Esther Elizur, *Infants Who Become Enuretics: A Longitudinal Study of 161 Kibbutz Children*, Monographs of the Society for Research in Child Development 42, whole no. 170 (1977).

76. Adele Faber and Elaine Mazlish, *Liberated Parents/Liberated Children*, (New York: Avon, 1975).

77. Dreikurs with Soltz, *Children*.

78. Krumboltz and Krumboltz, *Changing Children's Behavior*.

79. Stanley Turecki and Leslie Tonner, *The Difficult Child* (New York: Bantam Books, 1985).

80. Haim G. Ginott, *Between Parent and Child* (New York: Avon, 1969).

81. Rudolf Dreikurs, *The Challenge of Parenthood*, rev. ed. (New York: Hawthorn, 1958).

82. Robert Eimers and Robert Aitchison, *Effective Parents/Responsible Children* (New York: McGraw-Hill, 1977).

83. Dorothy C. Briggs, *Your Child's Self-Esteem* (Garden City, NY: Doubleday, 1975).

84. Ellen Galinsky, *Between Generations: The Six Stages of Parenthood* (New York: Times Books, 1981).

85. Ibid., pp. 126–137.

Chapter 8

1. Rima Shore, *Rethinking the Brain* (New York: Families and Work Institute, 1997).

2. Jean Piaget and Barbel Inhelder, *The Psychology of the Child* (New York: Basic Books, 1969).

3. Ross A. Thompson, "Early Sociopersonality Development," in *Handbook of Child Psychology*, ed. in chief William Damon and vol. ed. Nancy Eisenberg, vol. 3: *Social, Emotional, and Personality Development*, 5th ed. (New York: Wiley, 1997), pp. 25–104.

4. David Elkind, *Children and Adolescents*, 2d ed. (New York: Oxford University Press, 1974), p. 32.

5. Piaget and Inhelder, *Psychology of the Child*.

6. Frances Fuchs Schacter et al., *Everyday Preschool Interpersonal Speech Usage: Methodological, Development, and Sociolinguistic Studies*, Monographs of the Society for Research in Child Development 39, whole no. 156 (1974).

7. Sally K. Donaldson and Michael A. Westerman, "Development of Children's Understanding of Ambivalent and Causal Theories of Emotions," *Developmental Psychology* 22 (1986): 655–662.

8. Richard A. Fabes et al., "Preschoolers' Attributions of the Situational Determinants of Others' Naturally Occurring Emotions," *Developmental Psychology* 24 (1988): 376–385.

9. Gertrude Nunner-Winkler and Beate Sodian, "Children's Understanding of Moral Emotions," *Child Development* 59 (1988): 1323–1338.

10. Frank A. Zelko et al., "Adult Expectancies about Children's Emotional Responsiveness: Implications for the Development of Implicit Theories of Affect," *Developmental Psychology* 22 (1986): 109–114.

11. William Roberts and Janet Strayer, "Parents' Responses to the Emotional Distress of Their Children: Relations with Children's Competence," *Developmental Psychology* 23 (1987): 415–422.

12. Michael Lewis, Catherine Stanger, and Margaret Sullivan, "Deception in Three-Year Olds," *Developmental Psychology* 25 (1989): 439–443.

13. Pamela M. Cole, "Children's Spontaneous Control of Facial Expressions," *Child Development* 57 (1986): 1309–1321.

14. Kurt W. Fischer and Daniel Bullock, "Cognitive Development in School Age Children: Conclusions and New Directions," in *Development during Middle Childhood: The Years from Six to Twelve*, ed. W. Andrew Collins (Washington, DC: National Academy Press, 1984).

15. Nancy Eisenberg et al., "The Relations of Emotionality and Regulation to Preschoolers' Social Skills and Sociometric Status," *Child Development* 64 (1993): 1418–1438; Nancy Eisenberg at al., "Emotional Responsivity to Others: Behavioral Correlates and Socialization Antecedents," in *Emotion and Its Regulation in Early Development*, ed. Nancy Eisenberg and Richard A. Fabes, New Directions for Child Development, no. 55 (San Francisco: Jossey-Bass, 1990), pp. 57–73.

16. Florence L. Goodenough, *Anger in Young Children* (Minneapolis: University of Minnesota Press, 1931).

17. Nancy Eisenberg et al., "The Relations of Emotionality and Regulation to Children's Anger-Related Reactions," *Child Development* 65 (1994): 109–128.

18. John M. Gottman and Lynn F. Katz, "Effects of Marital Discord on Young Children's Peer Interaction and Health," *Developmental Psychology* 25 (1989): 373–381.

19. E. Mark Cummings, "Coping with Background Anger in Early Childhood," *Child Development* 58 (1987): 976–984.

20. Jerome Kagan and Nancy Snidman, "Temperamental Factors in Human Development," *American Psychologist* 46 (1991): 856–862.

21. Anders Broberg, Michael E. Lamb and Philip Hwang, "Inhibition: Its Stability and Correlates in Sixteen- to Forty-Month-Old Children," *Child Development* 61 (1990): 1153–1163.

22. Jerome Kagan and Howard A. Moss, *From Birth to Maturity* (New York: Wiley, 1962).

23. Fabes et al., "Preschoolers' Attributions."

24. David Matsumoto et al., "Preschoolers' Moral Actions and Emotions in Prisoner's Dilemma," *Developmental Psychology* 22 (1986): 663–670.

25. Susan Harter, "The Development of Self-Representations," in *Handbook of Child Psychology,* ed. Damon and Eisenberg, vol. 3, pp. 553–617.

26. Margaret Beale Spencer and Carol Markstrom-Adams, "Identity Processes among Racial and Ethnic Minority Children in America," *Child Development* 61 (1990): 290–310.

27. Deborah Stipek, Susan Recchina, and Susan McClintic, *Self-Evaluation in Young Children,* Monographs of the Society for Research in Child Development 57, serial no. 226 (1992).

28. Deborah J. Stipek, Theresa A. Roberts, and Mary E. Sanborn, "Preschool-Age Children's Performance Expectations for Themselves and Another Child as a Function of the Incentive Value of Success and the Salience of Past Performance," *Child Development* 55 (1984): 1983–1989.

29. Sandra Lipsitz Bem, "Genital Knowledge and Gender Constancy in Preschool Children, *Child Development* 60 (1989): 649–662; Michael Siegal and Judith Robinson, "Order Effects in Children's Gender Constancy Responses," *Developmental Psychology* 23 (1987): 283–286.

30. Susan Golombok and Robyn Fivush, *Gender Development* (New York: Cambridge University Press, 1994).

31. Kay Bussey and Albert Bandura, "Self-Regulatory Mechanisms Governing Gender Development," *Child Development* 63 (1992): 1236–1250.

32. Ibid., p. 1247.

33. Golombok and Fivush, *Gender Development* p. 111.

34. Marni H. Frauenglass and Rafael M. Diaz, "Self-Regulating Functions of Children's Private Speech: A Critical Analysis of Recent Challenges to Vygotsky's Theory," *Developmental Psychology* 21 (1985): 357–364.

35. Claire B. Kopp, "Antecedents of Self-Regulation: A Developmental Perspective," *Developmental Psychology* 18 (1982): 199–214.

36. J. Heidi Gralinski and Claire B. Kopp, "Everyday Rules for Behavior: Mothers' Requests to Young Children," *Developmental Psychology* 29 (1993): 573–584.

37. Leon Kuczynski and Grazyna Kochanska, "Development of Children's Noncompliance Strategies from Toddlerhood to Age Five," *Developmental Psychology* 26 (1990): 398–408.

38. Jeanne H. Block and Jack Block, "The Role of Ego-Control and Ego Resiliency in the Organization of Behavior," in *Minnesota Symposia on Child Psychology* vol. 13, ed. W. Andrew Collins (Hillsdale, NJ: Erlbaum, 1980), pp. 29–101.

39. Dante Cicchetti et al., "An Organizational Perspective on Attachment Beyond Infancy," in *Attachment in the Preschool Years: Theory, Research, and Intervention,* ed. Mark T. Greenberg, Dante Cicchetti, and E. Mark Cummings (Chicago: University of Chicago Press, 1990), p. 11.

40. Thompson, "Early Sociopersonality Development."

41. Ibid.

42. Edward Mueller and Elizabeth Tingley, "The Bears' Picnic: Children's Representations of Themselves and Their Families," in *Children's Perspectives on the Family,* ed. Inge Bretherton and Michael W. Watson, New Directions for Child Development, no. 48 (San Francisco: Jossey-Bass, 1992), pp. 47–65.

43. Martha F. Erickson, L. Alan Sroufe, and Byron Egeland, "The Relationship between Quality of Attachment and Behavior Problems in Preschool in a High Risk Sample," in *Growing Points of Attachment Theory and Research,* ed. Inge Bretherton and Everett Waters, Monographs of the Society for Research in

NOTES

Child Development 50, serial no. 109 (1985): 147–166.

44. Judith A. Crowell and S. Shirley Feldman, "Mother's Internal Models of Relationships and Developmental Status: A Study of Mother-Child Interaction," *Child Development* 59 (1988): 1273–1285.

45. Michelle L. Kelley, Thomas G. Power, and Dawn D. Wimbush, "Determinants of Disciplinary Practices in Low-Income Black Mothers," *Child Development* 63 (1992): 573–582.

46. Nancy B. Miller et al., "Externalizing in Preschoolers and Early Adolescents: A Cross-Study Replication of a Family Model," *Developmental Psychology* 29 (1993): 3–18.

47. Hiram E. Fitzgerald et al., "Predictors of Behavior Problems in Three-Year-Old Sons of Alcoholics: Early Evidence for the Onset of Risk," *Child Development* 64 (1993): 110–123.

48. John M. Gottman, Lynn Fainsilber Katz, and Carole Hooven, "Parental Meta-Emotion Philosophy and the Emotional Life of Families: Theoretical Models and Preliminary Data," *Journal of Family Psychology* 10 (1996): 243–268.

49. Thomas Gordon, *Teaching Children Self-Discipline* (New York: Times Books, 1989).

50. Judy Dunn, *Sisters and Brothers* (Cambridge, MA: Harvard University Press, 1985).

51. Brenda L. Volling and Jay Belsky, "The Contribution of Mother-Child and Father-Child Relationships to the Quality of Sibling Interactions: A Longitudinal Study," *Child Development* 63 (1992): 1209–1222.

52. Dunn, *Sisters and Brothers*.

53. Volling and Belsky, "The Contribution of Mother-Child and Father-Child Relationships."

54. Gene H. Brody, Zolinda Stoneman, and Michelle Burke, "Child Temperaments, Maternal Differential Behavior, and Sibling Relationships," *Developmental Psychology* 23 (1987): 354–362; Robert B. Steward et al., "The Firstborn's Adjustment to the Birth of a Sibling: A Longitudinal Assessment," *Child Development* 58 (1987); 341–355; Clare Stocker, Judy Dunn, and Robert Plomin, "Sibling Relationships: Links with Child Temperament, Maternal Behavior, and Family Structure," *Child Development* 60 (1989): 715–727.

55. Judith F. Dunn, Robert Plomin, and Denise Daniels, "Consistency and Change in Mothers' Behavior toward Young Siblings," *Child Development* 57 (1986): 348–356; Judith F. Dunn, Robert Plomin, and Margaret Nettles, "Consistency of Mothers' Behavior toward Infant Siblings," *Developmental Psychology* 21 (1985): 1188–1195.

56. Tiffany Field, Louis De Stefano, and John H. Koewler, III, "Fantasy Play of Toddlers and Preschoolers," *Developmental Psychology* 18 (1982): 503–508.

57. Willard W. Hartup et al., "Conflict and the Friendship Relations of Young Children," *Child Development* 59 (1988): 1590–1600.

58. Donald S. Hayes, "Cognitive Bases for Liking and Disliking among Preschool Children," *Child Development* 49 (1978): 906–909.

59. Michael P. Leiter, "A Study of Reciprocity in Preschool Play Groups," *Child Development* 48 (1977): 1288–1295.

60. Kenneth H. Rubin, William Bukowski, and Jeffrey G. Parker, "Peer Interactions, Relationships, and Groups," in *Handbook of Child Psychology*, ed. Damon and Eisenberg, vol. 3, pp. 619–700.

61. Ibid.

62. Ibid.

63. Diana Baumrind, "The Development of Instrumental Competence through Socialization," in *Minnesota Symposia on Child Development,* vol. 7, ed. Ann D. Pick (Minneapolis: University of Minnesota Press, 1973), pp. 3–46.

64. Patricia M. Greenfield and Lalita K. Suzuki, "Culture and Human Development: Implications for Parenting, Education, Pediatrics, and Mental Health," in *Handbook of Child Psychology*, ed. in chief William Damon and vol. ed. Irving E. Sigel and K. Ann Renninger, vol. 4: *Child Psychology in Practice,* 5th ed. (New York: Wiley, 1997), pp. 1059–1109.

65. Ibid.

66. Ibid.

67. Haim G. Ginott, *Between Parent and Child* (New York: Avon, 1969).

68. Thomas Gordon, *P.E.T.: Parent Effectiveness Training* (New York: New American Library, 1975); Thomas Gordon with Judith Gordon Sands, *P.E.T. in Action* (New York: Bantam, 1978).

69. Rudolf Dreikurs with Vicki Soltz, *Children: The Challenge* (New York: Hawthorn, 1964).

70. Richard Ferber, *Solve Your Child's Sleep Problems* (New York: Simon & Schuster, 1985).

71. Ibid., p. 49.

72. Daniel Goleman "Gene Link Found to Bed-Wetting, Proving Problem Isn't Emotional," *New York Times,* July 1, 1995.

73. Nathan Azrin and Victoria Besalel, *A Parent's Guide to Bedwetting Control* (New York: Pocket Books, 1979).

74. Ibid.

75. Frances L. Ilg and Louise Bates Ames, *Child Behavior* (New York: Harper & Row, 1955).

76. Benjamin Spock, *Baby and Child Care,* rev. ed. (New York: Pocket Books, 1976).

77. Adele Faber and Elaine Mazlish, *Liberated Parents/Liberated Children* (New York: Avon, 1975).

78. David M. Buss, Jeanne H. Block, and Jack Block, "Preschool Activity Level: Personality Correlates and Developmental Implications," *Child Development* 51 (1980): 401–408.

79. Charles H. Halverson and Mary Waldrop, "Relationship between Preschool Activity and Aspects of Intellectual and Social Behavior at Age Seven and a Half," *Developmental Psychology* 12 (1976): 107–112.

80. Kagan and Moss, *Birth to Maturity.*

81. David M. Buss, "Predicting Parent-Child Interactions from Children's Activity Level," *Developmental Psychology* 17 (1981): 59–65.

82. Russell A. Barkley, "The Use of Psychopharmacology to Study Reciprocal Influences in Parent-Child Interaction," *Journal of Abnormal Child Psychology* 9 (1981): 303–310.

83. Russell A. Barkley, *Attention Deficit Hyperactivity Disorder: A Handbook for Diagnosis and Treatment* (New York: Guilford Press, 1990).

84. Donald H. Meichenbaum and Joseph Goodman, "Training Impulsive Children to Talk to Themselves: A Means of Developing Self-Control," *Journal of Abnormal Psychology.* 77 (1971): 115–126.

85. Robert Eimers and Robert Aitchison, *Effective Parents/Responsible Children* (New York: McGraw-Hill, 1977).

86. Dorothy Rogers, *Child Psychology* (Monterey, CA: Brooks/Cole, 1969), p. 453.

87. Rosemary S. L. Mills and Kenneth H. Rubin, "Parental Beliefs about Problematic Social Behaviors in Early Childhood," *Child Development* 61 (1990): 138–151.

88. Ginott, *Between Parent and Child.*

89. Gordon, *P.E.T.*

90. Dreikurs with Soltz, *Children.*

91. Mills and Rubin, "Parental Beliefs."

92. Ginott, *Between Parent and Child.*

93. Gordon, *P.E.T.*

94. Dreikurs with Soltz, *Children.*

95. Eimers and Aitchison, *Effective Parents/Responsible Children.*

96. David M. Harrington, Jeanne Block, and Jack Block, "Intolerance of Ambiguity in Preschool Children," *Developmental Psychology* 14 (1978): 242–256.

97. Wesley C. Becker, *Parents Are Teachers* (Champaign, IL: Research Press, 1971).

98. Eimers and Aitchison, *Effective Parents/Responsible Children.*

99. Stanley Turecki and Leslie Tonner, *The Difficult Child* (New York: Bantam, 1985).

100. John E. Bates, Christine A. Maslin, and Karen H. Frankel, "Attachment Security, Mother-Child Interaction and Temperament as Predictors of Behavior Problem Ratings at Age Three Years," in *Growing Points of Attachment Theory and Research,* ed. Bretherton and Waters, pp. 167–193; Carolyn L. Lee and John Bates, "Mother-Child Interaction at Age Two Years and Perceived Difficult Temperament," *Child Development* 56 (1985): 1314–1325.

101. Keith A. Crnic and Cathryn L. Booth, "Mothers' and Fathers' Perceptions of Daily Hassles of Parenting across Early Childhood," *Journal of Marriage and the Family* 53 (1991): 1042–1050.

102. Kay Donohue Jennings, Vaughan Stagg, and Robin E. Connors, "Social Networks and Mothers' Interactions with Their Preschool Children," *Child Development* 62 (1991): 966–978.

103. Patricia Y. Hashima and Paul R. Amato, "Poverty, Social Support, and Parental Behavior," *Child Development* 65 (1994): 394–403.

104. Kelley, Power, and Wimbush, "Determinants of Disciplinary Practices."

Chapter 9

1. W. Andrew Collins, Michael L. Harris, and Amy Susman, "Parenting during Middle Childhood," in *Handbook of Parenting,* ed. Marc H. Bornstein, vol. 1: *Children and Parenting* (Mahwah, NJ: Erlbaum, 1995), pp. 65–89.

2. Ibid.

3. Ibid.

4. Deborah A. Phillips,, "Socialization of Perceived Academic Competence among Highly Competent Children," *Child Development* 58 (1987): 1308–1320.

5. Karl L. Alexander and Doris R. Entwisle, *Achievement in the First Two Years of School: Patterns and Processes,* Monographs of the Society for Research in Child Development 53, serial no. 218 (1988).

6. Lynn Okagaki and Robert J. Sternberg, "Parental Beliefs and Children's School Performance," *Child Development* 64 (1993): 36–56.

7. Harold W.. Stevenson, Chuansheng Chen, and David H. Uttal, "Beliefs and Achievements: A Study of Black, White, and Hispanic Children," *Child Development* 61 (1990): 508–523.

NOTES

8. Okagaki and Sternberg, "Parental Beliefs and Children's School Performance."

9. Harold W. Stevenson and Shin-ying Lee, *Contexts of Achievement,* Monographs of the Society for Research in Child Development, 55, serial no. 221 (1990).

10. Jacquelynne S. Eccles, Allan Wigfield, and Ulrich Schiefele, "Motivation to Succeed," in *Handbook of Child Psychology,* ed. in chief William Damon and vol. ed. Nancy Eisenberg, vol. 3: *Social, Emotional, and Personality Development,* 5th ed. (New York: Wiley, 1997), pp. 1017–1095.

11. Diane McGuiness, "How Schools Discriminate against Boys," *Human Nature,* February 1979.

12. Eccles, Wigfield, and Schiefele, "Motivation to Succeed."

13. Alexander and Entwisle, *Achievement in the First Two Years of School.*

14. Gary W. Ladd and Joseph M. Price, "Predicting Children's Social and School Adjustment Following the Transition from Preschool to Kindergarten," *Child Development* 58 (1987): 1168–1189.

15. Karin S. Frey and Diane Ruble, "What Children Say about Classroom Performance: Sex and Grade Differences in Perceived Competence," *Child Development* 58 (1987): 1066–1078.

16. Karen Klein Burhans and Carol S. Dweck, "Helplessness in Early Childhood: The Role of Contingent Worth," *Child Development* 66 (1995): 1719–1738.

17. Eccles, Wigfield, and Schiefele, "Motivation to Succeed."

18. Patricia M. Greenfield and Lalita K. Suzuki, "Culture and Human Development: Implications for Parenting, Education, Pediatrics, and Mental Health," in *Handbook of Child Psychology,* ed. in chief William Damon and vol. ed. Irving E. Sigel and K. Anne Renninger, vol. 4: *Child Psychology in Practice,* 5th ed. (New York: Wiley, 1997), pp. 1059–1109.

19. Stevenson, Chen, and Uttal, "Beliefs and Achievements."

20. Deborah J. Stipek and Karen M. DeCotis, "Children's Understanding of the Implications of Causal Attributions for Emotional Experiences," *Child Development* 59 (1988): 1601–1616.

21. Sally K. Donaldson and Michael A. Westerman, "Development of Children's Understanding of Ambivalence and Causal Theories of Emotions," *Developmental Psychology* 22 (1986): 655–662.

22. Paul L. Harris et al., "Children's Understanding of the Distinction between Real and Apparent Emotion," *Child Development* 57 (1986): 895–909.

23. Jackie Gnepp and Debra L. R. Hess, "Children's Understanding of Verbal and Facial Display Rules," *Developmental Psychology* 22 (1986): 103–108.

24. Dayna Fuchs and Mark H. Thelen, "Children's Expected Interpersonal Consequences of Communicating Their Affective State and Reported Likelihood of Expression," *Child Development* 59 (1988): 1314–1322.

25. Nancy Eisenberg et al., "The Relations of Children's Dispositional Prosocial Behavior to Emotionality, Regulation, and Social Functioning," *Child Development* 67 (1996): 974–992.

26. Charles L. McCoy and John C. Masters, "The Development of Children's Strategies for the Social Control of Emotion," *Child Development* 56 (1985): 1214–1222.

27. Nancy Eisenberg and Paul H. Mussen, *The Roots of Prosocial Behavior in Children* (Cambridge, England: Cambridge University Press, 1989).

28. G. R. Patterson, Barbara D. DeBaryshe, and Elizabeth Ramsey, "A Developmental Perspective on Antisocial Behavior," *American Psychologist* 44 (1989): 329–335.

29. Steven R. Asher et al., "Peer Rejection and Loneliness in Childhood," in *Peer Rejection in Childhood,* ed. Steven R. Asher and John D. Coie (Cambridge, England: Cambridge University Press, 1990), 253–273.

30. Michael Rutter, Jack Tizard, and Kingsley Whitmore, eds., *Education, Health and Behavior* (Huntington, NY: Kruger, 1981).

31. Kaoru Yamamoto et al., "Voices in Unison: Stressful Events in the Lives of Children in Six Countries," *Journal of Child Psychology and Psychiatry* 28 (1987): 855–864.

32. Elaine Shaw Sorensen, *Children's Stress and Coping* (New York: Guilford, 1993).

33. Eve Brotman-Band and John R. Weisz, "How to Feel Better when It Feels Bad," *Developmental Psychology* 24 (1998): 247–253.

34. Jennifer L. Altshuler and Diane N. Ruble, "Developmental Changes in Children's Awareness of Strategies for Coping with Uncontrollable Stress," *Child Development* 60 (1989): 1337–1349.

35. Denise F. Hardy, Thomas G. Power, and Susan Jaedicke, "Examining the Relation of Parenting to Children's Coping with Everyday Stress," *Child Development* 64 (1993): 1829–1841.

36. Sorensen, *Children's Stress and Coping.*

37. Molly Reid et al., "My Family and Friends: Six- to Twelve-Year-Old Children's Perceptions of Social Support," *Child Development* 60 (1989): 907.

38. Mary J. Levitt, Nathalie Guacci-Franco, and Jerome L. Leavitt, "Convoys of Social Support in Childhood and Early Adolescence," *Developmental Psychology* 29 (1993): 811–818.

39. Martin E. P. Seligman, *Learned Optimism* (New York: Pocket Books, 1990).

40. Susan Harter, "The Development of Self-Representations," in *Handbook of Child Psychology,* ed. Damon and Eisenberg, vol. 3, pp. 553–617.

41. Phyllis A. Katz and Keith R. Ksansnak, "Developmental Aspects of Gender Role Flexibility and Traditionality in Middle Childhood and Adolescence," *Developmental Psychology* 30 (1994): 272–282.

42. Frances E. Aboud, "The Development of Ethnic Self-Identification and Attitudes," in *Children's Ethnic Socialization,* ed. Jean S. Phinney and Mary Jane Rotheram (Beverly Hills CA: Sage, 1987), pp. 32–55.

43. Mary Jane Rotheram-Borus and Jean S. Phinney, "Patterns of Social Expectations among Black and Mexican-American Children," *Child Development* 61 (1990): 542–556.

44. James P. Connell and Barbara C. Ilardi, "Self System Concomitants of Discrepancies between Children's and Teacher's Evaluations of Academic Competence," *Child Development* 58 (1987): 1297–1307.

45. Albert Bandura, "Regulation of Cognitive Processes through Perceived Self-Efficacy," *Developmental Psychology* 25 (1989): 729–735.

46. Mariellen Fischer and Harold Leitenberg, "Optimism and Pessimism in Elementary School-Aged Children," *Child Development* 57 (1986): 241–248.

47. Hazel J. Markus and Paula S. Nurius, "Self-Understanding and Self-Regulation in Middle Childhood," in *Development during Middle Childhood,* ed. W. Andrew Collins (Washington, DC: National Academy Press, 1984), pp. 147–183.

48. Tamara J. Ferguson, Hedy Stegge, and Ilse Damhuis, "Children's Understanding of Guilt and Shame," *Child Development* 62 (1991): 827–839.

49. Markus and Nurius, "Self-Understanding and Self-Regulation in Middle Childhood."

50. Susan Harter, "Developmental Perspectives on the Self-System," in *Handbook of Child Psychology,* ed. Paul H. Mussen and E. Mavis Hetherington, vol. 4: *Socialization, Personality and Social Development,* 4th ed. (New York: Wiley, 1983), pp. 275–385.

51. Grazyna Kochanska, "Socialization and Temperament in the Development of Guilt and Conscience," *Child Development* 62 (1991): 1379–1392.

52. Judith G. Smetana, Melanie Killen, and Elliot Turiel, "Children's Reasoning about Interpersonal and Moral Conflicts," *Child Development* 62 (1991): 629–644.

53. Lawrence Kohlberg, "The Development of Children's Orientations toward a Moral Order: I Sequence in the Development of Moral Thought," *Vita Humana* 6 (1963): 11–33.

54. Collins, Harris, and Susman, "Parenting during Middle Childhood."

55. Ibid.

56. Ibid.

57. Judith G. Smetana, "Adolescents' and Parents' Reasoning about Actual Family Conflict," *Child Development* 60 (1989): 1052–1067.

58. Graeme Russell and Alan Russell, "Mother-Child and Father-Child in Middle Childhood," *Child Development* 58 (1987): 1573–1585.

59. Frances K. Grossman, William S. Pollack, and Ellen Golding, "Fathers and Children: Predicting the Quality and Quantity of Fathering," *Developmental Psychology* 24 (1988): 822–891.

60. Russell and Russell, "Mother-Child and Father-Child in Middle Childhood."

61. Molly Reid, Sharon Landesman Ramey, and Margaret Burchinal, "Dialogues with Children about Their Families," in *Children's Perspectives on the Family,* ed. Inge Bretherton and Malcolm W. Watson, New Directions for Child Development, no. 48 (San Francisco: Jossey-Bass, 1990), pp. 5–28.

62. Eleanor E. Maccoby, "Middle Childhood in the Context of the Family," in *Development during Middle Childhood,* ed. Collins, pp. 184–239.

63. Michael C. Thornton et al., "Sociodemographic and Environmental Correlates of Racial Socialization by Black Parents," *Child Development* 61 (1990): 401–409.

64. Ibid.

65. Algea O. Harrison et al., "Family Ecologies of Ethnic Minority Children," *Child Development* 61 (1990): 347–362; Margaret Beale Spencer and Carol Markstrom-Adams, "Identity Processes among Racial and Ethnic Minority Children in America," *Child Development* 61 (1990): 290–310.

66. Judy Dunn, *Sisters and Brothers* (Cambridge, MA: Harvard University Press, 1985).

67. Rona Abramovitch et al., "Sibling and Peer Interaction: A Final Follow-up and a Comparison," *Child Development* 57 (1986): 217–229.

68. Gene H. Brody, Zolanda Stoneman, and Michelle Burke, "Child Temperaments, Maternal Differential Behavior, and Sibling Relationships," *Developmental Psychology* 23 (1987): 354–362.

69. Gene H. Brody, Zolanda Stoneman, and J. Kelly McCoy, "Associations of Maternal and Paternal Direct and Differential Behavior with Sibling Relationships: Contemporaneous and Longitudinal Analyses," *Child Development* 63 (1992): 82–92.

70. Gene H. Brody et al., "Contemporaneous and Longitudinal Associations of Sibling Conflict with Family Relationship Assessments and Family Discussions about Sibling Problems." *Child Development* 63 (1992): 391–400.

71. Kenneth H. Rubin, William Bukowski, and Jeffrey G. Parker, "Peer Interactions, Relationships, and Groups," in *Handbook of Child Psychology*, ed. Damon and Eisenberg, vol. 3, pp. 619–700.

72. Willard W. Hartup, "The Company They Keep: Friendships and Their Developmental Significance," *Child Development* 67 (1996): 1–13.

73. Rubin, Bukowski, and Parker, "Peer Interactions, Relationships, and Groups."

74. Ibid.

75. Ibid.

76. Shelley Hymel et al., "Children's Peer Relationships: Longitudinal Prediction of Internalizing and Externalizing Problems from Middle to Late Childhood," *Child Development* 61 (1990): 2004–2021.

77. Gary Ladd, "Having Friends, Keeping Friends, and Being Liked by Peers in the Classroom: Predictors of Children's Early School Adjustment," *Child Development* 61 (1990): 1081–1100.

78. Shelley Hymel, Esther Wagner, and Lynda J. Butler, "Reputational Bias: View from the Peer Group," in *Peer Rejection in Childhood*, ed. Asher and Coie, pp. 156–186.

79. Lori J. Connors and Joyce L. Epstein, "Parent and School Partnerships," in *Handbook of Parenting*, ed. Marc H. Bornstein, vol. 4: *Applied and Practical Parenting* (Mahwah, NJ: Erlbaum, 1995), pp. 437–458.

80. Ibid.

81. Adele Faber and Elaine Mazlish, *Liberated Parents/Liberated Children* (New York: Avon, 1974).

82. Thomas Gordon, *P.E.T.: Parent Effectiveness Training* (New York: New American Library, 1975); Thomas Gordon with Judith Gordon Sands, *P.E.T. in Action* (New York: Bantam, 1978).

83. Rudolf Dreikurs with Vicki Soltz, *Children: The Challenge* (New York: Hawthorn, 1964).

84. Sherri Oden and Steven R. Asher, "Coaching Children in Social Skills for Friendship Making," *Child Development* 48 (1977): 495–506.

85. Philip G. Zimbardo and Shirley Radl, *The Shy Child* (Garden City, NJ: Doubleday, 1982).

86. Hymel et al., "Children's Peer Relationships."

87. Gerald R. Patterson et al., *A Social Learning Approach to Family Intervention*, vol. 1: *Families with Aggressive Children* (Eugene, OR: Castalia, 1975).

88. Gerald R. Patterson, *Families: Applications of Social Learning to Family Life*, rev. ed. (Champaign, IL: Research Press, 1975).

89. Gerald R. Patterson, *Living with Children*, rev. ed. (Champaign, IL: Research Press, 1976).

90. Haim Ginott, *Between Parent and Child* (New York: Avon, 1969).

91. Dreikurs with Soltz, *Children*.

92. John D. Krumboltz and Helen B. Krumboltz, *Changing Children's Behavior* (Englewood Cliffs, NJ: Prentice-Hall, 1972).

93. Faber and Mazlish, *Liberated Parents/Liberated Children*.

94. Krumboltz and Krumboltz, *Changing Children's Behavior*.

95. Aletha C. Huston and John C. Wright, "Mass Media and Children's Development," in *Handbook of Child Psychology*, ed. Damon, Sigel, and Renninger, vol. 4, pp. 1042–1043.

96. Patricia Marks Greenfield, *Mind and Media: The Effects of Television, Video Games, and Computers* (Cambridge, MA: Harvard University Press, 1984), p. 51.

97. Huston and Wright, "Mass Media and Children's Development," p. 1043.

98. Ibid., p. 1027.

99. Ibid.

100. Marites F. Pinon, Aletha C. Huston, and John C. Wright, "Family Ecology and Child Characteristics That Predict Young Children's Educational Television Viewing," *Child Development* 60 (1989): 846–856.

101. Robert Kubey, "Media Implications for the Quality of Family Life," in *Media, Children and the Family: Social Scientific, Psychodynamic and Clinical Perspectives*, ed. Dolf

Zillmann, Jennings Bryant, and Aletha C. Huston (Hillsdale, NJ: Lawrence Erlbaum, 1994), pp. 61–69.

102. Ibid, p. 64.

103. Aletha C. Huston, Dolf Zillmann, and Jennings Bryant, "Media Influence, Public Policy and the Family," in *Media, Children, and the Family: Social Scientific, Psychodynamic and Clinical Perspectives,* ed. Zillman, Bryant, and Huston, pp. 3–18.

104. Aimee Dorr and Beth E. Rabin, "Parents, Children, and Television," in *Handbook of Parenting,* ed. Bornstein, vol. 4, pp. 323–351.

105. Ellen Galinsky, *Between Generations: The Six Stages of Parenthood* (New York: Time Books, 1981).

Chapter 10

1. Jeanne Brooks-Gunn and Edward O. Reiter, "The Role of Pubertal Processes," in *At the Threshold: The Developing Adolescent,* ed. S. Shirley Feldman and Glen R. Elliott (Cambridge, MA: Harvard University Press, 1990), pp. 16–53.

2. Ibid.

3. Diane N. Ruble and Jeanne Brooks-Gunn, "The Experience of Menarche," *Child Development* 53 (1982): 1557–1566.

4. Jeanne Brooks-Gunn and Diane N. Ruble, "The Development of Menstrual-Related Beliefs and Behaviors during Early Adolescence," *Child Development* 53 (1982): 156–157.

5. Christy Miller Buchanan, Jacquelynne S. Eccles, and Jill B. Becker, "Are Adolescents the Victims of Raging Hormones? Evidence for Activational Effects of Hormones on Mood and Behavior at Adolescence," *Psychological Bulletin* 3 (1992): 62–107.

6. Jacquelynne S. Eccles, Allan Wigfield, and Ulrich Schiefele, "Motivation to Succeed," in *Handbook of Child Psychology,* ed. in chief William Damon and vol. ed. Nancy Eisenberg, vol. 3: *Social, Emotional, and Personality Development,* 5th ed. (New York: Wiley, 1997), pp. 1017–1095.

7. Grayson N. Holmbeck, Roberta L. Paikoff, and Jeanne Brooks-Gunn, "Parenting Adolescents," in *Handbook of Parenting,* ed. Marc H. Bornstein, vol. 1: *Children and Parenting* (Mahwah, NJ: Erlbaum, 1995), pp. 91–118.

8. Jane Norman and Myron Harris, *The Private Life of the American Teenager* (New York: Rawson Wade, 1981).

9. Ibid.

10. Jean Piaget and Barbel Inhelder, *The Psychology of the Child,* (New York: Basic Books, 1969); Herbert Ginsburg and Sylvia Opper, *Piaget's Theory of Intellectual Development* (Englewood Cliffs, NJ: Prentice-Hall, 1969).

11. Eccles, Wigman, and Schiefele, "Motivation to Succeed."

12. Jacquelynne Eccles et al., "Development during Adolescence: The Impact of Stage-Environment Fit on Young Adolescents' Experiences in Schools and in Families," *American Psychologist* 48 (1993): 90–101.

13. Edward Seidman et al., "The Impact of School Transition in Early Adolescence on the Self System and Perceived Social Context of Poor Urban Youth," *Child Development* 65 (1994): 507–522.

14. James Patrick Connell, Margaret Beale Spencer, and J. Lawrence Aber, "Educational Risk and Resilience in African American Youth: Context, Self, Action, and Outcomes in School," *Child Development* 65 (1994): 493–506.

15. Seidman et al., "The Impact of School Transition."

16. Gene H. Brody et al., "Financial Resources, Parent Psychological Functioning, Parent Co-Caregiving and Early Adolescent Competence In Rural Two-Parent African American Families," *Child Development* 65 (1994): 590–605.

17. Barbara D. DeBaryshe, Gerald R. Patterson, and Deborah M. Capaldi, "A Performance Model for Academic Achievement in Early Adolescent Boys," *Developmental Psychology* 29 (1993): 795–804.

18. Mihaly Csikszentmihalyi and Reed Larson, *Being Adolescent* (New York: Basic Books, 1984).

19. Reed Larson and Mark Ham, "Stress and 'Storm Stress' in Early Adolescence: The Relationship of Negative Events and Dysphoric Affect," *Developmental Psychology* 29 (1993): 130–140.

20. Ibid.

21. Buchanan, Eccles, and Becker, "Are Adolescents the Victims of Raging Hormones?"

22. David Elkind, *Children and Adolescents,* 2d ed. (New York: Oxford University Press, 1974), p. 91.

23. Larson and Ham, "Stress and 'Storm Stress' in Early Adolescence."

24. Anne C. Petersen et al., "Depression in Adolescence," *American Psychologist,* 48 (1993): 155–168.

25. Ibid.

26. Roberta G. Simmons et al., "The Impact of Cumulative Changes in Early Adolescence," *Child Development* 58 (1987): 1220–1234.

27. Mary J. Levitt, Nathalie Guacci-Franco, and Jerome L. Levitt, "Convoys of Social Support in Childhood and Early Adolescence: Structure and Function," *Developmental Psychology* 29 (1993): 811–818.

28. Susan Harter, "The Development of Self-Representations," in *Handbook of Child Psychology,* ed. Damon and Eisenberg, vol. 3, pp. 553–617.

29. Erik H. Erikson, *Childhood and Society,* 2d ed. (New York: Norton, 1963).

30. James E. Marcia, "Identity in Adolescence," in *Handbook of Adolescent Psychology,* ed. Joseph Adelson (New York: Wiley, 1980), pp. 159–187.

31. Harold D. Grotevant, "Adolescent Development in Family Contexts," in *Handbook of Child Psychology,* ed. Damon and Eisenberg, vol. 3, pp. 1097–1149.

32. William E. Cross, Jr., "A Two-Factor Theory of Black Identity: Implications for the Study of Identity Development in Minority Children," in *Children's Ethnic Socialization: Pluralism and Development,* ed. Jean S. Phinney and Mary Jane Rotheram (Beverly Hills, CA: Sage, 1987), pp. 117–133.

33. Nancy L. Galambos, David M. Almeida, and Anne C. Petersen, "Masculinity, Femininity, and Sex Role Attitudes in Early Adolescence: Exploring Gender Intensification," *Child Development* 61 (1990): 1905–1914.

34. Phyllis A. Katz and Keith R. Ksansnak, "Developmental Aspects of Gender Role Flexibility and Traditionality in Middle Childhood and Adolescence," *Developmental Psychology* 30 (1994): 272–282; Thalma E. Lobel et al., "The Role of Gender-Related Information and Self-Endorsement of Traits in Preadolescents' Inferences and Judgments," *Child Development* 64 (1993): 1285–1294.

35. Jean S. Phinney, "Stages of Ethnic Identity Development in Minority Group Adolescents," *Journal of Early Adolescence* 9 (1989): 34–49.

36. Margaret Beale Spencer and Carol Markstrom-Adams, "Identity Processes among Racial and Ethnic Minority Children in America," *Child Development* 61 (1990): 290–310; Michael C. Thornton et al., "Sociodemographic and Environmental Correlates of Racial Socialization by Black Parents," *Child Development* 61 (1990): 401–409.

37. Phinney, "Stages of Ethnic Identity Development."

38. Harter, "The Development of Self-Representations."

39. Susan Harter, "Self and Identity Development," in *At the Threshold,* ed. Feldman and Elliott, pp. 352–387.

40. Jane B. Brooks, "Social Maturity in Middle Age and Its Developmental Antecedents," in *Present and Past in Middle Life,* ed. Dorothy H. Eichorn et al. (New York: Academic Press, 1981), pp. 243–265.

41. Jack Block with Norma Haan, *Lives through Time* (Berkeley, CA: Bancroft Books, 1971).

42. John Janeway Conger and Anne C. Petersen, *Adolescence and Youth,* 3d ed. (New York: Harper & Row, 1984), p. 231.

43. Reed Larson and Maryse H. Richards, "Daily Companionship in Late Childhood and Early Adolescence: Changing Developmental Contexts," *Child Development* 62 (1991): 284–300.

44. Reed Larson and Maryse H. Richards, *Divergent Realities: The Emotional Lives of Mothers, Fathers, and Adolescents* (New York: Basic Books, 1994), p. 189.

45. Judith G. Smetana, "Concepts of Self and Social Convention: Adolescents' and Parents' Reasoning about Hypothetical and Actual Family Conflicts," in *Development during the Transition to Adolescence: Minnesota Symposia on Child Psychology,* vol. 21, ed. Megan R. Gunnar and W. Andrew Collins (Hillsdale, NJ: Erlbaum, 1988), pp. 79–122; Judith G. Smetana, "Adolescents' and Parents' Reasoning about Actual Family Conflict," *Child Development* 60 (1989): 1052–1067.

46. Smetana, "Concepts of Self and Social Convention."

47. Laurence Steinberg, "Impact of Puberty on Family Relations: Effects of Pubertal Status and Pubertal Timing," *Developmental Psychology* 23 (1987): 451–460;

48. Per F. Gjerde, "The Interpersonal Structure of Family Interaction Settings: Parent-Adolescent Relations in Dyads and Triads," *Developmental Psychology* 22 (1986): 297–304.

49. Laurence Steinberg, "Reciprocal Relation between Parent-Child Distance and Pubertal Maturation," *Developmental Psychology* 24 (1988): 122–128.

50. Gale Inoff-Germain et al., "Relations between Hormone Levels and Observational Measures of Aggressive Behavior of Young Adolescents in Family Interactions," *Developmental Psychology* 24 (1988): 129–139.

51. Andrew J. Fuligni and Jacquelynne S. Eccles, "Perceived Parent-Child Relationships and Early Adolescents' Orientation toward Peers," *Developmental Psychology* 29 (1993): 622–632.

52. Holmbeck, Paikoff, and Brooks-Gunn, "Parenting Adolescents."

53. Ibid.

54. Nancy Darling and Laurence Steinberg, "Parenting Style as Context: An Integrative Model," *Psychological Bulletin,* 113 (1993): 487–496.

55. Holmbeck, Paikoff, and Brooks-Gunn, "Parenting Adolescents."

56. James P. Comer, "What Makes the New Generation Tick?" *Ebony,* August 1990, p. 38.

57. Spencer and Markstrom-Adams, "Identity Processes."

58. David Elkind, *The Hurried Child* (Reading, MA: Addition-Wesley, 1981).

59. Bruce E. Compass et al., "Parents and Child Stress Symptoms: An Integrative Analysis," *Developmental Psychology,* 25 (1989): 550–559.

60. Rex Forehand et al., "Home Predictors of Young Adolescents' School Behavior and Academic Performance," *Child Development* 57 (1986): 1528–1533.

61. Norman and Harris, *Private Life of the American Teenager.*

62. Ibid.

63. Kenneth H. Rubin, William Bukowski, and Jeffrey G. Parker, "Peer Interactions, Relationships, and Groups," in *Handbook of Child Psychology,* ed. Damon and Eisenberg, vol. 3, pp. 619–700.

64. Lynne Zarbatany, Donald P. Hartmann, and D. Bruce Rankin, "The Psychological Functions of Preadolescent Peer Activities," *Child Development* 61 (1990): 1067–1080.

65. Maryse H. Richard et al., "Developmental Patterns and Gender Differences in the Experience of Peer Companionship during Adolescence," *Child Development* 69 (1998): 154–163.

66. Holmbeck, Paikoff, and Brooks-Gunn, "Parenting Adolescents," p. 95.

67. Richard Ferber, *Solve Your Child's Sleep Problems* (New York: Simon & Schuster, 1985).

68. Haim G. Ginott, *Between Parent and Teenager* (New York: Avon, 1969).

69. Thomas Gordon, *P.E.T.: Parent Effectiveness Training* (New York: New American Library, 1975), p. 252.

70. Don Dinkmeyer and Gary D. McKay, *STEP/TEEN Systematic Training for Effective Parenting of Teens* (Circle Pines, MN: American Guidance Service, 1983).

71. Robert Eimers and Robert Aitchison, *Effective Parents/Responsible Children* (New York: McGraw-Hill, 1977).

72. Ginott, *Between Parent and Teenager.*

73. Gordon, *P.E.T.*

74. Eimers and Aitchison, *Effective Parents/Responsible Children.*

75. Dinkmeyer and McKay, *STEP/TEEN Systematic Training.*

76. Ibid.

77. Adele Faber and Elaine Mazlish, *How to Talk So Kids Will Listen and Listen So Kids Will Talk* (New York: Rawson Wade, 1980), p. 165.

78. Kathryn R. Wentzel and Cynthia A. Erdley, "Strategies for Making Friends: Relations to Social Behavior and Peer Acceptance in Early Adolescence," *Developmental Psychology* 29 (1993): 819–826.

79. Sandra Graham, Cynthia Hudley, and Estella Williams, "Attributional and Emotional Determinants of Aggression among African-American and Latino Young Adolescents," *Developmental Psychology* 28 (1992): 731–740; Sandra Graham and Cynthia Hudley, "Attributions of Aggressive and Nonaggressive African-American Male Early Adolescents: A Study of Construct Accessibility," *Developmental Psychology* 30 (1994): 365–373.

80. Wentzel and Erdley, "Strategies for Making Friends."

81. Philip Zimbardo and Shirley Radl, *The Shy Child* (Garden City, NY: Doubleday, 1982).

82. Ginott, *Between Parent and Teenager.*

83. Eimers and Aitchison, *Effective Parents/Responsible Children.*

84. Ellen Galinsky, *Between Generations: The Six Stages of Parenthood* (New York: Times Books, 1981).

Chapter 11

1. Susan G. Millstein and Iris F. Litt, "Adolescent Health" in *At the Threshold: The Developing Adolescent,* ed. S. Shirley Feldman and Glen R. Elliott (Cambridge, MA: Harvard University Press, 1990), pp. 431–456.

2. Cathy Schoen et al., "The Commonwealth Fund Survey of the Health of Adolescent Girls" (New York: Commonwealth Fund, 1997).

3. Millstein and Litt, "Adolescent Health."

4. Ibid.

5. Ibid.

6. Schoen et al, "The Commonwealth Fund Survey."

7. Ibid.

8. Jerald G. Bachman et al., "Transition in Drug Use during Late Adolescence and Young

NOTES

Adulthood," in *Transitions through Adolescence: Interpersonal Domains and Context,* ed. Julie A. Graber, Jeanne Brooks-Gunn, and Anne C. Petersen (Mahwah, NJ: Erlbaum, 1996), pp. 111–140.

9. Millstein and Litt, "Adolescent Health."

10. Pam Belluck, "Black Youths' Rate of Suicide Rising Sharply," *New York Times,* March 20, 1998, p. 1.

11. Schoen et al., "The Commonwealth Fund Survey."

12. Barbara J. Tinsley and Nancy B. Lees, "Health Promotion for Parents," in *Handbook of Parenting,* ed. Marc H. Bornstein, vol. 4: *Applied and Practical Parenting* (Mahwah, NJ: Erlbaum, 1995), pp. 187–204.

13. Herant Katchadourian, "Sexuality," in *At the Threshold,* ed. Feldman and Elliott, pp. 330–351.

14. Joseph Lee Rodgers, "Sexual Transitions in Adolescence," in *Transitions through Adolescence,* ed. Graber, Brooks-Gunn, and Petersen, pp. 85–110.

15. Roger P. Weissberg and Mark T. Greenfield, "School and Community Competence-Enhancement and Prevention Programs," in *Handbook of Child Psychology,* ed. in chief William Damon and vol. ed. Irving E. Sigel and K. Ann Renninger, vol. 4: *Child Psychology in Practice,* 5th ed. (New York: Wiley, 1997), pp. 877–954.

16. Nancy J. Cobb, *Adolescence: Continuity, Change, and Diversity* (Mountain View, CA: Mayfield, 1992).

17. Rodgers, "Sexual Transitions in Adolescence."

18. James Jaccard, Patricia J. Dittus, and Vivian V. Gordon, "Parent-Adolescent Congruency in Reports of Adolescent Sexual Behavior and in Communications about Sexual Behavior," *Child Development* 69 (1998): 247–261.

19. Patricia Barthalow Koch, "Promoting Healthy Sexual Development during Early Adolescence," in *Early Adolescence: Perspectives on Research, Policy, and Intervention,* ed. Richard M. Lerner (Hillsdale, NJ: Erlbaum, 1993), pp. 293–307.

20. Lisa J. Crockett, "Early Adolescent Family Formation," in *Early Adolescence,* ed. Lerner, pp. 93–110.

21. Ibid.

22. Katherine Fennelly, "Sexual Activity and Childbearing among Hispanic Adolescents in the United States," in *Early Adolescence,* ed. Lerner, pp. 335–352.

23. Jeanne Brooks-Gunn and Frank F. Furstenberg, "Adolescent Sexual Behavior," *American Psychologist* 44 (1989): 249–257.

24. Melvin Zelnick and John F. Kantner, "Sexual Activity, Contraceptive Use, and Pregnancy among Metropolitan-Area Teenagers 1971–1979," *Family Planning Perspectives* 12 (1980): 230–237.

25. Daniel P. Keating, "Adolescent Thinking," in *At the Threshold,* ed. Feldman and Elliott, pp. 54–89.

26. Ibid.

27. Karen Bartsch, "Adolescents' Theoretical Thinking," in *Early Adolescence,* ed. Lerner, pp. 143–157.

28. Susan Harter and Ann Monsour, "Developmental Analysis of Conflict Caused by Opposing Attributes in the Adolescent Self-Portrait," *Developmental Psychology* 28 (1992): 251–260.

29. Jacquelynne S. Eccles, Allan Wigfield, and Ulrich Schiefele, "Motivation to Succeed," in *Handbook of Child Psychology,* ed. in chief William Damon and vol. ed. Nancy Eisenberg, vol. 3: *Social, Emotional, and Personality Development,* 5th ed. (New York: Wiley, 1997), pp. 1017–1095.

30. Ibid.

31. Sanford M. Dornbusch et al., "The Relation of Parenting Style to Adolescent School Performance," *Child Development* 58 (1987): 1244–1257.

32. Robert B. McCall, Cynthia Evahn, and Lynn Kratzer, *High School Underachievers* (Newbury Park, CA: Sage, 1992).

33. John Janeway Conger and Anne C. Petersen. *Adolescence and Youth,* 3d ed. (New York: Harper & Row, 1984).

34. Ibid.

35. Gary Alan Fine, Jeylan T. Mortimer, and Donald F. Roberts, "Leisure, Work, and the Mass Media," in *At the Threshold,* ed. Feldman and Elliott, pp. 225–252.

36. Ellen Greenberger and Laurence D. Steinberg, "The Workplace as a Contest for the Socialization of Youth," *Journal of Youth and Adolescence* 10 (1981): 185–210; Laurence Steinberg and Ellen Greenberger, "The Part-Time Employment of High School Students: A Research Agenda," *Children and Youth Services Review* 2 (1980): 161–185.

37. Ellen Greenberger, Laurence D. Steinberg, and Alan Vaux, "Adolescents Who Work: Health and Behavioral Consequences of Job Stress," *Developmental Psychology* 17 (1981): 691–703.

38. Ellen Greenberger and Laurence Steinberg, *When Teenagers Work* (New York: Basic Books, 1986).

39. Alan P. Bell, "Role Modeling of Fathers in Adolescence and Young Adulthood," *Journal of Counseling Psychology* 16 (1969): 30–35.

40. Lois Wladis Hoffman, "Material Employment: 1979," *American Psychologist* 34 (1979): 859–865.

41. Mihaly Csikszentmihalyi and Reed Larson, *Being Adolescent* (New York: Basic Books, 1984), p. 234.

42. Csikszentmihalyi and Larson, *Being Adolescent.*

43. Michael Windle, "A Longitudinal Study of Stress Buffering for Adolescent Problem Behaviors," *Developmental Psychology* 28 (1992): 522–530.

44. Suniya S. Luthar, "Vulnerability and Resilience: A Study of High Risk Adolescents," *Child Development* 62 (1991): 600–616.

45. Brooks-Gunn and Michelle P. Warren, "Biological and Social Contributions to Negative Affect in Young Adolescent Girls," *Child Development* 60 (1989): 40–55.

46. Albert Bandura, *Self-Efficacy: The Exercise of Control* (New York: Freeman, 1997).

47. Susan Harter, "The Development of Self-Representations," in *Handbook of Child Psychology,* ed. Damon and Eisenberg, vol. 3, pp. 553–617.

48. Jack Block and Richard W. Robins, "A Longitudinal Study of Consistency and Change in Self-Esteem from Early Adolescence to Early Adulthood," *Child Development* 64 (1993): 909–923.

49. Jack Block, "Some Relationships Regarding the Self from the Block and Block Longitudinal Study" (paper presented at the Social Science Research Council Conference on Selfhood, October 1985, Stanford, CA).

50. Susan Harter, "Self and Identity Development," in *At the Threshold,* ed. Feldman and Elliott, pp. 352–387.

51. Koch, "Promoting Healthy Sexual Development during Early Adolescence."

52. Katchadourian, "Sexuality."

53. Koch, "Promoting Healthy Sexual Development during Early Adolescence."

54. Nancy Eisenberg et al., "Prosocial Development in Adolescence: A Longitudinal Study," *Developmental Psychology* 27 (1991): 849–857.

55. Harold D. Grotevant, "Adolescent Development in Family Contexts," in *Handbook of Child Psychology,* ed. Damon and Eisenberg, vol. 3.

56. Richard Jessor et al., "Protective Factors in Adolescent Problem Behavior: Moderator Effects and Developmental Change," *Developmental Psychology* 31 (1995): 923–933.

57. Bachman et al., "Transitions in Drug Use."

58. Jane Norman and Myron Harris, *The Private Life of the American Teenager* (New York: Rawson Wade, 1981).

59. Diana Baumrind, "The Influence of Parenting Style on Adolescent Competence and Problem Behavior" (paper presented at the American Psychological Association Meetings, August 1989, New Orleans, LA).

60. Ibid., p. 16.

61. Laurence Steinberg et al., "Authoritative Parenting and Adolescent Adjustment: An Ecological Perspective," in *Examining Lives in Context,* ed. Phyllis Moen, Glen H. Elder, Jr., and Kurt Lusher (Washington, DC: American Psychological Association, 1995), pp. 423–466.

62. Grace M. Barnes and Michael P. Farrell, "Parental Support and Control as Predictors of Adolescent Drinking, Delinquency, and Related Problem Behaviors," *Journal of Marriage and the Family* 54 (1992): 763–776.

63. Brian K. Barber, "Parental Psychological Control: Revisiting a Neglected Construct," *Child Development* 67 (1996): 3296–3319.

64. Lori L. D'Angelo, Daniel Weinberger, and S. Shirley Feldman, "Like Father, Like Son? Predicting Male Adolescents' Adjustment from Parents' Distress and Self-Restraint," *Developmental Psychology* 31 (1995): 883–896.

65. Nina S. Mounts and Laurence Steinberg, "An Ecological Analysis of Peer Influence on Adolescent Grade Point Average and Drug Use," *Developmental Psychology* 31 (1995): 615–622.

66. Brooks-Gunn and Furstenberg, "Adolescent Sexual Behavior."

67. Ibid.

68. Greenberger and Steinberg, *When Teenagers Work.*

69. Andrew Billingsley, *Climbing Jacob's Ladder: The Enduring Legacy of African-American Families* (New York: Simon & Schuster, 1992).

70. Judith G. Smetana, "Concepts of Self and Social Convention: Adolescents' and Parents' Reasoning about Hypothetical and Actual Family Conflicts," in *Development during the Transition to Adolescence,* Minnesota

NOTES

Symposia on Child Psychology, vol. 21, ed. Megan R. Gunnar and W. Andrew Collins (Hillsdale, NJ: Erlbaum, 1988), pp. 79–122. Judith G. Smetana, "Adolescents' and Parents' Reasoning about Actual Family Conflict," *Child Development* 60 (1989): 1052–1067.

71. Joseph P. Allen et al., "Longitudinal Assessment of Autonomy and Relatedness in Adolescent-Family Interactions as Predictors of Adolescent Ego Development and Self-Esteem," *Child Development* 65 (1994): 1179–1194.

72. R. Rogers Kobak et al., "Attachment and Emotion Regulation during Mother-Teen Problem Solving: A Control Theory Analysis," *Child Development* 64 (1993): 231–245.

73. DeWayne Moore, "Parent-Adolescent Separation: The Construction of Adulthood by Late Adolescents," *Developmental Psychology* 23 (1987): 298–307.

74. S. Shirley Feldman and Thomas M. Gehring, "Changing Perceptions of Family Cohesion and Power across Adolescence," *Child Development* 59 (1988): 1034–1045.

75. David Elkind, "Growing Up Faster," *Psychology Today,* February 1979.

76. Duane Buhrmester and Wyndol Furman, "Perceptions of Sibling Relationships during Middle Childhood and Adolescence," *Child Development* 61 (1990): 1387–1398.

77. Csikszentmihalyi and Larson, *Being Adolescent.*

78. B. Bradford Brown, "Peer Groups and Peer Culture," in *At the Threshold,* ed. Feldman and Elliott, pp. 171–196.

79. Ibid.

80. Duane Buhrmester, "Intimacy and Friendship, Interpersonal Competence, and Adjustment during Preadolescence and Adolescence," *Child Development* 61 (1990): 1101–1111.

81. Norman and Harris, *Private Life of the American Teenager.*

82. Brown, "Peer Groups and Peer Culture."

83. Aaron Hogue and Laurence Steinberg, "Homophily of Internalized Distress in Adolescent Peer Groups," *Developmental Psychology* 31 (1995): 897–906.

84. Brown, "Peer Groups and Peer Culture."

85. Conger and Petersen, *Adolescence and Youth.*

86. Ibid.

87. Ibid.

88. Ibid.

89. Robert C. Sorenson, *Adolescent Sexuality in Contemporary America: Personal Values and Sexual Behavior Ages 13–19* (New York: Abrams, 1973).

90. Salvador Minuchin, Bernice L. Rossman, and Lester Baker, *Psychosomatic Families: Anorexia Nervosa in Context* (Cambridge, MA: Harvard University Press, 1978).

91. *The World Almanac and Book of Facts: 1994,* ed. Robert Famighetti (Mahwah, NJ: Funk and Wagnalls, 1993), p. 692.

92. Cobb, *Adolescence.*

93. Baumrind, "The Influence of Parenting Style on Adolescent Competence"; Jonathan Shedler and Jack Block, "Adolescent Drug Use and Psychological Health: A Longitudinal Inquiry," *American Psychologist* 45 (1990): 612–630.

94. Michael Windle et al., "Adolescent Perceptions of Help-Seeking Resources for Substance Abuse," *Child Development* 62 (1991): 179–189.

95. Beth Polson and Miller Newton, *Not My Kid: A Parent's Guide to Kids and Drugs* (New York: Avon, 1985).

96. Ibid.

97. McCall, Evahn, and Kratzer, *High School Underachievers.*

98. Fitzhugh Dodson, *How to Discipline with Love* (New York: Rawson, 1977), p. 410.

99. Ibid, pp. 410–411.

100. Haim G. Ginott, *Between Parent and Teenager* (New York: Avon, 1969).

101. Thomas Gordon, *P.E.T.: Parent Effectiveness Training* (New York: New American Library, 1975).

102. John D. Krumboltz and Helen B. Krumboltz, *Changing Children's Behavior* (Englewood Cliffs, NJ: Prentice-Hall, 1972).

103. Dorothy C. Briggs, *Your Child's Self-Esteem* (Garden City, NY: Doubleday, 1970).

104. Shirley Gould, *Teenagers: The Continuing Challenge* (New York: Hawthorn, 1977).

105. Krumboltz and Krumboltz, *Changing Children's Behavior.*

106. Katherine B. Oettinger, *Not My Daughter* (Englewood Cliffs, NJ: Prentice-Hall, 1979).

107. Thomas Gordon with Judith Gordon Sands, *P.E.T. in Action* (New York: Bantam, 1978).

108. Phyllis York, David York, and Ted Wachtel, *ToughLove* (Garden City, NY: Doubleday, 1982).

109. William Damon, *The Youth Charter: How Communities Can Work Together to Raise Standards for All Our Children* (New York: Free Press, 1997).

110. Ibid., p. ix.

111. George E. Vaillant, *Adaptation to Life* (Boston: Little, Brown, 1977), p. 225.

112. Laurence Steinberg with Wendy Steinberg, *Crossing Paths: How Your Child's Adolescence Triggers Your Own Crisis* (New York: Simon & Schuster, 1994).

Chapter 12

1. Urie Bronfenbrenner, "Ecology of the Family as a Context for Human Development," *Developmental Psychology* 22 (1986): 723–742.
2. Melvin L. Kohn, *Class and Conformity: A Study in Values* (Homewood, IL: Dorsey Press, 1969).
3. Adele Eskeles Gottfried, Allen W. Gottfried, and Kay Bathurst, "Maternal and Dual-Earner Employment Status and Parenting," in *Handbook of Parenting,* ed. Marc H. Bornstein, vol. 2: *Biology and Ecology of Parenting* (Mahwah, NJ: Erlbaum, 1995), pp. 139–160.
4. Ibid.
5. John L. Cotterell, "Work and Community Influences on the Quality of Child Rearing," *Child Development* 57 (1986): 362–374.
6. Gottfried, Gottfried, and Bathurst, "Maternal and Dual-Earner Employment Status and Parenting."
7. Ann C. Crouter, Mary C. Maguire, and Heather M. Helms-Erikson, "Daily Diaries: A Window into How Families Divide Work" (paper presented at the Society for Research in Child Development Meetings, Washington, DC, April 1997).
8. Elizabeth Menaghan and Toby Parcel, "Parental Employment and Family Life: Research in the 1980s," *Journal of Marriage and the Family* 52 (1990): 1079–1098.
9. Ann C. Crouter, "Processes Linking Families and Work: Implications for Behavior and Development in Both Settings," in *Exploring Family Relationships with Other Contexts,* ed. Ross D. Parke and Sheppard G. Kellam (Hillsdale, NJ: Erlbaum, 1994), pp. 29–47.
10. Ibid., p. 21.
11. Personal communication to author.
12. Ibid.
13. Rand D. Conger et al., "A Family Process Model of Economic Hardship and Adjustment of Early Adolescent Boys," *Child Development* 63 (1992): 526–541; Rand D. Conger et al., "Family Economic Stress and Adjustment of Early Adolescent Girls," *Developmental Psychology* 29 (1993): 206–219; Constance A. Flanagan, "Change in Family Work Status: Effects on Parent-Adolescent Decision-Making," *Child Development* 61 (1990): 163–177; Constance A. Flanagan and Jacquelynne S. Eccles, "Changes in Parents' Work Status and Adolescents' Adjustment at School," *Child Development* 64 (1993): 246–257.
14. Ronald L. Simons et al., "Support from Spouse as Mediator and Moderator of the Disruptive Influence of Economic Strain on Parenting," *Child Development* 63 (1992): 1282–1301.
15. Ronald L. Simons et al, "Social Network and Marital Support as Mediators and Moderators of the Impact of Stress and Depression on Parental Behavior," *Developmental Psychology* 29 (1993): 368–381.
16. Niall Bolger et al., "The Contagion of Stress across Multiple Roles," *Journal of Marriage and the Family* 51 (1989): 175–183.
17. Ibid.
18. Ellen Galinsky, "Families and Work: The Importance of the Quality of the Work Environment," in *Putting Families First,* ed. Sharon L. Kagan and Bernice Weissbourd (San Francisco: Jossey-Bass, 1994), pp. 112–136.
19. James A. Levine and Todd L. Pittinsky, *Working Fathers: New Strategies for Balancing Work and Family* (Reading, MA: Addison-Wesley, 1997).
20. Lois Wladis Hoffman, "Effects of Maternal Employment in the Two-Parent Family," *American Psychologist* 44 (1989): 283–292.
21. Grace G. Baruch and Rosalind C. Barnett, "Fathers' Participation in Family Work and Children's Sex Role Attitudes," *Child Development* 57 (1986): 1210–1223.
22. Crouter, "Processes Linking Families and Work."
23. Sandra Scarr, *Mother Care/Other Care* (New York: Warner, 1985).
24. Gottfried, Gottfried, and Bathurst, "Maternal and Dual-Earner Employment Status and Parenting."
25. Ann C. Crouter and Susan M. McHale, "The Long Arm of the Job: Influences of Parental Work on Child Rearing," in *Parenting: An Ecological Perspective,* ed. Tom Luster and Lynn Okagaki (Hillsdale, NJ: Erlbaum, 1993), pp. 179–202.
26. Cynthia A. Stifter, Colleen M. Coulehan, and Margaret Fish, "Linking Employment to Attachment: The Mediating Effects of Maternal Separation Anxiety and Interactive Behavior," *Child Development* 64 (1993): 1451–1460.
27. Cheryl D. Hayes, John L. Palmer, and Martha J. Zaslow, eds., *Who Cares for America's Children?* (Washington, DC: National Academy Press, 1990).
28. Crouter and McHale, "The Long Arm of the Job."

29. Ann C. Crouter and Susan M. McHale, "Temporal Rhythms in Family Life: Seasonal Variation in the Relation between Parental Work and Family Processes," *Developmental Psychology* 29 (1993): 198–205.
30. Martha J. Moorehouse, "Linking Maternal Employment Patterns to Mother-Child Activities and Children's School Competence," *Developmental Psychology* 27 (1991): 295–303.
31. Maryse H. Richards and Elena Duckett, "The Relationship of Maternal Employment to Early Adolescent Daily Experience with and without Parents," *Child Development* 65 (1994): 225–236.
32. Crouter, "Processes Linking Families and Work."
33. Gregory Pettit, "After-School Experience and Social Adjustment in Early Adolescence: Individual, Family, and Neighborhood Risk Factors" (paper presented at the Meetings of the Society for Research in Child Development, Washington, DC, April 11 1997).
34. Jean L. Richardson et al., "Substance Use among Eighth-Grade Students Who Take Care of Themselves after School," *Pediatrics* 84 (1989): 556–566.
35. Baruch and Barnett, "Fathers' Participation in Family Work and Children's Sex Role Attitudes."
36. Joan E. Grusec, Jacqueline J. Goodnow, and Lorenzo Cohen, "Household Work and the Development of Concern for Others," *Developmental Psychology* 32 (1996): 999–1007.
37. Jacqueline J. Goodnow and Jennifer M. Bowes, *Men, Women and Household Work* (Melbourne, Australia: Oxford University Press, 1994).
38. Hoffman, "Effects of Maternal Employment."
39. Ibid.
40. Ellen Greenberger and Robin O'Neil, "Spouse, Parent, Worker: Role Commitments and Role-Related Experiences in the Construction of Adults' Well Being," *Developmental Psychology* 29 (1993): 181–197; Ellen Greenberger and Robin O'Neil, "Parents' Concerns about Their Child's Development: Implications for Fathers' and Mothers' Well Being and Attitudes toward Work," *Journal of Marriage and the Family* 52 (1990): 621–635.
41. Ellen Hock and Debra K. DeMeis, "Depression in Mothers of Infants: The Role of Material Employment," *Developmental Psychology* 26 (1990): 285–291.
42. Anita M. Farel, "Effects of Preferred Maternal Roles, Maternal Employment and Sociodemographic Status on School Adjustment and Competence," *Child Development* 50 (1980): 1179–1186.
43. Hoffman, "Effect of Maternal Employment."
44. Greenberger and O'Neil, "Spouse, Parent, Worker"; Greenberger and O'Neil, "Parents' Concerns about Their Child's Development."
45. Levine and Pittinsky, *Working Fathers.*
46. Greenberger and O'Neil, "Spouse, Parent, Worker"; Greenberger and O'Neil, "Parents' Concerns about Their Child's Development."
47. Arlie Russell Hochschild, *The Time Bind: When Work Becomes Home and Home Becomes Work* (New York: Holt, 1997).
48. Greenberger and O'Neil, "Spouse, Parent, Worker"; Greenberger and O'Neil, "Parents' Concerns about Their Child's Development."
49. Michael E. Lamb, "Nonparental Child Care: Context, Quality, Correlates," in *Handbook of Child Psychology,* ed. in chief William Damon and vol. ed. Irving E. Sigel and K. Ann Renninger, vol. 4: *Child Psychology in Practice,* 5th ed. (New York: Wiley, 1997), p. 116.
50. Crouter, "Processes Linking Families and Work."
51. Lamb, "Nonparental Child Care."
52. Tiffany Field, "Quality Infant Day-Care and Grade School Behavior and Performance," *Child Development* 62 (1991): 863–870.
53. Bengst-Erik Andersson, "Effects of Day Care on Cognitive and Socioemotional Competence of Thirteen-Year-Old Swedish Schoolchildren," *Child Development* 63 (1992): 20–36.
54. Rebecca Maynard and Eileen McGinnis, "Policies to Enhance Access for High-Quality Child Care," in *Child Care in the 1990s: Trends and Consequences,* ed. Alan Booth (Hillsdale, NJ: Erlbaum, 1992), pp. 189–208; Hayes Palmer, and Zaslow, *Who Cares for America's Children?*
55. Carollee Howes, Claire E. Hamilton, and Catherine C. Matheson, "Children's Relationships with Peers: Differential Associations with Aspects of the Teacher-Child Relationship," *Child Development* 65 (1994): 253–263.
56. Carollee Howes and Claire E. Hamilton, "Children's Relationships with Child Care Teachers: Stability and Concordance with Parental Attachments," *Child Development* 63 (1992): 867–878.
57. Carollee Howes, Catherine C. Matheson, and Claire E. Hamilton, "Maternal, Teacher, and Child Care History Correlates of Children's Relationships with Peers," *Child Development* 65 (1994): 264–273.
58. Carollee Howes, "Can the Age of Entry into Child Care and the Quality of Child Care Predict Adjustment in Kindergarten?" *Developmental Psychology* 26 (1990): 292–303.

59. Lamb, "Nonparental Child Care," p. 115.
60. Jay Belsky, "Consequences of Child Care for Child Development: A Deconstructionist View," in *Child Care in the 1990s,* ed. Booth, pp. 83–94.
61. Lamb, "Nonparental Child Care."
62. Ibid.
63. Ibid.
64. Alison Clarke-Stewart, "Consequences of Child Care for Children's Development," in *Child Care in the 1990s,* ed. Booth, pp. 63–82; Alison Clarke-Stewart, "Consequences of Child Care — One More Time: A Rejoinder," in *Child Care in the 1990s,* ed. Booth, pp. 116–124.
65. Belsky, "Consequences of Child Care for Child Development."
66. Ron Haskins, "Public School Aggression among Children with Varying Day-Care Experience," *Child Development* 56 (1985): 689–703.
67. Deborah Lowe Vandell and Mary Ann Corasaniti, "The Relation between Third-Graders' After-School Care and Social, Academic, and Emotional Functioning," *Child Development* 59 (1988): 868–875.
68. Hayes, Palmer, and Zaslow, *Who Cares for America's Children?*
69. Richardson et al., "Substance Use among Eighth-Grade Students."
70. Hoffman, "Effects of Maternal Employment."
71. Ibid.
72. Ibid.
73. Ramon G. McLeod, "U.S. Study Finds Big Shift in Child Care," *San Francisco Chronicle,* August 15, 1990.
74. Carollee Howes, Deborah A. Phillips, and Marcy Whitebook, "Thresholds of Quality: Implications for the Social Development of Children in Center-Based Child Care," *Child Development* 63 (1992): 449–460.
75. Harriet B. Presser, "Child Care Supply and Demand: What Do We Really Know?" in *Child Care in the 1990s,* ed. Booth, pp. 26–32.
76. Sally Provence, Audrey Naylor, and June Patterson, *The Challenge of Daycare* (New Haven, CN: Yale University Press, 1977).
77. Edward F. Zigler and Mary E. Lang, *Child Care Choices* (New York: Free Press, 1991).
78. Sandra L. Hofferth, "The Demand for and Supply of Child Care in the 1990s," in *Child Care in the 1990s,* ed. Booth, pp. 3–25.
79. Zigler and Lang, *Child Care Choices.*
80. Lynette Long and Thomas Long, *The Handbook for Latchkey Children and Their Parents* (New York: Arbor House, 1983).
81. Zigler and Lang, *Child Care Choices.*
82. Hofferth, "The Demand for and Supply of Child Care in the 1990s."
83. Zigler and Lang, *Child Care Choices.*
84. Ellen Galinsky, "The Impact of Child Care on Parents," in *Child Care in the 1990s,* ed. Booth, pp. 159–171.
85. Stifter, Coulehan, and Fish, "Linking Employment to Attachment."
86. Stanley Greenspan, "After the Baby: The Best Time to Go to Work," *Working Mother,* November 1982.
87. Debra K. DeMeis, Ellen Hock, and Susan L. McBride, "The Balance of Employment and Motherhood: Longitudinal Study of Mothers' Feelings about Separation from Their First-Born Infants," *Developmental Psychology* 22 (1986): 627–632.
88. Susan McBride and Jay Belsky, "Characteristics, Determinants, and Consequences of Maternal Separation Anxiety," *Developmental Psychology* 24 (1988): 407–414.
89. Stifter, Coulehan, and Fish, "Linking Employment to Attachment."
90. Dorothy C. Briggs, *Your Child's Self-Esteem* (Garden City, NY: Doubleday, 1975), p. 64.
91. Ellen Greenberger and Wendy Goldberg, "Work, Parenting, and the Socialization of Children," *Developmental Psychology* 25 (1989): 22–35.
92. Levine and Pittinsky, *Working Fathers.*
93. Gloria Norris and JoAnn Miller, *The Working Mother's Complete Handbook* (New York: Dutton, 1979).

Chapter 13

1. U.S. Bureau of the Census, *Statistical Abstract of the United States: 1996,* 116th ed. (Washington, DC: Government Printing Office, 1996).
2. E. Mavis Hetherington and W. Glenn Clingempeel, *Coping with Marital Transitions: A Family Systems Perspective,* Monographs of the Society for Research in Child Development 57, serial no. 227 (1992): 2–3.
3. Marsha Weinraub and Marcy B. Gringlas, "Single Parenthood," in *Handbook of Parenting,* ed. Marc H. Bornstein, vol. 3: *Status and Social Conditions of Parenting* (Mahwah, NJ: Erlbaum, 1995), pp. 65–87.
4. Ibid.
5. Ibid.
6. U.S. Bureau of the Census, *Statistical Abstract: 1996.*
7. Weinraub and Gringlas, "Single Parenthood," p. 66.
8. Ibid.

NOTES

9. Robert Fauber et al., "A Mediational Model of the Impact of Marital Conflict on Adolescent Adjustment in Intact and Divorced Families: The Role of Disrupted Parenting," *Child Development* 61 (1990): 1112–1123.

10. E. Mark Cummings and Patrick Davis, *Children and Marital Conflict: The Impact of Family Disputes and Resolution* (New York: Guil-ford Press, 1994).

11. Brian E. Vaughn, Jeanne H. Block, and Jack Block, "Parental Agreement on Child Rearing during Early Childhood and the Psychological Characteristics of Adolescents," *Child Development* 59 (1988): 1020–1033.

12. Jeanne H. Block, Jack Block, and Per F. Gjerde, "The Personality of Children prior to Divorce: A Prospective Study," *Child Development* 57 (1986): 827–840.

13. Bruce D. Perry, "Incubated in Terror: Neurodevelopmental Factors and the 'Cycle of Violence,'" in *Children in a Violent Society*, ed. Joy D. Osofsky (New York: Guilford, 1997), pp. 124–149.

14. E. Mavis Hetherington, "An Overview of the Virginia Longitudinal Study of Divorce and Remarriage with a Focus on Early Adolescence," *Journal of Family Psychology* 1 (1993): 39–56.

15. E. Mavis Hetherington and Kathleen A. Camara, "Families in Transition: The Process of Dissolution and Reconstruction," in *A Review of Child Development Research*, vol. 7, ed. Ross D. Parke (Chicago: University of Chicago Press, 1984), pp. 398–439.

16. Judith S. Wallerstein and Sandra Blakeslee, *Second Chances* (New York: Ticknor & Fields, 1989), p. 286.

17. Ibid.

18. Ibid, p. 287.

19. Judith S. Wallerstein and Joan B. Kelly, *Surviving the Breakup* (New York: Basic Books, 1980).

20. Ibid, p. 66.

21. Ibid.

22. Wallerstein and Blakeslee, *Second Chances*.

23. M. Janice Hogan, Cheryl Buehler, and Beatrice Robinson, "Single Parenting: Transitioning Alone," in *Stress and the Family*, vol. 1: *Coping with Normative Transitions*, ed. Hamilton I. McCubbin and Charles R. Figley (New York: Brunner/Mazel, 1983), pp. 116–132.

24. Hetherington, "An Overview of the Virginia Longitudinal Study."

25. Hetherington and Camara, "Families in Transition."

26. Wallerstein and Kelly, *Surviving the Breakup*.

27. Ibid.

28. Hetherington and Camara, "Families in Transition."

29. Hetherington and Camara, "Families in Transition"; Wallerstein and Kelly, *Surviving the Breakup*.

30. Ibid.

31. Ibid.

32. Wallerstein and Kelly, *Surviving the Breakup*.

33. E. Mavis Hetherington, "Coping with Family Transitions: Winners, Losers, and Survivors," *Child Development* 60 (1989): 1–14.

34. Wallerstein and Blakeslee, *Second Chances*.

35. Carol E. MacKinnon, "An Observational Investigation of Sibling Interactions in Married and Divorced Families," *Developmental Psychology* 25 (1989): 36–44.

36. Wallerstein and Blakeslee, *Second Chances*, p. 110.

37. Hetherington, "An Overview of the Virginia Longitudinal Study."

38. James H. Bray and E. Mavis Hetherington, "Families in Transition: Introduction and Overview," *Journal of Family Psychology* 7 (1993): 3–8.

39. Sanford L. Braver et al., "A Longitudinal Study of Noncustodial Parents: Parents without Children," *Journal of Family Psychology* 7 (1993): 9–23.

40. Hetherington, "An Overview of the Virginia Longitudinal Study."

41. Eleanor E. Maccoby et al., "Postdivorce Roles of Mothers and Fathers in the Lives of Their Children," *Journal of Family Psychology* 7 (1993): 24–38.

42. E. Mavis Hetherington and Kathleen M. Jodl, "Stepfamilies as Settings for Child Development," in *Stepfamilies: Who Benefits? Who Does Not?* ed. Alan Booth and Judy Dunn (Hillsdale, NJ: Erlbaum, 1994), pp. 55–79.

43. Hetherington, "An Overview of the Virginia Longitudinal Study."

44. Stanford M. Dornbusch et al., "Single Parents, Extended Households and the Control of Adolescents," *Child Development* 56 (1985): 326–341; Judith G. Smetana et al., "Adolescent-Parent Conflict in Married and Divorced Families," *Developmental Psychology* 27 (1991): 1000–1010.

45. Hetherington and Clingempeel, *Coping with Marital Transitions*.

46. Dornbusch et al., "Single Parents."

47. Christy M. Buchanan, Eleanor E. Maccoby, and Sanford M. Dornbusch, "Caught between Parents: Adolescents' Experience in

Divorced Homes," *Child Development* 62 (1991): 1008–1029.

48. Hetherington, "An Overview of the Virginia Longitudinal Study."

49. Paul R. Amato and Brian Keith, "Parental Divorce and the Well Being of Children: A Meta-Analysis," *Psychological Bulletin* 110 (1991): 26–46; Dornbusch et al., "Single Parents."

50. Nicholas Zill, Donna Ruane Morrison, and Mary Jo Coiro, "Long-Term Effects of Parental Divorce on Parent-Child Relationships, Adjustment, and Achievement in Young Adulthood," *Journal of Family Psychology* 7 (1993): 91–103.

51. Weinraub and Gringlas, "Single Parenthood."

52. Ibid.

53. Charlotte J. Patterson, "Gay and Lesbian Parenting," in *Handbook of Parenting*, ed. Bornstein, vol. 3, pp. 255–274.

54. Weinraub and Gringlas, "Single Parenthood."

55. Ibid.

56. James A. Levine with Edward W. Pitt, *New Expectations: Community Strategies for Responsible Fatherhood* (New York: Families and Work Institute, 1995).

57. Ibid, p. 41.

58. Ibid, p. 108.

59. Earl Grollman, "Prologue," in *Explaining Death to Children*, ed. Earl A. Grollman (Boston: Beacon Press, 1967), p. 15.

60. Ibid.

61. John Bowlby, "Childhood Mourning and Its Implications for Psychiatry," *American Journal of Psychiatry* 118 (1961): 481–498.

62. Grollman, "Prologue."

63. Thomas Gordon with Judith Gordon Sands, *P.E.T. in Action* (New York: Bantam Books, 1978).

64. Grollman, "Prologue," p. 27.

65. Monica McGoldrick and Betty Carter, "Forming a Remarried Family," in *The Changing Family Life Cycle*, ed. Betty Carter and Monica McGoldrick, 2d ed. (New York: Gardner Press, 1988), pp. 399–429.

66. Wallerstein and Blakeslee, *Second Chances.*

67. Hetherington and Clingempeel, "Coping with Marital Transitions."

68. Fitzhugh Dodson, *How to Discipline with Love* (New York: Rawson Associates, 1977).

69. Hetherington and Jodl, "Stepfamilies as Settings for Child Development."

70. W. Glenn Clingempeel and Sion Segal, "Stepparent-Stepchild Relationships and the Psychological Adjustment of Children in Stepmother and Stepfather Families," *Child Development* 57 (1986): 474–484.

71. Hetherington and Jodl, "Stepfamilies as Settings for Child Development."

72. Ibid.

73. Hetherington, "An Overview of the Virginia Longitudinal Study."

74. Hetherington and Clingempeel, "Coping with Marital Transitions."

75. Hetherington and Jodl, "Stepfamilies as Settings for Child Development."

76. Hetherington and Clingempeel, "Coping with Marital Transitions."

77. Hetherington and Jodl, "Stepfamilies as Settings for Child Development."

78. Ibid.

79. Ibid.

80. Lynn White, "Stepfamilies over the Life Course: Social Support," in *Stepfamilies,* ed. Booth and Dunn, pp. 109–137.

81. Brenda Maddox, *The Half Parent* (New York: New American Library, 1975), p. 167.

82. Paul R. Amato, "The Implications of Research Findings on Children in Stepfamilies," in *Stepfamilies,* ed. Booth and Dunn, pp. 81–87.

Chapter 14

1. David Finkelhor and Jennifer Dziuba-Leatherman, "Victimization of Children," *American Psychologist* 49 (1994): 173–183.

2. Ibid, p. 173.

3. Jay Belsky, "Etiology of Child Maltreatment: A Developmental-Ecological Analysis," *Psychological Bulletin* 114 (1993): 413–434.

4. Jody Todd Manly, Dante Cicchetti, and Douglas Barnett, "The Impact of Subtype, Frequency, Chronicity, and Severity of Child Maltreatment on Social Competence and Behavior Problems," *Development and Psychopathology* 6 (1994): 121–143.

5. Kathleen A. Kendall-Tackett, Linda Meyer Williams, and David Finkelhor, "Impact of Sex Abuse on Children: A Review and Synthesis of Recent Empirical Studies," *Psychological Bulletin* 113 (1993): 164–180.

6. Belsky, "Etiology of Child Maltreatment," p. 413.

7. Robert E. Emery and Lisa Laumann-Billings, "An Overview of the Nature, Causes, and Consequences of Abusive Family Relationships: Toward Differentiating Maltreatment and Violence," *American Psychologist* 53 (1998): 121–135.

8. Ibid.

9. Ibid.

10. Bruce D. Perry, "Incubated in Terror: Neurodevelopmental Factors in the 'Cycle of

NOTES

Violence,'" in *Children in a Violent Society,* ed. Joy D. Osofsky (New York: Guilford, 1997), pp. 124–149.

11. Dante Cicchetti and Michael Lynch, "Toward an Ecological/Transactional Model of Community Violence and Child Maltreatment: Consequences for Child Development," *Psychiatry* 56 (1993): 96–118.

12. Fred A. Rogosch et al., "Parenting Dysfunction in Child Maltreatment," in *Handbook of Parenting,* ed. Marc H. Bornstein, vol. 4: *Applied and Practical Parenting* (Mahwah, NJ: Erlbaum, 1995), pp. 127–159.

13. Glenn D. Wolfner and Richard J. Gelles, "A Profile of Violence toward Children: A National Study," *Child Abuse and Neglect* 17 (1993): 199–214.

14. Finkelhor and Dziuba-Leatherman, "Victimization of Children."

15. Penelope K. Trickett, Catherine McBride-Chang, and Frank W. Putnam, "The Classroom Performance and Behavior of Sexually Abused Females," *Development and Psychopathy* 6 (1994): 183–194.

16. Patricia J. Mrazek, "Maltreatment and Infant Development," in *Handbook of Infant Development,* ed. Charles H. Zeanah, Jr. (New York: Guilford Press, 1993), pp. 159–170.

17. Belsky, "Etiology of Child Maltreatment."

18. David A. Wolfe, "The Role of Intervention and Treatment Services in the Prevention of Child Abuse and Neglect," in *Protecting Children from Abuse and Neglect,* ed. Gary B. Melton and Frank D. Barry (New York: Guilford Press, 1994), pp. 224–303.

19. Ibid.

20. Ibid.

21. Ibid.

22. Sally Zierler, "Studies Confirm Long-Term Consequences of Childhood Sexual Abuse," *Brown University Child and Adolescent Behavior Newsletter* 8, November 1992, p. 3.

23. Ibid.

24. Diana E. H. Russell, "The Incidence and Prevalence of Intrafamilial and Extrafamilial Sexual Abuse of Female Children," in *Handbook on Sexual Abuse of Children,* ed. Leonore E. Auerbach Walker (New York: Springer, 1988), pp. 19–36.

25. Karin C. Meiselman, *Resolving the Trauma of Incest* (San Francisco: Jossey-Bass, 1990).

26. Kendall-Tackett, Williams, and Finkelhor, "Impact of Sex Abuse on Children."

27. Ibid.

28. Ibid.

29. David Finkelhor and Angela Browne, "Assessing the Long-Term Impact of Child Sexual Abuse: A Review and Conceptualization," in *Handbook on Sexual Abuse of Children,* ed. Walker, p. 62.

30. Ibid, pp. 62–63.

31. Kendall-Tackett, Williams, and Finkelhor, "Impact of Sex Abuse on Children."

32. Ibid.

33. Trickett, McBride-Chang, and Putnam, "Classroom Performance and Behavior of Sexually Abused Females."

34. Leonore E. A. Walker and Mary Ann Bolkovatz, "Play Therapy with Children Who Have Experienced Sexual Assault," in *Handbook on Sexual Abuse of Children,* ed. Walker, pp. 249–269.

35. Robert E. Emery, "Family Violence," *American Psychologist* 44 (1989): 321–328.

36. Richard J. Gelles, "Physical Violence, Child Abuse, and Child Homicide: A Continuum of Violence or Distinct Behaviors?" *Human Nature* 2 (1991): 59–72.

37. Wolfner and Gelles, "A Profile of Violence toward Children."

38. Ibid.

39. Emery and Laumann-Billings, "An Overview of the Nature, Causes, and Consequences of Abusive Family Relationships."

40. David A. Hamburg, *Today's Children* (New York: Times Books, 1992).

41. Wolfner and Gelles, "A Profile of Violence toward Children."

42. Rogosch et al., "Parenting Dysfunction in Child Maltreatment."

43. Gail S. Goodman, Robert E. Emery, and Jeffrey J. Haugaard, "Developmental Psychology and Law: Divorce, Child Maltreatment, Foster Care, and Adoption," in *Handbook of Child Psychology,* ed. in chief William Damon and vol. ed. Irving E. Sigel and K. Ann Renninger, vol. 4: *Child Psychology in Practice,* 5th ed. (New York: Wiley, 1997), pp. 775–874.

44. Rogosch et al., "Parenting Dysfunction in Child Maltreatment."

45. Belsky, "Etiology of Child Maltreatment."

46. Goodman, Emery, and Haugaard, "Developmental Psychology and Law."

47. Wolfner and Gelles, "A Profile of Violence toward Children."

48. Cicchetti and Lynch, "Toward an Ecological/Transactional Model."

49. Emery, "Family Violence."

50. Dante Cicchetti et al., "Resilience in Maltreated Children: Processes Leading to Adaptive Outcome," *Development and Psychopathology* 5 (1993): 629–647.

51. Richard J. Gelles, "Abandon Reunification

Goal for Abusive Families and Replace with Child Protection," *Brown University Child and Adolescent Behavior Newsletter* 8, June 1992, p. 1

52. Goodman, Emery, and Haugaard, "Developmental Psychology and Law."

53. Ibid.

54. Rogosch et al., "Parenting Dysfunction in Child Maltreatment."

55. John E. Richters and Pedro Martinez, "The NIMH Community Violence Project: I. Children as Victims of and Witnesses to Violence," *Psychiatry* 56 (1993): 7–21.

56. Pedro Martinez and John E. Richters, "The NIMH Community Violence Project: II. Children's Distress Symptoms Associated with Violence Exposure," *Psychiatry* 56 (1993): 22–35.

57. John E. Richters and Pedro Martinez, "Violent Communities, Family Choices, and Children's Choices: An Algorithm for Improving the Odds," *Development and Psychopathology* 5 (1993): 609–627.

58. Ibid, pp. 622–623.

59. Ibid.

60. Lenore Terr, *Too Scared to Cry* (New York: Harper & Row, 1990).

61. James Garbarino et al., *Children in Danger* (San Francisco: Jossey-Bass, 1992).

62. Peter A. Wyman et al., "The Role of Children's Future Expectations in Self System Functioning and Adjustment to Life Stress: A Prospective Study of Urban At-Risk Children," *Development and Psychopathology* 5 (1993): 646–666.

63. Garbarino et al., *Children in Danger,* p. 110.

64. Ibid.

65. Terr, *Too Scared to Cry.*

66. Alexandra Okun, Jeffrey G. Parker, and Alytia A. Levendosky, "Distinct and Interactive Contributions of Physical Abuse, Socioeconomic Disadvantage, and Negative Life Events to Children's Social, Cognitive and Affective Adjustment." *Development and Psychopathology* 6 (1994): 77–98.

67. Sam Howe Verhovek, "In Arkansas Jail, One Boy Cries and the Other Studies the Bible," *New York Times,* March 27, 1998, p. 1.

68. Perry, "Incubated in Terror," p. 144.

69. Katherine Kaufer Christoffel, "Firearm Injuries Affecting United States Children and Adolescents," in *Children in a Violent Society,* ed. Osofsky, pp. 42–71.

70. John P. Murray, "Media Violence and Youth," in *Children in a Violent Society,* ed. Osofsky, pp. 72–96.

71. Steven J. Wolin and Sybil Wolin, *The Resilient Self* (New York: Villard Books, 1993).

72. Ibid, pp. 5–6.

73. Grace Hechinger, *How to Raise a Street-Smart Child* (New York: Ballantine Books, 1984).

Chapter 15

1. William Morris, ed., *The American Heritage Dictionary of the English Language* (New York: American Heritage, 1969).

2. Gail S. Goodman, Robert E. Emery, and Jeffrey J. Haugaard, "Developmental Psychology and Law: Divorce, Child Maltreatment, Foster Care, and Adoption," in *Handbook of Child Psychology,* ed. in chief William Damon and vol. ed. Irving E. Sigel and K. Ann Renninger, vol. 4: *Child Psychology in Practice,* 5th ed. (New York: Wiley, 1997), pp. 775–784.

3. David M. Brodzinsky, Robin Lang, and Daniel W. Smith, "Parenting Adopted Children," in *Handbook of Parenting,* ed. Marc H. Bornstein, vol. 3: *Status and Social Conditions of Parenting* (Mahwah, NJ: Erlbaum 1995), pp. 209–232.

4. Ibid.

5. Ibid.

6. Ibid.

7. Ibid.

8. David M. Brodzinsky,. Leslie M. Singer, and Anne M. Braff, "Children's Understanding of Adoption," *Child Development* 55 (1984): 869–878.

9. Brodzinsky, Lang, and Smith, "Parenting Adopted Children."

10. Ibid., p. 216.

11. Ibid.

12. Ibid.

13. Goodman, Emery, and Haugaard, "Developmental Psychology and Law."

14. Brodzinsky, Lang, and Smith, "Parenting Adopted Children."

15. Ibid.

16. Ibid.

17. Ibid., p. 220.

18. Ibid.

19. Ibid.

20. Goodman, Emery, and Haugaard, "Developmental Psychology and Law."

21. Ibid.

22. Ibid.

23. Ibid.

24. Judith Schaffer and Christina Lindstrom, *How to Raise an Adopted Child* (New York: Crown, 1989).

512

NOTES

25. Brodzinsky, Lang, and Smith, "Parenting Adopted Children."

26. Schaffer and Lindstrom, *How to Raise an Adopted Child.*

27. Brodzinsky, Lang, and Smith, "Parenting Adopted Children."

28. Susan Goldberg and Barbara DiVitto, "Parenting Children Born Preterm," in *Handbook of Parenting,* ed. Marc H. Bornstein, vol. 1: *Children and Parenting* (Mahwah, NJ: Erlbaum, 1995), pp. 209–232.

29. Robin Marantz Henig and Anne B. Fletcher, *Your Premature Baby* (New York: Ballantine, 1983).

30. Ibid.

31. Goldberg and DiVitto, "Parenting Children Born Preterm."

32. Rachel Levy-Shiff, Haya Sharir, and Mario B. Mogilner, "Mother- and Father-Preterm Infant Relationship in the Hospital Preterm Nursery," *Child Development* 60 (1989): 93–102.

33. Henig and Fletcher, *Your Premature Baby.*

34. Anneliese F. Korner et al., "Stable Individual Differences in Developmentally Changing Preterm Infants: A Replicated Study," *Child Development* 60 (1989): 502–513.

35. Levy-Shiff, Sharir, and Mogilner, "Mother- and Father-Preterm Infant Relationships."

36. Goldberg and DiVitto, "Parenting Children Born Preterm."

37. Ibid.

38. Mark T. Greenberg and Keith A. Crnic, "Longitudinal Predictors of Developmental Status and Social Interaction in Premature and Full-Term Infants at Age Two," *Child Development* 59 (1988): 554–570.

39. Virginia A. Rauh et al., "Minimizing Adverse Effects of Low Birthweight: Four Year Results of an Early Intervention Program," *Child Development* 59 (1988): 544–553.

40. Greenberg and Crnic, "Longitudinal Predictors."

41. Marilyn Stern and Katherine A. Hildebrandt, "Prematurity and Stereotyping: Effects on Mother-Infant Interaction," *Child Development* 57 (1986): 308–315.

42. Cynthia L. Zarling, Barton J. Hirsch, and Susan Landry, "Maternal Social Networks and Mother-Infant Interactions in Full-Term and Very Low Birthweight, Preterm Infants," *Child Development* 59 (1988): 178–185.

43. Glenn Affleck et al., "Effects of Formal Support on Mothers' Adaptation to the Hospital-to-Home Transition of High Risk Infants: The Benefits and Costs of Helping," *Child Development* 60 (1989): 488–501.

44. John E. Schowalter, "The Chronically Ill Child," in *Basic Handbook of Child Psychiatry,* vol. 1, ed. Joseph D. Noshpitz (New York: Basic Books, 1979), pp. 432–436.

45. Elizabeth Gellert, "Children's Conceptions of the Content and Functions of the Human Body," *Genetic Psychology Monographs* 65 (1962): 293–405.

46. Ibid.

47. Ibid.

48. Roger Bibace and Mary E. Walsh, "Developmental States of Children's Conceptions of Illness," in *Health Psychology,* ed. George C. Stone, Frances Cohen, and Nancy E. Adler (San Francisco: Jossey-Bass, 1979), pp. 285–301.

49. Michael Siegal, "Children's Knowledge of Contagion and Contamination as Causes of Illness," *Child Development* 59 (1988): 1353–1359.

50. John D. Campbell, "Illness Is a Point of View: The Development of Children's Concepts of Illness," *Child Development* 46 (1975): 92–100.

51. Lee Salk, *What Every Child Would Like His Parents to Know* (New York: Warner, 1972), p. 116.

52. Arthur H. Parmelee, Jr., "Children's Illnesses: Their Beneficial Effects on Behavioral Development," *Child Development* 57 (1986): 1–10.

53. Jerome L. Schulman, *Coping with Tragedy* (Chicago: Follett, 1976).

54. Elizabeth F. Loftus, "Words That Could Save Your Life," *Psychology Today,* November 1979.

55. Susan M. McHale and Wendy C. Gamble, "Sibling Relationships of Children with Disabled and Nondisabled Brothers and Sisters," *Developmental Psychology* 25 (1989): 421–429.

56. Dante Cicchetti and Sheree L. Toth, "The Development of Depression in Children and Adolescents," *American Psychologist* 53 (1998): 221–241.

57. Ibid.

58. Ibid.

59. Donald H. McKnew, Leon Cytryn, and Herbert Yahraes, *Why Isn't Johnny Crying?* (New York: Norton, 1983).

60. Anne C. Petersen et al., "Depression in Adolescence," *American Psychologist* 48 (1993): 155–168.

61. Cicchetti and Toth, "The Development of Depression."

62. Petersen et al., "Depression in Adolescence."

63. Ibid.

64. W. Brian Barr, "Child Behavior Professionals

Are Not Untouched by Family Suicides," *Brown Child and Adolescent Behavior Newsletter,* March 1998, p. 1.

65. Roger P. Weissberg and Mark T. Greenfield, "School and Community Competence-Enhancement and Prevention Programs," in *Handbook of Child Psychology,* ed. Damon, Sigel, and Renninger, vol. 4, pp. 877–954.

66. Susan Harter, "Visions of Self Beyond the Me in the Mirror" (University lecture, University of Denver, 1990).

67. Ibid., p. 16.

68. Petersen et al., "Depression in Adolescence."

69. Martin E. P. Seligman, *The Optimistic Child* (New York: Houghton Mifflin, 1995).

70. *Diagnostic and Statistical Manual of Mental Disorders,* 4th ed. (Washington, DC: American Psychiatric Association, 1994).

71. Stephen P. Hinshaw, *Attention Deficits and Hyperactivity in Children* (Thousands Oaks, CA: Sage, 1994).

72. Ibid.

73. Ibid.

74. Mary Jane Gandour, "Activity Level as a Dimension of Temperament in Toddlers: Its Relevance for the Orgasmic Specificity Hypotheses," *Child Development* 60 (1989): 1092–1098.

75. Deborah Jacobvitz and L. Alan Sroufe, "The Early Caregiver-Child Relationship and Attention Deficit Disorder with Hyperactivity in Kindergarten," *Child Development* 58 (1987): 1488–1495.

76. Duane Buhrmester et al., "Mothers and Fathers Interacting in Dyads and Triads with Normal and Hyperactive Sons," *Developmental Psychology* 28 (1992): 500–509.

77. Hinshaw, *Attention Deficits and Hyperactivity.*

78. Carol K. Whalen et al., "Peer Perceptions of Hyperactivity and Medication," *Child Development* 58 (1987): 816–828.

79. Barbara Henker and Carol K. Whalen, "Hyperactivity and Attention Deficits," *American Psychologist* 44 (1989): 215–223.

80. Sally L. Smith, *No Easy Answers: The Learning Disabled Child at Home and at School,* rev. ed. (New York: Bantam, 1995).

81. Byron P. Rourke and Jerel E. Del Dotto, *Learning Disabilities: A Neurological Perspective* (Thousand Oaks, CA: Sage, 1994).

82. Ibid.

83. Diane McGuinness, *When Children Don't Learn* (New York: Basic Books, 1985).

84. Betty B. Osman, *Learning Disabilities: A Family Affair* (New York: Random House, 1979).

85. Smith, *No Easy Answers.*

86. Jeanne Brooks-Gunn and Greg J. Duncan, "Poor Families, Poor Children: The Well Being of Children and Youth," *Family Psychologist* 14, no. 2 (1998): 16–19.

87. Vonnie C. McLoyd, "Children in Poverty: Development, Public Policy, and Practice," in *Handbook of Child Psychology,* ed. Damon, Sigel, and Renninger, vol. 4, pp. 135–208.

88. David M. Betson and Robert T. Michael, "Why So Many Children Are Poor," *Future of Children* 7, no. 2 (1997): 25–39.

89. Ibid.

90. Mary E. Corcoran and Ajay Chaudry, "The Dynamics of Poverty," *Future of Children* 7, no. 2 (1997): 40–54.

91. Ibid.

92. McLoyd, "Children in Poverty."

93. Ibid.

94. Ibid.

95. Corcoran and Chaudry, "The Dynamics of Childhood Poverty."

96. Ibid.

97. McLoyd, "Children in Poverty."

98. Corcoran and Chaudry, "The Dynamics of Childhood Poverty."

99. McLoyd, "Children in Poverty."

100. Jeanne Brooks-Gunn and Greg J. Duncan, "The Effects of Poverty on Children," *Future of Children* 7, no. 2 (1997): 55–71.

101. Ibid.

102. Janet M. Currie, "Choosing among Alternative Programs for Poor Children," *Future of Children* 7, no. 2 (1997): 113–131.

103. Eugene M. Lewit, Donna L. Terman, and Richard E. Behrman, "Children and Poverty: Analysis and Recommendations," *Future of Children* 7, no. 2 (1997): p. 11.

104. Corcoran and Chaudry, "The Dynamics of Childhood Poverty."

105. Benjamin S. Bloom, ed., *Developing Talent in Young People* (New York: Ballantine, 1985).

106. Ibid., p. 538.

107. Mihaly Csikszentmihalyi, Kevin Rathunde, and Samuel Whalen, *Talented Teenagers: The Roots of Success and Failure* (New York: Cambridge University Press, 1993).

108. Alexinia Y. Baldwin, "Programs for the Gifted and Talented: Issues Concerning Minority Populations," in *The Gifted and Talented: Developmental Perspectives,* ed. Frances Degen Horowitz and Marion O'Brien (Washington, DC: American Psychological Association, 1985), pp. 228–249.

109. Robert H. Bradley, Betty M. Caldwell, and Richard Elardo, "Home Environment, Social Class and Mental Test Performance," *Journal of Educational Psychology* 69 (1977): 697–701; William J. Van Doorninck et al.,

"The Relationship between Twelve-Month Home Stimulation and School Achievements," *Child Development* 52 (1981): 1080–1083.

Chapter 16

1. Urie Bronfenbrenner, "Ecology of the Family as a Context for Human Development," *Developmental Psychology* 22 (1986): 723–742.
2. Moncrieff Cochran, "Parenting and Personal Social Networks," in *Parenting: An Ecological Perspective,* ed. Tom Luster and Lynn Okagaki (Hillsdale, NJ: Erlbaum, 1993), pp. 149–178.
3. Ibid.
4. Moncrieff Cochran et al., "Personal Networks and Public Policy," in *Extending Families: The Social Networks of Parents and Their Children,* ed. Moncrieff Cochran et al. (New York: Cambridge University Press), pp. 307–314.
5. Moncrieff Cochran, "Factors Influencing Personal Social Initiative," in *Extending Families,* ed. Cochran et al., pp. 297–306.
6. Ibid., p. 297.
7. Cochran, "Parenting and Personal Social Networks."
8. Moncrieff Cochran and Charles R. Henderson, Jr., "Illustrations," in *Extending Families,* ed. Cochran et al., pp. 58–64.
9. Moncrieff Cochran and Starr Niego, "Parenting and Social Networks," in *Handbook of Parenting,* ed. Marc H. Bornstein, vol. 3: *Status and Social Conditions of Parenting* (Mahwah, NJ: Erlbaum, 1995), pp. 393–418.
10. Ibid.
11. Brenda K. Bryant, *The Neighborhood Walks: Sources of Support in Middle Childhood,* Monographs of the Society for Research in Child Development 50, whole no. 210 (1985).
12. Moncrieff Cochran and David Riley, "The Social Networks of Six-Year-Olds: Context, Content, and Consequence," in *Extending Families,* ed. Cochran et al., pp. 154–177.
13. Cochran, "Parenting and Personal Social Networks."
14. Emmy E. Werner and Ruth S. Smith, *Overcoming the Odds* (Ithaca, NY: Cornell University Press, 1992).
15. Judy Dunn, *Sisters and Brothers* (Cambridge, MA: Harvard University Press, 1985), p. 163.
16. Barbara J. Tinsley and Ross D. Parke, "Grandparents as Support and Socialization Agents," in *Beyond the Dyad,* ed. Michael Lewis (New York: Plenum, 1984), pp. 161–194.

17. Timothy F. J. Tolson and Melvin N. Wilson, "The Impact of Two- and Three-Generational Family Structure on Perceived Family Style," *Child Development* 61 (1990): 416–428.
18. Jane L. Pearson et al., "Black Grandmothers in Multigenerational Households: Diversity in Family Structures on Parenting in the Woodlawn Community," *Child Development* 61 (1990): 434–442.
19. Peter K. Smith, "Grandparenthood," in *Handbook of Parenting,* ed. Bornstein, vol. 3, pp. 89–112.
20. Ibid., p. 96.
21. Ibid.
22. Ibid.
23. Cochran, "Parenting and Personal Social Networks."
24. Moncrieff Cochran and Charles R. Henderson, Jr., "Formal Supports and Informal Social Ties: A Case Study," in *Extending Families,* ed. Cochran et al., pp. 230–261.
25. Cochran, "Parenting and Personal Social Networks."
26. Cochran and Riley, "The Social Networks of Six-Year-Olds."
27. Steven J. Wolin and Linda A. Bennett, "Family Rituals," *Family Process* 23 (1984): 401–420.
28. Linda A. Bennett et al., "Couples at Risk for Transmission of Alcoholism: Protective Influences," *Family Process* 26 (1987): 111–129.
29. Werner and Smith, *Overcoming the Odds,* p. 178.
30. Eigel Pedersen and Theresa Annette Faucher with William W. Eaton, "A New Perspective on the Effects of First-Grade Teachers on Children's Subsequent Adult Status," *Harvard Educational Review* 48 (1978): 1–31.
31. Ibid., p. 20.
32. Michael Rutter et al., *Fifteen Thousand Hours: Secondary Schools and Their Effects on Children* (New York: Cambridge University Press, 1979).
33. Cochran, "Parenting and Personal Social Networks."
34. Carolyn Pape Cowan and Philip A. Cowan, *When Partners Become Parents* (New York: Basic Books, 1992).
35. Bruce Cedar and Ronald F. Levant, "A Meta-Analysis of the Effects of Parent Effectiveness Training," *American Journal of Family Therapy* 18 (1990): 373–384.
36. Paul C. Burnett, "Evaluation of Adlerian Parenting Programs," *Individual Psychology* 44 (1988): 63–76.

37. Anthony M. Graziano and David M. Diament, "Parent Behavior Training: An Examination of the Paradigm," *Behavior Modification* 16 (1992): 3–39.

38. Gerald R. Patterson and Carla M. Narrett, "The Development of a Reliable and Valid Treatment Program for Aggressive Young Children," *International Journal of Mental Health* 19 (1990): 19–26.

39. Amy Wolfson, Patricia Lacks, and Andrew Futterman, "Effects of Parent Training on Infant Sleeping Patterns, Parents' Stress, and Perceived Parental Competence," *Journal of Consulting and Clinical Psychology* 60 (1992): 41–48.

40. Philip A. Cowan, Douglas Powell, and Carolyn Pape Cowan, "Parenting Interventions: A Family Systems Perspective," in *Handbook of Child Psychology,* ed. in chief William Damon and vol. ed. Irving E. Sigel and K. Ann Renninger, vol. 4: *Child Psychology in Practice,* 5th ed. (New York: Wiley, 1997), 3–72.

41. Ibid., pp. 59–60.

42. Deborah Stipek and Jacquelyn McCroskey, "Investing in Children: Government and Workplace Policies for Parents," *American Psychologist* 44 (1989): 416–423.

43. Ellen Galinsky, "Families and Work: The Importance of the Quality of the Work Environment," in *Putting Families First,* ed. Sharon L. Kagan and Bernice Weissbourd (San Francisco: Jossey-Bass, 1994), pp. 112–136.

44. Urie Bronfenbrenner and Peter R. Neville, "America's Children and Families: An International Perspective," in *Putting Families First,* ed. Kagan and Weissbourd, pp. 3–27.

45. Edward A. Zigler and Mary E. Lang, *Child Care Choices* (New York: Free Press, 1991).

46. David A. Hamburg, *Today's Children* (New York: Times Books, 1992).

47. Ibid., p. 331.

48. Zigler and Lang, *Child Care Choices.*

49. Norman B. Rice, "Local Initiatives in Support of Families," in *Putting Families First,* ed. Kagan and Weissbourd, pp. 321–337.

50. Gary B. Melton and Frank D. Barry, "Neighbors Helping Neighbors: The Vision of the U.S. Advisory Board on Child Abuse and Neglect," in *Protecting Children from Abuse and Neglect: Foundations for a New National Strategy,* ed. Gary B. Melton and Frank D. Barry (New York: Guilford Press, 1994), pp. 1–13.

51. Ibid., p. 8.

52. Frank D. Barry, "A Neighborhood-Based Approach: What Is It?" in *Protecting Children from Abuse and Neglect,* ed. Melton and Barry, pp. 14–39.

53. Claudia Dreifus, "We Have a Future Now," *Parade Magazine,* June 2, 1992, p. 20.

54. Roger P. Weissberg and Mark T. Greenberg, "School and Community Competence-Enhancement and Prevention," in *Handbook of Child Psychology,* ed. Damon, Sigel, and Renninger, vol. 4, pp. 877–954.

55. Werner and Smith, *Overcoming the Odds,* p. 177.

56. Joan Beck, *Effective Parenting* (New York: Simon & Schuster, 1976).

57. Robert Coles, *The Spiritual Life of Children* (Boston: Houghton Mifflin, 1990).

58. Ibid., pp. 119–120.

59. Ibid., p. 128.

60. Ibid., p. 127.

61. Felicia R. Lee, "Memories of Youths in Harlem," *New York Times,* July 10, 1993, p. 16.

62. Amy Arner Sgarro, "A Surgeon and Her Community," *Vassar Quarterly,* Spring 1993, pp. 10–13.

63. Ibid., p. 13.

INDEX

517